D1607955

Moral Theology for the Twenty-First Century

Kevin Kelly (image courtesy of Jan Jans)

Moral Theology
for the
Twenty-First Century

Essays in Celebration of Kevin Kelly

**Edited by
Julie Clague
Bernard Hoose
Gerard Mannion**

t&t clark

Published by T&T Clark
A Continuum imprint
The Tower Building, 11 York Road, London SE1 7NX
80 Maiden Lane, Suite 704, New York, NY 10038

www.continuumbooks.com

British Library Cataloguing-in-Publication Data
A catalogue record for this book is available from the British Library

Typeset by Free Range Book Design & Production Limited
Printed on acid-free paper in Great Britain by Biddles Ltd, King's Lynn, Norfolk

ISBN-10: 0-567-03285-X (hardback)
ISBN-13: 978-0-567-03285-0 (hardback)

Contents

Contents

Contents

Contributors

JOHN BATTLE has been Member of Parliament for Leeds West since 1987. He was Minister of Science and Energy at the Department of Trade and Industry following Labour's 1997 election victory, and from 1999 to 2001 was Minister of State at the Foreign Office. He chairs the All-Party Parliamentary Groups on Poverty and on Overseas Development. Before becoming an MP, John Battle was National Coordinator for Church Action on Poverty from 1983.

TINA BEATTIE is a reader in Christian studies at Roehampton University, London, and she has published widely in the fields of Catholic theology, Marian theology and devotion, gender and feminism, and human rights. She is currently researching questions of natural law, human rights and women's rights. She has also written on the clash between militant atheism and Christian creationism (*The New Atheists*, London: Darton, Longman and Todd, 2007).

JULIE CLAGUE lectures in the department of theology and religious studies at the University of Glasgow and is co-editor of the journal *Political Theology*. Julie has published widely in the areas of moral theology, Catholic social thought, bioethics and gender studies. She works as a theologian with the Catholic international development agencies, CAFOD and SCIAF.

CHARLES E. CURRAN, a Roman Catholic priest of the Diocese of Rochester, New York, is the Elizabeth Scurlock University Chair of Human Values at Southern Methodist University. He was the first recipient of the John Courtney Murray Award for Theology, and in 2003 received the Presidential Award of the College Theology Society for a Lifetime of Scholarly Achievements in Moral Theology. He has served as president of three national academic societies: the Catholic Theological Society of America, the Society of Christian Ethics and the American Theological Society. His latest books are: *Loyal Dissent: Memoir of a Catholic Theologian* (Washington D.C.: Catholic University of America Press, 2006); *The Moral Theology of Pope John Paul II* (London: T&T Clark, 2006); and *Catholic Social Teaching 1891–Present* (Washington DC: Georgetown University Press, 2002).

PROFESSOR CELIA DEANE-DRUMMOND has worked for many years at the interface of biology and theology. Her recent publications include *Wonder and Wisdom: Conversations in Science, Spirituality and Theology* (Philadelphia: Templeton Foundation Press, 2006); *Genetics and Christian Ethics* (Cambridge: Cambridge

Contributors

University Press, 2006); *Future Perfect: God, Medicine and Human Identity*, edited with Peter Scott (London: Continuum, 2006); and *Teilhard de Chardin on People and Planet* (ed.) (London: Equinox Publishing, 2006). She is director of the Centre for Religion and the Biosciences at the University of Chester.

DR JOHN ELFORD is Pro-Rector Emeritus of Liverpool Hope University and Canon Theologian Emeritus of Liverpool Cathedral. He writes on Christian ethics and pastoral theology. Recent publications include *The Pastoral Nature of Theology* (London: Cassell, 1999) and *The Ethics of Uncertainty* (Oxford: Oneworld, 2001). He edited *The Foundation of Hope* (Liverpool: University of Liverpool Press, 2003).

PATRICK HANNON is an emeritus professor of moral theology at the University of Maynooth. He holds doctorates in theology (Maynooth) and law (Cambridge), and is a member of the Irish Bar. He is a former chairman of the Irish Commission for Justice and Peace and of the Irish Commission for Prisoners Overseas. His most recent monograph is *Making Moral Decisions* (Dublin: Veritas, 2006).

NICHOLAS PETER HARVEY taught moral theology at Downside Abbey and Newman College, Birmingham. He also taught Christian ethics at Queen's College, Birmingham and the University of Birmingham. His first book, *Death's Gift* (London: Epworth, 1985) was republished this year. He is also the author of *The Morals of Jesus* (London: Darton, Longman and Todd, 1991). He belongs to the Association of Teachers of Moral Theology, and is a past president of the Society for the Study of Christian Ethics.

RUDOLF BRANKO HEIN OPraem has been a member of the Order of Canons Regular of Prémontre (Norbertines) since 1992. He studied theology and philosophy in Münster, Germany and at Heythrop College, London. After his novitiate, he embarked on a doctoral programme with Professor Autiero, Münster on the concept of conscience, graduating as doctor of moral theology in 1999. After his ordination, he joined the Association of Teachers of Moral Theology in 2002. Currently he is a part-time hospital chaplain and is working on a habilitation project in normative ethics.

LINDA HOGAN is professor of ecumenics at the Irish School of Ecumenics, Trinity College Dublin, teaching a range of courses, including ethics in international affairs and the ethics of human rights. She is the author of *Confronting the Truth: Conscience in the Catholic Tradition* (New York: Paulist Press; London, Darton, Longman and Todd, 2000) and *From Women's Experience to Feminist Theology* (Sheffield: Sheffield Academic Press, 1995).

BERNARD HOOSE lectures in moral theology at Heythrop College, London, and has written widely on various aspects of moral theology and ecclesiology. He is the editor of *Authority in the Roman Catholic Church: Theory and Practice* (Aldershot: Ashgate, 2002) and, more recently, with Philomena Cullen and Gerard Mannion, he co-edited *Catholic Social Justice: Theological and Practical Explorations* (London: Continuum, 2007).

Contributors

JAYNE HOOSE was formerly a senior lecturer at Canterbury Christ Church University, and currently works as a freelance writer and lecturer. She has published a range of articles, book chapters and books in the two disciplines of leisure and moral theology. She is the editor of *Conscience in World Religions* (Leominster: Gracewing, 1999). With Chris Bull and Mike Weed, she co-authored *An Introduction to Leisure Studies* (Harlow: Pearson Education, 2003).

GERARD J. HUGHES is a Jesuit priest. He studied classics and philosophy at Oxford, and did a doctorate in philosophy at the University of Michigan. He taught philosophy at Heythrop College, London from 1970 to 1998, and was master of Campion Hall, University of Oxford, from 1998 until 2006, where he remains as tutor in philosophy. He has written several books and many articles on ethics, Aristotle and philosophy of religion.

JAN JANS studied theology at the Katholieke Universiteit Leuven, Belgium, where he graduated in 1990. Since 1991 he has been assistant professor at Tilburg University in the Netherlands, where he is currently director of the Centre for Intercultural Ethics. Since 2002, he has been visiting professor at St Augustine's College, South Africa. He has published on issues of fundamental moral theology, medical ethics, media ethics and the way they interface. His current focus of research is Transparticular Love as Neighbour.

FR JAMES KEENAN SJ is professor of theological ethics at Boston College. He entered the New York Province of the Society of Jesus in 1970 and was ordained a priest in 1982. He studied moral theology at the Gregorian University in Rome with Josef Fuchs and Klaus Demmer, and received a licentiate (1984) and a doctorate (1988). *The Works of Mercy: The Heart of Catholicism* (Lanham MD: Sheed and Ward, 2005) is his latest book. He is the chair of Catholic Theological Ethics in the World Church and has just finished editing the plenary papers (to be published by Continuum Press) from the First International Crosscultural Conference for Catholic Theological Ethicists which was held in July 2006 in Padua, Italy. He is planning for the next conference: 'In the Currents of History: From Trento to the Future', to be held 24–27 July 2010 in Trent, Italy.

DR MICHAEL G. LAWLER is professor emeritus of Catholic Theology and director of the Center for Marriage and Family at Creighton University. He is the author of 20 books and some 150 scholarly essays in both systematic theology and ethics. Among his most recent publications are (with Dr Todd Salzman) *The Sexual Person: Toward a Renewed Catholic Anthropology* (Washington DC: Georgetown University Press, 2008); *What Is and What Ought to Be* (New York and London: Continuum, 2005); *Marriage in the Catholic Church: Disputed Questions* (Collegeville: Liturgical Press, 2002). Dr Lawler is a well-known international lecturer. He is married with three children and three grandchildren.

JACK MAHONEY SJ MA DD(Hon) is emeritus professor of moral and social theology in the University of London and a former principal of Heythrop College, London. Currently he is a teaching member of the Mount Street Jesuit Centre, London. His latest book is *The Challenge of Human Rights: Origin, Development and Significance* (Oxford: Blackwell, 2007).

Contributors

GERARD MANNION who studied at the Universities of Cambridge and Oxford, previously lectured at Church Colleges of the Universities of Oxford and Leeds, and was associate professor of ecclesiology and ethics at Liverpool Hope University. Chair of the Ecclesiological Investigations International Research Network and director of the Centre for the Study of Contemporary Ecclesiology, he has authored, edited and co-edited some ten volumes to date. Co-chair of the Ecclesiology Program Unit of the American Academy of Religion, he is editor of the T&T Clark Publications series Ecclesiological Investigations, and serves on the UK Catholic Theology Commission on Social Justice.

ENDA McDONAGH was professor of moral theology at the Pontifical University of Maynooth, Ireland, 1958–95, and has been a visiting professor, fellow and lecturer at various universities in the UK, USA, Canada, Europe, Africa and Australia. He is a consultant to Caritas Internationalis, CAFOD (London) and Trocaire (Ireland) on development issues, and is chair of the governing body of the University of Cork, 1999–2007, as well as being Ecumenical Canon at St Patrick's Cathedral, Dublin. He is the author of 17 books, the latest being *Immersed In Mystery* (Dublin: Veritas, 2007), and is editor of and contributor to 18 books, the latest being *Remembering to Forgive: A Tribute to Una O'Higgins O'Malley* (Dublin: Columba Press, 2007).

BARRY McMILLAN is Jubilee Doctoral Scholar in the department of theology and religious studies, Mary Immaculate College, University of Limerick, Ireland. Co-editor of *Technology and Transcendence* (Dublin: Columba Press, 2003), he has also published articles on sexual ethics and theology and film, and been consultant and contributor to a number of radio series on feminist theologies and theology and culture. His dissertation research is in feminist theological ethics – specifically, theological anthropologies and their implications for theological ethical method.

JUDITH A. MERKLE SNDdeN is professor of religious studies at Niagara University, New York. She lectures and writes in the areas of social ethics, Church and culture and contemporary religious life. She is the author of *From the Heart of the Church: The Catholic Social Tradition* (Collegeville: Liturgical Press, 2004), as well as articles and books on issues of faith, justice and contemporary Catholic life. She is a member of the Sisters of Notre Dame de Namur, an international community of religious women.

DR SUZANNE MULLIGAN is the Finlay Fellow in theology at the Milltown Institute, Dublin and is also a lecturer in the department of moral theology at Milltown. Recent publications include 'Women and HIV/AIDS', *Furrow* 57/4 (April 2006) and 'Moral Discourse in a Time of AIDS', in Amelia Flemming (ed.), *Contemporary Irish Moral Discourse: Essays in Honour of Patrick Hannon* (Dublin: Columba Press, 2007).

LADISLAS ÖRSY SJ is professor of jurisprudence and canon law at Georgetown University Law Center in Washington, DC He did his studies at the Gregorian University in Rome, at College St Albert in Louvain and at Oxford University. He taught at the Gregorian University, Fordham University in New York City and the

Catholic University of America in Washington DC. He has published widely in the fields of theology and law.

TODD SALZMAN is associate professor and chair of the department of theology at Creighton University, USA. He has published articles in *Theological Studies*, *Louvain Studies*, *Heythrop Journal* and *Studia Moralia*. His recent books include *The Sexual Person: Toward a Renewed Catholic Anthropology*, co-authored with Michael Lawler (Washington DC: Georgetown University Press, 2008) and *What Are They Saying about Catholic Ethical Method?* (New York: Paulist Press, 2003).

JOSEPH A. SELLING STD is *hoogleraar* (professor-in-ordinary) of theological ethics and chair of the department of theological ethics at the faculty of theology of the Katholieke Universiteit Leuven, Belgium. Between 1993 and 2007 he was also coordinator of a masters programme in applied ethics. His principle areas of interest and publication are in sexual ethics and fundamental ethics.

REVD DR STEVEN SHAKESPEARE is the Anglican Chaplain of Liverpool Hope University and associate director of the Centre for the Study of Contemporary Ecclesiology. Born in Walsall, UK, he studied theology at Cambridge University. His publications include *Kierkegaard, Language and the Reality of God* (Aldershot: Ashgate, 2001); *The Inclusive God. Reclaiming Theology for an Inclusive Church*, with Hugh Rayment-Pickard (London: Canterbury Press, 2006); and *Radical Orthodoxy: A Critical Introduction* (London: SPCK, 2007).

JACQUI STEWART holds an honorary lectureship in theology at the University of Leeds, and is presently a visiting fellow in the Department of Theology at the University of Exeter. Her first PhD and initial research career was in genetics. In 1990 she started her PhD in theology and changes subject. She has published a critical book on Pannenberg's theological anthropology. She is interested in the theological suspicions raised by social sciences as well as philosophy – for example, the work of Zygmunt Baumann and Paul Ricoeur.

Preface

Bernard Hoose

There has for some years now been a liking in moral-theology circles for multi-authored collections. Some, like those in the *Readings in Moral Theology* series launched by Charles Curran and Richard McCormick, tend to be devoted to particular themes. Others deal with numerous themes in one volume, and Festschriften are usually found in this latter category. A Festschrift can normally be described as a collection of writings put together in honour of a prominent scholar. The collection is usually then presented to that scholar to mark some significant event in his or her life. If the said collection is also published, it may attract a good deal of interest within the discipline concerned, especially if a fair number of the contributors to the collection are themselves scholars of some note. In the case of this particular collection of essays in honour of Kevin Kelly, the list of contributors includes scholars who have already had books published in their own honour, others who are widely regarded as being eligible for such an honour, some other well-established, international 'names', and a number of scholars who can fairly be described as 'up and coming'.

Some of the essays included in this collection will, no doubt, soon appear on numerous lists of bibliographies handed out to students in various parts of the English-speaking world, and perhaps beyond. These and a number of others may be described as thought-provoking, some as uplifting and a few, perhaps, as controversial. They do, however, have something in common. In their Introduction to a compilation put together some years ago, Ronald Hamel and Kenneth Himes commented that most of the Catholic theologians represented in their book reflected what they considered to be a 'mainstream' perspective. The word 'mainstream' was there used to indicate that those scholars shared in the theological vision of most moral theologians of their day. This 'mainstream perspective', said Hamel and Himes, could be termed 'revisionist' inasmuch as 'it has taken seriously the mandate of Vatican II to reform the discipline'.[1] Although not all of them are Roman Catholics, the same sort of terminology could be applied to the authors of this present volume.

The book is divided into five parts. The first four parts are devoted to traditional themes: fundamental moral theology, medical and sexual ethics, social and political ethics, and issues within the sphere of ecclesiology. Part Five, however, consists of commentaries of various kinds on the work of Kevin Kelly, plus an autobiographical chapter by the man himself. This section of the book has a peculiar importance of its own in that it highlights the pastoral approach to moral theology adopted by Kelly. Regardless of whether or not it will be open to younger generations of moral theologians to adopt a similar approach to the subject, what this section, along with a number of other chapters in the book, highlights is the importance of not allowing moral theology to be separated from what is generally referred to as 'the real world', as opposed to a world of unconnected theories, unsupported rules, and claims to the backing of 'authority'. This book is certainly mainstream.

Notes

1. Ronald P. Hamel and Kenneth R. Himes (ed), *Introduction to Christian Ethics: A Reader* (New York: Paulist Press, 1989).

Introduction[1]

Julie Clague

A good case could be made for characterizing the last 50 years of moral theology as the most dramatic in the discipline's long history. During this time there have been seismic changes in the structure and shape of the subject. The scope of the discipline has expanded, and the working principles, categories and approaches used to investigate it have changed in substance or in kind. Moral theology has become an extraordinarily broad, interdisciplinary enterprise, incorporating not just theological and philosophical tools and methods, but a panoply of resources from the full range of the human, social, political and life sciences. In creative conversation with Christian tradition, these resources have opened up new directions in moral theology and, as this branch of theology has grown, it has become increasingly differentiated into sub-specialisms, each requiring its own specific expertise.

Intimately linked to these changes has been the rapid transformation in who is studying and writing moral theology. The number of people engaged in study of the subject has grown to its highest ever level and these scholars are more diverse than at any other time in history. The demographics of moral theologians have changed. Whereas previously moralists tended, almost exclusively, to be priests teaching in an apologetic mode in seminary and clerical contexts, today's moral theologians are much less homogeneous. Many are lay people and many are female, having been introduced to the subject not through an ordination training programme but through tertiary academic study of theology. Large numbers of moral theologians are now based in university settings, many teaching students of all faiths and none, and publishing research in a climate of academic freedom of enquiry. As vibrant cultures of Christianity continue to develop their identities in non-Western contexts, moral theology is further enriched and resourced as new voices contribute their own distinctive experiences and insights to the ongoing conversations and, where necessary, correct previous, culturally blinkered, assumptions and categorizations. With this influx of moral theologians and the proliferation of writings on the topic, moral theology has entered a new phase of burgeoning growth. In this relatively short time period, therefore, one sees the remarkable diversification of the discipline and its practitioners into the variegated venture we recognize today. Moral theology is now better able to reflect upon and represent the multiplicity of ways of being human. For the first time in its history, moral theology has the chance to become truly catholic and ecumenical. This volume aims to reflect some of these changes and capture something of the variety and vitality of moral theology in the twenty-first century.

1

'There is no doubt that the single most influential factor in the development of the practice and of the discipline of moral theology is to be found in the growth and spread of "confession" in the Church.' With these words, John Mahoney SJ encapsulates the gradual emergence of moral theology as a particular sort of theological response to a particular sort of pastoral need.[2] Fifty years ago it could still plausibly be claimed that in Catholic Christianity the *raison d'être* of the discipline remained the care of souls in an ecclesial context in which, with the practice of auricular confession, the priest assumes responsibility for legal, moral and pastoral judgements concerning matters such as personal wrongdoing, culpability and sin. However, moral theology is no longer anchored in the confessional tradition which, in its sacramental manifestation – at least in the West – while not extinct is certainly endangered. In the intervening years, catalyzed by the reforms of the Second Vatican Council, the locus and focus of moral theology has changed.

By the time of the council the moribund nature of seminary-based moral theology was apparent, rooted as it was in a non-Christological, overly negative and pessimistic theological anthropology that owed its pathology to distorted genuflections to Augustine and Aquinas. The Council Fathers diagnosed a need for theological supplements and prescribed accordingly: theological education should have 'more living contact with the mystery of Christ and the history of salvation'. A renewed moral theology was created through a scripturally enriched, revivified anthropology that saw the human person's vocation in glorious theological technicolour:

> Special care must be given to the perfecting of moral theology. Its scientific exposition, nourished more on the teaching of the Bible, should shed light on the loftiness of the calling of the faithful in Christ and the obligation that is theirs of bearing fruit in charity for the life of the world.[3]

The council's call for a renewal of moral theology came in the Decree on the Training of Priests, betraying traces of the old school even as the new one was heralded. This was before moral theology was devolved to and made the joint responsibility of the whole people of God, rather than reserved, occult-like, to an initiated clerical caste.

This plural people of God have produced, not surprisingly, moral theologies in the plural. And this *de facto* plurality – while potentially one of the most fruitful opportunities for the Church – has become one of the major challenges of the post-conciliar era. That education in moral theology could be envisaged as the council imagined it, in terms of a 'scientific exposition' of the discipline, evoking images of a uniform and universally applicable syllabus offering a standardized account based on select authors, now seems unrealistic and naively wishful. Today's teachers of moral theology, confronted with a wider, more confusing and loosely structured subject, face no easy task in selecting appropriate material that will offer a fair and sufficiently comprehensive introduction to the discipline. However, approaches that view the task of theology in terms of constructing, maintaining and delivering overarching and often grandiose intellectual systems, and view the task of theological education as one of merely inculcating ecclesiastically sanctioned formulae that support such constructions, hark back to the indoctrinating manuals of moral theology (confessors' textbooks) that belong to an overly confident, rationalistic era largely discredited. Theological pluralism gives rise to many difficulties but few theologians would wish to turn the clock back and deny its existence.

Regrettably, with such varied readings of Christian tradition and vastly differing theological agendas, moral theology is as characterized by disagreements and divisions as its parent religion, Christianity. All too often, factiousness rather than fellowship is the default tendency, as moral theologians discover that they are working with markedly different models of the Church. As a result – and as several of the chapters in this collection indicate – the questions and issues that pertain to moral theology are frequently inseparable from questions and issues that pertain to ecclesiology. While the existence of moral disagreement is a source of concern for moral theologians, it is an even more acute challenge for a religious leadership entrusted with the task of preaching and teaching the Word. However, that Church authorities continue to respond to such disturbing pluralism through attempts to control the content of moral theology and the writings of moral theologians damages the state and health of the discipline. Moral theology – indeed, all theology – can only ever thrive and bear fruit when it is an open conversation (rather than a last word) and a communal enterprise of discernment in which all are invited to participate, listen and respond in fellowship as the people of God. Just as Christians must recognize the Holy Spirit's gift of *koinonia* in their midst, and actively work towards realizing its potential, so too should one consider the *koinonia* of moral theology that unites in fellowship – across space and time – those who through its study have engaged in the search for truth and the eschatological *koinonia* that this involves. Moral theology in the twenty-first century must renew its commitment to making this search for truth as constructive as it can for the life of the Church and for humanity as a whole.

And this brief retrospective brings us to the person whose contribution to moral theology occasions this volume; for Kevin Kelly's ministry as Catholic priest and moral theologian spans the half-century during which the discipline has changed most dramatically. In an understated but influential way he has helped contribute to the renewal of the subject in the English-speaking world and beyond. And because the touchstone of Kevin Kelly's moral theology has been the personalist spirit of Vatican II, he has kept his theology rooted in pastoral reflection on the joys and the hopes, the griefs and the anxieties of the human person.[4] Kevin Kelly has devoted himself to serving his parishioners and his theological public in a deeply committed and non-partisan expression of fellowship.

Kelly's mode of doing theology begins with the participatory act of listening: listening to what people are saying about their experience. His next move is to reflect upon what he has heard and, in a pastoral capacity, to act upon it. These moments are set out in his writings as he reflects upon what theological lessons he has learned from his encounter. Kelly's whole method of approach therefore follows the pastoral cycle of see, judge and act, followed by a return to the same reflective pastoral cycle in the new situation that has developed. In the same way, he conducts his theological discourse as if in the round, in an open circle to which all are invited to participate. This model of doing theology is mirrored in the pioneering, seminar-style working methods of the Association of Teachers of Moral Theology which Kevin Kelly co-founded with John Mahoney SJ as a means of reflecting upon and implementing the reforms of the council; and the same approach was applied at the New Directions In Moral Theology scholarly colloquium held in Kevin

3

Kelly's honour at Liverpool Hope University in March 2007, where most of the contributions to this collection began life. Although the colloquium occurred as a means of celebrating Kevin Kelly's contribution to moral theology, what emerged – as he himself identified – was a celebration of an approach to doing theology by hearing one another into speech through an inclusive model of listening and learning in the round.

This volume gathers those papers together as a Festschrift in Kevin Kelly's honour and as an exercise of communal learning and teaching. Many of the articles work at the interface of moral and pastoral theology, and a number of them focus on what is distinctive about Kevin Kelly's contribution to the subject, including the key commitments that shape his approach. Many of Kelly's writings have pushed the frontiers of Catholic treatment of issues in sexual, medical and social ethics, and many of the papers in this collection build on his contribution. Others concentrate on issues in fundamental moral theology. And, because Catholic moral theology is so connected to questions of ecclesiology, a number of authors consider the ramifications of a renewed moral theology for the life of the Christian Church.

A collection of this kind should not be read as a textbook; still less as a manual of moral theology. This is not an attempt to summarize the whole of a discipline or to offer a comprehensive overview of its key themes. Neither can this volume hope to capture entirely the discipline's diversity. These are writings by people who have worked with Kevin Kelly. This means the contributions are drawn solely from the Northern hemisphere and are largely, though not entirely, limited to the English-speaking world. As such, this anthology of writings can only offer a snapshot of contemporary work in moral theology. Nonetheless, the reader will find sufficient evidence of the diversity that has forever changed the discipline. What follows is a flavour of some of the central themes that drive Kevin Kelly's pastoral approach to moral theology. It should be seen as part of an ongoing reflection on aspects of moral and pastoral theology prompted by and written in the spirit of openness that Kelly's writings exemplify. It is an open conversation, rather than a last word, to which all are invited to listen and respond in fellowship. Whatever its shortcomings, we hope that it demonstrates that moral theology in the Catholic tradition has an academic importance and social significance beyond the confines of its own ecclesial context.

Notes

1. With thanks to the Derwent Consultancy, *The Furrow*, Billy Hardacre, Liverpool Hope University and the Tablet Trust for their generous support of the scholarly colloquium that made this volume possible.
2. John Mahoney SJ, 'The Influence of Auricular Confession', in *The Making of Moral Theology: A Study of the Roman Catholic Tradition* (Oxford: Clarendon Press, 1987), pp. 1–36 (1).
3. Decree on the Training of Priests, *Optatam totius* (Vatican II, 1965), 16.
4. Pastoral Constitution On the Church in the Modern World, *Gaudium et spes* (Vatican II, 1965), 1.

'It's Great to Be Alive':
Kevin Kelly –
A Brief Introduction to a Very Special Person

Gerard Mannion

As this is a collection where moral theology forms the focus of much of the proceedings, it is perhaps fitting to open with a brief case study. This volume has emerged as a result of a conference held in Liverpool, UK in March 2007. The organizers of the conference were faced with a crisis of conscience for the duration of the lengthy planning process until the week of the gathering itself. The ethical dilemma to consider then was this: whether or not it is morally permissible for a large group of people collectively to deceive an honourable and noble man for whom truthfulness has always been such a core virtue. Absolutist deontological moral reasoning did not help here at all. Utilitarian perspectives fared little better. Virtue ethics offered much more hope but, above all else, it was with much gratitude that we had two people at the heart of the organizing of this weekend whose expertise might come to the rescue. Julie Clague's work on changing perspectives in the Christian moral tradition proved invaluable at fending off the deontological pangs of conscience. And Bernard Hoose has not only published highly influential arguments as to why lying is not always morally wrong, but, well, let us just say that he wrote *the* book on our most convincing grounds for defence. In sum, then, let's just say 'thank God for proportionalism' and 'sorry, Kevin, that you were kept in the dark for so long'. Kevin himself closes his very first book by arguing that 'moral theology, therefore, to see sin through the eyes of God, so to speak, must view sin not as an "unlawful" act but as a "disordered" act'.[1] At times there was much disorder, even chaos, to the preparations for the Festschrift conference and celebratory weekend, more than most will ever know! But if that weekend, in the final reckoning, was not a disordered act, then the collective cloud of secrecy proved to be a virtuous, as opposed to a sinful, course of action. Our consciences thus assuaged, let us turn to our guest of honour.

During the course of that weekend, numerous guests from all over the world came together to pay tribute to one of Liverpool's favourite sons in the Church, university and charity sectors, the Revd Dr Kevin Kelly. As invitations went out for this Festschrift (a not uncomplicated task given the fact that the guest of honour was kept in the dark about it!), without exception, we were overwhelmed by the response of delight from those we communicated with: a great delight that there was finally to be a much overdue celebration of Kevin's enormous achievements and loving service. All could relate personal stories of the way in which Kevin had touched and inspired their lives. This lad was born in Crosby, just north of Liverpool, on 27 June 1933, to Patrick and Winifred Kelly, from the north of Ireland. No mean footballer, rugby player and cricketer in his day, he came to be known and admired the world over, although not primarily, it must be said, for his sporting prowess. The list of his friends and those who have been taught by, learned from and consulted him over five decades of his service to the Church and academic community alike, means that the challenge facing the organizers was how to do justice to the wealth of Kevin's contribution. That spring weekend of orations, reflections, liturgy, prayer and what turned out to be the most wonderful party and experience of true communion, was our response to that challenge. One weekend alone could not ever hope to do justice to Kevin Kelly's enormous gifts and qualities, nor to the full story of how he has moved and indeed, as many have testified, transformed the lives of those who have come into contact with him. But we hope that weekend and now this volume go some way towards serving as a fitting tribute and, of course (Kevin being Kevin), a most joyful *celebration* of his great gifts and achievements.

It is, indeed, incredible that Kevin did not find out about or guess that a celebratory weekend would be taking place in his honour, in advance. But that is so quintessentially Kevin: he would never presume that such an occasion should or would be held in his honour. During the course of the weekend, we heard much about his empowering humility, and others bear testimony to such in later chapters of this volume too, but let us here capture its essence by reference to a personal dedication that Kevin wrote to his then Archbishop (George Beck), on the flyleaf of his very first book, *Conscience: Dictator or Guide?*, which was the outcome of Kevin's doctoral research. There Kevin simply wrote: 'In gratitude for having been given the opportunity to pursue these studies – and with apologies for having so little to show at the end.' Well, either Archbishop Beck did not much care for moral theology or he profoundly disagreed with Kevin's assessment of the worth of those studies and of their outcome, for Beck presented the book as a gift to the newly established Christ's College – one of the forerunner constituent colleges of what is now Liverpool Hope University. Indeed, the Festschrift conference took place on the very site of that college.

In fact, we know Beck rated Kevin's expertise very highly indeed: so highly, in fact, that, in 1968, he chose Kevin to draft for him a communication to all the priests of the Archdiocese of Liverpool explaining how and why the Church had decided to change its teaching on artificial contraception and to allow its use in certain circumstances. This was because many expected the Vatican would follow the will of the majority of the Papal Birth Control Commission and lift the ban. Archbishop Beck wished his priests to be as pastorally prepared, in advance, as possible for so dramatic a change in official teaching. Kevin duly obliged and wrote a communication that was a fine piece of moral theologizing and pastoral sensitivity at one and the same time – characteristics that would be found in his many later writings also. Every priest was duly sent this articulate, insightful and carefully nuanced advice heralding a fundamental shift in the position of the official Magisterium. Of course we know that the Archbishop was just a little *too* ahead of developments here, and that teaching was not so transformed. Quite the reverse!

Indeed, when the Vatican wrote to Beck to ask him to explain this communication, Beck said it was not his own pen that had drafted the document and mentioned he had instead consulted one moral theologian in Ireland and two in Britain. One of the latter took a very hard-line conservative stance against artificial contraception. The other was Kevin Kelly! Despite being duly fingered, Kevin heard nothing more about it. The Vatican told Beck they recognized his intentions had been purely pastoral and advised him not to circulate the communication any further!

So let us explore the fruits of Kevin's assiduous studies in a little more depth. Kevin Kelly has been a pioneering priest and theologian, nurturing a compassionate approach to Catholic morality from the 1960s down to the present day. In his groundbreaking academic and pastoral work, he has tackled some of the most pressing issues facing the Church today – human conscience, HIV/AIDS, divorce and second marriage, bioethics, sexual ethics and, of course, pastoral theology in general. Kevin is undoubtedly one of the most influential experts in ethics of his generation. He has transformed the way in which Catholics approach moral dilemmas, always bringing human sensitivity and pastoral realism to those in difficult situations.

After formative years at the Upholland Senior Seminary, Lancashire, where he would later return to work, Kevin was further educated at Fribourg University, Switzerland and at the Gregorianum University, Rome. He enjoyed the former much more than the latter. This provides much insight into Kevin's character, theology and ministry itself, for it was at Fribourg that he completed a doctorate in moral theology and in Rome he gained a licentiate in canon law! The author of seven books and well over 100 articles and chapters elsewhere, he has worked tirelessly in urban parishes and academic settings alike, from the very outset of his priestly calling.

He began his academic career at St Joseph's Seminary, Upholland (1965–75), during which time he also served as a visiting lecturer at Manchester University, looking after the students of the late, great Ronald Preston, no less, and further honing his ecumenical vision and commitment. Kevin embarked upon that tireless combination of being an academic moral theologian at one and the same time as being a pastor at the 'coalface' when he was appointed to serve as assistant priest at St Clare's Parish in Liverpool from 1963 to 1965.

In 1975 Kevin took on the enormous task of being the founding director of the Upholland Institute, a centre and professional team for adult Christian education and in-service training for clergy. In this role he initiated pioneering educational and formational programmes, and the staff and students there may not have realized just how privileged they were, as Kevin would bring over visiting lecturers to speak to them of the calibre of Bernard Häring and Charles Curran. Under Kevin's leadership, this institute was something unique and very much an attempt to live out the spirit of the teaching of Vatican II. As his close friend Sr Mary McCallion writes, 'these insights opened up a new vision of the role of the laity in the mission of the Church. From the very beginning, therefore, Kevin saw it as vital to involve the laity, women and men, in a variety of ways and to use their skills, expertise and commitment to promote renewal.' Rumour has it that it became as legendary for its social activities as it did for its educational and formational ones!

In 1980 Kevin was a Visiting Fellow at St Edmund's College, Cambridge University, where pressing pastoral and ethical questions concerning divorce and second marriage preoccupied much of his research. During this time he also embarked on a tour of countries where major ethical challenges were being responded to through grass-roots activism and the newly emerged theologies of liberation. His travels took him to India, the Philippines and Peru. Kevin went out to learn about the experiences of people living amongst the harshest challenges of the times. Again, this was characteristic both of the man and of his methodology.

Kevin then played a leading role in the experimental 'Team Ministry' that was developed in the new town of Skelmersdale, serving from 1981 to 1985. The 'Thatcher Years' of UK government were pressing times for the northern regions of England in particular. And the early optimism that followed the founding of this new town soon turned to harsher realities for many in this part of the country. This innovative, dynamic and yet most challenging appointment left Kevin with many ideas he wished to explore in those hours of the week he gave over to his continuing academic studies. These questions pursued him so much that he eventually took leave to take up a research fellowship at Queen's College, Birmingham, where he completed his pioneering book on bioethics (1985–86).

Kevin did not put his pastoral ministry on hold for very long at all, and he was back in parish ministry at Our Lady's, Eldon Street in inner-city Liverpool as soon as 1986, continuing there until 1998. Again this brought him many rich experiences, and he lived through some of the toughest years for the city, and stood with the local community as they fought for self-determination and decent community facilities.

This full-time ministry was actually carried out in only half of Kevin's 'real' time, as he soon began a regular commute to London, where he had been asked to teach a 'few hours a week' at Heythrop College, the specialist theology and philosophy college of the University of London, by Jack Mahoney. Jack very soon after moved on to an elevated calling himself, at King's College in the same university, and Kevin found himself covering much of the moral theology at Heythrop and utilizing his train journeys to great effect as a makeshift study. Kevin continued this bi-locatory dual existence from 1986 until 1993. A close friend, Sr Liz Stinson, sums up his enormous dedication to both sides of that existence when she recalls that parish: 'I saw there how utterly devoted he was to the people of the parish and especially to the sick and the bereaved families, despite having to commute to Heythrop several days a week, for much of his time there. They still talk about him and have never stopped "wanting him back".'

Kevin's most recent educational attachments were at Liverpool Hope University, first of all as a part-time lecturer in Christian ethics at its former incarnation as the Liverpool Institute of Higher Education between 1993 and 1994. He then returned when it became a university college to be senior research fellow (again part-time) between 1996 and 1998. Finally, he was elevated to emeritus senior research fellow status in 1998. Kevin always says that he thinks 'emeritus means past it', but anyone who has seen how he has energetically remained involved in the life of that university community – taking part in numerous educational, research and pastoral initiatives, continuing to travel into the office he shares with John Elford for at least one or two days each week – will know that, in Kevin's case, 'emeritus' certainly does not mean 'past it' in the slightest shape or form! He has been a great friend, mentor and supportive colleague to so many of the staff and students in Liverpool and, of course, he often combines his trips into the university with visits to his many, many friends in the communities of Notre Dame de Namur who live on both sides of the Woolton Road, by the campus.

Kevin Kelly has contributed to research initiatives, conferences and international gatherings on almost every continent of the world. His researches and pastoral antennae have also taken him on numerous further visits to places such as the United States, Canada, Ireland and Continental Europe. In 1967, he was a co-founding member of the Association of Teachers of Moral Theology which thrives as a uniquely hospitable professional and supportive association, not least of all due to Kevin's continued support and involvement, to this day. In 1995, Kevin visited Thailand and the Philippines, taking part in an Asian theological consultation on the challenges of HIV/AIDS, and interviewing many people in connection with research for his forthcoming book on the subject, particularly to inform his reflections on the impact of these conditions upon women and upon how the position of women in society exacerbated the dilemmas posed by HIV/AIDS. In 1997, Kevin was also a co-founding member of the International Catholic Theological Coalition for HIV/AIDS Prevention, and in 1999 he spent the summer in Zimbabwe and Zambia, helping to run two National Winter Schools in the former which sought to educate people on the moral and pastoral issues concerning the care of those whose lives are affected by HIV/AIDS. Whilst there, he sought out further experiential 'research' opportunities through visiting partners of the UK Catholic aid agency (CAFOD), responsible for the care of AIDS orphans and also for AIDS home-care initiatives. Africa and the plight of those whose lives have been touched by HIV/AIDS have remained uppermost in Kevin's thoughts and prayers.

His pastoral achievements, however, were yet to take a further turn after his inner-city work and weekly sessions in the 'library on wheels' that the train to and from London became for him. Kevin's doctoral dissertation explored the work of Anglican moral theologians of the seventeenth century, and his ecumenical sensitivity and commitment, as indicated, have been amongst the most constant features of his life and career. Thus it was with great relish (once the joint parish committee had interviewed and accepted him for the job, that is!), that Kevin took up the post as Catholic pastor of the ecumenical Anglican and Roman Catholic Church of St Basil's and All Saints, at Hough Green near Widnes. So much of the daily life, worship, charity work and celebrations here are testimony to the true communion that lies at the heart of the Christian faith. Kevin's ministry here, with each of his Anglican partner priests, has served to enhance the exemplary ecumenical sign that this parish has become for the rest of the churches and the wider society alike.

Thus Kevin has always believed in doing much of his research 'on the ground', whether in the midst of investigations in parish ministry, the enormous challenges presented by HIV/AIDS, or the promise of liberation theology: he has travelled to witness the realities of moral and human dilemmas and to hear the stories of those living in the midst of such challenges. Focusing upon human experience – 'where people are at' because that is where God, also, is to be found – has been the enduring character of Kevin Kelly's work.

One of Kevin's great friends, 'Charlie' to Kevin but the eminent moral theologian and author, editor or co-editor of around 60 books, Charles E. Curran, to the rest of the world, has said the following of his long-time pal: 'Kevin Kelly has played a unique role in contemporary Catholic moral theology by combining the theoretical aspects of the discipline with his own pastoral practice. As we celebrate his stellar accomplishments, we also realise that because of the growing depth and breadth in contemporary moral theology there will probably be no one in the future who will even attempt to do what Kevin has done so well.'

And Joe Harrington, one of Kevin's parishioners, has stated that: 'Kevin is truly a gift sent from heaven. I think I can safely say that anyone who comes into contact with him really believes they are in the presence of a deeply spiritual man who is a credit to the priesthood.' Sister Jane Khin Zaw, a Carmelite nun and dear friend of Kevin's for many years, sums up the feelings of us all when she prays that: 'we ourselves feel enormously privileged to have as our friend such a radiant, loving and lovable example of a priest after Christ's own heart. May his priestly life and ministry, utterly bound up as they are with his *human* life and ministry, continue to bring great blessings to his friends and to all God's people. THANK YOU, Kevin, you are a friend in a million.'

We could go on. But it would not be a Kevin-esque thing to embarrass and name all of those who have told us that Kevin literally transformed their lives. They are, however, many. The tributes for Kevin have literally flooded in. One former friend spoke of how he ministered with great compassion to the terminally ill who were, by and large, unchurched people. Kevin made no judgements, granting them pastoral care and absolution without judgement, she said, for 'everything was the kingdom to him'.

Many people, from all over the world, whose lives Kevin has touched and inspired, have written scholarly essays and tributes about his work and writings, and these were presented to him in the form of a 'Festschrift' – a 'celebration-writing' in his honour, during the weekend's celebrations. You hold those essays, now in final form, in your hands. Liverpool Hope University awarded Kevin an honorary doctorate at its graduation ceremony on 19 July 2007 and, on Friday evening, 9 March, The Centre for the Study of Contemporary Ecclesiology honoured Kevin by awarding him its very first Honorary Fellowship for his services to the Church, to pastoral care, to moral theology, to ecumenism and to the wider community in general.

Indeed, who could possibly hope to put it better than these words from those whose lives Kevin has touched along the way of an extraordinary journey of service, friendship, love and compassion? Kevin Kelly steadfastly believes in the truth of the statement that 'It's great to be alive'.[2] For so many of us, this is a prayer that Kevin's life itself, his tireless ministry, writings and companionship have taught us.

We hope that you enjoy this very special tribute to a deeply special man!

3 June 2007
Feast of St Kevin

Notes

1. Kevin T. Kelly, *Conscience: Dictator or Guide? A Study in Seventeenth-Century English Protestant Moral Theology* (London: Geoffrey Chapman, 1967), p. 188.
2. This was the title of an essay he wrote that was published in an earlier Festschrift in honour of one of his many great friends in Ireland, 'It's Great to be Alive!' in Linda Hogan and Barbara Fitzgerald (eds), *Between Poetry and Politics: Essays in Honour of Enda McDonagh* (Dublin: Columba Press, 2003).

Part One

Issues in Fundamental Moral Theology

1

The Way beyond Civilization:
The Holy Spirit and Moral Theology

Bernard Hoose

In discussing the state of preconciliar moral theology, Norbert Rigali observes that, in the tables of contents and indices of a typical three-volume manual, one finds no mention of 'Jesus' or 'Christ'.[1] He also notes Timothy O'Connell's statement in a book published as late as 1978 that 'in a certain sense, moral theology is not theology at all. It is moral philosophy'.[2] One could, of course, point out that philosophers would not normally incorporate into their work, in quite the same way, all those references to the Bible and teachings of the Magisterium that one often finds in books on moral theology published before or since that date. Nevertheless, it is probably true that many of those books deal, for the most part, with themes that are also dealt with by moral philosophers. One might still claim, of course, that the importance attributed to *agape* in theological works would clearly place them on a different plane from that of philosophical works. Taking up this theme of the centrality of the Christian conviction that God is love and the teaching that Christian life can be summed up in the commands to love God and neighbour, Edward Vacek comments that it would seem odd if theologians were to exhibit any hesitation about exploring the role of love in ethics. Nevertheless, he says, such hesitation is typical. 'Love has *not* been central in most Christian ethics and dogmatic theology.'[3]

Leaving aside Vacek's disturbing judgement about dogmatic theology, we can at least attempt to understand what has been happening in the sphere of moral theology, but first we need to deal with a central question. When a plea was made at the Second Vatican Council for special attention to be given to the development of that discipline, what precisely was meant by the term 'moral theology'? Rigali notes that, before the council, the sphere of interest of moral theology was the obligatory aspects of the commandments and the virtues. Movement in the Christian life beyond those matters, towards perfection, was dealt with by ascetical theology. In effect, two classes of Christians were envisaged. As Rigali puts it, 'moral theology dealt with the lower class and ascetical–mystical theology with the higher class'.[4] Today we tend not to think in terms of two classes. How far moral theology should expand beyond those matters dealt with in the days of the manuals, however, remains a question to be addressed. The arguments of some contributors to the debate about the distinctiveness of Christian ethics could give the impression that there is very little scope for such expansion. Some years ago, however, Josef Fuchs argued that, in the strict sense, morality is not directly related to the rightness of our *behaviour* in this world. Rather, it is directly related to the goodness of the *person*. Activity that is morally right is called 'moral', he says, 'only by analogy to the concept of morality in the strict sense'.[5] Whatever one may feel about Fuchs' attempt to add precision to language here, one thing is clear. He is talking about the deepest level of what most of us refer to as 'morality'. His main concern is salvation. In this sphere Christianity does indeed have a good deal to say that is distinctive. At this level, for instance, we can talk about conversion, the Holy Spirit and the role of love.

Civilization and Evangelization

Preaching the gospel is clearly connected to the themes of conversion and the indwelling Spirit. There is room for debate, however, concerning what precisely is involved in preaching the gospel. When I was seven years of age I had a teacher who adopted a somewhat enthusiastic approach to what she presumably regarded as evangelization. On Monday mornings she habitually interrogated some of the boys in my class with the purpose of ascertaining whether or not they had been to Mass on the preceding Sunday. As I recall things, she questioned them about such matters as the time of the Mass allegedly attended, the colour of the priest's vestments and the content of his homily. All of this was, of course, a tall order for seven-year-olds, but, if my teacher was not satisfied with the answers received from any of the boys interrogated, she caned them. Most of us, one assumes, take a less violent approach to evangelization than my teacher did. There are, however, reasons for thinking that much of what we do in the name of evangelization has little more connection with the Good News than had her interrogation technique. Indeed, although some people are excellent conduits of the gospel, it seems clear that much of what passes for evangelization is little more than a variety of attempts to control the behaviour of other people. Many of them do have a civilizing effect, but nothing more than that.

The word 'civilization' has a number of meanings. Here I am chiefly referring to cultural, moral and intellectual refinement. Although the good effects of such refinement upon our world have been remarkable and considerable, a major problem with it is the oft-stated one that, unless it is accompanied by a true conversion process, it is only skin deep. It might be objected at this point that civilization is linked to the acquisition of virtue and is therefore necessarily deep, for, in acquiring, virtue, one takes on a kind of second nature. Even if this were true (and there would indeed seem to be a case for saying that the truly civilized are virtuous), it would be useful to note Aquinas's assertion that the theological virtue of charity directs the other virtues to its own end.[6] One might take a step further and say that, without charity, even the acquired virtues are, in a sense, lifeless. In reality, however, the situation is likely to be even more problematical. To what extent many of those who have been through a civilizing process are virtuous in any sense is a matter for debate. We have evidence, for example, that, when the restraining effects of the cultural group are relaxed or are not physically present, some people behave in a far from civilized manner. Certain forms of tourism provide ample evidence of this phenomenon.

The main point being made here is that some of what we call evangelization is little more than this skin-deep civilization. When the superficies is scratched, what results can be far worse than the excesses of holidaymakers in Mediterranean seaside resorts. We have seen a good deal of this sort of thing in recent decades as apparently committed Christians have engaged in horrific episodes of ethnic cleansing. I recall that some years ago, a Catholic priest who was a member of a missionary congregation told me that, while he and a number of his colleagues were taking part in an international meeting some years ago, news reached them of one such massacre. Most, if not all, of those who had taken part in the killing spree, it seemed, were Christians – the majority of these being Roman Catholics. A terrible depression settled over their meeting, he told me, and the missionaries found themselves asking: 'What have we done?' In that particular case, they felt that they were in some way responsible because, as I understand things, some of their number had been acting as missionaries in the country concerned for a considerable period. They asked themselves if they had somehow preached the gospel in an inauthentic manner. Their reaction was understandable, and we do well to ask ourselves what might really happen in such cases? Is it that the gospel is watered down by the preachers, or is it that the preachers have completely lost sight of what they should be communicating? Is it that the gospel is preached authentically, but that sin somehow takes over again after reception? Is it that the preachers themselves were merely civilized in the first place and had nothing more than skin-deep civilization to communicate? In any particular case it could, of course, be any one of these or indeed a mixture of several that has occurred. The one thing they all have in common, however, is that they involve the essentials of the gospel either not being seen at all or being lost from sight after initial revelation. The final result in all cases is merely a form of civilization that is easily swept aside, or perhaps even something less than that.

Preaching 'the Way'

It is indeed common for the gospel message to be watered down by either the preacher or the recipients of the preaching. The reported sayings of Jesus about the need for his followers to embrace poverty, for instance, have often been presented (although perhaps less so in recent years) under the heading of an evangelical counsel of perfection for members of religious orders (members of Rigali's higher class), lesser mortals being seen as somehow exempt. It is not at all clear, however, that Jesus intended such a two-tier Christianity. The fact is that *nobody* can serve both God and money.

A similar two-tier vision of things is also evident in some presentations of the much used chapter 13 of First Corinthians – the so-called 'hymn of love'. When this is not being used in a purely sentimental way, it is sometimes presented as an optional extra – something for those extraordinary souls who seek perfection. Closer inspection of the letter, however, reveals that Paul was merely preaching the essential elements of Christianity in that chapter. The Corinthians, or at least many of them, seem not to have latched on to what had earlier been communicated to them about Christianity. There were signs of sexual impropriety and a lack of due consideration for one another. In splitting into factions ('I am for Paul; I am for Peter, I am for Apollos; and I am for Christ') they seem clearly to have missed the

15

point of what they had been told at some earlier stage. In 1 Cor. 12–14, moreover, we learn that they had been making unwise use of gifts of the Holy Spirit, notably the gift of tongues. The problem seems to have been that the gifts were sometimes being used in a way that damaged community. Paul urged the Corinthians to use those gifts that can build up community and to use them precisely to that end.

If Paul had left things thus, he would merely have been urging civilization upon the recipients of his letter, in spite of his reference to gifts of the Holy Spirit. He did not, however, leave things thus. At the end of 1 Cor. 12, we find him telling the Corinthians that he is going to show them a most excellent way. He then begins to talk about an alternative way of being human – in fact, the only way of being *truly* human. An important word in this last sentence of ch. 12 is, in fact, 'way' (in Greek: *hodos*). Metaphorical references to 'the way' in regard to matters religious and moral were, of course, far from unusual in the Greek world. Given their nomadic history, moreover, the concept of the way had rich resonances for the Israelites. In the Old Testament we often find mention of two ways (although both, it should be noted, are sometimes referred to in the plural): the good way(s) and the evil way(s). The good way is variously described as the way of justice, truth, peace, mercy, light and life. In the book of Wisdom, for instance, we find a case of the people straying from the 'way of truth' (*apo hodou aletheias*, Wis. 5.6), while in the book of Proverbs we are presented with instruction on the way of or to life (*hodos zoes*, Prov. 6.23). Various passages in books of the Old Testament describe the way as a following of the law. In Deuteronomy, for instance, Moses tells the people of Israel that they must not stray to right or left of the Lord's commandments. Instead, they should follow the way that God has marked out for them (Deut. 5.32–33). Psalm 119 contains numerous synonyms for the law, one of which is 'way' (*hodos* in the Septuagint, where the psalm is numbered 118).[7] Another instance occurs in the book of Baruch, where we are instructed that God alone knows wisdom, the 'way of understanding', and has communicated it to his people in the law (Bar. 3.37–4.1). When the people follow the way of evil, the way that leads to disasters of various kinds, and, eventually, captivity in Babylon, God sends prophets to call them back to the way of the Lord (Bar. 3.13; Ezra 18.25–32; 33.17–20).[8]

The ways of the Lord, were, first and foremost, those in which God walked. One could thus talk about following in the ways of the Lord, but, in Isaiah, we find mention of God's way or path to his people (Isa. 40.3). This theme is, of course, taken up in all four Gospels with reference to the mission of John the Baptist: 'Prepare the way of the Lord'. (Mt. 3.3; Mk 1.2–3; Lk. 3.4; Jn 1.23). God's destination is the hearts of humans – the heart being not merely the seat of the emotions, but the very core of the personality. People were urged to prepare for the action of God within them, to remove obstacles, so that the Spirit could be their guide, a guide from within. All of this accorded with God's promise, as transmitted through the writings of Jeremiah and Ezekiel. Through Jeremiah, God had promised his people a different heart and a different way (Jer. 32.39), a declaration that is expressed with slightly different imagery in the preceding chapter, where a promise is made that God's law (which, as we have noted, was seen as God's way) will be written on the hearts of the people (Jer. 31.33). Through Ezekiel, moreover, the promise is made that God's breath (which, of course, seen through New Testament eyes, is the Holy Spirit) will be placed in the hearts of God's people and will cause them to walk in God's laws (Ezra 36.27).

Without this indwelling and saving action of the Spirit in the core of his or her personality no one can walk in the way of the Lord (Jn 3.5). The Spirit, however, blows where the Spirit wills. There is therefore no reason to suggest that those who have not been baptized with water will inevitably walk in the way of death. Nevertheless, it is entirely understandable that the expression 'the way' (*he hodos*) is applied to the baptized in the Acts of the Apostles. Thus we learn that, prior to his conversion, Paul (or Saul as he was called in those days) had persecuted the way, and, on the day of his conversion, he had been travelling to Damascus with the intention of arresting any of the way that he could find (Acts 9.2). When he fell to the ground he heard a voice saying: 'I am Jesus whom you are persecuting'. If the way is persecuted, Jesus is persecuted. In fact, Jesus is the way, something that is clearly stated in the Gospel of John: 'I am the Way, and the Truth, and the Life' (Jn 14.6). Later Paul declares that he worships God 'according to the way' (Acts 24.14). Clearly, however, Paul does not see the law as synonymous with the way. In his Letter to the Romans he refers to two ways, one being the way of ruin and misery, and the other being the way of peace (Rom. 3.16–17).[9] A little further on, however, he says that no one will be declared righteous in the sight of God by observing the law (Rom. 3.20). Indeed, as he tells the Galatians, if it were possible to attain righteousness through observance of the law, Christ would have died for nothing (Gal. 2.21). Those whom Paul describes as being of the way, therefore, are clearly not merely observing the law. They are of that way to which he refers at the end of 1 Cor. 12.

What, then, does Paul mean by 'way' when he tells the Corinthians that he is going to show them a most excellent one? Immediately after saying this he bursts into his so-called 'hymn of love'. The way is therefore love (*agape*). God surely did not send Jesus so that he could demonstrate to us the way or ways of God, in order that we might learn by imitation. He is indeed a model, as Paul points out in this same letter (1 Cor. 11.1). No one, however, would be capable of imitating Jesus unless the Spirit dwelt in the core of his or her personality and became the source of his or her activity. God sends his Spirit, who pours the love of God into us (Rom. 5.5). Indeed, the Spirit *is* Love. Christians, however, do not always act under the influence of the Holy Spirit, as is evidenced in the case of the Corinthians themselves. Paul therefore points out that such cooperation is the way. Further on in the same letter, he says: 'Let everything you do be done in love' (1 Cor. 16.14). In short, then, love is the way because God is Love.

Thus far in this chapter I have translated the Greek words *kath hyperbolen* as 'most excellent' ('I am going to show you a most excellent way') and that translation is found in a number of English language versions of the Bible. In the *Traduction Oecumenique de la Bible*, however, the way referred to is described as infinitely superior.[10] Love is not just the greatest of the charisms. It transcends them. A translation of *kath hyperbolen* using words which transcend even the superlative is therefore more than justified. We are not concerned with mere civilization here. We are in a completely different dimension.[11] When Paul says that he is going to show the Corinthians a way, he is in effect saying that he is going to show them *the* way, which, one imagines, had already been indicated to them on at least one previous occasion, but had not been recognized.

17

Moral Theology and 'the Way'

Much has been said and written in recent decades about the distinctiveness or otherwise of Christian ethics. Most of such debate, as one might expect, has been confined to discussion about the rightness and wrongness of acts. If, however, we take up Fuchs's comments about morality being directly related to personal goodness, we find that there is a good deal in Christian moral theology that is distinctive. Personal goodness is all about moving towards authentic humanity, about letting the monsters that I have created die, and about the new me emerging, all under the influence of the Spirit. What we are discussing, however, is not a solitary search for perfection, and it is in this regard that some comments of Kevin Kelly prove to be insightful. Referring to Jesus's statement that he has come to call not the just but sinners (Mt. 9.13), Kelly notes that these words 'suggest our being called out from our sinfulness, rather than our attempting to live some kind of perfect life free from sin. They would seem to imply that our sinfulness is actually the starting point for our spirituality.'[12]

The process thus begun lasts throughout our lives on earth.[13] Yves Congar sees this in the context of the 'already' but 'not yet' of salvation. 'In Pauline terms,' he says, 'it is the struggle between the Spirit and the flesh.'[14] It also involves other people. In Kelly's vision of things, growth out of sin is not something that one achieves on one's own for oneself alone:

> For instance, where my woundedness is relational, the growth in healing must necessarily be relational too. Likewise, where my woundedness goes back to structural roots, growth towards healing may well demand of me some kind of personal involvement in working for structural reform.[15]

The way of love could not be otherwise. It is a journeying together, on a rough road, in and with the Spirit. A moral theology that teaches less than this is in danger of being only a moral philosophy that may or may not have a civilizing influence upon those who hear its message. Such a moral theology may be declared in the tongues of men and of angels, but, if it does not speak of the way, it may bear some resemblance to Paul's empty-sounding gong or clanging cymbal. The same is true of any loveless attempts at civilization. As Pope John Paul II noted, 'true development must be based on the love of God and neighbour, and must help to promote the relationships between individuals and society. This is the "civilization of love" of which Paul VI often spoke.'[16]

Notes

1. Norbert Rigali, 'On Theology of the Christian Life', in James Keating (ed.), *Moral Theology: New Directions and Fundamental Issues* (Mahwah: Paulist Press, 2004), pp. 3–23 (4). Bernard Häring's somewhat revolutionary work *The Law of Christ* does not fit into this 'typical' category.
2. Rigali, 'On Theology of the Christian Life'. See Timothy E. O'Connell, *Principles for a Catholic Morality* (New York: Seabury Press, 1978), p. 40. O'Connell goes on to say that we use the term 'moral theology' because our ethics are generated within the Christian community; we make use of insights

in our tradition; our starting point is a 'fundamentally Christian vision of human beings and their world' (*ibid.*, p. 41).

3. Edward Collins Vacek, *Love, Human and Divine: The Heart of Christian Ethics* (Washington, DC: Georgetown University Press, 1994), p. xiii.

4. Rigali, 'On Theology', p. 7. A similar point is made by William C. Spohn. Catholic moral theology, which was based on natural law, he writes, emphasized moral standards and values shared by Christians and non-Christians, and 'largely ignored Jesus Christ as God's gift that shapes a distinctive way of life. That aspect of faith was considered in "ascetical" or "mystical theology" and was thought to have little impact on the rules and virtues that guide ordinary life' (William C. Spohn, 'Jesus and Moral Theology' in James Keating, *Moral Theology*, pp. 24–42 [24]).

5. Josef Fuchs, *Christian Ethics in a Secular Arena* (Washington, DC: Georgetown University Press, 1984), p. 63.

6. Thomas Aquinas, *Summa theologiae*, 2a2ae. 23, 8.

7. See, for instance, Ps. 119.1–5, 32.

8. See also Jer. 5.4–6.

9. They appear in a series of quotations from several psalms and Isaiah.

10. *Et de plus, je vais vous indiquer une voie infiniment supérieure.*

11. See also Giuseppe Barbaglio, who comments that *kath hyperbolen* has a superlative value, and is used to indicate a way that transcends all others (*La Prima Lettera ai Corinzi* [Bologna, Edizioni Dehoniane, 1996], p. 700, n. 264).

12. Kevin T. Kelly, *From a Parish Base: Essays in Moral and Pastoral Theology* (London: Darton, Longman and Todd, 1999), p. 157.

13. *Ibid.*

14. *En termes pauliniens, c'est la lutte entre l'Esprit et la chair* (Yves Congar, *Esprit de l'Homme, Esprit de Dieu* [Paris: Les Editions du Cerf, 1983], p. 44).

15. Kelly, *From a Parish Base*, p. 160. See also Congar, *Esprit de l'Homme*, p. 45.

16. John Paul II, Encyclical Letter *Sollicitudo rei socialis* (1987), 33.

2

The World and Moral Theology

Judith Merkle

There is perhaps no category of thought more challenging in the field of Christian ethics than the subject of the world. Deep in the intuitions of the Christian life is a basic paradox. One is called to live authentically in this world, yet also called to follow Jesus whose 'kingdom was not of this world'. How can one be faithful, and live in the tension of being worldly and other-worldly in the right balance?

This ambiguity is increased when we ask what clues the world as we find it reveals to us about the meaning of faithfulness in our lives. In this chapter I want to explore five 'moments' in the history of Christian thought which revisit this tension in Christian morality, to ask how they illumine the current quest to be faithful in our Christian commitment in the world today.

The Greek Moment

The world, or the totality around us, was for the Greeks something well-ordered and beautiful. For them, the order of human life, individual or social, was patterned on the order of the world.[1] While Plato saw the sensible world as only the image of a true world accessible to the spirit, Aristotle saw nature as the principle of all things. The world was unconscious of nature, but God guaranteed the order of all things in the cosmos through his full self-consciousness. For the Greeks, cosmology not anthropology was the more fundamental of the sciences.[2] The perpetual revolutions of the stars in the universe more closely imaged the immutability of God than men and women. The Stoics saw God as the all-pervading reason (*logos*), the soul of the world, making his providence the law of the universe. The world for the Greeks is the ultimate divine space.

Yet, the Gnostics did not share this great appreciation for objective sensible reality. They focused on 'another world', one of the spirit, apart from the laws of nature, above the vicissitudes of early life. Such a world was above injustices. It was more resilient than the drives and decay of the body and its vulnerability to sickness and death. Since matter threatened the world, flight from the body and the sensible world became the road to salvation, or the life of the soul. Introspection rather than involvement in this world was emphasized as the key to new life. The core ambiguity in Greek thought regarding the world contributed to

Christian ambivalence regarding embrace of the world and flight from the world in spirituality and morality.

The Christian Moment

The early Christians were grounded in the Jewish sense of a created world. Gen. 1.31 named the world as non-divine but good. God, who lives beyond the world, guarantees its consistency. Creation is God's first saving deed which is continued in the covenant, and the election of key figures of the Hebrew Scriptures. The world of human beings and the cosmos is good, but it is also fallen creation. Christians recognized Jesus Christ as the light of this world. While the world is fully redeemed, it remains the realm of the evil one. Humankind's ambivalent experience of the world is mirrored in New Testament thought.

Paul presents a world where sin reigns as a power.[3] While created good, the world through sin has turned away from God. The individual person cannot escape this (Rom. 5–8). Insofar as the world is the context of the human condition, it is marked by the sin of the world.[4] Jesus came from another realm to be the light of the world and to save it (Jn 3.17). The cross of Jesus discloses the evil of the world, as well as the boundless absolute love of God for the world. Since the world was accepted by God in Jesus Christ; this brought a new age to the world. Christians are not to flee the world. They are to live in a world which is both open to and distant from God's acceptance of it. They are to use the things of this world and recognize the goodness of creation, yet also to bear in mind that the world is passing away.

St Augustine tried to synthesize the positive and negative attitudes towards the world which remained in both Christian and Greek thought. Augustine thought better of the world than the Greeks who admired the structure and order of the world, but who viewed its matter as deficient. Augustine knew the world was created by God and was in itself good. Human persons were not just to fit into the world as a niche in the cosmic order. They were to be persons before the face of God. The world was important, but it was more important to live in God, one's supreme good. This was done through faith, hope and love. Augustine recognized that God's creation of the material world gave it beauty and order. However, for him this order was perceived in contrasts.

Augustine's world was comprised of three dimensions: the world, which was external; the human soul; and that above the soul and in its depths, God.[5] The three existed in dynamic tension. The cosmos itself was divided into two realities, the city of God and the city of the earth. The *saeculum* is the realm in which the carriers of the two cities are intertwined.[6] It is important to note that, for Augustine, the earthly city has two dimensions, and is not limited solely to sinful humanity. On the one hand, it is the world which is profane and rejects God. It is the realm of the impious and reprobate. On the other hand, the earthly city is simply the material world. It is the actual space of life, the empirical city where good and bad mix. The earthly city and its institutions have a moral dimension; they can be better or worse in their service of human life. The care of the *saeculum*, or the realm in which the two cities intertwine, thus has importance for both the believer and the non-believer. It is the real world in which all have to live. Augustine's vision of the two cities both validates the institutions and activities of the earthly city and relativizes their importance and purpose. Both aspects of his synthesis have an impact on the understanding of Christian faithfulness..

The institutions of the earthly city are validated as remaining intact until the end of the world (Rom. 13). They are not morally neutral. Augustine holds that societies, institutions and practices are incapable of salvation or damnation, the realm of the heavenly city.[7] Because human intentionality marks all morality, impersonal institutions have no eschatological destiny, no intentions which can be directed to ultimate ends. Yet, shared meanings and consensus on a value system remain essential features of a society, and form part of what the heavenly city recognizes, sanctions and fosters for its own ultimate purpose, the true worship of the one God.[8] For Augustine, the only true *res publica* based on the only true justice is the heavenly city. The values to which human groups are committed in this way are relativized by this ultimate reality, but not invalidated. For practices, customs and institutions form a complex which shapes and conditions human action and behaviour, even though they do not determine it.[9] Thus they have a bearing on human welfare and ultimately on the options available to humans to work out their salvation. To this degree, they reflect a consensus which promotes response to salvation or negates it.

It is impossible, given Augustine's synthesis, to relate every aspect of the world directly to the sacred, even though he holds all creation is good. He states: 'In truth, these two Cities are entangled together in this world, and intermixed until the last judgment effect their separation.'[10] The *saeculum*, or the secular, the shared space in which Christian and non-Christian both have a stake, retains its own autonomy and validity in this ambiguity. It is not a third city between the earthly and the heavenly, rather their mixed, intertwined state is real life. This middle ground between the sacred and the profane can neither be included in the sacred, by Christians or non-Christians, nor repudiated as profane and demonic. Political institutions, social practices and customs can be directed either to the enjoyment of eternal peace by members of the heavenly city or wrongly directed to lesser goods, the earthly city. Between the two exists a sliding scale of better and worse. Augustine claims that if you want to discover the character of any people, you have only to observe what they love.[11] Political institutions, social practices and customs, even of non-Christian origin, can foster proper loves. In this they have value.[12] Augustine validates the world by noting the importance of these institutions in human life.

Augustine's world was one of great pluralism.[13] However, it turned into the sacral society of the Middle Ages or Christendom. An ascetic impulse fostered an other-worldly emphasis in Christian spirituality. The political transformation in Western Europe led to a society which was organized around religion in the form of the Church. The Church in this sense swallowed up the world. Instead of the tension in Augustine's world between those inside and outside the Church, the Middle Ages was a time when the conversion process of the Christian, who was to become perfect, was stressed.[14] Christianity was endangered by becoming too closely identified with the culture and social structure of its social matrix. The danger to the Christian was a spirituality which embraced 'flight from the world' yet had to face the inevitability of life in this world.[15] Physical withdrawal from the world became a symbol of the division between the perfect and the imperfect spiritually. The world lost ground as a viable place of Christian faithfulness, while Christendom was viewed by some as the growing together of the heavenly and earthly cities. The eschatological 'gap' between Christ's lordship and the world narrowed, in the paradoxical situation of the devaluing of the world.

However, the Middle Ages also held the tensions of this impossible synthesis. Aquinas opened the door to the independence of secular reason to the degree that 'the philosopher', Aristotle, is treated in his work as an authority with his own underivable principles.[16] Reason entered that incomplete but real space of human well-being which both the believer and the unbeliever had an interest in preserving. The state gradually emerged as independent from the Church. Nature itself became a field for human experimentation, made possible by its freedom from a quasi-mystical status of magic and taboos. Nature created by God was free to have its own laws which opened it up to human investigation and study.

As modern times dawned, the image of how the human person gained access to God shifted. One no longer had to sit passively seeking God by observing the movement from cause to effect, as the only faithful stance. Rather, human action changed nature, the world and lives in it. However, discerning how the world and its transformation entered into Christian faithfulness remained a question. How should the human person hold in balance both the obligation to become perfect through love and work and to transform the conditions by which others do the same, while also acknowledging one's finitude before the world?[17] Symbolized by the inevitability of death itself as a signature of human identity, the Christian community had to ask how their growing consciousness of freedom before this world called them to be both this worldly and other worldly. How were they to follow Christ in this world and through this world, and also to surrender to Christ in love and hope, whose promise of a kingdom not of this world was only his to fulfil?

The Moment of Modernity

For the theologian Reinhold Niebuhr, the problem of faithfulness in the Christian life is inextricably tied to the process of human freedom before the world. The problem of sin, or of lack of faithfulness, resided for Niebuhr, not in the world as we find it, or society, but rather in the contradictions within the human person. Niebuhr, living in the disillusionment between the World Wars, reflected on a new state of humankind before the world which had been developing since the Enlightenment. Human nature is unique in that it can envision new possibilities and achieve them in this world. However, this very freedom is prone to entertain the illusion that the human person is not limited, but rather is self-sufficient.

Human freedom has both creative and destructive elements which cannot be separated. He remarks:

> The two are inextricably bound together by reason of man being anxious both to realize his unlimited possibilities and to overcome and to hide the dependent and contingent character of his existence.[18]

When the person feels the power of the creative potential of being human in this world, they can also deny the contingent character of human existence in pride and self-love. Another response is to ignore the moral call of this creative power before the world. The person escapes from this freedom in sensuality.[19]

Pride or sensuality is involved in every human act. One falls into pride when one seeks to raise one's contingent life to unconditioned significance. One falls into sensuality to escape from the freedom and possibilities of the human spirit by becoming lost in the detailed processes, activities and lesser interests of life. The result is that human beings have unlimited devotion to limited values and apathy towards what is truly good, including the social good, the call to transform the world.[20] Human sinfulness is more than a sheer act of defiance of God. Sin involves blindness to limitation. Sin is the deception that covers up the insecurity and anxiety people feel as they stand before the potentials of their freedom vis-à-vis this world. This deception inevitability leads to actions that stretch human power beyond its limits.[21]

Since the person stands before God in the paradoxical situation of freedom and finiteness, the person never really knows the limits of his or her possibilities. Only a sense of God and God's will can provide a boundary where freedom can find a balance between its drive for self-transcendence and its inherent creatureliness.[22] Niebuhr's anthropological turn places the tension of Augustine's two kingdoms in the internal spirit of the person vis-à-vis this world. However, it leaves unanswered the paradox of faithfulness in this world.

For Niebuhr, Christian faithfulness is an impossible ideal, one taken on in faith and love, but never accomplished. Since it is impossible to achieve, it is better to focus on strategies to live with its challenge. He debates with his brother H. Richard Niebuhr, who sees faithfulness in a more other-worldly manner. It depends on the disinterestedness of love which trusts in God, and seeks pure intentions and methods, in the many limiting situations which frame modern living.[23] Reinhold is more this-worldly in his approach, and urges concrete action. Faithfulness involves the humble acknowledgement that we are never pure, and conflict and coercion are inevitable in face of the evil of this world. The kingdom of pure love in society is always partially expressed, and imperfectly practised. The cross of modern living is the willingness to invest in societal change even though imperfect results may follow. In Reinhold Niebuhr's words, 'love may qualify the social struggle of history but it will never abolish it, and those who make the attempt to bring society under the domination of perfect love will die on the Cross.'[24]

Reinhold Niebuhr's world emerged through the processes of modernity which challenged both the human capacity to know the world as it is, and to experience its 'givenness' as a normative element in the quest for faithfulness. The world of nature of the Greeks was now the world of culture, the world as we find it, plus the human element of re-making it. However the man-made world of technology, forces of domination and lost enchantments, appeared as threatening as the untamed nature appeared to primitive people. What did it mean to be faithful in a world where history recounted no longer the cyclic flow of the inevitable, but the consequences of the chosen?

The Moment of Vatican II

Pope John XXIII's vision of the value of this world liberated the Church from a Catholic cultural ghetto created as a retreat from modernity. The search for an enclave of faithfulness apart from this world ended.[25] Acknowledgement of the secular as an autonomous realm entered in a new way into Catholic spirituality. Encouragement to invest rather than withdraw from the world as a measure of discipleship caused members of the Church to re-examine priorities and strategies for expressing faithfulness. In contrast to the suspicion in the pre-Vatican II Church of developments in science, technology and modes of social organization associated with the modern world, the documents of Vatican II reflect an appreciation for the changes which were sweeping the world. The Church recognized the expansion of human capacities to act. There was a deepening confidence that humankind could face the challenges of the time through new forms of social and political organization.[26] These insights also energized the Church to face the possibilities of this new context.

However, the document on the Church in the Modern World acknowledged in its introductory paragraphs the ambiguous character of life in the modern world:

> Never has the human race enjoyed such an abundance of wealth, resources and economic power, and yet a huge proportion of the world's citizens are still tormented by hunger and poverty, while countless numbers suffer from total illiteracy ... Political, social, economic, racial and ideological disputes still continue bitterly, and with them the peril of a war which would reduce everything to ashes ... Finally, man painstakingly searches for a better world, without working with equal zeal for the betterment of his own spirit.[27]

Appreciation for the expansion of human agency at the heart of great changes sweeping the world was tempered by insight into misery which could be avoided with other priorities and modes of organizing human life. The 'peace' which for Augustine was the order and tranquillity sought in human life had to be found again in a new age of human agency and massive inequities marking global progress.[28] Concomitantly, how to take responsibility for this new context posed a new challenge to visions of Christian faithfulness.

Because of massive cultural changes, in its Decree on Priestly Formation, the council called for a renewal in the Catholic Church in the area of moral theology. It stated: 'Special care should be given to the perfecting of moral theology. Its scientific presentations should draw more fully on the teaching of Holy Scripture and should throw light upon the exalted vocation of the faithful in Christ and their obligation to bring forth fruit in charity for the life of the world.'[29] Bernard Häring's major work, *Free and Faithful in Christ* identified the acceptance of responsibility for creative freedom to love in fidelity to Christ as the starting point of the Christian life.[30] Moral theology's concern is not only with decision-making or with discrete acts, according to Häring. 'Its basic task and purpose is to gain right vision, to assess the main perspectives, and to present those truths and values which should bear upon decisions to be made before God.'[31] Freedom in moral theology, however, is always freedom in a particular context, a freedom in this world. The Christian therefore receives direction for moral decisions by attending to the Word of God, and in light of God's Word, reads the signs of the times.

The Church's social tradition, both in its social encyclicals and in the theological voices of Christians at the margins of global progress, illumined this reading of the signs of the times. A more just and fully human development was 'another name for peace'.[32] The moral challenge of Augustine's *saeculum*, that world of the human well-being that both the believer and non-believer share, was given the normative vision of the *humanum*, the dignity of the human person.

God's kingdom is ultimately God's final action at the end of time. However, in the in-between times, Christians are called to look at decisions in the social-political order not just expediently but in terms of their ultimate meaning for the other. In this way, the kingdom also enters into time to shape it. Pope John Paul II offered a measuring-stick of Christian faithfulness in an ambiguous world through the humanistic criterion. This is a standard for evaluating and choosing between social systems, institutional reforms or legal reforms in terms of how they enhance human dignity. In his words, the humanistic criterion is:

> The measure in which each system is really capable of reducing, restraining and eliminating as far as possible the various forms of exploitation of man and of ensuring for him, through work, not only the just distribution of the indispensable material goods, but also a participation, in keeping with his dignity, in the whole process of production and in the social life that grows up around the process.[33]

The coming of the kingdom in the *saeculum* is always partial and incomplete. In this sense the other-worldly dimension of Christian spirituality remains intact in the Christian imagination. However, the lack of ultimacy of the *saeculum* did not reduce the urgency of the quality of its decisions. To be a faithful Christian in an increasingly interdependent world, the maxim to do good and avoid evil was not enough. One had to search out how to embrace responsibility for the 'other' in a manner that respects the other and his or her good as carrying the face of one's own moral obligation.

The Postmodern Moment and the Challenge of Liberation

The challenge of Vatican II was to embrace the world without submitting to a false incarnational optimism. The Church had to take stock of how the world has not yet been 'divinized'. The eagerness to embrace the world and interpret salvation history itself as the growing divinization of the world by thinkers such as Teilhard de Chardin was tempered by voices from the margins. These lives were marked, not by the inevitable progress of the developmentalist mentality of the 1960s, but by situations of 'institutionalized violence'.[34]

Chardin saw the cosmos as a process which mirrors the inner life of God. Despite its pain, failure and apparent absurdities, all life is developmental and moving in a process of cosmogenesis. Chardin saw the universe as a cosmos or whole developing in a precise direction. It goes from the Alpha point to the Omega point, under the ever-present care of God, the creator and preserver.[35] However, as positive and inviting as Chardin's view of the world was, many used his optimism as a theological foundation for prevailing cultural views which overstated just how well the world was progressing. They drew an analogy between continuous evolutionary process in nature and economic, social and political systems in the *saeculum*. What for Chardin was a process which had to be discerned, became for others a belief in a mechanical vision of progress in this world which was inevitable and divinely sanctioned. Such an overly optimistic view of the international community understated the conflict and interests protected by the status quo and the countervailing histories of women, the poor, minorities and whole continents left out of the post-World War II prosperity experienced in First World countries. Such visions lost ground in the modern outlook as both postmodern and liberation thinkers held the inconsistencies of human progress and the intractability of human suffering before the Christian imagination.

Experience of massive cultural change in the *saeculum*, the world shared by believer and non-believer alike, raised questions of faith for the believer. Christians pondered the future of faith itself and the meaning of moral faithfulness. How was one to be faithful in this new world? How was one to pass on faith to new generations? Moral theology had long focused on faithfulness through the analysis of individual human acts in relation to God as humanity's ultimate end. Vatican II shifted to a more biblically based morality which stressed the following of Christ in the modern world. What can and should Christ mean, if anything, in the moral lives of Christians? Systematic theology probed the penetrating consequences of these questions in its own field of enquiry. How does the quest for emancipation, in all its forms, relate to the Christian life? In the words of Walter Kasper, 'it is a fundamental question for modern Christology to decide the relation between redemption understood in a Christian perspective and emancipation understood as the modern age understands it.'[36]

These questions were coupled by even more troubling ones surrounding the significance of human agency, its relevance to faith, and even to knowledge of God. Those from the Third World, for whom little movement seemed possible in the North–South divide, asked: 'What possibilities remain for Christian faith if Christians have no possibilities of changing their history?'[37] What is the meaning of Christian freedom if people cannot be free; have no concrete options, before the conditions of their lives?[38] Practices of Christian asceticism were questioned regarding their significance for the order of this world. Asian theologian Aloysius Pieris comments regarding voluntary poverty: 'the few who renounce their possessions are not "founded and rooted in Christ Jesus" if the many who have no possessions to renounce are not the beneficiaries of that renunciation.'[39] The debate ensued as to the nature of Christian spirituality. What part is the practical conclusion of theology and what part is the radical involvement with the poor and oppressed? Does one know and unite with Jesus Christ through faith seeking understanding or by following Jesus as the way, especially the way of the cross, in involvement in social and political change in this world?

The impact of modern society on the process of evangelization was profound, raising questions regarding the meaning of Christian faithfulness in the handing on of the gospel. Since influences on people's receptivity for faith were so different from pre-modern times, a type of 'shaping of culture' was imperative for believers. John Paul II alerted the Church to a world situation characterized by a 'culture of life' and a 'culture of death'. 'We find ourselves not only "faced with" but necessarily "in the midst of" this conflict.'[40] Here it is not enough simply to analyze the world or flee it in search of moral faithfulness. Rather, the future of the believing community depends on discernment and action that can actually mould cultural reality. Christian faithfulness is marked in the *saeculum*, the world both believers and non-believers share, by a sense of transcendence and co-penetration on the part of believers and the Church.[41]

The Church continually reiterated that growth of this world into God's kingdom is not a progressive development, nor arrived at solely through the modern theories of human power over nature, evolutionary progress, science and technology, or even modern liberal rights.[42] Rather, it is a process often marked by radical contradictions, violent transformations and death–resurrection experiences. Latin American theologian Jon Sobrino terms this as *epistemological rupture* – scripturally founded in the 'transcendence of the crucified God'.[43] Others, embedded in First World culture, stress that a non-conflictual encounter between faith and modernity is impossible in Christian faithfulness.[44] The encounter of God and humanity – the interplay of grace and liberty – is seen as the obligation to use all human potentialities to anticipate the kingdom, which nevertheless remains God's gratuitous gift. What is involved is not a passive solidarity with the poor but also a dynamic participation in their struggle for full humanity. What is called for is not a self-righteous denunciation of modernity but a transformative influence on aspects of its culture which do not serve the *humanum*.[45]

The path to Christian faithfulness which takes the *saeculum* seriously is one of solidarity, for John Paul II. Solidarity is 'a firm and persevering determination' to commit oneself 'to the common good; that is to say to the good of all and of each individual because we are all really responsible for all'.[46] Solidarity checks individualism, desire for profit, thirst for power, those forces which ignore the fundamental equality of all and the purpose of creation and the goods of the earth. These are more than destructive personal attitudes; they are structures of sin that reside in cultural visions of what it means to be an adequate human being. John Paul II sees these structures as rooted in personal sin and linked to the acts of individuals who socially reproduce them and make them difficult to remove.[47]

The thirst for power and the desire for profit 'at any price' make human attitudes absolute in a manner that is really religious in nature, argued the pope. They are a form of idolatry. To see them as human short-sightedness does not grasp their depth.[48] He remarks that 'hidden behind certain decisions, apparently inspired only by economics or politics, are real forms of idolatry: of money, ideology, class, technology.'[49]

If that which blocks development is not just inadequate theories or structures for human flourishing but human sin itself, genuine development requires a conversion. Development is more than economic; it includes the trajectory of human growth towards otherness and depth. For Christians, this process is integral to the meaning of Christian faithfulness in the modern world. It is a call to conversion on a moral, affective, intellectual and religious level. 'This conversion specifically entails a relationship to God, to the sin committed, to its consequences and hence to one's neighbour, either an individual or a community.'[50] For our purposes, it is important to note that the spiritual conversion is not just an interior one. It has concrete manifestations in the individual and in society. A sign of conversion is a growing awareness of interdependence among individuals and nations and evidence that people 'care' about injustices and violations across the world.[51] Such conversion is also linked to a responsible use of human agency. The spiritual path of solidarity is reflected in a new imagination that creates systems that are more interdependent in economic, cultural, political and religious ways. These moral changes reflect a deeper growth in the spiritual path of solidarity. Finally for the Christian, living the virtue of solidarity has a political–mystical dimension: it gives one access to God. As we find worth in our neighbour, respond to her or him as 'other', we find God. The bonds formed in this way are deeper than the natural or human bonds we hope bind the world.[52] These are the bonds of communion. Augustine might recognize this communion as that mix of the heavenly and earthly city, one that requires the structures of a healthy *saeculum* but also is dependent on that gift of faith, hope and love which is only God's to give.

Conclusion

Johannes Metz in his *Theology of the World* argues that the history of the person of Jesus Christ illuminates for us the question of this essay.[53] How does one follow Jesus Christ faithfully living in the tension of being worldly and other-worldly in the right balance?

Jesus accepted the world in the 'form of a servant' (Phil. 2.6–11). His death was accepted, an exposure to the fate which came to him from the outside. His life and mission involved both activity and the passivity of obedience before that which was contradictory. The wholeness of Christ did not protect him from human suffering and paradox. In his humanity Christ fully engages and accepts the world, but in its distance from God. His embrace of the world changed the world and its possibilities, but the world remained different from God, and not completely integrated and transparent. Christ in this sense revealed the transcendent God, not the God of the Greeks who was conceived more as a world principle or kind of cosmic reason and cosmic law. Rather God being God lets the world be the world. For the Christian, this means that the pursuit of God in this world follows the path of the cross, as no matter how many transformations the world receives through human ingenuity, the world remains the world, and other than God. Its capacity to resist and subvert the embrace of God remains. Metz puts it this way:

> With the Father's acceptance of the world in Jesus Christ we have the radical and original setting-free of the world, its own authentic being, its own clear, non-divine reality. This process operates in history on the basis of the modern secularization of the world. The world is now universally given over to what the Incarnation bestows upon it in a supreme way: secularity.[54]

The historical course of this process of engagement with secularity or the *saeculum* is not free from ambiguity. The human propensity for evil grows alongside its real progress.[55] The prophetic call of Micah 'to act justly, to love tenderly and to walk humbly with God' (Mic. 6.8) reminds Christians that faithfulness is neither a self-initiated project nor a flight from this world. Rather, Christians affirm that God gives a future to all the fragments of love and meaning they seek to bring into the world, even if it appears that their efforts are like footprints on a sandy shore, easily swept away by the currents of more powerful forces among them.

As they voice a 'no' to the world as they find it, and seek to build a 'yes' of a better *saeculum*, Christians take on the cross.[56] This is not the cross found only in one's own life, but the cross embraced for the sake of the others. Only love makes the cross possible, and sustains it in its meaning.[57] Trust is required to confront evil, sustain those who suffer and draw near to those who are vulnerable in this world.[58] Without it there is no entrance into the dynamism of hope and investment which marks Christian faithfulness in this world.

The cross is involved not only in the use of power for the good in this modern age of science and technology, arms and communications, but also when humans are impotent in the face of suffering. The choice which measures faithfulness is whether to turn to God in hope and trust and continued faithful investment, or to turn away. It was a characteristic of the ministry of Jesus that he invited people beyond the externals of his various healings to its source, relationship with God. Every miracle in the gospel required a change of heart. The problem in Nazareth was that people were asking for miracles which required no change of heart, no deeper fellowship with God. Today technical solutions to the world's problems are not enough without the heart and will which reflect change in the human spirit.

The meaning of the paschal journey in Christian life has too often been concentrated in the symbol of the cross taken out of context and raised up in an isolation that glorifies suffering and death for its own sake. This false asceticism plagues the Church at various times and leads to other-worldly spirituality which is non-productive for the world. The cross, on the other hand, must be seen in conjunction with Jesus's relationship with God as the defining experience of his life. Jesus's mission to proclaim the reign of justice and love was not a Stoic goal of self-determination; it was a loving response to his Father. Jesus shows Christians that the cross always involves God as the positive ground and horizon of all negative experience of suffering.

The assurance of salvation which Jesus proclaims arises from the unbroken communion with God in which he lived.[59] There is no possible ground in the human history of disaster for the assurance of salvation that Jesus imparts: no plan, no form of government, no system or success which humans can create. There is no basis for the hope of a future opened up by God, except in the experience of contrast which Jesus himself knows in the depths of his own being in relationship with God. It is Jesus's love to the point of death, rather than death itself, which is salvific. The experience of the defeat of God's plan in him was the beginning of his experience of death. His sustained trust in God in the face of all resistance was the beginning of his experience of resurrection and the vindication of God's plan.

In the face of the cross, or negative personal experiences, Christians are brought mysteriously to the heart of God's purposes for them and for the world. Faithfulness in the Christian life is woven with this inviolable thread of communion with God standing in resistance to evil in and of the world. This experience lies at the heart of Christian faith and is what resurrection faith proclaims. The communion which flows from such sharing is also a door to joy. Christian faithfulness calls for solidarity in both joy and suffering, a standing with one another in concrete communion in face of all the dimensions of human life.[60]

Fidelity to God and God's cause, which is the cause of the flourishing of humanity, especially suffering humanity, has also been named as the path of the Church. John Paul II stresses that the human person is the primary and fundamental way for the Church. In the encyclical *Redemptor hominis* (1979) he remarks that this 'way' is 'traced out by Christ himself', the mystery of the incarnation and the redemption is grounded in God's love for human beings.[61] Christ's own model of living through the paschal mystery is the model that the Church herself is to follow. The truth of Christian faithfulness is that we experience the resurrection only in light of our deaths. And these deaths are to be as Christ's, for the life of this world. Here Christians find the clues to true faithfulness.

Notes

1. See Gerd Haeffner, 'World', in Karl Rahner (ed.), *Encyclopedia of Theology: The Concise Sacramentum Mundi* (New York: Crossroad, 1975), pp. 1832–38.
2. Aristotle, *Nicomachean Ethics*, VI, 7.

3. See Judith A. Merkle, 'Sin', in Judith A. Dwyer (ed.), *The New Dictionary of Catholic Social Thought* (Collegeville, MN: Liturgical Press, 1994), pp. 883–88.

4. See Piet Schoonenberg, *Man and Sin* (Notre Dame, IN: University of Notre Dame Press, 1965), p. 20.

5. Augustine, *The Confessions of St Augustine* (trans. F.J. Sheed), (New York: Sheed & Ward, 1943), book X, vi.

6. Robert A. Markus, *Christianity and the Secular* (Notre Dame, IN: University of Notre Dame Press, 2006), p. 48.

7. *Ibid.*, p. 47.

8. *Ibid.*, p. 62.

9. *Ibid.*, p. 44.

10. Augustine, *The City of God* (trans. Marcus Dods), The Modern Library, (New York: Random House, 1950), book I, 35.

11. *Ibid.*, XIX, 14.

12. Markus, *Christianity and the Secular*, p. 38.

13. In his account of fifth-century life, he notes the variety of philosophies, schools of thought and visions of right living in Roman society. In his account, there were currently 288 varieties (*City of God*, XIX, 1). Here Augustine quotes Marcus Varro.

14. Markus, *Christianity and the Secular*, p. 86.

15. Philip Sheldrake SJ, *Spirituality and History* (New York: Orbis Books, 1998), pp. 68–70.

16. Jean Porter, *Nature as Reason: A Thomistic Theory of the Natural Law* (Grand Rapids, MI: William B. Eerdmans, 2005), p. 8.

17. See Sheldrake, *Spirituality and History*, pp. 213–17 for a typology of Christian spiritualities which address this tension.

18. Reinhold Niebuhr, *The Nature and Destiny of Man* (New York: Charles Scribner's Sons, 1941), vol. II, p. 186.

19. See also Erich Fromm, *Escape from Freedom* (New York: Avon Books, 1969).

20. Niebuhr, *Nature and Destiny of Man*, p. 185.

21. *Ibid.*, p. 181.

22. *Ibid.*, p. 57.

23. H. Richard Niebuhr, 'The Grace of Doing Nothing', *The Christian Century* 49 (23 March 1932): 378–80.

24. Reinhold Niebuhr, 'Must We Do Nothing?', *The Christian Century* 49 (30 March 1932): 415–17 (417).

25. Judith A. Merkle, *From the Heart of the Church: The Catholic Social Tradition* (Collegeville, MN: The Liturgical Press, 2004), pp. 110–18.

26. John XXIII, *Pacem in terris* (Vatican II, 1963), 44–45, in Walter M. Abbott SJ (ed.), *The Documents of Vatican II* (New York: Herder & Herder, 1966). All Vatican II documents are quoted from this source.

27. Pastoral Constitution on the Church in the Modern World, *Gaudium et spes* (Vatican II, 1965), 4.

28. Augustine, *City of God*, XIX, 11–13.

29. Decree on Priestly Formation, *Optatum totius* (Vatican II, 1965), 16, 452.

30. Bernard Häring, *Free and Faithful in Christ: Moral Theology for Priests and Laity* (3 vols, Slough: St Paul Publications, 1978–81).

31. Häring, *Free and Faithful in Christ*, vol. 1, p. 6.
32. Paul VI, *Populorum progressio*, nos. 76, 83. All social encyclicals are cited from David J. O'Brien and Thomas A. Shannon (eds), *Catholic Social Thought: The Documentary Heritage* (Maryknoll, NY: Orbis Books, 2002).
33. John Paul II, 'Address to the United Nations on the Declaration of Human Rights': *Acta Apostolicae Sedis*, 1156, para. 17, as quoted in Donal Dorr, *Option for the Poor, 100 Years of Catholic Social Teaching* (New York: Orbis Books, 1983), p. 275.
34. Medellin, 2.16. 'Medellin Documents', in *The Gospel of Peace and Justice: Catholic Social Teaching Since Pope John* (ed. Joseph Gremillion), (Maryknoll, New York: Orbis Books), p. 460.
35. Teilhard de Chardin, *The Phenomenon of Man* (London: Wm. Collins and Co., 1959). See also Denis Carroll, 'Creation', in Joseph A. Komonchak, Mary Collins and Dermot A. Lane (eds), *The New Dictionary of Theology* (Wilmington: Michael Glazier, 1987), pp. 246–58.
36. Walter Kasper, *Jesus the Christ* (London: Burns and Oates; New York: Paulist Press, 1976), p. 42.
37. Hugo Assman, 'Statement', in Sergio Torres and John Eagleson (eds), *Theology in the Americas: Documentation and Papers from the Theology in the Americas Conference, Detroit, MI, August, 1975* (New York: Orbis Books, 1976), p. 300.
38. Roger Haight, *An Alternative Vision: An Interpretation of Liberation Theology* (New York: Paulist Press, 1985), p. 34.
39. Aloysius Pieris SJ, *An Asian Theology of Liberation* (Maryknoll, NY: Orbis Books, 1988), p. 21.
40. John Paul II, Encyclical Letter *Evangelium vitae*, 28, in J. Michael Miller CSB (ed.), *The Encyclicals of John Paul II* (Huntington, IN: Our Sunday Visitor Publishing Division, 1996), p. 702. All quotes from the encyclicals of John Paul II are from this source.
41. Merkle, *From the Heart of the Church*, p. 236.
42. Herve Carrier SJ, *Evangelizing the Culture of Modernity* (New York: Orbis Books, 1993), p. 119.
43. Alfred T. Hennelly, 'Theological Method: The Southern Exposure', *Theological Studies* 38 (1977): 709–35 (721).
44. Michael Paul Gallagher, *Clashing Symbols: An Introduction to Faith and Culture* (New York: Paulist Press, 2003).
45. This concept would also include the totality of systems which foster the well-being of the human in its harmony with nature.
46. John Paul II, Encyclical Letter *Sollicitudo rei socialis* (1987), 38.
47. *Ibid.*, 36.
48. *Ibid.*, 36–37.
49. *Ibid.*, 37.
50. *Ibid.*, 38.
51. *Ibid.*
52. *Ibid.*, 40.
53. Johannes Metz, *Theology of the World* (New York: Herder & Herder, 1971).
54. *Ibid.*, p. 35.
55. *Gaudium et spes*, 40.

56. Edward Schillebeeckx, *Church: The Human Story of God* (New York: Crossroad, 1990), p. 22.

57. Benedict XVI, *Deus caritas est* (Vatican City: Liberia Editrice Vaticana, 2006), 18.

58. Cynthia D. Moe-Lobeda, *Public Church For the Life of the World* (Lutheran Voices Series), (Minneapolis: Augsburg Fortress, 2004).

59. Kathleen Anne McManus OP, *Unbroken Communion: The Place and Meaning of Suffering in the Theology of Edward Schillebeeckx* (Lanham: Rowman and Littlefield, 2003).

60. Christopher Lasch comments that the modern views of progress suggest life will get better and better with each succeeding generation. Success brings an upward mobility and individual autonomy which reward citizens with having to depend less and less on others or be influenced by their wills. Yet modern culture lacks a language of meaning when life's negative experiences occur. The rosy outlook of secular culture makes faith, salvation and Church extra baggage on a non-conflicted secular life journey (*The True and Only Heaven: Progress and its Critics* [New York: Norton, 1991], pp. 40–81, 529–32).

61. John Paul II, Encyclical Letter *Redemptor hominis* (1979), 14.

Conscience: Dictator or Guide? – Meta-Ethical and Biographical Reflections in the Light of a Humanist Concept of Conscience

Rudolf B. Hein

The 'Pontifical' Function of Conscience

In 1967, the year of my birth, a scholar from Upholland College named Kevin Kelly published a study in seventeenth-century English Protestant moral theology, entitled *Conscience: Dictator or Guide?*[1] as a revised version of his doctoral thesis of 1961. It seems not even necessary to consult more than the introductory page in order to get an insight into the leading interest of this remarkable Catholic study: 'Is there a native Anglican moral theology, and if so, how far is it reformed and how much does it owe to scholastic influence?'[2]

From my point of view, this double question not only reveals a genuine ecumenically motivated interest in the historical development of moral theology but also pays attention to the key role of the concept of conscience for this task.[3] Therefore, this core concept of moral theology not only acts as a catalyzing factor for the study of a neo-Thomist revival within the thinking of the early Anglican moralists, it also reveals true 'pontifical' (i.e. bridge-building) capacities. The notion of 'conscience' will always remain closely linked to the historical context from which it emerged and which serves as a primary base or paradigm even for most of the *contemporary* interpretations.[4] Furthermore, the empirical and practical dimensions of 'conscience' (however it may be defined in the particular case) transcend all the confessional or even religious barriers, making it a universal object of meta-ethical moral considerations. Thus, I may dare to state that it had been a wise decision of Kevin Kelly to show his ecumenical expertise in moral theology with a study on conscience.

In more than one instance, conscience had made an illustrious appearance on the stage of English Reformation history before, or, more precisely, while the Anglican Church was being formed by Henry VIII. It may be common historical knowledge but still worth noticing that the very event that triggered the separation of the Church of England from the Catholic Church, the 'King's great matter', is closely linked to an appeal to conscience. In 1529, Henry VIII instructed his ambassadors to the imperial court of Charles V to answer questions about the annulment of his marriage to Catherine of Aragon in the following way:

> That whereas the King for some years had noticed in reading the Bible the severe penalty inflicted by God on those who married the relicts of their brothers, he began to be troubled in his conscience and to regard the sudden deaths of his male children as a Divine judgement. The more he studied the matter, the more clearly it appeared to him that he had broken a Divine law. He then called to counsel men learned in pontifical law.[5]

On the other side, we listen to the prominent voice of the king's Lord Chancellor Thomas More, who shortly after his appointment in October 1529:

> Hvmbly besought his highnes to stand his gratious souveraigne, as he euer since his entry into his graces service had founde him; saying there was nothing in the world had bine so greiuous vnto his harte as to remember that he was not able, as he willingly wold, with the losse of one of his limbes, for that matter anything to finde wherby he could, with his consciens, safely serve his graces contentacion.[6]

The well-documented story of his arrest, trial and death[7] reveals Thomas More's concept of conscience which by far exceeds mere theoretical considerations and, even for later generations, served as an existential model for personal integrity and steadfastness. Theoretically, and thus meta-ethically, it mainly rests upon the elaborate scholastic system of Thomas Aquinas who also remains the major source of the early Anglican moralists,[8] as Kelly has shown in his study.[9] They continued to discuss this enduring concept which, in the Elizabethan and Stuart periods, developed into a universally respected, not to say venerated, authority, prone to simplified popularization and even prostitution.[10] To accomplish their task of a rectification of these popular notional aberrations, they referred to the common heritage of the Scriptures, the Fathers and the scholastics.[11] A closer look at this list of sources reveals that one group obviously seems to be omitted: the humanists, of whom Thomas More can be counted a prominent member in Tudor England and who may have been at that time (dis-)regarded as almost contemporary and somehow irrelevant. Another interpretation of this negligence could be that those humanist thoughts had already subconsciously become embedded into their own Reformation tradition.

This brief outline seeks to highlight some aspects of the humanist approach to conscience, which also rests upon the basis of a certain indispensable scholastic/ Thomist tradition (as can be seen with the early Anglican moralists), but is capable of enriching even modern discussions on the notion and evaluation of 'conscience', with some interesting and perhaps genuine contributions. They seem to have been included even in the early Anglican moral tradition, to a certain extent.

It needs more than a mere historical retrospection to accomplish even a fragmental analysis of the humanist notion of conscience. First of all, therefore, we must sharpen our methodological instruments.

Conflict or a (Timeless) Approach to Conscience

Both the dispute about the concept of conscience and the experience of this fundamental moral phenomenon itself involve conflict. But before exploring this conflict, in order to avoid terminological confusion, we have first to consider the modern usage of the term 'conscience'.[12] Observing the contemporary usage of the term 'conscience', one can differentiate between at least four different meanings:

Conscience meaning 'Moral' or 'Ethical'

- 'It's a matter of conscience' – which means: 'it's a moral matter, it's a matter of moral decision.'
- A duty of conscience – which means: a moral duty.

Unlike German, the English language generally refrains from using the word 'conscience' in this last sense and prefers the usage of 'moral duty' (which is avoided in German because of its negative, almost Victorian notion).

Conscience as 'Capacity of Moral Discernment'

- 'In a wonderful manner conscience reveals that law which is fulfilled by love of God and neighbour.'[13]
- Everyone has a conscience and has a (natural) grasp of what is right or wrong.[14]
- 'It is through his conscience that man sees and recognizes the demands of the divine law.'[15]

This usage points to a forum of moral cognition *before* a (final) judgement is made; it also opens up the meta-ethical aspects of the question. What are the sources of our moral judgements? Is it more an intellectual cognition (cognitivist approach), an emotion (emotivists) or just a decision (decisionism)?

Conscience as 'Juridical Authority'

The most common usage of the word 'conscience' can be encountered in expressions like 'having a bad conscience' or 'my conscience struck me'. There is something within ourselves that gives a morally relevant commentary to what we have done or what we intend to do. In most cases, we cannot consciously control this commentary, which can refer to intentions, feelings, utterances or the general behaviour of a person. We sometimes do not even notice the act of judgement itself. We just suffer from the emotional consequences (remorse, unease, pangs of conscience in the case of a guilty verdict and, in the opposite case, joy and inner peace). All of these phenomena point to an internal moral judgement with an inner moral conflict often involved in it:

- The judge (*conscientia consequens*): some inner moral authority passes a judgement on a past act of the agent (the self).
- The commander (*conscientia antecedens*): some inner moral authority commands, admonishes that something is to be done or prohibits its being done in the future. (In a way it also passes a judgement on a future planned act of the agent.)

'Heart'

Especially in biblical or Christian terminology, we speak of a conscience that needs cleansing[16], or of a burdened conscience.

This usage refers to an inner authority which seems to be distinct from the speaker but which is capable of being burdened with a verdict. Hence it cannot be identical with the juridical authority (proclaiming the verdict) or the capacity of moral discernment. It points to the agent him- or herself who has acted in free self-determination and now regards him- herself as morally qualified in a positive or a negative sense.

A good example is found in 1 Tim 1.5: 'This instruction has love as its goal, the love which springs from a pure heart, a good conscience and a genuine faith.' It seems obvious that the apostle used rhetorical repetition (pleonasm). All those expressions are basically synonymous. Thus, 'good conscience' means the same as 'pure heart', pointing to the free-acting self, conscious of its moral integrity.

It is not only biblical language that makes ample use of this synonymy. On the other hand, in modern usage it is not always clear in which sense 'a bad conscience' is being used. For example, this term can just as easily point to a 'burdened free-acting self – impure heart' as to the effects of a verdict of the juridical authority.

But still there is good reason to differentiate between the free-acting self in its morally sensitive capacity ('heart'), the human ability of moral discernment, and several psychic phenomena pointing to an inner moral verdict. Therefore, it is hardly possible to analyze a person's notion of 'conscience' without bearing these fundamental categories in mind.

The Humanist Contribution to the Notion of 'Conscience'

In the late 1300s, the northern Italian city states (Florence, Venice, Milan and Padua) found themselves in a pivotal position between the Eastern and Western worlds. Not only particular well-established families, but also many 'ordinary' medical doctors, lawyers, merchants and even craftsmen were profiting from an economic boom so that wealth was not again concentrated in the hands of the nobility or the clergy.[17]

Therefore, more and more lay people were financially enabled to send their sons to the universities recently founded, to France (Paris) for theology, to Bologna for (canon) law or to Padua for medicine or rhetoric.

However, many young men returned from their study trips totally frustrated. They were tired of dull scholastic distinctions, of the endless quarrels between Scotists, Ockhamists, Thomists and other scholarly factions, who were throwing

37

linguistic or logical missiles at each other, and so they joined their fellow countrymen in studying civil law, medicine or rhetoric.[18]

The latter subject, especially, sparked an interest in the aesthetic qualities of language, creating a desire to uncover the long forgotten beauties of classical poetry. In this respect, Francis Petrarch (1304–74) was a leading figure. He started out as a bibliophile, discovering antique texts that he acquired from book dealers in Constantinople. He could not conceal his criticism of the scholastic stiffness and inelegance concerning language.[19]

Raising him up on their intellectual and methodological banners, those highly motivated young intellectuals claimed 'back to the roots' as their slogan. All their efforts went into the rediscovery and rereading of those Greek and Roman manuscripts that they could get hold of.

Marsilio Ficino (1433–99)

In Marsilio Ficino, we encounter a typical representative of the Italian humanist movement. Born in Florence of a noble family, he was economically and also intellectually well-suited to study philosophy and medicine in Florence (1451).

He became fascinated with Platonism, learned Greek and, full of enthusiasm, translated Plato's dialogues and other works into Latin, financially backed by Cosimo de Medici, who bought him a villa at Careggi. Ficino invited many friends to join him in Platonic discussions, and his commentaries on the dialogues of Plato evolved out of this Platonic academy.

Ficino believed that (Platonist) philosophy should be a practical means to help and perfect people for their daily lives, not a mere source of vain speculation. Deeply rooted in Christian tradition (he was ordained priest in 1473), Ficino tried to establish a continuity between Christian and Platonist hermeneutics. So much for a brief biography. Let us now explore his concept of moral cognition (or reception of moral values):

Arguing from a cognitivist position, Ficino assumes three major normative sources:[20]

- *Lex divina* (divine law): revealed by God to various elected messengers (Moses, Osiris, Plato, Muhammad), it is accessible to everyone by written or oral tradition, initiated by those messengers.[21] Material content: divine truths.
- *Lex naturalis*: inherent in the human mind, it is accessible to the enlightened intellect. Material content: the first formal principle,[22] the Golden Rule, God is to be venerated.
- *Lex positiva*: set up by human authority as a radiation from the light of divine and natural law.[23]

His fundamental underlying anthropological assumption starts from the innate divine light which illuminates the human mind, which is then capable of realizing its position in the cosmos and the fundamentals of the natural law.[24] From there, one can establish a hierarchy of values (wealth serves body serves soul serves reason serves God) and, consequently, from this point it is not difficult to establish some principles of natural law by reasoning (e.g. social responsibility).[25]

It is rather interesting to observe that this typically humanist 'light' terminology of Ficino is echoed by Bishop Sanderson, who in his *Prealectio* states that the human mind enjoys a triple light, innate, infused and rational: the light of nature, of Scripture, of teaching.[26]

Regarding the habitual perfection of cognition in Ficino's writings, we see a similar concept to Thomas Aquinas's notion of *synderesis*: since natural appetite (*appetitus naturalis*) inclines the will and intellect towards God[27] – a very optimistic concept which is also based on the assumption that God infused his creation with a natural striving for virtue – Ficino assumes that the intellect has an innate disposition to discern the formal principle of morality.[28]

Conscience understood as *juridical authority* functions in a way that very closely resembles the practical syllogism of Thomas Aquinas (the intellect draws a conclusion from certain principles by applying them to a particular case).[29] Even though Ficino observes a close connection between will and intellect within the moral act, the latter plays the leading role. Therefore, intellect is the authority of judgement and of cognition – a very similar concept to Thomas Aquinas, whose principles like the *conscientia consequens* and its functional role seem to be mirrored here.

On the other hand, there are some very remarkable differences. Humanist teaching goes beyond meticulous observations of the structure of a human act. It proceeds from theory to practice, from the lust of mere speculation to a more pedagogic, parenetic approach. Thus Ficino describes the inner pain, unrest and unease of the soul tormented by its own images of fantasy. He compares this phenomenon with an anticipated final judgement.[30]

Talking of conscience as a judge, calling the different parties of cogitations into the witness stand,[31] his notion is that of a watchman for the dignity of the soul.[32] The soul is kept clean of bad thoughts by this innate *notio naturalis* and therefore it should be venerated.[33]

So, finally, one clearly notes his optimistic view of God's image within every human being and of conscience as a fine instrument to help man lead a life worthy of this dignity. It may be evident from his concept of so many good sources for moral (in)formation that there is little room for an erring conscience.

John Colet (1467–1519)

Our focus will now be on northern Europe. Inherent to humanism is the bond of friendship, the contact to many other like-minded fellows who share the same ideals (the love for poetry, the spreading of erudition and moral perfection), but it took the best part of a generation for those ideas finally to reach Germany and England.

Looking at the biography of John Colet, the similarity to Ficino's life is remarkable. Born in 1467 as a son of the Lord Mayor of the City of London, John Colet almost had the status of a nobleman. He was sent to Cambridge, received his boring scholastic training[34] and escaped. After his graduation (BA: 1488) he went to visit Italy (1493) and France (1495), quickly made friends with local humanist circles, including Ficino's Platonist academy in Florence, and started to read the works of his shining examples Pico and Ficino.

Back in England in 1495, he started his revolutionary lectures on St Paul's epistles, and so rediscovered the literal sense of the text (the Antiochene method).

For his captive audience, St Paul rose from the dust of pious devotion to become a vivid human being with problems, scruples and doubts.

Theologically, Colet, who later became a famous dean of St Paul's Cathedral, basically remained faithful to the Augustinian school. Thus he distrusted pagan philosophy (as he called it), openly opposed Thomas Aquinas and the syncretistic attempts of Pico and supported the neo-Platonic dualism of body and soul.[35] Human will consequently is attributed to the carnal sphere, and so all of its movements are to be suspected at first hand.[36] On the other hand, man must have at least some access to *moral cognition* which is performed by the aid of:

- Creation (sensual perception, open to everyone).
- Spiritual creation, that is, 'Heaven' (revealed to all monotheists by Moses).
- The Son of God (revealed to Christians by self-revelation).

Starting from this concept, it seems easy to imagine that with natural reason the full truth can never be found, because reason is always entangled in fallen nature and thus can never function properly.[37] But even so, Colet upholds the (Thomist) idea of an innate, inextinguishable flame of moral cognition which discerns the good from the bad.[38] In order for moral cognition to go beyond the first formal principle, Colet states that a person needs spiritual purification and again purification.[39] Colet proclaims this method as the only way to transcend the limits of reason, to attain illumination, and the perfection that finally leads to unification with God[40] – a method which can only be successful with the aid of divine grace, without which the material content of what is good can never be properly or fully perceived.

The dean of St Paul's is, of course, familiar with the concept of conscience as a judge, which he calls, following Ockham, *dictamen conscientiae*, but it does not acquit. It condemns the whole person in retrospect.[41] Such a judgement, therefore, can never claim to be final. It is always overshadowed by the ultimate judgement of God. Not human conscience, not moral insight, but Christ alone can see into the soul. He is authorized to judge effectively.[42] In Colet's Augustinian/neo-Platonist teaching, conscience, therefore, never really has a fundamental moral relevance, as in the case of Ficino. Seen as a judge, it is a mere rational instrument, spoiled and weakened by sin and moral deformation. So, in his evaluation of conscience as a juridical authority, we find Colet very close to a theonomic ethical positivism, and quite distanced from his model and former 'teacher' Ficino.

Desiderius Erasmus (1466/9–1536)

Desiderius Erasmus Roterodamus does not really fit into the humanist biographical scheme. His parents were not particularly wealthy, nor even reputable members of society. Erasmus first saw the light of the world on 28 October 1466/69 as the second son of a priest named Rotger Gerards who temporarily worked in Italy as a scribe, a copyist for (Latin) manuscripts. It is quite evident that Erasmus received or inherited two things from his father: his ardent love of books (during his whole life, he remained a bibliophile and a book collector) and manuscripts, and a bitter aftertaste from his tainted family background. His guardians, however, sent him to the best schools in the Netherlands: the young boy learned his Latin at the chapter school of Deventer (1475–84), and, through the mediation of his headmaster,

Alexander Hegius, he was brought into contact with classical poetry, as well as the ideas of Modern Devotion. Erasmus entered the Augustinian Canons in 1487.

During the night hours, the young canon started to study the manuscripts in the library, and it was there that he discovered several authors of classical Latinity (Sallust, Vergil, Lucian, Ovid, etc.), and also came across selected works of some Italian humanists. Together with his young confrères at the priory (he had a very amiable character and easily made friends because of his enthusiasm for literature), he formed something like a 'dead poets' society' which secretly met to read poetry, plays, satirical, rhetorical and other classical texts, and tried to imitate their shining examples.

From that very first moment, Erasmus's great idol became Lorenzo Valla (1407–57), who had brought forth a literary concept of stylistic elegance in his *Elegantiae*. After his ordination in 1492, Erasmus went to Paris, and, like most of the other humanists, was bored by Scotus, Thomas Aquinas and so on, and soon looked out for other humanist circles to join and to unfold his rhetorical talents. Later, in 1496, he worked as a private teacher for four upper-class boys (two of them, Thomas Grey and Robert Fisher, were from England), and started to write pedagogical works. So, in his early years, he moved from a mere admiration of linguistic elegance to a more educational aspect of classical literature.

On his first trip to England in 1499, the young Dutch humanist met Thomas More and John Colet, being especially impressed by the pedagogical concept of the dean of St Paul's.[43] Erasmus drifted along with his friend More. They translated Greek satirical texts into Latin, composed classical poetry and shared their thoughts on a more holistic, co-educative concept of individual formation.

Of the many works Erasmus wrote, a crucial one deserves to be mentioned by name: his *Novum instrumentum omne*, a critical edition of the New Testament from the Greek original. In this key work, Erasmus's genuine idea of *Christian humanism* can be captured: back to the pure sources of religion, seeking a renewal of Christianity by a rediscovery, a re-naissance of the original texts.

Of course, not all of his fellow scholars and contemporaries liked this approach and, even after he had been appointed privy counsellor to the emperor (Charles V), he was pressured by some conservative circles from Louvain University. Even though Erasmus was never the darling of the 'conservatives' (scholastic theologians, Thomists, Scotists or Occamists), he never really changed camps in support of the emerging Reformation movement. He always very carefully weighed up all the arguments, all the pros and cons of the various positions, trying to find a compromise. Erasmus, the scholar, the peacemaker, mediator, teacher – all of his character facets can be found in his conscience teaching.

Moral Cognition
Like Ficino and Thomas Aquinas, the 'Prince of Humanists' believed in the fundamental goodness of creation and by this his idea of moral cognition is influenced.[44]

Material Content
(a) The cosmos bears an intrinsic order, instituted by the creator, so that traces of this order, that is, the principles of divine law, can be found in every human being even after the fall.[45] These principles can be perceived by reason alone and are eternally valid. Erasmus compares this innate rational cognitive capacity

41

with a mental light (*lumen ingenii*).[46] Erasmus mentions the Golden Rule in its negative formulation which emanated from this order.[47] Other fundamental moral principles are not named expressly.

(b) There is also a positive law (*lex operum*), directly given by God in the Decalogue and the Mosaic law which does not bear an absolute obligation (not eternally valid).[48]

(c) Finally, in the Scriptures we can find positive rules promulgated by Christ himself (*lex fidei*) (e.g. love of God and neighbour) – defined as the perfection of law.[49] Erasmus states that these are an obligation for all those who believe in Christ.

Means of Moral Cognition

If we assume an indestructible moral principle that is intrinsic to human reason (close to the concept of *synderesis*[50]), a *divinitus insculpta lex*,[51] the best method to realize it would be self-knowledge. Of course, Erasmus is very well aware of the effects of (original) sin, resulting in the inclination to choose the evil in spite of a correct rational cognition.[52] But still he retains his hope that, nevertheless, there remains a spark of the innate cognitive light in every human being (here we encounter the Thomist concept of *synderesis*).[53] His typical humanist optimism rests upon various sources of moral cognition which facilitate a correct judgement (mentioned in chronological order):[54]

- Creation (which always points to the creator).
- Scriptures of the philosophers and prophets.
- Revelation in the Old Testament (which can be overruled by New Testament revelation).
- Christ as a teacher and example (best source, highest authority).
- The Church Fathers.

Erasmus strongly believed that training this human capacity of moral cognition, combined with a quest for correct information, will result in morally good judgement. Such a person cannot persist in viciousness.[55]

Juridical Authority

Concerning the structure of the human act, Erasmus's concept strongly resembles that of Thomas Aquinas, although it is much simpler.[56] More than the Angelic Doctor, Erasmus stresses the role of self-knowledge: the better I know myself, the better I know how to judge and react. My reason gains more and more control over my emotions.[57] More than that, reason has a parenetic function: it admonishes, warns, praises and so on.[58] Erasmus does not describe exactly in which way all those forces within a person function, but he clearly and repeatedly points out the importance of perfecting and training this authority.[59] As a means for perfection, he mentions prayer, training (repetition) and, finally, information (internalization of Christian teaching in the Bible, taking Christ himself as a personal example).[60] By practising this method, principles become *opinions*, that is, habitual correct judgements.[61] On the other hand, Erasmus is well acquainted with the opposite effect: reason becomes darkened by bad habits and wrong (or non-existent) education.[62]

Terminological Use of 'Conscientia'

For Erasmus as a linguist, *conscientia* points to a morally qualified self-consciousness, including its emotional consequences. For example, *cruciatus per infelicem consciae mentis* means crucified by the consciousness of a morally bad act, which cannot be avoided even by vicious people.[63] His notion of the term *conscience* usually remains within the horizon of a classical Latinist, denoting consciousness in most cases, sometimes with a morally positive (*conscientia recti*) or negative connotation.

So, through his practically rooted teaching, his unique concept of Christian humanism, Erasmus aims at the restoration of human nature (divinely) founded in goodness (*instauratio bene conditae naturae*).[64] To achieve this, morally guiding reason shall be restored to its leading position by training, example, self-knowledge and grace.

Humanist Impulses for Modern Concepts of Conscience

Thus far, this short chapter has attempted to show that the humanists indeed made a genuine contribution to the 'classical' (i.e. scholastic) teaching on conscience, regarding theoretical (meta-ethical) as well as practical (normative ethical) aspects, which also – more or less indirectly – had a certain impact on the early Anglican moralists. What can a twenty-first-century reader learn from these Renaissance reflections? Pre-eminently, the humanists teach us from their own personal biographical perspective to ask questions, to go back to the classical roots of our western heritage, in order to attain a more vivid, more life-centred approach to morality.

I would like to open up the forum for some humanist impulses that may be relevant in a contemporary discussion on conscience:

- The hermeneutical impulse: first of all, one has to be well aware of the homonymy of the term 'conscience' – it points to more than just one single phenomenon. Many of the Renaissance theologians used different terms for various phenomena that are summarized by the English term 'conscience': capacity of moral discernment, juridical authority (commander/judge), 'heart' (morally conscious self), and even (morally qualified) self-consciousness.
- The meta-ethical impulse: where exactly do we locate the roots of that inner judgement? Just in our emotions? Or just in a behavioural habit solely acquired from education or one's socio-cultural environment? The answer of the humanists, especially Erasmus, points towards a traditional (Thomist) intellectual foundation of both the capacity of moral discernment and of the inner juridical authority.
- On the other hand, their emphasis on education, formation and self-reflection points to the person-centred concept of 'practical truth', which takes into account both objective reality and right appetite, a pivotal concept for the early Anglican moralists.[65] Therefore, being guided by conscience does not mean being observant to the dictate of reason but acquiring a habitual moral competence by practical training, intellectual education, prayer and a balanced understanding of one's own inclinations/reaction schemes.
- The normative ethical impulse: we are always ready to claim freedom of

conscience for ourselves – but are we open to accept any negative consequences? The biographies of Thomas More and even of Erasmus can teach us practical lessons in this area.

• The ecumenical impulse: the ideas and concepts of Renaissance theologians like M. Ficino, J. Colet and Desiderius Erasmus clearly look beyond a typical late mediaeval scholastic approach, which has always been their genuine intention. Therefore, in their striving to rediscover the original purity of Christianity via their sources, they never lost the capability for holding dialogue with the Reformation movement. So, finally, the irenic concept of Christian humanism could serve an important 'pontifical function' today.

Notes

1. Kevin T. Kelly, *Conscience: Dictator or Guide? A Study in Seventeenth-Century English Protestant Moral Theology* (London: Geoffrey Chapman, 1967).
2. Cf. Kelly, *Conscience*, p. 9; quoting the introduction of H.M. McAdoo, *The Structure of Caroline Moral Theology* (London: Longmans, 1949), p. ix.
3. 'Accordingly, the only thing to be done was to choose some area of moral discussion which seemed to loom large in their [i.e., the early Anglican moralists] writings. It did not take long to realize that conscience would be the most profitable subject to study; moreover, it seemed a topic which was also very appropriate in the light of present-day debates on moral problems' (Kelly, *Conscience*, p. 11).
4. It is more than interesting to observe that even Bishop Robert Sanderson (1587–1663), who is the main focus of Kelly's study, starts his consideration of the nature of conscience with a close historical examination devoted to the etymology of the various terms linked to 'conscience' (cf. *ibid.*, pp. 54–55).
5. Raymond W. Chambers, *Thomas More* (The Bedford Historical Series, 2), (London: Jonathan Cape, 1936), pp. 225–26.
6. William Roper, *The Lyfe of Sir Thomas Moore, Knight* (ed. Elsie V. Hitchcock; EETS, orig. ser., 197), (London: EETS, 1935), pp. 49–50.
7. As an example of a meticulous study on the trial of Thomas More, cf. Ernest E. Reynolds, *The Trial of Thomas More* (London: Burns & Oates, 1964).
8. Kelly centres his study around the writings and sermons of Bishop Robert Sanderson (1587–1663), also analysing the contributions of William Perkins (1558–1602), William Ames (1576–1633), Jeremy Taylor (1613–67) and John Sharp (1645–1714) as members of the early Anglican 'school' of moral theology.
9. Cf. Kelly, *Conscience*, pp. 10–12, outlining his quest for the underlying Thomistic ideas in the teaching of the Carolines on conscience.
10. Cf. *ibid.*, p. 79.
11. Cf. *ibid.*, p. 80.
12. Based on Bruno Schüller, *Begründung sittlicher Urteile. Typen ethischer Argumentation in der Moraltheologie* (Düsseldorf: Patmos Verlag, 1987), pp. 40–52.
13. Pastoral Constitution on the Church in the Modern World, *Gaudium et spes* (Vatican II, 1965), 16; in Walter M. Abbott SJ (ed.), *The Documents of*

Vatican II (New York: Herder & Herder, 1966), pp. 213–14. All Vatican II documents are quoted from this source.

14. *Jedermann hat ein Gewissen und kann wissen, was gut und böse ist. Echte christliche Verkündigung hat in bezug auf die Ethik nicht besondere Forderungen vorzubringen* (Rudolf Bultmann, 'Echte und säkularisierte Verkündigung im 20. Jh', in *Glauben und Verstehen* (Tübingen: Mohr, 1965, Bd. 3, p. 125).

15. Declaration on Religious Freedom, *Dignitatis humanae* (Vatican II, 1965), 2.

16. 'His blood will cleanse our conscience from the deadness of our former ways' (Heb. 9.14).

17. Cf. Marvin B. Becker, 'Lay Piety in Renaissance Florence', in Charles Trinkaus and Heiko A. Oberman (eds), *The Pursuit of Holiness in Late Medieval and Renaissance Religion* (SMRT, 10; Leiden: Brill, 1974), pp. 177–99. Also see Paul O. Kristeller, *Medieval Aspects of Renaissance Learning*, DMMRS, 1 (Durham, NC: Duke University Press, 1974), p. 16.

18. Cf. Kristeller, *Aspects*, p. 4 and P.O. Kristeller, *Studien zur Geschichte der Rhetorik und zum Begriff des Menschen in der Renaissance*, Gratia 9 (Göttingen: Gratia Verlag, 1981), p. 54.

19. Cf. P.O. Kristeller, 'Florentine Platonism and Its Relations with Humanism and Scholasticism', *Church History* 8 (1939): 201–11.

20. Cf. Marsilio Ficino, *Epistolae I*, 95, in *Opera Omnia* (Basel: Heinrich Petri, 1576; reprint Turin: Bottega d'Erasmo, 1959), p. 652: *Tres autem hae leges, divina, naturalis, scripta singulos homines quod sit iustitia docent.*

21. Cf. *ibid.*, 6; pp. 611–12: *Quamobrem omnes legum conditores partim Mosen, tanquam simiae imitati, divinarum legum verissimum authorem, partim nescio quomodo veritate compulsi, a Deo leges se habuisse sub variis figmentis affirmaverunt. Aegyptiorum legumlator Osiris a Mercurio, Zautrastes apud Arimaspos a bono numine, Xamolxis apud Scythas a Vesta, Minos Cretensis et Solon Atheniensis ab Iove, Lycurgus Lacedaemonius ab Apolline ... noster Plato Legum libros exorditur a Deo, quem esse ait communem legum omnium conditorem, quod etiam in dialogo ... dicens, artes illas, quae ad victum pertinent, a Prometheo, hoc est humana providentia nobis traditas esse.*

22. *Quis primo gustavit bonum ? Intellectus, qui rationem concepit boni dormiente etiam volunte ... Primum propositum est in intellectu atque est eiusmodi: bonum quo caremus comparandum* (Marsilio Ficino, *Comm. in Phil.*, cap. 37, in *Marsilio Ficino: The Philebus Commentary* [ed. and trans. M.J.B. Allen; Berkeley, Los Angeles, London, 1975; reprint 1979, with corrections], p. 375).

23. *Ab hac naturali lege, quae divinae scintilla quaedam est, scripta lex proficiscitur, scintillae euismodi radius* (Ficino, *Epistolae I*, 95; p. 652; also cf. *ibid.*, 6; p. 611). *Nam legum civilium institutio nobis non aliunde monstrata est quam a dispositione divinarum legum, quam in se ipsa mens intueatur divina dum in se ipsa reflectitur* (Ficino, *Comm. in Phil.*, cap. 26; p. 243).

24. *Ipsi* [Ficino alludes to the pagans] *sibi sunt lex, id est, pro lege, quotiens videlicet et legem mentibus suis divinitus ab initio scriptam, quodammodo legentes observant. Profecto lux illa vera, illuminans omnem hominem venientem in hunc mundum, infudit lumen menti veridicum* (Marsilio Ficino, *In Epistolas D. Pauli Comm.*, cap. 15, in *Opera Omnia*, p. 450).

25. *Nempe Deus, quemadmodum in ipso lumine intellectus principia posuit*

speculationibus conducentia, sic et regulas actionibus, et officiis praesidentes, per quas quilibet mentis compos intelligere possit, modo diligenter examinaverit, quid in agendo, vel non agendo bonum, honestum, decorum, iustum. Quodve contra. Item Deum mundi Dominum, naturali quadam ad illum cognatione cognitum, consensuque omnium confirmatum, verendum esse prae caeteris, et colendum, suum cuique tribuendum, honorem superioribus exhibendum. Quod tibi fieri nolis, alteri minime faciendum, caeteraque generis eiusdem. Eiusmodi regulae quasi leges sunt inscriptae intellectui nostro iudici, per lumen veridicum, infusum a luce vera, iudice mundi (ibid.).

Meminisse vero debemus, Iudeaos a Deo per Mosem legem geminam accepisse. Unam quidem moralem praecipue decalogo comprehensam, perpetuo duraturam, nec solum Iudaeis, sed etiam Gentibus necessariam. Gentes autem euismodi legem non scriptis, sed mentibus acceperunt (ibid.).

26. Cf. Kelly, *Conscience*, p. 65. In his footnote referring to Sanderson's quotation, Kelly looks for parallel thoughts in the teaching of Thomas Aquinas, who, however does *not* use the same 'light' terminology.

27. *Totus igitur animae nostrae conatus est, ut Deus efficiatur. Conatus talis naturalis est hominibus non minus, quam conatus avibus ad volandum. Inest enim hominibus omnibus semper ubique, ideo non contingentem alicuius hominis qualitatem, sed naturam ipse sequitur speciei* (Marsilio Ficino, *Theologia Platonica XIII*, in *Opera Omnia*, p. 305).

28. *Omne autem verum, et omne bonum, Deus ipse est, qui primum verum est, primumque bonum. Ergo Deum ipsum appetimus ... Quare in sola Dei, sive cognitione, sive possessione ultimus finis consistit humanus, quae naturalem sola terminat appetitum* (Ficino, *Theologia Platonica XIV*, 2, in *Opera Omnia*, p. 307).

29. *Intellectus natura sua in universalium rationum conceptione versatur. Quapropter ut ex eius apprehensione aliqua proveniat actio, oportet universalem eius conceptionem ad particularia quaedam deduci. Universalis autem notio vi sua multa, imo infinita singularia continet, ut exercendi commune genus modos exercitationis innumerabiles. Igitur potest universalis illa notio ad diversa pariter singularia derivari. Derivarionem huiusmodi sequitur iudicium de agendis. Diversum igitur sequi potest iudicium* (Ficino, *Theologia Platonica IX*, 4, in *Opera Omnia*, pp. 206–207).

30. *Quemadmodum natura providentiae divinae ministra corpora intrinsecus levitate sursum movet, gravitate deorsum, ita et providentia intrinseca lege, et quasi naturali cuidam inclinatione persimili omnia ducit ... Hac similiter insita lege mentes humanae sese ad loca suae vitae convenientia ducunt* (Ficino, *Theologia Platonica XVIII*, 10, in *Opera Omnia*, p. 418). Cf. Paul Oskar Kristeller, *Die Philosophie des Marsilio Ficino*, Das Abendland, N.F. 1 (Frankfurt: Klostermann, 1972), p. 181.

31. *Iam vero conscientiae virtus causam pro anima, vel contra animam agitans coram intimo lumine, tanquam Iudice leges habente, testes producit in medium, cogitationes recordationesque frequentes, quae nonnunquam nos accusant, ratione quadam obijcientes aliquid male factum. Quandoque etiam cogitationes aliae surgunt contra defendentes illud, alia quadam ratione non esse damnandum. Atque ita saepe mutua quadam alteratione vicissim, donec his ista sub iudice recognoscente interim conscientia dirimatur* (Ficino, *In Epist. D. Pauli Comm.*, cap. 15; p. 451).

32. *Ut non modo aliorum hominum conspectum quasi divinorum, verum etiam propriae mentis conscientiam (quod praecipit Pythagoras) tanquam Dei faciem vereamur, quae nos assidue malefactorum poenitentia stimulat, etiam si poenam non metuamus. Bene autem factorum oblectat memoria. Quasi coelestis animus a terrenis vitiorum maculis semper abhorreat* (Ficino, *Theologia Platonica* XIV, 8; p. 317).

33. *Id agunt prudentes quatenus externa et corporalia animo tamquam principi subiugunt. Toti ex mente pendent tamquam ex Deo. Augustam quoque suae mentis maiestatem velut divinam statuam vilibus cogitationibus terrenisque sordibus temerare nefas existimant. Quae quidem notio naturalis humano generi pudorem verecundiamque ingenuit* (*ibid.*).

34. Joseph Burney Trapp, *Erasmus, Colet and More: The Early Tudor Humanists and Their Books* (London, 1991), p. 120.

35. *Nam si anima, spiritus noster vitalis, lucidus, bonus, eternus, et immortalis, potest esse in hoc corpusculo nostro finito, temporali, malo, tenebrecoso, et moribundo* (John Colet, *Enarratio in 1 Cor.*, cap. 7, in *John Colet's Commentary on First Corinthians: A New Edition of the Latin Text, with Translation, Annotations, and Introduction* [ed. B. O'Kelly and C.A.L. Jarrott; Medieval & Renaissance Texts and Studies 21; Binghamton, NY: Medieval and Early Renaissance Studies, 1985], p. 154).

36. Cf. John Colet, *Enarratio in Rom*, cap. 12, in *An Exposition on St Paul's Epistle to the Romans* (ed. Joseph H. Lupton), (London: Bell and Daldy, 1873; reprint Ridgewood, NJ: Gregg, 1965), pp. 185–86.

37. *Interea autem antequam venerat haec racio justificandi homines, et reformandi in justiciam intrinsicam, ut interna lege Dei juste vivant; profecto ubique humanum genus solutum, vagum, dispersum, sine ordine, deforme, sine bonitate, inefficax justitiae fuit; quum, deserti a Deo, quisque, quo sua se contulit natura, illuc decidit* (John Colet, *De corpore Christi mystico*, in *Opuscula quaedam theologica* [ed. Joseph H. Lupton; London: H. Bell and Sons, 1876; reprint Ridgewood, NJ: Gregg, 1966], p. 186).

38. *Habet enim unusquisque lumen et innatam quandam vivendi regulam ... Lex nihil aliud est quam lucida ratio, discernens equum et iniquum; hoc condemnans, illud approbans. Omnes habent legem innatam, conscientiam* (John Colet, *B. Pauli ad Romanos Expositio*, cap. 2, in *Opuscula quaedam theologica*, p. 219).

39. *Oportet ergo privetur his involucris, denudeturque omnino, simplexque extet simplicitate Dei; abscisa et longe abjecta omni carnalitate, omni rudiori imaginatione, denique omni rationatione vaga et fluenti; ut sic expedita et liber in se mens facilime coeat cum Deo, concipiatque ex Deo, in Deoque fecundata pareat copiosam prolem justiciae* (Ibid., pp. 224–25).

40. Cf. *ibid.*, cap. 8; pp. 155–57.

41. *Quia quicumque sine lege Judeorum peccaverunt, sine lege peribunt; condemnante eos lege rectoque dictamine conscientiae suae. Habet enim unusquisque lumen et innatam quandam vivendi regulam; a qua si exorbitaverit, conscientia illum condemnabit sua* (ibid., cap. 2; p. 219).

42. *Quamobrem dum hic vivitur, tuae nimium non conscientiae, sed time judicium Dei; qui altius inspicit penitrantiusque intuitur quam tumetipse* (ibid.).

43. Erasmus wrote a number of poems and a prayer exclusively for St Paul's School which had been founded by Colet. Cf. Richard J. Schoeck, *Erasmus*

grandescens. The Growth of a Humanist's Mind and Spirituality (Bibliotheca Humanistica & Reformatorica, 43; Nieukoop: De Graaf Publishers, 1988), pp. 118–19, 121. Many of his pedagogical writings were used in this model school.

44. *Solus deus vere potens est, qui nocere nec potest, si velit, nec vult, si possit, quippe cuius natura est benefacere* (Erasmus, *Enchiridion*, in *Desiderius Erasmus Ausgewählte Schriften* [8 vols; ed. Werner Welzig; Darmstadt: Wissenschaftliche Buchgesellschaft, 1968], vol. I, p. 260).

45. This fundamentally optimistic idea is mirrored (even terminologically) in Sanderson's concept of the 'three lights': '*That first Light which I have called innate arises from the Natural Law … In other words, God wished certain truths and practical principles to remain in us so that in the depths of our hearts he might have heralds of his Will*' (Sanderson, *Prael. IV*, n. 24 [IV, 80–81]; quotation from Kelly, *Conscience*, pp. 65–66).

46. *Addidit homino condito lumen ingenii, quo perspiceret quid esset fugiendum, quid expectendum. Id quum esset per inobedientiam obscuratum, reliquit tamen scintillam, veluti seminarium quoddam revocandae lucis* (Erasmus, *In Psalmum Quartum Concio*, in *Opera omnia Desiderii Erasmi Roterodami* [ed. Ch. Béné; Amsterdam: North-Holland, 1985], vol. V-2, p. 214, lines 579–682).

47. *Lex naturae penitus insculpta mentibus omnium tam apud Scythas quam apud Graecos dictat iniquum esse, si quis alteri faciat, quod sibi nolit fieri* (Erasmus, *De libero arbitrio* IIa 5, in *Desiderius Erasmus Ausgewählte Schriften*, vol. IV, p. 42).

48. Cf. Erasmus, *Ratio verae theologiae*, in *Desiderius Erasmus Ausgewählte Schriften*, vol. III, pp. 184–86.

49. *Debent humanae leges ab hoc archetypo peti. Ab eodem lumine legum humanarum scintillae sumuntur* (ibid., p. 200).

50. *Si ratio pugnat cum affectibus, ad inhonesta proclivibus, necesse est ut aliquousque prospiciat, probetque quod sit honestum. Hanc partem Scholastici haud scio unde hausto vocabulo synderesim appellant, quae manet etiam in sceleratissimis* (Erasmus, *Hyperaspistes II* in *Omnia Opera Desiderii Erasmi Roterodami* [10 vols; ed. J. LeClerc; Leiden, 1703–1706; facsimile Hildesheim: Olms, 1961], 1463 B).

51. *Lumen enim illud purissimum divini vultus, quod conditor infuderat super nos, cum non nihil obfuscavit culpa primorum parentum, tum corrupta educatio, improbus convictus, perversi affectus, vitiorum tenebrae, consuetudo peccandi tanta obduxit rubigine, ut divinitus insculptae legis vix vestigia quaedam appareant* (Erasmus, *Enchiridion*, in *Desiderius Erasmus Ausgewählte Schriften*, vol. I, pp. 148–50).

52. *Caecitas ignorantiae nebula rationis obscurat iudicium. Lumen enim illud purissimum divini vultus, quod conditor infuderat super nos, cum non nihil obfuscavit culpa primorum parentum, tum corrupta educatio, improbus convictus, perversi affectus, vitiorum tenebrae, consuetudo peccandi tanta obduxit rubigine, ut divinitus insculptae legis vix vestigia quaedam appareant* (ibid.).

53. *Quemadmodum in his, qui gratia carent (de peculiari loquor), ratio fuit obscurata, non extincta, ita probabile est in iisdem voluntatis vim non prorsus extinctam fuisse, sed ad honesta inefficacem esse factam* (Erasmus, *De libero*

arbitrio, IIa 4, in *Desiderius Erasmus Ausgewählte Schriften*, vol. IV, p. 42).

54. *Adversus haec certa quaedam decreta in albo mentis nostrae describenda sunt atque ea, ne desuetudine obsolescant, subinde renovanda. Veluti contra malum obtrectationis, turpiloquii, invidentiae, gastrimargiae et id genus reliqua. Hi soli sunt hostes militum Christianorum, in quorum assultum oratione, sententiis sapientum, dogmatibus divinae scripturae, exemplis piorum hominum et maxime Christi multo ante est praemuniendus animus* (Erasmus, *Enchiridion*, in *Desiderius Erasmus Ausgewählte Schriften*, vol. I p. 370).

55. *Porro si cui penitus persuasum sit ac iam veluti cibus in animi substantiam sit traiectum solam virtutem optimam esse, dulcissimam, pulcherrimam, honestissimam, utilissimam, contra turpitudinem unicum esse malum, cruciatum foedum, erubescendum, damnosum atque haec non opinione populari, sed ipsa natura rerum non metiatur, fieri non potest, ut a constante persuasione diu in malis haereat (ibid.*, p. 244).

56. *Primum enim quidam orthodoxi patres tres gradus faciunt operis humani: primus est cogitare, secundus velle, tertius perficere* (Erasmus, *De libero arbitrio*, IIIc 4, in *Desiderius Erasmus Ausgewählte Schriften*, vol. IV, p. 140).

57. *Haec igitur est unica ad beatitudinem via, primum, ut te noris. Deinde, ut ne quid pro affectionibus, sed omnia pro iudicio rationis agas. Sana sit autem et sapiat ratio, hoc est tantum honesta spectet* (Erasmus, *Enchiridion*, in *Desiderius Erasmus Ausgewählte Schriften*, vol. I, p. 122).

58. *At ratio monstrat compendio, quid sequendum, quid vitandum sit, nec illa post acceptum malum monet: Hoc male cessit, posthac caue. Sed priusquam aggrediare, clamat: Hoc si feceris, et infamiam, et exitium tibi parabis* (Erasmus, *Declamatio de pueris statim ac liberaliter instituendis*, in *Opera omnia Desiderii Erasmi Roterodami*, vol. I-2, p. 40, lines 10–13).

59. *Nihil imbecillius, qui a carne superatur. Si tuas perpenderis vires, nihil difficilius quam carnem subigere spiritui, si deum auxiliatorem respexeris, nihil facilius. Tu modo ingenti animo perfectae vitae propositum concipe, conceptum urge. Nihil unquam vehementer imperavit sibi humanus animus, quod non effecerit. Magna pars Christianismi est toto pectore velle fieri Christianum. Quod aditu videbitur inexpugnabile, id fiet successu mollius, usu facile, consuetudine demum etiam iucundum* (Erasmus, *Enchiridion*, in *Desiderius Erasmus Ausgewählte Schriften*, vol. I, pp. 122–24).

60. *Adeoque alienos a perfectione Christi, ut ne communibus quidem virtutibus sint praediti, quas etiam ethnicis vel ratio natura insita vel usus vitae vel philosophorum praecepta parant (ibid.*, p. 210).

61. *Neque satis est huiusmodi decreta tradere, quae vel a turpibus auocent vel inuitent ad honesta: infigenda sunt, infulcienda sunt, inculcanda sunt et alia atque alia forma renouanda memoriae, nunc sententia nunc fabella nunc simili nunc exemplo nunc apophthegmate nunc prouerbio; insculpenda anulis, appingenda tabulis, adscribenda stemmatis, et si quid aliud est, quo aetas ea delectatur, vt vndique sint obuia etiam aliud agenti* (Erasmus, *Institutio principis christiani*, in *Opera omnia Desiderii Erasmi Roterodami*, vol. IV-1, p. 140, lines 143–48).

62. *Quid nisi magnum malum expectes ab eo principe, qui quocunque natus ingenio ... statim ab ipsis incunabulis, stultissimis inficitur opinionibus, enutritur inter*

stultas mulierculas, adolescit inter lasciuas puellas, inter collusores perditos, inter abiectissimos assentatores, inter scurras et mimos, inter combibones ac aleatores ac voluptatem architectos juxta stultos ac nequam, inter quos nihil audit nihil discit nihil imbibit, nisi voluptates delicias fastum arrogantiam auaritiam iracundiam tyrannidem (*ibid.*, p. 139, lines 103–10).

63. *Quis enim usqueadeo scelestus est, ut non resiliat a vitiis, si modo penitus credat momentaneis his voluptatibus praeter infelicem illum consciae mentis cruciatum aeternos quoque emi cruciatus* (Erasmus, *Ratio verae theologiae*, in *Desiderius Erasmus Ausgewählte Schriften*, vol. I, p. 154).

64. *Quid autem aliud est Christi philosophia, quam ipse renascentiam vocat, quam instauratio bene conditae naturae? Proinde quamquam nemo tradidit haec absolutius, nemo efficacius quam Christus, tamen permulta reperire licet in ethnicorum libris, quae cum huius doctrina consentiant* (Erasmus, *Paraclesis*, in *Desiderius Erasmus Ausgewählte Schriften*, vol. III, pp. 22–24).

65. Cf. Kelly, *Conscience*, pp. 165–66.

4

Applying a Moral Principle

Gerard J. Hughes

More than 35 years ago, Kevin Kelly was one of the founding members of the Association of Teachers of Moral Theology (ATMT), and many are the contributions which he has made to its discussions over the years. Two of these stick in my memory, though the precise titles of either I can no longer recall. The first was a paper on 'We would prefer not to have to start from here'; and the second was a paper on invalid second marriages which eventually gave rise to his admirable *Divorce and Second Marriage*. In both, Kelly displayed his characteristic virtues of academic rigour, broad experience and deep pastoral concern. He was never unwilling to deal with situations in which moral principles seemed to be in conflict, and where acceptable practical solutions were not easy to find. When a situation has already got out of hand, or has already gone wrong, fair-weather principles do not seem to fit at all well. Just such issues saw him at his judicious and courageous best.

In this short paper I wish to give a brief account of moral principles and their application, which will cover not just the difficult cases in which principles conflict or in which we have to start from an already unhappy situation, but which is quite general and true of complex and apparently simple cases alike. In so doing, I hope to throw some light on such well-worn problems as: 'Are there any exceptionless moral principles?', 'How does one apply a moral principle?' and 'Do moral principles change?

Some General Remarks on the Sense of the Words We Use

The process of learning the meanings of words is a good deal more complex than might appear. Even apparently simple instances, such as teaching a young child the meaning of colour words, are far from straightforward. One can imagine pointing to things and saying, 'This is red' and 'This is blue'; but what am I pointing at? Indeed, how do I 'point' at the colour rather than the shape or the size? What this kind of 'pointing' presupposes is some shared interest, or, especially in early infancy, some shared tendency to grasp what is the salient, or important, or most interesting feature of the things in our environment. But even when their colour vocabulary has grown considerably, the child might not be too sure about pink or crimson or purple; and would an adult be making an obvious mistake in saying that the red kilts of the pipe band in Edinburgh made a brave show – since, after all, Scottish kilts are kilts of many colours?

With the possible exception of some of our logical and mathematical concepts, the concepts we use in adulthood all have fuzzy edges; the coincidence of interests upon which the initial learning is based is not to be taken as a perfect match either then or later in life. Thus, 'red' shades into 'crimson' and 'cerise' and in many contexts can properly be applied to something which is only predominantly red. Knowing how to apply the word 'red' is in fact a complex skill, and the adult's use will itself discriminate between different kinds of situation. 'Was the traffic light red?' is not a particularly nuanced question in the way in which 'What colour of paint do you want?' often would be.

Our moral concepts are no different. Consider 'brave'. Tommy falls, grazes his knee, but does not cry despite the involuntary tears in his eyes. 'There's a brave boy!' his mother might say. Were that the first time he had encountered the word 'brave', what would he learn? That 'brave' means 'not crying'? Perhaps: but he will later have to learn that 'brave' will also apply to situations in which the brave thing is not to run away or to refuse to jump. Later still, he will learn that bravery also involves not allowing oneself to be bullied; and in adult life he will have to learn about moral courage – being willing to stand up for an unpopular view or to challenge a group to think again and possibly change their minds. Two features of this process are of particular importance. The first is that Tommy, from the age of four when he first grazed his knee until the present day when he decides to blow the whistle about some corrupt practice among his colleagues in the company, will not have changed his view that courage is a virtue. Aristotle might hope that he will by now have learnt to distinguish courage from foolhardiness as well as from cowardice; but, as Aristotle is at pains to point out, drawing the lines between foolhardiness, courage and cowardice is not any kind of mathematical process – the 'mean' in which virtuous conduct is to be found must not be understood in any quasi-arithmetical sense, nor has it necessarily anything to do with moderation. There are occasions on which bravery might require someone to behave in an extremely hazardous manner.

So Tom's views about bravery will have undergone an enormous development. Even though he will still subscribe to the 'same' moral principle, his understanding of it will have changed considerably since his childhood. In that sense, all our moral principles are liable to change at any time, while yet retaining their identity. At any given moment, a moral principle encapsulates the experience we have had up until that point.

'Universals come from Particulars'

Aristotle quite generally holds that to learn the use of any universal term involves what might broadly be termed an induction from the characteristics of individual situations in which it is appropriate. It is not an induction in the strictest sense, since it need not be the case that each individual instance in which it is used is precisely the same as all the others. Coming to formulate the principle is therefore not exactly parallel to discovering that the boiling point of water is always a function of temperature and pressure, and that these are the only relevant features. In the moral case, the features which are involved are themselves less precisely definable than are temperature and pressure. More radically, it is not possible to specify exactly which features will make a situation difficult in just the way that calls for courage, in contrast to the kinds of difficulties which might call for perseverance, or unselfishness. One just has to learn as one goes along.

The process is complex. One comes to any situation in possession of a battery of moral concepts – 'courage', 'perseverance', 'generosity' for instance – most of which can be contrasted with their related failure-concepts, ' foolhardiness' and 'cowardice', 'stubbornness' and 'laziness', 'coldness' and 'sentimentality' or some such. These offer the possibility of categorizing some of the means whereby we might 'read' the ways in which one might respond to that situation. Sometimes the particular instance will have no features which would leave us uncertain about how we should apply one or other of the concepts we already have. Just as we do not have to deliberate carefully before we describe one of the traffic lights as red or green, so there are many moral situations in which there is only one thing to be said – someone's behaviour was mean, or cowardly, or very generous, no two ways about it. But there are others in which it is not so clear. Just as 'red' can shade into 'cerise' or 'crimson' or 'purple', so in the moral case one might wonder whether a particular action really was generous, or might not better be seen perhaps as trying to ingratiate myself, or as an attempt at some form of manipulation. I can similarly wonder whether what I did yesterday really was being courageous, or was I simply unreasonably stubborn? Ways of behaving which are not central and straightforward instances of this or that moral property will make it hard for us to know what to say about them. In such cases, we will perhaps have to refine the way in which one or other of our moral concepts is to be understood. The sense of the universal term will be enriched by incorporating the insight gained from this particular instance.

I would argue that this account describes how our universal terms develop quite generally. The most explicitly annotated and detailed account of this development is surely to be found in our legal system, in which decisions made in particular cases modify in various ways the sense of the terms in which legal discussion subsequently must take place. Terms such as 'fraud', 'publish', 'public nuisance' or 'reasonably foreseeable' would be obvious examples. Just recently, it was claimed that to spend many hours continuously reading Harry Potter stories to prisoners in Guantanamo might amount to 'cruel and inhuman punishment' within the terms of the American Constitution. We do not have tight, unalterable legal definitions to determine without further reflection whether a mentally ill patient is 'a danger to others', nor even to determine the application of such a key notion as 'dead'. This is not a defect in the legal system; it is of the nature of any concept that it is susceptible of and often demands development in the light of further experience. In this respect our moral concepts are no different.

There is an important implication of this which is not always taken seriously enough; the attempt to solve particular issues simply by appealing to 'the definition of X' will always be radically question-begging, precisely because previous usage cannot be *presumed* to be adequate to deal with the case in point. Whether the concept should be used to cover this instance or not depends upon many complex considerations; and in the last analysis how we should determine the proper use of our moral concepts depends upon decisions about how we wish to behave, not the other way round. When we come to examine any situation, we bring our past experience to bear upon it in the shape of the concepts which we already have learnt to apply. So, of course, the traffic light is red, and using someone else's credit card without their consent is theft; but whether discontinuing the provision of nourishment in this case is murder, or whether it is justifiably letting die, or even whether we should rather say that the patient in fact died some months ago and that the functions artificially sustained do not amount to 'being alive' at all – those are not issues which can be determined simply by appeal to the sense of terms as hitherto used: firstly because that sense itself will be unclear in the limit cases, as will any concept; and secondly because we need to decide whether, and if so how, the sense in which the concept has hitherto been used should be extended to take into account this case, and if so how that is to be done. That kind of decision is complex, and not simply to be made by invoking the current use of words.

Changes and Exceptions

It is surely uncontroversial that our moral principles have changed and will continue to change over time, in the light of the many experiences which we as individuals have to confront, and which will face all of us as a community when we are dealing with the civil and criminal law. Such gradual developments (at least those outside the legal context where vigilance is a professional necessity) can often escape our notice, because we will usually be content to state the principle by repeating the same set of words throughout the period of change; Tom can continue to believe that courage is a good thing, despite the fact that as he grows in experience that principle will change its scope and even its central focus. Similarly we can continue to repeat the fifth commandment, even if the small print of casuistry quite properly enriches and modifies the sense in which we understand it. At most, invoking such a principle serves to point out an area of constant and serious concern to us; it does not and cannot delineate that area in such a way that no further judgement will ever be required in order to decide about how it applies here and now. Even uncontroversial judgements ('We have had five instances of wrongful killings in Ipswich in the last three months') are still judgements, however implicit, that there is no reason for questioning the hitherto accepted application of the term 'wrongful killing'. That such a judgement is often obvious does not mean that it is 'automatic'. The question whether previous usage is adequate to this case still has to be answered, even if the answer to it is not contentious.

Take the traditional term 'living in sin', one example of the controversial issues about which the ATMT was once consulted by the bishops, and on which Kevin Kelly himself was subsequently to write. If one asks whether a couple living in a canonically invalid marriage are living in sin, the question cannot be answered one way or the other *simply* by citing a definition of the term as previously used; for it is the moral adequacy of seeing the matter in the terms expressed in that definition which is in question. And if, as is surely the case, there are examples in which such couples should not be described as sinning (if, for instance, it would be morally irresponsible to suggest that their second family be broken up), then the sense of the term 'living in sin' will have been adapted to deal with such an instance. I would suggest that this is not a case of an *exception* to the principle, but rather a development in the way in which that self-same principle is properly to be understood. If someone wishes to contest the view that such a development is justified, the debate cannot be settled simply by appeal to 'the' definition of the terms in which it is conducted.

Exceptions to moral principles are, I would suggest, rather different. Consider an uncontroversial decision: an elderly person, just back from hospital after a serious operation, decides not to try to get to Mass on a bitterly cold Sunday. How is such a decision to be described? Consider three different proposals: 'looking after one's health, and permitting but not intending to fail to keep the Sabbath holy'; 'deciding not to keep the Sabbath holy in order to look after one's health'; and 'trying to look after one's health as best one can'. None of these three versions need involve questioning the central feature of the traditional Catholic sense given to the phrase 'keeping the Sabbath holy' – participating in the Eucharist. That is not in contention. But the rationale the elderly person might give can vary. The first analysis offered sounds a bit like an application of the so-called 'Principle of Double Effect': at least it is no more far-fetched than several other such invocations of that principle. The action itself consists in staying warmly wrapped up in bed; and this action has two effects, one intended, the other permitted. In the second version, it sounds as if the person has accepted the view that the end justifies the means: the person intends not to go to Mass, in order not to risk their health. In the third case, the person argues that, given the state of their health, they simply should not worry about not going to Mass at all. One can easily imagine pastoral advice being given to an over-scrupulous parishioner in just those terms. 'Don't you worry about that. You just make sure you look after yourself and get better soon!' In my own view, the first analysis of this case is unrealistic, since I do not think that there is a coherent account of 'intend' which will justify such an analysis. The second analysis does indeed sound as if the person is doing something wrong, which surely is not how we would wish to describe their behaviour. I would suggest that the third account is the correct one: and that involves saying that a consideration which is indeed usually a decisive consideration concerning one's religious duty is obviously overridden in the present circumstances. It is easy, though perhaps strictly inaccurate, to say, 'Just think about your health, and don't worry about not getting to Mass' when the correct course of action is obvious.

In other types of case one might have to say something different. Consider the Chancellor trying to decide on the allocation of funds to the health service and to education. He would not wish to deny that here and now both have claims upon him; his decisions will all have to be of the form 'I shall give X this amount despite the claims of Y'; both claims have to be considered, and Y would have been given more had it not been for X, and so on. Such moral principles are all of the 'other things being equal' form, since it is normally the case that they express moral claims which usually will have to be assessed together with other competing moral claims. I think that all morally important considerations are of this form. There are some circumstances, however, often involving regulations of public behaviour, in which we would regard the need to override a particular principle as comparatively rare. We would often mark these cases by saying something like, 'But I think we should make an exception in this case'. It need not be the most important principles which are overridden 'rarely' in this sense. 'We don't usually allow readers to renew books more than once, but I think we can make an exception for you, since nobody else has asked for this book in the last two years. Just give us your phone number.' This is a straightforward case of one principle (this particular customer's need) overriding another (the need to maximize availability to customers generally) which one does not want to incorporate into the general understanding of the principle itself.

This paper has not offered any detailed discussion of the process by which an individual would assess a situation in the course of applying to it one or other moral principle. Whether this instance is to count as an instance of falling under the principle, whether the principle has to be understood in a slightly different sense in order to accommodate this instance, and how decisions involving several possibly applicable principles are arrived at – these are not problems for which there is any automatic method of resolution. What I have tried to show is why attempts to short-circuit this process by appeal to the definitions of terms, or to allegedly exceptionless principles, or by the implicit suggestion that principles can and should be applied without further discussion by anyone who correctly understands them, fail to grasp the nature and origins of the very principles to which they appeal. There is in the end no substitute for emotional balance, correct information, honesty and experience of life.

5

Dialogue as Tradition

Jayne Hoose

Christianity arises out of a Jewish tradition which is seen to be in constant dialogue with Scripture. We see Christ engaged in this process at a very early stage in Luke's Gospel. His parents, having lost him, find him involved in discussions in the temple: 'After three days they found him in the temple, sitting among the teachers, listening to them and asking them questions' (Lk. 2.46). *Gaudium et spes*, *Ecclesiam suam* and *Laborem exercens*[1] call us all to follow his example and involve ourselves in this tradition of dialogue. *Gaudium et spes* states that:

> The Church sincerely professes that all men, believers and unbelievers alike, ought to work for the rightful betterment of this world in which all alike live; such an ideal cannot be realized, however, apart from sincere and prudent dialogue.[2]

Gaudium et spes 'deliberately set out to engage in dialogue with the contemporary world and, within that process, attempted to read the "signs of the times"',[3] which, according to Kevin Kelly, involves 'intelligently listening to the deepest hopes and desires, sufferings and anxieties, of the human family today'.[4] We should perhaps also include interpretations, opinions and beliefs, encouraging the broader reciprocal education to which Vatican II calls us.

Vatican II reversed the tendency towards drawing ideas for respectful living principally from religious leaders, particularly the pope and the bishops who had been assumed to have special gifts of wisdom and love. It pointed us back towards God's invitation for all to share in God's work through the wisdom of personal experience and love. This relies upon human persons treating themselves and others with respect. Such respectful behaviour 'can often only be discovered by a wise and loving heart as it learns from experience, listening to other wise and loving hearts'.[5] We are thus required to engage seriously in dialogue with the whole Church.

This draws upon the concept of the *sensus fidelium*,[6] which recognizes dialogue as a prerequisite of a living faith and Church. The *sensus fidelium* leads to reciprocal recognition of truth and discernment. It recognizes the need for the person teaching to understand the position of those they are teaching, and the need for continued mutual learning. The *sensus fidelium* is the means by which we recognize that the whole Church needs to be given a voice.

For Valadier,[7] the failure to take note of the *sensus fidelium* leads to official teaching becoming sterile and non-credible, and, in turn, leads to dissent because of a lack of recognition by the faithful. Faith is not about consuming what is given out. Recognizing the *sensus fidelium* and promoting dialogue is important in preventing us from falling into the trap of seeing the members of the Church as consumers. Debate and dialogue are essential in making it possible for the faithful to express consent because they recognize what they believe in the message. They recognize the message as a reflection of the gospel and their faith.

We need to promote a process which facilitates the recognition of the 'signs of the times' and the expression of a gospel of love and life in Christ in the current time and culture.[8] This is about recognizing and valuing the living of the gospel by all, where they are. It means engaging in a long and constant process that places the institution of the Church at the service of truth and love, and developing the responsibility of the faithful by promoting their 'need to understand their faith and take seriously the charisms of intelligence, knowledge and faith'.[9]

The fact that we are human means that we are all part of the teaching ministry and, hence, also all part of the learning ministry. A teaching Church by its nature must be a learning Church. The Church can only stay credible as a teaching authority if it is centred on learning. Effective learning and teaching occur through dialogue, which is a vital part of the teaching tradition of the Roman Catholic Church. A teaching Church, moreover, cannot be credible if it does not understand the wider society. Dialogue with *today's* society is therefore essential.

Those in teaching roles within the Church can only teach what is truly the faith of the Church having genuinely engaged with where the Church is in the context of today's society. It is when there is a lack of dialogue that we are likely to see questions arising regarding the credibility of what the Church teaches, and an increasing need to use the authority of governance to enforce teaching.

Recent Events

Recently, however, the approach to dialogue has been of particular concern because of a seemingly increased tendency for the Magisterium[10] to exercise control over or even close down certain areas of dialogue in the name of preserving and protecting tradition. Some recent events have led to questions regarding the Magisterium's commitment to dialogue.

One of these is that of the forced resignation of the editor of *America*, Thomas Reese SJ, in 2005. It appeared to many that this resulted from the Vatican finding an approach which invited dialogue on disputed issues to be inappropriate. It seemed that the discussion of key contemporary issues facing the Church by the publication of articles expounding different viewpoints was not acceptable.

Following the resignation of Reese, Robert Mickens wrote:

> And truth, it seems, has become a casualty in a clash of views between the Vatican and the Society of Jesus over what is open to discussion among ordinary Catholic believers and what is not.[11]

Jose de Vera (chief press officer for the Society of Jesus in Rome) indeed said that the Congregation for the Doctrine of the Faith wanted Jesuits to write articles 'defending whatever position the Church has manifested, even if it is not infallible'.[12]

Baumann challenged this approach stating that:

It's hard to imagine how any Church authority can shut down the sorts of debates that thinking Catholics are engaged in. What's most troublesome is that for the ordained, for those theologians who are priests, and for people working in Catholic universities, this will inhibit the honest exchange of views.[13]

It is true that some of the issues, debated in *America*, including AIDS prevention, homosexuality and same-sex marriage, and religious pluralism, cause great difficulty for many. Simply preventing the questions being asked and the debate taking place will not, however, change this. These difficulties will only be resolved when the questions raised by current doctrines are adequately addressed. A move to prevent such dialogue which publicly engages with all sides will simply mean that such dialogue will take place outside of the Catholic institutions which apply such restrictions.

As McCloskey noted:

I'm afraid a move like this one will cause more and more Catholic thinkers to say that they want to write for publications that are not identified as Catholic and to teach at schools not identified as Catholic, because there is more freedom there.[14]

The Thomas Reese affair has resulted in damage to the teaching credibility of the Magisterium, giving rise to such questions as: how can we be open to the Church today and to revelation in the absence of such dialogue? If the alternative positions put forward are so contrary to the truth, then why not simply resolve the debate by clearly outlining the flaws in the positions being proposed? If the Church's teaching does not stand up to such scrutiny, then why not?

A second recent example where the Magisterium stepped in to halt debate is on the issue of women priests. In response to the dialogue taking place within the Church, Pope John Paul II issued the apostolic letter *Ordinatio sacerdotalis* in which he states:

Although the teaching that priestly ordination is to be reserved to men alone has been preserved by the constant and universal Tradition of the Church and firmly taught by the Magisterium in its more recent documents, at the present time in some places it is nonetheless considered still open to debate, or the Church's judgement that women are not admitted to ordination is considered to have a merely disciplinary force.

Wherefore, in order that all doubt may be removed regarding a matter of great importance, a matter which pertains to the Church's divine constitution itself, in virtue of my ministry of confirming the brethren (cf. Lk. 22:32), I declare that the Church has no authority whatsoever to confer ordination on women and that this judgement is to be definitively held by all the Church's faithful.[15]

The final part of this statement caused confusion as to whether 'to be definitively held' was to be understood as belonging to the deposit of faith, and led to the release of a statement by the Congregation for the Doctrine of the Faith stating:

> This teaching requires definitive assent, since, founded on the written Word of God, and from the beginning constantly preserved and applied in the Tradition of the Church, it has been set forth infallibly by the ordinary and universal Magisterium (cf. Second Vatican Council, Dogmatic Constitution on the Church *Lumen Gentium* 25, 2). Thus, in the present circumstances, the Roman Pontiff, exercising his proper office of confirming the brethren (cf. Lk. 22:32), has handed on this same teaching by a formal declaration, explicitly stating what is to be held always, everywhere and by all, as belonging to the deposit of the faith.[16]

Such statements, however, which are to be 'definitively held by all the Church's faithful', must be recognized for their truth by the Church as a body. Whilst many of the faithful still have genuinely held questions about these statements, continued dialogue is a requirement for a sound *sensus fidelium* and *fides quaerens intellectum*. The whole body of the Church must be allowed a voice and respectful engagement where genuine dialogue is sought. All doubt is not removed by using the authority of governance where genuinely held questions are not addressed.

Moreover, had this approach been taken and statements which challenged the validity of debate and dialogue been applied and not challenged in the cases of slavery and religious liberty, we would not have rectified the errors previously made in these areas. We would still allow slavery and deny religious liberty. Similar arguments could also be made where teaching has changed on issues like torture and burning heretics at the stake.[17]

It is, indeed, stated in the Pontifical Council for Social Communications' document *Communio et progressio* that: 'Catholics should be fully aware of the real freedom to speak their minds which stems from a "feeling for the faith" and from love'.[18] It seems that the sense of the faithful, for example, regarding the issue of women priests, and the need for a vehicle where open and honest debate can be pursued, has at best been misread. If there is continued debate within the Church to such an extent as to draw institutional attention and require an authoritative statement to close it, it would seem that there are still genuinely held questions to be explored and answered before the teaching on such a matter can be declared to be 'set forth infallibly by the ordinary and universal Magisterium'.

Denying the tradition of dialogue through closing the debate discredits the teaching authority of the Magisterium and appears at odds with its own teaching. It removes the credible grounds for claiming women priests to be against tradition and damages teaching credibility through opting out of the learning process. As Archbishop Weakland pointed out, in 1990: 'listening is an important part of any teaching process; the Church's need to listen is no exception'.[19]

Without this there is an inevitable weakening of the moral position of the Church and its moral teaching. The omission of such dialogue also seems to confirm the observation of some theologians that the concept of the *sensus fidelium* has come to be treated with suspicion, and validates the call for a reinstatement of this concept recognizing that the faith is shared by all the faithful. Without this reinstatement, there is no recognition of the requirement for the teaching Church to be a learning Church which needs to be informed of all the complexities of a problem and engage in addressing such complexities.

In order to understand and be understood, we need to both listen and be listened to. We need time to work through issues. There is often a need for a long, mutual work of exchange to take place in order to facilitate understanding.[20] A lack of acceptance of an area of teaching does not necessarily mean that the teaching itself is in error, but may mean that the process of teaching has been inadequate. A message may still contain truth but may have been badly expressed. When a message is poorly accepted we need to take note and try to establish why it is poorly accepted. To close the debate, however, prevents us from recognizing and rectifying any errors in either approach or teaching. Surely the most effective way of safeguarding and promoting Church doctrine is to allow it to stand the test of the broadest and widest scrutiny.

Effective Dialogue: Some Pointers

The normal flow of life and the smooth functioning of government within the Church require a steady two-way flow of information between the ecclesiastical authorities at all levels and the faithful as individuals and as organized groups.[21]

This should not, however, be about dialogue for the sake of the process of dialogue but about a genuine searching and seeking, a genuine pursuit of discernment of right from wrong. It is vital that dialogue be pursued not simply as a process but as a process with clear intent. This includes respecting the virtues of truth-telling and honesty and hence requires transparency. Without this, the essential element of trust is no longer present and dialogue becomes an issue of control and power play, as opposed to a process of mutual exploration and discovery.

Dialogue, including dialogue with *today's* society, is essential. The Church cannot be a credible teaching Church if we do not understand society. Tradition must dialogue with what is contemporary in order to be credible. We can only maintain (preserve and protect) the integrity of tradition if we continue the common search on which it is based. This is a search which recognizes the wisdom of personal experience and love. It acknowledges the humanity of the Church and continues to seek out that which, through a previous lack of discernment, is built upon a lack of wisdom and love. In this way, we continue to discern the movement of the Spirit and remain alive as a Church. This requires that we respect the Spirit's moving through the whole family of the Church.

There is a need for us to respect the equity of status of all as God's children, showing equal respect for different forms of expertise and learning. Expertise should not be viewed from a limited perspective as lying in the hands of the Church hierarchy and academia. This can lead to the very real expertise of experience being overlooked. Experience, as well as qualifications and status, needs to be respected. This is essential if we are genuinely to seek 'the signs of the times' by being in touch with the issues raised through the different circumstances in which individuals are called to live the gospel. Ability to engage in such a dialogue which respects where others are is identified by *Ecclesiam suam* as proof of:

61

Consideration and esteem for others, understanding and kindness. It shows the detesting of bigotry and prejudice, malicious and indiscriminate hostility and empty boastful speech.[22]

Such an approach helps to avoid the human temptation for power play:

Our dialogue must be accompanied by that meekness which Christ bade us learn from Himself: 'Learn of me, for I am meek and humble of heart'.[23] It would indeed be a disgrace if our dialogue were marked by arrogance, the use of bared words or offensive bitterness. What gives it its authority is the fact that it affirms the truth, shares with others the gifts of charity, is itself an example of virtue, avoids peremptory language, makes no demands. It is peaceful, has no use for extreme methods, is patient under contradiction and inclines towards generosity.[24]

It is tempting to consult with groups we know to be broadly in agreement with us and which we expect to confirm an already held viewpoint. Confining dialogue within a certain school of thought or elite group does not honestly respect the intent to explore the issues fully in a bid to discern the truth. We need to avoid 'dialogue' as a public-relations exercise which seeks to add weight to a position already decided upon; that is, dialogue is not dialogue without a genuine openness in its pursuit. Dialogue does not start with a point to prove, and seek confirmation. It is not about confirming expectations.

While there is a need to seek consistency of outcome and agreement, this does not mean that lines of argument must be incorporated without being challenged or dismissed, disregarding genuine explorations. It means that different viewpoints and lines of argument must be genuinely engaged with:

Respect and love ought to be extended also to those who think or act differently than we do in social, political, and even religious matters. In fact, the more deeply we come to understand their ways of thinking through such courtesy and love, the more easily will we be able to enter into dialogue with them.[25]

There is also need to avoid a dialogue within a dialogue. We must avoid a private dialogue among the privileged few which is fronted by a public-relations exercise to the many. This is disrespectful of the Church as one body. At best, it patronizes 'the many' who are excluded from such private dialogues. At worst, it leaves problems of conscience for 'the many' which the few privately resolve within such dialogues. Alternatively, there may be a hidden resolution of conscience which results in both parties holding the same position but not publicly acknowledging the fact. This leads to the practice of deception between different groups within the Church and lacks the openness and honesty required to discern what is truly the movement of the Spirit.

This means eradicating the practice of saying one thing in certain contexts whilst publicly saying another, avoiding the issue, avoiding publicly saying quite the same thing or playing verbal gymnastics in public. Transparency is essential and requires us to avoid the mental and verbal gymnastics used to avoid public acknowledgement of what is spoken in private or to enable things to fit (however uncomfortable the fit) in order to convince the Church of the existence of an unbroken tradition. Contrived arguments and the use/misuse of language to deceive or hide true meaning[26] are both dishonest and contrary to the tradition of seeking the truth through genuine dialogue. How can we discern what the Church believes if beliefs are not openly and clearly spoken?

> Clarity before all else: the dialogue demands that what is said should be intelligible ... It is an invitation to the exercise and development of the highest spiritual and mental powers a man possesses.[27]

This requires a different approach from those who, in good conscience, question the Church's teaching. We need to start from the point of view of simply regarding such questions as part of a continuing and essential dialogue. Surely a living Church could not continue as such without this input to dialogue. Where the truth is genuinely discerned, it will stand up to scrutiny and the arguments will speak for themselves.

At times there may be a need to admit publicly that, at present, there is no clear route because of a lack of knowledge. This means a different educational process which avoids the temptation to tell individuals exactly what is required when this is not clear – even if that is what they want and find easiest. There is a need to invest in an educational process that draws all into the dialogue, despite its difficulties, and gives individuals the confidence as adults to make decisions, given the current knowledge, conflicts and contradictions. We all need to face and accept that honestly held differences of opinion can occur even between individuals with the same value systems.[28] There is no claim that dialogue will be easy and that there will not be strong feelings involved, but we must not let these facts cloud the issue of the need to respect each individual in the process of dialogue.[29]

When genuine dialogue leads us somewhere uncomfortable, it is not sufficient simply publicly to close the debate or ignore it in preference for the safety of history. Simply resorting to pointing to a long-standing tradition and the deposit of faith in a purely historical sense does not respect the need for the past to dialogue with the present. Such an approach is, therefore, contradictory in denying the tradition of dialogue and the need to be continually open to discernment through the Spirit. Dialogue allows us to stay open to revelation in the present:

> This free dialogue within the Church does no injury to her unity and solidarity. It nurtures concord and the meeting of minds by permitting the free play of variations of public opinion. But in order that this dialogue may go in the right direction it is essential that charity is in command even when there are differing views. Everyone in this dialogue should be animated by the desire to serve and to consolidate unity and cooperation. There should be a desire to build and not to destroy. There should be a deep love for the Church and a compelling desire for its unity. Christ made love the sign by which men can recognize His true Church and therefore His true followers.[30]

A living Church can only continue to exist through dialogue, revelation itself being the result of dialogue between God and humanity

We cannot close our eyes and minds to what may be a need for change due to development of understanding. We must be constantly on the alert, challenging and being challenged to address this shadow side. Admitting error and apparent lack of consistency is not contrary to and disrespectful of tradition; it is indeed an important part of respecting tradition, particularly the tradition of dialogue, and being continually open to revelation. We must engage with the deposit of faith in order to achieve a full, open and honest dialogue. Simply to accept historical interpretations of the deposit of faith without question, however, denies the need for the continued search for truth and the possibility of error. Change is about continuing the journey, not about denying the past. Tradition does not lie in the consistency of outcome but in the process and intent of the dialogue and engagement with the past, present and future.

Conclusion

By virtue of her mission to shed on the whole world the radiance of the gospel message, and to unify under one Spirit all men of whatever nation, race or culture the Church stands forth as a sign of the brotherhood which allows honest dialogue and gives vigour.

Such a mission requires in the first place that we foster within the Church herself mutual esteem, reverence and harmony, through the full recognition of the lawful diversity. Thus all those who compose the one People of God, both pastors and the general faithful, can engage in dialogue with ever abounding fruitfulness. For the bonds which unite the faithful are mightier than anything dividing them. Hence, let there be unity in what is necessary, freedom in what is unsettled, and charity in any case.[31]

If we accept human experience as an 'indispensable and fundamental source'[32] of developing moral knowledge, how can we not regard dialogue as key? This does not mean that morality is an entirely moveable feast. There is at its heart the unchangeable feature of the dignity of the human person. This is not the easy option. It means we must all take responsibility for placing the Church in the service of truth and love, not only recognizing the validity of our own personal experience but also that we are part of a wider teaching and learning community. Those with teaching authority in the community have a particular responsibility to value this as a gift, and recognize that they hold only a partial truth. Such a gift must be exercised in a way which respects the need for the learning and listening essential to credible teaching, and respects the involvement of the whole family in the process of maintaining a living tradition. Humble recognition of our own humanity and lack of grasp of the whole truth should lead us to search together in gentleness and respect.

Dialogue should not be about 'watering down or whittling away'[33] the truth but about establishing it and moving towards it together.

Truth, however, is to be sought after in a manner proper to the dignity of the human person and his social nature. The enquiry is free, carried on with the aid of teaching or instruction, communication and dialogue, in the course of which men explain to one another the truth they have discovered, or think they have discovered, in order thus to assist one another in the quest of truth. Moreover, as the truth is discovered, it is by personal assent that men are to adhere to it.[34]

Tradition must dialogue with what is contemporary in order to be credible. We must face the changes required by advancing knowledge and be open to the movement of the Spirit in recognizing that which has been historically accepted through a previous lack of discernment and built upon a lack of wisdom and love. Challenges to Church teaching need to be made and addressed openly through the genuine dialogue which forms a key part of the heart of tradition.

Notes

1. *Laborum exercens*, when addressing the issue of new social groups, particularly women in work, calls for 'movements of solidarity in the sphere of work – a solidarity that must never mean being closed to dialogue and collaboration with others' (John Paul II, Encyclical Letter *Laborem exercens* [1981], 8).
2. Pastoral Constitution on the Church in the Modern World, *Gaudium et spes* (Vatican II, 1965), 21.
3. Kevin T. Kelly, *New Directions in Moral Theology* (London: Geoffrey Chapman, 1992), p. 21
4. *Ibid.*, p. 22.
5. *Ibid.*, pp. 1–2.
6. The *sensus fidelium* ('sense of the faithful') refers to what the faithful believe and profess.
7. *Sensus Fidelium and Moral Discernment: Papers & Discussion* (Intercontinental Panel II, Catholic Theological Ethics in the World Church, International Conference, Padua, Italy, 8–11 July 2006).
8. *Ibid.*
9. *Ibid.*
10. The word Magisterium, unless otherwise qualified, is used throughout this text in the narrow sense of meaning the official teaching authority of the Roman Catholic Church, as represented by the pope and the bishops.
11. R. Mickens, 'The Thomas Reese Affair', *The Tablet* (14 May 2005), p. 8.
12. *Ibid.*
13. Michael Poulson (*Globe* Staff), 'Editor's Ouster worries Catholic Publications', *The Boston Globe* (10 May 2005).
14. *Ibid.*
15. John Paul II, Apostolic Letter *Ordinatio sacerdotalis* (1994), 4.
16. *Responsum ad dubium*: Concerning the Teaching Contained in *Ordinatio Sacerdotalis* (Congregation for the Doctrine of the Faith, 1995).
17. For further details see Bernard Hoose, *Received Wisdom? Reviewing the Role of Tradition in Christian Ethics* (London: Geoffrey Chapman, 1994), pp. 4, 20, 63; and John F. Maxwell, *Slavery and the Catholic Church* (London: Barry Rose Publishers, 1975).
18. *Communio et progressio* (Pontifical Council for Social Communications, 1971), 116.
19. Archbishop Weakland, 'Listening Sessions on Abortion: A Response', *Origins* (31 May 1990), p. 35; cited in Kelly, *New Directions in Moral Theology*, p. 69.
20. *Sensus fidelium.*

21. *Communio et progressio*, 120.
22. Paul VI, Encyclical Letter, *Ecclesiam suam* (1964), 79.
23. Mt. 11.29.
24. *Ecclesiam suam*, 81.
25. *Gaudium et spes*, 28.
26. Kelly, *New Directions in Moral Theology*, p. 18.
27. *Ecclesiam suam*, 81.
28. See Kelly, *New Directions in Moral Theology*, pp. 17–19 for further discussion of dealing with disagreement.
29. *Ibid.*, p. 65
30. *Communio et progressio*, 117.
31. *Gaudium et spes*, 92.
32. Kelly, *New Directions in Moral Theology*, p., 66. See pp. 66–69 for further information on the importance of human experience.
33. *Ecclesiam suam*, 88.
34. Declaration on Religious Liberty, *Dignitatis humanae* (Vatican II, 1965), 3.

6

Moral Theology and Doctrinal Change

Julie Clague

Our First Morality Tale: Slavery

Liverpool, birthplace and home of Kevin T. Kelly and location of the Festschrift colloquium that took place in Kelly's honour, was chosen as European Capital of Culture 2008. That designation arose in no small part because of the architectural heritage of this famous port. It was the commercial success of the port of Liverpool that built the city's wealth, making it one of the richest places in the British Empire. But beneath the façades of Liverpool's municipal buildings there lie stories not only of humanity's achievements but of its failures too. The story of Liverpool – like the story of humanity – is an ambiguous one, of happiness and of sadness, of triumphs and of tragedies, of winners and of losers, of virtue intermingled with vice. For, wherever one turns in Liverpool, one sees reminders of a city built on the slave trade – often by devout Christians who, if challenged, would rely on warped biblical and natural-law argumentation and the silent consent of their religious tradition to justify support of a commercialization of human trafficking that made merchants rich and undergirded the economic and imperial might of the not-so-morally-great Great Britain. Christians the world over had accomplished a suspension of belief with regard to the humanity of those several million who were traded that seemingly insulated them from their own Christian responsibilities. Thus, Baron de Montesquieu could observe with irony: 'It is impossible for us to suppose these [enslaved] creatures to be men, because, allowing them to be men, a suspicion would follow that we ourselves are not Christians.'[1]

The ambivalence of Liverpool's history was never more apparent than in 2007, which marked the two-hundredth anniversary of Britain's Abolition of the Slave Trade Act 1807 that brought to an end the lucrative trade by the worst-offending nation. It was when Thomas Clarkson learnt second-hand of the inhumanity of slavery that he saw its incompatibility with his Christian faith and was moved to campaign with William Wilberforce and others for its abolition. Crucial in mobilizing public support were the personal testimonies of those such as Olaudah Equiano, Quobna Ottobah Cugoano and Mary Prince, who had experienced slavery first-hand and could speak of its horrors. Just like the proverbial poacher turned gamekeeper, a reformed Britain would subsequently use its powers of influence and pragmatic diplomacy to persuade Catholic countries to end their part in the trade in humans. The weight of Christian tradition was against change. From the apparent acquiescence of the biblical Jesus to the slave-owning popes, slavery was part of the social fabric. It took the patient application of gentle and ecumenically sensitive diplomatic pressure on the Holy See by a non-Catholic nation to create the context for an official Catholic statement condemning the trade which could influence Catholic countries such as Portugal and Brazil.[2] Church teaching and practice changed, but the Church's theological reflection on the wrongness of slavery came later, as it too changed from culpable poacher to moral gamekeeper.

Christianity's historical blindness to the wrongness of slavery gives every contemporary Christian pause for thought; for Christian teaching now condemns what was previously approved, and moral repulsion at the practice has replaced moral equanimity. Which Christian can remain untroubled by the existence of past failings in the tradition they have inherited and by the present possibility that moral blind spots continue to lurk within it? Slavery is one of a number of stark examples where moral attitudes and evaluations have changed dramatically, necessitating a revision of Christian teachings to reflect this. In truth, though the changes are often less dramatic, the Church's moral doctrines are constantly subject to frequent if less obvious updating and fine-tuning as humanity learns more about how to be human. So numerous now are the instances of changed Church teaching, and so aware are Christians of the historical and cultural contingency of humanity's moral values, that doctrinal change has itself become an object of theological reflection and hermeneutical scrutiny. Changed teachings have changed our understanding of Church teaching itself and its relation to humankind's search for the truth.

A Cautionary Tale: *Veritatis Splendor*

These discussions of doctrinal change sometimes come from surprising quarters. In 1993 Pope John Paul II published the encyclical *Veritatis splendor* 'Regarding Certain Fundamental Questions Of The Church's Moral Teaching', in which he suggests that while 'Sacred Scripture remains the living and fruitful source of the Church's moral doctrine' the Catholic Church 'has achieved a *doctrinal development* analogous to that which has taken place in the realm of the truths of faith'.[3] By this John Paul reminds his readers that the moral teaching of the Church is not simply a comprehensive list of prescriptions and proscriptions that can be read from Scripture and applied unproblematically in every new era. Moral teaching takes shape in every age as Christians seek to make faithful sense of the biblical witness in their own historical and cultural context. The Catholic moral tradition – precisely as tradition – is subject to the same historical forces that shape any other tradition. As such, John Paul draws an analogy with the dynamic model of Christian tradition that was given expression in the Vatican II Dogmatic Constitution on Divine Revelation.[4] In this way there is a suggested parallel between the notion of development in theological doctrine (matters pertaining to faith) and development in moral doctrine (matters pertaining to morals).[5] Just as the Church grows in its knowledge of the faith, so too there is a corresponding growth in the knowledge of the moral law:

At all times, but particularly in the last two centuries, the popes, whether individually or together with the college of bishops, have developed and

68

proposed a moral teaching regarding the *many different spheres of human life* ... With the guarantee of assistance from the Spirit of truth they have contributed to a better understanding of moral demands in the areas of human sexuality, the family, and social, economic and political life. In the tradition of the Church and in the history of humanity, their teaching represents a constant deepening of knowledge with regard to morality.[6]

While couched in more positive terms than historians might expect, *Veritatis splendor* concedes that there is a history to morality and therefore to Church teaching.

The explicit papal mention of the existence of doctrinal development in relation to moral truths is significant. Such a statement does away with a Catholic tendency to see new formulations of doctrine in terms merely of a restatement, albeit better expressed, of a fundamental insight that of itself remains unchanged. In other words, the achievement which is claimed when speaking of a development of doctrine is not to be understood solely in terms of semantic refinement, but also in terms of improved knowledge and/or understanding of reality. This is all somewhat ironic, given that it occurs in an encyclical letter to bishops that emphatically stresses the existence of timeless (absolute) moral truths that are not subject to historical revision and that are authoritatively taught by the Church's Magisterium. Furthermore, it is mentioned in an encyclical that warns of the systematic calling into question and denial of those truths by large numbers of the Catholic faithful and (worse) by dissident moral theologians who should know better.[7] The internal disagreement arises from the widespread view that moral norms claimed to be exceptionless by the Church's Magisterium are time-bound proscriptions that are either no longer valid or no longer universally applicable.

In light of John Paul's assertion of doctrinal development in moral theology, one is inevitably confronted with the question of how and according to what criteria this development of moral doctrine has taken place. By what process does the Catholic Church discern which moral developments are authentic reflections of the good news of the gospel and in truthful accord with what God wills for humanity? In what ways is the Church's Magisterium an authority in such matters? What are Catholics to make of the fact that new moral teachings sometimes appear to render redundant or flatly contradict previously held norms? Such questions are often clustered under the general heading of 'the problem of doctrinal development'. Two interesting case studies in this respect are the theological discussions that preceded the change that took place in Catholic teaching on religious freedom in Vatican II's Declaration on Religious Freedom (1965) and Pope Paul VI's shoring up of Pope Pius XI's teaching on artificial contraception in *Humanae vitae* (1968); both make interesting modern morality tales.

The Declaration on Religious Freedom: An Abridged Morality Tale

The story begins with the nineteenth-century condemnations of religious liberty that were promulgated in the context of the aftermath of the eighteenth-century French and American constitutional declarations that asserted such a right. For example, Pope Pius IX's encyclical *Quanta cura* (1864) described as an 'erroneous opinion' the view that liberty of conscience and religion should be constitutional rights.[8] His infamous *Syllabus of Errors* (1864) specifically anathematized the following:

Error 77 'In our time it is no longer expedient to recognize the Catholic religion as the sole religion of the state, to the exclusion of any other forms of worship.'

Error 78 'Hence it is laudable in certain Catholic countries to provide by law for the people immigrating thither to be allowed publicly to practise their own religion, of whatever form it may be.'

Error 79 'For it is false that civil liberty for any kind of cult and likewise the full power granted to all of proclaiming openly and publicly any kind of opinions and ideas easily leads to corruption of the minds and morals of nations and to the propagation of the plague of indifferentism.'

Error 80 'The Roman Pontiff can and should reconcile and harmonize himself with progress, with liberalism, and with modern civilization.'

The reality on the ground was that some states were identifiably Catholic whereas, in others, Catholics were a minority religious population. In both scenarios Catholics demanded the right to confess the (true) Catholic faith. However, in Catholic states the same freedom of religion was not always extended to non-Catholics. The Church's stance at that time is succinctly summarized by Pietro Pavan: 'it demands freedom for itself in those political communities where Catholics are in the minority, while refusing the same freedom to non-Catholics in political communities where Catholics are in the majority.'[9] By the time of the Second Vatican Council the double standard had become something of an embarrassment to the Church, and a major stumbling block to the furtherance of ecumenism. Change, however, was not inevitable. On what basis could the Council Fathers overturn the body of previous papal teaching that error has no rights? In the *aula* of St Peter's, opponents of change expressed their misgivings:

> In the debate, 25 to 29 September, Cardinal Ruffini posed the question: How can the Catholic Church, which is the true Church and bearer of the truth, abandon the fostering of this faith, wherever possible, even with the help of the state? Toleration – yes; freedom – no! Cardinal Ottaviani raised the question: Will not the concordats concluded by the Holy See, for example, with Italy and Spain, which allow to the Catholic Church a privileged position, come to nothing through this declaration?[10]

However, a strong lobby emerged in favour of religious freedom, including the American bishops (supported by the arguments of John Courtney Murray SJ), who saw the positive rapprochement that it would allow with American Protestants, and Archbishop Karol Wojtyła of Krakow (later Pope John Paul II), who recognized the necessity of religious liberty as a means of countering religious persecution under atheistic communism in Eastern Europe. The debates during the second and third sessions of the council grew more heated, and the manoeuvrings of the minority opponents of change became increasingly Machiavellian.[11]

The argument for change was won, in no small part, due to the impassioned and persuasive rhetoric of bishops such as Emile Joseph de Smedt, Bishop of Bruges (briefed by Louis Janssens), who acted as *relator* of the draft text.[12] It was perhaps de Smedt more than any other speaker who convinced the Council Fathers that change was justified, and he did so by persuading them that the text of the declaration did not constitute a break with the Church's tradition. In his speech during the second session he sketched out the argument for change on the basis of a progress of doctrine that remains substantially consistent and in continuity with previous papal teachings that appear to condemn religious liberty: 'the doctrine [of religious liberty] must be understood as the contemporary terminus of a process of evolution both in the doctrine on the dignity of the human person and in the Church's pastoral solicitude for man's freedom.'[13] According to de Smedt, one can trace in the statements of earlier popes such as Leo XIII and Pius XI an emerging vision of human dignity and freedom found more explicitly in John XXIII's encyclical *Pacem in terris* (1963). The condemnations of religious liberty were made in the context of religious indifference and the rationalist position that conscience is subject to no higher law – views that Catholicism would still hold to be false. Historical analysis reveals that the political context that led to these papal condemnations no longer applies. To suggest that the teachings of previous popes undermine the current text would be 'to force the text to speak outside of its historical and doctrinal context'.[14]

While opponents of change pointed to the lack of scriptural warrant for religious liberty, the final version of the declaration (which bears the unmistakable imprint of Courtney Murray) establishes its position on the basis of the gospel and natural law. The New Testament offers the example of Christ and the apostles who never coerced followers but offered the gospel in truth and love. God has a regard for the dignity of the human person who stands under no compulsion. This allows the Church to concede that it has not always followed the spirit of the gospel but has sometimes opposed it.[15] The declaration was finally accepted by a large majority vote on the penultimate day of the council and became an object lesson in the historically conscious methodology of Vatican II. In the words of Jan Jans, the council had resisted the 'temptation to paint over new questions with old answers'.[16] The opening statement of the declaration states:

> This Vatican Council pays careful attention to these spiritual aspirations and, with a view to declaring to what extent they are in accord with the truth and justice, searches the sacred tradition and teaching of the Church, from which she draws forth new things that are always in harmony with the old … Furthermore, in dealing with this question of liberty the sacred Council intends to develop the teaching of recent popes on the inviolable rights of the human person and on the constitutional order of society.[17]

Thus, in Article 2, 'The Vatican Council declares that the human person has a right to religious freedom', Archbishop Marcel Lefebvre, vociferous opponent of change, was convinced that the Church's previous teaching had been trumped by the values of the secular Enlightenment.[18] In his view the declaration had more in common with the philosophies of Hobbes, Locke and Rousseau than with Pius IX and Leo XIII: 'The revolutionary slogan "Liberty, Equality and Fraternity"', Lefebvre famously said, 'had finally triumphed: liberty was religious liberty, equality equalled collegiality, and in fraternity he spotted ecumenism.'[19] Lefebvre's baneful assessment remains a minority view. The doctrine of religious freedom has become assimilated into the Catholic moral tradition. Hindsight, to most Catholics, makes it seem as though it always belonged there. Pius IX's *Syllabus* is more likely to inspire incredulity to the modern eye and scandalize those Christians who read it. The Declaration on Religious Freedom sent a powerful signal to the world that the Catholic Church is a fellow participant in humanity's moral history, and that doctrinal change is sometimes possible and desirable. Nonetheless, that considerable achievement came at a price, because it limited Catholicism's understanding of moral change to a cautious notion of doctrinal development based on continuity with and growth out of previous magisterial teachings; and, while this has the merit of retaining the prudence of an inherent conservatism, it also betrays an uncritical confidence in the content of official Church statements and the process of their composition.

Humanae Vitae: An Abridged Morality Tale

Four Catholic statements encapsulate the 'problem of development' as it impacted on the birth-control debate in the 1960s.

Paul VI, Allocution to the Sacred College of Cardinals, 23 June 1964

As the Commission on the Problems of Marriage and Family established by Pope Paul VI debated the merits and demerits of the case for artificial birth control, and public debate and speculation grew, Paul VI issued an unconvincing Allocution to the Sacred College of Cardinals:

> We say frankly that so far we do not have sufficient reason to consider the norms given by Pope Pius XII on this matter as out of date and therefore as not binding. They must be considered as valid, at least until we feel obliged in conscience to change them. In a matter of such seriousness it seems well that Catholics should wish to follow one single law, that which the Church puts forward with authority. It therefore seems opportune that, for the present, no one take it upon himself to make pronouncements in terms which differ from the prevailing norms.[20]

In this statement, Paul understandably asks the cardinals to sing from the same song-sheet on a matter of such seriousness. However, the statement concedes that norms proposed by a pope may become 'out of date' and subject to change on the basis of better knowledge.

During the course of its deliberations, the papal commission produced two working papers that represented the differing views and theological approaches of its members. As is well-known, a minority of the commission's participants strongly resisted a change to the Church's teaching on birth control, whereas a large majority favoured and recommended change. These working papers offer important insights into how the possibility of doctrinal change had become a major preoccupation and theological challenge in and of itself. Fortunately these documents came into the public arena when they were leaked to *The Tablet* and *National Catholic Reporter* in 1967.

Minority Working Paper, 23 May 1966

The four theologians on the papal commission who believed that the Church must retain the traditional condemnation of contraception could produce no convincing moral arguments in favour of a continued ban. Under the general heading: 'Why does the Church teach that contraception is always seriously evil?' the minority working paper states: 'If we could bring forward arguments which are clear and cogent based on reason alone, it would not be necessary for our commission to exist, nor would the present state of affairs exist in the Church as it is'.[21] Given this startling admission, the minority set out the real reasons for its concerns:

> The Church cannot change its answer *because this answer is true* ... It is true because the Catholic Church, instituted by Christ to show men a secure way to eternal life, could not have so wrongly erred during all those centuries of its history ... If the Church could err in such a way, the authority of the ordinary magisterium in moral matters would be thrown into question. The faithful could not put their trust in the magisterium's presentation of moral teaching, especially in sexual matters.[22]

The authors also appealed to moral slippage: if the teaching were to change on birth control, the natural-law prohibitions against other forms of sexual activity (such as masturbation, oral intercourse and direct sterilization) would be weakened. The notion of error in Magisterial teaching inevitably raised questions about the role of the Holy Spirit in guiding the Church. If Pius XI had been mistaken in his encyclical *Casti connubii* (1930), in which he describes contraceptive sex as 'grave sin', that would surely imply that the Anglican Communion's decision at the Lambeth Conference earlier that year to permit birth control within marriage had been right and that the Spirit was blowing through the wrong Church![23]

> This change would inflict a grave blow on the teaching about the assistance of the Holy Spirit, promised to the Church to lead the faithful on the right way towards their salvation ... Is it nevertheless now to be admitted that the Church erred in this its work, and that the Holy Spirit rather assists the Anglican Church? ... For the Church to have erred so gravely in its grave responsibility of leading souls would be tantamount to seriously suggesting that the assistance of the Holy Spirit was lacking to it.[24]

It seems extraordinary that, during a council in which ecumenical relations were high on the agenda, theologians could demonstrate such limited horizons and go so far as to express them in print. In the same vein, Bernard Häring records the well-known conversation between Fr Zalba SJ and Mrs Patty Crowley that illustrates the theological gulf between commission members:

> Zalba argued emotionally: 'What then about the millions of souls which according to the norms of *Casti connubii* we have damned to hell, if those norms were not valid?'
> The lovable Mrs Crowley answered casually: 'Do you really believe that God has carried out all your orders?'[25]

As leaders of the Christian Family Movement, American husband and wife team Pat and Patty Crowley had been invited to become members of the papal commission in 1964. It was their initiative of canvassing the members of their organization through questionnaires that allowed the voices and experiences of married couples to be taken on board by the commission members, and that provided a reliable body of evidence beyond anecdotal tales from the confessional, of the difficulties that married couples utilizing the rhythm method of birth control were facing in their efforts to combine responsible parenthood with fidelity to Church teaching. These almost unanimous stories of anguish conscientized the Crowleys and, when made public, catalyzed the case for change.[26]

Majority Working Paper, 27 May 1966

The majority position argued that Church teaching was in a period of evolution in which inadequate concepts of nature and natural law were in the process of being refined. While a change in teaching would require an admission of error on the part of the Church's Magisterium, the fact that the Church had conceded teaching errors in the past (for example, that sex must always have a procreative intention) meant that a future change need not be seen to undermine the credibility of the Church's teaching office:

> Such a change is to be seen rather as a step towards a more mature comprehension of the whole doctrine of the Church. For doubt and reconsideration are quite reasonable when proper reasons for doubt and reconsideration occur with regard to some specific question.[27]

The Theological Report of the Pontifical Commission, 26 June 1966

The final report of the commission, submitted to Paul VI, represented the view of a large majority of the commission's members and proposed the permissibility of regulating conception by artificial means. The arguments set out to justify a change in teaching follow a methodological and strategic template which mirrors that used in the drafts of the Declaration on Religious Freedom. Drawing on the teachings of Leo XIII's *Arcanum* (1880) Pius XI's *Casti connubii* and Pius XII's Address to the Midwives (1951), a careful account is constructed in order to illustrate how the proposed new vision for marriage and fecundity shares strong elements of continuity with the established teaching. Tradition has always sought to protect the good of procreation and the rightness of marital intercourse. A contraceptive mentality would therefore be wrong. However, the report claims that to allow contraception would contradict neither the tradition nor the purpose of previous doctrinal condemnations:

> A further step in the doctrinal evolution, which it seems now should be developed, is founded ... on a better, deeper and more correct understanding of conjugal life and of the conjugal act when these other changes occur. The doctrine on marriage and its essential values remains the same and whole, but it is now applied differently out of a deeper understanding.[28]

The 'Pastoral Approaches' section at the beginning of the report states: 'The whole of this developed doctrine can only appear to those who reflect on it as an enrichment, in full continuity with the deep, but more rigorous, moral orientations of the past'.[29] It took some two years of careful and even anguished deliberations on the part of Paul VI to consider the evidence of the papal commission and, suffering from what one could call *kairos*-blindness, to conclude that a change in the Church's moral teaching on contraception was not possible. Or, more strictly speaking, perhaps one should say that the prohibition was reasserted. Change had occurred in the arguments adduced to support the ban. *Humanae vitae* introduces the so-called 'inseparability principle' of the unitive and procreative dimensions of intercourse into Catholic teaching, thereby cementing a restrictive, biologically structured understanding of the natural law into sexual ethics and favouring the type of pre-Vatican II stoical approach to sex that had been studiously ignored in favour of the more covenantal language of marriage as a partnership of life and love in *Gaudium et spes* during the council (which will surely provide the theological escape route for future doctrinal change when *Humanae vitae* is overturned). Aware of the lack of persuasive force in the arguments adduced, Paul VI called on moral theologians to provide further reasons in support of the doctrine on biblical, ethical and personalistic grounds, a call that was reasserted by John Paul II in *Familiaris consortio* and attempted by him in his writings on the theology of the body.[30]

What can we Learn from these Morality Tales?

On Error and Change

> Suppose the test of orthodoxy were, Would Augustine or Thomas be surprised if he were to return and see what Catholic theologians are teaching today? By this criterion, the entire development of the purposes of marital intercourse would have been unorthodox. But it is a perennial mistake to confuse repetition of old formulas with the living law of the Church. The Church, on its pilgrim path, has grown in grace and wisdom.[31]

Perhaps there is a lesson here in how Christians understand the way that their tradition shapes their response to moral questions. The Catholic tendency has been to justify current teachings by appeal to continuity with previous teachings. Inevitably such a process is conservative in nature. The theological method this requires also creates an ambivalent and often uncritical attitude towards historical context. The Vatican tends to select and cite Magisterial texts as illustrations of the constancy and consistency of permanently valid teaching. In such moves, the historical context of statements is generally downplayed. The social, political, cultural and historical conditions that shaped the formulation of a statement are seldom cited. When reference is made to the historical conditions at the time of the text's composition, it is almost always as a means of offering mitigating circumstances that are supposed to reduce the degree of culpability for Church error.[32] It is perfectly possible and even likely that there is no ill-intent in the employment of these strategies. In which case, the degree of denial at work in Vatican reluctance to concede that not all its teachings are guaranteed error-free can only be described as institutionally pathological.

75

Catholic reluctance to admit of the existence of error in Church teaching is vividly demonstrated by the fear bordering on paranoia demonstrated by the theologians representing the minority position on the Papal Birth Control Commission. However, their fears were surely based on lack of due attention to the history of doctrine. As Hans Küng points out, citing a raft of Catholic U-turns including the condemnation of Galileo, the eleventh-century excommunication of Patriarch Photius and the Greek Church that formalized the schism with the Eastern Church, the prohibition of usury, condemnations of historical-critical methods of reading the Bible and the condemnations of evolution: 'it would be thoroughly naive to assume that an error in the question of birth control is the first serious error that has crept into the church's *magisterium*'.[33] Perhaps John Paul II's readiness to apologize for the past wrongs of the Church in terms of its sins against women, aboriginal peoples and Jews are the first fruits of a growing readiness to acknowledge the existence of institutional sin on the part of the Catholic Church in addition to the personal sin of individual believers, thus taking more seriously the maxim *ecclesia semper reformanda* – the Church always in need of reform.

The Catholic Moral Tradition as Participant in History

The Catholic moral tradition is not a dusty deposit of doctrinal documents. It is first and foremost something that is embodied and lived out in the concrete lives of people participating in human history. The way that they do so is according to the Vatican II principle of 'scrutinizing the signs of the times and of interpreting them in the light of the gospel'.[34] In this way, Scripture is continually reactivated and made alive in the lives of successive generations of Christians. This is the arena in which moral theology becomes meaningful and why Kevin Kelly's contribution to it rings true. He states:

> Christian moral theology must not be reduced to an exploration of moral concepts, however interesting that might be. An essential feature of it must be an involvement in reading the signs of the times for our world today so that these signs can be appropriately responded to ... That is why moral theology must be experience-based. The signs of the times are not restricted to the world of ideas. They include the joys and hopes, the sufferings and fears of human persons and the human family. The signs of the times have to be *felt*. They are the way the human spirit, moved by God's own Spirit, recoils in horror from whatever is dehumanizing and violating respect for persons in our world today. The signs of the times are *movements* of the human spirit. They embody human emotions of anger, repugnance, horror, fear, anxiety as well as the positive emotions of hope, expectation, determination, courage, etc. A disembodied moral theology will be oblivious to the real signs of the times.[35]

Johan Verstraeten describes this process in terms of a hermeneutical relation between the living community historically situated and the formative texts of the tradition.[36] This two-way process of mutual interrogation is the essential nutrient that keeps Christian tradition flourishing and, as John Mahoney notes, 'it is from the continuing dialectic, for the Church as for all believers, between belief and experience that there results what theology has come to term the development of doctrine'.[37] Of course, doctrinal formulation is only one of many Christian tasks – and one that has been emphasized by the hierarchy (especially during its more authoritarian phases) to the detriment of many more pressing Christian imperatives. It is salutary to recall that large numbers of Catholics remain oblivious to many elements of Church teachings – both theological and moral – and to the internal wrangles that surround particular texts.

On the Enduring Presence of the Holy Spirit in the Life of the Christian Church

Perhaps Heisenberg's Uncertainty Principle should be more readily invoked when humans attempt to predict with certainty both the location and the action of the Spirit in the life of the Church. If one examines the frequent appeals to the work of the Holy Spirit in Catholic Church teaching, one could be forgiven for concluding that the Spirit spends a rather disproportionate amount of time operating within the bounds of the doctrinal formulations and pronouncements of the Magisterium. Could there be a reason for this? Would it be appropriate to suggest a more devolved understanding of the Spirit's operation? In a passage in *Humanae vitae* (which is quoted approvingly in *Veritatis splendor*), it states: 'We hold it as certain that while the Holy Spirit of God is present to the Magisterium proclaiming sound doctrine, he also illumines from within the hearts of the Faithful and invites their assent.'[38] My point is that the Spirit of Truth might be prompting a quite different response.[39]

The title of this paper is expressed in terms of change in, rather than development of, moral doctrine. The term *doctrinal development* can be too easily misunderstood to refer to an effortless organic (and always faithful) unfolding of what has gone before. There are no a priori laws that can be advanced in order to project into the Christian future on the basis of what has been taught in the past. We should not be surprised, therefore, to find that the necessary human struggle in history to search for the truth of the gospel is flourishing in lively debates within Catholicism. What an unexpected lesson to learn from *Veritatis splendor*.

Notes

1. Charles de Montesquieu, *The Spirit of the Laws* (trans. Thomas Nugent: rev. J.V. Prichard), (London: G. Bell & Sons, 1914 [1748]), book XV.5. In the same ironic vein, and not irrelevant to our discourse, he writes: 'I would as soon say that religion gives its professors a right to enslave those who dissent from it, in order to render its propagation more easy' (*ibid.*, book XV.4). The Catholic Church placed *The Spirit of the Laws* on the Index of Forbidden Books.
2. This episode is brilliantly captured by John T. Noonan Jr in his work on moral change in the Catholic tradition, *A Church That Can and Cannot Change: The Development of Catholic Moral Teaching* (Notre Dame, IN: University of Notre Dame Press, 2005), pp. 102–109.
3. Pope John Paul II, Encyclical Letter *Veritatis splendor* (1993), 28.
4. Dogmatic Constitution on Divine Revelation, *Dei verbum* (Vatican II, 1965), 8; cf. *Veritatis splendor*, 27.

5. Cf. *ibid.*, 53.
6. *Ibid.*, 4.
7. Cf. *ibid.*, 4.
8. Pope Pius IX, Encyclical Letter Condemning Current Errors *Quanta cura* (1864), 3.
9. Pietro Pavan, 'Declaration on Religious Freedom' in H. Vorgrimler (ed.), *Commentary on the Documents of Vatican II* (London: Burns & Oates, 1969), vol. IV, pp. 49–86 (51).
10. H. Jedin, 'Chapter 4: The Second Vatican Council', in Hubert Jedin *et al.* (eds), *History of the Church Volume X: The Church in the Modern Age* (London: Burns & Oates, 1984), pp. 96–151 (127–28).
11. For a less 'airbrushed' account of events than that provided by Pavan, see Jedin, 'Second Vatican Council'.
12. For an account of Janssens' role in the composition of the declaration see Jan Jans, 'Enjoying and Making Use of a Responsible Freedom: Background and Substantiation of *Human Dignity* in the Second Vatican Council's in *Sustaining Humanity Beyond Humanism* (Societas Ethica Jahresbericht; Aarhus, Denmark: Societas Ethica, 2002), pp. 101–12; for Janssens' theological position on religious freedom see Louis Janssens, *Freedom of Conscience and Religious Freedom* (trans. Brother Lorenzo CFX), (Staten Island, NY: Alba House, 1965).
13. Emile Joseph de Smedt, Bishop of Bruges, '*relatio*' during the second session of the council, in H. Küng, Y. Congar and D. O'Hanlon (eds), *Council Speeches of Vatican II* (New Jersey: Deus Books and Paulist Press, 1964), pp. 237–53 (245).
14. *Ibid.*, p. 253.
15. Declaration on Religious Freedom, *Dignitatis humanae* (Vatican II, 1965), 12.
16. Jans, 'Enjoying and Making Use of a Responsible Freedom', pp. 101–12, 102.
17. *Dignitatis humanae*, 1.
18. Lefebvre, 'Intervention', 20 September 1965, in *Acta Synodalia Sancti Concilii Oecumenici Vaticani II* (Rome, 1976), 4.1, p. 409.
19. Michael Walsh, 'U-turn on Human Rights', *The Tablet* (14 December 2002): 7–9 (8).
20. Paul VI, Allocution to the Sacred College of Cardinals, 23 June 1964, *Acta Apostolicae Sedis* 56 (1964): 588–89.
21. In Peter Harris *et al.*, *On Human Life: An Examination of Humanae Vitae* (London: Burns & Oates, 1968), p. 178; see also *The Tablet* (29 April 1967): 485.
22. In Harris *et al.*, *On Human Life*, pp. 181–82.
23. Pope Pius XI, Encyclical Letter on Christian Marriage, *Casti connubii* (1930), 56; Anglican Communion, Lambeth Conference 1930, resolution 15. The text is available at the Lambeth Conference website: <http://www.lambethconference.org/resolutions/1930/1930-15.cfm>.
24. In Harris *et al.*, *On Human Life*, pp. 201–202.
25. Bernard Häring, *My Witness for the Church* (trans. L. Swidler), (New York: Paulist Press, 1992), p. 74.
26. Cf. Robert McClory, *Turning Point: The Inside Story of the Papal Birth*

Control Commission, and How Humanae Vitae *Changed the Life of Patty Crowley and the Future of the Church* (New York: Crossroad, 1995); Robert Blair Kaiser, *The Encyclical That Never Was: The Story of the Pontifical Commission on Population, Family and Birth, 1964-66* (London: Sheed & Ward, 1987).

27. In Harris *et al.*, *On Human Life*, p. 207.
28. In *ibid.*, p. 234.
29. In *ibid.*, p. 221.
30. Pope John Paul II, Apostolic Exhortation 'On the Role of the Christian Family in the Modern World' *Familiaris consortio* (1981)31; Cf. Karol Wojtyła, *Love and Responsibility* (San Francisco, CA: Ignatius Press, rev. edn, 1993).
31. John T. Noonan Jr, *Contraception: A History of Its Treatment by the Catholic Theologians and Canonists* (New York: A Mentor-Omega Book, 1965), p. 630.
32. For a discussion of papal appeals to historical conditioning, see J. Clague, 'Assessing Our Inheritance: John Paul II and the Dignity of Women', in Julian Filochowski and Peter Stanford (eds), *Opening Up: Speaking Out in the Church* (London: Darton, Longman and Todd, 2005), pp. 41–55.
33. Hans Küng, *Truthfulness: The Future of the Church* (London: Sheed & Ward, 1968), p. 178.
34. Pastoral Constitution on the Church in the Modern World, *Gaudium et spes* (Vatican II, 1965), 4.
35. Kevin T. Kelly, *New Directions in Moral Theology: The Challenge of Being Human* (London: Geoffrey Chapman, 1992), p. 91.
36. Cf. Johan Verstraeten, 'Re-thinking Catholic Social Thought As Tradition', in J.S. Boswell *et al.* (eds), *Catholic Social Thought: Twilight or Renaissance?* (Bibliotheca Ephemeridum Theologicarum Lovaniensium, 157; Leuven: Leuven University Press, 2000), pp. 59–77, esp. 70–71.
37. John Mahoney, *The Making of Moral Theology: A Study of the Roman Catholic Tradition* (Oxford: Clarendon Press, 1987), p. 218.
38. Pope Paul VI, Encyclical Letter *Humanae vitae* (1968), 29.
39. Cf. John Mahoney, *The Making of Moral Theology*, p. 295.

7

The Good News in Moral Theology:
Of Hospitality, Healing and Hope

Enda McDonagh

When Kevin Kelly began to study and then to teach moral theology, it was not notable for its 'Good News'. Professional moral theologians and the textbooks of that era were not what is termed in other contexts 'gospel-greedy'. Indeed Jesus and his joyous message of the imminent reign of God were scarcely mentioned. The 'bad news' of sin in number and kind predominated. In the subsequent transformation of moral theology and its rediscovery of Jesus's Good News, Kevin Kelly has played a very significant role. For students and colleagues, lay and clerical, Kelly has himself become 'Good News', but not without paying a price exacted by those whom Pope John XXIII dubbed, at the beginning of Vatican II, 'the prophets of doom'.

Without attempting any serious evaluation of either the developments in moral theology over the last half-century or Kelly's splendid contribution to them, this short essay seeks to elaborate some aspects of the Good News implied, if seldom made explicit, in these developments. Given some previous efforts to address similar issues and a certain weakness for alliteration, it did not surprise me to find these aspects listed in my mind as 'Hospitality, Healing and Hope', although in some other contexts the order might be different.

Of Hospitality in Moral Theology

Beyond the Inhospitable Discipline and its God

Whatever may be the origins of the human male, according to popular lore, morality, in its Hebrew, Greek and even Christian forms, and in various combinations of these, too often seemed to be from Mars; too often a cold military-style code of behaviour, demanding total obedience and lacking any concessions to the varieties and vagaries of real human beings. That form and style inevitably suggested a warrior, punitive, even vindictive God, certainly not the Hebrew God of loving kindness (*hesed*) or the God who is love (*agape*), the Abba-Father God of Jesus and the New Testament. Out of that distortion of Jewish-Christian morality and of its God grew the inhospitable discipline known as moral theology or, in this last half-century, more correctly as manual moral theology. Not that we should or can dismiss the justice and judging dimensions of the God and morality of Israel and of Jesus, but that we must integrate them, nay, subordinate them to the two great commandments of love of God and love of neighbour and their divine author. Justice continues to give love its cutting edge without dehumanizing or de-divinizing that love. It is in such a theological framework that hospitality, as characteristic/ virtue of the creating, saving and sanctifying God and of the human creature as image, child and temple of the same God, may raise its lovely head.

The Garden Party of Creation and its Divine Host/Artist

Although there are numerous examples of the practice and value of hospitality in both the Hebrew and Christian Scriptures, from the father of Hebrew and Christian faith, Abraham, to the centre of Christian faith, Jesus (and to these Scriptures we shall return), the heart of divine hospitality and the source of its human counterpart lie in the originating and continuing divine act of creation, continuing in the face of persistent human refusal of that divine graciousness. In face of that human refusal called sin, the continuing divine hospitality emerges as new creation in Jesus. To appreciate the depth and range of the human call to hospitality, its centrality to Christian life and to the examined Christian life in moral theology, it is necessary to begin at the beginning, with the God who created the Heavens and the Earth, saw that they were good and invited man and woman, created in the divine image, to share, enjoy and care for them.

The Genesis accounts of creation combine some of the features of a celebratory garden party given by a generous host with those of an artistic exhibition in which the artist also displays the earlier stages of his now completed work. The host/ artist is, of course, the creator/God. And the artworks of creation, as well as the celebratory food and drink, are available as free gifts for the enjoyment of all the guests: in this context, all generations of the human race. Jahweh, the God of Israel, appears as generous host and creative artist right through the history of Israel, as that history is recorded, prophetically judged and anticipated, celebrated and lamented in the Hebrew Scriptures.

The divine host/artist sets the tone as he recognizes the good and celebrates the goods of his creation-party offerings and welcomes the first human guests as reflections of his own goodness, and encourages them both to enjoy and care for what has been provided. Even at this first mythological but truth-bearing party, when the host's back is turned, the guests are tempted to get above themselves and to misbehave. It is ever so, but this host, at first offended, reaches more deeply into his resources of creative hospitality and loving kindness to maintain divine–human friendship in forgiveness, renewal of promise and celebration. East of Eden, in which land of Cain all human beings still partially reside with all their tragic failures and scandals, the role of divine host and the rule of divine hospitality persist. At their best the human guests recognize the role and accept the rule to the point of employing role and rule to act as hosts and guests of one another. As carers and sharers of the offerings of the divine creation, they behave in what prophets from Isaiah to Jesus might call a just and loving way.

In its more conventional and restricted sense, the language and practice of hospitality recur in biblical narrative and prophetic injunction. Abraham's reception of the strangers in Gen. 18 is the most notable example. The inhospitality of others, such as the people of Sodom, prepares the way for the condemnations by Amos and his prophetic colleagues of the neglect of the needy, the poor, the widow, the orphan and the stranger. Strangers as the Israelites were in Egypt, and beneficiaries as they were in their hunger and thirst in their exodus in the desert through the generosity of their God with manna from the heavens and water from the rock, they are called to show similar hospitality to the neighbour and visitor in need. The messianic land and age of promise, flowing with milk and honey, will typify the fullness of divine and human hospitality.

That fullness filters ambiguously through the nativity stories in the Gospels of Luke and Mark. The re-creative generosity of God in sending his own Son meets with the hospitable responses of Mary and Joseph, of Zachariah and Elizabeth, of the angels and the shepherds, of the wise men from the east, but suffers the rejection of the innkeeper and the murderous hostility of Herod, all this in parallel to the glory and the tragedy of Genesis. In the more nearly biographical sections of all four Gospels, the hospitality of God in Jesus, particularly towards the poor and excluded, and the return of hospitality by these to Jesus, are key to understanding the new divine–human relationship already in being and yet to be completed.

This active table-fellowship hospitality finds vivid expression in Jesus's teaching through parable and exhortation. In John, the most abstract of the evangelists in so many ways, Jesus's active ministry opens and closes with a party, the wedding party at Cana and the farewell party in the upper room in Jerusalem. It is unnecessary, and would be tedious for Gospel readers, to rehearse all the events from the feeding of the 5,000 to the parables of Luke to the final judgement account in Matthew to be aware of how deeply hospitality enters into the ministry and teaching of Jesus and how it is still invoked in the post-resurrection stories. With all that taken for granted, one may move on to how hospitality relates to the accepted major characteristics of Christian living, and so shapes that living, to how it may provide the basic guidance for that living to which moral theology also aspires.

Hospitality and Justice

Although charity/love played a pivotal role in the recent renewal of moral theology, justice in various forms may be more relevant here; partly because theological discussion of it too has developed in remarkable ways over the last decades, and partly because, at first inspection anyway, it may prove more challenging than charity to any central position for hospitality in moral theology. The harder edges of justice in morality, law and theology, with their retributive, retaliative and punitive echoes, seem far removed from the generous and forgiving spirit of hospitality. *Fiat justitia, ruat coelum* may be of secular rather than religious origin, but few religious traditions have escaped its influence, and that influence operated, sometimes at least, to organized religion's benefit. The injustices practised within the Christian tradition, for example, even against its own believers, including theologians, were not often overcome by the Church's formal adherence to the two great commandments. Such injustices were and are violations of hospitality, of the openness to the other involved in giving each person her due.

There is clearly a danger here that the violation of any moral virtue or moral commandment may be redescribed as a violation of hospitality without any additional light being shed on moral reality at issue. In the case of justice, it might be argued that hospitality is a broader and richer moral category which restores justice to its proper place as a quality of interpersonal relations and not simply a duty to be done. In such a context, for example, the preference for the poor so wonderfully illustrated in the Parable of the Feast in Lk. 13 would enjoy both the hard edge of justice and the *sans frontiers* thrust of the biblical and divine outreach. In a different fashion, the controlling value and virtue of hospitality would at once endorse the protection of society's vulnerable through the legal and court system while replacing the punitive and vindictive dimension of that system with a serious attempt at restorative justice for the offended party, at real rehabilitation for the offender and at mutual reconciliation in the society itself. Very little of these dimensions is evident in our present legal, court and prison systems. The messianic promise of liberation to prisoners in Isaiah and Lk. 4 as well as Jesus's self-identification with the prisoner you came to visit in Mt. 24 call for such hospitality justice and not in the satirical sense of regular usage with prisoners described as guests of Her Majesty.

A more obvious central role for hospitality may be found in the whole area of medical ethics. How far it would provide fresh insight into the usual boundary cases including abortion, IVF, embryonic stem-cell research, drug experimentation and assisted suicide would be open to question by certain proponents of these practices. It would at least provide a richer human context for their discussion than that of the purely autonomous, unrelated, individual human being. It should also deepen the motivation and commitment of all those engaged in both medical care and research. The origins of medical hospital and the more recent development of hospice and hospice care for the dying are eloquent testimony to the role of hospitality in the service of the sick. Beyond this, a hospitable society would be more aware of its obligations to all its sick and pressure its government to provide fair and adequate care for all.

One last and very difficult example is that of international relations. For most statesmen and commentators, the first and often the only realistic demand is to look after the national interest. A collective egoism predominates and is defended as the primary duty of leaders, whose responsibility is to their own people, whether or not they elected them. It has become increasingly difficult to confine or define the national interest of any particular state, however powerful it may appear by the usual criteria of military and economic strength. So the international interest has almost always to be considered. Unilateralism and exceptionalism, even by the very powerful, appear increasingly self-defeating. However, to identify the international interest with that of a coalition of the willing and powerful, as seems the present trend, may be successful in the shorter and more limited terms of realpolitik, but it can never be entirely stable and enduring. More significantly, in moral terms, it is deeply oppressive of the poorer and weaker nations. It is profoundly inhospitable to so many of its own kind, other human beings. Only when international relations and international law are rooted in a universal hospitality for the stranger, the poor, the weak and the sojourner, to invoke biblical categories, will there be a real prospect of a genuine united nations and of a just and peaceful world.

Other difficult domains of moral discourse and practice would, I believe, benefit from reintegration into the hospitable range of the creating and redeeming God, and of the created and redeemed human community. Sexuality may be one of the more difficult domains, as it is in every moral vision. Saving the Earth should be one of the easier ones, given creator/God as host, humans as the pre-eminent guests of creator and creation, hosts as well as guests of one another and of the rest of creation. And all this founded in the engagement of the triune God, whose reign is at hand but not complete.

Of Healing

The hospitality stories and their moral insights from Eden to Emmaus have their limitations as they also reveal the failures of their human protagonists. Divine hospitality in creation and salvation is destined to be a healing hospitality as well. The messianic promises, their fulfilment in the life and ministry of Jesus and their earlier partial anticipation in the history of Israel focus on that healing hospitality. However pure the divine or even human invitation and welcome may be as they face their guests, in establishing and developing personal, social or political relationships, human weaknesses, flaws and failures are endemic. We humans are sinners all, not only in relation to God, but in relation to one another. The Good News moral theology, however, includes healing in the hospitality, as so many of Jesus's actions and parables demonstrate. 'Which is it easier to say, Thy sins are forgiven thee or Take up thy bed and walk' (Mk 2.9).

In elaborating a Christian moral vision and any moral code derived from it, healing and forgiveness must be intrinsic to it. An idealistic moral system based on virtue (Aristotle), duty (Kant) or law (Decalogue, manuals) is not adequate to the human condition and its relationships because the healing and forgiveness are extrinsic and come after the fact, the fact of the inherently limited human condition as physically and morally vulnerable, as sinful and mortal. And, despite the perduring goodness of creator and creation and crucial healing accomplished in Jesus Christ, the holistic healing of the divine hospitality is yet to be. The historical earnest (*arrabon*) of which Paul speaks in 2 Cor., and which we already enjoy, reaches its fulfilment only in the eschaton. The interaction between hospitality and healing in all moral understanding and moral endeavour underlines the eschatological dimension of moral theology, which is, in itself, always flawed and incomplete, always in search of the fuller truth and practice, indeed the fuller truth through practice, including mistaken practice. That fuller, more healed moral truth and practice reflects the moral progress of the past in the exclusion of slavery, torture and capital punishment, for example, in the restrictions on warfare through the developing criteria for just war over the past centuries and the possibility of a total moral ban on war in the centuries ahead. In all these, better moral understanding and practice have benefited from the interaction. In the case of slavery, for example, whereas, in the nineteenth century, simple liberation could not satisfy the demands of hospitality, so grievously violated by the system, healing was necessary of both master and slave and of the destructive impact of the system. Such healing and hospitality are far from complete in social terms while new forms of the old oppression continue to surface.

In other moral areas, practice and understanding worthy of hospitality are not attainable without a great deal of healing. Sexuality provides many and difficult examples of this. Sexual development of young people depends on the hospitable care, support and understanding of adults, parents and mentors, who are often far from being open and integrated, healed and mature guides and companions in their own sexual lives. More progress could be made in morally good sexual understanding and practice if the hospitality which must always include justice and respect for the other were offered in a healing way by somebody aware of his own continuing need of healing. As in other moral relationships, the creative interaction between hospitality, the loving welcome of the other and healing care are essential to the followers of him who spent so much time with prostitutes and sinners. The insights of the moral theology of sexuality into masturbation, homosexuality and contraception, to take a few recently controverted examples, will continue to develop effectively only in such a hospitable and healing context, with all the intellectual, emotional and practical implications which that involves.

Of Hope

The final H-word in this brief excursus into Christian moral theology is the final historical H-word, indeed the final word of all Christian theology, Hope. In the human understanding and practice of the Christian moral life, the limitations of creatureliness and failure are endemic. As Paul expresses it, we are saved in hope; we see now through a glass darkly, and so the call to perfection of mind and morality remains out of reach. Not that we are not called to seek perfection and do not have some real grasp of moral truth. But the fullness is beyond us. The eschatological dimension of our very being is at once the source of our frustration and the basis of our striving. In affecting to teach the world and to bear witness to the life and love of God in Jesus, Christians are necessarily dependent on the Spirit who will finally lead them into all truth. But it will be finally so that their present moral understanding and practice is subject to that eschatological restraint as they attempt to follow the Spirit in the hope that protects from the arrogance and presumption of certain absolutist positions and from the despair and disintegration of certain relativist positions.

Even with this summary account of hospitality, healing and hope as integral to a theology of the Christian life or moral theology, the Good News of moral theology, to which Kevin Kelly so effectively witnessed, may be clarified a little further.

Part Two

Issues in Medical and Sexual Ethics

8

Embryo, Person and Pregnancy:
A New Look at the Beginning of Life

Jacqui A. Stewart

'Reverence for life is an attitude of wonder before the ultimate mystery of life. The whole process of the beginning of life culminating in the birth of a child is one of those privileged occasions when human consciousness feels that it is in the presence of this mystery.' Thus writes Kevin Kelly in his book on *in vitro* fertilization (IVF).[1] Reverence for life might well be said to be a guiding theme of his work, and this paper is a small attempt in a related area to honour his contribution to moral theology and ethics. Recent developments in medical technology, particularly in respect of embryonic stem cells, suggest that the question of the beginning of life might usefully be revisited, and some of the issues raised in Kevin Kelly's *Life and Love* are pertinent, as is his discussion of human dignity in ethics.[2]

Central to the debate about embryonic stem-cell research is the same question that underlies discussion of abortion and of IVF. It is the question of when human life begins. In a recent review of ethics and stem-cell research in a Catholic context, David Kelly summarizes some of the relevant arguments. The first difficulty is to define the question adequately. For example, blood cells can be human and alive, but there is no moral concern about the disposal of such isolated tissue. David Kelly gives two alternative formulations of the question. One may ask, when is there a human life with full basic human rights? Or, when is there a person? Official Catholic teaching distinguishes between these positions, arguing that the former is the appropriate question to be asked in the case of the human embryo, which must be treated as if it were a person. David Kelly observes that the logical consequence of this is that the terms become equivalent, while he prefers to speak about the presence of human personhood. He notes several traditional ways of defining this. Personhood has been defined by the possession of properties such as reason. It has also been defined in terms of potentiality to become free, autonomous, rational beings. And it has been defined simply by classification; any member of the human species is said to be a person.

David Kelly observes that, in human history, none of these approaches has avoided solutions with unacceptable conclusions, such as excluding particular races, people with brain damage, etc. He follows the typology suggested by Daniel Callahan in summarizing current ways of describing the earliest point at which human personhood can be thought to be present, and characterizes the approaches as the 'firm', the 'free' and the 'fickle'.[3] The 'free' approach is to say that personhood is completely socially constructed, and persons begin when adult humans choose to identify them as such. The 'firm' approach is what David Kelly calls the Catholic geneticist school. The human person is said to be instantly present at the moment of fertilization. The 'fickle' approaches are the developmental ideas, including arguments for 'delayed hominization'. These suppose that there must be some development, for example, to a phase of individuation after the point of twinning, before persons can be definitively said to be present. David Kelly notes, as do Kevin Kelly and John Mahoney, that official Catholic Church teaching does not give a definitive answer about the point at which human personhood begins.[4] Later in this paper, I will suggest an alternative way of thinking about human personhood which may avoid some of the difficulties with these existing approaches, and which meets some of the requirements Kevin Kelly describes in his account of personhood in terms of dignity,[5] in keeping with the tradition of Catholic moral theology.

The Developmental Nature of Human Beginnings

The difficulties experienced may be made clearer by addressing the nature and status of the questions actually being asked. Certainly, the question of what is human can be itself a human classification if it is reduced to a biological or philosophical categorization, and I am not aware of any work looking at the implications of this. It has, of course, long been observed that, in biological terms, the appearance of a human being is a developmental matter. From the point of fertilization, the zygote spends six to nine days suspended in fluid in the reproductive system, and the majority of such zygotes are lost from the body because they are rejected at the implantation stage. Those that successfully implant in the uterine wall, thus getting the support for continued survival, may then divide so that twin embryos develop. Very rarely, embryos with severe malformations incompatible with life, such as an absence of brain tissue, develop to the stage of birth, but the majority of malformed embryos are rejected in the process that has come to be known as 'spontaneous abortion'. The exact timings for all the observable developmental stages in human embryonic growth are variable. Under all these circumstances, it is very difficult to mark a point on the development spectrum and assert that, on biological grounds, this is when a human being becomes present.

There is also another aspect of biology that seems to be very much neglected in the literature discussing the beginning of life. The biological changes in the mother are also highly significant, and ought to be considered along with those in the embryo. At the end of the free-floating phase, the zygote exhibits immunological markers on the trophectoblast cells from its outer cell layer. These attach to receptor molecules on the inner surface of the uterus. The binding of these molecules is associated with a chemical cascade causing maternal cells to release stimulating factors for various kinds of cell growth and other hormones. The immediate consequence of all this is the invasion of the uterine wall by the embryonic trophoblast cells and their growth into what will become the placenta. The blood vessels and muscle of the uterine wall become radically changed anatomically and physiologically. Both the embryonic tissue and the uterine tissue actively contribute to this process, and the maternal body also produces the necessary progesterone and prostaglandins.[6] These events in turn trigger a physical transformation in the maternal body which would be astonishing if it were to be seen in some other context. The appearance of high levels of certain hormones, such as human chorionic gonadatrophin, cortisol, aldosterone, etc., and the reduction in levels of other hormones, mark changes in almost every system of the body – particularly renal, cardiovascular and endocrine – and in metabolism as well as macro- and micro-anatomy[7].

These changes, spread out over the approximately nine months of gestation, represent a reciprocal biological relationship between the mother and the foetus. In plain, non-biological terms, from the moment of implantation, the mother's body changes physically, some of the changes are irreversible, and all of them contribute to the mother's sensation of her own metamorphosis. Any account of the beginning of life ought surely to consider the significance of this. And certainly, if ethical discourse is to meet the challenge of being truly inclusive, consideration of the biology should not exclude the mother. Kevin Kelly presents evidence and arguments to show that women's perspectives must be included in these discussions, not only because their natural role should give them an influential voice, but also because, up until recently, they have not had that voice.[8] In biological terms, then, the beginning of life is a developmental matter involving relationship between the nascent human being and its mother, and, even at this level, the interactions between the mother's biology and the environment contribute to her own future state as well as that of the foetus.

The Developmental Nature of the Human Person

But there are, of course, other frames of reference for considering human life. Theological anthropologies have long taken into consideration insights from the psychological and social sciences, which also show how human beings are affected and formed by their experiences.[9] The contemporary understanding of the person takes into account the constant change and accumulation of experiences over time in human life. Theological anthropology also has to reckon with philosophy, literature and history, and the changing content of concepts such as the self (that is to say, human persons as subjects and agents capable of reflexive thought).[10]

In *Life and Love*, Kevin Kelly identifies the significance of the possibility of a specifically Christian contribution to the ethical questions about recognition of the human being.[11] Classically, much theological anthropology was related to theological construction around the idea of the image of God, the *imago Dei*. This sometimes neglected other implications of theology of creation, and the overwhelming significance of the incarnation of Jesus Christ.

In a recent account of theological anthropology in the context of health care ethics, Robert Dell'Oro points out that Vatican II promoted a renewed recourse to biblical sources of moral thinking, after a period of perhaps too much stress on rationalist natural-law philosophy. The resulting account of humanity is Christocentric; human moral life is a response to the call of Christ, rather than a following of an order of nature.[12] On this reading, moral knowledge and reason are not complete or given. They develop and work towards a future, requiring an 'intersubjective communal engagement'. And, when moral life is seen as such a response, the implication is that personhood is a process of actualization, of experience and interpretation which lead to an elaboration of the relationship between the human being and God, 'that finds its completion in love'.[13]

From a liberation-theology perspective, José Comblin locates the essential dimension of the human person in the Pauline concept of the new humanity in Christ. He says that this is not a historical example for us to follow, but a concrete presence down the generations in Christian communities as they struggle to bring in the kingdom. The new human being lives in the community that is the body of Christ, empowered by the Spirit to respond to God's mission of liberation and fulfilment.[14] A developmental concept of theological anthropology is also implied by William Schweiker in his recovery of the concept of responsibility and his constructive engagement between theological ethics and contemporary thought.[15] These examples of distinctive Christian contributions to the question of what it is to be human focus on receptivity and response to the call of God as it is instantiated in the human community as the body of Christ. On this reading, human being may be being human, a process of becoming and responding to the call of God, rather than a nature or essence capable of definition. In his discussion of IVF, Kevin Kelly observes that all churches argue both for the essence of Christian marriage and against perceived negative consequences of IVF. He argues that this use of both essentialist and consequentialist arguments raises the question of the relation between action and intention. He asks, 'Do our actions merely "reveal" or "conceal" our true selves ... or are our actions sometimes the very "raw material" from which our real selves are fashioned?'[16] One may respond to this by suggesting that the evidence from biology, psychology, social science and philosophy supports the kind of theological anthropology I have sketched out here, and that our actions do indeed form our selves as fully human in a theological sense. The immediate problem is that this is all very well for the conscious responsible adult, but how can it apply to a baby, much less a human embryo? In what sense can the human being at birth, or before it, be said to be responding to the call of Christ? Or engaging in the new community's Spirit-empowered mission of liberation and fulfilment?

The Relation between Embodiment, Community, Address and Personhood

There may be a clue to a possible answer to these questions in Hilde Nelson's reflection on the personhood of her sister Carla, who was born with hydrocephaly, and who died when 18 months old.[17] Nelson explores the question of how someone can be seen as a human person, who is apparently not active in constructing that personhood, and what limitations there are to the recognition of such personhood. She refers to the importance of narrative in human identity, noting that in Carla's case, the narratives were told from before Carla's birth by her family, friends and health care professionals, and Carla could play no active role in creating or critiquing these narratives. She argues that Carla was not arbitrarily being treated as if she were a human being, but that she was being addressed as a moral being, as 'who'. The practices of interpersonal relationships between human beings were engaged with by those who knew Carla. They include the body-based attention that allows recognition of human psychological states in another, and the equally bodily-based responses to the 'other'. Nelson uses the language of soul, drawn from Wittgenstein, to ground her claim that personhood is not conferred solely by the capacities of the individual, but is constituted – and limited – by the embodied relationships between individuals. She considers the question of the foetus in pregnancy, and concludes that the mother alone has a bodily experience on which to base such a relationship, since the foetus cannot normally be seen by others. The weakness in this kind of argument is that it can be reduced to a claim for the social construction of personhood, since it depends on the application of interpersonal 'practices' in social relations.

However, something like Nelson's approach can be interpreted in terms more capable of theological expression. The modified argument might run thus. A human being is spoken of in the narratives of his or her mother, father, family, friends and carers, when a physical or biological presence has been established to allow those narratives to be meaningfully created. One can follow Paul Ricoeur's philosophical anthropology, in which the embodied person has a narrative identity. This is elucidated by interpretation, and witnessed by attestation, the 'intention to', in an implicit social context.[18] The interpretation of narratives both of the self and of others is inherently ethical because it is always responsible to something over and against itself.[19] In *Oneself as Another*, Ricoeur delimits the other, the not-self in the context of the situated self, and shows that the ethical, the good, implies solicitude for the other as well as self-esteem for ourselves. He disagrees with Levinas in that he does not give the other ontological priority, and so makes ethics as the pursuit of the good foundational, rather than morality as the requirement of responsibility and the regulation of norms. In his discussion of human capabilities, he argues that interpersonal language is distinguished by qualifiers which assume value, the recognition of the good. 'I can' means both 'I have the power to' and also 'I am allowed to'. For Ricoeur, recognition of a person is not a social convention, but a recognition of the profound reality of the good.[20] Interpersonal language has meaning because it recognizes that truth includes the ethical dimension, and this mutual recognition of the good, and the need to act on it, is a condition necessary for communication and relationship[21].

On such an account, the individual's contribution to the narrative of themselves is made initially by the limitations their own physical particularity imposes, including the necessity of gender.[22] The related human community can narrate the story of the emerging person because it shares the recognition of, and response to, the ethical reality actualized in each human life.[23] As a human being develops, becomes able to act and respond, able to communicate and able to tell his or her own story, so the human person grows and a reflexive self emerges. The identity of the human person is an identity of continuity, not a static essence, that is, the person is historical. The presence of the human person is established by a correlation of embodied physical presence and narratives arising out of a network of relationships which make concrete God's call.

On this view, the human being is not constituted purely socially[24] and the argument is not subject to Charles Curran's objections to purely relational accounts,[25] but neither is the person defined by an individual essence. Similar considerations may lie behind Kittay's application of the position of Alasdair MacIntyre in this context[26].

At this point I wish to apply an argument made by Jean Porter, who points out that contemporary developmental arguments of 'delayed hominization' are not making the same argument as the mediaeval theologians made for the late 'infusion' of soul. The soul cannot be put into a body that lacks the capacities the soul needs; that is, a rational soul needs a rational body. So, for the mediaeval theologians, the question was, when was the body ready for the soul? But the present arguments for delayed hominization are about identifying a point when the foetus 'may be said to be identical with the person which will eventually be born'.[27] I suggest that the question the mediaeval theologians asked may be more appropriate. The human person is not a static essence, but a process of continuity which depends on interactions between the physical development of the individual and relationships expressed in narratives supplied by those around him or her. At no point is the foetus identical in terms of equivalence with the child to be born; the identity is one of continuity. Insofar as the question may be asked in such isolated terms, the proper question may indeed be, when is the body ready for the interactions that start the narrative of a person and recognize the moral element of personal presence? At what point do the representatives of the human community recognize the physical warrant for speaking of another human being? If this is the right question, it is clear that the answer may vary in time, and with respect to the community's knowledge of whom or what it speaks. Quite early on in normal pregnancy, mothers begin to speak of the child to be born as a human person, in response to their growing physical awareness of the child's presence. Family narratives of a child begin before birth. Conversely, an anencephalic foetus may grow to a late stage, and yet, when knowledge of the situation is obtained by health professionals, not be perceived as physically able to sustain the narrative of continuity as a person. On the other hand, an embryo that aborts in the first weeks of pregnancy because of chromosome abnormality may do so before any such narrative can be established. Such a conclusion does not provide a simple rule with which to judge situations. Instead, it suggests that considerable practical wisdom and skill must be used to evaluate each concrete problem as it arises. Given the manifest individuality of human beings, this is not surprising. In the case of embryonic stem cells obtained from pre-implantation embryos, it is the case that their physical, embodied state does not call forth address as persons. I would therefore agree with David Kelly that research on embryonic stem cells should be permitted, but for different reasons.[28] And, it should hardly be necessary to say, I do not advance my argument as in any way dispensing with the need for attention to be paid in practical situations in order that proper reverence for the dignity of the human person be not carelessly abandoned.

The important features of any theological anthropology, derives from the incarnation of God as a human being, and the resurrection of Jesus Christ as the foundation for a new relationship between humanity and God, can be reflected in this kind of claim for human personhood. The unique condition of personhood arises from the interaction between humans as embodied spirits, which recognize, by means of personal language, the call of God in the ethical claim of the 'other', and respond in love and justice to that call, creating a community which is grounded in God as the source of goodness. Such an anthropology meets the personalist criteria described by Kevin Kelly for an account that recognizes the human as subject, embodied, material, related to others, interdependent, historical and equal but unique. It also meets the need to take women's experience more seriously, since the maternal voice is often the initiator of the personal narrative. The requirement for justice implied by the narrative of personhood also implies that this inclusion of women's perspectives calls for appropriate social justice. Lisa Sowle Cahill describes this clearly in her critique of contemporary debates about abortion and reproductive medicine.[29] In the case of the potential use of embryonic stem cells, this will raise specific questions about commodification.

I hope this brief sketch will provoke debate and responses from those more familiar with this field than myself, and encourage further exploration of the various approaches discussed in Kevin Kelly's writings.

Notes

1. Kevin T. Kelly, *Life and Love: Towards a Christian Dialogue on Bioethical Questions* (London: Collins, 1987), p. 153.
2. Kevin T. Kelly, 'The Dignity of the Human Person: A Common Starting Point', in *New Directions in Moral Theology: The Challenge of Being Human* (London: Geoffrey Chapman, 1992), pp. 27–60.
3. David Kelly, *Contemporary Catholic Health Care Ethics* (Washington DC: Georgetown University Press, 2004), pp. 252–55 and Daniel Callahan, *Abortion: Law, Choice and Morality* (London: Macmillan, 1970).
4. David Kelly, 'Embryonic Stem Cells and the Beginning of Personhood', in *Contemporary Catholic Health Care Ethics*, pp. 252–53 (252); Kelly, *Life and Love*, pp. 51–52; John Mahoney, 'The Beginning of Life', in *Bioethics and Belief* (London: Sheed & Ward, 1984), pp. 67–69.
5. Kelly, 'The Dignity of the Human Person', summarized on page 30.
6. For example, see A.O. Trounson, M.F. Pera and A.H. Sathanathan, 'Fertilisation, Early Development and Implantation', in G. Chamberlain and P. Steer (eds), *Turnbull's Obstetrics* (London: Churchill Livingstone, 3rd edn, 2001), pp. 21–32.
7. For example, see F.B. Pipkin, 'Maternal Physiology in Pregnancy', in Chamberlain and Steer (eds), *Turnbull's Obstetrics*, pp. 71–91; and Y.L. Loke and Ashley King, 'Immunology in Pregnancy', in Chamberlain and Steer (eds), *Turnbull's Obstetrics*, pp. 93–104. See also F.G. Cunningham, N.F. Gant, K.J. Leveno, L.C. Gilstrap, J.C. Hauth and K.D. Wenstrom, 'Maternal Adaptations to Pregnancy', in *Williams Obstetrics* (New York: McGraw-Hill, 21st edn, 2001), pp. 167–200.
8. See Kelly, *Life and Love*, pp. 83–104, 143.
9. See Pannenberg's monumental *Anthropology in Theological Perspective* (Edinburgh: T&T Clark, 1985) or, for example, Alistair McFadyen's use of Rom Harre's psychology in *The Call to Personhood: Christian Theory of the Individual in Social Relationships* (Cambridge: Cambridge University Press, 1990).
10. For a definitive history of this, see Charles Taylor, *The Sources of the Self: The Making of Modern Identity* (Cambridge: Cambridge University Press, 1992).
11. Kelly, *Life and Love*, p. 149.
12. R. Dell'Oro, 'Theological Anthropology and Bioethics', in C. Taylor and R. Dell'Oro, *Health and Human Flourishing: Religion, Medicine and Moral Anthropology* (Washington DC: Georgetown University Press, 2006), p. 21.
13. *Ibid.*, pp. 22–23.
14. José Comblin, *Retrieving the Human: A Christian Anthropology* (New York: Orbis Books, 1990).
15. W. Schweiker, *Responsibility and Christian Ethics* (Cambridge, Cambridge

University Press, 1999), pp. 160–81; see also W. Schweiker, *Theological Ethics and Global Dynamics* (Oxford: Blackwell, 2004), esp. ch. 10.

16. Kelly, *Life and Love*, p. 148.
17. Hilde Nelson, 'What Child is This?', *Hastings Center Report* 32, no 6 (2002): 29–38.
18. For a summary see F. Dallmayr, 'Ethics and Public Life: A Critical Tribute to Paul Ricoeur', in J. Wall, W. Schweiker and W. David Hall (eds), *Paul Ricoeur and Contemporary Moral Thought* (London and New York: Routledge, 2002), pp. 215–20.
19. R. Kearney, *On Paul Ricoeur: The Owl of Minerva* (Aldershot: Ashgate, 2004), pp. 99–114, esp. p. 112.
20. P. Ricoeur, *Oneself as Another* (Chicago: University of Chicago Press, 1994), esp. Studies 5, 6 and 7. See also F. Dallmayr, 'Ethics and Public Life' and Don Browning, 'Ricoeur and Practical Theology', in Wall, Schweiker and Hall (eds), *Paul Ricoeur and Contemporary Moral Thought*, pp. 256–63.
21. Ricoeur, *Oneself as Another*, Studies 8 and 10. Also see P. Ricoeur, 'Ethics and Human Capability: A Response', in Wall, Schweiker and Hall (eds), *Paul Ricoeur and Contemporary Moral Thought*, pp. 279–90.
22. See Stiver's discussion of Ricoeur's embodied self in D. Stiver, *Theology After Ricoeur* (Louisville: Westminster/John Knox Press, 2001), pp. 165–66.
23. For Ricoeur, narratives of the self and those of others necessarily intersect because they seek to interpret the same reality. See Stiver, *Theology After Ricoeur*, p. 174.
24. This is in distinction to the position argued with impressive courage by Marjorie Maguire in 'Personhood, Covenant and Abortion', *Annual of the Society of Christian Ethics* (1983): 117–46.
25. Charles Curran, 'Abortion: Its Moral Aspects' (1973), reprinted in L. Steffen (ed.), *Abortion: A Reader* (Cleveland, OH: The Pilgrim Press, 1996), pp. 250–53.
26. Alasdair MacIntyre, *Dependant Rational Animals: Why Human Beings need Virtues* (Chicago: Open Court, 1999). For an application of some of this, see Eva Kittay, 'Disability, Equal Dignity and Care', in *The Discourse of Human Dignity* (Concilium 2003/2: London: SCM, 2003), pp. 105–15.
27. Jean Porter, '*Quaestio Disputata*: Delayed Hominization. Individuality, Personal Identity and the Moral Status of the Preembryo: A Response to Mark Johnson', *Theological Studies* 56 (1995): 763–70 (764).
28. David Kelly argues for a principle of remote material cooperation which allows Catholics to tolerate acts where the good outweighs the bad. This would only apply to embryonic stem-cell research, and has no bearing on the basic questions about personhood and human dignity. See Kelly, 'Embryonic Stem Cells and the Beginning of Personhood', pp. 256–57.
29. Lisa Sowle Cahill, *Theological Bioethics: Participation, Justice, Change* (Washington: Georgetown University Press, 2005), pp. 170–208.

9

The Moral Status of the Human Embryo according to *Donum Vitae*: Analysis of and Comment on Key Passages[1]

Jan Jans

Introduction

The human being must be respected – as a person – from the very first instant of his existence ... The human being is to be respected and treated as a person from the moment of conception.[2]

Although the manner in which human conception is achieved with IVF and ET cannot be approved, every child which comes into the world must in any case be accepted as a living gift of the divine Goodness and must be brought up with love.[3]

These two quotations are taken from the Roman Catholic Church's moral teaching statement on reproductive technologies, *Donum vitae*, drawn up by the Vatican's Congregation for the Doctrine of the Faith and published on 10 March 1987. The first quotation is a repetition of the well-known teaching of the same congregation issued in its 1974 Declaration on Procured Abortion on the immorality of any direct interruption of pregnancy. The conclusion of the second quotation might come as a kind of surprise – who would claim something different? – but it gains a special weight because it places the Church's argumentation with regard to the immorality of interventions in human procreation in a new light.

In this contribution, these quotations are my guidelines for an analysis of the moral status of the human embryo according to *Donum vitae*. From the perspective of this instruction, however, it is important to remark that the temporal difference between 'from the very first instance of his existence' and 'every child which comes into the world' does not signify any moral difference, as is made clear in an explanatory note added to the Foreword of *Donum vitae*:

The terms 'zygote', 'pre-embryo', 'embryo' and 'foetus' can indicate in the vocabulary of biology successive stages of the development of a human being. The present Instruction makes free use of these terms, attributing to them an identical ethical relevance, in order to designate the result (whether visible or not) [*sic*: whether viable or not] of human generation, from the first moment of its existence until birth. The reason for this usage is clarified by the text (cf. I, 1).

In the first part, I will focus on a clarification of 'the moment' from which the status as a person is applicable, according to *Donum vitae*. In the second part I assess the logic by which *Donum vitae* seems to claim that artificial reproduction reduces the child who is born to the status of a technological product, thereby possibly corroding her or his very moral status.

'As a Person – From the Very First Instant of Existence'

In my introduction, I remarked that the first quotation is known from the position on procured abortion taken by the Magisterium in 1974. Now what is puzzling to at least some extent – especially for 'outsiders' but also for convinced defenders – is the contrast or the distance between, on the one hand, what looks like a rather weak affirmation that the human embryo be treated '*as* a person' (as opposed to the affirmation that it *is* a person) and, on the other hand, the absoluteness of the strong moral prescriptions urged by *Donum vitae*, extending into behavioural norms for medical personnel and even the request that these become part of civil law. It is both interesting and confusing that the Magisterium itself is aware of this lack of a 'solid' foundation. Instead of an unequivocal ontological or an unambiguous natural-law statement such as 'the embryo *is* a person', the Magisterium limits itself to a practical-rhetorical position – the strength of which is at the very same time the impossibility of refuting it.

The reasoning employed by *Donum vitae* is called 'tutiorism' (from the Latin *via tutior*, meaning the safer way): the inviolability of each and every human is given with the biological uniqueness of a new human individual, and the theological way of framing this is through the category of 'ensoulment'. *Donum vitae*, however, is very reticent in the use of this theological category:

> Certainly no experimental datum can be in itself sufficient to bring us to the recognition of a spiritual soul; nevertheless, the conclusions of science regarding the human embryo provide a valuable indication for discerning by the use of reason a personal presence at the moment of this first appearance of a human life: how could a human individual not be a human person?[4]

The same Congregation for the Doctrine of the Faith was a lot less rhetorical in its argumentation offered in the Declaration on Procured Abortion, but this passage for some reason does not return in *Donum vitae*: 'it suffices that this presence of the soul be probable [Latin: *probabile*] (and one can never prove the contrary) in order that the taking of life involve accepting the risk of killing a man, not only waiting for, but already in possession of his soul'.[5] Here, the theological tutiorism is clear: if there were certainty about the ensoulment of this life, there would be no doubt about the prohibition on taking it. However, given the seriousness of what is at stake – the *risk* of killing a human – such certainty is not required and it is sufficient that there is a 'probability' – which is irrefutable – taking its moral weight from the 'risk' one has to avoid by all means.

Paradoxically, however, *Donum vitae* seems not to be satisfied to leave things there. On the one hand, the discussion with regard to 'the moment' is avoided because of the claim that a precise determination is not necessary for its normative position. On the other hand, an effort is made to demarcate this 'moment' with more precision then ever. This effort does not rely on reopening the toilsome theological debate on ensoulment – by its selective quotations from the 1974 declaration, *Donum vitae* gives the impression that this matter has been solved, but according to this declaration itself, such is not the case:

> This declaration expressly leaves aside the question of the moment when the spiritual soul is infused. There is not a unanimous tradition on this point and authors are as yet in disagreement. For some it dates from the first instant; for others it could not at least precede nidation. It is not within the competence of science to decide between these views, because the existence of an immortal soul is not a question in its field.[6]

The 'moment' which *Donum vitae* tries to determine is framed in terms of conception and the moral significance attributed to this event. However, the differences between the terminology in the original texts from 1987 and the later and official Latin translation of 1988 show that this effort again has its own difficulties.

According to the explanatory footnote mentioned in my introduction, *Donum vitae* claims that the same moral value must be affirmed for the various stages of biological development. The first stage mentioned is 'zygote', itself explained further down in the original 1987 texts as: 'The zygote is the cell produced when the nuclei of the two gametes have fused'. The context of this definition is again the quotation taken from the Declaration on Procured Abortion as given in *Donum vitae*, I, 1:

> 'From the time that the ovum is fertilized, a new life is begun which is neither that of the father nor of the mother; it is rather the life of a new human being with his own growth. It would never be made human if it were not human already' ... This teaching remains valid and is further confirmed, if confirmation were needed, by recent findings of human biological science which recognize that in the zygote resulting from fertilization the biological identity of a new human individual is already constituted.

By this definition, *Donum vitae* seems to bring precision to 'from conception onwards' and takes the position that 'the moment' has to be understood as completed syngamy – the two nuclei each with 23 chromosomes have fused and now there is one cell with 46 chromosomes. In other words: the 'moment' from which respect as for a person is due is the end of the formation of the zygote. This is confirmed by a comment made by Angelo Serra – the *de facto* chair of the subcommittee of this part of *Donum vitae*: 'Once the reconstitution (of a complete genetic apparatus of 46 chromosomes) has taken place we are in the presence of a new cell called the *zygote*. This cell is the *neo-conceptus*.'[7] *Donum vitae* itself draws the normative conclusion: 'Thus the fruit of human generation, from the first moment of its existence, that is to say from the moment the zygote has formed, demands the unconditional respect that is morally due to the human being in his bodily and spiritual totality'.[8]

The later official Latin text[9] contains two changes which lead to 'the moment' becoming vague again. The first change is in the very definition of the zygote: *Zygotum est cellula orta a fusione duorum gametum* ('The zygote is the cell coming from the fusion of two gametes') – a change by which 'the nuclei' have disappeared. The second change is an interpretation of 'the moment of conception' and goes as follows: *hoc est a momento quo formatio zygoti inchoatur* ('This is from the moment the formation of the zygote takes a beginning'). What are the reasons for these changes?

Because the official English text of *Donum vitae* defined the moment from which respect as for a person was due as 'the moment the zygote has formed', the question was raised by some as to what the 'status' was during the so-called pro-nucleus state, meaning the period (about 22 hours on average) between the head of the sperm entering the ovum and the constitution of one new cell composed of the chromosomes of the nuclei of the two gametes. In response to the speculation of some Australian researchers that during this period the neo-conceptus was not yet there – meaning no genetical individuality and probable ensoulment – and that therefore experiments such as cryopreservation might be allowed by *Donum vitae*, the Australian bishops' conference asked for a clarification. The response which came from Cardinal Ratzinger, then Prefect of the Congregation for the Doctrine of the Faith, referred to the forthcoming and authoritative Latin text with the two changes, without giving the reasons for these changes. By leaving out 'the nuclei', the definition of the zygote becomes more vague; by adding '*inchoatur*', the 'moment' becomes – again – speculative. The whole led the Australian moral theologian Norman Ford to the following: 'The Latin text removes the impression that the Church teaches that the zygote is not present before syngamy without denying that this might well be the case'.[10]

By way of conclusion of this analysis, I think that the position of the Magisterium reflects a practical wisdom which invites reticence – no more but no less. However, this prudential tutiorism leaves the ethicist with the further theological question of whether, over against some kind of practical agnosticism, the efforts to define as precisely as possible 'the moment' are not the consequence of a quantitative approach with regard to the question of ensoulment: *when* is the soul created or infused by God? I wonder if a hermeneutical approach aimed at grasping the meaning of what we express with the notion of ensoulment would not allow us to see the question of 'the moment' as a pseudo-problem.[11] More concretely, and following the lead of theologians such as Karl Rahner[12] and Josef Fuchs,[13] I would suggest that our self-understanding as truly being created 'in the image of God' could result in a positive and rich notion of humans as 'co-creators'. Exactly as being God's image, our human actions are always also more than mere facts. From this self-transcendence, thereby, ensoulment could be understood not as a separate 'act of God' but as immanent in the process of the self-transcendence of genetically being human and of moving towards becoming a human person in the unity of body and soul. As the Catechism of the Catholic Church declares: 'The human body shares in the dignity of "the image of God": it is a human body precisely because it is animated by a spiritual soul ... The unity of body and soul is so deep that one should consider the soul as "the form" of the body.'[14] Underneath this position one finds the Thomistic reasoning of 'gradual' or 'successive' ensoulment in which formal potentiality is actualized from within if the material internal and external conditions allow for development and growth.

Every Child 'as a Living Gift of Divine Goodness'

Those familiar with *Donum vitae* cannot but notice the difference between the rather careful moral methodology of Part I, discussing the respect due to human embryos, and the contrasting tone and approach in Part II, discussing interventions in human procreation. The so-called 'fundamental morality' proposed by Part II does not show any trace of tutiorism, and, instead of an argumentation looking for a careful and nuanced reflection on the risks one might encounter in assisted procreation, the approach chosen uses 'objective' properties and laws.

The rejection of the use of third-party reproductive interventions (such as a sperm or egg donor or surrogate gestational mother) standing outside of marriage is, according to *Donum vitae*, based on the objective characteristics of marriage itself:

> Respect for the unity of marriage and for conjugal fidelity demands that the child be conceived in marriage; the bond existing between husband and wife accords the spouses, in an objective and inalienable manner, the exclusive right to become father and mother solely through each other.[15]

In the subsequent rejection of so-called homologous artificial fertilization (usually artificial insemination by the husband) – meaning that the gametes used are those of the married couple – this objective approach is extended and radicalized by the focus on the moral connection, which is mandatory, between procreation and 'the act of marriage'. The argumentation of *Donum vitae* presents itself as analogous to the argumentation of the 1968 encyclical *Humanae vitae* on the immorality of contraception:

> Contraception deliberately deprives the conjugal act of its openness to procreation and in this way brings about a voluntary dissociation of the ends of marriage. Homologous artificial fertilization, in seeking a procreation which is not the fruit of a specific act of conjugal union, objectively effects an analogous separation between the goods and the meanings of marriage.[16]

This means, on the one hand, that the child may only be conceived by sexual intercourse between the spouses and, on the other hand, that '[the child] cannot be desired or conceived as the product of an intervention of medical or biological techniques; that would be equivalent to reducing him to an object of scientific technology'.[17] *Donum vitae* explicitly mentions other considerations such as the effort to avoid risking the loss of embryos, the rightful desire of infertile couples for children and the totality of sexuality within marriage, but only to turn these down as being of no moral relevance for its judgement: 'The process of IVF and ET must be judged in itself'.[18] In line with such an intrinsic judgement, the answer to the question 'Is homologous *in vitro* fertilization morally licit?' therefore goes as follows:

> Conception *in vitro* is the result of the technical action which presides over fertilization. *Such fertilization is neither in fact achieved nor positively willed as the expression and fruit of a specific act of the conjugal union. In homologous IVF and ET, therefore, even if it is considered in the context of*

101

'de facto' existing sexual relations, the generation of the human person is objectively deprived of its proper perfection: namely, that of being the result and fruit of a conjugal act in which the spouses can become 'cooperators with God for giving life to a new person'.[19]

The immediately following, seemingly relativizing, remark that the homologous techniques do not suffer from all the negativity present in extra-conjugal procreation really functions to stress the latter's double immorality, because it constitutes an infringement both of the objective laws of marriage and of the objective properties required for engendering a child. If one ponders the weight of this explicit line of reasoning, it is hard to escape the growing doubt whether such objective and intrinsic disabilities, which reduce the neo-conceptus to a product, can remain without influence on the moral status of such an embryo, and/or the child which is born later. I am led to believe that this question was raised during the deliberations of the committee drafting the second part of *Donum vitae*. This and the strict analogy with the argumentation of *Humanae vitae*, and especially its later interpretation by John Paul II, who condemns contraceptive marital intercourse as being 'a lie',[20] is the context for the way this question is reformulated by Janet Smith: 'It seems to me inescapable that if the Church is right, that you are really *making a product* when you make a child outside of the mother's womb and not creating a new life, then the nature of the act really has been changed'.[21] Furthermore, the reference in *Donum vitae* to the task and the mission of the parents to become cooperators with God in order to bring about the gift of life obtains a particular colour if one knows that the *de facto* chairman of this subgroup was Carlo Caffarra. Preceding the publication of *Donum vitae*, he repeatedly voiced his opinion that the theological core of the absolute demands in the teaching of *Humanae vitae* – and subsequently *Donum vitae* – resides in the special and exclusive rights of God with regard to 'the method' and 'the place' of conception.[22] Concretely with regard to 'the method': in a potentially fertile act of intercourse, it belongs in the last resort to God to decide if a new life will come into being, and therefore contraception is an objective infringement on this right of God. Concretely with regard to 'the place': because God has decided that a woman's body is the place for engendering new life, any extra-corporal conception is an infringement of this objective order.

Whatever one may think of these and similar positions, *Donum vitae* itself does not analyze such consequences[23] but seems to be satisfied by countering them with the apodeictic sentence I quoted at the beginning of this article by which the Magisterium decrees that the objective moral defects in terms of 'the child as product' do not result in an objective defect in the status of the child. To what degree this itself has an influence on the 'objective' degree of the argumentation is not thematized, but, in my opinion, it offers at least some kind of entrance to revisit again all the objections mentioned by a more tutioristic approach. The fact that *Donum vitae* itself tables the disvalues of marital infertility, and thereby confirms their seriousness, should not just be answered by the pseudo-theological stopgap: '[those spouses] are called to find in it an opportunity for sharing in a particular way in the Lord's Cross, the source of spiritual fruitfulness'.[24] An alternative more in line with the approach of Part I would ask for the real and possible risks and disvalues, and, in a careful – and thereby moral – approach, raise the real question with regard to the quality of intentions and concrete circumstances which would make the whole of what is actually done un/acceptable. This by no means boils down into a situation ethics or some kind of intentionalism. Imagine that a couple, through IVF–ET, would indeed have the intention of reducing the neo-conceptus to nothing but a product. This would, however, not factually result in the neo-conceptus being a product because its status as a human reality is independent of the underlying intention connected to the method of conception. After all, just as in the case of a couple practising periodic continence in which they are not oriented towards procreation but if they do conceive against their intention this does not lead to the result being 'a product', so it is also the case that, if people deliberately aim by sexual intercourse or IVF–ET 'to make a baby', they are not able effectively to produce 'a product'.[25] The quoted conclusion of Donum vitae is, therefore, in my opinion correct; its argumentation for the intrinsic immorality of the procedure has become, however, opaque.

Conclusion

A couple of remarks by way of a brief conclusion. The status of the embryo, according to Donum vitae, is clear in terms of the material norms for action which this instruction posits. However, from the moment one tries to deepen the line of argumentation – for example in order to favour the theological discussion between the Congregation for the Doctrine of the Faith and those Catholic universities and especially hospitals which practise some of the rejected interventions – all kinds of unevenness appear. By the refusal to incorporate those into its own reasoning or in later elaborations, Donum vitae undermines its own goal formulated in the Foreword: 'to offer, in the light of the previous teaching of the Magisterium, some specific replies to the main questions being asked in this regard'. Also by giving in to the temptation of replying to emerging controversies by authoritarian interventions such as the notorious anonymous editorial on the front page of the Vatican newspaper L'Osservatore Romano of 24 December 1988 with the telling title Sull' autorità dottrinale della Instruzione 'Donum vitae' ('On the doctrinal authority of the Instruction Donum vitae'),[26] the chances of offering guidance in the necessary formation of conscience on these difficult matters has become practically nil. What remains is a feeling of disappointment because – the risk of – medical-technological fundamentalism is not confronted with a vision and an approach in service of the cause of ethics, but with – at least the risk of – an anthropological and theological fundamentalism not going beyond the level of 'a particular opinion' and thereby hardly of significance for the content of the ongoing ethical investigations and discussions.[27]

Notes

1. A former slightly different Dutch version of this text was published as 'De status van het embryo in "Donum vitae". Kritische analyse van enkele sleutelpassages', in Theo Boer and Angela Roothaan (eds), Gegeven. Ethische essays over het leven als gave (Zoetermeer: Boekencentrum, 2003), pp. 78–94.

    A good reason to offer it in this collection of essays in honour of Kevin Kelly is the fact that I was reading his Life and Love: Towards a Christian Dialogue on Bioethical Questions (London: Collins, 1987) at the same time as Donum *vitae* appeared, thereby learning how his profound ecumenical look at the issues at hand and his attention to and incorporation of the views of women on the issues of what today is understood under the heading of 'reproductive health' leads to very different moral theological understandings.

2. Instruction on Respect for Human Life in its Origin and on the Dignity of Procreation. Replies to Certain Questions of the Day, *Donum vitae* (Congregation for the Doctrine of the Faith), (Vatican City: Polyglot Press, 1987), I, 1.

3. *Ibid.*, II, B, 5. IVF and ET are shorthand terms for the process of *in vitro* fertilization followed by embryo transfer from petri dish to uterus.

4. *Ibid.*, I, 1.

5. Declaration on Procured Abortion (Sacred Congregation for the Doctrine of the Faith, 1974), note 19.

6. *Ibid.*

7. Angelo Serra, 'The Human Embryo, Science and Medicine. Commentary on a Recent Document', in *Human Life: Its Beginnings and Development. Bioethical Reflections by Catholic Scholars* (International Federation of Catholic Universities, Paris: L'Harmattan/Louvain-la-Neuve: CIACO, 1988), pp. 47–65 (48).

8. *Donum vitae*, I, 1.

9. Congregatio pro Doctrina Fidei, *Instructio de observantia erga vitam humanam nascentem deque procreationis dignitatae tuenda. Responsiones ad quasdam quaestiones nostris temporibus agitatas*, in *Acta Apostolicae Sedis* 80 (1988): 70–102.

10. Norman Ford, 'When Does Human Life Begin? Science, Government, Church', *Pacifica* 1 (1988): 298–327 (315). In this article, Ford documents the whole discussion, including the letter from Cardinal Ratzinger.

11. This and other pseudo-problems in *Donum vitae* result from the hierarchical antagonism between God and human agents which permeates *Donum vitae*. Cf. Jan Jans, 'God or Man? Normative Theology in the Instruction *Donum Vitae*', *Louvain Studies* 17 (1992): 48–64.

12. Karl Rahner, 'Die Hominisation als theologische Frage', in Paul Overhaeghe and Karl Rahner, *Das Problem der Hominisation* (Freiburg, Basel and Vienna: Herder, 1961), pp. 13–90. The English translation of this text is *Hominization: The Evolutionary Origin of Man as a Theological Problem* (trans. W.T. O'Hara), (New York: Herder & Herder, 1965).

13. See, for example, Josef Fuchs, 'Seele und Beseelung im individuellen Werden des Menschen', *Stimmen der Zeit* 114 (1989): 522–30.

14. Catechism of the Catholic Church (1994), 364–65.

15. *Donum vitae*, II, 2.

16. *Ibid.*, II, 4a.

17. *Ibid.*, II, 4c.

18. *Ibid.*, II, 5.

19. *Donum vitae*, II, 5; italics in original.

20. Cf. John Paul II, Apostolic Exhortation *Familiaris consortio* (1981), 32: 'Thus the innate language that expresses the total reciprocal self-giving of husband and wife is overlaid, through contraception, by an objectively contradictory language, namely, that of not giving oneself totally to the other. This leads not only to a positive refusal to be open to life but also to a falsification of

the inner truth of conjugal love, which is called upon to give itself in personal totality.'

21. Janet E. Smith, 'Communicating the Values of the Instruction', in D. McCarthy (ed.), *Reproductive Technologies, Marriage and the Church* (Proceedings of the Bishops' Workshop on Reproductive Technology, Marriage and the Church held 1–5 February, Dallas, Texas), (Braintree: The Pope John Centre, 1988), pp. 68–83 (71).

22. Carlo Caffarra, 'The Demographic Question in the Magisterium of the Church', in *Demographic Policies from a Christian Point of View: Proceedings of the Symposium* (International Federation of Catholic Universities – Center for Coordination of Research), (Rome: Franco Biffi/Herder, 1984), pp. 33–46; Carlo Caffarra, 'Les droits de Dieu et le bien des hommes', in *L'Osservatore Romano* (French) (3 January 1984): 9. For a more elaborate discussion on the aporia of such a theological anthropocentrism, cf. Jan Jans, 'God or Man?', pp. 59–63.

23. One could, for example, speculate on the effect of *Donum vitae*'s teaching on the various 'rights' of Jesus and Mary (and maybe Joseph).

24. *Donum vitae*, II, 8.

25. Cf. the remark by Josef Fuchs: *Darum ist auch für die personale Menschwerdung das Wie der Ermöglichung einer Fusion der Gameten – aufgrund von Geslechtsverkehr, künstliche Insemination, In-vitro-Befruchtung – ohne Bedeutung* ('Therefore, the how of the fusion of the gametes – by intercourse, artificial insemination, fertilisation *in vitro* – is for the personal becoming-human unimportant') in Josef Fuchs, 'Seele und Beseelung im individuellen Werden des Menschen', *Stimmen der Zeit* 114 (1989): 522–30 (526). In my opinion, the same would apply for a child born as the result of somatic-cell nuclear transfer or so-called reproductive cloning: *homo generat hominem.*

26. 'Sull' autorità dottrinale della Instruzione "Donum vitae"', *L'Osservatore Romano* (24 December 1988): 1–2.

27. The announcement of *Donum vitae II*, on 30 January 2007 by the International News Agency ZENIT, does not offer an indication that, in dealing with 'the different bioethical and biotechnological questions posed today', a different approach can be expected. Cf. <http://www.zenit.org/english/visualizza.phtml?sid=102073> (accessed 12 February 2007).

10

On a Human Right to Die

Jack Mahoney

The idea of human rights has emerged and developed in the history of Western ethics to give increasingly powerful voice to the claims of justice when these are denied to individuals or groups or are under serious threat.[1] The doctrine of human rights therefore seems particularly appropriate to matters affecting life and death, and my purpose in this essay is to explore what light it might throw on our approach to dealing with death.

The Human Right to Die

The human right to die, as a claim to a moral entitlement, can be understood in two ways. One way is to view it as a right in certain circumstances to be allowed or permitted to die, as is envisaged in the growing practice of drawing up an advance directive, or a 'living will', which can require medical and nursing staff to refrain from applying what one judges will be unacceptable measures adopted to keep one alive once the process of dying has begun. Understood in this way, the human right to die can be viewed as what is often called a negative right, that is, a right not to be prevented from something, in this case, from dying. By contrast, the alternative understanding of a right to die is a much more positive one, as a right to take one's own life; and by extension a right to be actively helped to die by others, whether in a form of assisted suicide or by being put to death in an act of euthanasia. The simplest synonym for euthanasia in response to this positive right to die is to see it as 'mercy killing', that is, putting someone to death from a motive of mercy, although some advocates of euthanasia feel uncomfortable with such an unflinching description of the practice.

Reflecting on the latter understanding of a right to die, in the sense of having a positive right to end one's life and a claim on others for their active cooperation in this, one might usefully start from David Hume's rhetorical question in his essay on suicide, 'has not every one ... the free disposal of his own life?'[2] Confirmation of such personal autonomy can be made by appealing to John Stuart Mill's famous libertarian principle which has become so rooted in the political thought of western society, 'the very simple principle ... that the only purpose for which power can be rightfully exercised over any member of a civilized community, against his will, is to prevent harm to others'. As a consequence Mill concluded that 'the only part of the conduct of any one, for which he is amenable to society, is that which concerns others. In the part which merely concerns himself, his independence is, of right, absolute. Over himself, over his own body and mind, the individual is sovereign.'[3] There is, however, at least one relevant observation in the context of human rights which can be offered to the claim of Hume and the justification of Mill for the individual's personal autonomy when this is applied to suicide. Respecting another person's autonomy of action and refraining from preventing them taking their own life does not necessarily imply that one morally agrees with their acting in this way, far less that they would be entitled to demand one's cooperation or that one would be obliged to provide assistance to help them perform the action. Much depends on whether they are morally justified in undertaking the action in the first place, in this case in taking their own life.

The Point of Human Rights

One common ethical objection against suicide, whether committed personally or with assistance from others, arises from the point of view held by religious believers, although not by any means unanimously, that, as Hamlet expressed it, the Everlasting has 'fixed his canon 'gainst self-slaughter'.[4] Putting such religious prohibition to one side, one can consider a more rational line of argument affecting a claimed human right to commit suicide, whether as a liberty which others should refrain from impeding, or as a claim for assistance in the pursuit of one's action. That is to ask what in general is the purpose of human rights, and how these relate to human responsibilities. What is in question here is not the standard discussion of the logical priority between moral rights and responsibilities, in terms of whether other people have responsibilities arising from my possessing certain rights, or whether I have certain rights arising from other people's responsibilities. As I have argued elsewhere, it makes much more sense to begin with human rights belonging to the person and to see these as generating corresponding responsibilities on the part of others, rather than vice versa.[5] The connection between rights and responsibilities raised here is to enquire why I have any moral rights and claims in the first place which give rise to other people's responsibilities, the suggestion being that there is a close connection between my personal rights and my own moral responsibilities. Why do human beings have moral rights, beginning with the human right to life? What gives every one of us the moral authority to claim, even to demand, to be treated by all our fellows in certain ways, and not in other ways?

The common approach to recognizing and proclaiming the existence and power of human rights is to point to the dignity of individual human beings, which, for Christians, is explained and confirmed by the belief that all human beings are created in God's own 'image and likeness' (Gen. 1.26–27). David Hollenbach has analyzed in detail the history of the Catholic approach to human rights, and concluded that 'the Roman Catholic tradition answers the question of the foundation of human rights with a single phrase: the dignity of the human person'.[6] What also emerges from Hollenbach's study, however, is that almost no sustained attention is given in the Catholic tradition on human rights to considering what is the reason for human beings possessing them. All the stress is on the ground and justification of such rights, namely, the dignity of human beings; nothing is said of the purposes of such rights or, within the Christian context, of the reason why God has granted such rights to human creatures.

An almost passing comment of Pope John Paul II hints at the answer to this question of the purpose of human rights when he refers to 'the rights based on the transcendent vocation of the human being', that is, he subordinates one's rights to one's overall purpose and destiny in life.[7] More detail is provided by the Second Vatican Council's analysis of the right to religious freedom, in which it first noted that, in accordance with their dignity as persons, human beings have a moral obligation to seek the truth and to live by it. From this the council drew the general conclusion that humans 'cannot discharge these obligations in a manner in keeping with their own nature unless they enjoy immunity from external coercion as well as psychological freedom'. And, spelling this out in detail, the council declared: 'Wherefore everyone has the duty, and therefore the right, to seek the truth in matters religious';[8] that is, one's rights follow from one's duties. Moreover, in the early days of the council, when Pope John XXIII provided a detailed exposition of human rights in his encyclical *Pacem in terris*, he highlighted this intimate connection between a person's duties and their rights when he noted that 'the natural rights with which we have been dealing are, however, inseparably connected, in the very person who is their subject, with just as many respective duties'; and he instanced that 'the right of every man to life is correlative with the duty to preserve it; his right to a decent standard of living with the duty of living it becomingly; and his right to investigate the truth freely with the duty of seeking it ever more completely and profoundly'.[9]

From such passages it is possible to conclude that at the core of the Catholic approach to human rights is the recognition that the reason for human beings possessing personal moral rights is because they possess personal moral responsibilities; and that the purpose of their having human rights as moral claims on other people is precisely to make it possible for them to discharge those responsibilities. This point may be considered almost too elementary to make; yet the logical link and priority which it establishes between personal obligations and personal rights seems to throw valuable moral light on some situations. Nor is this intrinsic connection peculiar to Catholic or religious thinking. From a purely rational viewpoint also it is reasonable to hold that it is because I have certain moral duties concerning myself as well as others in society that I possess certain moral rights or claims on others, whether in the sense of rights or liberties not to be hindered in discharging my duties (e.g. the right to freedom of worship, the right to follow my conscience) or in the sense of claims for assistance to discharge those duties (e.g. the right to health, work, education, etc.). Human rights, then, are not ends in themselves; they have an inbuilt finality, and are means to a human end. My claims upon other people relating to certain values, such as life, freedom and truth, are precisely to make it possible for me to express those values in my life as I ought.

It appears to follow, then, that I possess my right to life precisely because now, or in the future, I have, or will have, a personal responsibility to safeguard and develop my own life; that is, to realize its potentialities to as full a maturity of autonomous self-fulfilment as I can achieve or can be helped by others to achieve. If this is the case, then, where suicide and voluntary euthanasia are concerned, the basic question becomes the self-contradictory one of how I can consider myself morally free to destroy myself in pursuit of my duty to protect myself. In the precise context of human rights, if their purpose is to enable me to fulfil my personal responsibilities, as I have argued, it does not make sense for me to claim to be ethically justified in requiring others to refrain from preventing me destroying myself, and, even more problematically, in requiring others to share in my self-destruction by helping me to annihilate myself.

It is difficult to reconcile any idea of free-floating, or purposeless, human freedoms, including Hume's 'free disposal of my own life', with the idea maintained here, that personal freedom has always a purpose which includes one's duty to respect, develop and fulfil one's own self. In Roosevelt's famous four freedoms which had such an influence on the modern development of human rights, two of the freedoms – freedom from want and freedom from fear – were freedoms from certain states of affairs, aimed at liberating or protecting people from hindrances to their due development as human persons; while the other two freedoms – freedom of speech and expression and freedom of worship – were to enable people to express themselves in ways they considered appropriate to their status as human persons.[10] In other words, in each case, being free is not an end in itself; it has a moral purpose, which is to provide room and resources for the expansion and development of one's human potentialities in concert with others, and in so doing to be enabled to discharge one's personal moral responsibilities.

Hence, particularly if one considers the foundation of human rights as being intrinsic human dignity and its moral acceptance in one's person as in others, it is difficult to see how studiedly destroying that person, including oneself, can be seen as a morally justifiable action, far less how one would be entitled to require others to cooperate in the action. It does not appear, then, to make sense to claim to possess a human right to bring about one's own death, either in the sense that others are precluded from aiming to prevent this, or in the sense that they are obliged to help one bring it about. By extension it follows that any legislation introducing a right to die in the form of legally countenancing assisted suicide or voluntary euthanasia would not be reflecting a previous moral human right, and would carry no intrinsic ethical warrant or justification.

Allowing to Die

Quite different, in fact as well as ethically, from suicide or voluntary euthanasia is the claiming of a right to die in the other sense which I have identified, that one is morally entitled to require others not to prevent one from dying once the natural process of one's dying has begun to take effect. The moral purchase of claiming such a right, or of expressing it beforehand in a living will, is that it is for the individual person to decide, before all others, what medical treatment may be provided him or her in such a terminal situation and what medical procedures are to be avoided or to be discontinued. Recognition in principle of such a right to die, in the sense of a human right for the process of one's dying not to be suspended or prolonged unprofitably, seems largely undisputed, and has a long history of support from the Catholic Church and other religious bodies, which seemed contradicted by the unwise decision in December 2006 of the Diocese of Rome to deny Christian burial on the grounds of suicide to a long-suffering patient who had successfully asked for his ventilator to be removed.

Much more ethically problematic is the situation of a patient who is defined as being in a persistent vegetative state (PVS), but who is not judged to be dying, nor diagnosed as brain dead. Such patients are apparently not, or not yet, in the process of dying, but it appears that the 'pause' button has been pressed on their life, which is, as it were, held frozen in time, going neither forward nor backward, yet requiring continuous medical support and care just to remain in a state of unconscious equilibrium. To what extent, it is regularly asked, may one claim for such a person that they have an ethical right to move on, to be allowed to die, and therefore that the procedures which are keeping them alive may morally be discontinued? Controversy here, both moral and legal, centres mainly on whether, or when, it is permissible to withdraw from such patients treatments such as the application of an artificial ventilator and the tubal provision of hydration and nourishment; treatments which are keeping them alive, but which provide no hope of reversing their situation and have no foreseen benefit to them.

The debate about the morality of continuing or discontinuing such treatment for PVS patients has intensified in recent years as a consequence of recurring court cases as well as a comment of Pope John Paul II in 2004 in which he insisted that patients in a permanent comatose state must always be provided with hydration and nutrition.[11] The pope's statement aroused considerable surprise and concern among even Catholic moral theologians and has been explored by various authors.[12] Most recently it was characterized by one respected bioethicist as being a one-off remark, delivered to a private audience, never repeated, and having 'no theological basis'.[13] Looked at from the point of view of human rights, the argument against discontinuing such treatment appears to be that doing so will inevitably result in the patient's death and, as such, will be an infringement of their basic right to live. The standard, and traditional Catholic, moral argument in favour of discontinuing such treatment has been that to persist in what appears a futile treatment is a refusal to accept human mortality, doing no more than holding at bay indefinitely and with no benefit to the unconscious patient the further deterioration of their condition which will, if unimpeded, inevitably result in death. The death which will follow on the discontinuing of treatment, it is maintained, is not due to ceasing to treat, but is actually brought about by the illness which was being held in check now proceeding to run its course and engulf the patient.

The argument for each of the above positions depends on an ethical analysis of human causality and the way in which treatment or non-treatment results or does not result in the death of the patient. A different line of approach could be offered, however, based on the way in which I have analyzed the human right to live. Following this line of reflection suggests that, in the case of PVS patients, the discontinuing of treatment is not, strictly speaking, an infringement of their right to life, since they no longer possess this right. If, as I have argued above and as appears to be latent in Catholic thinking, the purpose of an individual possessing moral rights is as a means to discharge their personal moral responsibilities, it follows logically that being able to discharge one's responsibilities is a necessary condition for continuing to possess human rights. If an individual is no longer in a position to exercise those personal responsibilities, then those rights have lost their purpose and have ceased to exist, and there is no basis for insisting that others respect those rights. In the case in point, a patient who has succumbed to a persistent vegetative state is no longer conscious of having any personal moral obligations, and therefore no longer has any such obligations, which, as a consequence of their state, have ceased to apply or to exist. As a result, other people are no longer morally required to help them in the now impossible task of fulfilling those obligations; and discontinuing treatment of that patient is not an infringement of their right to life, which logically they no longer possess.

Proceed with Caution?

An old scholastic axiom warns us that *qui nimis probat, nihil probat*: 'if you prove too much, you prove nothing'. The conclusion I have reached about the human right to live no longer strictly applying to the PVS patient appears to follow from considering that the purpose of human rights is to enable one to fulfil in the company of others the personal moral responsibilities of which one is aware. There is, however, a great deal more to human morality than matters of human rights. Values such as friendship, love, sympathy, forgiveness, magnanimity, affection and gratitude form a rich and necessary part of any truly human account of how people should regard each other and behave towards each other, and none of these has in itself any necessary connection with what Thomson calls the realm of rights.[14] Perhaps the reasoning worked through in this article, producing conclusions which are counter-intuitive or unwelcome, shows that the centuries-old tradition of human rights is not adequate to cope with the new moral complexities which are being created by modern medicine's ability to prolong human physical survival. Or perhaps applying the rationale of human rights logically should invite us to contemplate the possibility that new technologies of prolonging life may call for new approaches to the new dilemmas which result.

Notes

1. J. Mahoney, *The Challenge of Human Rights: Origin, Developments and Significance* (Oxford: Blackwell, 2007).
2. D. Hume, 'Of Suicide', in Alasdair MacIntyre (ed.), *Hume's Ethical Writings* (Notre Dame, IN: University of Notre Dame Press, 1965), pp. 297–306 (301).
3. J.S. Mill, 'On Liberty', in Mary Warnock (ed.), *Utilitarianism* (London: Collins, Fontana, 1962), pp. 126–250 (134).
4. William Shakespeare, *Hamlet*, I, ii, 132.
5. Mahoney, *The Challenge of Human Rights*, pp. 85–90.
6. D. Hollenbach, *Claims in Conflict. Retrieving and Renewing the Catholic Human Rights Tradition* (New York: Paulist Press, 1979), p. 90.
7. Pope John Paul II, Encyclical Letter *Sollicitudo rei socialis* (1987), 33.
8. Declaration on Religious Freedom, *Dignitatis humanae* (Vatican II, 1965), 2–3.
9. Pope John XXIII, Encyclical Letter, *Pacem in terris* (1963), 28–29.
10. F.D. Roosevelt, *The Public Papers and Addresses* (1940 volume), (London: Macmillan & Co., 1941), p. 672.
11. Cf. L. Sowle Cahill, 'Catholicism, Death and Modern Medicine', *America* (April 2005): 14–17.
12. See Thomas A. Shannon and James J. Walter, 'Assisted Nutrition and Hydration and the Catholic Tradition', *Theological Studies* 66 (2005): 651–62; and John

J. Paris, James F. Keenan and Kenneth R. Himes, 'Did John Paul II's Allocation on Life-Sustaining Treatments Reverse Tradition?', *Theological Studies* 67 (2006): 163–74.
13. J. Paris, 'A Life too Burdensome', *The Tablet* (6 January 2007): 10.
14. J.J. Thomson, *The Realm of Rights* (Cambridge, MA: Harvard University Press, 1990).

11

Contraception and Sin

Joseph Selling

Nearly 40 years after the publication of *Humanae vitae*, the Roman Catholic Church is still struggling with the issue of regulating human fertility by means that have been designated 'artificial'. The so-called contraception question has divided the community. It has served as a test case for 'orthodoxy'. Perhaps worst of all, it has been carried as a serious burden in the consciences of sincere, loving couples who are trying to do nothing more than practise responsible parenthood.

Attempting to explain the contraception issue to students or a genuinely inquisitive public has always been something of a challenge. For starters, the exposition of the broader question of regulating fertility within which the contraception issue is located usually proves to contain a few revelations. First, there is the issue of periodic continence. Most people are unaware of the fact that this technique was not admitted to be morally licit until 1951. I would venture that the vast majority of Catholics believe that this has always been the 'Catholic solution' to birth control and that the policy dates back to time immemorial, while the more informed or reflective thinkers presume that it originated with Pius XI's teaching in *Casti connubii* (1930). A close reading of that text, however, not to mention the moral debate that followed it, reveals something quite different.

A second revelation comes forth from that close reading of the 1930 encyclical where we find the pope voicing his approval of engaging in marital sexual intercourse known beforehand to be infertile because these acts are also capable of realizing the secondary ends of marriage, namely 'mutual aid, the cultivating of mutual love and the quieting of concupiscence'.[1] What is striking about this statement is that it is the first time that any official statement of the hierarchy had admitted a connection between sexual relations and love. This represented a genuine innovation in papal teaching.

A third revelation is found in being attentive to the reasoning of Pius XII's Address to the Italian Midwives in 1951. Since his predecessor had already declared marital intercourse known to be infertile to be licit by reassigning the ends of marriage to become the ends of the act of sexual intercourse, the remaining issue was whether it was allowable intentionally to limit marital relations to the periods of infertility for the purpose of avoiding conception. To respond to this, Pius proposed that exercising the rights of the married state simultaneously imposes upon the couple the duty to contribute to the preservation of the human race by having children. This being a positive duty, however, it may admit of exceptions that, in this case, would amount to having 'serious reasons' for avoiding the accomplishment of this duty. Those reasons, which the pope listed as 'medical, eugenic, economic and social', exempt the couple from their obligation.

Flowing from this teaching is the inescapable conclusion that the Church clearly supports well-considered and explicitly intended planning for birth control. A number of people frequently use rather inappropriate expressions to the effect that the Catholic Church is or has taken a stand 'against birth control'. This is very much not the case. In fact, since the Church has always taught that the vocation of a Christian couple is to *both* procreation *and education* of children, it has always at least implicitly condoned the avoidance of having children in situations where it would be difficult to provide an appropriate upbringing. What changed in 1951 was that a method of doing this which did not have to include complete abstinence was finally endorsed. What followed was a further speculation upon the nature of the 'serious reasons' mentioned by Pius XII and a recognition that these reasons did not have to be personal to the couple themselves. Concern for rapid population increase could also be cited as a valid reason for limiting family size.

A fifth revelation for those who study the teaching of the hierarchy seriously is that the reasoning used by Paul VI in *Humanae vitae* was exceptionally innovative. When Section 12 of the encyclical states that its teaching 'is founded upon the inseparable connection, willed by God and unable to be broken by man on his own initiative, between the two meanings of the conjugal act: the unitive meaning and the procreative meaning', he was actually stating something that had never been said before. Nowhere in 'traditional' teaching does such a phrase exist. Nowhere can one find any references to 'meanings' (in Latin: *significationes*) being attached to the act of sexual intercourse, and, even in this papal letter itself, the so-called 'unitive meaning' appears to fall by the wayside when it is stated 'that each and every marriage act [*quilibet matrimonii usus*] must remain open to the transmission of life'. If both of the meanings are so important and inseparable, why must not 'each and every marriage act' also be an expression of the 'unitive meaning' of conjugal and sexual love?

Finally, one more revelation awaits the attentive reader of *Humanae vitae* and brings us to the principal topic of this essay. Whereas Pius XI in 1930 did not hesitate to state the opinion that the use of 'artificial contraception' was a grave sin, 38 years later Paul VI apparently remained unconvinced about that opinion and does not use the word 'sin', grave or otherwise, in his moral teaching.

The word 'sin' does occur in the encyclical, but only in the later, pastoral part of the document. While giving advice to couples he writes:

> Let married couples, then, face up to the efforts needed, supported by the faith and hope which 'do not disappoint ... because God's love has been poured into our hearts through the Holy Spirit, who has been given to us'; let them implore divine assistance by persevering prayer; above all, let them draw from the source of grace and charity in the Eucharist. And if sin should still keep its hold over them, let them not be discouraged, but rather have recourse with humble perseverance to the mercy of God, which is poured forth in the sacrament of Penance.[2]

A number of things are rather striking about this statement. For one, the pope seems to allow a rather wide berth for recidivism in his pastoral advice. This position contrasts sharply with the occasional rigorist practice of some confessors after the publication of the encyclical who would go so far as to refuse absolution to penitents who had not resolved to stop using contraception.

Another striking thing about this statement is that, even though Paul VI does use the word 'sin' in his pastoral reflections, nowhere does he repeat Pius XI's qualification of 'grave'. One could reasonably speculate, if the pope believed that a certain action genuinely constituted a 'grave sin' in and of itself, would he not have been quite explicit in warning the Catholic faithful about this? One could say the same thing about the teaching of John Paul II in his apostolic exhortation *Familiaris consortio* (1981) as well as the teaching of the Catechism of the Catholic Church, both of which repeat the approach taken by Paul VI on this issue.

Returning to the moral teaching proper, in paragraph 14, we do find that Paul copies Pius XI's designation of contraception as *intrinsece inhonestum*, an expression that one could translate as 'odious' or 'wicked' in itself. However, he does not couple the word sin with that description. So is there a meaningful distinction to be made between what is, in itself, or 'objectively', odious or wicked (*intrinsece inhonestum*) and what is a 'sin'?

The first thing we ought to do is to recognize that the word 'sin' is a theological and not simply a moral or legal concept. Moral philosophers and jurists speak of offences or crimes. These are descriptive terms that tell us primarily 'what happened', while the process of determining responsibility or intent for what happened is matter for another form of investigation. The word 'sin', on the other hand, implies a certain personal offensiveness that has an impact upon a relationship, and particularly, in a theological context, one's relationship with God. Therefore, in order to speak about sin, one needs to take into account something more than merely 'what happened'. Knowing all things, God is not about to be offended by something that happened accidentally, was brought about through ignorance or was, whether or not mistakenly, undertaken in good faith and with a genuinely good intention and a sincere sense of responsibility.

Looked at 'objectively' then, one must accept that simply describing 'what happened' is not an adequate way to account for the presence of sin, theologically speaking. One needs to account for circumstances and for the broader, more personal meaning of whatever took place. This 'meaning', in turn, can only be understood in terms of what the person was convinced they were trying to accomplish.

For instance, to strike someone or threaten someone with the imposition of something clearly distasteful is easily classifiable as odious. All things being equal, one should refrain from such action because of the harm or injury caused to another person. However, in certain circumstances and with a proper intention, one can understand such acts to be justified. Carrying out punishment or instilling discipline have been seen as worthy goals that can legitimate such actions as long as reasonable proportion is exercised.

There are, in fact, all sorts of physical actions that 'objectively' or in and of themselves are properly understood to be harmful for persons and thus classifiable as odious or even wicked. Cutting someone and exposing them to loss of blood and the risk of infection is certainly harmful, but in the context of a medical procedure it can easily be understood as legitimate. Mutilating a person would seem so wicked as to be unforgivable, unless of course one is speaking of the voluntary donation of a healthy organ by a living donor.

115

Simply describing physical activities may tell us what is happening, but this alone rarely provides sufficient information for making a complete moral judgement. Perhaps it is an extreme example, but in his *Summa theologica*, St Thomas even suggested that killing a person can be morally judged either as an act of satisfying anger and thus immoral, or as an act of safeguarding justice or a realization of the virtue of *vindicatio*.[3]

The Problem of Contraception

So a physical act of contraception, doing something that will ensure that a given act of sexual intercourse will not result in conception, may indeed be odious or wicked, but not necessarily a sin. This leaves us with two substantive questions and one practical one. The first substantive question is why it is appropriate to refer to the use of contraception as odious or wicked. In *Humanae vitae*, Paul VI suggested that this had something to do with breaking 'the inseparable connection, willed by God and unable to be broken by man on his own initiative, between the two meanings of the conjugal act: the unitive meaning and the procreative meaning'.[4]

In other words, this had nothing to do with the 'waste' of sperm or the suppression of ovulation. It had to do with the integrity of human sexual behaviour. Focusing as he did on the context of the marital encounter, the pope could clearly recognize the two 'meanings' that are uniquely brought together in the act of sexual intercourse, the relational ('unitive') meaning and the procreative one. But it was not his goal to elaborate upon the entire meaning of human sexuality at that time. Had he done so, he would probably have been able to say much more about what God had in mind when God created humankind as sexual beings.

In 1975, the Vatican 'Declaration on Certain Questions Concerning Sexual Ethics' brought our attention to the observation that human sexuality has a personal, individual meaning as well. In its opening words, we read:

> According to contemporary scientific research, the human person is so profoundly affected by sexuality that it must be considered as one of the factors which give to each individual's life the principal traits that distinguish it. In fact it is from sex that the human person receives the characteristics which, on the biological, psychological and spiritual levels, make that person a man or a woman, and thereby largely condition his or her progress towards maturity and insertion into society.[5]

So there is a personal 'meaning' to human sexuality as well as the unitive and procreative ones mentioned in the encyclical. A little more reflection will inevitably lead us to the observation that there is certainly a social meaning of human sexuality as well. Clearly, this is visible in just about every society's attempt to institutionalize sexual relationships in the context of what we generally refer to as marriage. In addition, during the past 30 years most of us have also become aware of the role that gender plays in justice questions and social ethics. There is an entire range of 'social meanings' to human sexuality that demand attention, not the least of which is its intimate role in the construction of kinship relationships or, in the extended meaning of the word, 'family'.

There are, therefore, a number of meanings bound up with or dimensions present within human sexuality that, from a theological point of view, we would recognize as being part of the gift that God has given to us. It is probably appropriate to say that to offend any one of these meanings or dimensions would threaten or diminish the integrity of human sexual behaviour and that, in the absence of some justifying or, as Pius XII wrote in 1951, 'serious' reason, this would be offensive to God. In and of itself, however, this does not yet determine the moral significance of what is happening.

What Constitutes Sin?

The second substantive question, then, is when does something 'odious' actually become a sin, that is, something for which one should seek repentance? The first and most appropriate answer to that would seem to be when a person actually intended or deliberately wanted to destroy the integrity of sexuality by setting out to obliterate one or more of its meanings. In regard to the contraception question, we see how Paul VI singled out this intention with his reference to an anti-life attitude; and later John Paul II referred to a certain culture of death.

These expressions of a bad attitude signify the root cause of any activity that is truly offensive. Regardless of what is actually done, such a bad intention is itself sufficient to speak of 'sinful' behaviour. For with a bad intention, one embraces the odious aspect of what is happening not simply as a side effect of reaching some other, perhaps urgently pressing goal, but because the person wishes for and plans some manner of achieving the damage precisely as damage. Returning to the example of doing physical harm to another person, the soldier, law-enforcement officer or executioner who pursues their work precisely because it gives them an opportunity to harm or even kill human beings is not only doing something that entails harm or offence but has accepted that harm or offence as the end or purpose of their activity.

Another way in which doing something offensive can become sinful is when there is a lack of proportion between the good being sought and the offensive aspect involved in the achievement of that goal. If moral uprightness involves a commitment to the pursuit of good and the minimalization of evil, then the toleration of disproportionate harm constitutes a certain collusion with evil that can be described as 'sinful'. Obviously, there is no formula that predetermines 'proportion' for every human situation. Thus we can appreciate the crucial role of conscience in all moral decision-making.

Sinfulness, or more specifically the actual commission of a sin, thus arises not simply from the presence of something humanly odious or harmful but depends upon one's intentional attitude towards that aspect of behaviour, or upon the perceived and accepted lack of proportion between the good accomplished and any harm done in the process.

Is Every Use of Contraception a Sin?

This brings us to the practical question: why do so many people automatically presume that every use of contraception is a sin? My spontaneous answer to this

117

question would be that this is due to a category mistake, that is, not making a sufficient distinction between action and motivated behaviour. Only the latter can genuinely be classified as a moral category, for the mere description of physical activity is insufficient to determine whether a human event in its unity and totality is moral or immoral, or to use theological language, sinful. To speak of motivated behaviour is to address all three issues of intention, circumstances and action.

The fact is, however, that many people consider contraception to be more than a simple, physical activity. One reason for this is because they presume that the engagement of that activity necessarily makes reference to some kind of attitude, for instance, the claim that all use of contraception is anti-life. Dragging that presumption into the light of day, however, makes us confront the example of the couple who already have children, possibly as many children as they believe they can cope with at the moment, who use contraception to keep the size of their family within reasonable limits. How could one say that these parents are anti-life?

Of course, if a couple are using contraception because they really do have an anti-life attitude, then it might be appropriate to consider that a sin is being committed – not, however, because contraception is being used but precisely because of the attitude that is being brought to realization.

There are other situations in which the circumstances do not proportionately warrant the use of some forms of contraception. One thinks of the couple who are merely attempting to put off the birth of the first or next child but who are using a contraceptive method that is injurious to health or severely disrupting the relationship. In causing more harm than necessary, one could seriously question whether the motive of such a couple is misplaced. But again, it is not the contraceptive act per se which renders this sinful but the perpetration of harm that could have been avoided.

Then there is the argument that using contraception in some manner renders the sexual act counterfeit, making it incapable of expressing the loving relationship. Again considering the argument in the light of day reveals that the test of whether a loving relationship is being served or harmed is to be found in the testimony of those who are actually engaged in the relationship. I do not believe that it even approaches exaggeration to suggest that the vast majority of couples would disagree with such a proposition. In fact, I would venture that most couples would say that greater harm is done to their relationship when they are forced to live with the anxiety of an inappropriate pregnancy.

Finally, we come to the idea that using contraception is somehow destroying the integrity of human sexuality as such. It is not insignificant that, immediately following Paul VI's rejection of contraception, we find his argument about the evil consequences he believed would follow upon taking the opposite position – a decrease of marital fidelity and general lowering of moral standards, loss of respect for women, and a weapon being placed in the hands of countries that wanted to impose a limit on the number of births.[6] He feared that the integrity of human sexuality would disintegrate and that all sexual behaviour would become hedonistic.

The problem with the consequentialist argument is that it fails to appreciate the position of those who are not turning against the good of procreation as one of the 'meanings' of human sexuality but rather are seriously pursuing the other meanings inherent in sexual behaviour, namely those that serve the needs of human relationship, the goods of personal flourishing, and the protection of the social dimensions of human sexuality within the institution of marriage. These are persons whose intention is directed to the realization of a genuine, realizable good, not primarily the denial of another potential, perhaps even unachievable good. The decision to sacrifice the realization of one good in the course of accomplishing another or even multiple other goods, perhaps in pressing circumstances, could constitute a justifiable loss.

As we consider one argument after the other, it becomes increasingly hard to substantiate the position that the mere physical description of using some artificial means for preventing conception from taking place is, in and of itself, sufficient to conclude that a sin is being committed. When confronted with such a proposition, I like to tell the story of the newly married couple who have considered very seriously that it would be prudent to wait for some time before beginning to raise a family. In the course, or at the end, of one fine day they spontaneously experience the desire to express their love for each other in a sexual manner. Since the decision has been made to postpone having children, however, they mutually decide to use contraception. If one believes that the use of contraception automatically entails the commission of a sin, then we have to speak of two sins being committed because both of them have agreed to do this.

The next day the same thing happens so that two more sins are committed, making a total of four sins. On the third day, another repetition brings the total to six sins. With some embellishment I like to drag out the story to amount to an entire year of contracepted love-making, so that we come to day 366, on which the couple, about to engage once again in marital coitus and carrying the combined burden of 730 sins decide that now, indeed, is an appropriate time to think about starting a family and thus refrain from using contraception. What should we call such people, I ask? In the minds of those focused upon the performance of physical acts as sufficient basis for committing a sin, the answer will be that they are both 'sinners'. In the minds of the vast majority of the faithful, however, I think the answer would simply be 'parents'.

Notes

1. Pope Pius XI, Encyclical Letter, *Casti connubii* (1930), 59.
2. Pope Paul VI, Encyclical Letter, *Humanae vitae* (1968), 25.
3. Thomas Aquinas, *Summa theologica*, I-II, 1, 3, ad 3; cf. II-II,. 108.
4. *Humanae vitae*, 12.
5. Declaration on Certain Questions Concerning Sexual Ethics, *Persona humana* (Congregation for the Doctrine of the Faith, 1975), 1.
6. *Humanae vitae*, 17.

12

Deconstructing and Reconstructing Complementarity as a Foundational Sexual Principle in Catholic Sexual Ethics: The (Im)Morality of Homosexual Acts

Todd A. Salzman and Michael G. Lawler

The evolution of Catholic sexual teaching throughout history resulted in the formulation in the late twentieth century of a unitive–procreative principle as the foundational principle of Catholic sexual ethics. According to this principle, there are two intrinsic meanings of the marital sexual act, a unitive meaning and a procreative meaning. The unitive meaning refers to the union of 'husband and wife in the closest intimacy'; the procreative meaning refers to their capability 'of generating new life'.[1] More recently, in his 1981 apostolic exhortation, On the Role of the Christian Family in the Modern World, Pope John Paul II introduced the term complementarity into official Magisterial sexual teaching.[2] Since its introduction, complementarity has become a foundational sexual–ethical principle defending the morality of heterosexual marital sexual acts of a reproductive kind and condemning as immoral homosexual unions and acts.

Kevin Kelly, to whom this essay is dedicated, notes that the concept of ontological complementarity, as developed by Pope John Paul II, is 'oppressive and deterministic', in large part due to the gender stereotypes reflected in that concept. While we concur with Kelly, we believe that it is not the concept itself that is problematic, but the formulation of that concept in Catholic sexual teaching, and the absolute prescriptive norms deduced from it. We propose a reconstructed complementarity that adequately considers the sexual human person. This essay argues in three cumulative sections that the Magisterium's complementarity principle is grounded in biological genitalia, the male and female sexual organs, and that this grounding is inadequate as a principle for the construction of a personalist, relationally centred, sexual ethic. First, we present the Magisterium's teaching on complementarity; secondly, we deconstruct this complementarity principle on the basis of historical and sexual anthropological considerations; thirdly, we reconstruct a principle of holistic complementarity that allows for the morality of *some* homosexual acts.

Magisterial Teaching and the Primacy of Biological Complementarity

The term 'complementarity' originated in *Familiaris consortio* but it has been adopted in other Magisterial documents, including the Universal Catechism (1994) and the Congregation for the Doctrine of the Faith's (CDF) Considerations Regarding Proposals to Give Legal Recognition to Unions between Homosexual Persons (2003). The CDF articulates the principle that 'sexual relations are human when and insofar as they express and promote the mutual assistance of the sexes in marriage and are open to the transmission of new life'.[3] This is the standard unitive–procreative principle. The CDF explains the term *sexual complementarity* in relation to this principle and, on this foundation, defends heterosexual marriage and condemns homosexual unions and acts.[4]

Complementarity: Biological and Personal

Though neither Pope John Paul II nor Magisterial documents specifically define complementarity, we offer the following definition that reflects its use in these documents. The term complementarity indicates that certain realities belong together in the created order and that they together produce a whole which neither produces alone. In these documents, complementarity has two general meanings, biological and personal, with subcategories within each (Table 1). The definition of what constitutes a moral sexual act depends on how biological and personal complementarity are defined in themselves and in relation to one another. We consider each of these definitions in turn.

Biological Complementarity	
Title	Definition
Hetero-Genital Complementarity	The physically functioning male and female sexual organs (penis and vagina) used in sexual acts.
Reproductive Complementarity	The physically functioning male and female reproductive organs used in sexual acts to reproduce biologically.
Personal Complementarity	
Title	Definition
Communion Complementarity	The two-in-oneness within a hetero-genital complementary marital relationship that is created and sustained by sexual acts.
Affective Complementarity	The integrated emotional, psychological, spiritual, relational dimensions of the human person grounded in hetero-genital complementarity.
Parental Complementarity	Hetero-genitally complementary parents who fulfil the second dimension of reproductive complementarity, namely, the education of children.

Table 1: The Meanings of Complementarity

Biological complementarity is divided into *hetero-genital* and *reproductive* complementarity. The CDF describes what we label hetero-genital complementarity this way: 'Men and women are equal as persons and complementary as male and female. Sexuality is something that pertains to the physical–biological realm'.[5] Hetero-genital complementarity pertains to the biological, genital distinction between male and female. While biological genitalia are necessary for moral sexual acts, however, they are not sufficient to realize such acts; they must also function properly. If they cannot function complementarily, neither hetero-genital nor reproductive complementarity is possible, and, in that case, canon law prescribes that a valid marriage and sacrament are also not possible. 'Antecedent and perpetual impotence to have intercourse, whether on the part of the man or of the woman, which is either absolute or relative, of its very nature invalidates marriage.'[6] Finally, only sexual acts where the penis is inserted into the vagina and (male) orgasm takes place in the vagina are suitable for moral sexual acts. All other sexual acts that lead to orgasm (e.g., masturbation, oral sex, sodomitical acts) are considered immoral sexual acts. Thus three biological criteria: genitalia, biologically functioning genitalia and spatial location of orgasm, must be met before one can even consider whether a sexual act can be a moral sexual act.

Hetero-genital complementarity is the foundation for human reproduction and 'therefore, in the Creator's plan, sexual complementarity and fruitfulness belong to the very nature of marriage'.[7] Hetero-genital and reproductive complementarity are to be distinguished, however. While the Magisterium teaches that a couple must complement each other genitally, it also teaches that it is not necessary that they biologically reproduce. Infertile couples and couples who choose not to reproduce for the duration of the marriage 'for serious reasons'[8] can still enter into a valid and sacramental marital relationship. Reproductive complementarity, therefore, necessarily entails hetero-genital complementarity, but hetero-genital complementarity does not necessarily entail reproductive complementarity. Hetero-genital complementarity is distinct from, and can stand alone from, reproductive complementarity in the service of personal complementarity.

The CDF also refers to complementarity on the 'personal level – where nature and spirit are united',[9] and divides this personal complementarity into several subcategories. First, there is what we call *communion complementarity* in the marital relationship: 'a communion of persons is realized involving the use of the sexual faculty'.[10] The use of male and female genitals contributes to the realization of a communion of persons in marriage expressed in moral sexual acts. Without hetero-genital complementarity, according to the CDF, communion complementarity is not possible, a point underscored in its statement on the morality of homosexual unions. 'There are absolutely no grounds for considering homosexual unions to be in any way similar or even remotely analogous to God's plan for marriage and family. Marriage is holy, while homosexual acts go against the natural moral law. Homosexual acts close the sexual act to the gift of life. They do not proceed from a genuine affective and sexual complementarity. Under no circumstances can they be approved.'[11]

Secondly, there is *affective complementarity*. Citing the Catechism of the Catholic Church, the CDF asserts without proof that affective complementarity is lacking in homosexual acts and, therefore, these acts can never be approved. It does not clarify here exactly what it means by affective complementarity, but we can glean some insight from other Magisterial sources. The Congregation for Catholic

Education teaches that 'affective-sex education must consider the totality of the person and insist therefore on the integration of the biological, psycho-affective, social and spiritual elements'.[12] Since affective sex education seeks to integrate the biological and the personal, affective complementarity must similarly integrate the biological and personal dimensions of two people in a moral sexual act.

In *Familiaris consortio* Pope John Paul II discusses 'natural complementarity', lauding biological and personal complementarity that creates 'an ever richer union with each other on all levels – of the body, of the character, of the heart, of the intelligence and will, of the soul – revealing in this way to the Church and to the world the new communion of love, given by the grace of Christ'.[13] There are two important points to note in Pope John Paul's explanation of 'natural complementarity'. First, there is the standard Catholic intrinsic relationship between the two principles of being, body and soul, here specifically between genital and personal complementarity. Secondly, given the Magisterium's teaching on the immorality of homosexual acts, it is clear it regards hetero-genital complementarity as a *sine qua non* for personal complementarity in moral sexual acts. Without hetero-genital complementarity, 'natural complementarity' in the sexual act is not possible.

Thirdly, the CDF refers to what we call *parental complementarity*.[14] Parental complementarity designates hetero-genitally complementary parents who fulfil the second dimension of reproductive complementarity, namely, the education of children. It argues against same-sex union, based on the unsupported claim that, 'as experience has shown, the absence of sexual complementarity in these unions creates obstacles in the normal development of children who would be placed in the care of such persons'.[15] The congregation provides no scientific evidence, here or elsewhere, to substantiate this claim and, since there is substantial social-scientific data that challenges it, the question remains unresolved whether or not parental complementarity is as intrinsically linked to hetero-genital complementarity as the Magisterium claims. Parental complementarity does, however, remind us that moral sexual acts have implications beyond the immediate sexual act between the couple, and facilitates caring, nurturing and authentic relationships within the family and in the broader community. Social-scientific data strongly support the claim that communion and affective complementarity greatly facilitate parental complementarity.

Interrelationship between Hetero-Genital and Personal Complementarity

Hetero-genital complementarity alone is insufficient to justify moral sexual acts. Rape, incest and adultery all take place in a hetero-genitally complementary way, but no one would claim they are also personally complementary. Complementarity is not either/or, either hetero-genital or personal, but both/and, both hetero-genital and personal. The Magisterium posits an intrinsic relationship between biological (hetero-genital and possibly reproductive) and personal (communion, affective and parental) complementarity. There is a prioritization, however, of hetero-genital over personal complementarity; male and female genitals are the point of departure for personal complementarity and, therefore, moral sexual acts. When hetero-genital complementarity is assured, it must be situated within the appropriate marital, interpersonal and relational context to assure moral sexual acts. If hetero-genital complementarity is not assured, as it is not assured in homosexual acts, the act is by definition 'intrinsically disordered',[16] and there is no possibility of either personal complementarity or moral sexual acts.

An important question for the theological understanding of a moral sexual act is whether or not there can be such acts without hetero-genital complementarity. Is hetero-genital complementarity the essential, foundational and *sine qua non* component of moral sexual acts, established by God and recognized in the natural law, or must genital and personal complementarity be more thoroughly integrated to serve as foundational principles for defining a moral sexual act? If the latter is the case, then a loving homosexual act might fulfil the criteria for a moral sexual act. We approach these questions from two perspectives: first historically, investigating other 'divinely established' complementarities, and secondly anthropologically, exploring the Magisterium's evolution in its understanding of human sexuality.

The Deconstruction of 'Complementarity'

Divinely Instituted Complementarities

Throughout history, there have been religious, racial and social dimensions of the human person, which were posited as necessary, complementary realities, instituted by God or justified by natural law, which must be present to justify marital relationships and the sexual acts within those relationships. These include religious complementarity, denominational complementarity, racial complementarity and role complementarity.

Prior to the revision of canon law in 1983, religious and denominational complementarity, found only in the marriage between two Catholics, were required for valid marriage in the Catholic Church. Religious non-complementarity, that is, the marriage between a Catholic and a non-baptized person, and denominational non-complementarity, the marriage between a Catholic and a non-Catholic Christian, were strictly forbidden in the 1917 Code of Canon Law. 'The Church everywhere most severely prohibits the marriages between two baptized persons, one of whom is a Catholic and the other a member of a heretical or schismatic sect.'[17] A similar prohibition applied to interreligious marriage.[18] In the conceptual world of early-twentieth-century theology and canon law, it would be correct to say that 'religious complementarity' and 'denominational complementarity' were instituted by God and were strict requirements for any valid Catholic marital relationship. In the revised code (1983), however, these canons were revised. '*Without the express permission of the competent authority*, marriage is forbidden between two baptized persons, one of whom was baptized in the Catholic Church ... and the other of whom is a member of a Church or ecclesial community which is not in full communion with the Catholic Church.'[19] The revised code continues to declare that interreligious marriages are invalid,[20] but they can be validated and permitted if certain prescribed conditions are fulfilled.[21] What was strictly forbidden in the 1917 code was more readily acceptable under certain conditions in the 1983 code. Strict religious complementarity and denominational complementarity were relaxed in the Catholic tradition and in other traditions.

Though the Catholic Church never explicitly condemned interracial marriages, other Christian denominations did and, in the United States up to 1967, racial-complementarity in marriage was enforced through miscegenation laws which prohibited interracial marriage as 'unnatural' and prohibited by divine sanction. For example, in 1878 the Virginia Supreme Court declared the following: 'the moral and physical development of both races ... require that they should be kept distinct and separate ... that connections and alliances so unnatural that God and nature seem to forbid them, should be prohibited by positive law, and be subject to no evasion.' Racial complementarity was defended both legislatively and religiously for many Christian denominations as a reflection of God's will and the natural order. Such complementarity is now seen for what it truly is, racist bigotry.

Finally, throughout most of history, the Catholic tradition posited a strict role-complementarity in marriage justified by the Genesis creation story, which accepted biologically, historically and socially conditioned interpretations of gender. Wives were nurturing childbearers, subservient to the husbands, who were protectors and providers. These traditional roles have been challenged in recent Magisterial teaching, but residual influences remain. While admitting that women's roles have been too narrowly defined historically 'as wife and mother, without adequate access to public functions, which have generally been reserved for men',[22] John Paul II goes on to note the following: 'On the other hand, the true advancement of women requires that clear recognition be given to the value of their maternal and family role, by comparison with all other public roles and all other professions'.[23] Men's roles are not defined primarily in terms of husband and father; more emphasis is given to their social roles. Positing role-complementarity in marriage perpetuates imbalances in power and social structures that limit women's creativity and contributions in the public realm. Contemporary gender analysis suggests that such distinctions between feminine and masculine roles in marriage and family life are more socio-historically constructed than ontologically determined. For this reason, most Catholic theologians now argue that traditional perceptions of role-complementarity should be abandoned.

Since these seemingly 'divinely instituted' complementarities, once required for valid marriage, have been redefined or abandoned in light of the historical evolution of human understanding and theological reflection, one can reasonably ask if seemingly 'divinely instituted' hetero-genital complementarity might be similarly redefined or abandoned in light of a more profound theological reflection and sexual anthropology? We ask, what would warrant the displacement of hetero-genital complementarity as the *sine qua non* and primary consideration for moral sexual acts in Magisterial teaching?

Historical Developments in Catholic Teaching on Marriage

Though historically, biological (hetero-genital and reproductive) complementarity *may* be accepted as the foundational principle for Catholic teaching on marriage and human sexuality, several developments in that teaching necessitate redefining its status. First, Pius XI in *Casti connubii* affirms the primary and secondary ends of marriage. 'The primary end of marriage is the procreation and the education of children.'[24] The secondary end includes 'mutual aid, the cultivating of mutual love, and the quieting of concupiscence'.[25] There is in this encyclical, however, a deepening appreciation for the secondary end. The mutual love of spouses 'can in a very real sense ... be said to be the chief reason and purpose of matrimony

125

provided matrimony be looked at not in the restricted sense as instituted for the proper conception and education of the child, but more widely as the blending of life as a whole and the mutual interchange and sharing thereof'.[26] In addition, Pius XI concurs with St Augustine that 'it is wrong to leave a wife that is sterile in order to take another by whom children may be had'.[27] Infertile marriages are still sacramental and valid. The renewed emphasis on the secondary end of marriage and the recognition of the sacramentality of infertile marriages combine to challenge the primacy of biological complementarity over personal complementarity.

Secondly, Pius XII[28] and Paul VI[29] acknowledged that even a fertile couple could choose not to reproduce for the duration of the marriage for 'serious reasons'. In such cases, the marital act does not 'cease to be legitimate even when, for reasons independent of their will, it is foreseen to be infertile'.[30] On the basis of this teaching, a couple can intentionally eliminate the possibility of reproduction in the marital act through responsible parenthood and periodic abstinence and these acts are morally licit.

Thirdly, the vast majority of bishops of Vatican II affirmed what was logically implicit in earlier Magisterial teaching, namely, since reproduction was not essential for a sacramental and valid marriage, it was illogical to continue to teach procreation as the primary end of marriage. *Gaudium et spes* eliminated the primary end–secondary end terminology; procreation is no longer the primary end of marriage. Marriage and conjugal love 'are by their very nature ordained to the generation and education of children', but that does not make the other ends of marriage of less account.[31] In addition, the bishops designate marital love in the sexual act 'noble and worthy'[32] and affirm Catholic teaching that 'marriage is a communion of life' even when reproduction is impossible.[33] Finally, *Gaudium et spes* replaced the traditional, juridical term 'contract', describing the marital relationship with the biblically based, interpersonal term 'covenant'.[34] These shifts are significant in that they emphasize personal complementarity and the personal and relational dimensions of human sexuality and marriage.

Fourthly, Paul VI's *Humanae vitae* abandons the primary end–secondary end terminology, and defines the marital act as having two intrinsic *meanings*, one procreative and the other unitive.[35] Procreation is not equivalent to *actual* reproduction in *Humanae vitae* or earlier Magisterial documents; rather, it is defined as being 'capable of generating new life'.[36] An important question for *Humanae vitae* and its act-centred approach to human sexuality is whether or not it is logical to claim that 'each and every marriage act must remain open to the transmission of life'.[37] In the case of infertile couples, couples who practise natural family planning specifically to avoid the transmission of life, and couples where the wife is post-menopausal, this statement is morally ambiguous. In such cases, it seems that the procreative meaning of the marital act, if indeed it exists at all, is merely elided into the unitive meaning of the marital act whereby personal complementarity is the primary meaning of the sexual act.

This evolution in sexual teaching with its growing appreciation for the centrality of conjugal love in the marital relationship and the sexual act, and the elimination of procreation as the primary end of marriage and the sexual act, have conflicting implications for complementarity. On the one hand, they justify displacing the primacy of biological complementarity over personal complementarity. These teachings combined seem to indicate the *de facto* primacy of personal complementarity in marriage and the marital act since a marriage is sacramental and valid when a couple cannot reproduce or choose not to reproduce for the duration of the marriage. On the other hand, they affirm the primacy of hetero-genital complementarity as the foundational principle of Catholic sexual teaching, since marriage is only possible between a man and a woman. Elsewhere, however, the Magisterium provides sexual anthropological insights that further warrant the displacement of hetero-genital complementarity's primacy.

An Evolution in Sexual Anthropology

The Magisterium's sexual anthropology, in dialogue with the scientific community, has evolved in recent years. According to the CDF:

> The human person, present-day scientists maintain, is so profoundly affected by sexuality that it must be considered one of the principal formative influences of a man or woman. In fact, sex is the source of the biological, psychological and spiritual characteristics which make a person male or female and which thus considerably influence each individual's progress towards maturity and membership of society.[38]

An important dimension of the human sexual person is the person's integrated relationship to self and, therefore, to be moral, a sexual act ought to be integrated with the whole self. The Congregation for Catholic Education asserts that sexuality 'is a fundamental component of personality, one of its modes of being, of manifestation, of communicating with others, of feeling, of expressing and of living human love. Therefore it is an integral part of the development of the personality and of its educative process.'[39] The integration of the sexual self and its moral expression in sexual acts requires that we know the sexual self. Magisterial teaching on sexual orientation has furthered this self-knowledge.

The Magisterium's recognition of the distinction between homosexual acts and homosexual orientation, and the further recognition that homosexual orientation is a given factor in personal sexuality, has profound implications for any discussion of the primacy of hetero-genital complementarity as a foundational, sexual–ethical principle. The meaning of the phrase 'sexual orientation' is complex, but the Magisterium provides Catholics with a concise description. It distinguishes between 'a homosexual "tendency", which proves to be "transitory", and "homosexuals who are definitively such because of some kind of innate instinct"'.[40] In light of this distinction, it judges that 'it seems appropriate to understand sexual orientation (heterosexual or homosexual) as a *deep-seated* dimension of one's personality and to recognize its relative stability in a person. A homosexual orientation produces a stronger emotional and sexual attraction toward individuals of the same sex, rather than toward those of the opposite sex.'[41] We define sexual orientation as an innate condition characterized by a psychosexual and emotional attraction to persons of the opposite or same sex, depending on whether the condition is heterosexual or homosexual.

Concerning the genesis of homosexual and heterosexual orientations, the bishops note what is agreed on in the scientific community, namely, there is as yet no single isolated cause of a homosexual orientation. The experts point to a variety of factors, genetic, hormonal, psychological, social, that may give rise to it. Generally, homosexual orientation is experienced as a given, not as something freely chosen and, therefore cannot be considered sinful, for morality presumes the freedom to choose. This judgement is not to be understood as a claim that a homosexual orientation is morally good or even morally neutral, for elsewhere the Magisterium teaches that 'this inclination ... is objectively disordered' and, therefore, homosexual acts, which flow from the orientation, are intrinsically disordered.[42] They are intrinsically disordered because 'they are contrary to the natural law. They close the sexual act to the gift of life. They do not proceed from a genuine affective and sexual complementarity.'[43]

Biological Complementarity's Deconstruction

The Magisterium condemns homosexual acts because they violate both hetero-genital and reproductive complementarity and, *because of this violation*, also personal complementarity, regardless of the meaning of the act for a homosexual couple. Since the sexual act is frequently closed to reproductive complementarity, often even intentionally for fertile heterosexual couples, hetero-genital complementarity is established as *the* litmus test for determining whether or not a sexual act can fulfil personal complementarity, and thus be moral. Certainly moral sexual acts necessarily include personal complementarity but, for the Magisterium, personal complementarity is not sufficient for a moral sexual act. Hetero-genital complementarity is the necessary, foundational, *sine qua non* condition for what defines a moral sexual act. Since homosexual acts lack hetero-genital complementarity, they can never be moral. All of which is true *if* the Magisterium has sufficiently defended its claims on the 'intrinsically disordered' nature of homosexual acts.

While it clearly condemns homosexual acts on the grounds that they violate hetero-genital complementarity, the Magisterium does not explain its justification for the condemnation, other than to state that homosexual acts 'do not proceed from a genuine affective ... complementarity'. This statement, however, begs the question whether or not such acts can ever be moral on the level of personal complementarity. Though the Magisterium has made no effort to confront this question, monogamous, loving, committed homosexual couples have confronted it experientially, and they tell all who will listen that they do experience personal complementarity in and through homosexual acts. They add that these acts also facilitate the integration of their human sexuality and bring them closer to self, to neighbour and to God.

The Reconstruction of Complementarity

Sexual Orientation Complementarity

As we noted, the relationship between biological and personal complementarity is both/and. Sexual orientation is a fundamental dimension of the human sexual person, which draws that person relationally, emotionally, biologically, spiritually and sexually to persons of the same or opposite sex. Sexual orientation complementarity fully integrates genital and personal complementarity. In the case

128

of persons of homosexual orientation, male–male or female–female orientational complementarity and genitality, in the context of a just, loving, committed, faithful relationship, facilitate personal complementarity and are essential for a moral sexual act. In the case of persons of heterosexual orientation, male–female orientation and genitality, in the context of a just, loving, committed, faithful relationship, facilitate personal complementarity and are essential for a moral sexual act. To judge moral sexual acts on the primacy of hetero-genital complementarity inadequately considers the sexual human person.

Holistic Complementarity and the Moral Sexual Act

In light of the various senses of complementarity explored in the foregoing, we argue that a moral sexual act must be an authentic *expression* of holistic complementarity (see Diagram 1).

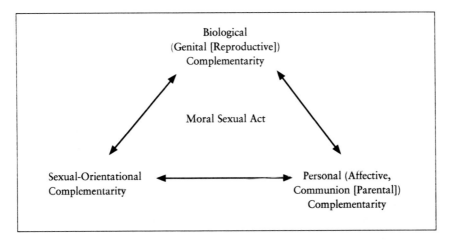

Diagram 1: Holistic Complementarity

Holistic complementarity is the authentic *integration* of biological, personal and orientational complementarity. In holistic complementarity, genital complementarity alone is an insufficient foundational principle for moral sexual acts; personal and orientational complementarity are the foundational principles. It is only in light of these foundational principles that one can assess the appropriate nature of genital complementarity within a sexual relationship and morally assess a sexual act. Certainly genitalia are essential in human sexual acts; their moral use, however, must be assessed in terms of the human sexual person adequately considered. It is this personalist interpretation of genital complementarity, which sees the physical genitals as organs of the whole person, including his or her sexual orientation, which allows us to expand the definition of a moral sexual act to include both heterosexual and homosexual sexual acts. In couples of heterosexual orientation, personal complementarity is manifested, nurtured and strengthened through male and female genital activity; in couples of homosexual orientation, it is equally manifested, nurtured and strengthened through male and female genital activity. If one takes hetero-genital complementarity as the *primary* principle for a moral sexual act, one defines a person's potential for a moral sexual act in terms of a single, physical dimension, namely, the genitals. This mono-dimensional perspective, we argue, does not acknowledge the complexity of the human sexual person. Holistic complementarity embraces the entirety and complexity of the human person, and understands genitality to be in dialogue with and at the service of personal and orientation complementarity.

While biological complementarity *may* include reproductive complementarity in the case of heterosexual couples who are capable of reproduction and who choose to reproduce, it does not necessarily include reproduction. Similarly, while personal complementarity *may* include parenthood, in the case of heterosexual couples who choose to reproduce or heterosexual or homosexual couples who choose to adopt or foster, it does not necessarily include parenthood.

Moral sexual acts can be defined only in the context of this complex biological, personal and orientational interrelationship. As it would be an immoral and unnatural sexual act for a heterosexual person to engage in sexual acts with a person of the same sex, so also it would be an immoral and unnatural sexual act for a homosexual person to engage in sexual acts with a person of the opposite sex. It would be immoral and unnatural, not because of physical genitals alone, but because of the individual's personhood, sexuality and sexual orientation. Recognizing, embracing and internalizing his or her sexuality facilitates a deeper realization of self in relation to not only that other with whom he or she enters into intimate sexual acts, but also to God. If we shift the *sine qua non* foundation for a moral sexual act from hetero-genital complementarity to an integrated holistic personal, sexual-orientational and genital complementarity, the principle for what constitutes a moral sexual act becomes more personal and can be formulated as follows. A moral sexual act is an authentic expression of holistic complementarity. Such acts are in accord with a person's sexual orientation and facilitate a deeper appreciation, integration and sharing of a person's relational embodied self with another relational embodied self, which may or may not result in reproduction.

Conclusion

Holistic complementarity recognizes the complexity of the human person and of her or his sexuality, and facilitates the integration of human sexuality in light of the interrelationship between personal, sexual-orientational and biological complementarity. This integration allows the person to love God, neighbour and self in a more just and committed way, and to express this love in sexual acts that are perfectly moral. The principle of holistic complementarity allows for the morality of *some* homosexual sexual acts and *some* heterosexual sexual acts, depending on the interrelationship of its three dimensions and their meaning for human persons and human relationships. It also may allow for other sexual acts that are absolutely prohibited by the Magisterium, such as artificial contraception and reproductive technologies. We believe that this reconstruction of the complementarity principle more accurately reflects a personalist, Christian sexual ethic.

Notes

1. Pope Paul VI, Encyclical Letter, *Humanae vitae* (1968), 12.
2. Pope John Paul II, Apostolic Exhortation, *Familiaris consortio* (1981), 19.
3. Considerations Regarding Proposals to Give Legal Recognition to Unions between Homosexual Persons (Congregation for the Doctrine of the Faith, 2003), 7.
4. *Ibid.*, 2–4.
5. *Ibid.*, 3.
6. *Codex iuris canonici* (1983), can. 1084, 1.
7. Considerations Regarding Proposals to Give Legal Recognition to Unions between Homosexual Persons, 3.
8. *Humanae vitae*, 10.
9. Considerations Regarding Proposals to Give Legal Recognition to Unions between Homosexual Persons, 3.
10. *Ibid.*
11. *Ibid.*, 4.
12. Educational Guidance in Human Love (Congregation for Catholic Education,1983), 35.
13. *Familiaris consortio*, 19.
14. Considerations Regarding Proposals to Give Legal Recognition to Unions between Homosexual Persons, 3.
15. *Ibid.*, 7.
16. Catechism of the Catholic Church (1994), 2357.
17. *Codex iuris canonici* (1917), can. 1060.
18. *Ibid.*, cann. 1070, 1071.
19. *Codex iuris canonici* (1983), can. 1124, emphasis added.
20. *Ibid.*, can. 1086.
21. *Ibid.*, cann. 1125, 1126.
22. *Familiaris consortio*, 23.
23. *Ibid.*
24. Pope Pius XI, Encyclical Letter, *Casti connubii* (1930), 17.
25. *Ibid.*, 59.
26. *Ibid.*, 24.
27. *Ibid.*, 36.
28. See Pope Pius XII, Apostolate of the Midwife (1951).
29. See *Humanae vitae*, 10.
30. *Ibid.*, 11.
31. Pastoral Constitution on the Church in the Modern World, *Gaudium et spes* (Vatican II, 1965), 50.
32. *Ibid.*, 49.
33. *Ibid.*, 50.
34. *Ibid.*, 48.
35. *Humanae vitae*, 12.
36. *Ibid.*
37. *Ibid.*, 11.
38. Declaration on Certain Questions Concerning Sexual Ethics, *Persona humana* (Congregation for the Doctrine of the Faith, 1975), 1.
39. Educational Guidance in Human Love, 4.

40. Unites States Conference of Catholic Bishops, 'Always Our Children', *Origins* 28/7 (2 July 1998): 100; *Persona humana*, 8.
41. 'Always Our Children', 100.
42. 'Vatican List of Catechism Changes', *Origins* 27/15 (25 September 1997): 257.
43. Catechism of the Catholic Church, 2357.

13

Dissecting the Discourse: Homosexuality and Same-Sex Unions

Barry McMillan

Introduction

One of the distinguishing characteristics of Kevin Kelly's published theological work is its combination of, on the one hand, theological rigour and, on the other, particular sensitivity to the concerns arising in the real, lived lives of people. His is, then, not a theology that addresses the pastoral, so much as one that emanates from the pastoral. In works such as *New Directions In Moral Theology*,[1] *New Directions In Sexual Ethics*[2] and *Divorce and Second Marriage*[3], amongst others, what can be seen is the result of his having looked unflinchingly at the real pain of people he has encountered in his ministry, and of his interrogation of, and challenge to, the theologies which cause, contribute to or sustain that pain. For Kevin Kelly, the *pastoral* is the political (and the political the theological). As a consequence, he is more likely to ask, as a starting point in any given instance, if it is the theology that is flawed, rather than assume that it is the people who are flawed and the theology unassailable.

This paper, as part of this collection, seeks to follow his example – by having as its focus a source of pain in the real, lived lives of people, and by interrogating and challenging the theology which causes, contributes to and sustains that pain. The pivot around which the paper rotates is the Catholic Church's condemnation of same-sex unions. This is for two reasons. First, because condemnation is the totality of what the hierarchical Church offers on the matter, and such a singularly barren position constitutes a theological and pastoral privation of such degree as to demand having attention focused on it; and secondly, the theology which underpins and drives the condemnation is based on such a series of long-held, unreflected-upon stereotypes and jaundiced perceptions as to warrant the highlighting of the extent of their inadequacy.

A Moral Taxonomy of Abstraction

Magisterial and hierarchical discourse on homosexuality is characteristically conducted in terms of 'condition', 'acts', 'disorder' and 'depravity'. The abstractionism

133

which powers such rhetoric serves an important function in that it enables the discourse to operate in a clinical, disinterested fashion, where the attribution of descriptions such as 'objective disorder'[4] and 'strong tendency ordered toward an intrinsic moral evil'[5] can be carried out as the efficient exercise of a moral taxonomy of abstraction. Conducting discourse about 'homosexuals' or 'homosexual persons' in terms of organs and orifices and presumed sexual behaviours maintains decontextualization and dehumanization, and allows the discourse to continue – indeed, enables it to replicate itself and its ill-informed presuppositions and stereotypes – at a safe, self-sustaining, distance from the real, lived lives of the gay men and lesbians who are its object. Characteristically, in Magisterial and hierarchical discourse on homosexuality, if there is one thing notable by the starkness of its absence, it is advertence to gay men and lesbians simply as people:[6] people – with hopes, aspirations, needs, failings and feelings; people – who are fathers, mothers, sons and daughters, brothers, sisters and friends; people – who seek, amidst the ordinariness of daily life, to live, love and, importantly, experience the fulfilment that committed loving relationship can bring. It seems unnecessary to point out that, in these regards, homosexuals are just the same as heterosexuals, yet this is not a conclusion one would draw were one's perspective and experience to be confined to Magisterial and hierarchical Catholic teaching and writing on homosexuality and same-sex unions.

That the idea of relationship, and its correlates such as love, commitment, fidelity, trust and devotion, are fundamentally threatening to the maintenance of the nature and content of traditional Catholic discourse on homosexuality is illustrated by the push to clarification and correction which follows upon the perception of any senior hierarch's having ceded such qualities to homosexual relating. In February 1995, in his Note on the Teaching of the Catholic Church Concerning Homosexual People,[7] Cardinal Basil Hume of Westminster stated:

> Love between two persons, whether of the same sex or of a different sex, is to be treasured and respected ... When two persons love, they experience in a limited manner in this world what will be their unending delight when one with God in the next. To love another is in fact to reach out to God, who shares his lovableness with the one we love. To be loved is to receive a sign or share of God's unconditional love ... To love another, whether of the same sex or of a different sex, is to have entered the area of the richest human experience.[8]

Cardinal Hume's reflection, rich and beautiful, also apparently treated manifestations of love, *qua* love, on equal terms. However, subsequent to the publishing of the note, it was deemed necessary that a clarification be issued – a clarification which emphasized that, despite what had been stated here, it was to be reiterated that physical expression of homosexuality remained contrary to the teaching of the Church.[9]

In a not dissimilar fashion, in November 2004, in an interview with the *Irish Independent*, Archbishop Diarmuid Martin of Dublin commented:

> I recognize that there are many different kinds of caring relationships and these often create dependencies for those involved. The State may feel in justice that the rights of people in these relationships need to be protected ... I

have a wide range of relationships in mind. I do not exclude gay relationships but my main concern is with all caring relationships where dependencies have come into being.[10]

Some days later, a press release from the Dublin Diocese Communication Office was deemed necessary in order to offer clarification:

Nothing in Archbishop Martin's actual comments ... supports the claims that he was advocating 'spousal rights' for gay persons, much less marriage or civil unions.[11]

The point to which attention is drawn here is that the notion of loving, stable relationship (and its correlates), employed in the context of homosexuality, threatens and subverts the standard dehumanizing and decontextualizing discourse of traditional Catholic moral theology in this area, and the stereotypes that it evokes and sustains. Traditional Catholic discourse on homosexuality trades both explicitly and implicitly on the stereotype of the promiscuous homosexual man, indulging in multiple, narcissistic, self-gratifying, hedonistically motivated, random sex acts. It is a stereotype readily conjured up by a discourse of 'tendency',[12] 'disorder',[13] 'lack',[14] 'depravity',[15] etc., but it is a stereotype which is simply exploded if the terms of the discussion should become commitment, compassion, care, loyalty, monogamy and fidelity.

In discussing the film *Brokeback Mountain*, in 2006, *Sunday Times* columnist Andrew Sullivan observed:

Where once they were identified entirely by sex, now more and more [people] recognize that the central homosexual experience is the central heterosexual experience: love – maddening, humiliating, sustaining love.[16]

Gareth Moore, in similar vein, observes that:

It is becoming clear to more and more people that homosexuals are capable of loving devotion and self-giving in their personal relationships, including their sexual relationships, and that they, as well as everybody else, should have the chance to taste the fulfilment that such relationships can bring.[17]

In Magisterial and hierarchical discourse, the nature of the discussion of homosexuality as yet, however, shows no signs of such evolution. Discussion of homosexuality is almost always (explicitly or implicitly) taken to infer a discussion about, and the presumed sexual activities of, gay men. Lesbians – in a manner reminiscent of Queen Victoria's mystification regarding them and her incapacity to acknowledge them – might as well not exist. Thus, the characterization of, and the reduction of, 'homosexuality' as referring to gay men and to a focus in particular on the act of anal penetration – designated the *homosexual* act – remain to the fore. This combined disregard of female experience and typical presentation of gay men as so fixated upon, and so engaged in, the act of anal penetration such that it is their *defining* characteristic, is revealed therefore as, rather, the defining characteristic of the *discourse* about homosexuality. In such light, the emphases in the discourse would seem to reveal more about the concerns of those authoring the discussions than about those about whom the discussions are authored. On the evidence, and given the extent of the emphases, there seems little way of understanding the skewed nature of the discourse other than that it is primarily informed and driven by some foregrounded melding of phallocentrism, penetratocentrism and coprophobia in the perceptions and sensibilities of those dictating the terms of the discussion. It also, moreover, declares a startling lack of awareness about, or acknowledgement of, the range of sex acts in which heterosexuals engage. As it stands, therefore, Magisterial and hierarchical discourse on homosexuality declares little more than its own impoverishment and the degree of its inadequacy for addressing its subject.

Drawing attention to the foregoing is important because the unreflected-upon stereotypes and jaundiced perceptions highlighted, and the conceptual legacy they sustain, constitute the stultifying parameters of traditional Catholic discussion of homosexuality and related matters. Clearly, hedonistic and narcissistic gay men exist, but the reification of such individuals into the defining archetype of an entire diverse subsection of humanity is simply as indefensible, as unethical and as misleading as predicating a discussion of heterosexuality on the basis that it is typified by the behaviour of hedonistic and narcissistic heterosexual men. The purpose of drawing attention to the functioning of the archetypes and stereotypes and the conceptual legacy they bequeath is to acknowledge them, and in that acknowledging to set them aside. In the purview of this paper, gay men and lesbians are not reduced to abstracted organs, orifices or orgasms, but are considered people – three-dimensional, sexual, spiritual, relational, embodied persons, with three-dimensional, sexual, spiritual, relational, embodied lives and loves.

The Condemnation of Same-Sex Unions

There are, at this point in time numerous and continuing examples and occurrences of Magisterial and hierarchical condemnation of same-sex unions. The Congregation for the Doctrine of the Faith's June 2003 Considerations Regarding Proposals to Give Legal Recognition to Unions Between Homosexual Persons (issued during the prefecture of the then Cardinal Ratzinger) states:

> Legal recognition of homosexual unions or placing them on the same level as marriage would mean not only the approval of deviant behaviour, with the consequence of making it a model in present-day society, but would also obscure basic values which belong to the common inheritance of humanity.[18]

It also instructs Catholic politicians that they have, under pain of grave sin, 'a moral duty ... to vote against it', elaborating:

> When legislation in favour of the recognition of homosexual unions is proposed for the first time in a legislative assembly, the Catholic law-maker has a moral duty to express his opposition clearly and publicly and to vote against it. To vote in favour of a law so harmful to the common good is gravely immoral.

When legislation in favour of the recognition of homosexual unions is already in force, the Catholic politician must oppose it in the ways that are possible for him and make his opposition known.[19]

In June 2005, the by-then Pope Benedict XVI, at an address in the Basilica of St John Lateran in Rome stated:

The various forms of the dissolution of matrimony today, like free unions, trial marriages and going up to pseudo-matrimonies by people of the same sex, are rather expressions of an anarchic freedom.[20]

In January 2006, in a speech to political leaders from the Rome area, the pope spoke against government recognition of same-sex unions, calling it a grave mistake:

It is a serious error to obscure the value and function of the legitimate family founded on matrimony, attributing to other forms of unions improper legal recognition, for which there really is no social need.[21]

Other hierarchs, in other territories, have been still harsher in their condemnation. In March 2004, Bishop Nicholas DiMarzio of Brooklyn, New York, discussed the Church's position in an interview on radio station WROW-AM, condemning same-sex marriage as something that might, by extension, be compared to a legal union of people with their pets:

I will give you an example, O.K.? You want to reduce something to the absurd, which is basically rhetorical use of an image: Why can't we have marriages between people and pets? I mean, pets really love their masters and why can't we have a marriage so they could inherit their money? ... There is no end to it ...[22]

In February 2006, in the Spanish Diocese of Ciudad Real, Bishop Antonio Algora, in light of Spain's move to recognize same-sex unions, likened the Spanish Prime Minister Jose Luis Rodriguez Zapatero to the notoriously depraved Roman Emperor, Gaius Caligula:

If Zapatero wants to become Caligula, it's up to him, but without doubt people will have to learn who Caligula was and what customs he imposed on Rome, it's as simple as that.[23]

Conspicuously, none of these statements, and most obviously the latter two, was deemed to warrant additional subsequent clarification or correction. The Magisterial and hierarchical condemnation of same-sex unions is, plainly, complete and total. Regrettably, it is also tainted with wholly unnecessary disparagement and ignorance, and, as is illustrated, in some instances a particularly invidious strain of splenetic hyperbole.

Such collective and forceful condemnation, however, raises key questions. In the face of such resistance to state-endorsed same-sex relationships, and in light of such intractable condemnation, what option or alternative does the hierarchical Church offer to gay men and lesbians? The weight of pastoral responsibility comes to the fore at such a juncture. Condemnation, in and of itself, is insufficient. What 'good news' is to be offered to gay and lesbian people in place of the legally sanctioned and societally supported same-sex unions that they seek?

The Imperative to 'Chastity'

With all homosexual sexual activity condemned, and formal recognition of same-sex relationships actively resisted and condemned, the Catechism of the Catholic Church states the course of action thereby decreed for gay men and lesbians:

> Homosexual persons are called to chastity. By the virtues of self-mastery that teach them inner freedom, at times by the support of disinterested friendship, by prayer and sacramental grace, they can and should gradually and resolutely approach Christian perfection.[24]

Patently this is an uncompromising assertion that demands interrogation and evaluation. To return to an earlier consideration – might it possibly be the case that it is the theology which is flawed, rather than the people?

In the Christian tradition, chastity is traditionally understood as being manifest in a number of ways. Given that heterosexuality is presumed normative for sexual relationship, it is heterosexual experience which is traditionally cited to illustrate and illuminate these ways. The first expression of chastity is that way in which it is embraced as a vow or evangelical counsel – as a radical form of sexual continence or virginity performed as an act of Christian witness. The aspect of note for our purposes is that such chastity is personally chosen by individuals as a vocational expression of religious conviction or of their relationship with God witnessed to the Church. A second expression of chastity is as the virtue by which the married conduct their sexual lives, described by Vincent Genovesi (citing Donald Goergen) as that way which 'moderates one's sexuality and enables a person to place genitality's intense physical pleasure at the service of love'.[25] As with the first expression, such chastity is freely embraced by those with whom it resonates as the appropriate mode of their sexual be-ing. In the third expression, traditionally delineated as the chastity of the single person, living chastely is (for the vast majority of those who embrace it) that choice to live in a non-genital fashion until such time as, a change in relational situation arising, acting genitally becomes appropriate and, in the new context, chaste in its own way.[26] Again here, a key element of the character of chastity is that it is entered into freely as the individual's chosen and elected appropriate mode of sexual be-ing.

Such outline leads to consideration of the injunction that 'homosexual persons', as a class of person, should 'lead a chaste life'.[27] For many, or even most, gay men and lesbians,[28] it is not the case that living without physical sexual expression is what resonates with them as the appropriate God-given living out of their relational lives. The choice of chastity, as outlined in the first and third expressions above, does not accord with their sense of who they are, and are called to be, as persons. In the core of their being they have no sense that God will find any joy in their living lives of reluctant loneliness and isolation. However, given that their sexual expression is condemned, and their relationships and unions condemned and opposed, these gay men and lesbians are denied by Church teaching any principle or mode by which they might live and manifest loving, committed, faithful relationship. They seek to live sexual relationship chastely but are told that this is simply not possible for them to do.

In light of the content of Church teaching on homosexuality and same-sex unions, the chastity demanded of gay men and lesbians is, consequently, categorically different from that of the assumptively heterosexual categories of the tradition, and different, especially, from the category of the chastity of the single heterosexual person – the category into which they are conventionally directed and consigned. The reasons why are threefold. First, the gay and lesbian people here described are either not single, or not drawn to singleness as their mode of living and sexual being. Secondly, for the vast majority of single heterosexuals who choose to live chastely, their lack of genital expression is elected, comprehended and adopted, as a temporary mode of living, a transitional mode on the way to another, namely marriage, where physical sexual expression is both foundational and central. In contrast, given Church teaching, the chastity advocated for homosexual people is not, and cannot be, a stage on the way to a sexually active chastity, but is, in contrast, a fixed, lifelong state without transitional character. Fundamentally, therefore, the state being entered into by both groups cannot be said to be the same. Thirdly, and most significantly, key to the character and nature of all three of the expressions of chastity found in the tradition is the element of election. Choice, as it must be, is a fundamental element of the pursuit of virtue. Without the element of choice, what would be enacted would not be virtue, but merely behaviour. Action demanded and undertaken without freedom or without election is simply coercion. In the matter under discussion, therefore, what is being prescribed as chastity for homosexuals is not in fact chastity – this is a misnomer. What is being prescribed is, more correctly, an impelled and imposed celibacy. In real terms, gay men and lesbians are, rather, being *instructed* by the Church to be lifelong celibates. In light of the combined condemnations of homosexual sexual expression and same-sex unions, the only possibility the Church presents to gay men and lesbians is an imperative to lifelong imposed celibacy.

To have arrived at this point is to have arrived at the heart of the matter. Is an imposed lifelong celibacy a viable concept, either theologically or pastorally? The sources best suited for enquiry into the characteristics and qualities of celibacy are the Church decrees, exhortations and encyclicals concerning or addressing Catholic priesthood.[29]

Presbyterorum ordinis,[30] *Sacerdotalis caelibatus*,[31] *Pastores dabo vobis*[32] and *Veritatis splendor*[33] all go to some lengths to emphasize and reiterate that celibacy is a charism gifted by God, but a charism not given to everyone, and unsustainable by purely human endeavour.

Sacerdotalis caelibatus, 5 describes celibacy as 'a special spiritual gift', while *Presbyterorum ordinis*, 16 describes it as freely received 'as a grace of God'. Illustrating that the charism of celibacy is not given to everyone, not even to those who have very good reason to desire it, *Sacerdotalis caelibatus*, 7 highlights the question of 'whether it is right to exclude from the priesthood those who, it is claimed, have been called to the ministry without having been called to lead a celibate life', and goes on to answer in the affirmative.

According to *Sacerdotalis caelibatus*, 62, in the embracing of celibacy, a free choice must arise within the individual: 'In virtue of such a gift ... the individual is called to respond with free judgement and total dedication, adapting his own mind and outlook to the will of God who calls him.'

139

Veritatis splendor, 22 highlights the unsustainability of celibacy by purely human endeavour:

> And Jesus, referring specifically to the charism of celibacy 'for the Kingdom of Heaven' (Mt. 19:12), but stating a general rule, indicates the new and surprising possibility opened up to man by God's grace ... To imitate and live out the love of Christ is not possible for man by his own strength alone. He becomes *capable of this love only by virtue of a gift received*.[34]

To sum up, Donald Cozzens, who has written extensively on the subject of celibacy, draws an unequivocal conclusion, illuminating to the argument herein. According to Cozzens, if we accept 'that healthy, life-giving celibacy is a charism given by God to relatively few individuals', then 'mandatory celibacy emerges as an oxymoron. Gifts that are grounded in the grace of God simply cannot be legislated.'[35]

It is clear that the charism of celibacy is described in Church teaching as something which cannot be implemented by warrant of authority alone, nor just adopted at will – even by those strongly motivated to do so. In other words, gritting one's teeth and being determined to be celibate because one has been told to, not only cannot work, but is never going to work. Nevertheless, and despite its own teaching on celibacy, the Magisterial and hierarchical Church continues to pursue its insistence that gay men and lesbians must be denied the flourishing of long-term, committed relationship and live by a celibacy not of their choosing but which is demanded from, and imposed upon, them. It is a desiccated logic, with tragically painful consequences for countless people.

Such, then, is the paradox with which the Magisterial and hierarchical teaching presents gay men and lesbians: physical sexual expressiveness is denied them as deviant and disordered; the fulfilment of committed relationship is denied them as anarchic and false; the imposed celibacy as a lifelong vocation demanded of them is unsustainable. In the light of such contradiction, one is left with thoughts of experts in the law who load people down with burdens and do nothing to assist them,[36] and of bread being sought but stones being offered.[37]

Conclusion

Others, elsewhere, have dealt sufficiently with the finer points of whether the fact of something's being considered sinful by the Catholic Church should warrant its not being made legal in democratic, multicultural civil societies, such that it is not here necessary for me to rehearse those arguments. My own point is a simpler, and more strictly theological, one. In its proscription of same-sex sexual expression and same-sex unions, on the one hand, and its prescription of an imposed lifelong celibacy, on the other, what the teaching of the Church has to offer gay men and lesbians is a rock and a hard place, and, moreover, a rock and a hard place that make no apparent sense, even on the Church's own theological terms. The Magisterium and hierarchy are actively, determinedly working to restrict and undermine the flourishing of the committed, loving relationships of homosexual people that already exist and for which they seek social recognition and support. Such interference in, and imposition upon, the flourishing of human relationships in such a dogged and determined manner, of necessity, must require the provision of a profoundly meaningful and utterly persuasive case. Certainly, it requires a great deal more than theological contradictions and inconsistencies, and the blank inarticulacy of blanket condemnation. One is left with the conclusion that, as part of an operative theology of sexuality, the teaching of the Church on same-sex sexual expression and unions is ultimately contradictory theologically and untenable pastorally.

Notes

1. Kevin T. Kelly, *New Directions in Moral Theology: The Challenge of Being Human* (London: Geoffrey Chapman, 1992).
2. Kevin T. Kelly, *New Directions in Sexual Ethics: Moral Theology and the Challenge of AIDS* (London: Geoffrey Chapman, 1998).
3. Kevin T. Kelly, *Divorce and Second Marriage: Facing the Challenge* (new and expanded edn), (London: Geoffrey Chapman, 1997).
4. Letter to the Bishops of the Catholic Church on the Pastoral Care of Homosexual Persons, *Homosexualitatis problema* (Congregation for the Doctrine of the Faith, 1986), 3.
5. *Ibid.*
6. Even a document entitled in the manner of the New Zealand Catholic Bishops' Conference's People in Homosexual Relationships (2000), by its halfway point, descends into the rhetoric of 'condition' and of being resigned to an 'inclination'. Though not beyond criticism either, the United States Conference of Catholic Bishops' pastoral message 'Always Our Children' (*Origins* 27/17 [2 July 1998]), in its distinctive approach, represents something of an exception to the general rule outlined here.
7. This document was an expansion of an earlier document, published in 1993, entitled, Some Observations on the Teaching of the Catholic Church Concerning Homosexual People.
8. Basil Hume, 'A Note on the Teaching of the Catholic Church Concerning Homosexual People' (February 1995), 9–10 (*Origins* 24/45 [27 April 1995]: 765–69).
9. The amended text of the 1995 document, dated April 1997, is available on the website of the Catholic Bishops' Conference of England and Wales at <http://www.catholicchurch.org.uk/citizenship/mfl/homosexuality/hs970400.htm> (Accessed 8 February 2007).
10. David Quinn, 'Archbishop Backs Legal Rights for Gay Couples', *Irish Independent* (16 November 2004).
11. Dublin Diocese Communication Office, 'Press Release: Archbishop Martin's Comment on Gay Marriage' (22 November 2004).
12. Declaration on Certain Questions Concerning Sexual Ethics, *Persona humana* (Congregation for the Doctrine of the Faith, 1975), 8.
13. *Homosexualitatis problema*, 3.
14. *Persona humana*, 8.
15. Catechism of the Catholic Church (1994), 2357.
16. Andrew Sullivan, 'Gay Cowboys Embraced by Redneck Country', *The Sunday Times* (26 February 2006).
17. Gareth Moore, 'Sex, Sexuality and Relationships', in Bernard Hoose (ed.), *Christian Ethics: An Introduction* (London: Cassell, 1998), pp. 223–47 (224).

18. Considerations Regarding Proposals to Give Legal Recognition to Unions Between Homosexual Persons (Congregation for the Doctrine of the Faith, 2003), 11.

19. *Ibid.*, 10.

20. Pope Benedict XVI, Address of His Holiness Benedict XVI to the Participants in the Ecclesial Diocesan Convention of Rome (6 June 2005).

21. Pope Benedict XVI, Address of His Holiness Benedict XVI to Members of The Regional Board of Lazio, the Municipal Corporation of Rome and the Province of Rome (12 January 2006).

22. Cf. Thomas J. Lueck, 'Bishops Assail Gay Marriages as a Threat', *The New York Times* (10 March 2004).

23. 'El Obispo de Ciudad Real Compara a Zapatero con Caligula por Impulsar el Matrimonio Gay', *El Pais* (14 February 2006). *Si Zapatero vuelve a ser el Caligula de la época del siglo II, allá él. Sin duda alguna, la gente tendrá que aprender quién era Caligula y las costumbres que impuso en Roma, as' de sencillo.*

24. Catechism of the Catholic Church (1997), 2359.

25. Cf. Vincent J. Genovesi, 'Sexuality', in Joseph A. Komonchak, Mary Collins, Dermot A. Lane (eds), *The New Dictionary of Theology* (Dublin: Gill and Macmillan, 1990), pp. 947–54 (953). Genovesi is citing Donald Goergen, *The Sexual Celibate* (New York: Seabury Press, 1974).

26. There will, of course, be those heterosexuals for whom subsequent committed sexual relationship simply does not occur, but the point remains, that the choice to be, or remain, chaste is a free one, with an ongoing potential openness to transitioning to the sexually active chastity of the second expression outlined.

27. *Homosexualitatis problema*, 13.

28. It is acknowledged that it might be the case that any individual gay man or lesbian might, of course, choose to pursue vowed or consecrated chastity, or to live singly and non-genitally.

29. The content of the summary that follows is reiterated and underpinned in canons 247 and 277 of the code of canon law.

30. Decree on the Ministry and Life of Priests, *Presbyterorum ordinis* (Vatican II, 1965).

31. Pope Paul VI, Encyclical Letter on the Celibacy of the Priest, *Sacerdotalis caelibatus* (1967).

32. Pope John Paul II, Apostolic Exhortation on the Formation of Priests in the Circumstances of the Present Day, *Pastores dabo vobis* (1992).

33. John Paul II, Encyclical Letter Regarding Certain Fundamental Questions of The Church's Moral Teaching, *Veritatis splendor* (1993).

34. Emphasis in the original.

35. Donald Cozzens, *Freeing Celibacy* (Collegeville, MN: Liturgical Press, 2006), p. 33.

36. Lk. 11.46

37. Mt. 7.9.

Part Three

Issues in Social and Political Ethics

14

'A Strange Sort of Freedom':
HIV/AIDS and Moral Agency

Suzanne Mulligan

Figures released by UNAIDS in December 2006[1] illustrate the severity of the global AIDS pandemic, and in particular point to the grip that this disease has on poorer countries in the Developing World.[2] Of all people infected with HIV/AIDS, 90 per cent reside in the Developing World, and sub-Saharan Africa remains the worst affected region. Two-thirds of all adults and children infected with HIV live in sub-Saharan Africa – an estimated 24.7 million people. When one examines the statistics even further, one notices that women emerge as the group that are especially vulnerable to infection; figures for sub-Saharan Africa for 2006 show that 13.3 million women are infected – that is, 59 per cent of the infected adult population.

And a closer inspection reveals that, in this region, South Africa contains the greatest number of people infected. Until recently South Africa was dubbed the 'AIDS Capital' of the world, a title which has more recently been accorded to India.[3] The epidemic in South Africa, Mozambique and Swaziland continues to grow. An estimated one in three adults in Swaziland is HIV-positive. South Africa has one of the highest prevalence rates among women attending public antenatal clinics (35 per cent).[4] It is interesting to note that, although in South Africa HIV-infection rates among young pregnant women appear to be stabilizing, they continue to increase among older pregnant women.[5] In overall terms, there are approximately 5.5 million people currently living with HIV and AIDS in South Africa, and the epidemic here disproportionately affects women. For example, young women in South Africa (15–24 years) are four times more likely to become infected than their male counterparts; in 2005 prevalence rates among young women within this age category stood at 17 per cent compared to 4.4 per cent for young men.

These statistics are certainly sobering, and remind us of the enormity of the problem within poorer countries. But statistics can often appear cold and detached. It can be difficult to visualize in real terms exactly what such data represent. At the heart of the pandemic lie people living with this disease and suffering in ways that most of us cannot imagine. Perhaps as a means of visualizing this crisis a little more easily I may recall a visit to South Africa in 2003.

Freedom Park, South Africa

The diocese and town of Rustenburg is located in the North West Province of South Africa. Rustenburg is an important platinum-mining area, and, as you drive through the countryside, you see mining shafts and mining plants at regular intervals. One consequence of the emergence of mining for Rustenburg has been the influx of migrant workers to the region in search of work, and this in turn leads to the existence of squatter camps where the majority of poor emigrants live. One such place that I visited during a trip to South Africa in 2003 is called Freedom Park.

Camps such as Freedom Park offer little to their inhabitants. There are no public facilities or services for the people living here; in fact, the most basic provisions that we in the West take for granted are a distant dream in places like Freedom Park. There is no electricity supply for example, no toilet facilities or running water. Water is available for purchase from delivery tanks that call at the settlement twice a week. Personal security can easily be threatened; people live in poorly constructed shacks which are often overcrowded and fail to provide much by way of privacy or security for the occupants.

The relationship between poverty and the spread of HIV/AIDS has been well documented. As the above statistics indicate, it is the poorest regions and countries of the world that are experiencing the highest incidence of HIV infection. My account here of the living conditions in Freedom Park, brief though it is, may help illustrate the nature of the deadly relationship between poverty and AIDS.

As mentioned, a major source of employment in Rustenburg is platinum mining. Mining communities throughout South Africa are known to experience particularly high rates of HIV/AIDS infection. The social conditions in such locations allow for the easy transmission of STDs such as HIV. It is common for men to migrate long distances in search of work, and, in many cases, they begin new relationships in these places of employment. They return home a couple of times a year and often bring infection with them.

Women, too, migrate to the squatter camps that have emerged around the mines, but they are in search of a different type of work. They know that there is a greater likelihood of finding men here who have a secure income, and they hope that they can establish a relationship with one of these men. Women may also avail themselves of the ever-present need for sex workers around squatter camps and male hostels. So they often deliberately move to places like Freedom Park in the hope that life will be a little better. It seldom is.

Poverty remains a major challenge for the South African government, and for most poor black women there is little chance of conventional employment. Women's dependence on men is therefore strengthened, since men may provide the financial and social security that a woman needs. However, should that relationship break up, survival for many women often involves quickly finding another partner who is willing to provide food and shelter in exchange for sex. The fact that there are few (if any) recreational facilities for most people living in poor mining communities means that men generally spend their wages on alcohol and sex. These conditions provide a fertile environment for the spread of HIV.

On my first day in Freedom Park I met a lady called Tseidi, one of the day-care nurses who work in Freedom Park Clinic. We arranged to meet the following day when she would bring me into the camp itself to meet some families living there. As we spoke that first morning, Tseidi told me of events the previous week. Two young girls, one aged 10 and the other aged 14, were kidnapped by a taxi driver as they went to the shops. The two girls were killed and mutilated. Their reproductive organs were taken out, their kidneys removed, fingers and ears chopped off, and tongues cut out. Their body parts were sold to a sangoma for *muti*, a ritual where the body parts of children are sacrificed to gain spiritual power and prosperity.[6] This brutal killing left the community in considerable shock.

When I enquired about the police response to this crime, Tseidi replied that it was unlikely that the perpetrator would be brought to justice even though a number of people suspected who it was. She explained that the police were not interested in what happens here, and that most people would be too afraid in any case to cooperate with them for fear of reprisal. The horrific nature of this crime made me question why someone would do something so cruel to young children. Perhaps it was a 'simple' case of lack of respect for anyone. But the nature of the crime was horrific, and it had a specific purpose – selling these body parts for money. Poverty was surely a factor here.

The following day, Tseidi and I went into the squatter camp, where we visited some people living there. One woman I met had three young children, one of whom was an infant whom she carried on her back. This woman had migrated from the KwaZulu Natal region to Rustenburg in the specific hope of finding a man who would support her. She left behind 11 children in KwaZulu Natal who were now young adults. Here in Freedom Park this woman had begun a new family with another man.

The youngest infant was visibly ill. Since the woman was HIV-positive and was breastfeeding, Tseidi concluded that the baby was most likely infected too. This woman's partner had recently left her and the family upon discovering her HIV status. She was now left with the responsibility of feeding and caring for her children alone with no income and no family in the area to support her. The hut in which the family lived was empty, and they had no food at all. The children were all hungry, and Tseidi discovered that they had not eaten in days. Naively I asked Tseidi where the family would get food – I thought there must be a soup kitchen or a food programme in the area. Tseidi replied that the best way for her to secure food for her family was to find another boyfriend quickly. Without a man to give them food and/or money, this family would not survive. The trap which many women and young girls find themselves in became starkly clear to me in that instance. As we walked on towards the next family, Tseidi explained the mechanism by which most children in the area were 'tested' for HIV. 'If a child reaches 5 years of age then they are unlikely to be infected. If they die before that age it is probably AIDS-related.'

Later we visited a woman who had TB. She was not HIV-positive. She had four small children and their living conditions were also very poor. Tseidi asked to see her medication card to ensure she was taking her daily dose of tablets. It emerged that this women had not taken her medication for a number of days. Tseidi enquired why this was the case and the woman explained that the medication must be taken with food, but since they had nothing to eat she was unable to take her tablets. The family, we discovered, had not eaten in three days. Again, this woman had no partner and the future of the family was precarious.

Unfortunately, these cases were representative of most people's struggle in Freedom Park. Before I left, Tseidi drew my attention to the name of the squatter camp – 'Freedom Park'. 'No one here is free,' she said. The truth of that statement had indeed been borne out by the experience of my visit to the camp. Statistics tell us that the poor are most vulnerable to infection, and that poverty drives people to engage in high-risk practices that increase the likelihood of exposure to HIV. Poverty locks millions of people in a daily struggle for survival, and takes away many of the freedoms that others enjoy. Freedom Park is but one illustration of this reality.

Gender and HIV

Experiences in places like Freedom Park serve to confirm that women are particularly vulnerable to infection, as well as illustrating the major challenges for those working in the area of HIV prevention and containment. Gender stereotypes are placing women at risk of infection. Women are often unable to access the same social, economic and educational opportunities as men, which in turn means that their social security is intimately connected with a male partner, spouse or male relative.

This, of course, has real implications for women's sexual health. Women in unequal or abusive relationships are less likely to be able to negotiate when, if and how they have sex with their partner. Sexual and physical violence within the relationship is not uncommon, should a woman try to resist or restrict the sexual advances of her spouse/boyfriend. In addition, women who experience violence within a relationship are at greater risk of infection with STDs such as HIV. Studies carried out in Rwanda, Tanzania and South Africa indicate that women who have experienced sexual violence are up to three times more likely to become infected with HIV than women who have not experienced such violence.[7] It must be noted at this point, however, that gender stereotypes not only affect how men perceive women, but also how women themselves view their 'role' within a relationship. For example, in Kenya, the 2003 Demographic and Health Survey showed that 68 per cent of women interviewed agreed that a man was justified in beating his wife if she refused to have sex with him.[8]

Equally, male gender stereotypes can expose men to infection. Traditional characteristics which portray the man as the sexually experienced partner within the relationship, or attitudes that may accept and even encourage pre- and extra-marital sex, often encourage men to engage in high-risk sexual practices. Once infected, it is highly probable that these men will in turn infect their wives or girlfriends. Indeed, many women now believe that marriage poses the greatest risk of becoming infected with HIV. For, although a woman's abstinence and fidelity may well be demanded by prevailing cultural norms, and she may indeed live up to such norms, it is unlikely that the same standards would be demanded of men.

If we return to the South African context, we see that a major concern for those working in the area of HIV prevention is the high level of violence, particularly sexual violence, directed towards women and girls. Although rape and sexual violence is a crime that any woman can fall victim to, poorer women are more likely to experience this form of abuse than wealthier, more independent women.[9] The reasons for this are varied, but poverty is a major factor increasing women's risk of attack.[10]

It is almost impossible to calculate how many women are affected by rape and sexual abuse in South Africa, since the South African Police Service (SAPS) and professional groups working with survivors of sexual attacks, such as Rape Crisis

Cape Town, agree that the vast majority of rapes go unreported to the relevant authorities.[11] The reasons for this are varied; it is usually the case that the victim knows her assailant and she may be fearful of a reprisal attack should she report her attacker; she may be socially or economically dependent on her attacker; many poor black women in South Africa remain suspicious of the police service and this in turn affects levels of reporting; and, in the case of attacks on young children, the child may not be able to identify her attacker. Because of such extensive under-reporting, as well as numerous shortcomings within the South African legal system, many rapists go unpunished.[12] Fewer than one-third of reported rapes ever reach court, and, of those cases that do make it to court, fewer than half result in conviction.[13] It is estimated that a woman is raped every 23 seconds in South Africa, and that between one in three and one in two women or girls will be raped in their lifetime, most of whom will know their attacker.

A more recent and very disturbing development in South Africa is the number of young girls and children who are becoming victims of rape and sexual assaults. Again, the South African authorities are struggling to cope with the scale of the problem. As in the case of adult rape, the reasons for such attacks are many, and can vary, depending on the specific situation. But one likely motivating factor here is the 'virgin myth'. This myth initially suggested that sex with a virgin would cure a man of AIDS. Men tended to target younger girls in the belief that they were less likely to be sexually active. But this myth appears to have mutated into one now suggesting that sex with a child or infant will cure someone of AIDS. Increasing numbers of very young children in South Africa are falling victim to various forms of sexual violence. Between January 2000 and October 2001, over 31,000 cases of child rape and attempted child rape were reported to the South African police.[14]

Not all agree that the 'virgin myth' sufficiently answers why so many young children are falling victim to attacks of this nature.[15] Some believe that the problem is related more to the general inferior status of women and girls than to sexual myths. It is probable that both of these explanations offer insights into the nature of the problem. Clearly sexual myths heighten the vulnerability of young children and infants and are likely to be a motivating factor in many sexual attacks on the young. But the discrimination and inequality that many women and young girls encounter in their lives inevitably makes them targets for sexual abuse and violence. Attitudes towards women and gender stereotypes must be addressed before basic rights for women and girls will be protected.

Kevin Kelly's Contribution to this Debate

In his message for the World Day of Peace 2007, Pope Benedict stated:

> Inadequate consideration for the *condition of women* helps to create instability in the fabric of society. I think of the exploitation of women who are treated as objects, and of the many ways that a lack of respect is shown for their dignity; I also think – in a different context – of the mindset persisting in some cultures, where women are still firmly subordinated to the arbitrary decisions of men, with grave consequences for their personal dignity and for the exercise of their fundamental freedoms.[16]

These are indeed welcome words from Pope Benedict. Unfortunately, there has been a tendency within Catholic moral theology to restrict discussion of the AIDS pandemic to the issue of condom use. Yet this pandemic is making us rethink our approach to sexual ethics, as well as asking us to consider the broader justice and human-rights dimensions of the problem.

A number of moral theologians have helped to broaden discussions on HIV/AIDS by looking at some of the fundamental justice issues that lie at the heart of the crisis. Kevin Kelly has written about HIV/AIDS with this in mind, and, when one reads his work, one notices from the outset that his treatment of the HIV/AIDS pandemic is not confined to the much-debated question of condom use. In *New Directions in Sexual Ethics*, Kelly calls for a new approach to the way we think about sexuality, and, in particular, the way we perceive gender relations and the role of women. The women I met in Freedom Park were at risk of HIV infection mainly because of their social and economic subordination. In his work, Kelly argues that preventive measures focusing on behavioural change alone will not succeed – change, he reminds us, must also occur at a deeper social level.[17]

One of the biggest problems when trying both to contain HIV transmission and assist behavioural change in sexual relations is what Kelly calls the 'double-standard morality'. In many parts of the world women are treated as second-class citizens, and are not afforded equal rights within marriage. In addition, owing to their economic vulnerability as well as inferior social status, women are often unable to negotiate safe sexual practices within a relationship. Kelly therefore concludes that:

> In the light of the picture presented above, it would seem unrealistic and even harmful to suggest that the only real solution to the HIV/AIDS pandemic lies in the traditional 'faithful to one partner' sexual ethic. That offers no help to many women. For them, what is lacking is the very foundation without which such a sexual ethic is virtually meaningless. As long as their full and equal dignity is not accepted in theory and in practice, many of the norms of this traditional sexual ethic are likely to work against the well-being of these women and may even prove to be the occasion of their becoming infected by HIV.[18]

This point is rarely, if ever, acknowledged by the Magisterium, but its truth has profound implications for the way we think about and teach Catholic sexual ethics in a time of AIDS. A more person-centred sexual ethic, one which affirms and protects the dignity of women, is essential if Catholic sexual teaching is to respond in a more positive way to the lives of millions of women affected by this pandemic.

Kelly takes the point further and suggests that, given the current crisis and the sexual exploitation often endured by so many women, Christian sexual ethics ought to be 'pro-person' or 'pro-women' before it is 'pro-marriage'. As the account of Freedom Park illustrates, a sexual ethic that emphasises the faithful-to-one-partner 'solution' is unlikely to offer hope to women in abusive or exploitative relationships or to women who depend on sex work for survival. The abstinence and fidelity approach can only succeed if women are viewed as *equal partners* within the relationship and if they receive the same opportunities and freedoms that men enjoy. This will involve a major change in mindset, as well as ensuring greater economic freedom for women. And, as with any long-term strategy, attitudinal change will require time and education. The results will not be seen immediately, and, in the intervening period, Church teaching on HIV/AIDS needs to respond with credible alternatives that address the needs of those most affected by this disease.

Perhaps the need for new approaches to sexual ethics arises because, traditionally, the starting point has been wrong, as Kelly argues in his work. The traditional ethic has placed considerable emphasis on the sexual act and on trying to define when and in what circumstances it is/is not acceptable. Kelly notes that, for many women, this is not the main priority. Rather, their concern rests more with the quality of the relationship; women want to be fully respected and their dignity as human persons acknowledged.[19] Systems, therefore, that oppress women, be they economic, political or cultural, fail to allow for their full realization, and deny basic freedoms that we should all be able to enjoy.

One of the striking aspects of places like Freedom Park is the lack of freedom afforded to people, especially women, owing to the socio-economic realities of the place. 'No one here is free.' Yet we know that freedom is an essential component of our decision-making capabilities, something that has been long recognized within the Catholic moral tradition. In fact, as Richard Gula suggests, 'freedom is so central to the moral life that without it we cannot properly speak of being moral persons at all.'[20]

Within the moral tradition, the importance of knowledge and freedom in our decision-making has always been central. But what happens when one's freedom, and therefore one's choices, are diminished by factors such as poverty? And what happens when the approach to the AIDS pandemic advocated by those in authority lies beyond the capabilities of many worst affected by the disease? What if people simply lack the freedom or the capability to choose a particular course of action due to social and/or economic reality? It would appear that attempts to contain existing levels of HIV and attempts to prevent future infections must recognize the debilitating impact of poverty on people's lifestyle choices, especially their sexual choices.

These are themes taken up by Amartya Sen in his book *Development as Freedom*.[21] Here, as elsewhere, Sen draws attention to the importance of understanding poverty as more than just the absence of income. Poverty manifests itself through the lack of freedoms and opportunities and the inability to make free choices that would otherwise be available to people. Poverty then takes away our freedom to decide who we wish to become; or in other words it destroys our basic freedom. Basic freedom can be understood as our freedom to make something of ourselves, to flourish as human beings, to fulfil our potential, to decide the sort of person we wish to become; poverty often destroys this most fundamental of freedoms.

If this is the case, then development must also be understood in a broader way than in the more commonly held economic perceptions. Sen tells us that true *human development* implies that people are free in their choices and are not constrained by the crippling effects of poverty:

Development requires the removal of major sources of unfreedom: poverty as well as tyranny, poor economic opportunities as well as systematic social deprivation, neglect of public facilities as well as intolerance or overactivity of repressive states. Despite unprecedented increases in overall opulence, the contemporary world denies elementary freedoms to vast numbers – perhaps even the majority – of people. Sometimes the lack of substantive freedoms relates directly to economic poverty, which robs people of the freedom to satisfy hunger, or to achieve sufficient nutrition, or to obtain remedies for treatable illnesses, or the opportunity to be adequately clothed or sheltered, or to enjoy clean water or sanitary facilities. In other cases, the unfreedom links closely to the lack of public facilities and social care, such as the absence of epidemiological programmes, or of organized arrangements for health care or educational facilities, or of effective institutions for the maintenance of local peace and order. In still other cases, the violation of freedom results directly from a denial of political and civil liberties by authoritarian regimes and from imposed restrictions on the freedom to participate in the social, political and economic life of the community.[22]

For Sen, any adequate theory of development must go beyond considering solely the accumulation of wealth. Development must also incorporate freedom. It is interesting that concepts of development that traditionally placed emphasis on economic progress alone without considering broader issues were found wanting.[23]

When one visits camps such as Freedom Park, it becomes immediately clear how poverty acts as a barrier to people's development. And there are many 'Freedom Parks' across the Developing World. If we are to talk about true human development, our discussions and understanding must move beyond simply concentrating on eliminating financial or material inadequacies. The elimination of financial barriers in people's lives is of course part of the process, but history has shown that, when one concentrates solely on economic progress, the needs of many, especially the most vulnerable within our societies, can easily be forgotten. Development, if it is to serve the flourishing of the human person, must include the restoration of an individual's freedom to make choices, to secure his/her rights, and to have access to the opportunities that poverty otherwise denies.

Conclusion

Given the situation described above, it seems unrealistic to speak about HIV prevention or containment without considering the ways in which the oppression and discrimination of women assist the spread of HIV. It appears unlikely that efforts to reduce transmission will succeed in the long term unless women achieve a level of social and economic freedom. Gender discrimination is placing increasing numbers of women and girls at risk of infection, and, in many cases, these women and girls are powerless to change the situations in which they find themselves.

Economic independence for women is therefore perhaps the most crucial element for women's overall well-being. Economic independence allows individuals to have a greater say in the decisions that most intimately affect them. For example, there seems little point advocating the ideals of abstinence and fidelity to the many women I met in Freedom Park since sex was their only means of survival. Credible economic alternatives need to be created for women if they are to attain social and economic independence. And, without such independence, women are unlikely to be able to control their sexual lives and sexual health. Initiatives designed to create economic alternatives to sex work are emerging throughout South Africa, but more needs to be done.

Through his work, Kelly has drawn attention to these problems and has made invaluable contributions to debates on HIV/AIDS. His work displays a deep concern and commitment to the issues involved, shaped no doubt in part by his experiences in Kenya and Uganda. Kelly borrowed the phrase 'The body of Christ has AIDS', a powerful and challenging image.[24] There is a difficult truth to those words. Approaching the AIDS pandemic in a manner which fails to move beyond debates about condom use, or which promotes a sexual ethic which is only act-centred, offers little hope to the many members of this body who are infected with HIV/AIDS. The starting point for us, as we face this time of AIDS, must always be the human person – the suffering and dying body of Christ.

Notes

1. See the UNAIDS 'AIDS Epidemic Update' (December 2006): available at <www.unaids.org> (accessed 15 January 2007).
2. Many commentators are unhappy with the term 'Developing World' since it is commonly accepted that many countries in this part of the world are not in fact developing at all. Many of the poorest countries are instead regressing in economic development terms. While noting these difficulties I will, for convenience, retain this usage here.
3. Estimates for India suggest that between 6 and 8 million people are HIV positive. Owing to the stigma and silence that is attached to AIDS in India, these figures are likely to be conservative in their predictions. See the UNAIDS website for regional data on HIV/AIDS infection rates.
4. Swaziland is struggling with an even more severe situation. Figures issued in 2005 show that HIV prevalence among women attending antenatal clinics rose from 4 per cent in 1992 to 43 per cent in 2004.
5. See UNAIDS 'AIDS Epidemic Update' (December 2006).
6. *Muti* is based on the belief that there is only a certain amount of luck in the world and everyone is allocated a portion of that luck. It is believed that very young children have not yet used up their supply of luck which can be transferred to whoever takes the medicine derived from their remains. The younger the child, the more potent the medicine. More potent still, if the child's organs were removed while the victim was still alive, since it is thought that the body parts are rendered more potent by the child's screams. Not all *muti* involves the use of body parts. Plants and shrubs are also used for this 'medicine'.
7. See The Global Coalition on Women and AIDS, 'Stop Violence Against Women – Fight AIDS': available at <http://womenandaids.unaids.org/publications.html> (accessed 9 April 2007).
8. *Ibid.*
9. I do not wish to imply that women are the only group that are exposed to these types of attacks. Rape and sexual violence is not confined to any one sex, class, race or age group. In fact, within the South African prison system, there is a serious rape crisis among male prisoners. It has become such a problem that many men now believe that, if sent to prison, they will become infected within a short time of their incarceration. However, for the purpose of this paper I wish to examine the high incidence of rape experienced by South African women and girls.
10. For example, poorer women may not have access to public transport and

may have to walk longer distances to work or for food. This increases their vulnerability to attack. Also, poorer areas tend to have less lighting, and poorer women often live in less secure housing. These factors assist in making poorer women 'easier targets' for sexual attacks.

11. It is believed that perhaps as few as 1 in 35 sexual assaults are reported. See Catholic Institute for International Relations (CIIR), *Tamar's Cry: Re-reading an Ancient Text in the Midst of an HIV/AIDS Pandemic* (London: CIIR, 2002), p. 17; The Pietermaritzburg Agency for Christian Social Awareness, *Rape* (PACSA Factsheet no.44; June 1998), p. 1.

12. For example, the definition of rape under South African law is very narrow. 'Rape' refers to unlawful and intentional sexual intercourse with a woman without her consent. It applies therefore only to sexual intercourse between a man and woman, and there must be penetration by the penis into the vagina. Acts of forced oral or anal sex do not qualify, nor does penetration by foreign objects such as bottles or sticks. These acts are criminalized instead as 'indecent assault', but are not defined as rape. The South African Law Commission is currently working to amend this narrow definition of rape, but, at the time of writing, the definition under South African law remains confined to that given here.

13. For these figures see Binaifer Nowrojee, *Violence Against Women in South Africa: State Response to Domestic Violence and Rape* (New York: Human Rights Watch, 1995), p. 90.

14. CIIR, *Tamar's Cry*, p. 17.

15. See, for example, Rachel Jewkes, Lorna Martin and Loveday Penn-Kekana, 'The Virgin Cleansing Myth: Cases of Child Rape are not Exotic', *The Lancet* 359 (23 February 2002): 711.

16. Message of His Holiness Pope Benedict XVI for the Celebration of the World Day of Peace, 1 January 2007: available at <www.vatican.va> (accessed 9 April 2007), emphasis in original.

17. Kevin T. Kelly, *New Directions in Sexual Ethics: Moral Theology and the Challenge of Aids* (London: Geoffrey Chapman, 1998), p. 3.

18. *Ibid.*, pp. 8–9.

19. *Ibid.*, p. 139.

20. Richard Gula, *Reason Informed by Faith* (New York: Paulist Press, 1989), p. 75.

21. Amartya Sen, *Development as Freedom* (Oxford: Oxford University Press, 1999).

22. *Ibid.*, pp. 3–4.

23. It is worth noting that much of what Pope Paul VI warned against in his social writings on this matter was only properly understood and acknowledged by leading economists in the late 1990s. Amartya Sen and Joseph Stiglitz are two economists who have long advocated a new way of thinking about development and a new way of devising and implementing economic policies that meet *all* the needs of the human person and which would therefore allow for the true development of peoples.

24. See Kevin T. Kelly, 'A Moral Theologian Faces the New Millennium in a Time of AIDS', in James F. Keenan (ed.), *Catholic Ethicists on HIV/AIDS Prevention* (New York: Continuum, 2000), pp. 324–32 (324).

15

Animal Ethics: Where Do We Go from Here?[1]

Celia Deane-Drummond

Kevin Kelly's book *New Directions in Moral Theology: The Challenge of Being Human*, published in 1992, set out important parameters for considering what it means to be human in an ethical sense.[2] There are a number of considerations that are relevant to ethical analysis in general, but I suggest that they have particular poignancy when considering animal ethics. I am not intending to argue that the similarity between animals and humans automatically means that human ethics could be extended to include animals. This has, it seems to me, been the assumption behind much talk of animal ethics in terms of 'rights', by extension from human rights.[3] My intention here is much more modest, namely, to draw insights from the way Kelly *approaches* ethical issues in human persons in order to enlighten the discussion of animal ethics, without presupposing that this supports the view that animals and humans are, in fact, directly comparable in ethical terms. In other words, it is the *methodological* issues that most interest me here, rather than simple ethical transfer across different ethical fields.

The first aspect that is important is his somewhat controversial belief that all truth statements are provisional and that we need to be courageous enough to voice what we think is true, even if it means critically assessing the position of the Church, for the sake of building up wisdom and love in the Church.[4] This is particularly the case for animal ethics, for, historically, Roman Catholic perspectives on animals have included views which are highly instrumental in tone, largely excluding animals from moral consideration at all. For example, a book entitled *Moral Philosophy* by Joseph Rickaby, written at the turn of the twentieth century, although not official Church teaching, was commonly adopted in seminaries and refers to animals as 'brute beasts' without understanding, not being persons and, therefore, not having rights.[5] This lacuna was astonishingly reinforced by the Vatican, under Pius IX, actually opposing the establishment of a Society for the Prevention of Cruelty to Animals.[6]

Since Vatican II there has been an upsurge of interest in ecological and environmental issues emerging in Catholic social teaching, but there has still been a surprising lack of adequate treatment of animal ethics. Kevin Kelly recognizes that the post-Vatican II climate favoured consideration of ecological issues as an important response to the 'signs of the times'.[7] This is reflected, for example, in

Pope John Paul's recommendation of the need for 'ecological conversion' that influences at the deepest level practices of the individual and the Church.[8] It is a pity, perhaps, that similar concern for animals at both the secular level and among some lay groups, such as the Catholic Circle for Animal Welfare, has yet to impinge sufficiently on official Church teaching.[9] As Kelly suggests, moral theology must have 'some persuasiveness in general experience' and *Gaudium et spes* 'attempts to listen to the movements of God's Spirit in the heart of the human family and through this listening tries to discern "the signs of the times"'.[10] I suggest, therefore, that the time is ripe for serious Catholic scholars to reconsider the place of animals and press for its subsequent inclusion in official Church teaching.

Another issue that Kelly raises is how to view disagreement in moral issues in such a way that such disagreement leads eventually to a positive outcome. This perspective is formed on the basis of a 'common humanity' that enables us to appreciate the 'richness of our diversity', leading to a 'plurality of moral stances'.[11] This is not, he argues, the equivalent of an endorsement of moral relativism, where any opinion could be as good as any other; rather, it is an acknowledgement that, when it comes to making claims about the truth, it may be that one's own particular culture and experience leads to alternative positions, but all have their own integrity and need to be respected as such. He uses the example of the radical public disagreement about experimentation on human embryos offered by leaders of the Roman Catholic Church and the Anglican Church respectively at a time when the Human Fertilization and Embryology Bill was being debated in the House of Commons. The Roman Catholic bishops, led by Cardinal Hume, insisted that from the beginning of the fertilization process the embryo is new human life, which gives it special status, dignity and rights under the law, and means that justice requires that equality of respect be given to all human life, whatever its stage of development. Cardinal Hume suggested that those who favoured such experimentation had 'abandoned fundamental aspects of Christian morality'. He then went on to insist that those holding such views 'have dispensed with the traditional Christian vision of the sanctity of human life. We can no longer claim to be a truly Christian society'.[12] The Archbishop of York at the time was John Habgood, who, on the other hand, was more concerned that scientific evidence could not be brought to bear on precisely when the individual human life should be given unique moral status, arguing in favour of limited experimentation where this was essential for research. Kelly suggests that many Christians would find it hard to believe that the Roman Catholic bishops were implying that Archbishop John Habgood had 'abandoned fundamental aspects of Christian morality' and 'dispensed with the traditional Christian vision of the sanctity of human life'.[13] I think this is a generous reading of the Roman Catholic bishops' statement, as it seems to me that this *is precisely* what they were saying, namely that Habgood should not be in a position to influence Christians in this way, even though his name was not specifically mentioned. Also, how far they could also claim to 'respect' Habgood's *position*, after claiming that his view is incompatible with Christian faith, is open to some doubt, even though it may have been said courteously: that is, they were highly respectful of Habgood on a personal level. Yet, Kelly is quite correct to suggest that the *reasonable* approach is one that admits the good intentions of the other party. Certainly, to my reading of the discussions that went on, the goodwill was on the part of Habgood, who resisted any claim that his opponents were somehow not Christian because of their views on the status of the embryo. Kelly also suggests that diversity should be considered not so much a 'scandal', but a 'valuable stage on the road towards better understanding'.[14] Of course, whether we agree with this statement depends on whether we believe there is genuine room for disagreement. It applies, most specifically, where there is room for different perceptions by Christian believers, not in unambiguous cases, such as a rejection of paedophilia.[15]

I have included a discussion about the disagreements on the embryo for a number of reasons. In the first place it offers a sharp contrast with the somewhat varied positions, where they have been aired, that Roman Catholic leaders have held in relation to animals. While they have been highly conservative about experimentation on early embryos, in particular, campaigning for the protection of embryos from the first moment of conception through to full gestation, they have been deafening in their relative silence in recent years on the treatment of animals and their use in medical research. Kelly, in places, seems to approve of the use of animals in medical research by claiming that 'it may be impossible to have accurate information regarding the treatment's long-term effects on human subjects unless one is prepared, having exhausted whatever experimentation might be helpful on non-humans, to take the risk of using this treatment on humans'.[16] To be fair, he did not discuss the extent of experimentation on animals; the point is that there is a contrast between animals in their usefulness to humans and embryos, which, as human, are deemed to deserve or be considered for a completely different order of protection. The emotionally charged and heated debate about the use of embryos is related to deeply held philosophical positions about the status of the human embryo and its moral significance.

Much the same could be said about divergent views on the status of animals. Those Christians who are now campaigning for animal rights in the name of justice for animals are doing so on the basis of the status of animals, arguing for a moral priority of the weak as a fundamentally Christian perspective. Campaigns for the rights of the embryo are couched in terms of the moral priority of the weakest members of human society, those who cannot speak for themselves. Andrew Linzey, for example, strongly argues from a Christian perspective for the protection of animals against any form of destructive use by humans, which includes, for example, experimentation, genetic engineering, meat-eating and hunting.[17] He speaks of those who oppose his views in somewhat derogatory tones.[18] The olive branch of a more conciliatory attitude is most likely to come from those who are less wedded to animal rights, for rights language is more commonly campaigning in its tone. Those who oppose animal-rights campaigns do so on the basis of potential benefits to humanity, in this case, for example, through the development of medical treatments that would be impossible without *some* use of animals. Of course, a middle ground also exists, as in embryo research, where there is careful scrutiny of the necessity of using animals, and allowance only in those cases where it would not be achievable by other methods.[19]

Another contrast with embryo research is the lack of open public disagreement about animal issues by different Church leaders, even though it is quite clear from the literature that there are widely diverse views held on the subject. Yet the treatment of animals could hardly be thought of as tangential to moral concerns, given that human lives are inextricably bound up with that of animals, whether through agriculture, pet ownership, ecosystem stability or scientific research. Given the strength of feeling for animals, the use of violence *against* humans in

157

the name of animal rights shows some chilling parallels with violence by more fundamentalist conservative groups towards human-abortion clinics. This shows that consideration of animal ethics is a political and public matter that needs to be taken with utmost seriousness and discussed as *public* theology. In other words, it is no longer enough just to be silent on this issue. There are, of course, many other important reasons why the Roman Catholic Church needs to take animal ethics more seriously, to do with the inherent value of animals as God's creation. My point here is this: even given the view that animals can be used by human beings for experimental purposes, the violent and political dimension of this issue is enough to challenge those in positions of authority to take stock, certainly not as a way of becoming conciliatory to such violence, but in speaking out against it, based on clear ethical analysis of animals in their relationships with human beings.

Of course, one of the reasons why Kelly suggests that there may be disagreements relates to ignorance about the issues at hand. Now both parties in the embryo debates will claim that they are knowledgeable about the scientific aspects of reproduction and the *in vitro* creation of embryos, though both groups tend to load the facts to suit their particular positions. In the case of animals, I have the suspicion that there is a certain amount of ignorance about the sophistication of animal intelligence and social behaviour that is being discussed in the scientific community, in particular, among ethnologists interested in animal behaviour.[20] Of course, those who have had particular experiences with animals, through either pet ownership or animal husbandry, may have more insights compared with those city dwellers living in relative isolation from animals. It is here that I suggest that ordinary members of the Church need to be encouraged to speak out and claim what is deservedly their particular view on the treatment of animals. There are lay pressure groups in the Roman Catholic Church that actively support animal welfare, including, for example, the Catholic Study Circle for Animal Welfare that publishes a journal committed to discussion of views about animals from a Roman Catholic perspective, endorsed by some active bishops who are its patrons. It actively seeks to encourage those strands in the Roman Catholic tradition that do exist which promote a more compassionate attitude towards animals.

Kelly also suggests that there may be disagreement because it would be too disturbing to consider the consequences of the truth. If, for example, animals are to be integrated into the human family in some way, does the consequence in terms of our own lifestyle seem too challenging to be dealt with at the practical level? I suspect, however, that it is possible to argue the case for some measure of moral pluralism in the treatment of animals, based on the experience and practices of different human communities and religious affiliations. We need to be able to cope with what Kevin Kelly calls 'graceful disagreement', rather than accusing those with different views of being guilty of 'scandal'. The question that remains to be thought through is what might be acceptable *limits* in terms of treatment of animals where disagreement exists.

Kelly suggests that morality is about the goodness and badness of persons and how they are orientated, their 'heart' or 'fundamental option', as well as their actions.[21] As social beings we need to see our relationships extending outwards to include the wider ecological community, including 'the rest of God's creation', so that our relationships are directed to the well-being of humans as well as the rest of creation.[22] In other words, human social relationships in their widest sense could stretch so as to consider animals and their treatment by human persons. As *God's creation*, animals could not be treated in a purely instrumental way for human benefit.

Drawing on the work of Gerry Hughes, Kelly suggests that moral pluralism should be linked with cultural pluralism, where we find a variety of acceptable moral codes alongside coherent patterns of beliefs and desires. Yet underlying these differences there is a common rationality and desires that constitute human nature as such, leading to a 'Principle of Humanity' that allows us to engage with cultural traditions other than our own.[23] I suggest that this is especially relevant to animal ethics for two reasons. The first is that the diversity of approaches to animals in different cultures, including their link with particular religious traditions, needs to be recognized and acknowledged. As Hughes states, understanding why a cultural tradition holds such an attitude 'is a task requiring painstaking empirical study in order to discover just how a particular pattern of behaviour functions in the life of a culture or an individual, just how it is related to the desires and beliefs that are held by that culture'.[24] Secondly, traditional ways of casting 'human nature' as unique in terms of reason and language that offer a radical distinction from the 'rest of creation' are now beginning to be cast into doubt. Any 'Principle of Humanity', if it exists, is unlikely to relate to rationality as such, for the level of rationality in social animals shows a remarkable degree of sophistication that those who speak in these terms need to consider. The real question is what is it that *really* distinguishes human beings from other animals, and this requires a much more detailed appreciation of anthropological palaeontology and the origins of humanity.[25] According to this account, the image of God, or distinctiveness in humans, emerges in the human community, rather than appears suddenly or all at once. Of course, this challenges more rigid traditional interpretations of the Genesis account of Adam and Eve and the question of ensoulment. The parallels with animals are interesting to consider here, for what does it mean for animals to have souls?[26] And what place might animals have in future redemption?[27] Or even more specific, how far do traditional accounts of the Fall, atonement and redemption need to be modified in the light of our knowledge of animal behaviour and evolutionary science?[28]

The question now becomes, how might we approach animal ethics in a way that is alternative to the more extreme views expressed through, for example, campaigns for animal rights? The first point to reinforce in entering this difficult area is to affirm a theology of creation that recognizes humanity as integrated with the material, created world. Kelly suggests much the same in his statement that:

> Humanity is bound up in an intrinsic and essential relationship with the rest of creation. There are not two separate and independent ethical criteria operating in ecological issues: what is good for humanity and what is good for creation as a whole. To consider creation as a whole is to consider it as including humanity. It is to recognize humanity as creation reaching a higher level of existence, the level of personal and social consciousness. This level of existence does not constitute a breaking away from the rest of creation. Creational health remains an integral element of the good of humanity, just as does bodily health ... For humanity to distance itself from the rest of creation and lord it over it would be a form of alienation from an integral part of ourselves.[29]

While this reflects a concern for animals on the basis of ecological issues, as applied to animal ethics, it shows the importance of viewing humanity not as distant from the creaturely world, but existing in mutual relationship. Margaret Atkins has contrasted three different ways of loving an animal: the conservationist, expressed through ecotheology, the animal liberationist and the farmer or agriculturalist.[30] I suggest that the second and third need to be considered in the light of the first, that is, animal liberation does not make sense if it works against the interest of ecological concerns. Much the same applies to agriculture. That is, it needs to become more aware of the pressures on the Earth's carrying capacity. Yet consideration of animals also needs to go further than just regarding them as another aspect of an ecosystem, which tends to be the case where ecological concerns take hold. The ongoing tension between holistic and more individualist approaches comes to the fore. Hence, disagreement exists on how we are to love an animal, even among those who support compassionate treatment of animals.

More promising, perhaps, are Kelly's hints at another approach that is relevant to consideration of animals where he describes approaches to IVF in the following terms: 'Reverence for life is an attitude of wonder before the ultimate mystery of life ... Does the intrusion of scientific technology and research into the reproductive process destroy this sense of wonder or can it provoke wonder in a new way?'[31] Much the same ideas could be used in consideration of animals. In the first place, it is important to have reverence for life, but life as inclusive of all life, along with an attitude of wonder towards life in its richness and diversity. Animals can also, like persons, be treated as individuals. While I would not go as far as to say they are 'persons', the human relationship to at least some animals, especially those domesticated through pet ownership, is one that is best described in terms of friendship and love, reflecting that reverence which Kelly speaks about. The kind of friendship that might be possible is clearly different from that which pertains in the human community.[32] Also, I am rather more sceptical about the value of liturgical rites that deliberately include the physical presence of animals, for the benefit seems in this case to be one-sided, that is, it is helpful for the humans taking part in this ceremony, not the animals themselves.[33]

Kelly also recognized, importantly, that the natural world, in the light of the processes of evolutionary science, is not a fixed 'given'. Rather, we should think of ourselves as being 'gifted' to respond appropriately to ethical dilemmas.[34] This means for him being wise and loving. I suggest that wisdom on the part of the human community, held in alignment with love, is particularly relevant in consideration of animals. For the extremes of instrumentalism or animal rights are not the only options open to human beings. Rather, the human community needs to develop the virtue of practical wisdom or prudence, alongside *appropriate* forms of justice for non-human species.[35] Kelly also believes that natural law is not 'natural', meaning that which contrasts with the 'artificial', but, rather, natural law simply reflects what is most reasonable. In this he offers a form of moral realism that is not content just to oppose those practices which seem 'artificial' in any way. I suggest that a version of natural law understood as reasonable is particularly important when considering ways forward in the treatment of animals through agricultural practices, an area remarkably neglected by Christian theologians.[36]

This essay has tried to show that Kelly's work is not just fruitful in the areas in which he has discussed ethical dilemmas, but also reaches beyond this to newly emerging areas of ethical concern that were unforeseen at the time when he wrote. I have argued that one of the most important areas that deserves our moral attention is that of animal ethics. Not only does this impinge on political activism and lay concern, it also serves to draw attention to where the Church could do more to develop its social teaching in this area. Kelly has provided us with some pointers about how to navigate the maze that forms complex debates in animal ethics. His work on human nature is prophetic in the sense that many issues relevant to this debate are pertinent here. In particular, ways forward through disagreements need to include a more conciliatory tone, one that puts emphasis on the giftedness of humanity in its wisdom and love, not in order to downgrade the status of the animal world, but to put emphasis on those attributes of moral character that are necessary for the building up of a flourishing society that includes rather than excludes animals from moral concern.

Notes

1. I am grateful for critical comments from David Clough and Margaret Atkins to an early draft of this paper.
2. Kevin T. Kelly, *New Directions in Moral Theology: The Challenge of Being Human* (London: Geoffrey Chapman, 1992).
3. A discussion of the ethical basis for animal research on the basis of similarity with humans is, of course, one that could be defended, but equally it could be argued that both animals and humans are significantly different to be treated in different ways from an ethical viewpoint.
4. Kelly, *New Directions in Moral Theology*, p. viii.
5. Joseph Rickaby, *Moral Philosophy*, (London: Longman, 1901), vol. 2. This book went through many editions and was, in the past, widely adopted in seminaries. See especially pp. 248–56. The most recent statements in the Catechism of the Catholic Church (1999), 2416–18, show a much more nuanced view that differs significantly from Rickaby. Historically, leading Roman Catholic churchmen have had varied views, including, for example, statements of Pope Pius V on bullfighting or Cardinal Manning on vivisection (Margaret Atkins, personal communication).
6. For discussion, see James Gaffney, 'Can Catholic Morality Make Room for Animals?', in Andrew Linzey and Dorothy Yamamoto, *Animals on the Agenda* (London: SCM, 1998), pp. 100–12.
7. Kelly, *New Directions in Moral Theology*, p. 3.
8. See, for example, Catholic Bishops' Conference of England and Wales, *The Call of Creation: God's Invitation and the Human Response; The Natural Environment and Catholic Social Teaching* (London: Department of International Affairs: Catholic Bishops' Conference of England and Wales, 2nd edn, 2003 [1st edn, 2002]), esp. p. 5.
9. Roman Catholic teaching on animals does exist, as in the Catechism, but I suggest it is not sufficient.
10. Kelly, *New Directions in Moral Theology*, pp. ix, 3.
11. *Ibid.*, pp. 4–5.
12. Cited in *ibid.*, p. 9.
13. *Ibid.*, p. 10
14. *Ibid.*, p. 11

15. Of course, part of the difficulty here is that, for many conservatives, there is only one Christian option, even in what seem to others to be ambiguous cases. One of the tasks of ethics is to try and discern where there is room for disagreement from a Christian perspective and where there is not. I suggest that both the status of the embryo and consideration about animals fall into this category, but, in both, there would be limits to what might be done, even according to the position that affords both beings the lowest status.

16. Kelly, *New Directions in Moral Theology*, p. 19.

17. He argues, for example, that animals should be treated as especially worthy of protection because they are unable to defend their own interests. He has campaigned for a Christian endorsement of animal rights for some years. See A. Linzey, *Animal Theology* (London: SCM, 1994).

18. For example, while he claims moderation by resisting naming those who approve of practices such as hunting and genetic engineering from a Christian perspective as a 'source of all evil', by comparing genetic engineering with human slavery and eugenic practices in the Nazi era, and describing animal experimentation as 'ungodly sacrifices', he rejects the idea that it could be morally reasonable (and responsible) to hold a different view. See *Animal Theology*, pp. 95–113, 138–55. This compares with his far more obviously strident approach in his earliest work, such as *Animal Rights: A Christian Assessment* (London: SCM, 1976).

19. Campaigners for animal rights in their more absolute moral stance might argue that, if it were not for their protests, nothing would have changed with respect to the use of animals for medical purposes. The fact that there have been significant changes to more humane practices shows that those who have argued for the use of animals in research have listened to public concerns. For discussion of the historical changes see, for example, Mark Berkoff (ed.), *Encyclopedia of Animal Rights and Animal Welfare* (London: Fitzroy Dearborn, 1998).

20. See, for example, Frans de Waal and Peter Tyack, *Animal Social Complexity: Intelligence, Culture and Individualized Societies* (Cambridge, MA: Harvard University Press, 2003); also Frans de Waal, *Good Natured: The Origin of Right and Wrong in Humans and Other Animals* (Cambridge, MA: Harvard University Press, 1996).

21. Kelly, *New Directions in Moral Theology*, p. 17. This draws in particular on Karl Rahner's idea of the fundamental option.

22. Kelly, *New Directions in Moral Theology*, p. 17

23. *Ibid.*, p. 20

24. Citing a paper by G. Hughes presented to the Association of Teachers of Moral Theology entitled 'Is Ethics One or Many?', in Kelly, *New Directions in Moral Theology*, p. 20.

25. Such a discussion is thrashed out in J. Wentzel van Huyssteen, *Alone in the World: Human Uniqueness in Science and Theology* (Grand Rapids: Eerdmans, 2006).

26. Margaret Atkins has discussed this in her article, 'Could There be Squirrels in Heaven?', *Theology in Green* 4 (October 1992): 17–27.

27. These issues are too broad to be discussed in detail in the present context. The point I am making is that theological beliefs about animal ensoulment and animal destiny in the reign of God will have implications with respect to how

they are treated on Earth. Some theologians, such as Ruth Page, are prepared to suggest that the idea of imaging God needs to be extended to include animals. See, for example, Ruth Page, 'The Human Genome and the Image of God', in Celia Deane-Drummond (ed.), *Brave New World: Theology, Ethics and the Human Genome* (London: Continuum, 2003), pp. 68–85.

28. I discuss this in more detail in 'Shadow Sophia: The Evolution of Evil and the Redemption of Nature', *Theology and Science* (forthcoming). A book that is particularly relevant to a discussion of Roman Catholic teaching on the Fall in relation to evolutionary theory is Daryl P. Domning and Monika K. Hellwig, *Original Selfishness: Original Sin and Evil in the Light of Evolution* (Basingstoke: Ashgate, 2006).

29. Kelly cites work he has previously published in *New Blackfriars*, on 'The Changing Paradigms of Sin', *New Blackfriars* 70 (1989): 489–97 (497), cited in Kelly, *New Directions in Moral Theology*, p. 38.

30. She gives the three positions memorable names: Connie, Libbie and Aggie. For her discussion see Margaret Atkins, 'Three Ways to Love an Animal', *New Blackfriars* 81 (2000): 108–23. Also spread over three issues in *The Ark: Bulletin of the Catholic Study Circle for Animal Welfare* 185 (Summer 2000): 47–52; 186 (Winter 2000): 51–56 and 187 (Spring 2001): 30–34.

31. Kevin T. Kelly, *Life and Love: Towards a Christian Dialogue on Bioethical Questions* (London: Collins, 1987), p. 153, cited in Kelly, *New Directions in Moral Theology*, p. 57.

32. For a fuller discussion of different aspects of friendship and how far they may or may not be applied to animals, see ch. 9, 'Genetics and Environmental Concern', in Celia Deane-Drummond, *Genetics and Christian Ethics* (Cambridge: Cambridge University Press, 2006), pp. 220–44.

33. This view contrasts, for example, with that of Andrew Linzey, who has actively sought to encourage liturgical rites that include animals. I am not saying that animals should be excluded in the verbal sense from Christian liturgy. Rather, 'funeral' rites that, for example, commemorate an animal's death are still very much human inventions entirely for the sake of those in the human community. One could say, 'So what, if this helps humans to be more compassionate?' Yet, it also has the danger of actually deceiving ourselves into thinking that animals are identical to human beings, which clearly they are not. Their differences, in other words, need to be respected.

34. Kelly, *New Directions in Moral Theology*, pp. 69–72.

35. I began a discussion of this issue in Celia Deane-Drummond, *The Ethics of Nature* (Oxford: Blackwell, 2004), pp. 54–85.

36. This point has also been noted by Margaret Atkins. See, for example, 'Three Ways to Love an Animal'. I am arguing for much more than just a reflection on professional ethics of farmers and their practices, but careful theological reflection on the merits or otherwise of such approaches in the light of beliefs about animals and their status before God and humanity. Clearly, further work needs to be done in this area. That is, we need to extend moral consideration not just to animal experimentation and hunting, for example, but also to farming practices that are routine, as well as those that are more exotic, such as the use of biotechnology.

16

Gott's Law:
Thou Shalt Not Blaspheme

Patrick Hannon

The last person in England to be put in jail for blasphemy was John William Gott in 1922.[1] Gott's case was also the last initiated by public prosecution; and, although the offence has come up in the courts twice since then by way of a private prosecution, one might have thought that Lord Denning had to be right when nearly 60 years ago in the first Hamlyn Lecture he declared that the law concerning blasphemy was a dead letter.[2] Or at any rate one might surmise that no one could seriously think it necessary or useful to maintain a law against blasphemy in the UK still. Yet, within the past two years, a motion in the House of Lords to abolish the crime of blasphemous libel was defeated; and this was but the most recent defeat in a series that reaches back over several decades.[3]

The persistence of the crime of blasphemy in the law of England and Wales has its own interest, and we shall look at it in a moment. But what probably comes to mind is the international furore occasioned in 2006 by the publication in Denmark of cartoons depicting Muhammad; for a key objection was that the cartoons were blasphemous and deeply offensive to Muslim believers. And this recalls another controversy in which English law concerning blasphemy became an issue, the *fatwa* imposed by the Ayatollah Khomeini on Salman Rushdie because of his novel *The Satanic Verses*.[4]

In the UK, as elsewhere, the debate surrounding publication of the cartoons raised questions at several levels: questions about morality and law, and the right to freedom of expression; about religion and law, and the meaning of religious freedom; and questions about cultural and religious diversity, and the extent to which the full implications of Britain's and, more widely, Europe's experience of this phenomenon have yet to be grasped. And of course there are questions for the churches and their leaders and for Christian theology.

Kevin Kelly's repertoire of interests and expertise as a moral theologian is extensive, though he has not written about blasphemy, nor has he dealt at length with the right to freedom of speech or the right to religious freedom. But his doctoral work was concerned with conscience, and his life's work, as well as his writing, reflects appreciation of conscience's primacy and rights. And, in his practice as a Catholic moral theologian and as a parish priest, he has exemplified signally the virtues which these freedoms bespeak. It is not inappropriate therefore, I hope, that a paper intended as part of a tribute to Kelly should have as its theme some of the issues which recent debates about blasphemy have raised. Nor perhaps is it inappropriate that the paper concerns itself with the bearing of Catholic theology on debates which, for all that their ostensible subject matter is widely seen as a legal and religious archaism, continue to generate deep feeling and obviously touch a nerve. Kevin Kelly has always displayed a sensitivity to the signs of the times, and he has seen his own theological inheritance not as providing ready and conclusive answers to our time's problems but as contributing to their resolution, in dialogue and cooperatively with other churches and other faiths, and indeed with all who are of goodwill.

The questions raised by the blasphemy debates go far beyond the usual purview of moral theology or Christian ethics, and ultimately they have to do with the nature of religious truth and the conditions under which it is to be sought and expressed. But two issues arise in the debates which are commonly discussed in terms of rights and hence are of concern to moral theology: the principle of freedom of expression and the principle of religious freedom. And it is the first of these which is the focus of this paper. It was Karl Barth who said that theology is best done with the Bible in one hand and a newspaper in the other. A Catholic version of this is that one might have in one hand not the Bible but Magisterial teaching: surely a defensible adaptation of the great Protestant theologian's advice, if only because the Bible says nothing (or nothing directly, if I must be absolutely careful) about rights to freedom of expression or freedom of religion, whereas the Magisterium does. And as regards the other hand, the Law Reports and Hansard are doubtless more reliable than the newspapers, though, as it happens, I make use here also of newspaper articles by two prominent philosophers of morality and law, Ronald Dworkin and Onora O'Neill.

The legal proscription of blasphemy is not confined to the UK; anti-blasphemy statutes are found also in the laws of Austria, Denmark, Finland, Germany, the Netherlands, Spain and Switzerland, to name only European countries. It may be of interest, too, that in several of these countries, attempts to have the statute repealed have failed. Finland, for example, witnessed unsuccessful attempts to rescind its anti-blasphemy law in 1914, 1917, 1965, 1970 and 1998; and the most recent failed attempt in Denmark was in 2004. Those familiar with United States jurisprudence, thinking of the First Amendment, may find this and everything that follows here astonishing. But that will be only if they remain unaware of Chapter 272, Section 36 of the General Law of Massachusetts, and the debates about hate speech which continue to rage.[5]

The statement of Lord Denning already mentioned is: 'The reason for this law was because it was thought that a denial of Christianity was liable to shake the fabric of society, which was itself founded on the Christian religion. There is no such danger to society now and the offence of blasphemy is a dead letter.'[6] Not quite a dead letter, however, as the editor and publishers of a paper called *Gay News* discovered when in 1977 a private prosecution against them was brought by the well-known campaigner Mrs Mary Whitehouse in respect of a poem and a drawing which had appeared in that journal, entitled 'The Love that Dares to Speak its Name'. By ten votes to two a jury found the defendants guilty, the editor Denis Lemon was given a suspended sentence of nine months' imprisonment and fined £500, and the publishers were fined £1,000. An appeal against conviction was dismissed by the Court of Appeal, though the court quashed Lemon's jail sentence, and, in the House of Lords, the conviction was upheld by a majority of three to two.[7]

R. v. Lemon is now the leading case on blasphemy in English law, and Lord Scarman – regarded in his time, incidentally, as one of the more progressive members of the House of the Lords – introduced his judgment as follows:

> I do not subscribe to the view that the common law offence of blasphemous libel serves no useful purpose in the modern law. On the contrary, I think that there is a case for legislation extending it to protect the religious beliefs and feelings of non-Christians. The offence belongs to a group of criminal offences designed to safeguard the internal tranquillity of the kingdom. In an increasingly plural society such as that of modern Britain it is necessary not only to respect the differing religious beliefs, feelings and practices of all but also to protect them from scurrility, vilification, ridicule and contempt.[8]

And it was this view – that the scope of the common-law offence of blasphemous libel should be extended to protect sensibilities other than Christian – that was central in the plaintiffs' submission on the last occasion on which blasphemy was considered in the English courts. In 1989 a group of Muslims sought to have the blasphemy law invoked against Salman Rushdie and his publishers Viking-Penguin for Rushdie's novel *The Satanic Verses*, but they were unsuccessful at first instance and on appeal. The court held that, even if it or a higher court had power to extend the law, it should not do so. For, as Lord Justice Atkins in his judgment put it: 'extending the law of blasphemy would pose insuperable problems and would be likely to do more harm than good.'[9]

The Law Now

Be that as it may, blasphemy in the law of England and Wales according to *R. v. Lemon* is 'any contemptuous, reviling, scurrilous or ludicrous matter relating to God, Jesus Christ or the Bible, or the formularies of the Church of England as by law established'. It is not blasphemous to speak or publish opinions hostile to the Christian religion so long as the language is 'decent and temperate'. The question is not one of the *matter* expressed, but of its *manner*, that is, 'the tone, style and spirit' in which it is presented.[10] Moreover, the offence is one of strict liability. This means that the presence or absence of an intention to commit an act of blasphemy is irrelevant; what matters is whether a defendant *did in fact publish the material* that is the subject of the prosecution. It means, in other words, that it is possible to be found to have committed the crime without having the slightest idea of the wrongness of what one has done.

A little reflection will no doubt suggest that, in present-day circumstances, the retention of a law in these terms is not merely anachronistic but also dangerous and indeed unjust, and it is no surprise to discover that from the *Gay News* case onwards there have been repeated attempts to have it changed. An additional reason since 1998 is that, with the passing into UK law of the Human Rights Act, English judges are bound to ensure compatibility between their interpretation of the law and the provisions of the European Convention on Human Rights. Article 9 of the convention protects religious freedom, and Article 10 freedom of expression, and it seems likely that, if a case were taken under the blasphemy law now, it would fail for breach of the convention, on the threefold ground that it is, in many respects, uncertain, that it is unduly restrictive of freedom of expression, and that it is religiously discriminatory.

Which, as it happens, are the three reasons for change given by the Law Commission in 1985, after it had undertaken a review of the law in the wake of the *Gay News* trial.[11] And they are again presented, along with numerous others – as well as arguments against a change – in several parliamentary debates in the 20 or more years since then. A restatement of the arguments pro and con is to be found in the 2003 Report of a Select Committee of the House of Lords set up in the context of a Private Member's Bill on Religious Offences;[12] and the arguments received yet another official outing in the debates on what has become the Racial and Religious Hatred Act 2006.[13] Meanwhile there have taken place also the more public debates that surrounded the publication in Britain of *The Satanic Verses*, and the controversy which followed the publication in Denmark of cartoons depicting Muhammad, whose depiction is regarded in Islam as itself a blasphemy, leaving aside the additional offensiveness of one of the cartoons in particular. Meanwhile the law on blasphemy remains unchanged.

Part of the explanation for this doubtless lies in the vagaries of practical politics; one thinks, for example, of the absence of the Prime Minister, with the concurrence of his Whip, from a vote on the Racial and Religious Hatred Bill, in which a Government measure was defeated by one vote. Media coverage generally leaves the impression of the thwarting of the forces of progress by reluctance on the part of establishments to change something deeply ingrained. And no doubt there is something to that, too: see the contributions to the Lords debates of (say) the Bishop of Oxford,[14] and the submission made to the Select Committee on behalf of the Catholic Bishops of England and Wales.[15]

But there is, on the whole, a sense of tiredness about parliamentary and related discussion of the blasphemy laws. When you look at the debates in the Lords, for example, there is an impression of standard liberal and conservative responses. In a speech in the 2005 debate on Lord Avebury's motion to abolish the offence of blasphemy the Conservative peer, Baroness O'Catháin, offers a textbook illustration of the views that we associate with Lord Devlin and of his antecedent Fitzjames Stephen.[16] And Lord Lester QC provides invariable reassurance of the continuing influence of H.L.A. Hart and of *his* antecedent J.S. Mill.[17] Nor does any other peer open new ground.

One may ask whether both liberal and conservative thinking needs to move beyond the patterns that have taken hold over decades of discussion and debate, not least in view of the sheer persistence of the offence in English law. Such a development is perhaps more likely in academe than in the courts or Parliament and, as it happened, the cartoons provoked reaction among academics also, albeit in the media rather than in scholarly journals. It was interesting to read the views of two philosophers, each of whom is commonly taken to be a liberal thinker, though – as with Hart and Devlin – the second more conservatively so. The focal question was the rightness or wrongness of the decision of mainstream British media not to publish the cartoons. In newspaper articles Ronald Dworkin offered a vigorous and uncompromising defence of the principle of freedom of expression, but Onora O'Neill took a more questioning line.

Academics

Though he accepted what he called the wisdom of the decision not to publish in Britain, Dworkin feared that the decision would be taken as an endorsement of 'the widely held opinion' that freedom of speech has limits: 'that it must be balanced against the virtues of multiculturalism, and that the Government was right after all to propose that it be made a crime to publish anything "abusive or insulting" to a religious group'.[18] Freedom of speech is more than just 'a special and distinctive emblem of Western culture that might be generously abridged or qualified as a measure of respect for other cultures that reject it, the way a crescent or menorah might be added to a Christian religious display'. Free speech for Dworkin is nothing less than a condition of legitimate government.

As for the contention that a right to freedom of expression cannot imply the freedom to offend the sensibilities of religious believers, Dworkin's reply is that, in a democracy, 'no one, however powerful or impotent, can have a right not to be insulted or offended'. He notes that it is sometimes said that, because people's religious convictions are so central to their personalities, 'they should not be asked to tolerate ridicule in that dimension'. But he contends that we cannot make an exception for religious insult if we want to use law to protect the free exercise of religion in other ways.

Onora O'Neill's contribution[19] is, in the main, a criticism of the defence put forward by Flemming Rose, the cultural editor of *Jyllands-Posten*, the Danish paper that published the cartoons in the first place. Rose had expressed regret at what happened in consequence of the decision but insisted on the paper's right to publish. The decision, he said, had been a deliberate challenge to what he and his colleagues saw as a climate of self-censorship among Danish writers and artists. O'Neill observes that Rose's account reflects the standard liberal view, a view about which she has some reservations.

She points out first that even committed liberals do not hold that rights to free speech are unlimited: 'Nobody thinks that a right to free speech confers an unconditional licence to intimidate, to incite hatred, to defraud, to deceive or the like, and nobody thinks that the law should protect speech acts that harm, injure or put others at risk'. 'Speech acts' is O'Neill's preferred term, and she is wary of what she describes as the modern tendency to equate freedom of speech and freedom of expression: 'Freedom of expression sounds so harmless: merely a matter of expressing oneself, seemingly no more than an aspect of individual privacy'. Yet, she says, most speech acts are not merely expressive, for they are intended to communicate, and so may affect others, and even harm them.

O'Neill reminds us that Kant called free speech 'the most innocuous freedom', and Mill seems to have been the first to equate free speech with freedom of expression, and therefore 'as no more than self-regarding action', as O'Neill puts it. Yet both accepted that most speech acts are not mere self-expression, and that many are far from innocuous. Each argued that some speech acts have the capacity to harm, and so must be restricted in order to protect the rights of others. For Kant it was the free speech of officials, clergy and others in authority that may need to be limited. Mill's argument was that free speech does not entitle one to perform speech acts that harm others, or to think that there is a right to defame, or to shout 'fire!' in a crowded theatre, causing panic and perhaps death.

O'Neill thinks it regrettable that 'the Millian conflation of (seemingly innocuous) freedom of expression with (sometimes injurious) freedom of speech has now been entrenched in the vocabulary of human rights conventions, and in wider discussions of free speech'. In the European Convention on Human Rights, for example, Article 10 proclaims a right to freedom of expression, characterized as the 'freedom to hold opinions and to receive and impart information and ideas without interference by public authority and regardless of frontiers'.

This suggests, as O'Neill says, that free speech is a matter for individuals, whose self-expression it protects against state power and in particular against censorship. But the article applies also to speech and publication by those with power to influence the world at large, including, of course, the media. To accord the local press the same freedom of expression as belongs to individuals may, in Mill's day, have been uncontroversial; and indeed a free press was then often seen as the champion of the weak and a voice for the powerless. But O'Neill believes that to grant the same freedom of expression nowadays to more powerful organizations, including media organizations, is less easily justified.

The convention does in fact confer a right of freedom of expression on institutions as well as on individuals, but it also sets out a basis for possible restriction:

> The exercise of these freedoms, since it carries with it duties and responsibilities, may be subject to such formalities, conditions, restrictions or penalties as are prescribed by law and are necessary in a democratic society, in the interests of national security, territorial integrity or public safety, for the prevention of disorder or crime, for the protection of health or morals, for the protection of the reputation or rights of others, for preventing the disclosure of information received in confidence, or for maintaining the authority and impartiality of the judiciary.[20]

So, while the convention assigns a right to freedom of expression both to individuals and to institutions, it balances that freedom with the possibility of setting conditions on its use. In effect, as O'Neill puts it, 'it proclaims not an unrestricted right to freedom of expression, but a defeasible right – essentially, one that may be overridden to protect other important rights'.

O'Neill remarks that it is usual to say that free speech must include a right to say things that are offensive or provocative, but not rights to defame, insult, let alone intimidate. But she considers that these distinctions are in practice inevitably unclear, since interpretations of speech acts vary with audiences: 'Danes might read the cartoons as no more than mildly provocative and offensive; many Muslims have read them as insulting and defamatory'.

A conflation of the notions of free speech and free expression will influence thinking, too, O'Neill says:

> If we think of speech as mere self-expression, we are likely to think that what has happened is in no way the responsibility of *Jyllands-Posten* or of Flemming Rose. But if we think of free speech as exercised in communicating with audiences, and remember that audiences vary greatly in the way they will read what is said and written, we may find reason to be more circumspect.

O'Neill thought that Rose and the paper should have sought other ways of communicating legitimate worries about self-censorship in Denmark, 'ways that would have found resonance and respect'.

In fairness to Ronald Dworkin (or for that matter Onora O'Neill), it should be said that a short piece in a newspaper is hardly a basis for criticizing a philosophy of law, and one can see in Dworkin's most recent book,[21] as well as his earlier writings, that, of course, he is aware of the need to harmonize the exercise of rights, and of the need for some legal regulation of what may be said and expressed. It is no cause for surprise, however, that, in this piece, he explicitly rejects the privileging of religious sensibility, nor is it inconsistent that he is unpersuaded by the claims of 'multi-culturalism'. It is perhaps not entirely clear what is meant by saying that 'we cannot make an exception for religious insult if we want to use law to protect the free exercise of religion in other ways'. At any rate it is fair to say that, had Dworkin's article appeared first, his view on the cartoons controversy is what Onora O'Neill might have had in mind as standard liberal.

With O'Neill's article, we have a more nuanced approach. No doubt her preference for the term 'speech acts' already invokes a philosophy not to everyone's taste, though it has perhaps the advantage of being home-grown. But her disinclination to 'conflate' freedom of speech and freedom of expression is worthy of discussion. In the end it is not clear whether she would favour some *legal* restraint on speech acts of the sort represented by the cartoons. Her criticism of *Jyllands-Posten* and Flemming Rose may be better understood as implying that they were in breach of an *ethical* responsibility.

Catholic Theology

Which is perhaps what should be said also of the Vatican's official response to the cartoons controversy. In a brief statement, the Vatican spoke of the caricatures as an 'unacceptable provocation'. The right to freedom of thought and expression, said the statement, 'cannot entail the right to offend the religious sentiment of believers'.[22]

There is little enough discussion in Catholic moral theology of matters such as freedom of speech or expression, or even of the right to religious freedom, which is still envisaged mainly within the terms set by the work of John Courtney Murray. And Catholic or other Christian theologians have not engaged much with media ethics, notwithstanding the worldwide proliferation of centres of applied ethics in whose programmes it prominently features. Unexpectedly perhaps, but fortunately, a starting point for Catholic moral theologians is available in a corpus of documents beginning with the Decree *Inter mirifica* of the Second Vatican Council. These documents have received little attention from theologians or religious affairs commentators, and the distinction formerly accorded Catholic social teaching – that it was the Church's best-kept secret – might now more aptly pass to its teaching on the media for social communications. This is regrettable, for the work of the Pontifical Council for Social Communications has been constructive, as well as remarkable in its range.

In terms of our interest here, what is available is largely in the form of generalities but – just as in the social doctrine – these are useful in shaping a general approach. *Inter mirifica* itself is commonly (and rightly) regarded as one of the weakest of the Council's documents, moralistic in content and patronizing in stance and tone. But its attitude to the media is positive: it sees them as gifts of God which have a capacity to promote true community, and so bring about God's purposes for humanity. And this positive appraisal has been carried over into the work of the Council for the Media and has informed its approach to the concrete questions which it has addressed. Here I shall confine attention to the first of that Council's statements, but what this says is replicated, explicitly or by implication, both in the Council's treatment of particular questions and in its return to basic conceptions, in its various subsequent documents.

The opening words of the Instruction *Communio et progressio* (1971) are indicative: 'the unity and advancement of people living in society: these are the chief aims of social communication and of all the means it uses'.[23] The Christian vision of man, says the Instruction, sees modern technological development as a response to the divine command to possess and master the world, and as an act of cooperation in God's work of creation and conservation. Moreover, social communications 'tend to multiply contacts within society and to deepen social consciousness. As a result the individual is bound more closely to his fellow men, and can play his part in the unfolding of history as if led by the hand of God'.[24]

In the light of Christian faith, 'the unity and brotherhood of man are the chief aims of all communication, and these find their source and model in the central mystery of the eternal communion between the Father, Son and Holy Spirit who live a single divine life'.[25] It is also relevant that 'communication is more than the expression of ideas and the indication of emotion. At its most profound level it is the giving of self in love'.[26] The Instruction links this potential of communication with the revelation made in Christ ('Christ's communication was, in fact, spirit and life'); with the Eucharist (communion with God and with each other) and the Church ('Christ's mystical body'); and with the eschatological hope of 'that last unity where "God will be all in all"'.[27] This exalted view of the media's place is tempered by an awareness of the dangers of their misuse; the Instruction makes it clear that a Christian understanding includes the insight that we are sinful and in need of salvation and of the redemption achieved in Jesus Christ. But it seems worthwhile drawing attention here to the point that, in the Instruction's perspectives, Catholic thinking is not meant to be negative or defensive or closed.

Freedom of expression is discussed primarily in the context of the right to information, the importance of which is, in turn, seen in terms of its contribution to the formation of public opinion. The means of social communication are indeed 'a public forum' where people may exchange ideas: 'the public expression and the confrontation of different opinions that occur within this dialogue influence and enrich the development of society and further its progress'.[28] According to the Instruction, public opinion is 'an essential expression of human nature organized in a society'.[29] It cites Pope Pius XII, who described it as 'the natural echo of actual events and situations as reflected more or less spontaneously in the minds and judgements of men'.[30] And freedom of speech is 'a normal factor' in the development of public opinion.[31]

It is therefore 'absolutely essential' that there be freedom to express ideas and attitudes. 'In accordance with the express teaching of the Second Vatican Council it is necessary unequivocally to declare that freedom of speech for individuals and groups must be permitted so long as the common good and public morality be not endangered.'[32] The Instruction amplifies:

In order that men may usefully cooperate and further improve the life of the community, there must be freedom to assess and compare differing views which seem to have weight and validity. Within this free interplay of opinion, there exists a process of give and take, of acceptance or rejection, of compromise or compilation. And within this same process, the more valid ideas can gain ground so that a consensus that will lead to common action becomes possible.[33]

All of this requires that the public have free access to the sources and channels of information, and be allowed freely to express their own views. 'Freedom of opinion and the right to be informed go hand in hand. Pope John XXIII, Pope Paul VI and the Second Vatican Council have all stressed this right to information which today is essential for the individual and for society in general.'[34]

No doubt it has been noticed that in recalling the teaching of Vatican II – the reference is to *Gaudium et spes*[35] – the Instruction introduces a qualification: the common good and public morality must not be endangered. Naturally a great deal depends on what is to be considered as necessitated by the common good and what is to count as public morality. A full discussion would, of course, require that we move now to the terrain mapped by Hart and Devlin and traversed by their numerous commentators. But, for our purposes, it must suffice to attend to some pointers in the Instruction. Three specific grounds of restriction are mentioned: the right of truth, 'which guards the good name both of men and of societies',[36] the right of privacy[37] and the right to confidentiality.[38] But the document stresses that 'the role of the civil authorities is essentially a positive one. Their chief task is not to create difficulties or to suppress, though, at times, corrective measures may become necessary.'[39] It again invokes the teaching of Vatican II, that human freedom is to be respected as far as possible, and curtailed only when and as far as necessary; and it affirms that 'censorship therefore should only be used in the very last extremity'.[40]

And So?

It will, I hope, be plain from the foregoing that at the level of broad principle and general orientation there is an abundance of material in Catholic thinking about the right to freedom of expression. It will be apparent also that the teaching's commitment to the values of free expression is wholehearted. One is therefore justified, I think, in questioning whether a reliance on restrictive law, either in the form of a blasphemy law or of prior (or any) censorship, is in these perspectives an appropriate response to the issues raised in the cartoons controversy or those that were at stake in the Rushdie case. The stance of the Vatican, like that articulated by Onora O'Neill, is a proper challenge to standard liberal pieties. But the challenge is to moral sensibility, and it is about values such as prudence and reverence and respect, values that will never be engendered or engineered by the making of law.

Notes

1. *R. v. Gott* (1922) 16 Cr App R 87.
2. Lord Denning, *Freedom Under the Law* (Hamlyn Lectures, 1; London: Sweet and Maxwell, 1949), p. 46.
3. Racial and Religious Hatred Bill 2005.
4. An account, with references, is at <www.csulb.edu/~bhfinney/SalmanRushdie. html> (accessed 14 June 2007).
5. General accounts are found in Leonard Levy, *Blasphemy: Verbal Offense Against the Sacred, from Moses to Salman Rushdie* (Chapel Hill: University of North Carolina Press, 1993); David Lawton, *Blasphemy* (Philadelphia: University of Pennsylvania Press, 1993). On hate speech in US law more generally see <www.law.umkc.edu/faculty/projects/ftrials/conlaw/hatespeech. htm> (accessed 14 June 2007).
6. See note 2 above.
7. *R. v. Lemon; R. v. Gay News Ltd* (1979) 1 All ER 898.
8. *R. v. Lemon.*
9. *R. v. Chief Metropolitan Stipendiary Magistrate ex parte Choudhury* (1991).
10. *R. v. Lemon.*
11. 'Offences against Religion and Public Worship' (Report: LAW COM. No. 145; London: HMSO, 1985).
12. See Religious Offences Bill (HL Bill 39 53/1): available at <http://www. parliament.the-stationery-office.co.uk/pa/ld/ldrelof.htm> (accessed 14 June 2007).
13. Available at <http://www.opsi.gov.uk/acts/acts2006/20060001.htm> (accessed 14 June 2007).
14. The Hansard text of the speech in the House of Lords on 8 November 2005 is available online at <http://www.publications.parliament.uk/pa/ld200506/ ldhansrd/vo051108/text/51108-08.htm> (accessed 14 June 2007).
15. Select Committee on Religious Offences in England and Wales, Written Evidence, Submission from the Catholic Bishops' Conference of England and Wales. Available at <http://www.parliament.the-stationery-office.co.uk/pa/ ld200203/ldselect/ldrelof/95/95w10.htm> (accessed 14 June 2007).
16. The Hansard text of her speech on 8 November 2005 is available at <http://www.publications.parliament.uk/pa/ld200506/ldhansrd/vo051108/ text/51108-10.htm> (accessed 14 June 2007).
17. The Hansard text of his speech on 8 November 2005 is available at <http://www.publications.parliament.uk/pa/ld200506/ldhansrd/vo051108/ text/51108-08.htm> (accessed 14 June 2007).
18. Ronald Dworkin, 'Even Bigots and Holocaust Deniers must have Their Say', *The Guardian* (14 February 2006): http://www.guardian.co.uk/comment/ story/0,,1709372,00.html> (accessed 14 June 2007). All quotations from Dworkin are from this piece.
19. Onora O'Neill, 'A Right to Offend?', *The Guardian* (13 February 2006). All quotations from O'Neill are from this piece.
20. European Convention on Human Rights (Article 10.2).
21. Ronald Dworkin, *Is Democracy Possible Here? Principles for a New Debate* (New Jersey: Princeton University Press, 2006).
22. Cf. Anon., 'Arson and Death Threats as Muhammad Caricature Controversy

Escalates', *Der Spiegel* (4 February 2006). Available online at: <http://www.spiegel.de/international/0,1518,399177,00.html> (accessed 14 June 2007).

23. Pastoral Instruction On the Means of Social Communication, *Communio et progressio*, (*Acta Apostolicae Sedis* 63 [1971]: 593–656). The translation used here is that given at the Vatican website: <http://www.vatican.va/roman_curia/pontifical_councils/pccs/documents/rc_pc_pccs_doc_23051971_communio_en.html> (accessed 14 June 2007).
24. *Communio et progressio*, 8.
25. *Ibid.*, 8.
26. *Ibid.*, 11.
27. *Ibid.*, 11.
28. *Ibid.*, 24.
29. *Ibid.*, 25.
30. Pius XII, Allocution to Catholic Journalists, 17 February 1950 (*Acta Apostolicae Sedis* 42 [1950]: 251).
31. *Communio et progressio*, 25.
32. *Ibid.*, 26.
33. *Ibid.*, 26.
34. *Ibid.*, 33.
35. Pastoral Constitution on the Church in the Modern World, *Gaudium et spes* (Vatican II, 1965), 59.
36. *Communio et progressio*, 42.
37. *Ibid.*, 42.
38. Called here secrecy, following the usage of the manuals of moral theology and of canon law; cf. *ibid.*, 42.
39. *Ibid.*, 86. Cf. also 87: 'Therefore it is right that, in the light of these principles, freedom of communication and the right to be informed be established in law and guarded from excessive economic, political and ideological pressures that might weaken them. There should be legislation to guarantee to citizens the right to criticize the actual working of the communications media. This is particularly desirable where the media are conducted as a monopoly. This is all the more necessary if the monopoly is exercised by the civil authorities themselves.
40. *Ibid.*, 86.

17

Same-Sex Relationships and the Common Good: A Theological Comment

Linda Hogan

In the English-speaking world, few moral theologians have had so significant an impact on the way in which the ethics of sex is approached as Kevin Kelly. One of the most striking aspects of his work is the way he attends, resolutely and seamlessly, to the three publics of theology: the Church, the academy and society. By way of tribute to his remarkable corpus of pastoral, theological and political writing on the matter of sexual ethics, I shall take this opportunity to reflect on one of the enduring areas of moral concern for both Church and society today: that is, whether and how same-sex unions should be given political recognition. I offer these reflections without the expectation that our honourand would share or endorse the view for which I am going to argue. Rather, they are offered as a way of connecting with some of the themes with which he has been occupied and in the knowledge that he has always approached sensitive issues in a spirit of justice and care.

In the past two decades in the Western world, no issue has divided churches more than the question of whether there ought to be legal recognition of same-sex unions, and if so, what form that recognition ought to take. The terminology varies from one jurisdiction to another, with the language of civil unions, civil partnerships, registered partnerships, reciprocal beneficiary relationships, life partnerships and civil pacts being used to refer to the form of recognition that these relationships are given. Thus, in many European countries and elsewhere, same-sex couples can enter into unions that carry rights, benefits and responsibilities that are comparable to those enjoyed by opposite-sex couples who marry. Currently, however, only in five countries, that is, Belgium, Canada, Spain, South Africa and The Netherlands, and in the US state of Massachusetts, can couples enter into same-sex marriage. In the United Kingdom, same-sex couples now enjoy rights and responsibilities identical to civil marriage, and, in the Republic of Ireland, the Dá' is currently debating the issue. The most immediate context for the discussion in Ireland is an All-Party Oireachtas Committee on the Constitution which, after a wide consultation process, reported to Government in late January 2006. It considered whether the *constitutional* recognition and protection of the family based on marriage should be extended to all family forms and, although it proposed that there be no change to the definition of the family based on marriage in the constitution (Article 41), it did recommend that legislation to give 'some marriage-like rights' to same-sex couples be enacted. It further noted that same-sex couples are also entitled to social protection on the same practical basis as with other relationships of dependence.

The Contribution of the Catholic Church to the Current Debate

In the background, of course, is the substantive issue of the morality of homosexual 'acts', with the hierarchical Magisterium promoting its unambiguous condemnation of homosexual activity, so that, when homosexual persons 'engage in sexual activity they confirm within themselves a disordered inclination which is essentially self-indulgent'.[1] Moreover, although 'the particular inclination of the homosexual person is not a sin, it is a more or less strong tendency ordered towards an intrinsic moral evil; and thus the inclination itself must be seen as an objective disorder'.[2] The case for this position is made with arguments from natural law (which include claims about the natural complementarity of the sexes, the nature of marriage as founded on this natural complementarity and the significance of the reproductive function of sex); arguments from Scripture (based on particular interpretations of key texts); and arguments from tradition (based on the claim that there has been an unchanging and constant tradition of condemnation). It is not necessary to rehearse here the significant and sustained theological critiques of each of these positions. Suffice it to acknowledge that each of the arguments is contested, with theologians from every Christian denomination disputing elements of each of these claims.[3] The language of condemnation of homosexual acts, together with the ambivalent approach to homosexual persons, has inevitably been the context in which the hierarchical Magisterium has framed its response to the proposals regarding same-sex unions in the various jurisdictions.[4] For the most part, we find a reluctance to advocate for any form of social protection for same-sex unions, on the basis that it will wound the body politic and trivialize the respect due to marriage. However, there is a degree of variation in the responses of the different episcopal conferences throughout the world. All the episcopal conferences share a conviction that marriage, in both its sacramental and legal forms, should be reserved for heterosexual couples. Yet there are some small divergences among the conferences regarding whether there should be some protection for same-sex unions, with the caveat that they would only accept a form of protection that did not imply equivalence with heterosexual marriage. Thus the Irish Episcopal Conference in its submission to the All-Party Oireachtas Committee on the Constitution says: 'it may, in certain circumstances, be in the public interest to provide legal protection to the social, fiscal and inheritance entitlements of persons who support caring relationships which generate dependency, provided always that these relationships are recognized as being qualitatively different from marriage and that their acceptance does not dilute the uniqueness of marriage.'[5] The submission is ambiguous, however, since it makes these comments in a section entitled 'Is it Possible to give Constitutional Protection to Families other than those Based on Marriage?', and, in the following section entitled 'Should Gay Couples be Entitled to Marry?', it advocates a system of private legal provision rather than formal recognition.

Relationships not Acts: The Need for a Change of Focus

What strikes one when reading such interventions is that the hierarchical Magisterium seems to have no framework within which it can talk about the morality of homosexual relationships, and thus no coherent way of contributing to the debate about legal recognition for same-sex couples. Rarely if ever do the texts that issue from the teaching offices of the Church speak about homosexual relationships or construe the question in relational terms. Instead, typically in the Catholic tradition, the moral concerns are discussed in terms either of the orientation of persons, of homosexual acts or of homosexual activity. Even the Irish bishops' submission, while it wishes to allow for some legal protections, can only speak in the veiled language of 'persons who support caring relationships which generate dependency'. There is a deep-seated reluctance to acknowledge that homosexuality is essentially about sexual desire contextualized in particular relationships. Moreover, this reluctance to accept a relational rather than a mechanistic definition of homosexuality means that the tradition has no way of conceptualizing, and therefore no way of evaluating, homosexual desire in its natural context, that is, in the context of relationships. Of course, some relationships are permanent and faithful and others are more transient, and, within the Christian tradition, these elements have a bearing on whether sexual expression within such relationships is regarded as praiseworthy or not. Thus far, however, the hierarchical Magisterium has not been able even to raise the questions about the moral quality of particular relationships because it has failed to acknowledge that the moral questions that relate to homosexuality arise not simply in relation to persons or acts but rather in terms of relationships. Moreover, it is for this reason that the issue of recognition for same-sex relationships has been so difficult; that is, this is the first time that the Church has really had to face the reality that the moral questions pertaining to homosexuality involve us in a discussion about committed, mutual, faithful relationships.

The acknowledgement that there may be a moral case for the protection of certain rights for same-sex couples is indeed welcome. Without doubt the language is grudging and the characterization of these relationships is sufficiently obscure so as not to undermine the hierarchical Magisterium's more fundamental claim about the immorality of homosexual sex. Nonetheless, this modified position does provide a way for the Church to take some steps towards supporting a social ethic that guarantees some protections for gay and lesbian people, if it feels challenged to do so. It must surely be regarded as a positive development that the Church now has a range of possible responses to political initiatives that give some protection to same-sex couples. Yet, it is difficult to see how the equal dignity of all persons can be promoted or guaranteed while the hierarchical Magisterium's official position on the morality of homosexuality remains intact.

Just Love: A Reordering of the Moral Question

In her magisterial *Just Love: A Framework for Christian Sexual Ethics*,[6] Margaret Farley constructs a normative framework for a sexual ethic that puts justice at its core. This approach, which echoes some of the insights of theologians like James

Alison, Beverly Wildung Harrison and Grace Jantzen, dislodges the question of sexual orientation from the central place it has traditionally occupied and replaces it with a question about the relationship between sexuality and justice in all forms of sexual expression. Homosexuality is thus no longer characterized as an incomplete or less perfect expression of human sexuality. Rather, a person's sexuality is recognized as being part of one's embodied identity. As such it is endlessly evolving. It is an aspect of our lives that we experience as complicated, thrilling and sometimes difficult. Moreover, this is true of sexual desire whether it is expressed in the context of heterosexual or homosexual relationships. The moral questions are thus raised in terms of the quality of the relationships within which sexual desire is expressed. Relationships, especially sexual relationships, are never simple and unambiguous. They can be both affirming and undermining at different times; they usually involve a dialectic of joy and pain. Nor is longevity an unequivocal indication of a relationship's strength or integrity, since security and comfort can sometimes trump mutuality and love. Thus the questions we ask as we try to understand the moral quality of sexual relations need to be nuanced. As we probe the ethics of same-sex relationships, therefore, the issues that ought to concern us are: whether a relationship enhances the dignity of each of the individuals involved; whether the relationship is a mutual one; whether it is a committed and faithful one; whether it is a truthful one; whether it is generative (either in a biological or a social sense); and whether it aspires to embody the values of justice and care. With such normative language there is a risk of theological idealization, and thus it is important that one avoids the kind of over-inflated rhetoric about sexuality that has been characteristic of some Christian writings. However, in cautioning against the idealization of sexuality, it is important to affirm the basic contention of this discussion: that is, that both heterosexual and homosexual relationships have the capacity to reflect the best of our humanity and to embody those aspects of our relationality that connect us with the 'spark of the divine' in our world.

Enhancing the Common Good

Thus far, the question of recognition for same-sex couples has been concerned exclusively with the civil sphere. However, there are theological and sacramental implications of the view of same-sex relationships for which I have argued above. Of course, there are people in same-sex unions who, just like some heterosexual couples, will not want to marry, who will either wish to cohabit or to contract civil rather than sacramental unions. Indeed the feminist critique of the patriarchal nature of Christian marriage has been so resonant that many same-sex couples see no potential in the institution as it is currently conceptualized. Nonetheless, there are many same-sex couples who do wish to marry, or, as is the case currently in Ireland, who wish to have their lawfully contracted marriages recognized in jurisdictions where the existing law does not recognize same-sex marriage. In this regard, it is interesting that, in the legal campaign to gain constitutional recognition for their Canadian registered marriage, Ann Louise Gilligan and Katherine Zappone mention 'our parents [who] have provided us with exceptional models of love and married life and we are inspired by them and grateful to them'.[7] In my view, the argument for ecclesial recognition of lifelong relationships of love and care is a strong one. I believe that same-sex couples do indeed have the capacity to gift 'the mutual self-bestowal that is caught up into divine love'[8] and to make 'a clear and public commitment to live together and to support each other, with the intention of their union being for life'.[9] Moreover, far from being an attack on the common good, I believe that such a change in our understanding of both the sacramental and the legal dimensions of marriage would enhance rather than threaten the common good.

A notoriously ambiguous concept, the common good is a central component of Catholic theological approaches to the question of the proper relationship between recognizably Catholic norms and the values that originate from other religious communities or from the liberal (often secular) state. If one analyzes how it is invoked in modern political debate, however, it becomes apparent that it is often mistakenly regarded either as an endorsement of a long-standing social order, or as a kind of majoritarianism that is anathema to the common good. In fact the common good is not about a trade-off between the rights of minorities and those of majorities or about a utilitarian calculus of some kind. Rather, the concept of the common good focuses on trying to harmonize different values in the attainment of a just and cohesive society. It involves 'construing the relationship of the individual to society so that the limits and possibilities of both individual and communal well-being are preserved, and in which the appropriate responsibilities and obligations that exist among individuals are clarified and articulated'.[10] A more thorough analysis of how legal recognition for same-sex unions would enhance rather than undermine the common good is much needed. However, in the first instance, one might mention legal recognition of faithful, mutually committed relationships, social protection and recognition for the models of family life that exist in the state, the equality of citizens, the sense of dignity experienced by those whose relationships, though not conforming to the dominant social patterns, are valued in their diversity, and the political stability that arises from the equal treatment of all citizens as components of the common good that are assured with legal recognition for same-sex relationships.

Setting and Keeping High Standards in Public Debate on Moral Issues

All religious groups, including the churches, not only have a right, they also have a duty to participate in public debate on matters of social significance. Moreover, I believe that there is no violation of the public sphere when the Catholic Church employs religious language as its preferred idiom in public debate. Thus I do not accept Rawls's public-reason requirement, nor do I accept his modification of the proviso.[11] It is not only legitimate, but good for our democracies that groups of various kinds can participate in public debate using arguments and in languages that embody best each group's deepest-held convictions. What is clear, however, is that, in a democracy, the Church has to be prepared to take its place alongside other interest groups that similarly will want to express their deeply held convictions about how what is true and good can best be embodied in the social sphere. Thus dialogue, together with robust but respectful debate, is likely to be the means by which we may hope to come to a consensus about how best to protect human dignity in the social context.

In its attempt to set and keep high standards in its contribution to the public debate on recognition for same-sex relationships, the Catholic Church faces at least two challenges. The first relates to the potential damage that its assessment of homosexuality may cause. The categorical distinction that the hierarchical Magisterium makes, between homosexual acts on the one hand, and homosexual persons on the other, is not easily communicated or understood. Moreover, even when it is understood it is often not accepted. Thus the language of condemnation that accompanies discussions of homosexuality can leave the Church open to charges of homophobia and discrimination. Indeed, commenting on the European Parliament's Resolution on Homophobia, Cardinal Ratzinger suggested that 'the concept of discrimination is ever more extended, and so the prohibition of discrimination can be increasingly transformed into a limitation of the freedom of opinion and religion. Very soon it will not be possible to state that homosexuality, as the Catholic Church teaches, is an objective disorder in the structuring of human existence.'[12] Although the hierarchical Magisterium is now increasingly sensitive to the negative impact that the language of 'objectively disordered inclination' may have, it has as yet not found a convincing way of mitigating the negative social consequences of that language. Thus, if the hierarchical Magisterium continues to affirm this moral evaluation of homosexuality, then it is essential that it find a way of minimizing the corrosive effect that this language may have on the norms of civility in public life.

A second challenge relates to the manner in which the Church manages the internal diversity on this matter. In every Christian denomination there are radically different views on how and where the good is to be found, and this is no less true in the Catholic Church. However, the responses to these internal divisions vary radically so that the Roman Catholic Church has sought to achieve unity-in-diversity by denying or underplaying the fact of this diversity and thus risking authoritarianism, whereas the Anglican Communion has given voice to the diversity within but risks fragmentation. Over the years, our honourand has made an important contribution to the question of how the Church can recognize and manage the diversity that exists within. His insight that 'dissent' is usually motivated by 'respect for tradition, concern for the truth, love of the Church, [and a sense of] shared responsibility for the Church's mission in the world'[13] suggests a position where diversity ought not to be feared but rather, to be welcomed as a potential site of prophetic insight. We inhabit a tradition that is dynamic and discursive, one that develops and changes as our knowledge and understanding change. As a result, the Church ought to be capable of modelling for the society a form of community of unity-in-diversity, wherein new insights are approached in an open and generous manner, and wherein a shared sense of vocation ameliorates any damage that disagreement on serious moral issues brings. Thus far the Church has not risen to this challenge. A good first step, however, would be to give public voice to the diversity within on the issue of same-sex unions.

Debates of this kind always return to the question of pluralism, minority rights and the common good, with the phrase 'the common good' usually invoked as a restriction on the rights of same-sex couples to have legal recognition. However, to reiterate my argument by way of conclusion, I believe that, far from being an attack on the common good, extending legal recognition for same-sex couples and opening the existing definition of marriage so as to include same-sex couples would enhance rather than threaten the common good.

Notes

1. 'Letter to the Bishops on the Pastoral Care of Homosexual Persons' (Congregation for the Doctrine of the Faith, 1986), 5.
2. *Ibid.*, 3.
3. In the interests of brevity I will not provide a detailed bibliography here. One can be found, however, in James Keenan, 'The Open Debate: Moral Theology and the Lives of Gay and Lesbian Persons', *Theological Studies* 64 (2003): 127–50.
4. An important early text in this regard, of course, is 'Responding to Legislative Proposals on Discrimination Against Homosexual Persons' (Congregation for the Doctrine of the Faith, 1992).
5. Joint Submission of the Committee on the Family of the Irish Episcopal Conference and the Office for Public Affairs of the Archdiocese of Dublin (February 2005), 7–9.
6. Margaret Farley, *Just Love: A Framework for Christian Sexual Ethics* (New York: Continuum, 2006).
7. Statement, 9 November 2004: available at <http://www.kalcase.org> (accessed 24 August 2007).
8. Pastoral Constitution on the Church in the Modern World, *Gaudium et spes* (Vatican II, 1965), 48.
9. Joint Submission of the Committee on the Family of the Irish Episcopal Conference and the Office for Public Affairs of the Archdiocese of Dublin, 5. The document does not argue for the extension of the definition of marriage to same-sex couples. However, I am arguing here that the definition of marriage it endorses can indeed apply to same-sex relationships.
10. James Donahue, *Religion, Ethics and the Common Good* (Mystic, CT: Twenty-Third Publications, 1996), p. x.
11. See John Rawls, 'The Idea of Public Reason Revisited', in *The Law of Peoples* (Cambridge, MA: Harvard University Press, 1999). With his idea of public reason Rawls proposed that, when citizens support laws and policies that invoke the coercive powers of government concerning fundamental political questions, they ought to do so, not on the basis of ideas of truth or right based on comprehensive doctrines, but on the basis of 'an idea of the politically reasonable addressed to citizens as citizens'. Arguments based on religious convictions therefore should be translated into language that all citizens can understand. Rawls modified this claim somewhat with the introduction of the concept of the 'proviso', meaning that religious language could be used in public debate provided that, in due course, these religious reasons are replaced by 'public' reason.
12. Cf. 'Cardinal Ratzinger on Europe's Crisis of Culture' at http://www. catholiceducation.org/articles/politics/pg0143.html (accessed 8 October 2007).
13. Kevin T. Kelly, 'Obedience and Dissent, 2. Serving the Truth', *The Tablet* (1986): 647–49; reprinted in C.E. Curran and R.A. McCormick, *Readings in Moral Theology No. 6, Dissent in the Church* (New York: Paulist Press, 1988), pp. 478–83 (480).

Part Four

Issues in Ecclesiology

18

Has Ecumenism a Future?[1]

Ladislas Örsy

More than 40 years have passed since 21 November 1964, when the bishops assembled at Vatican Council II – after much argument and among great rejoicing – approved solemnly the Decree on Ecumenism. Ever since, time after time, we pause and ponder, trying to assess our progress towards the one and only Church of Christ. How far have we come? How much remains to be done?

The recounting of some recent facts and events may well put us into a sombre mood: the progress is slow and much remains to be done. The goal, the blessed unity of all Christians, appears as elusive as ever – if not more so. We are tempted to say with a heavy heart – like the two disciples on the road to Emmaus – 'We had hoped' (cf. Lk. 24.21).

Here are some findings – they can hardly be contested.

- The dialogues are increasingly revealing their limits. True, as appointed groups of experts meet each other, they succeed in creating friendly relationships. They raise pertinent questions and listen to learned answers. They apologize for past wrongs and, time and again, on a (subtle) point of doctrine, they reach a consensus. Yet, no matter how much they may accomplish, they leave more undone. Judging by what they have achieved over some 40 years, by any reasonable estimate, centuries more of conversations are needed to reach the communion of minds and hearts that Christ prayed for.
- While the groups of experts are doing their selfless work, large segments of ordinary Christian folk of different denominations remain content to be as they are and feel no pressing need for a greater unity. Bad memories may hamper them or unconsciously absorbed prejudices may withhold them. Yet, committees of specialists cannot achieve full communion: a mass movement of the faithful alone can bring it about. The one and only Church of Christ cannot exist without the people (saints and sinners) from all corners of the earth crowding into it – all *being of one heart and soul* (cf. Acts 4.32). The lesson of the aftermath of the Council of Florence (1439–45) must not be forgotten. Although at the Council the representatives of the Eastern Church consented to the union, when they returned home with the agreement, the people rejected it. And that was the end of the reconciliation.
- In spite of the efforts expanded for union, new disagreements are emerging in various communities. The Episcopalian (Anglican) Church is struggling with centrifugal forces. The autonomous churches of the East are searching – not

185

without trying crises – for the correct relationships among themselves. There is disunity among the Lutheran synods. Behind the present apparent calm in the Roman Catholic communion strong conflicting dynamics are testing the strength of unifying forces.

- Reliable witnesses, be they detached observers or engaged workers, keep reporting signs of tiredness, indifference, even despair in the cause of unity. Admittedly, it may be difficult to prove such hearsay by hard evidence; yet, the witnesses are too numerous and their voices too strong to be ignored.

Such appears to be the state of the ecumenical movement. Facts and events do not lie; on no account should we deny them, or cover them up with an irrational rhetoric of 'optimism'. No serious thinking or effective work can be done in God's kingdom without utmost respect for verifiable facts and occurring events: God is in the real.

But if God is in the real, we should take a second look at the whole extent of 'the real': God's plan is broader than our senses can perceive. Hence the question: is our interpretation of the facts and events correct? Have we grasped their *full* meaning? Remember how the two disciples left Jerusalem and took the road to Emmaus because (as they were told by the stranger who joined them) they failed to understand the Scriptures? Are we like them: 'We had hoped', we say, and walk away from God's plan because we do not understand the grace-filled time of God?

Could it be that God's plan is unfolding precisely through the facts and events narrated, but we are not reading his plan correctly?

What follows is an attempt to penetrate into the deeper meaning ('the mystery', I should say) of the ecumenical movement within the horizon of faith, hope and love; the only way we can enter into God's plan. My intent is not to deny or to cover up sobering facts and events; it is to discover how they are part of a greater project. If there is a way of overcoming the crisis, it is not in trying to change occurrences over which we have no power, but in changing our attitudes in handling them.

The One Church of Christ in Focus:
The Goal and Measure of Ecumenical Efforts

The ecumenical movement makes sense because we believe that the one and only Church of Christ exists in God's plan. Christ prayed for it at the solemn night of his *transitus*: his prayer could not have been in vain. Hence, our duty is to build this Church, even if – as yet – we have no glimpse of its internal harmony in unity and diversity; even if we have not seen its 'glory'.

When Vatican Council II declared that the Church of Christ *'subsists' in the Roman Catholic Church*,[2] *the council meant that we are in possession of the fullness of revelation, but in no way did the council affirm that we understand what we have in all its breadth and depth. Hence we can believe in both the present fullness and the future unfolding of riches.*

Further, in our 'theological imagination' we should never see this future Church of Christ as a merely 'religious phenomenon', isolated from the rest of human history. It is God's gift to the whole human family: the very 'threshold of salvation' for all generations to come. St Paul writes: 'For the creation waits with eager longing for the revealing of the children of God' (Rom. 8.19) and 'the whole creation has been groaning in travail together until now' (Rom. 8.22). In a mysterious way, the one Church of Christ is instrumental in the redemption and exaltation of the whole creation.

When we position the future Church of Christ as the goal and measure of the ecumenical movement, the very nature of the movement reveals itself with a clarity and simplicity that otherwise we cannot have. Ultimately, the goal of the movement is not to reach mutual agreements among the churches, but for each community to transform itself to the image of the one Church of Christ – as far as they can discern it. The ecumenical task consists of a continuous effort to know the mystery better and to move towards it. Then, agreements among the separated communities are bound to follow.

The dialogues should be seen as forms of 'mutual assistance' among believing people to help each other to penetrate the word of God to a greater depth. *There*, they will find unity; *there*, they will cease to disagree.

The ecumenical dialogues should be common efforts to receive the gift of unity from God. We are disposed to receive this gift through the theological virtues of faith, hope and love.

In the Light of Faith

Faith reveals that (1) the Spirit of God alone has the power to create or restore the one Church of Christ, and the divine Spirit, the creator, alone can give us the vision and energy to build it; (2) such work of the Spirit is discernable in recent developments; (3) in fact, the Spirit has already created a substantial unity among the Christian people.

(1) We believe, on the authority of our tradition, reaffirmed by Vatican Council II, that only the Spirit, the creator, has the power to establish the one and only Church of Christ. The conciliar texts amount to a profession of faith:

> It is the Holy Spirit, dwelling in those who believe and pervading and ruling over the entire Church, who brings about that wonderful communion of the faithful and joins them together so intimately in Christ that he is the principle of the Church's unity.[3]

> Further, this council declares that it realizes that this holy objective – the reconciliation of all Christians in the unity of the one and only Church of Christ – transcends human powers and gifts.[4]

The council says, with no ambiguity, that the Holy Spirit is the originator of the movement for union and communion, and the Spirit remains in charge of it. We, humans, can be cooperators but not creators. For its course we cannot lay down our own laws and conditions.

(2) The history of the last 40 years offers quasi-empirical evidence that the Holy Spirit is indeed in charge and active. All we need is to put side by side what happened (or did not happen) in the last four centuries and what happened in the recent decades. Attitudes of extreme rigidity that pervaded generations of persons and communities have literally melted away, if not everywhere, certainly

187

far and wide, and have given place to a disposition of openness and flexibility. Christians who once refused to say even the 'Our Father' together have learned to praise the Lord with one voice – even if they have not come so far as to share the Eucharistic table. We must admit that such deep transformation of attitudes could not have happened without an immensely strong injection of healing grace into the communities.

(3) Through faith we know that a substantial unity already exists among the Christian communities. Admittedly, the language we use daily is misleading us into thinking otherwise. We speak of 'our separated brothers and sisters', but the fundamental truth is that our brothers and sisters in their gatherings outside the Roman communion are united to us as we are united to them through our common baptism and profession that 'Jesus is the Lord' (Cf. 1 Cor. 12.3).

Ordinarily, the fact of historical separation dominates our discourse. Yet, the ontological reality (what is really real) is that the Spirit, in whom they dwell and who dwells in them, holds all baptized believers together. Now, it makes some difference if the ecumenical movement consists in working for the reconciliation of separated bodies, or if it is a healing process within one sacramental but internally lacerated body. In the former case negotiations take primary importance; in the latter case the liberating of the internal healing forces does the real work.

Hope Divine

The theological virtue of hope is often misunderstood: we conceive it on the pattern of human hope. On an earthly level, 'to hope' is to define expectations (variously grounded) for the future, and then cling to them – happen what may. Obviously, to hope in this manner may lead to a disregard of facts and events and to a stubborn pursuit of a fallacy that can bring only disaster at the end.

Divine hope is radically different. It regards more the present than the future. It is 'to surrender' to God who is in charge of the events. It is 'to blend' into his plan, here and now. It creates an unbounded optimism (and a well-grounded one) in the one who hopes: God guarantees a good outcome but without telling us what it will be. Divine hope installs a human person into the flow of God's project; it is to join him in his creative activity.

In this prospect the sobering and depressing facts and events reveal their true nature: they are part of God's plan – a plan of which we see only some fragments. Considered in isolation from their broader context, they may be disappointing, but, as parts of a whole, they are bound to make sense.

A comparison comes into my mind. Let the reader use it or discard it. Imagine a mediaeval architect who was asked to design a cathedral, all of it in its magnificence, the soaring towers, the flying buttresses, the rose windows – also the impish gargoyles on the roof. He, the architect, sees the entire project, but then – sensibly – he portions out the work among his apprentices. They will be in charge of the parts assigned to them; some of them will be given no more than the ugly shapes of the gargoyles.

God has designed his own cathedral. We are the apprentices – at times allowed to see only the gargoyles.

The theological foundation for this understanding of the virtue of hope is in the Scriptures (and the following should not be taken as a mere pious statement).

When Mary of Nazareth pronounced the sentence 'Let it be to me according to your word' (Lk. 1.38), she signalled that she was willing to surrender herself to a plan that she did not know, still less could direct in any way. As she found out later, the plan was full of sombre facts and events. Her participation in God's project was perfect; she never said, 'I had hoped'.

We have reached a point where the assessment of the ecumenical movement in function of faith, hope and love reveals its internal cohesiveness and essential soundness. Faith brings an intelligence that no human insight could give, Hope opens the door to enter and blend into the dynamics of a divine plan. Love leads to action that no human strength could sustain.

Love Divine: Magnanimity

Love does not consist in words but in deeds. Christ repeatedly stated it, saints practised it, sages affirmed it and doctors explained it.

Love in God, then, is synonymous with giving, but 'this inclination to give' is not a mere attribute. When Moses asked God speaking in the burning bush, 'What is your name?' God responded, 'I am who I am.' God could have said, '*I am who gives*'; that is '*I am Goodness effusive.*' God's very nature is to communicate himself. Within him and inwardly there *are* the communications that *is* the Trinity of persons. Within him but outwardly, there is the effusion of life – the act of creation – that brings us existence and sustenance.

Let us call this divine giving 'magnanimity' – a word borrowed from the philosophy of Aristotle where it has a finite meaning but is a word that can be stretched to reach into the infinite. Magnanimity is divine when it means to give from an inexhaustible internal resource without expecting any reward.

Such love must be the operating principle of the ecumenical movement. Its source is the living Spirit that all communities possess through their baptism and their gift of faith. It follows that their prime concern should not be '*what could we do?*' but, '*how can we remove the impediments surging from our narrow humanity and let the dynamics of the Spirit prevail?*'

The acceptance of the vision of faith and the surrender in hope lead to the operation of love. A divine manner of life.

So much for a sublime theory. But how to apply it? Without finding a way of practising it in our daily work for unity, beautiful as our words may be, they are no more than the sounds of 'an empty gong or a tinkling cymbal' (1 Cor. 13.1).

In recent years, two practical proposals emerged for effectively promoting the cause of unity among Christian churches – no matter what the observers may report. Both are demanding and both demand the communities 'to give' – perhaps in a somewhat metaphorical sense, but still 'to give'. Both ask for giving in a divine manner; that is, from the internal resources of each community and for reward. Both are radical requests for down-to-earth manifestations of magnanimity.

Above all, both are immediately feasible.

One is *the way of kenosis*, proposed by the *Groupe des Dombes* in France; the other is *the way of learning and receiving*, suggested by the participants of the Durham Colloquium in January 2006. The former speaks of giving up, or giving away what hampers unity; the latter speaks of giving space in our midst to gifts of grace and wisdom coming from others.

The Way of Kenosis

The way of kenosis has been suggested first by the *Groupe des Dombes*, a permanent association of ecumenists founded by Paul Couturier and meeting since 1937. Their method of seeking ecumenical understanding through intense periods of prayer and the reading of early Christian sources could serve as a model for all.

Their proposal is grounded in the analysis of the identity of Christian churches. They see it as composed of three elements. In its core, each communion has a substantial Christian identity, which is not negotiable. Then, in the course of history, each developed a unique 'personality', for instance, Orthodox, Roman, Lutheran, etc., which should not be abandoned since it may represent due diversity. Finally, each denomination has confessional characteristics, accretions by historical accidents, devotional customs and ritual observances, all of which are not indispensable and – to some and varying degrees – could be sacrificed for the sake of unity.

The ecumenical task for each Church is, then, to turn inward and ask: what is in our manner of life that does not belong to the Christian core? What is not part of the beauty of our unique personality? What among our unnecessary heirlooms could be sacrificed for the sake of unity?

Not to cling to precious possessions but to enter a world of poverty can be the correct path towards unity. This is how Christ enriched the world: 'though he was in the form of God, he did not count equality with God a thing to be grasped, but emptied (*ekenosen*) himself' (Phil. 2.5–6). This is how individual communities can build the one Church of Christ.

A potential misunderstanding should be discarded: in no way does the Groupe des Dombes *suggest that the exercise of kenosis should ever allow anyone to abandon the truth for some comfortable common denominator. The way of kenosis requires a sharp intelligence of faith to discern what it is that all must hold for truth in unity, what each must preserve as part of legitimate diversity, and what can be left behind for the sake of harmony.*

The Way of Learning and Receiving

The way of learning and receiving has been proposed by the participants of an ecumenical meeting held in January 2006 at Durham University and Ushaw College in England, close to the hallowed resting place of St Cuthbert. Cardinal Walter Kasper gave the keynote address and participated in the works.

It was a new initiative. Catholics were simply asking the representatives of their sister communities, Anglicans, Orthodox, Methodists and others, what, in their view, Catholics could learn from them. The three days of conversation revolved around some principal issues of convergences and divergences: the role of the laity, the meaning of collegiality, the practice of primacy and so forth.[5]

The inspiration came from Vatican Council II:

Catholics must gladly acknowledge and esteem the truly Christian endowments from our common heritage which are to be found among those separated from us ...

Nor should we forget that anything wrought by the grace of the Holy Spirit in the hearts of our separated brothers and sisters can contribute to our own edification. Whatever is truly Christian is never contrary to what genuinely belongs to the faith; indeed it can always bring a more perfect realization of the very mystery of Christ and the Church.[6]

Of course, any learning and reception should be done wisely, without endangering the substance of our faith or the specific diversity and beauty of our Roman communion. In truth, such 'enrichment' on the Catholic side has already taken place; for instance, we learned and received much in the field of biblical studies from the Protestant communities.

If we have become dejected by hearing the sombre news about the ecumenical movement, and if we were tempted to leave it as the two disciples left Jerusalem, the proposals coming from France and England show us new vistas. They may *open our eyes* to see new opportunities, *and may burn our hearts* with new hope (cf. Lk. 24.31–32) and let us resume the work with a love that only the Spirit can grant.

Conclusion

The issue of Christian unity is mostly thought of – by believers and non-believers alike – as an internal matter for Christian communities. In truth, much more is at stake. Christ has come, and died, and has risen for the whole human family. In this immense work of redemption his Church is called to play an indispensable role: it is the keeper of the Good News; it is the eminent source of divine energy through the blessed play of sacred actions.

But the very sacrament of the world, the community of Christians held together by the Spirit, is torn internally, and much of its energy is burned up by dissensions. It is handicapped in announcing God's saving message; it is hampered in dispensing God's exhilarating graces.

Yet, if ever, in our days, the human family is in extreme need to hear the life-giving news and receive the infusion of fresh force – divine news and divine force. Never before has evil had so much power to put science and technology into its own service. Violence is rampant in numerous places; it may even appear that God has abandoned his creation and *the Spirit is not moving over the face of the planet Earth* (cf. Gen. 1.2).

The world needs a Church that proclaims with one clear voice the message of peace – God's peace. There is no time to waste 'for the creation waits with eager longing for the revealing of the children of God' (Rom. 8.19).

Notes

1. This essay was first published in *America* (5 February 2007): 14–19.
2. Dogmatic Constitution on the Church, *Lumen gentium* (Vatican II, 1964), 8.
3. Decree on Ecumenism, *Unitatis redintegratio* (Vatican II, 1964), 2.
4. *Ibid.*, 24.
5. Oxford University Press will publish the findings of the 'Group of Durham' in the Spring of 2008 under the title *Catholic Learning: Explorations in Receptive Ecumenism*.
6. *Unitatis redintegratio*, 4.

19

The Paradox of the Inclusive Church: Can Ecclesiology Live with Questions?

Steven Shakespeare

Jesus said, 'But to what will I compare this generation? It is like children sitting in the marketplaces and calling to one another "We played the flute for you and you did not dance; we wailed and you did not mourn".' (Mt. 11.16–17)

Some things do not change. From the meetings of heavyweight bishops to the comments in the Church press, from bloggers on the web to campaigning groups of every stripe, we can hear the echo of these childish disputes: 'We appointed a flying bishop, but you did not get on board; we published a Latin Mass, but you did not face east; *we* bought *The Tablet* – but *you* read *The Universe*'.

Is the Church coming apart at the seams, unable to hold mature debate? That is one of the pressing questions that underlie this paper. I want to explore the issue of inclusivity in dialogue with conservative Anglicans who fear that the communion of the Church (Anglican, but also wider than that) is breaking down; that we have abandoned the living tradition which kept us Catholic. I will explore their arguments, and offer some criticisms, before briefly outlining an alternative approach.

I begin with a quotation:

In place of the complex God revealed in Christ Jesus, a God of both judgement and mercy, a God whose law is meant to govern human life, we now have a God who is love and inclusion without remainder. The projected God of the liberal tradition is, in the end, no more than an affirmer of preferences.[1]

Those words are taken from *The Fate of Communion: The Agony of Anglicanism and the Future of a Global Church*. Its authors are Ephraim Radner and Philip Turner, two theologians of the Episcopal Church of the USA, part of the Anglican communion. Until 2006 the Episcopal Church of the USA was known by the abbreviation ECUSA. It is now known as TEC, which stands for 'The Episcopal Church'. As the book's title suggests, TEC is at the centre of a crisis affecting the Anglican communion and raising the question of whether that communion has any future at all. The facts can be briefly told. It is important to note that in the USA, Episcopalian bishops are elected at a diocesan convention, at which each parish is represented by clergy and laity. In 2003 the Diocese of New Hampshire elected as its bishop Gene Robinson, a divorced man who was openly living with a partner of the same sex. That election was ratified by ECUSA's General Convention later in the year. In a separate development, the synod of the Canadian Anglican diocese of New Westminster (again a representative body) voted to ask its bishop to give permission to clergy to bless same-sex unions. This permission was given in May 2003. It is not the purpose of this paper to analyze in depth either these events or the subsequent controversy they have sparked across the whole Anglican communion. However, some points are worth briefly noting.

At the request of the primates (the heads of the various national Anglican churches), the Archbishop of Canterbury set up a commission to look at the issues raised by these events. The result of the commission is known as the Windsor Report. It found that ECUSA and the Canadian Church had acted in such a way as to damage the 'bonds of affection' that held the Anglican communion together. Decisions should have been taken with a view to how they would be received in other parts of the communion. ECUSA in particular was invited to express regret, and to withdraw its representatives from international Anglican bodies until it did so.

ECUSA did offer an expression of sorrow for hurt caused, but this fell short of the repentance demanded by some. Some parishes and dioceses within ECUSA have sought to separate themselves from its oversight, in some cases placing themselves under the oversight of African churches. Some national churches, including Nigeria and Uganda, have declared themselves out of communion with ECUSA. At a recent meeting of primates in Tanzania, some of the representatives of what has become known as the Global South movement of Churches from the Developing World refused to take Communion alongside ECUSA's presiding bishop, Katharine Jefferts Schori. The communiqué issued by the meeting called on ECUSA to make a commitment that it would not consecrate any more practising gay bishops, and that it would not authorize the blessing of same-sex unions.

It is also worth pointing out that the Anglican communion is an historic grouping of national churches, obviously linked to the British Empire. It does not have a supranational authoritative body or person. The ten-yearly Lambeth Conference of Bishops has only advisory power, and the Archbishop of Canterbury's position as first among equals has no element of jurisdictional power. The Windsor Report recommended that this lack of structure should be revisited, and proposals are under way to draw up a covenant spelling out conditions for membership and decision-making in the communion.

As I have said, this paper is not about the specifics of this Anglican civil war, but the particular character of the controversy does throw up questions that are at the heart of ecclesiology. What is the nature of the Church and in what does its identity consist? What unites it across different contexts? What is the nature of authority in the Church and how should it be exercised? What are the limits of acceptable diversity, beyond which the Church falls apart, or loses its integrity?

More immediately the agony of Anglicanism underlies the arguments put forward by Radner and Turner, arguments I want to use as a critical foil for developing an ecclesiology for an inclusive Church. Because – to declare my colours – I am a supporter of the movement in the Church of England called Inclusive Church, and jointly responsible (with Hugh Rayment-Pickard) for a book called

The Inclusive God, both of which make the case that neither gender nor sexual orientation should be a bar to office or ordination in the Church, and that faithful same-sex unions are a source of grace and blessing which should be affirmed.[2]

There are, of course, debates about whether this position is consistent with the Bible, which is in turn a question of how the Bible is interpreted. But the Bible does not exist in a vacuum. It is read in the context of the Church's worship and mission. It is a text that is always associated with a community, with traditions of interpretation, with a history of reception and application. Unless we are aware of this context, disputes about what the Bible says become arid stalemates, because those in debate are effectively talking different languages, making different assumptions about the kind of text the Bible is and the appropriate ways to read it.

Ecclesiology is therefore not an optional extra, but a way of giving attention to the context in which revelation is given, received and shared. For all its concern with structures and authorities, ecclesiology is earthed in the study of relationships, and what makes possible genuine communication, liberation and peace. It is also, of course, a study of those things that break and hinder communication, liberation and peace.

Those who are committed to exploring more inclusive forms of Christian faith cannot therefore simply leave the Church to one side. And it is when we press this question of the Church that the paradox referred to in my title emerges. I suggest that there are three dimensions to this paradox.

The first is a general point about any organization which claims a minimum of coherent identity. No such organization can simply be 'inclusive'. It must have boundaries which, however loosely, define what it is and what it is not. A football team is not a counselling service, a local council is not a university. Each institution will be located in narratives and contexts, and will develop its own responses to its conditions. An organization with no boundaries would not be organized in any meaningful sense. So making inclusion the primary mark of an institution's identity is a sure way to dissolve that identity.

Secondly, a specific point about the Christian Church. The way in which the Church has been understood has varied enormously through history and across traditions. However, what remains constant is that it is defined in some way with reference to the Bible, to worship, to doctrine, to structures of authority and governance. More particularly, its identity is always related to the purposes and nature of God revealed in Jesus Christ. You do not have to embrace the view that all non-Christians are on the path of damnation to recognize that the Church makes claims about the nature of God, the world and humanity which are shaped by this scandal of particularity. An inclusive Church looks suspiciously like a Church which has abandoned the reality of Christ for a vaguely well-meaning, inoffensive, generalized religion, which might be soothing but can hardly be called Christian.

The third point follows on from this. Christianity demands conversion, the transformation of our personal and communal lives, the call to follow Christ and grow into his full stature. An inclusive Church seems to abandon this call, heedlessly baptizing any and every person, group and culture with which it comes into contact. It has lost the sense in which God continues to protest against human sin, to draw lines and to judge those behaviours which bring only fear and death in their wake.

What I have called the paradox of the inclusive Church for many would simply be a contradiction. An organization without boundaries, a Christianity without Christ, a faith without calling and conversion, mercy without judgement: it all adds up to very little. A religious veneer to life as usual, a comfort blanket for our wearied world.

Turner and Radner would no doubt be sympathetic to this criticism of inclusion. The passage with which I began derides the liberal God, who has lost all complexity and forgotten that he is judge as well as saviour. But their opposition to the rhetoric of inclusivity is not just mockery. It is based on a diagnosis of the ills of modern culture, which, they claim, are particularly strong in US society. And they develop a remedy for this sickness – a form of conservative Christianity which cannot just be dismissed as reactionary. So I want to explore what they are saying in a little more detail, because they challenge those of us who wish to promote inclusion to take seriously issues of theological truth, authority and the nature of the Church. It is not good enough to use inclusion as a badge or slogan for our cause unless we are prepared to examine it critically.

Radner and Turner are heavily indebted to what has been called the 'new traditionalism' in theology, a loose alliance of theologians who are united by their rejection of contemporary liberal secularism. Among their ranks we find the Methodist Stanley Hauerwas, the Anglican John Milbank and the Catholic philosopher Alasdair MacIntyre (Hauerwas writes a glowing foreword for *The Fate of Communion*). MacIntyre is clearly a major influence on our authors. He has argued against the idea that there is any free-floating, universal reason which we can call upon to solve our intellectual and moral arguments. That idea is the product of the very specific ideology of modern liberalism. Liberalism is anti-traditional. It appeals to canons of reason which are supposed to be self-evident to any reasonable person, and to moral laws which apply to everyone in all situations. Liberalism seeks a consistent moral and rational framework for reality, independent of the limited, parochial and frankly superstitious traditions associated, in particular in Western Europe, with the Christian Church.

However, he argues that the framework which liberals produce is notoriously thin. It cannot deliver universal agreement. The best it can do is promote toleration and the rule of law, so that competing visions of reality can live side by side without coming to blows. Religion is tolerated as a private option, a preference, but not something that can be influential or persuasive in the public sphere. We can recognize in this the source of all sorts of contemporary controversies about whether people can wear religious symbols at work, whether society should fund faith schools, whether Catholic adoption agencies should have an opt-out from discrimination laws and so on.

MacIntyre argues that there is no easy way of resolving these disputes, because people are coming to them speaking different languages. They do not share a common moral universe. Disputes about abortion, for instance, might well take account of medical views of the viability of the foetus, the development of the central nervous system and so on, but the moral dispute cannot be settled by the accumulation of more and more facts. The problem is that liberalism separates facts and values. It assumes there is a real world out there which science discovers, and then we come along and project our values on to it. But, MacIntyre argues, that is not what actually goes on. Our values come first. They shape the kind of world we experience and the kind of things that count as evidence for us. And values are always rooted in stories and communities which articulate and sustain a moral vision of life.

We need community, with its standards of authority and belonging, its rituals, its stories, its moral examples, in order for people to be shaped as moral agents. Without this context, people become fragmented individuals, unable truly to connect with one another and vulnerable to whatever worldly powers happen to hold sway. Liberalism dethrones authority and tradition in the name of freedom, but its freedom is too abstract. It has no substance. And the suspicion arises that this is no accident. Liberal political thought and liberal religion in fact exist to serve liberal economics: the capitalist free market. Capitalism *wants* us to be individual consumers of reality; it wants to disperse all centres of opposition to its own hidden moral vision. It is happy with the kind of religious, tribal and ethnic identities that remain lifestyle options and private preferences, because this allows it to create niche markets. And the modern state exists to serve capital. It takes over the running of society, it claims a monopoly on the use of force, and so it creates an ordered setting in which our competitive, atomized lives can be lived out.

This critique is very much in the background of Radner and Turner's rejection of inclusivity. They argue that the American Episcopalian Church has been particularly prone to lose its distinctive identity, and adapt itself to the surrounding environment. This is partly to do with the broader story of American history. Those who came as pilgrims and immigrants to what is now the USA had what they call a 'primordialist' mentality. In other words, they were leaving their past communities and traditions behind, and starting over in a new land, a pristine wilderness (never mind the Native Americans). In religious terms, this has led to a particularly American temptation to proliferate sects and denominations, as Christians again and again split from one another, seeking a pure form. Catholicity is sacrificed for the expression of preferences.

Radner and Turner identify two opposing versions of this tendency. On the one hand are the liberals. Liberals embrace what is new and modern and progressive over what is traditional. They have an inbuilt bias in favour of change, a presumption that change equals progress. They declare themselves in favour of secular ideas of human rights and scientific reason, but they also accept the fact and desirability of pluralism – that there can be no single adequate interpretation of the world or of God, and that we should rejoice that we are fragmented into many competing visions. Let a hundred flowers bloom, say the liberals, and the fact that we can hear the accents of Chairman Mao speaking through that saying might indicate that the liberal vision hides conflict and oppression at its heart.

Over and against the liberals Radner and Turner set the radical conservatives. The radical conservatives want to reject modern liberal ways, but they too have lost any sense of Catholic tradition, and so they try to reinvent a pure Christianity from the bottom up. They call people back to a literal interpretation of the Bible, for example, or possibly to an ancient form of liturgy. But this return is a revolutionary one, which aims to sweep away all present structures in its apocalyptic fervour.

Liberals and radical conservatives might hate one another with a passion, but Radner and Turner claim that the most important thing about them is what they have in common. They both turn their back on the slowly accumulated wisdom of tradition and life in communion, to call for a new beginning. They set up a timeless principle (it might be the idea of freedom, or the words of the Bible taken as an immutable law) which takes on an importance and life of its own way above the tried and tested ways in which a community has apprehended the truth, known the world and worshipped God. They are both guilty of a violent gesture. The besetting sin of liberals is to surrender to the forces of capitalism. That of radical conservatives is to turn into fascists.

So, if these alternatives are both in thrall to modernity, what remains? Radner and Turner advocate a kind of conservatism, whose approach is fundamentally different from either liberalism or radicalism. It is a dynamic, community-based conservatism. It accepts that the history of the Church is often one of conflict and struggle. It accepts that whatever standards and rules of faith we have – the Bible, creeds, official doctrines – they have to be interpreted, their meaning has to be worked out by a living community. So this form of conservatism does not just say 'back to the Bible'. It accepts that change does happen and that the Church develops. But it can only develop faithfully and truly if it does so as a communion.

This means that for individuals and groups to break with the Church and set up their own counter-Church will be to break faith with what the Church is called to be. Disputes should be resolved through community discernment, which demands patience and humility and due obedience to authority. For Anglicans, that authority is invested in bishops, as a reminder that it is people and not books or rules which issue commands. Bishops should be the ones who exercise authority within the slowly evolving life of the communion – and they should exercise discipline over those who break communion.

This is clearly not a version of biblical fundamentalism, but the Bible still plays a central role. The Anglican tradition, it is argued, is that the community's life should be characterized by immersion in Scripture. The Bible is read in its entirety in the context of the Church's worship. Some Anglicans claim that they have several distinct sources of authority – Scripture, reason and tradition, and sometimes experience is also added. However, Radner and Turner disagree. Scripture is the primary reality that shapes the community's tradition and reason and experience. They have no being apart from the shared reading of the Bible and the way this shapes the Church's knowledge of God and God's world. There are not three or four sources of truth, but one, which is celebrated and reflected upon and lived out through history.

In the light of this, it comes as no surprise that the authors condemn ECUSA's introduction of novelties – like the consecration of a practising gay bishop – because these novelties have not arisen from a Catholic sense of the community's own discernment of truth, but are the actions of one part of a global fellowship in defiance of their brothers and sisters across the world.

The problem comes back to the critique of liberalism we looked at earlier. The liberals running much of the American Episcopal Church assume that progress according to secular standards of human rights is intrinsically a good thing. And they claim a prophetic authority to act in the name of justice. But this prophecy and this justice are cut off from the immersion in Scripture and bonds of common life and worship which should lead to caution and patience before introducing change. It is liberal arrogance, for liberals – like radical conservatives – are absolutely sure that God is on their side.

This is a subtle form of conservatism, which does not take refuge in fundamentalist certainties. It does not simply quote proof-texts from the Bible to settle arguments, because it accepts that the answers to our questions cannot simply be read directly off the pages of Scripture or the creeds. But it does reject the ideals of liberalism, and particularly any simplistic idea that the Church should be inclusive. Inclusivity does not resolve disagreements, it just manages them. It does not bring people into communion, it merely provides a setting in which irreconcilable differences co-exist – and that falls far short of the vision of the Church set out in, for example, the letter to the Ephesians.

Is this the death knell for inclusion? Is liberalism unmasked as a non-Christian ideology which spells ruin for the Church? It is easy to be seduced by the sweeping vision of the new traditionalists, whose plausible historical and cultural explanations seem to leave nothing out, and offer an attractive vision of the Church as an alternative community. But if we press the arguments a little, we soon find that cracks begin to appear.

Dynamic conservatism claims to take history and conflict seriously. But it has little to say about the churches' own investment in abusive forms of authority, except that they are passing anomalies. But this is where we can usefully learn from secular wisdom. In the wake of the racist murder of Stephen Lawrence, the 1993 MacPherson Report analyzed the role of the police, and introduced the idea of 'institutional racism' into popular consciousness. Although the idea remains controversial, it does seem to touch on a dimension of power which cannot be adequately described in terms of individual prejudices. It suggests that structures and processes of working suck individuals into an oppressive logic, over which no one person has control.

The MacPherson Report was a public event, which brought into consciousness dimensions of power and abuse which had previously not been named in quite the same way. It was not merely an exercise of liberal individualism, nor was it a radical call to sweep away the current police institutions and start again. In other words, it did not fall into the categories set out by Radner and Turner. But it did alter awareness and promote change in decisive, irrevocable ways.

I propose that the kind of analysis provided by the MacPherson Report needs from time to time to be directed towards the Church. For the Church is not an innocent transmitter of tradition. The conflict, pride and abuse in which it has been involved are not merely the result of individual wickedness. They are also structural. Attitudes to the authority of women are a clear example of how the Church as a structure has shaped itself and its members to exclude certain possibilities of human relationship and fulfilment on the basis of cultural prejudices. We might also mention racism and slavery, attitudes to dissenters and heretics, and the promotion of submission to feudal powers.

I am not claiming that these issues are simple and one-dimensional. I am not arguing that the Church is entirely corrupt, nor denying that there have been traditions and people who have questioned all of these structures of exclusion. But I do not see how Radner and Turner can either account for them or how they justify support for the movements which have campaigned for and won change in the Church and wider society.

Let me give two examples, one quoted by the authors, the other not. The first is the question of the ordination of women, as one way in which the Church affirms the full sacramental, public authority of women. Radner and Turner acknowledge that this has been hugely controversial, that in the Anglican communion, it is still disputed and that change came about without consensus. However, over time, the Anglican communion has accepted that the ordination of women need not divide churches from one another.

My question is simply: why? There are clear scriptural teachings that women should not have authority over men in Church and that they preferably should not speak and certainly not teach (1 Tim. 4). It was not the practice of the vast majority of the Church to ordain women, and it is still not the practice of the vast majority of Christians who are Roman Catholic and Orthodox. Given Radner and Turner's arguments, there could be no justification for making such an innovative move, unless the compromises of the Anglican Communion are arbitrarily insulated from the rest of the Church. Also missing from their account of the manoeuvres of Anglican bodies which tried to resolve this issue is any acknowledgement of either secular pressures to accept the equality of women, or the critiques offered by feminist theologians of the Church's patriarchal structures. The result is that the change is made to look less radical, less revolutionary and less questioning of the natural evolution of tradition.

A second example is that of the civil rights movement in the USA. For many who opposed the abolition of slavery in the nineteenth century and the end of segregation in the 1960s and 1970s, what was at issue was a community's slowly evolved form of life, based upon the created order of different races. One could make a plausible case that the supporters of segregation were only being true to their tradition and the way it unfolded.

Of course, this tradition was founded on a lie. And it was only handed on and sustained by communities which refused membership and a public voice to those who were considered alien, different and subhuman. Radner and Turner leave the reader with no clue how they would withstand the arguments of racists to maintain their cherished traditions, which were thought to be perfectly consistent with the Bible.

The conservatism they propose looks like a coherent, attractive vision of the Church patiently working out its calling and discerning its path under God's providential guidance. But patience can be a cloak for silencing dissent, and providence is a story written by those whom it seems to favour. Ideas like community and tradition and immersion in Scripture are actually abstractions, and they are used by conservatives to rule innovation out of court. In fact, I would put it more strongly than this. By ignoring the possibility that our most cherished traditions and forms of community might turn out to be based on nothing but a will to power, they exclude the possibility of conversion, the breaking of our hearts and the overturning of our tables which is the shocking, exposing effect of Christ in our lives.

Are we just left with chaos, then; with a liberal God who just affirms our preferences and prejudices? I suggest not, because that charge refuses to engage with the actual historical struggles and patterns of discernment and conversion which have shaped the contemporary call for inclusion.

One of the reasons Hugh Rayment-Pickard and I wrote our book was to suggest that inclusion cannot simply be dismissed as novelty. It is a response to Christian revelation, to the nature of God shown in creation, in Christ and in the outpouring of the Spirit. It is part of the dynamic that builds communion, but that also makes it possible for the limits of that communion to be identified, and its borders broken open from time to time.

For all the continuities of tradition and the accumulation of wisdom, there are also times of rupture, conversion and radical change not only for individuals but for the people of God. Creation itself represents a risk on God's part. To create what is other than God is to introduce the reality of change, frailty and mortality into the ultimate nature of things. Creation cannot be undone. But the risk also makes meaningful human life and response to God possible. The image of God is present in our created humanity. That is our primary identity, against which all inequalities on the basis of other identities have to be measured.

The identity of the people of God is forged through wandering, loss and exile, as much as through settlement and expansion. The idea that we find who we are by losing ourselves is confirmed by the teaching of Jesus and the pattern of his cross and resurrection. Identity is not a stable possession, a thing that is set in stone in creation. The risk of creation sets free a history of response to God in which our identity, tradition and sense of order are ever called into question.

And God's revealed response to this situation is one of incarnation, of embodied solidarity with the world, of dispossession. The gospel witness is that Jesus ate with sinners and tax collectors, with the unclean and the sexually and financially prostituted. This does not imply approval of any or all of these patterns of life, but it does suggest that the things that separate people from God are man-made structures of alienation, oppression and exclusion.

Perhaps most striking in the development of the Church's response to revelation is the mission to the Gentiles, without which the Church simply would not exist. The Gentiles are eventually admitted to the Church without having to become Jews. It is hard for us to recall how revolutionary this was. The New Testament itself cannot hide the bitter disputes that split the early community. At one point in his Letter to the Galatians, Paul wishes that those who oppose him on this point would castrate themselves, such is his anger (Gal. 5.12). And there continued to be communities of Jewish-Christians who would not accept the change. According to the book of Acts, those who did accept the revolution did so for a reason: they could discern the presence and activity of the Holy Spirit among the Gentile converts. The fruits of the Spirit were already in evidence.

In the light of these admittedly sketchy aspects of the biblical story and the revelation of God in Israel and in Christ, I believe there are grounds for affirming an inclusive dynamic at the heart of the Church's identity and story.

Inclusion is not the same as saying that 'anything goes'. Those who supported the consecration of Gene Robinson were not indifferent to the truth or to Scripture, but believed they were interpreting them with faithfulness for our time. Inclusion, like any word – liberal, conservative, traditionalist – is imperfect, and if it suggests the absurd idea that the Church should accept anything and everything, it needs to be challenged. But that is not where current arguments for inclusivity come from. They themselves have a tradition, rooted in revelation, shaped by secular and Church struggles. They challenge our institutions and communities to confront their patterns of exclusion, and to ask whether they are truly responsive to the biblical witness, the invitation of Christ and the evidence of the Spirit's presence. This form of inclusivity is demanding. It is a specific challenge to forms of exclusion from the Church on the basis that some people are defined as less than fully human, as less than perfectly made in the image of God. It is not a carte blanche to do what you will, but a faithful exercise of judgement.

Those who argue that gay and lesbian people should play a full and open part in the life of the Church do so because we have experienced the Spirit at work in them, and because their lives can be consistent with the faithfulness, gentleness, self-control, patience and love which the Bible puts at the heart of a Christian understanding of relationships. If these are present, as many conservatives admit, then why continue to exclude?

The answer given by Radner and Turner is weak. Apart from the innate conservatism which will not accept novelty (although this appears to be a matter of judgement), they appeal to the created order of male and female complementarity. Sexuality is the 'Rubicon' which cannot be crossed, because the male/female distinction is part of the created order of things, and it shapes our response to God. Marriage is a sign of the Son being given to the world by the Father, for example. The Church is the bride of Christ.

There is a stunning lack of critical evaluation in these assertions. There is a sleight of hand at work here. The male/female distinction is equated with a particular interpretation of that distinction. Imagery associating men with the divine, activity, initiative and the power of salvation has been used to uphold the submission of women to men, on the basis that women were created to be passive and secondary. But, even if the imagery is reinterpreted to fit modern ideas of equality, the idea that the complementarity of men and women translates into an exclusive affirmation of either marriage or celibacy is simply a way of reading a cultural prejudice into the text. Men and women do not have to be married to relate to each other in significant ways, nor does their complementarity exclude same-sex friendship and intimacy. Why then does it exclude sexual relationships between people of the same sex?

It is noteworthy that Radner and Turner do not quote the half a dozen proof-texts used to justify biblical opposition to homosexual practice. This is undoubtedly because they are subtle enough to know that these texts cannot be directly applied to our contemporary understanding of homosexuality without a lot of interpretative work and questionable judgements.

Creation, interpretation and commitment cannot happen without risk and without questions arising in their wake. But is this anything more than a recipe for the kind of fragmentation that the authors of *The Fate of Communion* fear, in which, to quote the book of Judges, everyone just does what is right in their own eyes (Judg. 17.6)? Are there communal bonds and disciplines which can prevent us simply walking apart?

Their answer is to call us back to ideas of communion and catholicity. But we can no longer be naive about such ideas. The temptation is to decide in advance who is part of our communion, and what the limits of our catholicity are. The result is that those whose bodies, desires, faces and voices do not fit are excluded a priori. And this is actually a lack of patience and humility, precisely those virtues lauded by Radner and Turner when it suits their own agenda.

For a Church to live with a continual questioning of the limits of diversity is a more uncomfortable path to take. Nevertheless, it may actually be less likely to lead to division than the current hardening of attitudes to orthodoxy, communion and purity we are witnessing in Anglicanism. If Anglicanism in its global form is to have any future, then individual churches will need to consult with others, and to ask themselves what the effect of changes they introduce will be. But this cannot be used to rule out in advance the possibility that local churches will, prayerfully, make changes appropriate to their context in order to be more hospitable to God and the stranger. And the Church will have to live with some open questions about the precise bounds of communion, about whether changes will prove to last and bear fruit. Anglicanism perhaps still has a chance of modelling the ability to share in communion even as we disagree.

Radner and Turner worry that this makes the Church a theological debating shop with no convictions of its own. But I would argue that a Christian inclusivity is rooted in the revelation that God deals with creation and humanity in a certain way – through risk, through incarnate vulnerability, through the excessive gift of the Spirit. The content of revelation cannot be divorced from the way it is given, and it is not given like a thunderbolt from the blue. It is given as enfleshed invitation, and we have a responsibility to work out in our time what that means.

I believe these themes are true to the spirit of Kevin Kelly's theological approach, and to what he has given to the Church from his own experience of parish ministry. He writes that, for a parish to be true to the spirit of the Second Vatican Council, it must be worldly, sacramental, inclusive, ecumenical and Catholic.[3] Kelly is a great example of a theologian and pastor whose vision of inclusivity is earthed in the worshipping life of a community that lives towards the kingdom of God where it is, and whose moral theology is firmly centred on persons, not abstractions. An 'inclusive Church' for Kelly is one in which there is real listening and sharing of power. *How* things are done matters as much as, if not more than, the explicit messages proclaimed.

I am particularly taken by Kelly's preface to *New Directions in Moral Theology: The Challenge of Being Human*, in which he states:

> I believe there is great wisdom and love in my Church. I recognize too that there is also unwisdom and unlove in my Church. To be afraid to voice what I think is true would be tantamount to saying that I believe that unwisdom and unlove is stronger than wisdom and love in my Church. And that I do not believe.[4]

And, he adds: 'I hope I am ready to recognize that there is a fair share of unwisdom and unlove in me.'[5] I believe this is an exercise of inclusive judgement in practice; an outspoken humility which disarms our resentments and exclusions.

A commitment to inclusion welcomes such questioning as intrinsic to our identity, not merely as a danger to it, because it is one way in which we learn the discipline of hospitality. Inclusion is not merely an abstracted liberal 'value', an empty exercise of non-judgementalism. It is a virtue, whose pattern and substance is shaped by the impress of revelation upon us. It is about who we are, about the kind of community we are: a community that always allows such questions of identity to tremble before the approach of one who alone defines who we are and how we belong. Inclusive truth is personal truth, not in the sense of being driven by individual taste, but because its measure is that full stature of maturity we are called towards in Christ. For he calls us to a life without fearful anxiety about the other.

Jesus teaches that we must become like children to enter the kingdom of God. Sometimes this passage is interpreted as referring to the innocence of children. But Jesus was not a sentimental fool. Remember the story with which we began, the children catcalling in the marketplace. He knew the darker side of childish behaviour, its tribalism and violence. Perhaps Jesus puts the child before his disciples as an example because he knew that children were not part of the public world of authority and teaching. They, like women, were meant to be passive recipients. It is yet another way in which the one who was rejected and crucified teaches us that our salvation will come from those we have excluded.

Notes

1. E. Radner and P. Turner, *The Fate of Communion: The Agony of Anglicanism and the Future of a Global Church* (Grand Rapids and Cambridge: William B. Eerdmans, 2006), p. 23.

2. Hugh Rayment-Pickard and Steven Shakespeare, *The Inclusive God: Reclaiming Theology for an Inclusive Church* (London: SCM Canterbury Press, 2006).

3. Kevin T. Kelly, *From a Parish Base: Essays in Moral and Pastoral Theology* London: Darton, Longman and Todd, 1999), p. 24.

4. Kevin T. Kelly, *New Directions in Moral Theology: The Challenge of Being Human* (London: Geoffrey Chapman, 1992), p. viii.

5. *Ibid.*, p. viii.

20

Church Leadership, Ethics and the Moral Rights of Priests

James F. Keenan

The first item that I read by Kevin Kelly was his *Conscience: Dictator or Guide? A Study in Seventeenth-Century English Protestant Moral Theology*. It had an enormous influence on me because at the time I was studying British casuistry, particularly the late-fifteenth- to mid-sixteenth-century Scottish theologian, John Major or Mair. I was completely disappointed with what I was finding, and Kelly introduced me to his splendid book on how the English Protestants produced a practical theology that integrated the more experiential ascetical or devotional theology within a moral theology.[1]

Of course, this was vintage Kelly, he was finding in his ancestors his theological roots, for Kelly has always been working out of a vision that brought together the spiritual and the moral, or as today, the pastoral and the moral. In fact, it is hard to separate his moral theology from his pastoral experience and, while there are some current models that maintain strong traditional morals mollified by a compassionate pastoral approach, Kelly keeps them in tandem: a good morals is read from and through the experience of a good pastoral. One finds this approach in his *New Directions in Moral Theology*, where he insists that the starting point of any morals is not the dignity of the human person objectively conceived but rather the dignity of the person as experienced subject.[2] This position would lead him to more inclusive sexual ethics[3] and, more recently, Kelly again brought himself as an experienced pastor encountering the experience of cohabiting, prenuptial couples and began to ask how we can accompany them.[4] Good pastoral equals good morals and good morals equals good pastoral.

Inevitably, Kelly would have to turn to the ethics of Church pastoral work and did so in *From a Parish Base*.[5] There, Kelly looked at the ethics of the Church rather critically and I want to follow up on those endeavours here. In particular I want to look at the life of the Church as in need of ethical training and then I want to look at a particular dimension of ethics in the Church. Inasmuch as, of late, priests have been insisting on greater prerogatives about their lives and the exercise of their ministry, I will ask what moral rights they have.

I

Occasionally for a variety of reasons Church leadership in some parts of the world finds itself in morally problematic situations. Whether it concerns religious, priests or bishops in Europe, North America, South America, Asia or Africa, scandals arise due to a variety of reasons. Some of these reasons rightfully put the fault with Church leaders. Such reasons could be simple human misjudgement or small-mindedness, a lack of transparency that masks itself as protective confidentiality, a failure to follow the code of canon law, or a deep consequentialism interested in protecting the image of the Church at any cost. Other reasons for the reporting of these scandals are not at all fair or just. These include anti-Catholic bigotry, anti-authoritarianism or a media sensationalism that needs to sell copy. We know many of the true and false reasons that prompt the reporting of a scandal. What I want to argue here is that a rarely cited cause for such scandals derives from the fact that we rarely ask ethical questions about the Church and its leadership.[6]

For instance, in whatever part of the world sexual-abuse scandals broke out, we saw an evident lack of ethics. Ethics was not only lacking among the predatory priests, but it was also noticeably absent in the decision-making by some bishops and their counsellors as they transferred such priests, as they failed to notify civil authorities, as they stonewalled, as some even defamed the reputations of concerned and aggrieved parents, and, most importantly, as they left children at profound risk. But ethics were also not evident even after the harm was done. As the crisis unfolded, some innocent priests were not protected, due process was often and still remains breached, financial mismanagement occasionally occurred, lay initiatives often were treated with derision, priests who protested episcopal mismanagement became targeted, and chanceries relied on certain types of lawyers who did little to promote the common good.

Why were ethics so absent in this scandal as well as other scandals? Why did no one in clerical life ask the simple question, 'Is this ethical?' Why was such a relevant question not more frequently invoked?

We need to realize that ecclesiastical leadership does not regularly promote for its own members an awareness of the ethical goods and benefits that are engaged by the practice of critical ethical thinking in routine decision-making. Unlike many other professions, religious leaders rarely turn to ethical norms to consider what constitutes right conduct in their field of leadership and service.

I do not mean by this that religious leaders or their decisions are always or necessarily unethical. In fact, in most instances I am sure they are not. That being said, however, when religious, clergy and bishops exercise routine decision-making, they turn to a multitude of considerations, for instance, canon law, common sense, long-standing practices, etc.; but articulated ethical norms, their specific values and goods, the virtues and the type of critical thinking that estimates the long-standing social claims that these values, goods and virtues have on us, are not explicitly, professionally engaged. In a word, ethical norms and critical ethical reasoning, which frequently aid other professionals in law, business, medicine, counselling, nursing and even politics, play a much less explicit role in ecclesial leadership practices.

For instance, here in the United Kingdom, is a discussion about priests and their 'so-called' employer. *The Tablet* ran an editorial on it in the 20 January 2007 edition and, in an article in the same issue, Isabel de Bertodano described the issues between the Government's Department of Trade and Industry and the Bishops' Conference. In the very limited amount of material I have read, the bishops are seeking expertise, it seems, exclusively from canon and civil lawyers. But could they not ask other questions, not about whether canonical and civil principles of due process are correctly and consistently applied, but whether the moral rights of priests are protected and promoted?[7] I was struck in both articles by how there is a good and healthy turn to canon law, but not a similar turn to ethical considerations.

Still, before I go further, let me be clear about a number of presuppositions with which I am operating. I will simply stipulate six of these that I have developed elsewhere.[8]

First, what I say about the Roman Catholic Church applies to other communities of faith. Many churches simply do not default to an explicitly ethical way of thinking in making leadership decisions. Likewise, what I say about Church leadership refers to bishops, clergy and lay administrators and is similarly found in other churches, mosques and synagogues. And, what I say about clergy is not solely about diocesan clergy. I have raised and published, for instance, questions about practices internal to the Society of Jesus, such as when some Jesuit provinces require HIV testing of candidates applying to the order; or how different Jesuit provinces, so as to evaluate Jesuit scholastics for advancement, use a procedure infelicitously called *informationes*.[9]

Secondly, I am not solely concerned with sexual boundaries, though these are very important, but also with financial responsibility, personal and social accountability, the claims of confidentiality, the importance of truth-telling, due process, consultation, contracts, fair wages, delations, adequate representation, appeals, conflicts of interests, etc.

Thirdly, this is not part of an ideological agenda, either progressive or conservative. I am simply proposing that such training in ethical reflection is necessary for those who exercise the various ministries of the Church. Nor am I saying (and this bears repeating) that the churches act unethically. I am simply saying that, unlike most other institutional spheres, the ethical question does not seem to be as in-play in Church leadership as it is elsewhere.

Fourthly, the lack of training in ethics has caused a greater vacuum than most of those outside of leadership recognize. Most, I believe, presume that we have attended to this training all along and that we routinely engage in professional ethical standards. Thus, for the most part, in the wake of sex-abuse scandals, the laity has rightfully insisted on talking about structures of governance, but does not focus on the related questions of ethics, such as whether Church leaders have been trained in ethics.

Fifthly, this lack of critical ethical training is evident not only in ministerial decisions but also in the practices internal to the clerical, religious and episcopal cultures.

Finally, I believe that mandating ethical training and subsequent ethical accountability ought not to be seen as inimical to the interests of the Church or her mission, but rather constitutive of it. As Yale University's Wayne Meeks notes in *The Origins of Christian Morality: The First Two Centuries*, 'making morals means making community'.[10]

So, why is there so little ethical professional insight within the leadership practices and lives of our clergy and episcopacy? I offer two answers.

The more immediate answer is that seminarians, religious men and women, lay leaders and bishops are not and have not been trained in professional ethics. Those who study at seminaries, divinity schools or schools of theology rarely receive the type of ethical training that those at most other professional schools receive. Persons admitted to business, medical or law schools take ethics courses that address specifically the ethical issues that are relevant to their particular profession. Those students are taught the responsibilities and rights specific to their profession, whether these deal with matters of representation, confidentiality, client expectations, privileges, promotions, evaluations, conflicts of interest, professional boundaries, etc. Their ethics courses in their professional schools aim to shape, if not the students' internal dispositions, then at least the students' external conduct so as to become acceptable colleagues in their particular professional field. Subsequent to this education, they join professional organizations which establish minimal codes of ethical conduct for their members. They become part of accountability structures from internal reviews to the Internal Revenue.

This type of professional ethical training and accountability is generally not found at most seminaries, divinity schools or schools of theology, even though many students take two, three or four courses of Christian ethics. What we find, instead, are courses that deal with the sexual lives of the laity, the social ethics of businesses, and the medical ethics of physicians and nurses. That is, those in ministry are taught how to govern and make morally accountable the members of their congregations with regard to their sexual, reproductive and marital lives, as well as being able to make claims about those in the medical and business profession. In fact, since they first started after the Council of Trent, seminary classes in moral theology were singularly focused on determining moral judgement for hearing confessions: seminary courses were designed for priests to help the laity who came to them as sinners in need of moral guidance.

Generally speaking, then, religious and seminarians are not taught by what ethical reasoning, insights or norms they should be held morally accountable as pastors, priests or bishops. They have no training in the keeping of confidences, in making assignments, in avoiding conflicts of interest, in professional evaluations, in the relevance of truth-telling, in crisis management, etc. You might be surprised at this, but just consider the question of keeping confidences. Certainly the priest knows to keep the confidence of the confessional absolutely, but what about other confidences? I studied, for instance, what the standards of confidentiality were when a priest or religious went for therapy, and their ordinary or superior believed they had a right to know what was said to the therapist.[11] I have often wondered, furthermore, what training in confidences retreat directors and spiritual directors have.

In the hierarchical structure in which priests exist, their accountability is solely to 'the man upstairs'. That is, a priest's or bishop's professional accountability is singularly vertical, but again that man upstairs has probably had no training in fairness or any other professional ethical standard. Thus a priest basically is singularly responsible to nothing but the bishop's own expectations and judgements. Quite apart from the absence of any ethical standards guiding the bishop's evaluation of his priests, religious and lay ministers, there do not seem to be any specific normative ethical standards to guide the bishop in his assessment of his diocesan personnel. Moreover, this vertical accountability is singularly unidirectional.

Furthermore, there is very little horizontal accountability in this very clerical world. A priest is not accountable either to a fellow priest, his community or even to his parish. This is the world of clerical culture that Michael Papesh tragically captures in his work, *Clerical Culture: Contradiction and Transformation*.[12]

It is worth noting that there is one other institutional culture that also fails to make professional ethics a part of their mode of proceeding and that is the academy. Like the clerical world, we professors teach ethics for others, but we have not been trained in it. None of us is really trained to be ethical in the standards we use for grading papers, for seeing students, for maintaining office hours, for evaluating colleagues or prospective hires. We have not been taught anything about professional boundaries with our students or about keeping our contracts. We have not really addressed the fact that our salaries are so disproportionate or that tenure decisions sometimes lack, what shall we call it, 'objectivity'. We do not have professional questions about our investments, our budgets, or about our boards of directors. Our accountability is solely vertical, to our chairs and deans, but not to one another and certainly not to our students.

Like the Church, our standards are fairly mediaeval and the standards of horizontal professional accountability noticeably lacking.

The second reason why there has not been any ethical training in Church leadership goes back to the Enlightenment. After the Wars of Religion, the Enlightenment attempted to establish a way of understanding the ethical as universally normative. After the Church validated, in the seventeenth century, the triple contract and allowed for money-lending, pensions, annuities, banks, pawn shops and a host of other financial innovations, it unleashed an industrialized world that needed moral guidance beyond the privacy of the confessional. The Enlightenment's engagement of reasoned argumentation in the eighteenth century left it freer than the Church, whose dependence on its tradition and its constant casuistry let it fall, if you will, behind the times. The Enlightenment moved in where the Church once was. Adam Smith's *Theory of Moral Sentiments*, for instance, provided a moral outline about how to proceed in the new markets of emerging democracies. Moreover, its democratic interests in horizontal accountability offered a new model of moral uprightness and accountability.

We know how strongly the Church resisted those democratic movements, preferring the palace to the senate. Progressively, it became a foreigner in the democratic world where normative standards were being articulated by lay judges rather than by clerical confessors. In a way the confessional remained the place for personal sin, but social guidelines were less and less regulated by Church dicta. Eventually, in the name of civil religion, the Enlightenment raised up the legislative conscience, seeking to regulate normative human commerce. Later on, in this past century, the term 'professional ethics' would enter a variety of mainline professions and their respective teaching institutions as well. But one place those standards never entered was the world of the Church, where the moral was once singularly determined by the theologian but now by the bishop and mediated by the priest confessor in a highly vertical, unidirectional, hierarchical accountability structure.

Today we see the Church wrestling with those democratic structures of governance. We see the Church in court, bishops being deposed, priests being arrested, affidavits being filed, audits being run. A new mode of accountability is being imposed on the Church. But this is an imposition from outside invoking minimalist standards that are sometimes fairly applied and sometimes not.

Do Church leaders need to be so passive in this ordeal? Could not Church leadership take a more aggressive stance and become not only regulated but also self-regulating, ethically self-regulating? Could not the Church put up its own standards, which are not only professionally ethically responsible but also have a form of transparent accountability that is predominantly horizontal? Could not these standards also be articulated and imposed from within? I believe so.[13]

II

The resources for this move are, already, considerable. For instance, in an essay about the sex-abuse crisis in the United States, entitled 'What the Bishops Failed to Learn from Corporate Ethics Disasters',[14] Kirk Hanson enunciates ten ethical principles that address the legitimate interests and welfare of Church stakeholders. These include: 'Take care of the victim', 'Express public apology quickly and often', 'Learn everything about the incident; know more than anyone else', 'Search for the causes of the crisis', 'Remove individuals who are responsible'. This essay builds on the normative principles elaborated in the corporate world, which are transposed into a Church setting and make evident the claim I have made here: the need for professional ethical standards in the Church that could train Church leaders for effective, moral leadership, particularly in moments of crisis.

While there is much to be learned from the corporate world (I helped host a conference of organizational managers and helped edit the conference papers bridging the world of organizational management and Church leaders: *Church Ethics and its Organizational Context: Learning from the Sex Abuse Scandal in the Catholic Church*[15]), Michael Buckley believes that, rather than going outside the Church to find resources for normative directions, we should dig deep into our own theological framework. Doing this, he offers four proposals that deal not with principles but rather with long-abandoned policies. Thus he begins, first we must 'restore to the local church – and hence to the laity – a decisive voice in the selection of its own bishop'. Secondly, 'the church should restore the enduring commitment of the bishop to his see'. Buckley insists that the 'church should reaffirm strongly and effectively the ancient canonical prohibition that forbids a bishop's leaving one see to obtain another'. Thirdly, 'the church needs to restore or strengthen Episcopal Conferences and regional gatherings of local bishops'. Finally, 'to counter the present excessive centralization within the church, certain institutions that may at one time have served a useful purpose need to be reconsidered and even abolished'. Among his suggestions: the College of Cardinals, the office of papal nuncio, the appointment as 'bishops' in the Roman Curia of those who have no local Church to administer, and honorific attachments to the papal court, such as 'monsignor'. Buckley's essay on policies keeps us alert to the theological warrants that could make our Church leadership a more ethically credible institution.[16]

Besides principles and policies, there are ethical pledges. Frank Butler, the president of Foundations and Donors Interested in Catholic Activities (FADICA) offered a code of ethics written specifically for Church members, entitled 'A Professional Code of Ethics Reflecting the Nature of a Christian Vocation and an Understanding of Leadership in the Church'. Let me list a few of his ten well-honed pledges:

209

I promise to do all in my power to deepen my understanding of the church as a community and, as such, the body of Christ, and I will evaluate my service in the church daily in the light of my relationship to the person of Jesus Christ and his command to love one another as he has loved us.

I will pledge to strengthen my understanding and practice of Catholicism, its teachings, principles and values on an on-going basis so as to apply them to church operations and thus to be a credible witness to the faith.

I will exercise the authority of my office in a way that empowers those whom I serve and work in a collaborative spirit of church leaders.

I will do all in my power to foster broad participation in the life of the church, to encourage public opinion, and to respect honest differences and the rights of others.[17]

Butler's pledges, along with Hanson's principles and Buckley's policies, offer us a glimpse of the horizon for where our Church could be as it pursues ethics.

III

Let me now turn to an initiative of my own, the rights of priests. I propose here not canonical rights, since I am not a canonist. Rather I use the word 'rights' as moral theologians and Christian social ethicists do when speaking of the right to food, or work, or health care, that is, as a moral right.

Ladislas Örsy, the canon lawyer, notes that moral theology differs from canon law in terms of purpose, nature and goal. But he argues that moral theology has a priority over canon law in this: moral theologians investigate the nature of the human person, society and the common good and examine the virtues, values and norms that are constitutive of the person, society and the common good.[18] We hope to see these virtues, values and norms as formative of the canonical precepts and prohibitions that canonists eventually articulate for the good of the Church and its members. Thus we articulate moral rights with the hope that, if need be, they will be eventually articulated canonically or civilly. In any event, whether they become articulated as canonical rights, they still are matters of moral rights. Yet, while I have no competency to develop them canonically and I do not claim that they have canonical force today, at least in the first two moral rights I will refer to the Code of Canon Law because the interests of the canons literally overlap with the interests of ethics.[19]

Let me also add that I do not consider rights as voluntaristic assertions of power over and against others; rather, I see rights language as springing from a community of faith looking to see how best its members can protect the good of the whole Church and its specific members. Following Brian Tierney,[20] I believe that rights were originally recognized by eleventh- and twelfth-century theologians and canonists who tried to articulate those that belonged to popes, bishops, clergy and other Church members, not as inimical to the life of the Church, but as constitutive of the Church. In other words, before the use of rights language appeared in the Enlightenment and in modern liberal democracies, they were first expressed as intrinsic to the good of the Church. That is where I locate myself and my use of the term rights.

Rights language developed in the twelfth century precisely as we became more interested in the nature of the person. Caroline Bynum points to the privileging of spiritual experiences of members of charismatic movements of the twelfth century that eventually led, in the next century, to the founding of the great religious orders by Dominic, Francis and Clare. In the twelfth century, mystics saw themselves in union with God and understood God as triune, that is, as three persons in one God. Bynum asks the very relevant question, 'Did the twelfth century discover the individual?'[21] Her question is pivotal, inasmuch as much of twelfth-century spirituality was an appreciation of God's love for the human in God's image and, inasmuch as that image was not predominantly Christological but Trinitarian, the Christian saw her/himself more and more like the Trinity, that is, as a person constitutively related to other persons.

Rights are for persons. The more we recognize someone's rights, the more we recognize their personhood and, the more we recognize their personhood, the more we recognize them as related to ourselves.

Rights language, therefore, does not alienate or individuate, divide or polarize, rather rights language incorporates into the human community those who are persons: upholding one's rights then is an act of upholding one's own participation in the goods of the community.

Over the past 50 years we have seen the language of rights being used precisely to build up the community by asserting particular rights to particular groups of people. First, the civil rights movement in the United States moved from asserting moral rights to articulating legal and constitutional ones so as to break down the predominant American mentality to keep African Americans segregated, that is, outside of the body politic. By recognizing their rights they became incorporated on to our buses, at our lunch counters, into our schools and, finally, into our neighbourhoods. Secondly, in the pro-life movement we have seen a vigorous attempt to restore to foetuses the rights that *Roe v. Wade* effectively suppressed. Each gain that the foetus makes of a right not to be terminated or of a right towards living, each time that we see a foetus being protected by the state, we see the community's growing recognition of the personal status of the foetus. Finally, in the gay rights movement, we see the search for parity about property, housing, health care and other issues as steps towards being treated more as persons and being more fully incorporated into the body politic.

Thus, as Aristotle taught us, ethics is for the community, and asserting the moral rights of priests is certainly not at the cost of the community, but rather for its benefit. To the extent that these rights are not respected, then, to that extent not only priests but the community of the Church, its own very *communio* suffers. Correlatively, to the extent that we withhold these rights, to that extent we exclude priests from being incorporated into the community and relegate to them a second-class status.

I am convinced that the process of recognizing, articulating and asserting the rights of priests is a deeply humanizing process for a group of men who have suffered a great deal these years. I believe that this work of rights not only helps restore to priests their incorporation into the community, but also occasions the possible restoration of much of their humanity.

Moreover, I believe that, if we can articulate and defend the rights of the clergy, we will with that mentality articulate and defend the rights of the laity and bishops as well. In fact, the laity is already doing that, and one reason why I am speaking about the rights of the clergy is precisely because so few do.

The six rights that I am proposing are not unrelated to one another. Taken together, they more fully comprehend the man in his humanity and in his priesthood.

The Code of Canon Law defines three canonical rights for priests: of association, to a vacation and to fitting and decent remuneration. Instead of these three canonical rights, I propose six 'moral' ones: the right to share in the episcopal ministry of the local ordinary; the right of association; the right to discern the proper exercise of their ministry; the right to their personal development; the right to privacy; and the right to fair treatment. Let me briefly comment on each of them.

The Right to Share in the Episcopal Ministry of the Local Ordinary

I invoke this first right after considering many recent actions by priests expressing concern about modes of episcopal governance. Do they have a right to do this? For instance, in the United States, 58 Boston priests sent a letter on 9 December 2002 calling for the resignation of Cardinal Bernard Law. On 1 October 2003, the priests of Rockville Centre wrote to meet with Bishop William Murphy over 'widespread dissatisfaction' with his leadership. Later the priests of Chicago wrote an open letter to the hierarchy about the tone and content of Church leaders' remarks about gay and lesbian persons, a letter subsequently adopted by priests from Rochester, New York. In August 2003, 160 priests in Milwaukee called for a married clergy. Do priests have a right to do this?

Thinking of these actions, I first turned to canon law and found in John Lynch's commentary the repeated assertion that the 'cleric shares in the Episcopal ministry'.[22] Lynch roots his claim precisely in canon 273 that specifically talks about the special obligation to show reverence and obedience to the ordinary. Lynch concludes: 'It should be noted, in sum, that the special obedience that the cleric owes his bishop is based on his sharing in the Episcopal ministry through the sacrament of orders and the bond of incardination'.[23] While Lynch acknowledges that this right is not yet a canonical right, even though it has been discussed as one, I believe it can be called a moral right.

Moreover, we find the moral right implicit in Vatican II documents. The Decree on the Ministry and Life of Priests states: 'Priestly obedience, inspired through and through by the spirit of cooperation, is based on the sharing of the Episcopal ministry which is conferred by the sacrament of order and the canonical mission.'[24] Similarly, in The Bishops' Pastoral Office, we find: 'All priests, whether diocesan or religious, share and exercise with the bishop the one priesthood of Christ.'[25] Finally, *Lumen gentium* declares: 'The Bishop is to regard his priests, who are his co-workers, as sons and friends, just as Christ called his disciples no longer servants but friends.'[26] It is also found in the rite of ordination. The first question the bishop asks the ordinand is:

> Are you resolved, with the help of the Holy Spirit, to discharge without fail the office of priesthood in the presbyteral order as a conscientious fellow worker with the bishops in caring for the Lord's flock?[27]

Then, in the prayer of consecration we hear the bishop say:

> Lord, grant also to us such fellow workers,
> for we are weak and our need is greater.
> Almighty Father, grant to this servant of yours the dignity of the priesthood.
> Renew within him the Spirit of holiness.

As a co-worker with the order of bishops
may he be faithful to the ministry
that he receives from you, Lord God,
and be to others a model of right conduct.[28]

In sum, priestly experience, the teachings of Vatican II, canonical commentary and the rite of ordination itself support the claim that a priest has a moral right to share in the exercise of Episcopal authority.

The Right of Association

The right of sharing in the ministry of the bishop leads to fostering right relations among the clergy through association. Canon 275.1 states: 'Since clerics all work for the same purpose, namely, the building up of the Body of Christ, they are to be united among themselves by a bond of brotherhood and prayer and strive for cooperation among themselves according to the prescripts of particular law.' Immediately after this paragraph, the code adds: 'Clerics are to acknowledge and promote the mission which the laity, each for his or her part, exercises in the Church and in the world.' Associations among the clergy are intimately tied, then, to promoting the laity's own involvement in the life of the Church. In fact, in the earlier draft of the code, the clergy were only called to recognize the laity's mission; according to the promulgated code, they must promote it.

Though canon 215 defined the right of all the Christian faithful to form associations, that is, both lay and clergy, canon 278 establishes it as the first canonical right for priests. The code reads: 'Secular clerics have the right to associate with others to pursue purposes in keeping with the clerical state.' This is the first time that canon law recognized this moral right.

In developing the revised code, the commission rejected a proposal that placed associations of priests under the local ordinary. To do so would be to infringe on the exercise of the very right that was being promulgated.

Throughout the United States, we have seen in the past few years free-standing priests' associations emerge, for example, the Boston Priests' Forum, the Milwaukee Archdiocese Priest Alliance or New York's Voice of the Ordained. This moral right and now articulated canonical right validates these groups. The recent innovations by priests to form local groups are congruent with good thinking within the Church. Moreover, these organizations do not replace presbyteral councils which are organized through the chancery and have different goals from these other less official and often more fraternal gatherings.

The Right to Discern the Proper Exercise of Their Ministry

While there is an obligation to exercise one's priestly ministry, there is also a right to exercise that ministry according to one's particular judgement. Here I think of pastors who must discern a variety of issues on a weekly basis: whether this particular couple is actually ready to get married in the Church, whether they should preach about the way the gospel applies to this particular local issue, or how these children in this parish should be prepared for confirmation.

In the United States Conference of Catholic Bishops document on Sunday homilies, 'Fulfilled in Your Hearing', the bishops call the pastor to listen to the Scriptures and to the congregation, and to respond to that listening. Is there something that happens existentially in that listening that could prompt the pastor to hear the needs of the laity of his parish in some way that the bishop has not yet addressed? If the priest, in all his listening, is also obliged 'to foster peace and harmony based on justice' as canon 287 states, he may find himself needing to obey his conscience as a preacher of the Word to the particular congregation he serves.

This is not advocacy for rebel priests. Rather, it recognizes both the context in which a priest exercises his ministry and the process by which he comes to preach the sermon and exercise other forms of ministry. Though by his faculties a priest exercises his ministry at the bishop's pleasure, there seems to be another claim on the priest that comes not from the bishop directly but from the people whom the priest serves. If the priest is to promote peace and justice and *communio*, it seems that, in order to discern how to do so, he needs to rely on something in addition to the bishops' particular perspective. Like other expressions of his ministry that he shares with the bishop and with the laity, a priest's preaching calls for a conscientious integrity to witness to the gospel as he sees it expressed in his midst. This too follows from the insight of Thomas Aquinas that, as we descend into a situation, specific circumstances need to be attended to in order to discern rightly what is actually acquired. That is, the priest, in being more proximate to his congregation, usually understands better than the ordinary many of the varying factors that make a particular congregation a particular congregation.

Certainly the bishop enjoys the right and has the duty to teach, but that right is in tandem with the moral right of the priest to discern the proper exercise of his ministry and the proper putting into effect of the specific teaching of the bishop. These rights are not limiting the freedom or obligation that each needs to perform; rather, they help enhance the entire ministry of building up *communio*.

The Right to Their Own Personal Development

While the previous right affirms the relevance of a priest's personal, though professional, experience with his congregation and encourages him to trust the development of a professional fealty with his parishioners that couples the fealty he enjoys with his ordinary through the orders which unite them, this right encourages the community and the priest to appreciate the priest as an embodied, personal relational agent. In many ways it expresses the insight that the priest must learn not only about his parish and his chancery, but also about himself. If the previous right is about him developing himself into a professional, this right recognizes that, to be a professional, one needs to be a person first.

Because of clericalism, most priests' personal affective experiences were often measured not with mature adult self-understanding and responsible affective conduct based on mutual respect, but rather on an intuited sense of what constituted 'proper discretion'. In other words, so long as a priest manifested decorum, he stayed within the boundary lines of acceptable clerical conduct.[29]

By this moral right, however, we see that affective experiences are good and necessary for personal growth and wisdom; this right recognizes what clericalism shadows. It proposes to say that priests need and have a right to the forms of friendship and responsible affective relations that make a person a mature adult and that he has a right to invoke these experiences as sources of wisdom.

The range of the right is broader than simply the development of affective relationships, since it includes intellectual and spiritual development as well. Thus, priests have a right to continuing education, leisure, sabbaticals, retreats, adequate time for daily prayer, etc. In other words, priests have duties in these areas and thereby should have rights as well. A more inclusive right to human development embraces affective experience (intimacy, friendship, etc.), while also calling for needed intellectual and spiritual development and their related goods as well.[30]

Rightly understood, these spiritual and intellectual developments happen within an affective context. Thus, the right could be expressed as I heard it from a fellow priest and friend: the right to our own affective experience and the wisdom that derives from it. Bernard of Clairvaux supports the claim: *Instructio doctos reddit, affectio sapientes.*[31] Instruction renders us learned, experience renders us wise. In my own life as a priest, I have received much wisdom about myself, my God, those I serve and my share as a disciple in the mission of Christ as a man precisely through the affective relationships that challenged, sustained and nurtured me.[32]

The Right to Privacy

This right turns inevitably to the right to privacy. The noted Roman moral theologian Brian Johnstone described privacy as the protected zone wherein a person can exercise self-determination, pursuing ends in a shared moral climate wherein the individual and society respect the claims of one another, that is, the individual's personal good and society's common good.[33]

The right to privacy is the right to exercise personal responsibilities and decisions. It is the right to be self-determinative, the right to be a mature adult whose movements are not subject to suspicion or intrusion without civil warrant. The right protects a person to be a person. In short, it allows a priest to have a place he calls his home, a circle of acquaintances to be called friends, and a conversation to be called confidential.

The assertion of the right to privacy not only shoulders the earlier rights stated above, but it also prompts us to recognize the relevance of the final right.

The Right to Fair Treatment

No less than Cardinal Avery Dulles has articulated, addressed and defended the rights of priests to due process.[34] Like him, others in Rome have responsibly reviewed and at times overturned a local ordinary's decision that effectively ignored a priest's right to due process. Similarly, I think of the Vatican's vigilance to protect the basic right of all priests to due process, especially when, in facing national scandals, episcopal conferences install new modes of proceeding that compromise priests' rights.

As we discern the rights of priests, it is this right more than any other that demands that an accused priest deserves to be treated as a human being, that is, as a person. This is the right that covers the question regarding the priest as an employee in the aforementioned *Tablet* articles. It is the same right that needs to be

215

reviewed in the United States with its way of proceeding in innumerable cases of accusations of child abuse. By analogy, it is the same right that needs to be better applied in the formation houses of religious orders and in seminaries, where, in some instances, a man or woman is dismissed without due cause. It is the basic right that effectively prompts us to consider the moral rights of priests in the first place.

It is on this right that I close. I propose these six rights – one about participatory leadership, another about association, a third about ministerial vocation, the fourth about personal growth, the fifth about basic civil liberties and the sixth about fairness – with the hope that these may further encourage the voice of the clergy. Throughout these recent years, the voice of the clergy, when it does occasionally, though not at all often enough, address either the harm and shame attached to the abuse of children or the rights of the laity and bishops, has done so most frequently in the place that they are called to be: the parish pulpit. I suggest that, if priests begin to recognize the rights due to them, they might in turn be more vocal from that pulpit in recognizing the rights of others and in fostering the *communio* that the Church so desperately needs. But, in order to get to those rights and better to foster *communio*, we need to get into the habit of raising and considering an even more important question about the way we as Church behave, and that is the lingering question that must be more habitually asked: 'but is it ethical?'[35]

Notes

1. Kevin T. Kelly, *Conscience: Dictator or Guide? A Study in Seventeenth-Century English Protestant Moral Theology* (London: Geoffrey Chapman, 1967).

2. Kevin T. Kelly, *New Directions in Moral Theology: The Challenge of Being Human* (London: Geoffrey Chapman, 1992).

3. Kevin T. Kelly, *New Directions in Sexual Ethics* (London: Geoffrey Chapman, 1998).

4. Kevin T. Kelly, 'Cohabitation: Living in Sin or Occasion of Grace?', *The Furrow* 56.12 (2005): 652–58.

5. Kevin T. Kelly, *From a Parish Base* (London: Geoffrey Chapman, 1999).

6. As in most works looking at the future of the Church, several essays in Julian Filochowski and Peter Stanford (eds), *Opening Up: Speaking Out in the Church* (London: Darton, Longman and Todd, 2005) take account of the need for ethical norms in Church conduct. They include: Enda McDonagh, 'Love and Justice: In God and Church, in Sexuality and Society', pp. 30–40; Julie Clague, 'Assessing Our Inheritance: John Paul II and the Dignity of Women', pp. 41–55; Jane Fraser, 'Teenage Pregnancy: Are the Churches to Blame?', pp. 81–94; Jeannine Gramick, 'Changing Hierarchical Structures', pp. 233–44; Conor Gearty, 'Keeping It Honest: The Role of the Laity in the Clerical Church', pp. 257–66; and Kevin Kelly, 'Do We Need a Vatican III?', pp. 267–79. For a survey of works on this topic, see James F. Keenan, 'Ethics and the Crisis in the Church', *Theological Studies* 66.1 (2005): 117–36.

7. 'Who is a Priest's Employer?', *The Tablet* 261 (20 January 2007): p. 2; Isabel de Bertodano, 'What About God's Workers?', *The Tablet* 261 (20 January 2007): pp. 14–15.

8. James F. Keenan, 'Toward an Ecclesial Professional Ethics', in Jean Bartunek, Mary Ann Hinsdale and James Keenan (eds), *Church Ethics and its Organizational Context: Learning from the Sex Abuse Scandal in the Catholic Church* (Lanham, MD: Sheed & Ward, 2005), pp. 83–96.

9. James F. Keenan, 'HIV Testing of Seminary and Religious-Order Candidates', *Review for Religious* 55 (1996): 297–314; James F. Keenan, 'Are Informationes Ethical?' *Studies in the Spirituality of Jesuits* 29 (September 1997): 1–33.

10. Wayne Meeks, *The Origins of Christian Morality: The First Two Centuries* (New Haven: Yale University Press, 1993), p. 5.

11. James F. Keenan, 'Confidentiality: Erosion and Restoration', *Review for Religious* 51 (1992): 882–94. See also, James F. Keenan, 'Confidentiality, Disclosure, and Fiduciary Responsibility in the Professions', *Theological Studies* 54 (1993): 142–59.

12. Michael Papesh, *Clerical Culture: Contradiction and Transformation* (Collegeville: Liturgical Press, 2004).

13. James F. Keenan and Joseph J. Kotva Jr, *Practice What You Preach: Virtues, Ethics and Power in the Lives of Pastoral Ministers and Their Congregations* (Franklin, WI: Sheed and Ward, 1999).

14. Kirk Hanson, 'What the Bishops Failed to Learn from Corporate Ethics Disasters', in Thomas Plante (ed.), *Sin Against the Innocents: Sexual Abuse by Priests and the Role of the Catholic Church* (Westport: Praeger, 2004), pp. 169–82.

15. See note 8 above.

16. Michael J. Buckley, 'Resources for Reform from the First Millennium', in Stephen Pope (ed.), *A Common Calling: The Laity and Governance of the Church* (Washington, DC: Georgetown University Press, 2004), pp. 71–86. Similarly, see the contributions by Bernard Hoose on this subject, especially *Authority in the Roman Catholic Church: Theory and Practice* (Aldershot: Ashgate, 2002); 'Authority in the Church', *Theological Studies* 63.1 (2002): 107–23. Also Gerard Mannion, 'A Haze of Fiction: Legitimation, Accountability, and Truthfulness', in Francis Oakley and Bruce Russett (eds), *Governance, Accountability, and the Future of the Catholic Church* (New York: Continuum, 2003), pp. 161–74; Gerard Mannion, Richard Gaillardetz, Jan Kerkhofs and Kenneth Wilson (eds), *Readings in Church Authority: Gifts and Challenges for Contemporary Catholicism* (Burlington, VT: Ashgate, 2003).

17. Francis Butler, 'A Professional Code of Ethics Reflecting the Nature of a Christian Vocation and an Understanding of Leadership in the Church', in Bartunek, Hinsdale and Keenan (eds), *Church Ethics*, pp. 137–45.

18. Ladislas Örsy, *Theology and Canon Law* (Collegeville: Liturgical Press, 1992), pp. 119–38.

19. James F. Keenan, 'Framing the Ethical Rights of Priests', *Review for Religious* 64.2 (2005): 135–51; 'The Ethical Rights of Priests', *Touchstone* 20 (2004): 6, 19–20; 'The Moral Rights of Priests', in Donald Dietrich (ed.), *Priests for the 21st Century* (New York: Crossroads, 2006), pp. 77–90.

20. Brian Tierney, *The Idea of Natural Rights: Studies on Natural Rights, Natural Law and Church Law, 1150-1625* (Atlanta: Scholars Press, 1997).

21. Caroline Bynum, 'Did the Twelfth Century Discover the Individual?', *Journal of Ecclesiastical History* 31 (1980): 1–17.

22. In this section I am indebted to John E. Lynch CSP, 'The Obligations and Rights of Clerics (cc.273–289)', in John Beal, James Corriden and Thomas Green (eds), *The New Commentary on the Code of Canon Law* (Mahwah: Paulist Press, 2000), pp. 343–81 (345).

23. Lynch, 'The Obligations and Rights of Clerics', p. 347.

24. Decree on the Ministry and Life of Priests, *Presbyterorum ordinis* (Vatican II, 1965), 7.

25. The Bishops' Pastoral Office, *Christus dominus* (Vatican II, 1965), 28.

26. Dogmatic Constitution on the Church, *Lumen gentium* (Vatican II, 1964), 28.

27. 'The Ordination of Deacons, Bishops and Priests', International Commission on English in the Liturgy (ed.), *The Rites of the Catholic Church* (New York: Pueblo Publishing Company, 1980), vol. II, pp. 64, 66–67.

28. *Ibid.*, pp. 66–67.

29. Michael Papesh, 'Farewell to the Club', *America* 186 (13 May 2002): 8–9; see also his *Clerical Culture: Contradiction and Transformation* (Collegeville: Liturgical, 2004). See also, David Gibson, 'Clericalism: The Original Sin', in *The Coming Catholic Church: How the Faithful Are Shaping a New American Catholicism* (New York: HarperCollins, 2003), pp. 197–219.

30. See Pope Paul VI, Encyclical Letter on the Development of Peoples, *Progressio populorum* (1967).

31. *Nec te moveat, quod initium sapientiae huic demum loco dederim, et non priori. Ibi quippe in quodam quasi auditorio suo docentem de omnibus magistram audimus Sapientiam, hic et suscipimus; ibi instruimur quidem, sed hic afficimur. Instructio doctos reddit, affectio sapientes. Sol non omnes, quibus lucet, etiam calefacit; sic Sapientia multos, quos docet quid sit faciendum, non continuo etiam accendit ad faciendum. Aliud est multas divitias scire, aliud et possidere; nec notitia divitem facit, sed possessio. Sic prorsus, sic aliud est nosse Deum, et aliud timere; nec cognitio sapientem, sed timor facit, qui et afficit. Tunc sapientem dixeris, quem sua scientia inflat? Quis illos sapientes nisi insipientissimus dicat, qui cum cognovissent Deum, non tanquam Deum glorificaverunt, aut gratias egerunt? Ego magis cum Apostolo sentio, qui insipiens cor eorum manifeste pronuntiat (Rom. I, 21). Et bene initium sapientiae timor Domini; quia tunc primum Deus animae sapit, cum eam afficit ad timendum, non cum instruit ad sciendum. Times Dei justitiam, times potentiam; et sapit tibi justus et potens Deus, quia timor sapor est. Porro sapor sapientem facit, sicut scientia scientem, sicut divitiae divitem* (Bernard of Clairvaux, *Sermones in Cantica Canticorum*, 23.14. J.-P. Migne, *Patrologia Latina*, 183, cols 0891d–0892a).

32. For valuable insights on this, see Donald Cozzens, *The Changing Face of the Priesthood: A Reflection on the Priest's Crisis of Soul* (Collegeville: Liturgical Press, 2000).

33. Brian Johnstone, 'The Right to Privacy: The Ethical Perspective', *The American Journal of Jurisprudence* 29 (1984): 73–94; Richard McCormick, 'The Moral Right to Privacy', in *How Brave a New World* (Garden City: Doubleday, 1981), pp. 352–61.

34. Avery Cardinal Dulles, 'The Rights of Accused Priests: Toward a Revision of the Dallas Charter and the "Essential Norms"', *America* 190 (21 June 2004): 19–22 (20).

35. Parts of this paper were presented in the fourth Alan Bray Memorial Lecture, London, 3 March 2007, 'Church Leadership, Ethics & the Future'. Earlier, I presented similar ideas as The Santa Clara Lecture, at the University of Santa Clara, 7 March 2006.

21

Kevin Kelly:
Establishment Man?

Nicholas Peter Harvey

Reflecting on the present predicament of his own discipline, Adam Phillips notes the anxious eagerness of psychoanalysis 'to entomb itself in definitives'.[1] This strikes me as a helpful epitome of a tendency in contemporary Catholicism in general and moral theology in particular. For instance, prevalent ecclesial hostility to legislation in favour of civil partnerships is expressed in terms of a particular understanding of marriage and family which excludes all others. Such partnerships are condemned not so much in themselves as because of what they are not: they do not fit the only authorized pattern of marital and familial relationship. This is perhaps a besetting sin of all aspirations to a timeless and transcultural orthodoxy in matters of belief and practice. Phillips writes of his discipline's 'desire for purifications, its desire to define itself by endlessly declaring what it is not'. Likewise with the Church, which, we are constantly told, is 'not a democracy'.

Just after his appointment to Westminster, Cormac Murphy-O'Connor was interviewed on TV by David Frost. To each contentious question from the usual checklist in the fields of medical and sexual ethics he gave the standard Catholic reply, following up with 'I am a man of the Church'. Here a particular set of 'definitives' have taken over. But there are other ways of being a man – or a woman – of the Church, Kevin Kelly being an outstanding example of one of these ways. He is a moral theologian who continues to consider each question on its merits. His story so far, while of interest in itself, also draws attention to a puzzling feature of Catholic life in Britain, of which more later.

It is impossible to imagine Kevin as other than a Roman Catholic. His whole life has been and is dedicated to the service of the Church, and he pays careful attention both to the pronouncements of its leaders and to the opinions of other moral theologians. Long ago he resolved neither to teach nor write any more on moral theology without keeping closely in touch with pastoral realities. He continues to honour that commitment. Any disagreement is conducted with notable moderation. He has no interest in polemics, seeking always to persuade rather than condemn. Kelly's eirenic tone and intent mark him out in a severely polarized field. Careful reading of his work nonetheless points up the trenchancy of many of his conclusions.

In a recent book review, Austen Ivereigh waspishly stereotyped Kevin Kelly as a member of 'the liberal Catholic establishment'.[2] Whether or not there is such a thing, it is inconceivable that Kevin should belong to it, or indeed to any establishment. He is sturdily independent. It is a reflection of the state of the Catholic Church in Britain that Kevin Kelly's work has neither been condemned nor taken with the seriousness it deserves. At the time of the first publication of his groundbreaking book on divorce and remarriage he found himself under the conditional and temporary protection of his archbishop, Derek Worlock, against the desire of at least one other bishop for his public condemnation. The sad thing is that this controversy did not lead to any shift in the bishops' public stance on marriage and its hazards. A recent reissue with corroboratory appendices from a range of other authoritative sources seems likewise to have fallen on deaf ears.

A similar and overtly scandalous test case is the question of condom use in prevention of the spread of HIV/AIDS. Here Kelly has provided a wonderful resource in his book, *New Directions in Sexual Ethics*. All the arguments deployed in recent years against condom use are dispassionately considered and found wanting. What is therefore strange is that the same repetitious and wearisome condemnations persist long after their inadequacy, and their seriously destructive consequences, have been exposed. Bishops still voice the opinion that condoms contribute to the spread of HIV by promoting promiscuity. It seems strange to blame an inanimate object, the condom, for human moral choices. More seriously, there is an abdication of leadership by bishops who hide behind a falsely objectified notion of 'the teaching of the Church'. The continuing marginalization of Kevin Kelly's work is a symptom of this impasse. Pope Benedict XVI's recent concession that, in some circumstances, condom use may be the lesser evil, is no more than a partial and inadequate corrective to all that has gone before.

The only defence of such episcopal attitudes that has come my way is that bishops are not in a position to disagree with the pope, or with the Curia, considered as an extension of papal authority. But how can human life and health be expendable in the interest of such a priority? Kevin Kelly's case is that, for all the remarkable work of Catholic agencies in caring for sufferers from HIV/AIDS, our Church contributes to the spread of the virus by colluding with patriarchal attitudes to women and marriage and forbidding condom use. This charge has never been answered, though the bishops of England and Wales insist in their teaching document, 'Cherishing Life', that the only safe way to avoid infection is continence. Given that this unhelpful truism is the only advice this document offers, the flight from reality is breathtaking.

Some years ago the seal of ecclesiastical approval was withdrawn from John Mahoney's book, *Bioethics and Belief*.[3] Following complaints from nameless Catholic sources, Basil Hume was prompted to act by the Vatican, and approval of the book was quietly withdrawn. At that time Mahoney would have had a credible claim to be considered the leading British moral theologian. The only significant national publicity given to this chilling sign of the times and the place was an article by Clifford Longley in *The Times*, praising what had happened as an example of the civilized English Catholic way of doing things. A very seasoned commentator, well known in other contexts for incisive and, at times, acerbic remarks, on this occasion Longley took an evasive and anodyne line.

How, I wonder, is the pursuit of truth supposed to be well served by a quiet act of censorship of this kind? Longley was right to draw attention to something characteristic of the contemporary Catholic Church in England, but wrong to regard what had happened as admirable. Not long afterwards, Mahoney, for whatever reason, refocused his considerable gifts of mind on business ethics, an area curiously uncontentious in our Church. Even in the case of Clare Richards, the Norwich schoolteacher whose censorship was much more up front, local clergy and laity in my neck of the woods seem strangely unexercised by what happened in their midst. Yet in the world of sixth-form religious instruction in Catholic schools throughout the land the Vatican's point was taken, a climate of fear prevailed, and Clare's textbook for Catholic sixth forms, now in consequence unsaleable, was pulped. I am by no means arguing that the less-than-serious approach to theology typical of contemporary British Catholicism is harmless!

This excursus touching on the censuring of Mahoney and Richards, in each case involving published work already cleared by the censor, is included here to illustrate the passive dysfunctionality of the Catholic Church in Britain in which Kevin Kelly has pursued his work as a moral theologian. Another Liverpool priest and theologian, Peter Wilkinson, used to say that Kelly wrote in such a way as to beg the Inquisition to condemn him. This remark by a friend was a tribute to Kelly's avoidance of the tortuous circumlocutions deployed so often in theology to avoid censure. Kevin Kelly remains undaunted, but the fact that he has not shared the fate of his friend Charles Curran in America has to do, at least in part, with the peculiar, limbo-like condition of British Catholicism. In honouring him we need to remember that he has continued to ply his trade in what has been described by another leading moral theologian as an 'ice age'.

This age features the annihilation of theology committed by the Polish Pope, John Paul II, and Joseph Ratzinger, with the collusion, quiet or otherwise, of many bishops and religious superiors, accompanied by widespread lay acquiescence, or at least inadvertence. I use the word 'annihilation' advisedly, to describe the ruling state of mind which says that the task of theology is to find better arguments to justify ecclesiastically predetermined conclusions. Theologians whose work does not conform to this pattern are either condemned or marginalized, leaving no scope for exploratory work. Pressing questions about the meaning and applicability of supposedly orthodox statements are left unanswered. Central to this approach is an appeal to unity which forgets that in theology unity is always an eschatological term. It is always future, so that any appeal to an achieved unity as adequate, much less as excluding other perspectives, is unacceptable. The situation of our Church, which Kevin Kelly so loves, is a parlous one as he faces retirement.

Notes

1. Adam Phillips, *Side Effects* (London: Hamish Hamilton, 2006), p. xiv.
2. Austen Ivereigh, 'Private Tributes', *The Tablet* (21 October 2006): 28.
3. John Mahoney, *Bioethics and Belief: Religion and Medicine in Dialogue* (London: Sheed & Ward, 1984).

22

From Rosaries to Rights –
Towards an Integrated Catholicism

Tina Beattie

It is a great privilege to be invited to contribute to this Festschrift for Kevin Kelly. He is somebody whose personal, intellectual and pastoral qualities combine to offer a glimpse into that most elusive and difficult-to-define enigma – the truly good person. Perhaps this is about integration as well as integrity – the integrated wholeness of the qualities which make up a rich and fruitful life.

Questions of integrity and integration concern me in this paper, because I want to ask how we might discover an integrated Catholicism – a Catholicism which allows us to worship with integrity, in spirit and in truth – through a renewed vision of the relationship between sacramentality and social justice. Since the Second Vatican Council, this relationship has fractured along conservative/liberal lines, although those terms are inadequate to describe the increasingly complex issues they involve and the fluidity of the positions they describe.

The papacy of John Paul II brought into sharp relief a crisis which had been simmering since the council. On the one hand, there were those who enthusiastically embraced the new social vision of a Church in conversation with the world, eager to be seen to embrace 'the joys and the hopes, the griefs and the anxieties of the people of this age'.[1] On the other hand, there was growing discontent among those who mourned the loss of the sacramentality and mysticism of the pre-conciliar rite in favour of what they saw as an excessively politicized process of modernization. To quote Hans Urs von Balthasar:

> What can one say of 'political theology' and of 'critical Catholicism'? They are outlines for discussion for professors of theology and anti-repressive students, but scarcely for a congregation which still consists of children, women, old men, and the sick ... May the reason for the domination of such typically male and abstract notions be because of the abandonment of the deep femininity of the Marian character of the Church?[2]

The realization that the sacramental life of the Church may have been depleted by the reforms of the council is no longer confined to conservatives, and not everybody would agree with von Balthasar that 'political theology' is necessarily in conflict with the 'Marian character of the Church'. The American feminist Charlene Spretnak criticizes post-conciliar, 'progressive' Catholics for their ongoing resistance to the mystical holiness of the Marian tradition. She cites her parents as examples of many pre-conciliar Catholics whose devotion to Mary went hand in hand with the kind of political ethos that informs post-conciliar liberal Catholicism. Spretnak describes the Catholic Church as 'a container and guardian of mysteries far greater than itself',[3] and she writes:

> When, forty years ago, the Roman Catholic Church deemphasized and banished an essential cluster of (Marian) spiritual mysteries, as well as the evocative expression of ritual and symbol that had grown around them, a profound loss ensued. Today, the theology and liturgy of the Catholic Church is less 'cluttered,' less mystical, and less comprehensive in its spiritual scope. Its tight, clear focus is far more 'rational' but far less whole. We who once partook of a vast spiritual banquet with boundaries beyond our ken are now allotted spare rations, culled by the blades of a 'rationalized' agenda more acceptable to the modern mindset.[4]

I think Spretnak speaks for many liberal-minded Catholics who share her concerns. However, if we are to reconcile those who have moved to different ends of the Catholic social and sacramental spectrum in order to bring about an integrated Catholicism, then we need to go beyond nostalgia to an informed appreciation of the risks as well as the riches of a sacramental theology, replete with nuptial and sacrificial imagery and redolent with a sublimated sexuality, in a Church which has never, in its 2,000-year history, learned to cope well with human sexuality and desire. The reason why there is an apparent stand-off between liberals and conservatives around these issues may be because the attempt under John Paul II to reinvigorate the Church's Marian life was deeply influenced – perhaps the word should be 'infected' – by von Balthasar's theology, and I think many liberal Catholics are quite properly wary of the sexual stereotypes and repressive attitudes which flow from such a theological vision. But a Church with a social conscience which is sustained through the repression of its mystical and devotional life is as dysfunctional as a Church whose devotional life is motivated by a Manichean impulse to condemn the world and all its ways through the assertion of an idealized spirituality which represses sexuality.

Psychoanalysis has taught us that the language of desire and death is deeply rooted in the human psyche, and psycholinguists such as Luce Irigaray, Julia Kristeva and Jacques Lacan have discovered in Catholic language and imagery a rich resource for the exploration of the Western unconscious and its discontents. My own study of von Balthasar's theology has led me to conclude that the poison also holds the clue to the cure: if we analyze his writings with the insights offered by psychoanalysis, we find ourselves confronted by a visceral rhetoric which transforms the lush sacramental vision of nuptial and Marian theology into a torrid sado-masochistic fantasy of sex and violence, what I would call theo-pornography.[5]

Before there can be a new sacramental awakening in the Church, we have to be willing to make a painful journey into the heart of spiritual darkness, and to recognize why our sacramental inheritance is so easily co-opted by those who use it as an instrument of control, censure and exclusion. The sacraments should never be used to police the Church, and only if we can go beyond the current climate of fear around issues such as homosexuality and the role of women, in particular, will we be able to celebrate a sacramental and liturgical life which speaks of an inclusive and open Church called to incarnate Christ's love in the world.

This is a time of *krisis* for the Church – I use the word '*krisis*' in the Greek sense, to describe a time of decision, a turning point. This means it is also a *kairos* moment, a time of particular grace which opens us to the possibility of revelation and transformation. It is a time of ambiguity and uncertainty, in which it is becoming more and more difficult to read the signs of the times, particularly during the papacy of Pope Benedict XVI. On the one hand, there are signs of a genuine opening up to a more dialogical and inclusive approach, but on the other hand there are worrying signs of an authoritarianism which is reminiscent of the Congregation for the Doctrine of the Faith under Cardinal Ratzinger. For example, Pope Benedict's willingness to enter into dialogue with Hans Küng led some of us to hope for a greater climate of intellectual freedom for Catholic theologians, but recent attempts to bring the teaching of theology in European Catholic universities more strictly under the control of Rome and the notification against Jon Sobrino in March 2007[6] suggest a move in the opposite direction. How are we to interpret such contradictory messages?

Perhaps there is a clue in Pope Benedict's first and to date only encyclical, *Deus caritas est*, which seeks to overcome centuries of suspicion by affirming the significance of bodily, erotic love for the Christian faith. The encyclical observes that '*eros* and *agape* – ascending love and descending love – can never be completely separated. The more the two, in their different aspects, find a proper unity in the one reality of love, the more the true nature of love in general is realized.'[7] But, argues Benedict, if *eros* is to find its rightful place in the Christian expression of personhood, then it must become part of 'a path of ascent, renunciation, purification and healing'.[8]

Deus caritas est is a revolutionary document in many ways, but it emerges in the context of a Church which is still riven with anxieties and fears about sexuality, particularly as far as its hierarchy is concerned. If *eros* truly is to be purified and healed, then we have to look inwards as well as outwards. We cannot simply point to a world in which people are abused and exploited through the commodification of sex and the unleashing of *eros* in an individualistic and self-gratifying culture. We also need to acknowledge that many of the problems associated with erotic love in Western culture can be traced back to the influence of Christianity, an influence that has been and continues to be malign in some contexts.

I want to spend the rest of this paper asking what this path of the purification and healing of *eros* might mean for those in the Church, and I am going to do this by focusing on von Balthasar. The general tenor of *Deus caritas est* suggests that the education and purification of *eros* is primarily to do with the expression of heterosexual desire, but a more urgent task may be to address the ways in which a celibate priesthood and a dysfunctional theology together can poison the erotic life of the Church so that it loses its sacramental capacity to nurture healthy and life-giving sexual love between its members. If we are to be a Church in which *eros* and *agape* are part of our wider vocation of *caritas* – care for the world – described in the last section of the encyclical, then we need to consider the ways in which a healthy and life-giving sacramentality nurtures the marriage between *eros* and *agape*, just as a fearful and repressive sacramentality distorts it.

We are discovering to our cost that the beauty of the pre-conciliar rite sometimes provided a miasma of mystification which masked a violent religious culture of sexual predation and abuse. There are feminist theologians who argue that Christian theology is violent through and through, from its central sadistic image of a Father–Son relationship, in which the Father takes pleasure in the Son's torture, through its long history of masochistic spirituality, misogyny and war. This verdict is one-sided and fails to do justice to the complex interweaving of sin and grace, light and shadow, in Christian history, but I do think that the widespread and uncritical reception of von Balthasar is cause for serious concern. Taking von Balthasar's popularity as symptomatic of a malaise which continues to afflict the development of Catholic spirituality, I suggest that the purification and healing of *eros* entails nothing less than the transformation of the Catholic theo-sexual psyche. To this end, a discerning theological engagement with the insights of psychoanalysis might contribute to the cultivation of a sacramental spirituality capable of nurturing a life of social justice and sexual wholeness, whether that takes the form of celibacy, marriage or other forms of faithful and holy sexual love.

Psychoanalysis involves an intimate stripping away of our public *personae* – the morally responsible, self-controlled individuals whom we seek to present to the world in our public roles and social relationships. It probes the soft underbelly of language and desire, where we discover ourselves to be vulnerable, alienated beings at the mercy of psychological forces which we do not entirely control, and which are largely focused around issues of sexuality, violence, death and bodiliness. The therapeutic process involves a journey into the heart of our own darkness, in order to recognize and learn from the hidden dimensions of the self and the not-self which we discover there. The unconscious is, suggests Lacan, closely associated with mysticism as the articulation of an absence that is both God and the Mother.[9] For Kristeva, the unconscious is where meaning becomes incarnate in the encounter between the body's impulses and the language of desire, a space of thunder and revelation, of love and horror, a space where new life emerges from the silence of abjection and dread.[10]

Kristeva argues that the post-Enlightenment man of reason derives his identity and values from the repression of this otherness that we discover within ourselves, and its projection on to others – women, non-Western races and cultures and, I would add today, religion, for the secular individual, incarnate in figures such as Richard Dawkins, increasingly derives his or her identity from the demonization of the religious other.[11] For Kristeva, it is through exploring and embracing our interior sense of otherness and alienation that we might learn to go beyond constructs of masculinity and femininity, identity and otherness, which structure the modern subject, to a new appreciation of the subject in the process of becoming, the multiple subject whose identity might better be understood in maternal metaphors of the body pregnant with and capable of giving birth to the vulnerable and dependent other, than in the metaphors of isolated and autonomous masculinity.[12] Catholicism, argues Kristeva, has sublimated rather than repressed the maternal other associated with bodiliness and desire, but it is in a move beyond both sublimation and repression to an integrated wholeness of being – paradoxically discovered in the embrace of difference, otherness, mourning and desire – that we might discover the transformation of both ethics and *eros*.

The Catholic tradition has been reluctant to affirm fully the potential of human sexuality to act as an expression of the life of Christ in a way which cannot be reduced to the procreative function alone – important though that is. But it has also found its richest expression in a sacramental life which is redolent with an eroticized sensuality shimmering beneath the surface of our liturgies and devotions, so that a sublimated and highly seductive sexuality plays through the texts and practices of Roman Catholicism. This gives rise to a double movement, perhaps particularly within a celibate priesthood which stands at the very heart of this fusion of *eros* and *agape*. On the one hand, it requires a stifling of the desire and yearning of the sexual being. On the other hand, it requires an appropriation of the language of erotic desire to describe the yearning of the celibate man for God – a yearning which has since the Middle Ages often been described in feminized language. But this double movement of desire and denial produces a fear of the seductive power of the bodily, sexual other – the otherness of one's own sexual body and the sexuality of the bodily other. This fear in turn produces violence turned in on the self in masochistic acts of mortification, and turned on the other in sadistic acts of condemnation, degradation and exclusion. The sexual other thus becomes the target of a furious and often futile denial of the body's vulnerability and desire.

Consider, for example, the case of Richard Rolle, a fourteenth-century English hermit. Borrowing the language of the Song of Songs, Rolle writes:

> The more I am raised above earthly thoughts the more fully do I enjoy the pleasure I long for; the more carnal longings are banished, so much the more truly do the eternal ones flare up. Let [Christ] kiss me and refresh me with his sweet love; let him hold me tight and kiss me on the mouth, else I die; let him pour his grace into me, that I may grow in love.[13]

But this eroticized relationship between the celibate male and Christ is premised upon the avoidance of women since, to quote Rolle again:

> A man who honestly wants to love Christ must not let his imagination toy with the love of women ... Loving women upsets the balance, disturbs the reason, changes wisdom to folly, estranges the heart from God, takes the soul captive, and subjects it to demons! ... Womanly beauty leads many astray. Desire for it can sometimes subvert even righteous hearts, so that what began in spirit ends up in flesh.[14]

'What began in spirit ends up in flesh': is that not what the doctrine of the incarnation is about? And what happens to the sacramental imagination when it both seduces and refuses desire at the same time? Let me consider that question by turning to von Balthasar and his growing influence on Catholic theology and spirituality – and here I use 'Catholic' in a broad sense, to encompass a movement that is wider than Roman Catholicism.

There seem to be two main responses to von Balthasar: there are those who have dipped into him just enough to be put off for life, and there are those who regard him as the greatest theologian of the modern Church. His influence extends far beyond conservative Roman Catholicism. He is the theologian of choice in many seminaries so that his ideas are having a formative influence on the next generation of priests, and he is also highly regarded among some Anglican thinkers, including those associated with the Radical-Orthodoxy movement.

I am not going to offer a survey of von Balthasar's thought here. I am simply going to pick out a few quotations to illustrate what I mean when I say that this is a misogynistic theology which feeds on sado-masochistic fantasies, stimulated and sustained by the dysfunctional relationship between von Balthasar and his mystic/hysteric soulmate, Adrienne von Speyr. Johann Roten is one of a number of theologians who insist on the inseparable connection between von Balthasar's life and work, describing his thinking and writing as 'a theological biography, where it would be impossible to separate the spiritual from the theological, the existential from the intellectual'.[15] Roten writes:

> If feminist concerns are not merely a matter of hierarchic functional uniformity, then the example of Hans Urs von Balthasar and Adrienne von Speyr could be a challenging illustration – not necessarily to be copied as such! – of the best possibilities the Church has to offer to men and women, granted that both be shaped and permeated by the common fundamental Marian personality structure.[16]

Those who admire von Balthasar cite several features of his work which I want to pick up on here: his understanding of kenosis, his interpretation of Christ's descent into Hell on Holy Saturday, and his theology of sexuality. I must stress that my task in the limited space available here is that of briefly calling into question von Balthasar's rhetoric, not of presenting his theology per se. So let me begin with a quotation from an early work, *Heart of the World*, written soon after meeting von Speyr, when von Balthasar writes about kenosis in the context of a nuptial ecclesiology. Here, in a chapter titled 'Conquest of the Bride', Christ addresses the Church:

> I, the strong God, have betrayed myself to you – my Body, my Church ... this simmering darkness, opposed to the Father's light ... I dared to enter the body of my Church, the deadly body which *you* are ... No wonder you realized your advantage over me and took my nakedness by storm! But I have defeated you through weakness and my Spirit has overpowered my unruly and recalcitrant flesh. (Never has woman made more desperate resistance!) ... Our wrecked covenant – our blood-wedding, the red wedding of the Lamb – is already, here and now, the white bridal bed of divine love.[17]

Kenosis, then, is the final overwhelming of a strong, masculine God by the seductions of the sexual female flesh. Christ enters that flesh as an act of marital rape. I do not need to spell out the implications for ecclesiology, Christology and the theology of marriage.

I often quote that passage because for me it effectively sums up why von Balthasar's theology is so poisonous for the spirituality of *eros* and for the representation of women in the Church. However, I have been asked if I risk taking passages out of context – particularly since this is an early and immature work. My own reading of von Balthasar leads me to conclude that this dynamic of sexual violence is a persistent theme running through his theology, and once one becomes attentive to it, it becomes almost inescapable. To give more examples, let me turn to his account of Christ's descent into Hell.

On Holy Saturday, von Balthasar sees 'the idea of a *struggle* between the divinity which descends into the underworld, and the power hostile to God which is vanquished there and must yield up either the menaced or imprisoned divinity itself, or some other prey'.[18] What is this power that is hostile to God; that imprisons God and must be vanquished, so that, in the resurrection, 'a voracious power is obliged to recognize its impotence to hold its prey'?[19] Von Balthasar argues that, in Hell, Christ enters 'the second "chaos"', 'the pure substantiality of "Hell" which is "sin in itself"'.[20] He goes on to search for images that might express something of the nature of this Hell that is the very substance of sin. He refers to 'mud', 'ordure', 'leprosy', 'phlegm' and, in apocalyptic imagery, to 'the great harlot of Babylon, as quintessence of the sin of the world' which is burned up in fire and smoke.[21] I am not going to inflict that whole ugly passage on readers, but we should note that, in von Balthasar's imagery, the incarnation is God being overwhelmed by the sexual female flesh, and the resurrection is the final burning up of the harlot body which held the dead Christ imprisoned. Elsewhere, he describes the Word coming from the Father into 'a menacing void, a chasm fitted with teeth. The light came into the darkness, but the darkness had no eye for the light: it had only jaws'.[22] The raped bride, the incinerated harlot, the *vagina dentata* – kenosis, Holy Saturday and sexuality – these are the great insights which von Balthasar offers to the modern Church, a daily diet of misogyny and violence on which our young seminarians are now being fed.

But of course, ask any theologian worth his salt, and he will say that I am reading von Balthasar too selectively. Yes, there are times when his choice of rhetoric is a little unfortunate, but every theologian slips up occasionally. The fact that he is occasionally a little over the top in his sexual imagery does not mean we should write him off altogether.

Since publishing *New Catholic Feminism*, it is interesting how much feedback I have received from women who have had a similar reaction to mine when reading von Balthasar, but who have felt unable to admit to this because of his great influence on contemporary Catholicism. But one of the more disturbing aspects of this whole experience has been the uncritical engagement of so many theologians with von Balthasar's work, which has led me to wonder how some of the finest theological minds in the modern Church are so anaesthetized to his pervasive rhetoric of sexual violence and misogyny. Perhaps the most startling example of this blindness is a paper by Aristotle Papanikolaou published in *Modern Theology*, in which he argues that, in situations of sexual abuse and violence against women, von Balthasar's 'understanding of *kenotic* personhood is the most adequate way to account for the healing of abused victims'.[23] It is hard to square this with my own reading of von Balthasar, which at times felt like being exposed to rhetorical acts of sexual abuse.

Those who translate and write about von Balthasar are mostly male theologians, but he has a growing following among women as well. They are developing what they call 'new Catholic feminism', based on Pope John Paul II's call for women to discover a new feminism which would celebrate feminine genius rather than modelling itself on aggressive patterns of masculinity.[24] The new Catholic feminists offer an uncritical affirmation of the theologies of both John Paul II and von Balthasar, and they are deeply antagonistic towards other feminisms on issues of sexual and reproductive rights, being anti-contraception, anti-abortion and anti-homosexuality.

229

I am suggesting that, when one reads von Balthasar from a psychoanalytic perspective such as that offered by some French feminist theorists, the violent sexual desires which shadow his theological language come into sharp relief. There are quite astonishing resonances between the psychoanalytic language of writers such as Kristeva and Irigaray, and von Balthasar's theological prose. The difference is, Kristeva and Irigaray are deliberately crafting their language to give an insight into the disturbed sexual psyche and its hauntings and seductions, whereas von Balthasar and his readers seem deadly serious in taking these as manifestations of theology of the highest order. But to read von Balthasar's nuptial theology in conversation with Irigaray's psycholinguistic theory of sexual difference, or to read his account of Christ in Hell in conversation with Kristeva's description of abjection and psychosis, is to discover that, in von Balthasar, as perhaps nowhere else, do we see the unveiling of the unconscious of Catholic sacramental theology.

This is a wounded psyche which needs to be healed. The fact that it resonates deeply with many in the Church is not evidence of its theological truth. It is rather evidence of the extent to which feminists are right when they point to the unacknowledged violence which continues to shape the theological enterprise. Von Balthasar's widespread popularity in some theological circles suggests that theology still has within it a proclivity to violence which too easily cultivates a spirituality of repression, misogyny and sado-masochistic desire.

Let me finish by bringing this paper into conversation with Jim Keenan's paper in this volume, 'Church Leadership, Ethics and the Moral Rights of Priests', in which Keenan points to the lack of ethics in the sexual-abuse crisis, both in the predatory behaviour of the priests themselves and in the response of the bishops. While organizations and businesses are now aware of the need for professional ethics, Keenan argues that the Church's practices are too seldom informed by ethical insight. He goes on to argue that recognizing the moral rights of priests is part and parcel of developing an ethically informed Church, and he includes among those rights the right to personal development.

I am suggesting that the formation of priests requires an ethical concern for the psychosexual well-being of priests, not only in helping them to live out their vocation to celibacy in an expressive rather than a repressive way, but so that they do not inflict their own unresolved sexual issues on those for whom they have pastoral responsibility, either through abusive relationships or through the cultivation of an excessively rigid sexual morality. If we want to see a healthy integration between sacramentality and ethics, uniting spirituality, sexuality and social justice, then we need to go beyond a Church with dark secrets and unacknowledged desires, a Church where the mysticism of the liturgy unleashes a cauldron of unconscious fears and fantasies, a Church where too many of our priests become sexual predators because they have never been given the insight they need with regard to understanding their own desires. Von Balthasar would in my opinion be an ideal choice for the sex education of priests if he were read against the grain – as an example of what can go wrong when these questions are not addressed in a spirit of honesty and self-awareness. But when his theology becomes the narrative which shapes our understanding of priesthood, personhood, gender and God, then I am afraid for the Church and for the next generation of priests.

Questions of sexual rights are among the most challenging facing the Church today. On issues of social and economic justice, the Catholic Church is living out her mission to the poor in a radical way. The Church's social teaching champions the cause of human rights and, since the collapse of Communism, offers the only sustained and coherent critique of global capitalism and its consequences. But an integrated Catholicism requires no less courage in the face of the new sexual and psychological questions facing humankind at the beginning of the twenty-first century. Christ brings life incarnate to our desire. He offers us *eros* without *thanatos*, desire without death. We achieve that, not by aspiring to 'supra-sex' (to use von Balthasar's expression)[25] above and beyond the body's vulnerabilities and yearnings, but by learning to express our sexuality in relationships focused on the delight of the beloved other. A sexuality which is truly a giving of self is an abundant, bodily, creative love, an expression not of sacrifice but of incarnation.

Having given readers a taste of some of what I am suggesting is the distortion of *eros* in the Catholic spiritual tradition, let me end with a passage which celebrates *eros* in a far less violent way, offering us not marital rape but a delightful secret encounter between lovers. The following meditation on the Song of Songs is by the thirteenth-century beguine, Mechthild of Magdeburg. She imagines her soul going into the bedroom of Christ the bridegroom, and this is the conversation that follows:

'Stay, Lady Soul.'
'What do you bid me, Lord?'
'Take off your clothes.'
'Lord, what will happen to me then?'
'Lady Soul, you are so utterly formed to my nature
That not the slightest thing can be between you and me.'

Then she says to him:

'Lord, now I am a naked soul
And you in yourself are a well-adorned God.
Our shared lot is eternal life
Without death.'
Then a blessed stillness
That both desire comes over them.
He surrenders himself to her,
And she surrenders herself to him.
What happens to her then – she knows –
And that is fine with me.
But this cannot last long.
When two lovers meet secretly,
They must often part from one another inseparable.[26]

Mechthild knew the risk of speaking about God like this. She knew that she risked being burned at the stake, but in prayer God told her, 'My dear One, do not be overly troubled. No one can burn the truth.'

231

Notes

1. Pastoral Constitution on the Church in the Modern World, *Gaudium et spes* (Vatican II, 1965), 1: on the Vatican website <http://www.vatican.va/archive/hist_councils/ii_vatican_council/documents/vat-ii_cons_19651207_gaudium-et-spes_en.html> (accessed 29 May 2007).
2. Hans Urs von Balthasar, *Elucidations* (trans. John Riches), (London: SPCK, 1975), p. 70. It is interesting that von Balthasar groups women with children, old men and the sick, over and against professors of theology: professors of theology include an abundance of old men and even a few women.
3. Charlene Spretnak, *Missing Mary: The Queen of Heaven and Her Re-Emergence in the Modern Church* (New York and Basingstoke: Palgrave Macmillan, 2004), p. 3.
4. *Ibid.*, p. 4.
5. In this paper I am summarizing ideas which are developed more fully in my book, *New Catholic Feminism: Theology and Theory* (London and New York: Routledge, 2006).
6. For the text of the notification see the Vatican website <http://212.77.1.245/news_services/bulletin/news/19850.php?index=19850&lang=it#TRADUZIONE%20IN%20LINGUA%20INGLESE> (last accessed 31 May 2007).
7. Pope Benedict XVI, Encyclical letter *Deus caritas est* (2005), 7: on the Vatican website <http://www.vatican.va/holy_father/benedict_xvi/encyclicals/documents/hf_ben-xvi_enc_20051225_deus-caritas-est_en.html> (accessed 29 May 2007).
8. *Ibid.*, 5.
9. Cf. Jacques Lacan, 'God and the *Jouissance* of/The Woman', in Juliet Mitchell and Jacqueline Rose (eds), *Feminine Sexuality: Jacques Lacan and the école freudienne* (Basingstoke and London: Macmillan Press, 1982), pp. 138–48.
10. Cf. Julia Kristeva, *Powers of Horror: An Essay on Abjection* (trans. Leon S. Roudiez), (New York: Columbia University Press, 1982) and Julia Kristeva, *Tales of Love* (trans. Leon S. Roudiez), (New York: Columbia University Press, 1987).
11. See Julia Kristeva, *Strangers to Ourselves* (trans. Leon S. Roudiez), (Hemel Hempstead: Harvester, 1991). For a discussion of religion as the 'other' of militant atheism, see Time Beattie, *The New Atheists: The Twilight of Reason and the War on Religion* (London: Darton, Longman and Todd, 2007).
12. See Julia Kristeva, '*Stabat Mater*', in *Tales of Love*, pp. 234–63.
13. Richard Rolle, *The Fire of Love* (trans. Clifton Wolters), (London: Penguin Books, 1972), p. 125.
14. *Ibid.*, p. 136.
15. Johann Roten, SM, 'The Two Halves of the Moon: Marian Anthropological Dimensions in the Common Mission of Adrienne von Speyr and Hans Urs von Balthasar', in David L. Schindler (ed.), *Hans Urs von Balthasar: His Life and Work* (San Francisco: Communio Books, Ignatius Press, 1991), pp. 65–86 (83).
16. *Ibid.*, pp. 85–86.
17. Hans Urs von Balthasar, *Heart of the World* (trans. Erasmo S. Leiva), (San Francisco: Ignatius Press, 1979), pp. 194–97.
18. Hans Urs von Balthasar, *Mysterium Paschale: The Mystery of Easter* (trans. Aidan Nichols OP), (Edinburgh: T&T Clark, 1990), p. 151.

19. *Ibid.*
20. *Ibid.*, p. 173.
21. *Ibid.*, pp. 173–74.
22. *Ibid.*, p. 39.
23. Aristotle Papanikolaou, 'Person, Kenosis and Abuse: Hans Urs von Balthasar and Feminist Theologies in Conversation', *Modern Theology* 19 (2003): 41–65 (42).
24. See the essays in Michele Schumacher (ed.), *Women in Christ: Toward a New Feminism* (Grand Rapids, MI and Cambridge: William B. Eerdmans Publishing Co., 2004).
25. The concept of supra-sexuality recurs in von Balthasar's writings. It refers to the eschatological dimension of sexuality symbolized by the relationship between Mary the bride and Christ the bridegroom, and finding its most perfect earthly manifestation in the virginal life of the celibate. Cf. Hans Urs von Balthasar, *Theo-Drama III: The Dramatis Personae: The Person in Christ* (trans. Graham Harrison), (San Francisco: Ignatius Press, 1992), pp. 325–27.
26. Mechthild of Magdeborg, *The Flowing Light of the Godhead* (trans. Frank Tobin), (The Classics of Western Spirituality, Mahwah: Paulist Press, 1997), p. 62.

Part Five

Kevin Kelly and the Interface of Moral and Pastoral Theology

23

Compassion as the Fundamental Basis of Morality

Gerard Mannion

On Bracketing 'Kelly's Heroes'

Rather forcefully, well for him at least, Kevin Kelly once admonished Liverpool Hope University for having listed him amongst its research groups in philosophy and ecclesiology. Kelly told me he was 'definitely *not* a philosopher' and 'neither, for that matter', did he consider himself to be an ecclesiologist. I would not dare disagree with Kelly's own assessment – for it is well known, as other contributions to this Festschrift have made very clear, that Kelly is a pastor/moral theologian. And although ethics, very often understood to be a branch of philosophy, preoccupies so much of Kelly's thinking, writing and acting, he is equally insistent that he is someone who approaches moral dilemmas from a *theological* standpoint. Theology – discourse about God – informs Kelly's ethical thinking and his assessment of what is the best course of action in a given situation.

However, I do wish to try and demonstrate that Kevin Kelly is, *de facto*, very much a *metaphysician*, that is, someone who ponders the fundamental questions and meaning behind our existence and what might lie 'behind' that existence or as the first principles for that existence. And, if I can show that he is a metaphysician, given how blurred the borderlands between philosophy and theology actually are, particularly in the Roman Catholic tradition, then we may yet get Kelly to yield a little and consider that his work at least has genuine philosophical relevance. Furthermore, given the approach I wish to take in illustrating the latter, we may even get Kelly to concede that he may very well be an 'anonymous' ecclesiologist.

How on Earth, I can hear Kelly asking, scratching his head as he does, can I demonstrate either of these positions? I will start with my conclusion and work backwards, borrowing a little natural theological methodology. Elsewhere in this Festschrift, John Elford states that *compassion* is the *key* to Kelly's moral theology, and I could not agree more. Kelly's firm commitment to the priority of compassion actually betrays a great deal about his understanding of the world we live in, indeed of reality itself. Compassion informs and shapes Kelly's understanding of being.

237

And his understanding of being, his ontology, is very much a *social* ontology. We are called to be persons-in-community. This, in turn, informs how Kelly believes we should exist together in communities, the Church being one very obvious and prominent means of striving to exist-in-community in a virtuous, particularly a *compassionate* manner.

Why? Because Kelly is obviously premising his ethics, as well as his social ontology, upon the fact that the ground of our existence, what Christians call God, is essentially a perfect and compassionate (here offering a further explanatory dimension of the term *perichoresis*) community of persons, a community of love. God calls us to mirror that community of love in our own social existence.

Thus Kelly is quite right in one sense: the Christian doctrine of God, that is, a *theological* basis, is his starting point. But that entails profound metaphysical statements, and the ethics and social ontology that proceed from his starting point obviously feed into serious debates that preoccupy both contemporary philosophy and contemporary theology. Consider the biblical sayings: 'Be compassionate as your Father in heaven is compassionate' (Lk. 6.36) and 'the Lord is compassion and love' (Ps. 103.8). The Father *is* compassionate, the Lord *is* compassion and love. Kelly's theology makes a profound claim about the nature and essence of the ground of existence, namely that the ground of existence *is* compassion and love. That is why *we* should be compassionate and loving towards one another. That is why we should strive to live as harmoniously in community as is humanly possible for such fallible creatures. That is why the mode of social being that we call Church is important (alongside other religious as well as non-religious forms of social ontology): the Church helps us strive to respond positively to the self-communication, that is, to use a technical theological term that would scare off many philosophers, the *revelation* of that ground of being who *is* compassion and love, that which Christians call God. Compassion has transcendental implications.

Let us explore not simply the parameters of what it entails to say that the ground of being *is* compassion and love, but let us also look at the sort of company that Kelly is keeping. One could point to countless examples of compassion as a leading theme in the Christian tradition, but here we are seeking to offer a philosophical argument first, before moving on to an ecclesiological one, so I shall choose some examples, initially, from outside the Christian tradition. For, although I am going to try and demonstrate that Kelly is more of a philosopher and ecclesiologist than he lets on, one might also thereby see that, in primarily understanding the nature of the ground of being as compassion and love, he actually rubs close shoulders with Buddhists, Jains, with particular branches of Islam, Judaism and Hinduism and even with so-called pessimistic philosophers disillusioned with the positivistic myth of progression that prevailed in the first half of the nineteenth century.

In order to take forward this contention about Kelly and philosophy, I will thus focus in the main on the latter. I will also mention at least one worldview that is antithetical to such a metaphysics in general and metaphysics of morals in particular. In the final analysis, I shall show that, in taking the starting point that he does, Kelly shares close affinities with another great Christian theologian of the twentieth century: and as that other theologian could very much be considered both a philosopher and an ecclesiologist, why not Kelly too? Furthermore, parallels with one of the Church's most compassionate souls of all will further support our conclusions. Indeed, I hope it will be seen that, in relation to his focus upon compassion, Kelly is, literally, very much a 'man of the world' as opposed to his typically humble delimiting of his expertise to being that remit of pastor/moral theologian.

The Metaphysical and Transcendental Significance of Compassion

First of all, let us explore what we actually mean by compassion. Compassion is often equated with, or at least closely associated with, the terms 'sympathy' and 'pity'. Compassion has a long history as a theme in the various philosophies and theologies of human history. In the modern era, two philosophers who focused in particular upon compassion/sympathy were Arthur Schopenhauer and Max Scheler. The modern philosopher who offered the sternest critique of compassion was Friedrich Nietzsche.

You will note that all three of the above-mentioned people are German. The Germans do not have such a problem with different words such as 'compassion', 'sympathy' and 'pity'. They usually employ the same word to signify the three meanings that we attach to these respective words in English. That word is *Mitleid*, literally 'suffering-with'. In his insightful analysis of the difficulty of translating the term *Mitleid* into English, David Cartwright has noted that the three words most frequently used – that is, 'compassion', 'sympathy' and pity' – are *not* synonymous, and, therefore, a misleading impression can be given if the wrong word is used in translation. Cartwright argues that the three words entail emotions which are considerably different in their moral significance. Hence 'sympathy' is not appropriate to translate Arthur Schopenhauer's idea of *Mitleid* because sympathy can also be a fellow-feeling with another's joy (akin to the German *Mitfreude*), whereas Schopenhauer's concept does not share such an affinity. Cartwright believes 'pity' focuses upon the suffering of another but actually implies superiority over the one who is pitied – it can be an expression of contempt and can enhance the pitier's own self-esteem, thereby introducing egoistic motives which are forbidden in Schopenhauer's basis for ethics.

Therefore, Cartwright settles upon 'compassion' as the most appropriate translation for the sense in which Schopenhauer employs *Mitleid* because the primary concern of an agent moved by compassion is the well-being of another. The agent adopts the interests of another as if they were the agent's own and, even if the agent enjoys helping the other, that is not the main motive behind the action but rather a side effect.[1]

Let us now turn to explore how, in delving into the nature of compassion or sympathy, we actually are brought into the realm of metaphysics and, indeed, there confronted with questions that touch upon the heart of *theological* enquiry. Such an interpretation was certainly offered by the earlier Max Scheler (who influenced the intellectually formative years of the Polish Pope, John Paul II). In his classic study, *The Nature of Sympathy*, Scheler suggests that:

> [Sympathy (or compassion or fellow-feeling)] necessarily requires an intelligence transcending all finite persons, to ordain this object and destiny; an intelligence which, in bringing persons into existence, at the same time conceives their individual diversities of character according to a pattern; if so, pure fellow-feeling, by the very fact of being inexplicable in genetic or associate terms, lends support to the conclusion that all persons intrinsically

capable of sharing in this feeling have one and the same creator. If fellow-feeling has a metaphysical meaning then it is that, in contrast to identification and infection which are also found in the animal kingdom, it points, not to pantheism or monism, but to a *theistic* metaphysics of ultimate reality.[2]

Arthur Schopenhauer proclaimed as the supreme ethical principle the following: *Neminem laede, imo omnes, quantum potes, juva*: 'Injure no one; on the contrary, help everyone as much as you can.'[3] On the subject of compassion (*Mitleid*) Scheler praised Schopenhauer in part, but criticized him in the main (not least of all because of what Scheler perceived to be an overtly monistic metaphysics and lack of theological attention). But I believe Scheler here perhaps did him a great disservice, and at least Schopenhauer maintained consistency on this topic, something which Scheler, alas, did not. But let us not dwell too long on this here as I have considered this debate at length elsewhere.[4]

Indeed Schopenhauer has described as 'Christianity's greatest merit' the theoretical identification and formulation as a virtue of philanthropy, loving-kindness, *caritas, agape* (all of which he equates).[5] For not even Plato, he tells us, proceeded thus far, getting 'only as far as voluntary, disinterested justice'.[6] It is the 'entire ethical content' of the New Testament, the virtue (following Paul) that contains all others.[7] But Schopenhauer only gives credit to Christianity here as far as Europe is concerned. 'For in Asia a thousand years earlier the boundless love of one's neighbour had been the subject of theory and precept as well as of practice, in the Veda and Dharma-Sastra, Itihasa and Purana, as well as the teaching of the Buddha Sakya-Muni, never weary of preaching it.'[8]

The true origin of such philanthropy, loving kindness, *caritas, agape*, etc., and hence of true justice, that 'first and fundamentally essential cardinal virtue',[9] Schopenhauer tells us, lies in *compassion* itself. Elsewhere, he declares that 'All love (ἀγάπη, *caritas*) is compassion or sympathy.'[10] It is through compassion that the *suffering* of another becomes my motivation for positive action towards helping that other at no gain to and perhaps at considerable cost to myself.[11] Schopenhauer sees something mystical in this, a direct participation in the being (here the suffering) of another. I and the suffering thou are united by compassion:

> The barrier between the ego and non-ego is for the moment abolished; only then do the other man's affairs, his need, distress, and suffering directly become my own. I no longer look at him as if he were something given to me by empirical intuitive perception, as something strange and foreign, as a matter of indifference, as something entirely different from me.[12]

Rather, in a manner beyond reason, I suffer *in* that other's person. The 'greatest lack of compassion' is what defines an act's depth of 'moral depravity and atrocity'.[13] Hence, for Schopenhauer, compassion is the one and the only source of truly disinterested actions. It is, therefore, the basis, the foundation of morality,[14] and it points to a metaphysical understanding of morality at that.

On the other hand, Friedrich Nietzsche tells us that compassion (*Mitleid*) is a pernicious thing to be shunned at all costs. Nietzsche was one of the foremost critics of Schopenhauer's idea of *Mitleid* and, indeed, of compassion in general.[15] His *Human All Too Human* was in many ways an attack upon Schopenhauer's ethics in its entirety.[16]

On the whole, Nietzsche believes Schopenhauer's *Mitleids-Moral*, his ethic of compassion, owing much to the Christian tradition of what is rendered in German as *Mitleid*, along with aspects of Buddhist thought, tends towards a negative evaluation and eventual rejection of human nature and even the world itself: a 'denial of life'.[17]

Nonetheless, as I have sought to argue elsewhere, at the heart of the criticisms of those who reject Schopenhauer's understanding of compassion as the basis of morality lies either a fundamental misunderstanding of his metaphysical thinking or, indeed, a failure either to engage with or to appreciate the full metaphysical significance of ethics itself.

Of course, Schopenhauer's ethical writings are far from being unproblematic. At times, despite their dependence upon his metaphysics, the ethical writings seem to contradict other aspects of the metaphysics and, along with Schopenhauer's doctrine of salvation, his ethics implies a more positive worldview than that with which he is often credited.[18] I wish to argue that this is due to the mystical and even, one might say, 'religious' character of some of Schopenhauer's writings in this sphere. Indeed, I suggest that Schopenhauer's ethics owes much to his researches into the various world religions, despite the fact that the early sections of his metaphysics of the will appear to challenge fundamental religious doctrines. Confirmation of the religious element in Schopenhauerian ethics may be afforded by Nietzsche, himself the one-time disciple of Schopenhauer, who turned against his 'educator' nowhere more virulently than in relation to ethics. Schopenhauer's essay *On Ethics* contains the following statement:

> That the world has only a physical and not a moral significance is a fundamental error, one that is the greatest and most pernicious, the real *perversity* of mind. At bottom, it is that which faith has personified as antichrist. Nevertheless, and in spite of all religions which one and all assert the contrary and try to establish this in their own mythical way, that fundamental error never dies out entirely, but from time to time raises its head afresh until universal indignation forces it once more to conceal itself.[19]

Yet Nietzsche was happy to embrace this title of *The Antichrist* in his work of the same name, along with the attendant worldview which Schopenhauer condemns in the above quotation. Not only does he rail against Schopenhauer's ethics per se, but he also criticizes Schopenhauer's affinity to Christian morals. In particular, Nietzsche's 'enemy' is the theological mindset which he believes has corrupted much of German philosophy. 'I make war on this theologian instinct: I have found traces of it everywhere. Whoever has theologian blood in his veins has a wrong and dishonest attitude towards all things from the very first'.[20] Thus compassion is not universally lauded as a good thing; for those such as Nietzsche, such loving-kindness towards our neighbour is not simply founded upon a delusional metaphysical or religious foundation, it is a debilitating and debasing virtue altogether.

Kevin Kelly on Compassion, Ethics and Ecclesiology

I wish to offer not simply Schopenhauer, but also Kevin Kelly, amongst others, as examples of those whose work can resist the arguments of Nietzsche and those other forces in our contemporary times that would seek to demean or indeed to constrict the empowering energy that compassion constitutes. For compassion forms the basis of an ethic that transcends faith and so can help inform a truly global ethic, and one that is attentive to context, being neither consequentialistic nor deontological in character. Given how central it has been to the traditions of so many belief systems, compassion, furthermore, allows religious belief and practice to continue to *inform* ethics in a postmodern world – whether in a context that is religious or secular.

Compassion encapsulates – indeed epitomizes – Kevin Kelly's work. If we are right to perceive compassion as the basis of morality, then it must also be the starting point for method in moral theology. If one reads through the works of Kevin Kelly, I think his attention to the experiences of 'ordinary people', particularly those, as the cover of the revised edition of his *Divorce and Second Marriage* states, who are marginalized by society or, indeed, by the Church, is in fact another way of saying that compassion is the starting point for moral theology. Let us consider a few examples.

Even in his very first book, a study of conscience with reference to Anglican moral theologians of the seventeenth century,[21] we already see an openness and ecumenical sensitivity displayed, along with a readiness to think 'outside the box' of the assumed modus operandi of Catholic moral theology that had been prevalent when Kelly pursued the doctoral studies that eventually found fruit in that volume. He hints already at the need for a tradition that is dynamic and attentive to the need for growth, development and even change. Already the seeds of a moral theology grounded in compassion are shown in his statements here about the fundamental nature of conscience, sin and indeed moral theology itself.

Thus, his *Divorce and Second Marriage* calls for the Roman Catholic Church to look again at the thorny issues of marriage, indissolubility and second marriage after divorce. Kelly commends a much more sympathetic understanding of the struggles and heartbreak involved in the breakdown of relationships, as well as of the joyous and grace-filled experiences to be enjoyed in second marriages. In particular, he calls for a major reconsideration of the sacramental provision offered to people in various relationship situations that previously have led to the Roman Catholic Church considering their situation to be irregular and/or sinful. So, for example, in reflecting upon the 1980 Synod on Marriage and the Family, Kelly suggests that, instead of the more prescriptive line of some synod documentation and the eventual apostolic exhortation that emerged from it (*Familiaris consortio*),[22] we should remember the Sabbath is made for people and not vice versa. 'If we are going to err in any direction, it seems to me that it is more in line with the climate of the Synod to err in the direction of pastoral openness towards persons seeking healing for the wounds of marriage breakdown.'[23]

In his *From a Parish Base*, Kelly speaks of how Vatican II allowed priests to move from being stern judges to being 'compassionate confessors' attentive to the realities of day-to-day struggles. Kelly there urges them to go further still and be yet more compassionate by not focusing upon people's sins primarily *at all*; instead pastors should look to the gifts and achievements in the ordinary lives of people.[24]

Only through such an approach can we understand that pastoral theology will obviously explore matters pertaining to morality and must do so compassionately but so, also, must moral theology be pastorally oriented and sensitive to moral growth and particular contexts. The parable of the wheat and darnel forms the basis for his reflection here. 'Sometimes what might look like a puny and undeveloped plant might, in fact, be a miracle of growth, given the adverse conditions under which it has had to struggle'.[25]

Indeed, in that same work, Kelly shows how the notion of 'sin' can actually be employed in a positive way, pointing towards the compassion of God that *is* the love of God. Indeed, Kelly suggests that those Christians who condemn, for example, people who are living in a second marriage, or couples utilizing artificial contraception, or those who are in 'life-giving' same-sex relationships, because they contradict the teachings of the Church, are missing the point entirely:

> In reality, what scandalizes many people outside the church, as well as within, is the fact that a church of sinners which professes belief in a God of forgiveness and compassion seems to condemn groups of people for whom most in our society would feel great compassion.[26]

People look less to the Church for clear moral principles, Kelly argues. Instead:

> [They look to the Church] for compassion and understanding and the assurance that they are not alone in their pain and in their suffering – and that there are grounds for real hope for them. Jesus heard the cry of people's suffering and pain. He was angered by the insensitivity of the religious leaders of his day and wept over their hardness of heart. If we are to share his outraged anger, we must not rest satisfied with living on the surface. We too must try to go to the roots of the evils causing pain in our society today.[27]

A realization of our own human limitations, including that of priests and religious leaders, Kelly argues, can actually teach us how to be more sensitive and compassionate. These are themes that one also finds throughout the pages of his *New Directions in Moral Theology: The Challenge of Being Human*,[28] a book that opens with typically self-effacing humility on Kelly's part and yet which goes on to deliver penetrating insights into the difficulties facing contemporary Catholics, and to offer profoundly constructive suggestions for how moral theology might better aid people in facing such challenges. Again, Kelly seeks to commend the Church to move away from an authoritarian emphasis upon norms and precepts and condemnations of sin, towards being a more responsive and humane Church. Such a response offers the key to successful evangelization in these postmodern times. He also offers polite suggestions as to how the Church, and in particular the official Magisterium, can live with questions and see the questioners as positive assets for the Church itself.

One might say that the dominant theme throughout each and every page of Kelly's groundbreaking and highly influential *New Directions in Sexual Ethics: Moral Theology and the Challenge of AIDS*[29] is the need for a more compassionate approach on the part of the Church itself, as much as of individuals, not simply towards those blighted by HIV/AIDS, but also towards those in relationships that the Church has vociferously condemned. He explores the linkage made between sexuality and sin in a refreshingly candid, constructive and, of course, ultimately compassionate way.

But he offers not simply a constructive, but also a joyful and empowering theology of sexuality for our times. This includes suggesting that the Church must bear the sinful consequences of its own teaching concerning the subjugation of women and concerning gay and lesbian people. Rooting his reflections in the factuality of our historical, social and cultural contexts, Kelly works towards offering a 'gay and lesbian theology and spirituality', embracing the 'woundedness' of gay and lesbian Catholics to enable their true healing, so that the Church might proclaim that the gospel is truly and fully 'good news' for gay and lesbian Christians too.

Furthermore, he discusses monumental moral dilemmas posed to religious congregations by the blight of HIV/AIDS and also suggests that a re-examination of Church teaching against the use of condoms might perhaps offer the most compassionate response to those contexts where HIV/AIDS is a daily fact of life. If the Church is to 'live positively' with AIDS, then compassion must lie at the basis of its teaching, witness and practice alike.

Needless to say, the title of Kelly's equally pioneering study into bioethical questions speaks volumes on the compassionate approach that informs his exploration into the moral dilemmas considered within – *Life and Love: Towards a Christian Dialogue on Bioethical Questions*.[30]

Thus Kelly's many writings are infused with compassion throughout, just as his ministry has been a ministry grounded on compassion. Whether it be compassion for those whose marriages have failed, for those cohabiting or in second marriages, for the victims of HIV/AIDS, for theologians who have respectfully disagreed with official Church teaching (and with both Church and university authorities), for those blighted by tragedy, poverty or illness, for those in same-sex relationships who are labelled as sinful by Church and society alike, for those human beings anywhere who are suffering in whatever way at all, Kelly *feels* their suffering and argues that the Church's key duty is to feel their suffering too. It is the Christian calling to *suffer with*: the meaning of compassion.

In all, then, it is demonstrable that Kevin Kelly has stood against the modern and postmodern heirs of Nietzsche in *not* forsaking compassion, in refusing to reject it as a decadent and life-denying virtue. Kelly has stood up for and suffered on behalf of the victims of the strong, the powerful, those who refuse to allow compassion to enter into their way of being; those who see only advantage to be gained by shutting out any compassionate sensibilities at all, and thereby easing the way of oppression and subjugation – and this, whether it be the powerful in our society, in far-off lands or *within* the Church itself. Kelly has always been and remains a *witness* for compassion. And in this his ministry and scholarship have been truly *prophetic*, for he has borne witness to the very reality of the being of the God of love itself. The Lord *is* compassion and love.

And, as throughout his writings Kelly ceaselessly calls the Church to be a Church of compassion, a further examination of his works illustrates that he is not simply a knowledgeable, realistic and gifted ecclesiologist but a truly visionary one at that.[31] Of this, more below.

Kelly, I hope, would not disagree here, for, if theology is his starting point, and theology, of course, begins and ends with God's very own self, then, if the Lord *is* compassion and love, if God is the source and end of all goodness, what else can the basis of morality be but compassion? Kelly's works help further demonstrate how, from such starting points as a metaphysical and ecclesiological approach grounded in compassion, can flow sure grounding for such moral theological approaches as personalism, proportionalism, virtue ethics and the like.

Compassion as Fundamental Existential and Moral Option: Individually, Ecclesially, Socially

It will help this attempt to argue that Kevin Kelly is not only a metaphysician but also an ecclesiologist if we now return to the modern Christian tradition and briefly examine the work of another great figure of post-Vatican II Catholic theology who might be described in a similar fashion.

For Karl Rahner and Kevin Kelly actually have a very great deal in common when one examines the existential, pastoral and theological starting points for their reflections upon morality and the Church alike. Rahner's famous 'fundamental option', whereby the shift in moral theology is away from concentration upon individual acts to a focus upon an existential commitment for or against a positive response to the gracious self-communication of God, an option actualized across the entire lifetime of a person, obviously has social and ecclesial consequences in many different ways.[32] Perhaps 'fundamental orientation' might be a better phrase here. Nonetheless, this is very similar to what Kevin Kelly says about moving away from looking at individual acts and instead looking at the wider context and broader life stories of particular individuals. The 'option' is really a cumulative building-up of character towards either selfish egoism or towards love of God which is manifested through love of other human beings.[33] One opts for a grounding of one's existence in a transcendent order of truth and values or one opts for self-love and its actualization in what traditionally has been called concupiscence. But how is the love of God to be actualized? Rahner states it is and must be actualized *through* nothing else but the love of others.[34] The supernatural theological virtue of *caritas*, of love or charity, is key to this. Recall that Schopenhauer told us that one of Christianity's greatest achievements was in making *caritas* such a fundamental virtue and ground for justice. Recall that he said the means by which we exercise *caritas* is *compassion*.

Hence what informed Rahner's groundbreaking anthropological development of this fundamental option was his great belief that the love of God and the love of neighbour are intertwined, indeed, can be viewed to be one and the same.[35] As Rahner states, 'the categorised explicit love of neighbour is the primary act of the love of God',[36] and hence the converse – failure to love neighbour equates to failure to love God – is true in an ontological sense and not simply in a moral or psychological sense. In loving neighbour we open ourselves to an 'opening in trusting love to the whole of reality'[37] – we transcend individual and selfish concerns, as Schopenhauer might have put it, and realize our transcendental unity with others, returning to a Christian moral ontology, as with God. The only way to love the invisible God, Rahner states, is by loving the visible neighbour.[38] Absolute selflessness towards another is not only an act of loving God, it is an actualization of our soteriologically significant fundamental option.[39] Rahner sums all this up most succinctly when he states the following:

If the word of God can be spoken in the world at all it can only be spoken as a finite word of man. And, conversely, the direct relation to God is necessarily mediated by inner-worldly communication. The transcendental message needs a categorial object, a support, as it were, in order not to lose itself in the void; it needs an inner-worldly Thou. The original relation to God is the love of neighbour. If man becomes himself only through the love of God and must achieve this by a categorial action then, in the order of grace, the act of neighbourly love is the only categorial and original act in which man reaches the whole categorially given reality and thus experiences God directly, transcendentally and through grace.[40]

And, as studies of Rahner by George Vass and Karen Kilby have shown, philosophical questions preoccupied Karl Rahner throughout his life, and we see this reflected in his enormous corpus of writings.[41] So, too, have Richard Lennan and Paul D. Murray illustrated in a convincing fashion that perhaps the true abiding significance of Rahner's work (here I would say most certainly so in terms of *practical* outcomes) are the ecclesiological implications of his writings – for it is throughout the Church that the lasting *human* implications of Rahner's theology can bear fruit.[42] And I believe we can say the same of Kevin Kelly. Thus here I would stress that this fundamental option and actualization of the love of God *as* love of neighbour is not something simply for Christian individuals to attend to. It is also an 'imperative' for the Church itself to *be* compassionate in every aspect of its existence.

The fundamental option, the unity of love of God and love of neighbour, is but another way of saying that we must reach out compassionately to where people are, in the midst of their suffering, for there God, also, is to be found. 'When I needed a neighbour, were you there?' is a question as much for the Church collectively, and for each Christian minister and leader, as it is for every Christian individual. And, as the Sydney Carter hymn which develops the theme of that parable continues, 'the creed and the colour and the name *won't matter*: were *you* there?' To the hymn Kelly might add 'and the marital status, sexual orientation, medical condition won't matter, were you there?'

Compassion as the Founding Principle of Ethics and Ecclesiology for the Twenty-First Century

This combination of metaphysics and morality grounded on compassion, of a theology made praxis, a theology articulated in the love of all others, an ontology of the fundamental unity, the interconnectedness of all livings things, of all reality itself, should recall to us another great figure of Christian history who believed in reaching out to people in the midst of their sufferings, in going out to learn from, to understand, to share their experiences of suffering, and who likewise believed in doing so for there God also is to be found. I speak, of course, of St Francis of Assisi – that embodiment of compassion, a selfless love that unlocked for him the secrets of reality itself and opened the door to the most profound understanding of and union with God's very self, the path to which, of course, was a fundamental option manifested in total commitment to love of neighbour, of the poorest, most oppressed, neglected and despised of neighbours above all else.

That great sometime Friar Minor himself, Leonardo Boff, in his profound and extended meditation on Francis, also draws upon Max Scheler's classic study of sympathy (read compassion), noting how Scheler asserted that: 'Never again in the history of the West does there emerge a figure marked with such a strength of sympathy and of universal emotion as that of Saint Francis'.[43] Boff himself speaks of how Francis is forever relevant, highlighting, particularly for today, his 'introduction of care, heartfelt reason and emotional intelligence',[44] his 'universal kinship', with Boff also emphasizing his especial kinship with 'the poor and excluded, such as lepers ... who were then the equivalent to those living with HIV today. He touched their skin and embraced them so that they would truly feel like members of the human family'[45] – a kinship that also embraced those Muslims that other Christians were busy putting to the sword at that time. Boff further highlights the ecological stance of Francis, his love for all nature. And, finally, for today, he notes the enduring significance of 'the joy, enthusiasm, and optimism' of Francis, 'especially in the face of the shadowy dimension of existence. Human weakness and even sin did not distance him from God. They were paths for reaching God with humility and compassion.'[46] Note that Kevin Kelly, in his study of HIV/AIDS, follows this Franciscan line, stating that:

> In New Testament times those who were sick tended to be marginalised by 'respectable' society who believed there was some kind of causal link between illness and sin. Jesus challenged this mentality. Consequently, the sick seem to have been drawn to him like a magnet. It is especially noticeable that contact with lepers seems to have played a major part in the healing ministry of Jesus. In our own day Christians who have felt themselves drawn to care for people living with HIV/AIDS believe that they should show the same compassion to people living with HIV/AIDS as Jesus did to the lepers of his day.[47]

And neither does Kelly shirk discussion of the difficult challenges involved in offering such compassion, particularly to those who feel marginalized by the Church on the grounds of the expression of their sexual orientation.

But perhaps the most significant point to remember in all this is that Francis was not primarily interested in being a model of heroic virtue through that extraordinary and limitless compassion that he embodied throughout his life, in other words, in being a saint for the sake of it. What was the primary motivating factor behind Francis' mission and service? It was primarily *ecclesiological*. First and foremost, Francis was called by Christ to rebuild his Church. The 'lesser brothers', and soon after the 'poor Clares', were founded to renew and rebuild the Church. Not far into a new millennium, Francis, Clare and their many companions sought to rebuild the Church itself through a way of life and a spirituality given to concrete practical outcomes in the form of service to the poor, the sick, the needy and oppressed. Their mission was grounded upon compassion: Francis realized that compassion offered a profound explication of the mysteries of the universe – it grounded his metaphysical sensitivities, his theological orientation, his moral and pastoral principles and activities alike and his all-embracing social ontology. *Compassion* became the starting point for the renewal of the Church.

At the dawn of the third millennium, the work of those such as Kevin Kelly shows us how compassion can and should become the starting point for our ecclesiology and ethics alike. Leonardo Boff speaks of the striking relevance of the vision of

St Francis of Assisi for our time, calling him 'Postmodern Brother', because he represents the 'Triumph of Compassion and Gentleness'.[48] In the twenty-first century we see aggression, domination, oppression and exclusion taking a strangulating grip on so much of our world. Sincere and genuinely effective care for others has become frowned upon in many quarters. The triumph of neo-liberal capitalism and the neo-imperial tendencies this further feeds, the triumph of dehumanizing globalization and the social decay and damage to communities that it brings with it, represent the antithesis to a metaphysics grounded upon compassion. And we see that domination and exclusivistic mentalities, indeed a net reduction in compassion, have become all too prevalent once more even within the Church itself.

Let the Church renew itself once again, to fulfil its sacramental mission to the world through attention, first and foremost, to compassion, to that absolute and unconditional love of God, which can only become manifest in the world through love of neighbour. Let the Church renew its own compassion within, spread that love without and engage in a universal coalition to make compassion and not domination the prevailing ontological energy for our times. Let us learn from the prophetic wisdom and example of those such as Kevin Kelly. Consider the following words from Leonardo Boff, who here describes Francis once more, and one may be led to consider whether there may be parallels here with Kevin Kelly:

> He demonstrated with his life that, to be a saint, it is necessary to be human. And to be human, it is necessary to be sensitive and gentle. With the poor man from Assisi fell the veils that covered reality. When this happens, it remains evident that human reality is not a rigid structure, not a concept, but rather it is sympathy, capacity for compassion and gentleness.[49]

Metaphysics once more – and a most fitting and illuminating metaphysical foundation for both morality and ecclesiology for the twenty-first century.

Conclusion

Kevin Kelly believes in a God who *is* compassion in the innermost depths of the divine being and in the outpouring love of the self-communication of that being. He *therefore* commends a vision of the Church that is true to the being of that compassionate God of love in its day-to-day teaching, ministry and practice. The Church must be both the sign and mediation, that is, must be sacramental, of that compassionate love of God. Hence, given the profundity of these metaphysical and ecclesiological statements, I am minded to suggest that Kevin Kelly is much more a philosopher and an ecclesiologist than he lets on.

Leonardo Boff said that 'people are moved not so much by ideas as by the witness of exemplary persons. Their meaning transcends the historic period in which they lived. They speak to all the ages.'[50] Kevin Kelly is one such figure, and what he says to all the ages is that in compassion lies the key to the answers to all our deepest and most pressing questions. As Boff goes on to state, Francis of Assisi 'rightly intuited that, from the downtrodden and the presence of God in them, one finds the intimate and secret heart of Christianity'.[51] For Francis, there was no distinction between theory and practice.[52] Neither is there any such distinction for Kevin Kelly.

Compassion is certainly a word that is richly evocative in so many ways but the Italians can go one better. As Schopenhauer remarked in the mid-nineteenth century, in Italian, 'sympathy and pure love are expressed ... by the same word, *pietà*'.[53] If you want the perfect word to describe not simply Kevin Kelly's approach to ethics but also his default character, then *pietà* is the word you should employ.

Notes

1. David E. Cartwright, 'Schopenhauer's Compassion and Nietzsche's Pity', *Schopenhauer-Jahrbuch* 69 (1988): 557–65. See esp. 558.

2. Max Scheler, *The Nature of Sympathy* (London: Routledge & Kegan Paul, 1954), p. 66.

3. Arthur Schopenhauer, *On The Basis of Morality* (Oxford: Berghahn, 1995), p. 69. This formula appears in Augustine's *City of God*, XIX, 14. Whilst Schopenhauer does not acknowledge Augustine's use of the same formula, he does quote from the *City of God*, XIX, 3 earlier in *On The Basis of Morality* (p. 45). This suggests some debt to Augustine is highly likely.

4. Cf. Gerard Mannion, 'Mitleid, Metaphysics and Morality – Interpreting Schopenhauer's Ethics', *Schopenhauer-Jahrbuch* 83 (2002): 87–117. (Also in a different form as chapter 6 of my *Schopenhauer, Religion and Morality – The Humble Path to Ethics* [New Critical Thinking in Philosophy Series, Aldershot: Ashgate Press, 2003], pp. 189–220). See also the works of Cartwright, note 6 below, and Patrick Gorevan, 'Scheler's Response to Schopenhauer', *Schopenhauer-Jahrbuch* 77 (1996): 167–69. On the notion of compassion in general and a discussion of its various philosophical and religious treatments, including by Schopenhauer, cf. Esmé Wynne-Tyson, *The Philosophy of Compassion* (London: Vincent Stuart, 1962).

5. Schopenhauer, *On The Basis of Morality*, p. 162, also p. 164.

6. *Ibid.* A similar point is made in his 'On Religion – A Dialogue', in *Parerga and Paralipomena* (Oxford: Clarendon, 1974), pp. 324–94 (348).

7. Schopenhauer, *On the Basis of Morality*, p. 167.

8. *Ibid.*, p. 163. He mentions that traces can be found also in Cicero and Pythagoras.

9. *Ibid.*, p. 162.

10. Arthur Schopenhauer, *The World as Will and Representation* (New York: Dover, 1969), vol. II, p. 374.

11. Schopenhauer, *On the Basis of Morality*, p. 163.

12. *Ibid.*, p. 166.

13. *Ibid.*, p. 170.

14. *Ibid.*, p. 183.

15. See David E. Cartwright's various writings concerning compassion in general, for example, and Schopenhauer and Nietzsche on *Mitleid* in particular: 'Scheler's Criticisms of Schopenhauer's Theory of Mitleid', *Schopenhauer-Jahrbuch* 62 (1981): 144–52; 'Compassion', in W. Schirmacher (ed.), *Zeit der Ernte* (Stuttgart: Frommann-Holzboog, 1982), pp. 60–69; 'Schopenhauer's Compassion and Nietzsche's Pity', in *Schopenhauer-Jahrbuch* 69 (1988) 557–65; 'Schopenhauer on Suffering, Death, Guilt and the Consolation of Metaphysics', in Eric von der Luft (ed.), *Schopenhauer – New Essays in*

Honour of His 200th Birthday (Lewiston: Edwin Mellen Press, 1988), pp. 51–66; 'Schopenhauer as Moral Philosopher', *Schopenhauer-Jahrbuch* 70 (1989): 54–65; 'Kant, Schopenhauer and Nietzsche on the Morality of Pity', *Journal of the History of Ideas* 45 (1984): 83–98; 'Editor's Introduction', in Arthur Schopenhauer, *On the Will in Nature* (Oxford: Berg, 1992); 'The Last Temptation of Zarathustra', *Journal of the History of Philosophy* 31 (1993): 49–69; 'Introduction', in Schopenhauer, *On The Basis of Morality*, pp. ix–xxxviii; 'Nietzsche's Use and Abuse of Schopenhauer's Moral Philosophy for Life', in C. Janaway (ed.), *Willing and Nothingness* (Oxford: Clarendon, 1998), pp. 116–50; 'Schopenhauer's Narrower Sense of Morality', ch. 8 of C. Janaway (ed.), *The Cambridge Companion to Schopenhauer* (Cambridge: Cambridge University Press, 1999), pp. 252–92. For Nietzsche (all references are to the section number and not the page number of the relevant texts) see, for example, *Human All Too Human*, book I, Preface, 1; 57; I: 99, 103; *Daybreak*, 63, 133–134, 139, 142; *The Gay Science*, 13, 14; *On the Genealogy of Morals*, 5; *Twilight of the Idols*, 1, 37; *The Antichrist*, 7.

16. As Nietzsche suggests, *The Genealogy of Morals* (trans. Francis Goffling), (London: Anchor, 1956; with *The Birth of Tragedy*), no. V.

17. Cf. Friedrich Nietzsche, *The Antichrist* (trans. R. Hollingdale), (Harmondsworth: Penguin, 1990), no. 7. One should guard against *Mitleid*, argues Nietzsche, for it stifles true self-actualization and is debilitating both to the one who pities and the one pitied: it 'makes them small'; cf. *Thus Spake Zarathustra* (trans. R.J. Hollingdale), (Harmondsworth: Penguin, 1969), esp. 'Of the Compassionate', pp. 112–14 and 'Of the Virtue that Makes Small', pp. 187–92.

18. I examine the character of Schopenhauer's worldview in detail in ch. 1 of *Schopenhauer, Religion and Morality*.

19. Schopenhauer, *Parerga and Paralipomena*, II, 201. Cf., also, his *On the Will in Nature*, pp. 3, 139–40.

20. Friedrich Nietzsche, *The Antichrist*, no. 9; see also nos 7–8. Ironically, Schopenhauer also condemns his philosophical contemporaries for their refusal to let go of theology, e.g., *On the Will in Nature*, pp. 7, 23.

21. Kevin T. Kelly, *Conscience: Dictator or Guide? A Study in Seventeenth-Century English Protestant Moral Theology* (London: Geoffrey Chapman, 1967).

22. John Paul II, Apostolic Exhortation On the Role of the Christian Family in the Modern World, *Familiaris consortio* (1981).

23. Kevin T. Kelly, *Divorce and Second Marriage* (London: Geoffrey Chapman, 1997), p. 74.

24. Kevin T. Kelly, *From a Parish Base: Essays in Moral and Pastoral Theology* (London: Darton, Longman and Todd, 1999), ch. 7, pp. 97–110.

25. *Ibid.*, p. 109.

26. *Ibid.*, ch. 6, 'Co-responsibility and Accountability within a Sinful Church', p. 90.

27. *Ibid.*, p. 154.

28. Kevin T. Kelly, *New Directions in Moral Theology: The Challenge of Being Human* (London: Geoffrey Chapman, 1992).

29. Kevin T. Kelly, *New Directions in Sexual Ethics: Moral Theology and the Challenge of AIDS* (London: Geoffrey Chapman, 1998).

30. Kevin T. Kelly, *Life and Love: Towards a Christian Dialogue on Bioethical Questions* (London: Collins, 1987).
31. e.g., see the 'Introduction' to his *From a Parish Base*.
32. See Karl Rahner, 'Theology of Freedom', in *Theological Investigations* (London: Darton, Longman and Todd, 1969), vol. 6, pp. 178–96.
33. The parallels with Schopenhauer here are also striking (save the overt theistic elements, of course).
34. Rahner frequently asserts this point. See, for example, Karl Rahner, 'Reflections on the Unity of the Love of Neighbour and of the Love of God', in *Theological Investigations* vol. 6, ch. 16, pp. 231–49 (246–47); Karl Rahner, *The Love of Jesus and the Love of Neighbour* (New York: Crossroad, 1983), pp. 69–71 (also cited in Karl Rahner, *The Practice of Faith* [London: SCM, 1985], pp. 113–14, and also in his 'Marxist Utopia and the Christian Future of Man', ch. 5 of *Theological Investigations*, vol. 6, pp. 65–66. See, also, his 'Love', in Rahner, *The Practice of Faith*, pp. 111–12 (112) (originally from his *Grace and Freedom* [London: Burns & Oates, 1969], pp. 215–18 [218]).
35. Rahner, 'Reflections on the Unity of the Love of Neighbour and of the Love of God', esp. pp. 246ff.
36. *Ibid.*, p. 247.
37. *Ibid.*
38. A point reiterated in 'Marxist Utopia and the Christian Future of Man', ch. 5 of Rahner, *Theological Investigations*, vol. 6, p. 5.
39. *Ibid.*
40. Rahner, 'Love', pp. 111–12.
41. George Vass, *A Theologian in Search of a Philosophy* (vol. 1 of *Understanding Karl Rahner*, London: Sheed & Ward, 1985); Karen Kilby, *Karl Rahner: Theology and Philosophy* (London: Routledge, 2004).
42. Richard Lennan, *The Ecclesiology of Karl Rahner* (Oxford: Oxford University Press, 1995); Paul D. Murray, 'The Lasting Significance of Karl Rahner for Contemporary Catholic Theology', *Louvain Studies* 29 (2004): 8–27.
43. Leonardo Boff, *Francis of Assisi* (New York: Orbis Books, 2006, first published in 1981), pp. 16–17; citing Scheler's German edition, *Wesen und Formen der Sympathie* (Bonn: Verlag von Friedrich Cohen, 1923), p. 110.
44. Boff, *Francis of Assisi*, p. ix.
45. *Ibid.*, p. x.
46. *Ibid.*, cf. Kelly's *From a Parish Base*, pp. 82–94.
47. Kelly, *New Directions in Sexual Ethics*, p. 68.
48. Boff, *Francis of Assisi*, p. 16.
49. *Ibid.*, p. 17.
50. *Ibid.*, p. ix.
51. *Ibid.*, p. 23.
52. *Ibid.*, p. 18.
53. Schopenhauer, *The World as Will and Representation*, vol. I, p. 376.

24

Kevin Kelly:
Priest and Moral Theologian

R. John Elford

Moral decision-making is a self-evidently complex human process which always has and ever will both fascinate and bewitch. Those, and there have been many over the centuries, who believe that it can be simplified are invariably proved wrong, right though they may well be in some aspect or other of what they are claiming. One of the best descriptions of this process uses the image of a prism. In this the elements of light can be separately discerned, but they are, at the same time, elusive as they blend, by refraction, into the wider spectrum. We might wish that just one colour would lead us to the inner mystery of the whole, but this cannot be the case. All the elements are inextricably part of a wider whole. Dorothy Emmet used this powerful and helpful image in her *The Moral Prism* which she concluded with these words: '[The prism] was but an image, pointing to complexity in our moral vision. The unseen white light can pass through the prism, but the complex of colours remains; we may fasten selectively on one at any given time, yet we see it as but one colour in the spectrum. It does not eclipse the others, and if we are fortunate it can even enhance them.'[1]

Religious moralities are perhaps, and sadly, invariably noted for their claims to be able to simplify this inherent complexity. These are often premised upon some claim to a superior knowledge. Most commonly, this is held to derive from either the Church or the Bible or both. At their most strident, these claims proffer certainty in an ever-uncertain world. For this reason alone, they bear an obvious allure to those afflicted by moral uncertainty on the one hand, and, on the other, to those who claim to be able to dispel it. Christians have often been and are to the fore in both of these groups. For them the Church and the Bible are both still all-sufficient in the face of moral uncertainty and they are never more so than when they are claiming to be expressing themselves in unison. It is, of course, axiomatic in Christian moral decision-making that the Church and the Bible are both supremely important. But just how important are they in this instance or that? And, is that importance all-sufficient, or are there other factors which have to be taken into account? Many such are pressed upon us by modernity with ever increasing urgency. Our burgeoning technologies, which proffer ever-new hopes of deliverance from some affliction or other, are a common source of them. We already know enough to know that these hopes are often well-founded as the quality and longevity of human life improves. We also know, however, that these technologies have their dark side and that for this reason alone we have to deploy them with respect and caution. Yet other factors which have to be taken into account when we want our moral endeavours to succeed are those arising from the ever-changing circumstances of our personal lives. Here, older traditions and conventions are breaking down and newer ones arising in their place. The traditions of family life are an obvious example of this. The seemingly ever-increasing instance of marriage breakdown and new approaches to sexuality with their liberation for many, including homosexuals, are all a challenge to older certainties and sensibilities.

Those who think that morality is cut and dried often struggle to come to terms with the world as we have briefly described it. For this reason they face immense challenges. For the rest, this description might just have touched upon what they find to be commonplace in their everyday lives. These latter are people much like ourselves and those we encounter around us, our loved ones and acquaintances. They are the people whom a priest meets in his, or her, daily round. They are also, of course, so often those for whom the Church and the Bible have little significance. This is where Christian ministry meets the modern world. It is nothing less than the coalface where its integrities are put to the test.

Kevin Kelly knows all this and more. For this reason his vocations as a priest and a theologian are as two sides of a coin. They are inseparable. To realize this is to begin to understand them both. But there is more, much more, to them. They are both hard-wrought. Kelly's ministry, which is written of elsewhere in this volume, is a testimony to his faithfulness to his Church and to the people he has served with affection, grace and integrity. His academic career is on a par with this. His teaching and writing have taken him to the heart of many institutions and from them back again into the wider world. All this has created, in his person, a flowing source of insight and spirituality. These two spheres of Kelly's work have been equally sustained. It would be easy, but misleading, to say that they have been sustained in parallel. This would suggest that they have not met, and nothing, as we have stressed, could be further from the truth. They have been sustained in their own right but have importantly been brought together in his person. This is more unusual than might be thought. For most of us, the rigours of one vocation or the other have to take precedence over the years. As this happens the neglect of the one has probably resulted in the weakness of both. Kelly has avoided this, by devoting his life to his continuing ministry and his moral theology. The part played in this by the celibacy of his calling, his selflessness and modesty is something that those who know him cherish and admire. I have been personally privileged to have seen and occasionally been part of this for nearly 40 years. Accordingly, I have benefited from Kelly's wisdom and, above all, his friendship.

In what follows, we will look at two examples of the way in which Kelly has both reconciled and given equal strength to these two sides of his continuing life's work: his ministry and his moral theology. The first is derived from his parish ministry and the second from his wider concern for human well-being. Following this we will draw out some of the common themes which hold these and other aspects of his work together. Here we will be guided by his own writing, so much of which has been focused on the importance of understanding what these aspects are.

Divorce and Second Marriage

In 1982 Kelly published the first edition of his *Divorce and Second Marriage*.[2] It was written whilst he was leader of the team ministry in Skelmersdale, Lancashire, a large new town settled by people displaced by inner-city regeneration in Liverpool and elsewhere. Here he discovered couples from previously divorced marriages who were 'among the best parishioners in the community. Their home is a truly Christian home, their family is exemplary, they are fully participating members of the Eucharistic community and there is evident prayer and goodness in their lives'.[3] Kelly responds to this by following the Vatican II observation that faith and life should not be separated. This leads him to two questions. First, is a person for whom a first marriage has failed to be denied the possibility of ever seeking and establishing a successful second one? Second, what about the well-being of similar couples who are living together in a new relationship, but who may not obviously exemplify the devout virtues? The gospel, he reflects, is as much good news for them as for anybody else, including the devout. These two pastoral challenges are then interpreted as being of divine origin and, for that reason, incapable of being ignored. (Yet another challenge which has motivated others to respond to this situation is the desire to do something about the illegitimate status of the children of unmarried couples, one or other of whom has previously divorced.) No pastor living amid such challenges can ignore them. They are further exacerbated for the faithful because they are often refused Communion following divorce, a practice also once common in the Church of England. It is to their credit that most pastors have now long since made progress with all these issues. We should remember, however, that this was not the widespread case in 1982. (The Church of England, for example, was a very long way from permitting second marriages officially, although the law did permit clergy to officiate at them if they so wished. The Methodist Church had already done better by allowing the subsequent marriage of divorcees for pastoral reasons.) Kelly's work in the field was at the time, therefore, largely pioneering.

It was also courageous. He realized that no progress could be made with the pastoral phenomenon he was confronting unless a second look was taken at the doctrine of the indissolubility of marriage. What he did was not to challenge the doctrine, but to reinterpret it in the light of the changing understanding of marriage. This change he observed to be good, because it embraced deeper meanings of marriage which included recognition of the place of both sexuality and commitment within it. Kelly, then, discusses, with great sensitivity, the possibility of interpreting the doctrine of the indissolubility of marriage in a way which neither denies the validity of a previous marriage nor precludes the possibility of creating a subsequent one. He achieves this by interpreting the word not as a description of what happens until one partner of a marriage dies, but as a reference to 'deeper levels of personal being'.[4] Of this he writes: 'I do not think that the position I have been outlining is a denial of indissolubility. It is merely a different way of understanding it. Admittedly, it accepts the possibility that some marriages (far too many at present) will not attain this inner indissolubility and instead will disintegrate and fall apart so that eventually they no longer exist. This is not to deny that these marriages were never indissoluble in any sense. They were, but their indissolubility during that initial stage drew its binding force from the pledged commitment they had made to become two-in-one at a deep personal level. It was not yet based on the achievement of that personal two-in-oneness.'[5]

In the light of all this, Kelly faces the, for him and for all other devout Roman Catholics, difficult problem of the work of the marriage tribunals and the grounds they use for the declaration of the nullity of some previous marriages. He welcomed the fact that, even in 1982, these tribunals were revising the grounds upon which nullity was granted. Of this he trenchantly observes that they were either wrong in the past or in the present! Far better, he concludes, to trust the 'sound native wit and intuition of a good honest person'.[6] From this he forcefully concludes that the Church should accept the true healing of a second marriage when it is established to have occurred.[7]

In 1997 Kelly published a new and expanded edition of *Divorce and Second Marriage*.[8] This includes a new Introduction and Appendix, along with other important documents which have appeared since the first edition was published. Here he thankfully acknowledges that, in the intervening years, the Roman Catholic Church at different levels has put a lot of thought and effort 'into trying to formulate and implement a much more positive pastoral approach to couples in a second marriage'.[9] He recognizes, however, that it remains to be asked how far this positive attitude can go. This is the question addressed by the second edition.

Kelly was surprised to discover that, on rereading his 1982 book, he still effectively concurred with it. This, recall, would have been after even more hardworking years ministering to the faithful in need. He acknowledges that the high incidence of failed second marriages presents a problem for those like him who want to do everything possible to make them possible and understand them. For this reason, he takes a second look at the statistics and, ever the pastor, enjoins that this is a further reason for extending compassion. Here he observes that the continuing refusal of the Church to admit divorcees to the Eucharist is a serious pastoral problem. He welcomes recent changes in canon law, which recognize the human dimensions of consummation and interprets this as indicating that the Church has adopted a two-tier approach to indissolubility. He reiterates his belief that informal changes in pastoral practice 'can be a healthy sign that the whole Church is beginning to play a more active part in theological reflection and pastoral discernment'.[10] One important amendment to the original text substitutes the word 'disagreement' for 'dissent' where he is critical of Church teaching. This is important because, as we will see below, Kelly's whole ministry and moral theology is exercised within the parameters of the Church as he carefully understands them. Another amendment replaces the previous use of sexist language.

New Directions in Sexual Ethics

In 1994 Kelly undertook a major tour of Uganda, Thailand and the Philippines to find out for himself, at first hand, how the AIDS pandemic was affecting the lives of ordinary people. He then subjected these experiences to a major theological analysis which was published as *New Directions in Sexual Ethics: Moral Theology and the Challenge of AIDS*.[11] The book focuses on the plight of underprivileged women and the way in which this exposes them to the disease. It claims that, if 'our understanding of the man–woman relationship is out of kilter, our sexual ethics is bound to be at best inadequate, if not misguided'.[12] Much of the discussion is based on and illuminated by moving first-hand experiences recorded in a diary. Themes, which are familiar throughout Kelly's writing, soon become apparent. The first is the need to place the ordinary experiences of afflicted folk in a wider historical and sociological context. The important point made here is that this context is a human construction and, for that reason, it should not be treated as sacrosanct. Also, for that reason, it can be changed by human beings themselves, even radically if necessary. (There are echoes of a philosophy of freedom here which are resonant with Karl Marx's outstanding pre-1848 philosophical writings, which have, sadly, been neglected, largely out of political prejudice against his later writings.) Kelly brings to this philosophical insight his belief in the gospel of good news. This stresses not only that things should be changed, but that, by the grace of God, they can be. Understood in this way, the notion of 'social construction' is not an end in itself, nor is it to be used as a licence for accepting unbridled human freedom. It is but a tool for understanding the proper and improper constraints on human flourishing.

Against the background of virtually 20 centuries in which Christians perpetuated notions of the subordination of women, Kelly welcomes the pro-women teaching in the encyclicals of Pope John Paul II.[13] Responding to the Irish theologian Enda McDonagh, Kelly agrees that the time of AIDS is a time for the reappraisal of the place of women in society. This is nothing less than a *kairos* time; one in which an initiative can and has to be seized. He writes: 'It is as though the experience-based theological reflection of women is fashioning a clearer lens, enabling the Church to see what needs to be done. In other words, if we are not living in an age in which God's Spirit is speaking in new ways through the voices of women interpreting their own experience, the Church might not be able to interpret accurately what God's spirit is saying in "the time of AIDS".'[14] This point is central to the argument of the book. It helpfully includes extended analysis of the many responses to Pope John Paul II's teaching on women, particularly by women who disagreed with it. This also includes analysis of reactions in the lesbian and gay community. A chapter is devoted to a discussion of what the churches are saying about the issue worldwide. From all this it is powerfully concluded that the Church needs to work towards a new sexual ethic. Two chapters are then devoted to discussing what this might entail. They understand sex as a gift from God and, as always, listen carefully to what people, particularly young people, are saying about their sexual experiences. This discussion has immense implications for understanding human sexuality, particularly in the churches. The issues that are taken up are those encountered in the AIDS pandemic.

This discussion is, again, rooted in a moving human experience. It is that of a Ugandan mother called Noerine, whose husband died of AIDS amid ignorance and superstition. It was from her that Kelly first heard the phrase 'living positively with AIDS'.[15] With others, Noerine was subsequently responsible for setting up an important support organization for sufferers.

Kelly appreciates that the churches are in many ways responding magnificently to the pandemic. He confines his comments to the responses made by CAFOD and other agencies in the Roman Catholic Church. Two specific issues are discussed. The first is the question about whether or not candidates for the priesthood and the religious life should be tested for AIDS. The conclusion here is that they should not be. This is not only because it might infringe on their privacy, it is for the much more powerful reason that HIV-positive persons who were seen to be serving in both of these vocations would themselves embody the spirit of 'living positively with AIDS'.[16]

Finally, the book turns to the discussion about the propriety of the use of condoms as a means of preventing the spread of AIDS. It is now accepted worldwide that such a use is effective, if short of preventing all transmitted infection. This is what has prompted the 'safe-sex' campaigns which have been one major way of trying to prevent the spread of the disease. The conviction that this is one of the actions which needs to be taken causes many non-Roman Catholics (the present writer included) to view with incredulity the official Roman Catholic opposition to such a use. As always, Kelly discusses this with humanity and sensitivity. He makes an important distinction between the use of condoms as promoted by governments as a component of their AIDS-transmission prevention schemes and their use within marriage where one partner is HIV-positive. Again, Kelly quotes and analyzes recent Roman Catholic Church pronouncements. His conclusion on the promotion of the use of condoms by governments is that, because they have an obligation to promote the health of their citizens, 'to oppose a government following this course of action would seem to be tantamount to obstructing a government in carrying out its moral obligation towards its citizens'.[17] He also observes that Church opposition to the use of condoms in marriage where the husband is HIV-positive is tantamount to perpetuating an injustice against women. This is a telling conclusion at the end of a book which decries such injustice.

We have now looked briefly at two central examples of Kevin Kelly's writing on pastoral issues. They are ones which are central to his ministry and to which he has devoted a great deal of attention as a moral theologian. We will now see if we can extract from them common concerns and principles. Here we are assisted, again, by Kelly's own writings. Continuous self-reflection and analysis runs throughout them. There is an understated passion in all this, which clearly derives from Kelly's vocation as a devout scholar-priest. Those of us who have known him over the years and who have also had the privilege of seeing him at work will have abundant further reason for understanding this. As mentioned above, this is remarkable in itself, as is the fact that it continues unabated in his work in the ecumenical parish (joint Anglican and Roman Catholic) of St Basil and All Saints in Widnes and as a senior research fellow at Liverpool Hope University. What follows is but the briefest account of something which deserves, and will no doubt receive in due course, much more analysis.

First of all, Kelly sees moral theology as something dynamic and exciting, because, at its best, it responds to its environment. He writes, 'my experience of combining pastoral work as a diocesan priest in an inner-city parish with teaching students at undergraduate and postgraduate level has convinced me that the role of moral theology will vary according to the context in which it is operating.'[18] This view is derived from the post-Vatican II emphasis on the use of the sacraments as a pastoral means of reconciliation and healing. This is in contrast to an older model which saw the sacramental ministry as one which served, albeit compassionately, to bring pastoral practice into line with preconceived ideas. Those ideas, as we shall see, remain important to Kelly because they have a continuing role to play, but it is not the *only* one. There are several others. However, throughout this change, the role of moral theology remains the same. It is to serve priests in their ministry.[19] Would that all theologians remembered this fundamental aspect of their craft. So much theology seems, at least, to exist for the purpose of its own artifice, as though it has long forgotten the reason for its necessity in the first place. The ugliness of this is never more obvious than when such theology then seeks to 'apply' itself to the world whence it had become artificially extracted by its own efforts. Such application is invariably as artificial as the source from which it comes. Far better, simpler and, as we shall see, more profound, to treat moral theology as Kelly does. As, that is, the servant of the faithful.[20]

A Humility of Risk and Adventure

While Kelly acknowledges that moral theology has always been contextualized to some extent, what he does is to give it a specific grounding in the everyday lives of ordinary folk. These lives are not there to be addressed or corrected (though there might be occasion for that); they are to be treated with respect and, above all, learned from because they are the bearers of wisdom. This seemingly simple observation is anything but. It is, in fact, profound in the extreme. The first thing that it does is to give moral theology a new and exciting humility, which requires it to be more catalyst than ever before. In this it has to risk its own vulnerability as it seeks to venture into the insecurities of those it serves. The 'it' here, of course, is not an impersonal 'it'. The person of the pastor/theologian is also embraced. The sort of humility this demands is not the all-too-common refuge of the pious. It is, rather, a humility of risk and adventure. It is summed up in the subtitle of Kelly's *New Directions in Moral Theology – The Challenge of Being Human*.[21] The challenge, of course, is as great for the pastor as it is for the pastored. This foundational aspect of Kelly's theology has, admittedly, been a bit laboured, but that has been necessary because it is so seemingly simple that it can be overlooked. It is what makes the life of a pastor/theologian so exciting and, ultimately, worthwhile.

In *From a Parish Base*, Kelly identifies nine aspects of this challenge. We will consider them, briefly, in turn. The first is the Second Vatican Council's insistence that the prime object of moral theology is the good of the human person. This 'good' is not an isolated good. If it were, it could lead to selfish reductionism. It is, rather, a good which has to be understood in the context of a wider whole, including the good of others, its wider social context, in which is to be discovered the dichotomy of sin and righteousness.

The second is the importance of the experience and reflection of women. To the extent to which all the Christian pastoral traditions have been patriarchal to some degree or other, this is profoundly important. Such experience and reflection has to be central and formative, rather than peripheral and token. The example of Noerine, mentioned above, is a moving enough case in point. Kelly clearly rejoices in the fact that women are becoming increasingly well established in careers as moral theologians. (What he does not here comment on is that fact that, in his own Church, they are denied the priestly pastoral responsibilities which are so formative for many of their male counterparts.) What we are also thankfully seeing is that the writing of women pastoral theologians is ceasing to exist as a separate genre, but becoming, rather, an integrated part of the wider literature.

The third aspect Kelly mentions is the ethical teaching and thinking found in non-Roman Catholic churches. Such recognition gives Roman Catholic moral theology a wider reference and context. The enrichment here is, of course, importantly two-way. As an Anglican, I readily and frequently attest the benefit I have received in my own career as a pastor and ethicist from my Roman Catholic colleagues. (Not a little of this has been enabled by privileged membership of the

Association of Teachers of Moral Theology, in my case now largely by association in retirement.)

The fourth aspect is the explosion in empirical knowledge, with its concomitant advances in technology. Such knowledge is now widely available, and has, for that reason, effectively become democratized. It is now so extensive that moral theologians cannot now be specialists in everything. Some choose to specialize and others choose to restrict themselves to general principles short of their detailed application. Here again the discipline has had to learn a new humility as it works with others to try and make sense of a rapidly emerging new world of threats and possibilities. Collaborative activities are now widespread, but it is timely to remember how comparatively recent they are.

The fifth aspect is what Kelly calls the 'historical consciousness'. He attributes this, again, to Vatican II, in which he sees 'a rediscovery of the vitality and dynamism of our living tradition through recovering a sense of historical consciousness'.[22] What this reveals is the extent to which all moral endeavour is historically conditioned and time-bound. Unless it is aware of this it becomes fossilized and, literally, useless in an ever-changing present. Accordingly, the institutions of morality have to be, and remain, dynamic if they are to go on serving human well-being.

The sixth aspect is, again, human experience. Kelly focuses here on the encyclical *Humanae vitae*. He was, like so many Roman Catholics at the time, disappointed that the encyclical did not follow the advice of the Papal Birth Control Commission, but reinforced traditional Roman Catholic teaching on the unacceptability of the use of any artificial means of contraception. For Kelly, this failed for the simple reason that it was not responsive to the experiences of faithful and committed Roman Catholic couples. He writes: 'For them the reasons given for the Church's prohibition were out of tune with their own lived experience of marriage and the ruling itself offered them no practical help.'[23] In other words, the encyclical failed because it did not take the givenness of faithful human experience seriously enough.

The seventh aspect is that of dialogue. This has to be, so to speak, with all-comers who have anything to say. It is as wide as that. Obviously, this requires a process of continuous learning and openness. Kelly laments the fact that this is often more difficult to achieve within his Church than it is outside it.

The eighth aspect is involvement in the public arena and media exposure. This is because moral topics have become an open subject for urgent and often passionate public debate. This is an aspect of what we referred to above as the democratization of knowledge. Everything is up for open debate, and that debate is often big news. Society is infinitely better for this than it was when conventional wisdom deferred with the belief that 'a little knowledge was a dangerous thing'. Moral theologians can no longer ply their trade by talking only to each other. When called upon, they have to enter the public arena and, in so doing, put their credibility and their vulnerability on the line.

The ninth and final aspect is the need for dialogue within the Roman Catholic community. When he wrote, this was expressed as a need for a dialogue with the immensely creative and hands-on pope, John Paul II. Kelly saw this as something which would strengthen papal teaching and, thereby, benefit the whole Church. It could not be achieved by displaying only an obligatory reverential silence.

These nine aspects of what is now required of moral theology are referred to throughout Kelly's writing. He will, doubtless, continue the discussion of them. We have rehearsed them here, however briefly, so that we can get an overall picture of his most passionate professional concerns. What remains now is for us, also briefly, to comment upon them.

It is again necessary to stress that Kelly's accomplishments and his international reputation as a moral theologian can easily cause us to overlook the important fact that he is essentially a priest. Those of us who know him well are never likely to forget this. In his many parish ministries, he has worked tirelessly not only to care for those in his charge but to care, also, for the well-being of the societies in which they live. Much of this work is not spectacular. It is everyday, commonplace and downright ordinary. Such is much of the work of a priest, particularly of one who blends into his or her environment and draws attention only to others. All this requires self-giving to an unimaginable degree, and it does this the more so when it is sustained, year in year out, for so long. Perhaps only those of us who have been privileged to experience something of this can know how difficult it can often be. The required physical effort alone is often enough to daunt the most energetic. The spiritual effort is even greater and can only be sustained in prayer by the grace of God. The other side of this coin is, of course, the blessing of seeing that grace makes a difference to people's lives, often when it is needed the most. It is always a privilege to see Kelly work in a parish, to see what a joy he takes in it and what a natural and much-loved priest he is. It is essential for us to appreciate this, if we are to understand just a little of the deep pastoral roots of Kelly's moral theology. His ministry is marked, above all, for the compassion he shows for those around him. This, I suggest, is the key to his moral theology. In the two examples we have looked at, the compassion felt for those in need is paramount. Moreover, it is evidently the greater when the need is most. All this, of course, is of the essence of the ministry of Jesus. His repeated insistence that those with the greatest needs, the outcast, were deserving of special care caused repeated offence. The theology of Jesus's whole ministry can be read off from this. The same is true of ministry in his name. However, not all moral theology needs to be grounded in pastoral care this way. Others can write importantly about issues which are more removed from all this, but none the less important. Moral theology needs its technicians as much as any other branch of theology. The point here being made is that Kelly is not one of them. He is a priest who turns to moral theology to make sense and improve the effectiveness of his ministry.

This compassion takes whatever is given with a radical seriousness. It does not take offence or make alienating moral judgements. It requires, rather, an open and empirical honesty. This is the simple reason why Kelly goes to great lengths to find out about and understand as fully as possible whatever he is confronted by. Wherever possible, he prefers to obtain this knowledge at first hand. Secondary analysis is resorted to only when it is necessary to dispel ambiguity and misunderstanding. All this is of immense importance as we endeavour, as we now invariably do, to make pastoral sense in the light of limited knowledge. No effort can be spared to make sure that pastoral practice is as accurately informed as it can possibly be. The two examples of Kelly's work we have looked at are, of course, exemplary in this important respect.

The next stage in Kelly's priestly moral theology is the realization that, in the face of need, something *can* and *must* be done. There is no turning away. No pretending that other things are more important. Hope must be sought where it is needed most. It is tempting to use the phrase 'brought to bear' of this hope.

In Kelly's theology this would be totally misleading. He seeks hope, rather, in the situations themselves, in the lives of the afflicted. Moreover, he often finds it through the guidance of those afflicted. The moving example of Noerine is, again, illustration of this. The lives of those who have sought remarriage after divorce is another.

A ministry and theology which achieved all this would be well-deserving of admiration in their own right. Their limitation, however, would be that they could degenerate into a relativism which could only become self-defeating. No priest or moral theologian is more aware of this than Kelly. Once he has immersed himself in some pastoral issue or other he always turns to the wider picture. That always means, in the first, but not the only, instance to the wisdom and experience of his Church. All Kelly's writing is redolent with scholarly and sensitive analysis of papal and Magisterial teaching. In this he is a sure guide, particularly to the outsider who seeks such understanding but does not have knowledge of the means to access it. Much has been written in recent years, by so-called 'virtue ethicists', on the importance of the communitarian aspects of virtue. They have pointed out, no doubt rightly, that there must be some essential correlation between doing the right thing and the community of hopes and aspirations in which such action is taken. It might be observed, however, that many such writers have overstressed this point. As a result, they have often both romanticized such communities and circumscribed within their boundaries the virtue they seek. Kelly clearly avoids these shortcomings. While he locates his quest for pastoral enlightenment deep in the bosom of his own ecclesial tradition, two things prevent him from ending it there. The first is his constant dialogue with that tradition. He always wants to tease it out, not by dissenting from it but by staying close to its heart, in respectful disagreement, if necessary. It is this very 'hanging in there' which creates Kelly's ability to balance his hands-on empiricism with the wider picture, which prevents that empiricism from imploding in a sea of well-meaning, but self-defeating, relativism. The other thing that prevents the dangers of relativism in Kelly's writing is his openness to the wisdom of the moral insight of other Christian churches and to such wisdom from wherever it comes.

Recall, again, the analogy of a prism with which we began these reflections. Reflect, on how well it enables us to understand Kelly's ministry and moral theology as we have briefly outlined it. All the separate elements are there and can even be distinguished from each other. But, and this is the important thing about the analogy, they all blend into one – at the same time. Once we begin to understand this, we can begin, also, to use the analogy to throw light on our quest for pastoral wisdom and practice. It does not, of course, solve all our problems. Far from it. What it does is more important; it enables us to live with them in the hope that, by the grace of God, we can sometimes do the right thing. Though he does not mention the analogy of the prism in his own writings, no priest or moral theologian understands it better then Kevin Kelly.

Notes

1. Dorothy Emmet, *The Moral Prism* (London: Macmillan, 1979), p. 158.
2. Kevin T. Kelly, *Divorce and Second Marriage: Facing the Challenge* (London: Collins, 1982).
3. *Ibid.*, p. 10.
4. *Ibid.*, p. 35.
5. *Ibid.*, p. 36.
6. *Ibid.*, p. 44.
7. *Ibid.*, p. 78.
8. Kevin T. Kelly, *Divorce and Second Marriage: Facing the Challenge* (London: Geoffrey Chapman, new and expanded edn, 1997).
9. *Ibid.*, p. xi.
10. *Ibid.*, p. xx.
11. Kevin T. Kelly, *New Directions in Sexual Ethics: Moral Theology and the Challenge of AIDS* (London: Geoffrey Chapman, 1998).
12. *Ibid.*, p. ix.
13. *Ibid.*, pp. 46–50.
14. *Ibid.*, p. 30.
15. *Ibid.*, p. 188.
16. *Ibid.*, p. 196.
17. *Ibid.*, p. 198.
18. Kevin Kelly, *From a Parish Base: Essays in Moral and Pastoral Theology* (London: Darton, Longman and Todd, 1999).
19. *Ibid.*
20. See John Elford, *The Pastoral Nature of Theology* (London: Cassell, 1999), ch. 1.
21. Kevin T. Kelly, *New Directions in Moral Theology: The Challenge of Being Human* (London: Geoffrey Chapman, 1992).
22. Kelly, *From a Parish Base*, p. 121.
23. *Ibid.*, p. 124.

25

Kevin Kelly and Political Humility

John Battle

After moral theology lectures by Fr Kevin Kelly at St Joseph's College, Upholland, in the post-Vatican II, late 1960s, it was often remarked that he 'left us with more questions' and 'had not given any easy clear-cut notable answers'. Since he had not seemed to have made up his own mind and fixed a view in aspic for others simply to reflect on, those who listened to him were left with work to do themselves, having perhaps been encouraged on how to think, but not told what to think.

His great works, *Life and Love: Towards a Christian Dialogue on Bioethical Questions* (1987) and *New Directions in Moral Theology: The Challenge of Being Human* (1992), are consistently characteristic of this questioning openness. Chapters entitled 'Dialogue and Self-Criticism' and 'Drafting the Agenda', for example, are a series of amplified shared questions, reminding us that:

> Pointing out weaknesses in another person's position is a valid exercise in the context of dialogue. However, unless it is accompanied by a willingness to be self-critical as well, it can easily turn dialogue into confrontation and polemics. The same is true at community level and between communities.[1]

This statement could go to the core of political debate, by defining a grossly neglected style of radical politics in the current postmodern era of politics as 'spectacle', in which presentation is all, as politicians struggle to perfect the tactics of survival from one news bulletin to the next, with little regard or time for underpinning moral values or developing a sense of the common good. It is now the digital age of 'ones and zeros' as the only acknowledged ciphers, of on–off switches and 'yes–no' answers, with no respected space between. 'Graceful Disagreement', a chapter title of Kevin Kelly's *New Directions in Moral Theology*, is a rare position or category in the twenty-first-century political landscape.

Yet patiently Kevin Kelly has spent a lifetime insisting on starting out with 'I may be wrong, but…', because, as he puts it:

> I believe that truth statements on some highly debated issues in the field of morality are difficult to arrive at and hence any attempt to articulate them must

be presented with due modesty and must lay itself open to critical questions. Moreover these truth statements have a certain note of provisionality about them. Insofar as they are true, they are a partial statement of truth. They are certainly not the whole truth, nor are they necessarily the best expression of this partial grasp of the truth.[2]

That courageous opening to a Roman Catholic book on moral theology seems remote not only from the present world of politics but also from the traditional understanding of the Catholic Church as a kind of deposit box of guarded 'truth'. Notably the martyred Algerian bishop Pierre Claverie, who was killed in 1996 after a lifetime of interfaith work with Muslims, went further, and in his last writings stated: 'I have come to the personal conviction that humanity is only plural. As soon as we start claiming to possess the truth or to speak in the name of humanity, we fall into totalitarianism. No one possesses the truth, each of us is searching for it.'[3]

To analyze the relationships between truth, diversity and dialogue in the context of the Church and in the work of moral theologians (a topic tackled in detail in *New Directions in Moral Theology*) is for other practitioners and specialists. But could Kevin Kelly's approach be of significance to the practice of politics in general?

For the much revered prophet of postmodern politics, Nietzsche, the one virtue that he attacked as fundamental – and fatally weakening – to Christianity, was humility. He regarded humility not just as humbug but as the great lie of public deception that suggested 'cowardice' could be a means of bringing about human improvement. For Nietzsche this central Christian virtue undermined the essence and purpose of politics; Christians, by stressing humility, were destroying the possibility of sensible politics. Perhaps it is surprising therefore that humility hardly features in modern summaries of the Catholic catechism. It did not feature in the *New Catechism, Catholic Faith for Adults* (the famous Dutch catechism published in the post-Vatican II, late 1960s), despite excellent sections on 'The Way of Christ' and 'The Business of Living', which spelt out the implications of *Gaudium et spes*, including 'Giving One's Life'. Nor is humility mentioned in the Dominican Herbert McCabe's excellent summary, *The Teaching of the Catholic Church* (1985). Even in the official catechism (the millennium edition, published in 1997), humility remains merely implicit in the list of the seven capital sins and their contrary virtues – set against 'pride' (1866). To be fair, humility finds its way into the index, where we are advised that 'the baptised person should train himself to live in humility' (2540) and that 'humility is the fountain of prayer'; 'only when we humbly acknowledge that "we do not know how to pray as we ought" are we ready to receive freely the gift of prayer' – 'Man is a beggar before God' (2559). But there is no public reference to this humility in prayer before God, except when it is hinted at in a reference to Jesus as he enters Jerusalem on a donkey, 'conquering ... by the humility that bears witness to the truth' (559).

Since most contemporary English dictionaries list, as synonyms for humility, 'obsequiousness', 'subservience', 'submissiveness' and 'self-abasement', it would certainly seem that Nietzsche has successfully seen off humility. What is more, Nietzsche was backed up in his assault on humility by Freud and Adler. As the Cistercian Dom André Louf puts it in his pamphlet 'Humility':

For Freud, it is a masochistic variant of the guilt complex. For Adler, it is close to a simple feeling of inferiority. Their interpretations have left their mark on our modern culture. How can humility be reconciled with the famous 'assertiveness' which is so extolled by psychologists from across the Atlantic and with some reason too? How is it possible to honour the last place preached by the Gospel, in a society which is only impressed by the success of 'young Turks' in politics, or 'golden boys' in economics?[4]

There certainly seems to be no space for humility in contemporary politics located in a go-getting culture in which success is all and 'failure is no success at all'. But this eradication of humility from the general culture not only leaves its mark on politics. The Jesuit David Hollenbach in his *Claims in Conflict* consistently fosters the concept of 'epistemological humility', suggesting that an intellectual dimension crucial to moral enquiry has been all too absent.[5]

To restore faith in humility, it is perhaps worth digging into the roots of the concept. Humility was regarded by the early Church Fathers and Mothers as a key virtue. John Cassian regarded *humilitas* as the 'mother and mistress of every virtue';[6] the Desert Mother Theodora advised her peers, 'it is not ascetic practice, nor vigils, nor any other work that can save us but only sincere humility'.[7] Isaac the Syrian regarded it as 'salt to the food' of good works.[8] St Augustine even went as far as to suggest that 'humility is the only thing required for the Christian life'.[9] But though Dom André Louf argues that Thomas Aquinas, in trying to accommodate Aristotle (who failed to include humility among his list of virtues), toned down humility with his emphasis on moderation and emphasized magnanimity instead, Aquinas is still keen to retain the emphasis on humility in his (still popular) post-Eucharistic prayers: 'May this Holy Communion be a helmet of faith and a shield of goodwill ... may it bring me charity, and patience, humility and obedience, and growth in the power to do good'.[10] In this context humility seems to be moving in the direction of a 'public virtue'.

The Latin root of humility (*humilis*) is in 'humus', and though often translated as 'lowly' or 'near the ground', could mean 'earthed' or 'rooted' in the ground. St Augustine's emphasis, 'human, know that you are human; your whole humility is to know yourself',[11] need not be confined to the Ash Wednesday reminder that 'we are all dust and to dust will return' in the sense of knowing our earthly, dirt-based place. Rather it could include a much greater awareness of our basic relationship of equality with our fellow human beings. In emphasizing Christ as the supreme model of humility, St Paul underlines the concept not as lowliness of human birth but as selflessness ('Greater love has no man ...') and self-emptying love for others.

In his work *The Global Face of Public Faith: Politics, Human Rights and Christian Ethics*, David Hollenbach explores the moral virtues for intellectual enquiry that seek 'to contribute to political and social life by advancing our understanding of human well-being', focusing on the 'virtue of humility' and 'the commitment of solidarity' in an attempt to resist current trends for 'excessive desire for social control, scepticism about the possibility of knowing anything significant about what is normatively human and ironic detachment that treats all claims to normative understanding as naive', themselves vices undermining the overall good of the human community.[12]

It is often remarked that the pace of modern technological change and development is outstripping our moral capacity to keep up with them, but perhaps the real challenge is the postmodern one of realizing that in our world of increasing global interdependence, the pursuit of individual 'mastery' or control of our universe is a chimera. Increasingly markets and economic integration (though still generating a widening gulf between rich and poor), instant telecommunications and far-reaching transport infrastructure are reducing our globe to an interconnected network of villages in which the global is now local – and vice versa. Nor is the Earth simply to be exploited for resources as the crisis of unsustainability has shown. While polluting and climate-destabilizing molecules cannot observe national borders, human beings increasingly have to work with a respect and understanding of natural orders. Dominating nature is now generally regarded, along with the forceful abuse of political power, as unacceptable, arrogant and disrespectful. Of course, the risk is that overplaying the need for a withdrawal from technological progress or political engagement, attached to a new kind of 'things should not or cannot be changed' mentality, can lead to a live and let live attitude that displaces the search for a more just and peaceful society. Politics itself becomes dismissed as the problem, disengagement the solution. At this point Hollenbach stresses the need to retrieve the virtue of humility from 'the confusion evident in the presuppositions of a social science rooted in the modern humanistic pursuit of human betterment that is at the same time sceptical about all judgements concerning what counts as better'.[13] He argues that 'humility leads to paying attention to the reality of other persons and the world of nature. It is the awareness that one is not the centre of the universe precisely because one feels reverence for the inherent worth of realities beyond the self.'[14]

The catechism's emphasis on 'humility' in prayer was graphically illustrated by a young British Muslim I encountered a while back. At a public meeting in inner city Leeds to discuss extending the local mosque to include a minaret and the muezzin – the call to prayer – to be on a par with the local church bell for the 11 o'clock Mass, the Muslim community was immediately challenged by an outspoken man who asserted that there should be a firm rejection of the proposals because Britain was by nature a Christian country. Invited to explain what the Muslim community wanted – and what the 'muezzin' was – a young Muslim came forward to spell out what his life was like in inner city Leeds: 'It's like falling into the filthy River Aire in winter when it's full of supermarket trolleys, tyres and rubbish, and sinking down into the dark mud and going under believing you are the cause of all the world's problems.' Pressed on whether he ever felt more positively, he replied: 'Sometimes it's like super-surfing on the River Aire in the rushing waters of springtime, when you feel on top, and in control – and the solution to all the problems.' And the call to prayer?

> So when I get out of bed in the morning and before I lie down at night, and three times during the day, I pause to reflect on the fact that there is a greater reality than me – and I am neither the cause nor the solution to all the problems, but I have to relate to greater realities.

His experience of prayer was underpinned by an understanding of humility as a relational virtue. As Hollenbach puts it:

> Humility is a bond of a certain kind with reality beyond the self. It forms the kind of connection with reality that is appropriate for persons who are finite and limited rather than demi-gods ... Authentic humility requires acceptance

of one's dependence and vulnerability to what is beyond oneself. It is a stance towards the world that regards relationships with nature, other persons, society and indeed with God as essential to authentic personhood.[15]

Prayer and genuine solidarity therefore converge in this revived definition of humility.

In a brief pamphlet *Living the Virtues* (1968), recommended by Kevin Kelly to his seminary students, the theologian John Foster wrote: 'If living the virtues means anything it means this: the opening up of new territory. In every human person there are huge areas of untapped energy and resources.'[16] Long before the introduction to public (and private) administration of the SWOT analysis (for assessing an organization's Strengths, Weaknesses, Opportunities and Threats), Foster stressed that 'living the virtues' meant 'to view one's own world as always open and disclosing new possibilities of action ... to judge reality as one sees it insofar as it reveals new creative opportunities for the human spirit to work within it'. In contrast to the optimism of the recent past (of the 1960s), he refers to 'a more healthy awareness of the precariousness of justice in every unique human situation', underlining that 'the religious accomplishment today is to know the precariousness of any just order and yet be able to decide and act'.[17]

There is one key passage in Foster's text that finds a regular echo in Kevin Kelly's work. It refers to the virtue 'which Christ excelled in, that of obedience ... the word itself means listening or being attentive to something that is being said'. The virtue of obedience, in other words, is about listening properly. Foster stressed:

Apart from the fact that the human ear is physically one of the least developed of the human organs, listening is one of the most difficult activities in life, as a game of consequences shows. In addition there is the tendency in most people to hear what they want to hear and not necessarily what the speaker has to say. Growth in obedience is simply a refining of one's faculty of hearing. As a virtue it could be said that only a mature person is capable of being obedient. We are speaking of hearing, here, not merely in the sense of being able to pick up the sounds but also of being able to interpret them and make them meaningful.[18]

'Obedience', he says in summary, 'is nothing less than a reverence for the other side of a relationship, a receptivity to everything that goes on around us, a feeling of oneness with the whole life of the world.'[19]

John Foster stresses that personal encounters are growth points:

At such-and-such a moment, I met this particular person, had this encounter. However trivial such a meeting was, I was not the same person afterwards. Another relationship has enriched my life. Certain meetings, of course, can change the whole direction and pattern of one's life.[20]

Kevin Kelly adds another dimension to encounter, stressing that it 'is not just a matter of listening to individuals. It also means listening to other communities, organizations or movements of committed people whose value systems may not be exactly the same as our own, or who may order their priorities differently to ourselves'.[21]

In the preface to *New Directions in Moral Theology*, Kevin Kelly modestly writes: 'I am a run of the mill teacher of moral theology who has read fairly widely in the field and who has tried to listen a lot.'[22] In practice, his approach and listening methodology have always characterized his style as he listens attentively, responding by gentle questions to engage and draw out a person more. As Hollenbach puts it, 'genuine solidarity is impossible among those who are not really equal. And humility is a condition for hearing what others have to say about themselves.'[23] But the preface reveals something of the context of Kelly's listening:

> There is no doubt in my mind that the people in whose midst I am privileged to live in Liverpool play an important role in my understanding for Christian ethics. The very down to earth love and wisdom that is evident in their everyday living, despite all its hardship and ambiguity, provides an important resource for Christian ethics. I am fortunate in being able to draw on their expertise crafted in the school of experience over many generations.[24]

There is an understated hint here of a context running throughout his work and life. As Hollenbach writes:

> The real challenge to political authority and economic systems will come from within the experience of solidarity and genuine 'listening', particularly to fellow suffering human beings, as well as setting out with the acknowledgement that one does not have ready answers to all questions of how people ought to live together.[25]

Kevin Kelly's work and life draw us back towards that over-neglected if not derided political virtue, humility.

Notes

1. Kevin T. Kelly, *Life and Love: Towards a Christian Dialogue on Bioethical Questions* (London: Collins, 1987), p. 105.
2. Kevin Kelly, *New Directions in Moral Theology: The Challenge of Being Human* (London: Geoffrey Chapman, 1992), p. viii.
3. Pierre Claverie, 'Humanité Plurielle', *Le Monde* (4–5 August 1996).
4. André Louf OP, *Humility* (London: Catholic Truth Society, 2005), pp. 5–6
5. David Hollenbach, *Claims in Conflict: Retrieving and Renewing the Catholic Human Rights Tradition* (New York: Paulist, 1979).
6. Cited in Louf, *Humility*, p. 9.
7. Cited in *ibid.*, p. 15.
8. cf. *ibid.*, p. 15.
9. Cited in *ibid.*, p. 9.
10. The prayer of St Thomas, that some Catholics recite after Mass.
11. St Augustine, *Tractates on the Gospel of John*, 25:16 [Jn 6.15-44].
12. David Hollenbach, *The Global Face of Public Faith: Politics, Human Rights and Christian Ethics* (Washington: Georgetown University Press, 2003), p. 40.
13. *Ibid.*, p. 45.

14. *Ibid.*
15. *Ibid.*
16. John Foster, *Living the Virtues* (London: Darton, Longman and Todd, 1968), p. 15.
17. *Ibid.*, p. 22.
18. *Ibid.*, p. 29.
19. *Ibid.*, p. 34.
20. *Ibid.*, p. 33.
21. Kelly, *New Directions in Moral Theology*, p. 4.
22. *Ibid.*, p. vii.
23. Hollenbach, *The Global Face of Public Faith*, p. 49.
24. Kelly, *New Directions in Moral Theology*, pp. vii–viii.
25. Hollenbach, *The Global Face of Public Faith*, p. 46.

26

Kevin T. Kelly and the Role of the
Pastoral Moral Theologian

Charles E. Curran

Kevin T. Kelly has done and continues to do moral theology by fusing together
the experience and concerns of a professional moral theologian and of a priest
engaged in pastoral ministry. Unlike academic moral theologians, he has one foot
in the academy and one foot in pastoral practice. Pastoral experience constitutes
an important part of his moral theology.[1] Kelly points out that his 1992 book
New Directions in Moral Theology owes at least as much to his belonging to
the universe-city of Liverpool as it does to his involvement in the University of
London.[2]

Kelly's understanding of his vocation as a moral theologian follows from
his understanding of what moral theology involves. Human experience is an
indispensable and fundamental source for developing moral knowledge. Most of
our ethical principles came into existence as the crystallization of the experience
of wise and loving persons. A continual dialectic exists between principles and
concrete situations and experiences. At times, in the light of experience, principles
have been changed and should be changed. Too often the natural law has been
understood as something that is given. In light of the contemporary emphasis on
historical consciousness, it is more accurate to say that we have been gifted by God
with our nature and our call to use our God-given gifts wisely and lovingly.[3]

Kelly's emphasis on experience and a historically and culturally conscious
approach to moral knowledge grounds his emphasis on the importance of
dialogue. Vatican II called for dialogue in many dimensions – dialogue with the
world, dialogue with other Christians and other religions, and even with all people
of good-will. Kelly hastens to point out that dialogue does not mean that one
embraces relativism, or denies the existence of some objective truth, or reduces
morality only to personal preferences.[4] Kelly's writings illustrate how important
dialogue is in his approach to moral theology. One aspect of this is the ecumenical
dialogue that so often comes through in his writings. His 1982 book *Life and Love*
involves a dialogue with other Christians and churches on bioethical issues that are
facing the world and the churches today.[5]

The emphasis on experience and dialogue as constitutive dimensions of moral theology has changed Kelly's understanding of his own role as a teacher of moral theology. He began teaching moral theology by handing over to his students the moral truths. But he later realized that this is the wrong frame of reference. Learning is the most important reality; and, if no learning occurs, there is in reality no teaching. The teacher is also very much a learner and the teaching role is to involve both the teacher and the students in the learning process.[6]

The hierarchical teaching office of the Roman Catholic Church should be seen in the same way. Learning is the primary process and teaching is seen as a leadership role within the learning process. The 'learning' teaching authority in the Church will be conscious that the primary teacher in the Church is the Holy Spirit. Such an approach recognizes the importance of dialogue in its many dimensions while still finding a place for the prophetic dimension.[7] Yes, the Catholic understanding recognizes a special divine assistance given to the Magisterium of the Church, but this divine assistance should not be understood in a fundamentalistic sense as some kind of directly revealed new and exclusive knowledge given to the pope and bishops. The hierarchical Magisterium has to carry out all the tasks of a good 'learner' teacher. Also, Catholic theology recognizes that the Holy Spirit is given to all people in the Church and even some outside the Church.[8]

In keeping with his own approach to moral theology, Kelly dialogues with the 1990 instruction of the Congregation for the Doctrine of the Faith, 'The Ecclesial Vocation of the Theologian'. In the process, he maintains that Catholic theologians are called at times to express timely public disagreement with 'non-irreformable' Church teaching.[9]

With this method and approach, Kelly has addressed many of the issues that have arisen in the Catholic Church in the post-Vatican II period. He quotes the 1995 National Conference of Priests in England referring to 'the growing gap between the official regulations of the Church and the demands of pastoral practice'. Kelly deals with some of these issues in a chapter entitled 'Mind the Gap'.[10]

His comparatively short 1982 book *Divorce and Second Marriage*, which was expanded in a new edition in 1997, calls for a change in the Catholic teaching on the indissolubility of marriage and recognizes that people involved in such second marriages at the present time, under certain conditions, should be allowed to participate fully in the Eucharistic liturgy and the life of the Church community.[11] The book itself is a response to challenges coming from experience. Kelly recognizes that experience alone can be flawed and does not by itself provide solutions. But his pastoral experiences challenged him to rethink the theory and practice of the Church with regard to the indissolubility of marriage.

Kelly has also been challenged by the experience of people and his ministry with them in the area of sexuality. Here too, in response to their challenge, he has rethought the Catholic approach to sexuality. Sex is not sinful; it is a gift of God. Casual and uncommitted sex is obviously wrong. There is a need to develop a growth ethic in sexuality similar to the growth ethic which is part of the entire Christian life. Foundational beliefs for a Christian sexual ethic include the following: the equal dignity of women; human freedom; friendship, intimacy and love; the goodness of the human body and sexuality; the giftedness of life; and respect for the conscience of the unique human person.[12] He has dealt in some depth with two particular issues – homosexuality and cohabitation.

How is the gospel good news to people who have a gay or lesbian sexual orientation? In trying to respond to that question he dialogues with the experience of gay and lesbian persons but also with what other churches, theologians and scientists have had to say about the issue. A fundamental factor in real growth for all people – heterosexual or homosexual – is the practical acceptance of themselves as sexual persons and the goodness that is involved in this. Kelly argues for a Christian sexual ethic which is the same for heterosexuals and homosexuals, seeing sexuality in the context of love and moral responsibility, while opposing the antinomian and individualistic tendencies often found in our culture.[13]

The experience of others and his pastoral ministry also brought him to question the Church's teaching and practice on cohabitation before marriage which he has dealt with in a number of places.[14] Here again he follows his method of trying to make 'faith-sense of experience' and 'experience-sense of faith'. Above all, we need to listen to the experience of those who are cohabitating before marriage. While acknowledging problems with cohabitation and the many different forms it takes, Kelly recognizes that, for some people, cohabitation is a good experience and involves their growth towards the commitment of marriage. This experience constitutes a challenge for theologians to make experience-sense for these people.

Many but not all of the issues Kelly has addressed come from the discrepancy between hierarchical moral teachings and the experience of people with whom he was ministering. Among the other issues Kelly addresses is the role of women in society and the Church. Kelly is highly critical of the patriarchy that has oppressed women in both society at large and the Church. To prove his point, he quotes from the textbook in moral theology he used as a seminarian. It states that a woman cannot receive holy orders in the Catholic Church because priesthood requires a certain superiority in ruling the faithful, but a woman by her very nature is inferior to a man and is subject to him.[15] Christian theology is substantially flawed because it has been constructed predominantly by men in light of men's experience of a world in which women were second-rate citizens and women's experience was not considered important for theology.[16]

Kelly has also dealt with spirituality in light of his pastoral experience. He maintains that growth out of sin can be a very helpful spirituality for Christians today. Christian spirituality is a lifelong growth process out of being victims of sin and agents of sin. The very experience of my woundedness and the inhumanity it brings into my life and that of others is the very stuff out of which repentance, healing and growth are fashioned. Such a spirituality also avoids the dangers of a one-sided individualism by recognizing the social and ecological dimensions of a spiritual growth out of sin.[17]

From his ministerial experience, Kelly has come to appreciate the sinful social structures that often influence individual lives. His book on sexual ethics was written in light of his experience in Africa with the AIDS pandemic. The book, in keeping with his method, is not an academic study but a Church-challenging and pastorally helpful study supportive of people committed to working in the AIDS field. The social structures, heavily influenced by patriarchy and poverty, have greatly influenced the AIDS pandemic. These structures need to be changed and transformed in order to overcome the pandemic, but so too the Church's sexual teachings need to be changed and transformed.[18]

The Pastoral Approach of St Alphonsus Liguori

Kevin Kelly is by no means the first Catholic moral theologian to do moral theology from the perspective of pastoral practice. Most moral theologians in the past have adopted such an approach. The best illustration of this tradition is Alphonsus Liguori (1696–1787), the patron saint of moral theologians. The very first sentence of the preface to his large four-volume moral theology explains the pastoral nature of his approach. Alphonsus Liguori founded a congregation of priests and brothers, popularly called the Redemptorists, with the purpose of working among the rural poor in giving missions, guiding consciences and hearing confessions. His textbook served to give these young Redemptorist students what they needed to carry out their apostolate.[19]

Alphonsus explicitly mentioned that his own pastoral experience changed his approach to moral theology. He was trained in the rigorism of the French author, Francis Genet.[20] Pastoral experience convinced him of the need for a more benign approach to moral theology. Alphonsus insisted that his own approach was the happy medium between rigorism and laxism. But most of his writings involved his disagreements with rigorism because he was often attacked by the rigorists. Marciano Vidal, the leading contemporary Spanish Redemptorist moral theologian, subtitled his book on the moral theology of Alphonsus 'From Rigorism to Benignity'. Vidal summarizes the entire moral theology of St Alphonsus with the following synthetic phrase: 'Pastoral benignity against moral rigorism'.[21]

In the preface to his moral theology, Alphonsus points out a twofold problem with rigorism – the forming of erroneous consciences and the desperation that comes when the faithful fear they cannot live in accord with what rigorism proposes. The rigorist approach confuses precepts with counsels; has no understanding of human weakness; forgets the particular human situation with all its differences of persons, places and circumstances; weighs conscience down with new commandments; and renders intolerable the burden that Jesus proclaimed as light.[22] The last reason points out an important theological difference between Alphonsus and the rigorists. The rigorists believed that only a comparatively few people were saved and the vast majority, even of Christians, would not be saved. Rigorists tended to cite the biblical phrase about the narrow gate, whereas Alphonsus cited Jesus as saying his burden is light. Alphonsus, in his theology and his writings, consistently emphasized the mercy of God. He chose as the motto of his congregation the passage from Ps. 130.7 (the famous *De profundis*) – *copiosa apud eum redemptio* – 'With Him there is plentiful redemption'.

Alphonsus was obviously a creature of his own time. He followed the approach of the manuals of moral theology with their emphasis on a legal model focusing on what constituted sin and the degree of sinfulness. However, within this perspective, the benignity of Alphonsus, based on his pastoral experience, came across in a number of areas. This paper will discuss only conscience and the sacrament of penance as instances of his more benign approach in opposition to the rigorists.

Domenico Capone points out what he claims has been forgotten by almost all those who think they follow Alphonsus. Alphonsus's first words on conscience assert that the divine law is the remote and material rule of human actions, while conscience is the proximate or formal norm. Conscience strives to conform itself to the divine law, but conscience ultimately determines the formal goodness or badness of the act. As a result of such an understanding, Alphonsus, in opposition to the rigorists, recognizes that one could be invincibly ignorant of the natural law. Alphonsus inserts the judgement of conscience into the dynamism of the human person moving towards her end in the glory of God and the love of neighbour.[23] Louis Vereecke points out that Alphonsus goes so far as maintaining that a person acting in invincible ignorance (the ignorance is not the fault of the person) performs a good and meritorious act. Thomas Aquinas did not go that far. Aquinas maintained that the act done by an invincibly erroneous conscience is not a sin, but he did not call it good.[24]

Much of the attention given to Alphonsus on conscience refers to the debate over what was called 'the moral systems'. What is one obliged to do when in doubt about the existence of a law? Tutiorism claimed you always had to follow the safest position favouring the law. Probabiliorism proposed that one could act against the law only if such a position was more probable (probable really means provable or rational) than the position in favour of the law. Laxism maintained that the position favouring freedom from the law needed only to be tenuously probable. Alphonsus adopted and defended a moderate probabilism (meaning that one could justifiably act against a law, provided that a good case could be made for doing so), especially in his extended controversy with Patuzzi who supported probabiliorism.[25]

Alphonsus's prudence, supported by his theological concerns and his pastoral experience, comes through clearly in his solution of particular cases. Here he avoided the extremes of rigorism and laxism, and his solutions appealed to many. He approached each individual question, striving to discern the truth in the particular situation. In his approach to specific issues he brought together his pastoral sensitivity and his theological understanding of a merciful God.[26]

Marciano Vidal speaks of the Copernican revolution that Alphonsus brought to the sacrament of penance by his option for benignity over rigorism.[27] Perhaps this judgement is somewhat exaggerated, but there is strong evidence for significant differences that Alphonsus brought to his understanding of the role of the confessor. Alphonsus wrote a number of books on the role of the confessor. He accepted the general understanding of the confessor as a judge, but in the very beginning of his discussion of the sacrament of penance in his moral theology, he points out the other roles of the confessor as father and doctor. Rigorism held that the confessor should never absolve the penitent unless he is certain that the penitent is properly disposed and will not sin again. In dealing with such a penitent, a penitent who is in a proximate necessary occasion of sin, a penitent who confesses a habit of sin, or a penitent who constantly falls into the same sin, Alphonsus tries to find a middle way between rigorism and laxism.

Thus, there is a long tradition in the Catholic approach for moral theologians to have one foot in the academy and one in pastoral practice. Likewise Kelly is following in the tradition of Alphonsus Liguori by his call for change in some aspects of moral theology in light of his pastoral experience. One can see in Kelly what Vidal has seen in Alphonsus – pastoral benignity struggling against moral rigorism.

The Future

Yes, Kevin Kelly is part of a long tradition of pastoral moral theologians, but this is a dying breed. Kelly in fact will probably be the last of the pastoral moral theologians writing in English in the Catholic tradition. Even today there is no one like him doing this kind of work. What explains this reality?

The discipline of moral theology has become much more academic than it was in the pre-Vatican II period. The number of people engaged in the study of moral theology has increased exponentially. The publications in moral theology in any one year at the turn of the century were greater than the publications in English in any 15-year period in pre-Vatican II times. The discipline of moral theology today is so complex that no longer can one person claim to be competent in all of moral theology. When Kevin Kelly and I started teaching moral theology in seminaries in the 1960s, one person was expected to cover all moral theology. In light of the breadth, depth and complexity of moral theology in the academy, it is practically impossible for a moral theologian to have one foot in the academy and one in pastoral practice.

What explains the dramatic change that has occurred in the discipline of Catholic moral theology in the last 50 years? I will briefly reflect on the changes that have occurred in my own country, which obviously have some parallels in other countries.[28] In the early to middle 1960s, the home of moral theology in the United States was the seminary, and the professors were all white, male, celibate, Catholic priests. Vatican II obviously affected the change in moral theology but also circumstances within the USA. The Catholic academic world had a significant role to play. For all practical purposes, before 1965 the Catholic University of America was the only institution offering doctoral degrees in moral theology.

What about the more than 200 Catholic colleges and universities that existed in the United States and taught courses in moral theology? Yes, Catholic colleges required undergraduate students at this time to take often as many as four different courses in theology. But in the 1950s there was general agreement that these courses were catechetical rather than theological and were taught not by qualified academics but by people who qualified by reason of their religious profession or their priestly ordination. The society now called the College Theology Society came into existence in 1955 with the aim of improving the academic nature of theology in Catholic colleges. Together with Vatican II, the need for a more academic approach to theology courses in Catholic colleges brought about a tremendous increase in the number of Catholic moral theologians and a more complex and in-depth academic approach to the discipline itself. Teachers of theology in Catholic colleges needed to receive PhD degrees. After Vatican II, major Catholic universities began to offer PhD degrees in theology so that today there are over ten Catholic universities in the USA offering such degrees.

Professors in these graduate programmes must meet the requirements found in any graduate and research university. Those who now teach in Catholic colleges are required to fulfil all the requirements for any academic, which include publishing scholarly articles and books. As a result, the number of professional moral theologians has increased dramatically in the past 50 years. Catholic theologians today are also a diverse lot. There are many more lay people than clerics or religious; many women have attained positions of leadership in the field of moral theology; Latino/a and African American theologians are also now part of the community of Catholic theologians in the United States.

In my judgement, the academic professionalization of moral theology and the much greater number and diversity of Catholic moral theologians makes a very significant contribution to the discipline. One of the negative consequences is that the discipline will no longer have the participation of the pastoral moral theologian. Academic moral theologians will obviously continue to recognize experience as one of the sources of moral wisdom and knowledge. But, because the direct experience of the pastoral moral theologian will be missing, practitioners of moral theology need to be open to other ways of learning from what happens in pastoral practice.

Notes

1. Kevin T. Kelly, *From a Parish Base: Essays in Moral and Pastoral Theology* (London: Darton, Longman and Todd, 1999), pp. 1–2.
2. Kevin T. Kelly, *New Directions in Moral Theology: The Challenge of Being Human* (London: Geoffrey Chapman, 1992), p. viii.
3. *Ibid.*, pp. 66–75.
4. *Ibid.*, pp. 3–6.
5. Kevin T. Kelly, *Life and Love: Towards A Christian Dialogue on Bioethical Questions* (London: Collins, 1987).
6. Kelly, *From a Parish Base*, pp. 75–76.
7. *Ibid.*, pp. 76–81.
8. Kelly, *New Directions in Moral Theology*, pp. 142–46.
9. *Ibid.*, pp. 138–59.
10. Kelly, *From a Parish Base*, pp. 6–8, pp. 69–74.
11. Kevin T. Kelly, *Divorce and Second Marriage: Facing the Challenge* (London: Collins, 1982; new and expanded edn, London: Geoffrey Chapman, 1997).
12. Kevin T. Kelly, *New Directions in Sexual Ethics: Moral Theology and the Challenge of AIDS* (London: Geoffrey Chapman, 1998), pp. 137–87.
13. *Ibid.*, pp. 64–95.
14. Kelly, *From a Parish Base*, pp. 99–110; Kelly, *New Directions in Sexual Ethics*, pp. 123–26, 144–45, 187; Kevin T. Kelly, 'Cohabitation: Living in Sin or Occasion of Grace?' *The Furrow* 56.12 (2005): 652–58.
15. Kelly, *New Directions in Sexual Ethics*, p. 45.
16. Kelly, *New Directions in Moral Theology*, pp. 86–94.
17. Kelly, *From a Parish Base*, pp. 157–72.
18. Kelly, *New Directions in Sexual Ethics*.
19. Alphonsus de Ligorio, *Theologia moralis* (ed. Leonardus Gaudé), 4 vols (Rome: Typographia Vaticana, 9th edn, 1905), 1:lv.
20. Alphonsus de Ligorio, *Dissertatio scholastico-moralis pro uso moderato opinionis probabalis* (Neapoli: 1749), p. 45.
21. Marciano Vidal, *La morale di Sant' Alfonso: Dal rigorismo alla benignità* (Rome: Editiones Academiae Alphonsianae, 1992), p. 253.
22. Alphonsus, *Theologia moralis*, 1:lv.
23. Domenico Capone, 'Per la norma morale: Ragione, coscienza, legge', in *Historia: Memoria futuri: Mélanges Louis Vereecke* (ed. Réal Tremblay and Dennis J. Billy), (Rome: Editiones Academiae Alphonsianae, 1991), pp. 199–225 (221).

24. Louis Vereecke, *De Guillaume d' Ockham à Saint Alphonse de Liguori: Études d'historie de la théologie morale moderne 1300-1787* (Rome: Collegium S. Alfonsi de Urbe, 1986), pp. 553–60.

25. Frederick M. Jones, *Alphonsus de Liguori: The Saint of Bourbon Naples* (Westminster, MD: Christian Classics, 1992), pp. 262–95.

26. Vereecke, *Ockham à Liguori*, pp. 579–85.

27. Vidal, *La morale di Sant' Alfonso*, pp. 270–72.

28. For a more detailed description of the US scene, see Charles E. Curran, *Loyal Dissent: Memoir of a Catholic Theologian* (Washington, DC: Georgetown University Press, 2006), pp. 219–28.

27

The Role of Personal Story in the Teaching of Moral Theology

Kevin T. Kelly

When I taught at Heythrop College in the University of London, I would always spend at least the first session sharing with the students my own life story and how I felt it would influence the experience of moral theology I hoped to provide for them. I also insisted that their own life experience was also an important factor and would inevitably colour their own interpretation of what moral theology was all about. I stressed that this was true, not just at an individual level, but also of the group experience we would share together. It would be a mutual learning experience. That was one of the reasons why I anticipated that my course would be different each year, partly because of what I myself had learned and how I had changed over the previous year, and partly because of the dynamic interchange that would take place in the current year.

A similar highlighting of personal story was reflected in a talk I gave to the theological faculty at Leuven University in 2003 and subsequently published under the title, 'Confessions of an Ageing Moral Theologian' in the Irish theological periodical, *The Furrow*.[1]

This essay is a third version of the same story, written at a later date and so coloured by my more recent experience and all those who have influenced me during this later period. Consequently, my own interpretation of my earlier story will probably also be different to some extent. Although I am basically still the same person I have always been, in many ways I have changed considerably, and in some ways even quite radically over the years. I hope I am still changing. The ageing process itself is a challenging and even enriching experience. And the world I am living in is certainly changing drastically and throwing up challenges, opportunities and threats which I would never have envisaged when I was younger.

So what follows is the same story, though longer in duration, which some of my students and friends have heard already. Yet it is not the same story since the storyteller is now seeing it from a different vantage point which brings with it a renewed focus.

Early Years

I was blessed with a very happy childhood. I felt loved and secure at home. Yet this was hardly a time of 'innocence'. Little did I realize how my childhood was also 'deprived'. I had no sisters, an impoverishment which deepened still further when, at the age of 14, I moved to the all-male establishment of the seminary at Upholland College. Unconsciously, I was being affected by an atmosphere of emotional deprivation and so not receiving the kind of well-integrated education in personal and sexual relationships which is now recognized as part of any young person's healthy development. This all-male environment encouraged a macho culture in the seminary. Discipline was strict. Feelings were not for public display. The image of priest put before us was of a man, strong, independent, able to control himself and others, and totally obedient to the will of God, which came through the voice of authority and the rules of the seminary. *Tintinabulum vox Dei est* ('The bell is the voice of God') was drilled into us. This was bound to have a negative influence on my early formative years studying moral theology – and, in fact, the whole of theology and spirituality. Moreover, this ethos of the seminary was itself a by-product of the kind of theology (especially moral theology) that held sway in the Church in those days.

My initial theological education was in a pre-Vatican II seminary. I was ordained in 1958, five years before the council began. Yet it would be unfair to present my seminary education as all doom and gloom. While I could not say it did me no harm, I am still grateful for much of the seminary experience. The senior seminary staff at Upholland College in those days included two outstanding biblical scholars, Alexander Jones and Tom Worden, both of whom played a major role in awakening the Catholic Church in the UK to the renewal in biblical studies that was beginning to emerge in places like the *Ecole Biblique* in Jerusalem. Moreover, their spirit of critical enquiry was infectious, and not restricted to biblical studies. It is worth mentioning one experience I have never forgotten and which, I suspect, had a long-term influence on my later theology. While I was in the sixth form we followed a course on St John's Gospel by Alexander Jones. He went to a lot of trouble explaining to us his particular interpretation of a passage in John 6. When it came to the end-of-year exam, I had the nerve to reject his interpretation and give my reasons why. That was totally against the ethos of seminary education. It was not just the bell which was the voice of God. The teacher was too! I was expecting to fail my exam because of my foolhardiness. Instead I was given top marks. Looking back, I feel sure that the case I argued was probably very flawed. I suspect that my high mark was for being prepared to approach the issue in a spirit of critical enquiry!

I had respect, even affection, for Paddy Hanrahan, the Irish priest who taught moral theology in the seminary. Yet much of his course was light years away from the approach to moral theology that emerged from Vatican II. The three-volume moral theology manual by Noldin was our text. Its subtitle was *Secundum mentem S. Thomae* ('according to the mind of St Thomas'). When, after ordination, I studied moral theology in Fribourg from the actual text of Aquinas, I discovered that Noldin was very far from the mind of Thomas. In addition, a great deal of the course was devoted to canon law – not unnaturally, since Noldin's treatment of the sacraments was largely based on canon law. The manual's coverage of sexual ethics was in a separate volume on the sixth and ninth commandments and said little about sexual maturity and healthy relationships. Its main aim was to specify as accurately as possible all the kinds of sins against chastity and to offer guidance on determining what guilt was involved.

Further Studies

After my ordination in 1958, I was sent to Fribourg University in Switzerland. My remit was to do a licentiate in (moral) theology there, and then go to Rome for a doctorate in canon law. That was seen as giving the necessary competence to teach moral theology. Even at that early stage this struck me as putting the cart before the horse, so I managed to get approval to reverse the priorities. I was able to complete the two-year licentiate in one year, which enabled me to stay on in Fribourg to do my doctorate in (moral) theology. So my canon law studies were reduced to a licentiate. I have since enjoyed describing myself as a lapsed, non-practising canon lawyer!

My theological studies at Fribourg were truly a liberating experience. Although we studied from the actual text of St Thomas's *Summa theologica*, that text was seen in its historical context, wrestling with the problems of its day. Its very methodology encouraged a critical approach to theology. The *questiones* (questions) in the text presented key problems that the contemporaries of Aquinas were struggling with. They were far from Aunt Sallies, deliberately set up to be knocked down. They actually engaged one's personal faith. The teacher was the leader of the exploratory expedition, rather than an oracle whose teaching had to be taken on faith. I and my fellow students were engaged in a struggle for meaning, delighting in any insights in the truth we achieved, though always conscious that the truth was something much bigger than we would ever grasp or understand. This approach gave us a respect for tradition. I learned to treasure the mediaeval saying: 'We see further than our forebears, we are dwarfs standing on the shoulders of giants.' However, that same text was a reminder that it is a living tradition, to be further enriched, and we all share responsibility to try to 'see further' and so develop this living tradition.

My appreciation of the complexity of this living tradition deepened as a result of my doctoral work on conscience and Caroline divines, a group of mainly Anglican theologians in seventeenth-century England who kept alive the very fertile insights of Aquinas on conscience and the virtue of prudence. This was at a time when the neo-scholastics were sucking the lifeblood out of this tradition and reducing prudence to a fearful cautiousness instead of seeing it as a virtue of creative initiative in the face of the exigencies of real life with all its particularity. My interest in this field was stimulated by my tutor, Cornelius Williams OP, an Irish Dominican who became a close friend. Though not a brilliant lecturer, our paths crossed at just the right moment. He also introduced me to the writings of his predecessor, Thomas Deman, a French Dominican who died in his early forties, but not before producing some magnificent writing on prudence and conscience. Although I never met Deman, his writings have inspired much of my later writings and practice.

What about my two years of canon law at the Gregorianum University in Rome? There were two redeeming features. The first was a course on the philosophy of law by the German Jesuit, Bertrams. Though the dullest of lecturers, he opened my eyes to the importance of exploring the philosophy of law. A sound philosophy of law frees moral theology from the shackles of legalism. Laws are no longer chains depriving us of our freedom. Rather, they are tools enabling us to live together, respecting each other's freedom and life commitments through a shared vision of the common good, while at the same time doing justice to the demands of the uniqueness of individual situations through the exercise of *epikeia*, part of the more general virtue of justice.

The second redeeming feature was a seminar with Ladislas Örsy. The subject matter of the seminar was not the important thing – in fact, I cannot remember what it was. What has affected me ever since was the way Örsy personified 'the human face of canon law'. For him – as for Jesus himself – laws are made for people, not people for the law. The impact of Bertrams and Örsy on my moral theology can be seen in a whole variety of ways. It probably comes out most clearly in my short piece entitled, 'Pastoral Care and Church Law: "Mind the Gap"',[2] where I describe *epikeia* as the 'gap virtue', playing on the well-known 'mind the gap' announcement on the London Underground.

Initial Parish Experience and Teaching in the Seminary

After completing my further studies, I spent two years as a curate in St Clare's, a very busy parish in Liverpool. Vatican II was in full spate at the time. I still remember my parish priest (also vicar general), Mgr Tommy Adamson, looking up from his breakfast table reading of *The Times* and saying to me with a note of puzzled excitement in his voice, 'What do you think of this? "The Church is a community of churches"'. The excitement in his voice told me that his heart was in the right place theologically. That moment has remained embedded in my mind. I felt I had experienced the energy released by the fusion of two very different mindsets.

From five to nine every weekday evening all four priests in the parish engaged in house-to-house visiting. Having covered every Catholic home in my district about three times in my first six months in the parish, I was feeling pretty desperate. I rang a good friend of mine, Jimmy Collins, a very inspirational priest, and asked him, 'Jimmy, what the hell do you talk about when you visit people in their homes?' I have never forgotten his reply. It has deeply influenced my moral theology ever since. 'You don't talk about anything,' he said, 'you listen to people's lives.' I am not opposed to the academic dimension of moral theology. However, if that becomes the be-all and end-all of moral theology and if moral theologians lose touch with people's lives, I think moral theology will lose its soul.

After my two years in the parish, I returned to the seminary to teach moral theology. I was struck by the unreality of the situation on my first night back. As the senior students, all aged from 18 to about 30, processed out of chapel on that first evening back, the thought came to me that, in many of the homes I had visited in St Clare's parish, young men of this age were already married, fathers of young children and holding down a job. As seminarians, any responsibilities they carried were fairly minimal and artificial, and, to all intents and purposes, they were treated as minors and subject to the rigid discipline of the institution. Such a situation was hardly conducive to their making their own an experience-based and pastorally sensitive moral theology.

Father Tom Worden, whom I have mentioned above as one of the lights shining in the darkness, had returned from being a *peritus* (expert adviser) at Vatican II. As dean of studies, he set about renewing the whole approach to theological and biblical studies. Formal lectures were reduced to a minimum. Great emphasis was placed for the students on writing regular essays, which enabled them to give their personal and reflective response to reading usually suggested by the tutor. Each essay would be evaluated by and discussed with the tutor for that particular course. In addition, weekly seminars were held at which the students shared with each other the fruits of their research. This was designed to inculcate in students a frame of mind in keeping with the spirit of Vatican II. It tried to equip the students to feel at home in a climate of radical change. In this way the seminary itself became a kind of laboratory of how changes occur. Staff and students had to cope with all the struggles and criticism that accompany any radical change. They had to learn to live with ambiguity, recognizing that, in any process of change, some good things are inevitably lost and new weaknesses are taken on board – something Rahner describes as 'compulsory alternatives'. Nevertheless, feeling at home with change, though disconcerting, is a better preparation for a Vatican II-style moral theology.

Early Writings

While I was at the seminary I took my first tentative steps in writing on moral theology for periodical publication. Again, the personal element comes in here. I had got to know Michael Richards while I was in Rome. We both lodged at the Beda College. It was Michael who made possible the publication of my doctoral dissertation, *Conscience: Dictator or Guide?* (1967) in a series he was editing for Geoffrey Chapman. When he became the editor of the *Clergy Review* he began to encourage me to publish in that periodical and later invited me on to its editorial board. I have never forgotten my first piece. It was in two parts and entitled 'The Authority of the Church's Moral Teaching'.[3] I showed it to my predecessor and former moral theology teacher, Paddy Hanrahan, who was still on the staff. When he returned my manuscript, he had corrected the spelling and punctuation errors but offered no other comment. On reflection, I appreciated what he had done. He was implicitly saying to me: 'It's up to you to get on with it now. I've done my bit.' That tied in with the attitude of historical consciousness that I had imbibed in my time at Fribourg. He had been true to his times. It was up to me now to be true to my times. And the times they were a-changing!

An example of the best of his times was the regular feature in the *Clergy Review* entitled, 'Questions and Answers'. In each issue practical problems raised mainly by priests in parishes were discussed and answers provided. Canon E.J. Mahoney was the expert over many years, eventually succeeded by Lawrence McReavy. Many, though far from all, the problems raised had a canonical basis to them. Mahoney's two volumes of *Questions and Answers* were prominent on the bookshelves of most priests and were frequently consulted. In the years leading up to Vatican II Karl Rahner had been writing on the importance of helping people in forming their own consciences so that they would be in a position to discern what they should do in any situation that presented itself. This will ring bells with anyone familiar with the Ignatian Exercises. The weakness with the 'questions and answers' approach was that, for most of the moral questions raised, answers were traced back to some kind of authoritative Church teaching, often papal statements or declarations of the then Holy Office. In the absence of such authoritative statements, a search was made of 'the approved authors'. These were the many manuals of moral theology written over recent centuries and used as textbooks in seminary training. Although these 'approved authors' would discuss the arguments for and against a particular position, at least as much weight was given to the 'authority' of the author as to the strength of his arguments.

Michael Richards asked me to take over the 'Questions and Answers' column. My reaction was that a totally different approach was needed for our post-Vatican II age. Consequently, I wrote an introductory article entitled, 'Do-it-Yourself Moral Theology'[4] and expressed the hope that the members of our recently formed Association of Teachers of Moral Theology (ATMT) would be able to supply a series of articles which would give readers a grounding for tackling their own problems. I have to confess that a trickle of such articles appeared for a couple of years and then the stream dried up. Whether this was a good thing or not, it is not easy to judge.

Over the years I have found the ATMT, founded by Jack Mahoney and myself almost 35 years ago, a great source of inspiration and on-going learning. At each meeting we would discuss papers submitted and read in advance. This encouraged a conversational methodology in which members were never out to score a point but were focused on trying to help each other deepen their understanding of the topic under consideration. In such a non-threatening climate we developed into a group of friends as well as professional colleagues. On a number of occasions we even had shared meetings with the bishops. The listening and learning approach was much in evidence in such a session held after the publication of John Paul II's encyclical, *Veritatis splendor* in 1993, which deals with fundamental moral questions. The meeting, carefully prepared by a small, joint planning group led by Bishop Jack Brewer, opened with bishops and moral theologians sharing how they felt when they first read the pope's letter. Only after we listened to each other's feelings did we move on to discuss some of the actual issues raised by the encyclical. This was very much a listening and learning exercise, a good model for a Church committed to a collaborative ministry in teaching authority.

Humanae Vitae

The issue of conscience came up with a vengeance with the publication of Pope Paul VI's encyclical, *Humanae vitae*, in 1968. After outlining a very person-centred approach to marriage and sexuality, the pope gave his decision on the very down-to-earth issue of birth control. He based it on a rationale that did not sit easily with the person-centred approach of the rest of the document. Moreover, his decision went against the advice of his so-called 'Birth Control Commission', which included moral theologians, social scientists and some extremely committed married people. Their report carefully argued that a change in the Church's teaching would do justice to the heart of what is contained in the Church's living tradition, and it even contained a supplement proposing a way this change could be presented to the Church at large. Three moral theologians on the commission broke ranks and submitted to the pope their own private document, arguing that such a change would harm the credibility of the Church. Sadly, it was their unofficial advice that was heeded.

Extensive reading and research had convinced me that there would be a change in the Church's teaching. Hence, *Humanae vitae* came as a great shock to me. I had actually supported Archbishop Beck in preparing the Liverpool clergy for such a change and in offering appropriate pastoral guidance to them. An inadequate grasp of ecclesiology and the role of authority in the Church led me to respond to the encyclical in a way which I can see, with hindsight, was a pastoral failure. I feel I let people down on this point. My good friend, the moral theologian Charles Curran, who has always been a great inspiration to me, and whom I admire for his great courage and integrity, had foreseen such an eventuality and had anticipated and worked through the ecclesiological issues raised by it. Hence, he was able to disagree publicly with the pope's teaching and supported people in their conscience decisions to continue using birth control. I argued rather feebly in long articles in the *Catholic Pictorial* and the *Clergy Review* that *Humanae vitae* presented the Church with something new and that we would need time to weigh up and wrestle with its teaching. I recognized that, though it was a word spoken by legitimate authority, it might not be the last word or even the best word. I felt we needed time to reflect on it before we could responsibly disagree with it and reject its teaching. However, I did recognize that it was a matter with immediate and practical consequences for the lives of married couples. Hence, their conscience decisions needed to be respected during this time of reflection and they should not be coerced into conduct they considered harmful to the good of themselves and their children.

A major learning experience for me in this matter occurred some months after the encyclical was published. I was asked to speak to a large group of married couples in Rock Ferry on the Wirral. They were very committed Catholics who used to meet regularly in cells to support each other in their married life. They asked me to explain the thinking of *Humanae vitae* to them. Believing that the lived experience of such committed couples was an important source for theological reflection on marriage, I thought that my meeting with them could be a good learning experience for me. Hence, in addition to speaking to them about the encyclical, I asked them – a group of about 200 – to write down for me how far the teaching of *Humanae vitae* tied in with their lived experience. I was taken aback – and chastened – to find that pretty well all of them said that it did not fit in with their understanding and experience of marriage. Their response comes back to me every time I read that challenging passage in Jack Mahoney's magnificent book, *The Making of Moral Theology*:

> In the case of *Humanae Vitae* ... Pope Paul may appear to imply that the reception of his teaching by the Church at large will have, through the complementary influence of the Spirit, at least a confirmatory value in establishing the truth of his teaching. The possibility cannot be ruled out, however, that in such non-infallible teaching on a matter which is not contained in revelation the response of the body of the faithful will be less than whole-hearted in agreeing with the papal teaching and the considerations underlying it. For the influence of the Holy Spirit in the hearts of the faithful, as described by Pope Paul, is envisaged purely as disposing them to be receptive, whereas it might be a more positive one of refining, qualifying, or even correcting the papal teaching.[5]

Cardinal Hume was surely right when, at the 1980 Rome Synod on the role of the Christian family, he said that the experience of married people can be 'an authentic source of theology from which we, the pastors, and indeed the whole Church can draw'.

Upholland Northern Institute and My Three-Pronged Sabbatical

My appreciation of the importance of human experience deepened still further when I was appointed director of the newly formed Upholland Northern Institute (UNI) after the Senior Seminary moved to the north-east and was amalgamated with Ushaw College, Durham. UNI was set up as a centre for Adult Christian Education and In-Service Training (IST) for clergy. Actually, our very first course was an IST course for the bishops of England and Wales on the theme 'The Bishop as Teacher'. My own talk to the bishops was precisely on that topic. My input was deeply influenced by a course of adult learning that our UNI team had recently undergone. That, combined with Brian Wicker's analysis of the 'seminar leader' model of teaching authority, led me to suggest that teaching authority in the Church is an exercise of collaborative ministry and that we all have our part to play in it. The Church is both a learning community and a teaching community. A fuller version of the kind of approach I put forward is found in Chapter 5 of my *From a Parish Base*.[6] Such an approach obviously has implications for an issue such as disagreeing with 'official' Church teaching. I tried to tackle that in the little piece 'Dialogue, Diversity and Truth: The Vocation of the Moral Theologian in the Roman Catholic Church Today', which I wrote as an epilogue to my *New Directions in Moral Theology*.[7] This is an issue that refuses to go away. I get the impression that the way many European bishops today are interpreting *Ex corde ecclesiae*, the Vatican document on Catholic universities, is leading to a situation where the only form of moral theology that seminarians will be exposed to is one of strict compliance with 'official' teaching. There will be no chance of their hearing the Spirit speaking through voices expressing loyal and responsible disagreement.

After five very fruitful and stimulating years as director of UNI, I enjoyed the great privilege of a seven-month sabbatical. Two separate blocks of two months were spent as a fellow of St Edmund's House, Cambridge. To broaden the learning experience, I asked a scientist friend to recommend a non-theology book that might open my mind to new horizons. His suggestion, Thomas Kuhn's *The Structure of Scientific Revolutions*,[8] blew my mind. Kuhn's analysis of 'paradigms' of knowledge enabled me to make sense of the changed approach to the theology of marriage found in Vatican II. It gave a solid basis to my book, *Divorce and Second Marriage*.[9] Though most of the writing was done at Cambridge, it was not finally completed until I became leader of the Skelmersdale Team Ministry. The learning experience at Cambridge was intensified through many stimulating personal contacts, most notably visiting fellows Ellen Leonard from St Michael's, Toronto, an expert on Modernism, especially in England, and Peter and Ann Pettifer Walsh, respectively from South Africa and England, but who manage to keep revolutionary fire blazing in their bellies in the hardly revolutionary setting of Notre Dame University, where Peter is professor of government and international studies and Ann edits an alternative campus newsletter entitled *Common Sense*. Their continuing friendship is a rich theological resource for me.

Two months of my sabbatical comprised visiting a number of developing countries, notably India, the Philippines and Peru. I had the privilege of seeing liberation theology and inculturation put into practice in real life. It was an experience that has marked me for life. In Peru I also had my eyes opened to the implications of denying priestly ordination to women. While still at UNI my research for a series of talks entitled *Being Human means being Sexual* had led me to face the unacceptability of the Church's negative line on this matter. In Peru I experienced at first hand how this position results in leaving isolated communities denied the Eucharist, apart from once or twice in the year. I accompanied a religious Sister of Notre Dame, Therese Hartley, on a three-hour drive from Tambogrande to an outpost mission where she regularly leads a Eucharistic service. A priest comes for Mass at most once or twice a year. I learned sufficient Spanish to say the second Eucharist Prayer. The rest of the Mass was led by Therese. The situation struck me as ludicrous and even obscene! It was making gender a higher priority than the Eucharist itself. A similar disordering of priorities (including celibacy as well as gender) mars the otherwise very inspiring and beautiful post-synodal letter, *Sacramentum caritatis*, published by Benedict XVI in February 2007.

The third component of my sabbatical was a 30-day Ignatian retreat at Dollymount in Dublin. One unforgettable insight from that retreat was to do with the will of God. I had always been attracted to the spirituality of Charles de Foucault and recited daily his well-known 'Prayer of Abandonment'. It came home very powerfully to me during this retreat that to pray 'Father, I abandon myself into your hands' lacked any real credibility if, in fact, I was not prepared to exercise my will. It was to give God nothing. I had tended to accept too passively whatever happened as God's will. I now realized that it was only by fully accepting responsibility for whatever lay in my control that I was enabling God's will to be truly realized. In a sense, it was up to me to 'create' God's will. God's will is not predetermined in some kind of divine database. This insight led me to write an article in *The Way*, entitled 'Towards an Adult Conscience'.[10] An abbreviated version is found in Chapter 10 of *From a Parish Base*. It is worth quoting the following passage:

> In a sense we create God's will; or better, God's will takes shape through our decisions. We are not puppets with the whole of our lives and everything we do already pre-programmed by God, the puppet-master. As each major decision looms before us in life, God's will is not already determined and filed away in some kind of divine computer programme. Discovering God's will is not a matter of discovering what God has already decided that we should do. Rather, discovering God's will lies in ourselves deciding what is the most loving and responsible thing for us to do. We discover God's will by actually bringing it into being ... It gradually dawned on me that abandonment to God's will was very closely linked with having the faith and courage to respond actively, not passively, to the situations in life. It meant being prepared to make decisions myself, and accepting responsibility for my own decisions.[11]

Skelmersdale Team Ministry and Queen's College, Birmingham

After my sabbatical I was appointed leader of the Roman Catholic Team Ministry in Skelmersdale New Town. This was a steep learning curve for me since the Team

Ministry had been in operation for a number of years. It was made up of priests, sisters and laity well experienced in collaborative ministry. I have written up some of the fruits of that experience in Chapter 3 of *From a Parish Base*. More than anything it taught me that any mission statement at any level of Church life has to be based on an analysis of the local situation in which the Church community in the area is called to live its life and exercise its ministry. A mission statement that could apply to any Church community, regardless of time, place or culture, will never put fire in our bellies. That is why, to my mind, the Liverpool archdiocesan mission statement produced a few years ago was a non-starter, despite its statement of the highest ideals: 'Taking to heart the last words of the Lord Jesus, we will go into the world to proclaim the Good News to the whole of Creation'.

At the end of five years in Skelmersdale I was becoming worried that there was very little writing taking place in the UK in the field of moral theology. Because of my training and experience I could not ignore such a lacuna. Although I had thoroughly enjoyed my years in the Team Ministry, I decided that I would make better use of my talents, such as they were, by re-engaging with teaching and writing in moral theology. To give myself time to catch up with developments, I accepted a one-year research fellowship at Queen's College in Birmingham, an ecumenical establishment for training for the ministry. Although Skelmersdale had been a rich ecumenical experience, Queen's College offered me a much broader form of ecumenical life, especially in the field of liturgy. With Queen's being an ecumenical foundation, free from the restraints of different denominational churches, I had the opportunity to experience the Eucharist celebrated by ordained Methodist and German Lutheran women. This was prior to the Church of England accepting women's ordination. I was happy to find myself feeling completely at home with a woman presiding at the altar.

Moreover, my research project was itself ecumenical. It was an examination of the position of different Christian churches on the new development of *in vitro* fertilization. It was eventually published by Collins in 1987 under the title *Life and Love: Towards a Christian Dialogue on Bioethical Questions*. My growing appreciation of the importance of women's contribution to the full life, ministry and teaching of the Church led me to include a specific chapter in this book entitled, 'What some Women are Saying about IVF'. By 1992, when my *New Directions in Moral Theology* was published, I had come to realize that the contribution of women to moral theology was not just important. It was absolutely essential. Hence, Chapter 5 of that book is entitled 'Moral Theology – Not Truly Human without the Full Participation of Women'.

Arriving in Birmingham a few weeks after the Handsworth riots, I had the enriching experience of helping out each weekend in St Francis parish, Handsworth, courtesy of its amazing and inspiring parish priest, Fr Tom Fallon, very much a man of the people. My experience in Birmingham also introduced me to the interfaith scene. I visited far more mosques than Catholic churches during my year there, and I made good friends with some delightful Muslims. Attending Muslim and Hindu prayer services never left me feeling that the God they were praying to was a foreign or alien God. Despite major differences, I could sense the truth in the expression 'We all believe in the same God'. Looking back years later, I would add: 'And the same God believes in us'.

Combining Parish and University:
Eldon Street, Liverpool and Heythrop College, London

After Birmingham I was determined to combine parish experience with teaching moral theology. My good friend, Jack Mahoney, offered me the opportunity to join him at Heythrop College in the University of London, while at the same time engaging in pastoral ministry in Our Lady's parish, Eldon Street in inner-city Liverpool. Although the original suggestion was that I involve myself in Heythrop as much as I felt able, by the time I arrived there Jack had been appointed professor of moral and social theology at King's College in London, and I was left with carrying the full teaching load in moral theology on a part-time basis! It was very hard work, but I enjoyed every minute of it. I would catch a Sunday evening train from Liverpool Lime Street station to London Euston so that I could start work at the crack of dawn on Monday morning. Thursday afternoon would see me dashing with a heavy bag of books on my shoulder to Oxford Circus tube station to get to Euston in time for my return train to Liverpool. I never once missed it, even though at times I had only minutes to spare! I found the twice-weekly, three-and-a-half-hour train journey a very valuable time to catch up with my theological reading.

Both sides of this 'double life' fed off each other. Eldon Street was a very privileged pastoral setting. The Eldonians, the incredible community and housing group in this area of multiple deprivations, were still in their early days, though they had already weathered their battle with Derek Hatton and his militant tendency on Liverpool City Council. The groundwork was solidly in place, due to the inspired leadership of former dock-crane operator, Tony McGann and the combined force of the local community, solidly supported by the two local priests, Jim Dunne and Michael Lane. To be dropped into such a situation was an immense privilege and one I will never forget. It would be impossible to attempt to summarize the theological richness of such an experience. I can only point readers to 'Struggling to Live the Gospel in Inner-city Liverpool: A Case Study', Chapter 2 of my *From a Parish Base*. There I have tried, very inadequately, to capture some of the inspiration and excitement of those early days. My ten years in Eldon Street parish offered me a theological 'source', which I was able to share in my theological teaching in Heythrop and which the students seemed to appreciate greatly. Heythrop possesses one of the best theological libraries in the UK. The Eldonians provided me with a library of a totally different kind. I was privileged to read the 'living Gospels' incarnated in their everyday lives. The remarkable thing is that the wonder of the Eldonians is as alive today as it was then. I am writing this in mid-June 2007, one week after the future Prime Minister, Gordon Brown, visited the Eldonians and was deeply inspired by what he saw.

HIV/AIDS and CAFOD

During my early days at Heythrop College I was introduced to a second experiential and theological 'source' which affected me deeply on my first encounter with it and which has continued to have a major influence on me as a moral theologian. In the early 1990s HIV/AIDS was beginning to make its presence felt. Initially considered to be restricted to the gay community, people soon recognized that it was affecting heterosexual people on a far wider scale, especially in sub-Saharan Africa. The

288

Roman Catholic development agency CAFOD quickly realized that HIV/AIDS, as well as being a terrible and, in those pre-ART days, terminal medical condition, was also a major development issue. CAFOD responded very quickly by setting up an HIV/AIDS section with its own advisory committee. A Medical Missionary sister, Dr Maura O'Donohue, headed the whole venture. Her medical expertise, combined with her extensive experience of Africa and her deep commitment to social justice and respect for the dignity of women, enabled her quickly to become a key figure in the Church's response to HIV/AIDS. She became an 'expert' in the fullest sense of the word. In other words, her knowledge and understanding of HIV/AIDS was based on grass-roots personal experience of how people were being infected and affected by this pandemic. Maura invited me to join her advisory committee and my eyes began to be opened to the enormity of HIV/AIDS, a process of personal enlightenment that continues to this day. Along with Dr Mary McHugh, chair of the advisory committee, and two CAFOD staff, Maura enabled me to have a three-week exposure experience of the grass-roots reality of HIV/AIDS in Uganda, a visit I shall never forget. I saw how poverty was a major factor in the spread of HIV/AIDS – and vice versa. I was also confronted with the feminization of poverty, while being bowled over by the extraordinary resilience of the women involved in one way or another. The slogan 'Living positively with AIDS' made a deep impact on me, and I had to face the startling truth that 'the body of Christ has AIDS'.

My contact with CAFOD also led to my being invited to share in theological reflection on the pandemic with moral theologians and people living with AIDS from the UK and Ireland, USA and Asia at conferences in New York, Dublin and Bangkok. After the Bangkok meeting, I stayed on for an additional two weeks to meet people working with and living with AIDS in Thailand and the Philippines. This was to ensure that the book on AIDS I was working on was firmly grounded in real life. Unfortunately, the publishers would not accept a book exclusively devoted to HIV/AIDS. They insisted on my discussing some wider issues of sexual ethics. Nevertheless, my primary emphasis on HIV/AIDS comes through very clearly in the subtitle: *New Directions in Sexual Ethics: Moral Theology and the Challenge of AIDS*.[12]

Part of 'living positively with AIDS' for me has been the great privilege of meeting many inspiring people such as Noreen Kaleeba, Ursula Sharp MMM, Archbishop Pius Ncube, Sister Mary Courtney, Father Bob Vitillo, Julian Filokowski, Martin Pendergast, Ann Smith and the very dedicated and multi-talented Jesuit moral theologians, Jim Keenan and Jon Fuller. Although I am not HIV-positive, HIV/AIDS is a key dimension of my personal story. In any teaching of moral theology I have been engaged in, it has certainly made its presence felt. I have never forgotten the words of a poor man in Thailand whose broken life was transformed and given purpose when he was diagnosed HIV-positive: 'AIDS is my gift'. I have kept detailed diaries of my three extensive exposure experiences in Uganda, Zimbabwe, Nairobi and Zambia. When I retire, one of my AIDS gifts will be to make these three diaries more widely available. An awareness of HIV/AIDS cannot only transform our own lives. It can also 'put fire in our bellies' to combat the many dehumanizing factors which fuel injustice in our world and which also lie at the roots of the pandemic. It was not without reason that the last subtitle I used in the final chapter of *New Directions in Sexual Ethics* was 'A Time of Grace: AIDS – A Window of Opportunity for Our Global Society'. In the words of Enda McDonagh, we are living in 'a time of AIDS'. I finish my book on a challenging and hopeful note:

Many individuals living with HIV/AIDS experience a conversion to living more fully and with more commitment to what life is all about. Our human family is now living with HIV/AIDS. Will that experience turn out to be a conversion experience for us? ... Theologically, I would suggest, our world is faced with a redemptive moment. If that is not a challenge to Christians and Christian churches, what is?[13]

Ecumenism – St Basil and All Saints, a Shared Church in Widnes – and Beyond ...

For the last ten years of my personal story I have been parish priest of a shared Roman Catholic/Anglican church in Hough Green, Widnes. This experience has served to deepen my conviction that the future is ecumenical – and more than ecumenical. As a Hindu priest said to me only last night, 'religion, though good, can also narrow our minds. God is not narrow. God is all-embracing.' Almost from its inception, the Association of Teachers of Moral Theology has been graced with a small but highly influential ecumenical membership. The faithful attendance of Professor Ronald Preston at our twice-yearly residential weekends until his death in 2001 was an outstanding example of that.

Chapter 2 of my *New Directions in Moral Theology* is entitled 'Graceful Disagreement'. In it I try to wrestle with the phenomenon of disagreement on moral issues between different Christian churches. This is a far cry from those early days when authoritative papal or Vatican statements were regarded as the final word on most moral questions. Even later, when the English-language version of the Catechism of the Catholic Church was published in 1994, I highlighted still further the ecumenical context in which that document needed to be read:

> Since Vatican II, any presentation of Catholic faith must have an ecumenical dimension to it. This entails more than a longing for the unity for which Christ prayed. It also involves a recognition that God's Spirit is at work in other Christian churches. It is in this spirit that the moral section of the Catechism needs to be read. This implies that, when there are particular issues of moral disagreement between the major Christian churches, the Catechism's presentation of the current authoritative Catholic teaching should not be presumed to be the final and definitive Christian position on this topic. The Catechism offers a helpful ecumenical service in presenting an authoritative Catholic position. However, it would be ecumenically harmful if such a presentation was understood to carry such authority that any other position must be rejected as unchristian. The importance of this point was brought out all the more through the publication in 1994 of *Life in Christ, an Agreed Statement by the Second Anglican–Roman Catholic International Commission* (ARCIC II). This agreed statement is a powerful witness to the fact that, even on those specific moral issues where these two churches disagree, they still share the same vision and are committed to the same common values.[14]

Sections 29 and 32 of the Agreed ARCIC II Statement, *Life in Christ*, referred to in the above quotation and authored by a body of which Cardinal Cormac Murphy-

O'Connor was co-chair, offer a challenging comment on the formation of conscience and how a well-formed conscience actually contributes to the development of the Church's moral teaching:

> (29) The fidelity of the Church to the mind of Christ involves a continuing process of listening, learning, reflecting and teaching. In this process every member of the community has a part to play. Each person learns to reflect and act according to conscience. Conscience is informed by and informs the tradition and teaching of the community. Learning and teaching are a shared discipline, in which the faithful seek to discover together what obedience to the gospel of grace and the law of love entails amidst the moral perplexities of the world.
>
> (32) Teaching developed in this way is an essential element in the process by which individuals and communities exercise their discernment on particular moral issues. Holding in mind the teaching they have received, drawing upon their own experience, and exploring the particularities of the issue that confronts them, they have then to decide what action to take in these circumstances and on this occasion. Such a decision is not only a matter of deduction. Nor can it be taken in isolation. It also calls for detailed and accurate assessment of the facts of the case, careful and consistent reflection and, above all, sensitivity of insight inspired by the Holy Spirit.

My personal story in the setting of our shared church of St Basil and All Saints has only made me more convinced of the truth and importance of the above quotations.

If God spares me, a new phase of my personal story will begin after I retire at the end of June 2008. Austin Smith CP, a good friend of mine, describes retirement as 'disengaging to re-engage'. I look forward to learning what impact that will have on my understanding and teaching of moral theology. I just hope it makes some allowance for my failing memory and diminishing hearing!

Notes

1. 'Confessions of an Ageing Moral Theologian', *The Furrow* (February 2004), pp. 82–91.
2. Cf. Kevin T. Kelly, *From a Parish Base: Essays in Moral and Pastoral Theology* (London: Darton, Longman and Todd, 1999), pp. 69–74.
3. Kevin T. Kelly, 'The Authority of the Church's Moral Teaching', *Clergy Review* (1967): 682–94, 938–49.
4. Kevin T. Kelly, 'Do-it-Yourself Moral Theology', *Clergy Review* (1970): 52–63.
5. John Mahoney, *The Making of Moral Theology* (Oxford: Clarendon Press, 1987), p. 295.
6. Kelly, *From a Parish Base*, pp. 75–81.
7. Kevin T. Kelly, *New Directions in Moral Theology: The Challenge of Being Human* (London: Geoffrey Chapman, 1992), pp.138–59.
8. Thomas Kuhn, *The Structure of Scientific Revolutions* (Chicago: University of Chicago Press, 1962).

9. Kevin T. Kelly, *Divorce and Second Marriage: Facing the Challenge* (London: Collins, 1982).
10. Kevin T. Kelly, 'Towards an Adult Conscience', *The Way* (1985): 282–93.
11. Kelly, *From a Parish Base*, pp. 148–49.
12. Kevin T. Kelly, *New Directions in Sexual Ethics: Moral Theology and the Challenge of AIDS* (London: Geoffrey Chapman, 1998).
13. *Ibid.*, pp. 212–13.
14. Kelly, *From a Parish Base*, p. 135.

Selected Bibliography of Kevin T. Kelly

Books Published

Conscience: Dictator or Guide? A Study in Seventeenth-Century English Protestant Moral Theology (London: Geoffrey Chapman, 1967).

Divorce and Second Marriage: Facing the Challenge (London: Collins, 1982).

Life and Love: Towards a Christian Dialogue on Bioethical Questions (London: Collins, 1987).

New Directions in Moral Theology: The Challenge of Being Human (London: Geoffrey Chapman, 1992).

Divorce and Second Marriage: Facing the Challenge (London: Geoffrey Chapman, new and expanded edn, 1997).

New Directions in Sexual Ethics: Moral Theology and the Challenge of AIDS (London: Geoffrey Chapman, 1998).

From a Parish Base: Essays in Moral and Pastoral Theology (London: Darton, Longman and Todd, 1999).

Unfortunately, *New Directions in Moral Theology*, *New Directions in Sexual Ethics* and *From a Parish Base* are out of print. Their publishers have given Kevin Kelly permission to make the texts available, free of charge, on the web. The following address gives access to them, plus a complete bibliography of his writings:

<http://www.hope.ac.uk/artsandhumanities/hopepark/theology/staff/kellyk.htm>.

Articles in Books

'The Role of the Moral Theologian in the Church', in R. Gallagher and B. McConvery (eds), *Conscience and History* (Dublin: Gill & Macmillan, 1989), pp. 8–23.

'Divorce and Remarriage', in Bernard Hoose (ed.), *Christian Ethics: An Introduction* (London: Geoffrey Chapman, 1998), pp. 248–65.

'Divorce', in Adrian Hastings (ed.), *The Oxford Companion to Christian Thought* (Oxford: Oxford University Press, 2000), pp. 172–73.

'A Moral Theologian Faces the New Millennium in a Time of AIDS', in James Keenan (ed.), with Jon Fuller, Lisa Sowle Cahill and Kevin Kelly, *Catholic Ethicists on HIV/AIDS Prevention* (New York and London: Continuum, 2000), pp. 324–32.

'Some Theological Reflections on the Parish Reports', in Noel Timms (ed.), *Diocesan Dispositions & Parish Voices in the Roman Catholic Church* (London: Ashgate, 2001), pp. 167–80.

'Divorce and Remarriage', in James J. Walter, Timothy E. O'Connell and Thomas A. Shannon (eds), *A Call to Fidelity: On the Moral Theology of Charles E. Curran* (Washington DC: Georgetown University Press, 2002), pp. 97–112.
'Resuscitation', in Peter Drury, Tony Flynn and Kevin T. Kelly, *Resuscitation: Whose Decision?* (Derby: Christian Council on Ageing, 2003), pp. 13–25.
'It's Great to Be Alive', in Linda Hogan and Barbara Fitzgerald (eds), *Between Poetry and Politics: Essays in Honour of Enda McDonagh* (Dublin: Columba Press, 2003), pp. 191–203.
'Do We Need a Vatican III?', in Julian Filochowski and Peter Stanford (eds), *Opening Up: Speaking Out in the Church* (London: Darton, Longman and Todd, 2005), pp. 267–80.

Articles Published since 1967

'Mortal Sin and Grave Matter', *Clergy Review* 52 (1967): 588–605.
'The Authority of the Church's Moral Teaching', *Clergy Review* 52 (1967): 682–94 and 938–49.
'Christian Morality', *Catholic Gazette* 59 (November 1968): 11–17.
'"Do It Yourself" Moral Theology', *Clergy Review* 55 (1970): 52–63.
'The Invalidly Married and Admission to Sacraments', *Clergy Review* 55 (1970): 136–41.
'A New Deal for Interchurch Marriages', *Clergy Review* 55 (1970): 621–45.
'Why Should Catholics Oppose Euthanasia Legislation?', *Catholic Gazette* 61 (April 1970): 3–8.
Christians and Injustice, CIIR Justice Papers, 1 (1970).
'A Positive Approach to Humanae Vitae', *Clergy Review* 57 (1972): 108–20, 174–86, 261–75, 330–48 and 803–808.
'The Bitter Pill', *Daily Express* (8 December 1972).
'A Chemist's Dilemma', *The Tablet* 229 (19 July 1975): 683.
'Human and Christian Values', *The Month* 9 (1976): 378–80.
'The Divorced-Remarried', *The Tablet* 234 (13 September 1980): 910–11.
'Adult Christian Education and Liberation', *Word in Life* (Australia) (August 1981): 121–27.
'The Priest Shortage and the Answer To It', *Clergy Review* 66 (1981): 61–63.
'How Just Can Violence Be?', *The Month* 15 (1982): 408–11.
'The Priest in Community', *Way Supplement* 47 (Summer 1983): 43–51.
'Towards an Adult Conscience', *The Way* 25 (1985): 282–93.
'Obedience and Dissent, 1. The Learning Church', *The Tablet* 240 (14 June 1986): 619–20.
'Obedience and Dissent, 2. Serving the Truth', *The Tablet* 240 (21 June 1986): 647–49.
'Sexual Ethics and the Vatican', *The Times* (30 August 1986).
'Formation for Collaboration', *Way Supplement* 56 (Summer 1986): 3–15.
'Viewpoint: Faith in Action', *The Tablet* 241 (26 September 1987).
'Conformity and Dissent in the Church', *The Way* 28 (1988): 87–101.
'The Eldonian Community in Liverpool', *The Month* (2nd n.s.) 21 (1988): 784–90.
'Tested and Found Wanting', *The Tablet* 242 (1 October 1988): 1117–20.
'The Changing Paradigms of Sin', *New Blackfriars* 70 (1989): 489–97.
'Embryo Research: The Ethical Issues', *The Month* (2nd n.s.) 32 (1990): 59–64.
'The Embryo Research Bill: Some Underlying Ethical Issues', *The Month* (2nd n.s.) 32 (1990): 115–22.
'Catholic Doctors, Philosophers and Moral Theologians in Dialogue', *The Month* (2nd n.s.) 32 (1990): 144–47.

'Sexual Ethics: Experience, Growth, Challenge', *The Month* (2nd n.s.) 32 (1990): 368–73.

'Christians and Linkage', *The Month* (2nd n.s.) 33 (1991): 66–68.

'Looking Beyond Failure: Life After Divorce', *The Tablet* 245 (3 August 1991): 935–37.

'Sin, Spirituality and the Secular', *The Way* 32 (1992): 13–22.

Letter re Tony Bland Case, *The Tablet* 246 (5 December 1992).

'Rest for Tony Bland' *The Tablet* 247 (13 March 1993): 332–35.

'Do We Believe in a Church of Sinners?', *The Way* 33 (1993): 106–16.

'A Medical Dilemma', *The Month* (2nd n.s.) 26 (1993): 138–44.

'A Great Pleasure', *Priests and People* 7 (1993): 361–65.

'The Spirit and the Letter', *The Tablet* 248 (4 June 1994): 722–23.

'The Catechism and Moral Teaching: 10 Tentative Tips for Readers', *The Month* (2nd n.s.) 27 (1994): 266–69.

'Moral Theology in the Parish', *Priests and People* 8 (1994): 367–73.

'Divorce and Remarriage: Conflict in the Church', *The Tablet* 248 (29 October 1994): 1374–75.

Series of four articles on HIV/AIDS in *Catholic Pictorial* (5, 12, 19, 26 March 1995).

'Living with HIV/AIDS', *The Tablet* 249 (13 May 1995): 597–99.

Letter re The Ordination of Women, *The Tablet* 249 (2 December 1995): 1548.

'Archbishop's Worlock's Legacy to Liverpool', *The Month* (2nd n.s.) 29 (1996): 129–36.

Letter re How to Fight Poverty, *The Tablet* 250 (29 June 1996): 854.

'Being a Moral Theologian Today', *Priests and People* 10 (1996): 318–23.

'The Challenge of AIDS', *Way Supplement* 88 (Spring 1997): 46–54.

'Obituary of Bernard Häring', *The Tablet* 252 (11 July 1998): 922–23.

'What Binds Marriage?', *Priests and People* 12 (1998): 157–59.

'A Prophet for the New Age', *The Tablet* 254 (8 January 2000): 6.

'Spirituality and the Parish', *Way Supplement* 101 (2001): 129–37.

'Retirement', *The Furrow* 54 (2003): 670–81.

'Confessions of an Ageing Moral Theologian', *The Furrow* 55 (2004): 82–91.

'A Eucharistic Dis-Service: A Personal Reading of "Redemptionis Sacramentum"', *The Furrow* 55 (2004): 397–400.

'The Passion of Christ', *The Furrow* 55 (2004): 442–43.

'Eucharist and Violence', *The Furrow* 56 (2005): 25–36.

'Vintage McDonagh', *The Furrow* 56 (2005): 114–18.

'One More Thing Needful', *The Tablet* 259 (2 July 2005): 19.

'The Body of Christ – Amen – Eucharist and Unity', *The Furrow* 56 (2005): 464–71.

'Cohabitation: Living in Sin or Occasion of Grace?', *The Furrow* 56 (2005): 652–58.

Index

Index

299

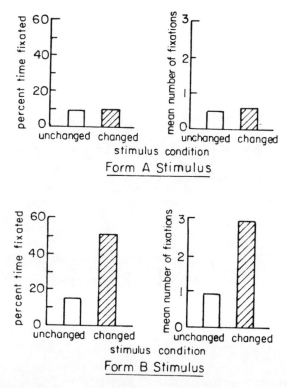

Figure 3. Presented separately for stimulus Form A and stimulus Form B: the average percent viewing time, and the mean number of fixations, devoted to the "sometimes changed" stimulus element when it had or had not changed.

dent that the significant effects shown previously in Figure 2 were carried entirely by the subjects who were exposed to the "easier" Form B stimulus (both of the Form B differences are significant at $p < .01$, U test). In sum, it appears that the change in form was detected only if it was in a nearby location. The implied corollary—that the infants did not regularly scan over the entire array on each presentation—will be documented in a later section. (Notice, incidentally, that a major assumption has been introduced into these anlayses: because the infants failed to direct saccades to a peripherally located discrepancy, it is assumed that the change had indeed gone unnoticed. The alternative—that the change was in fact

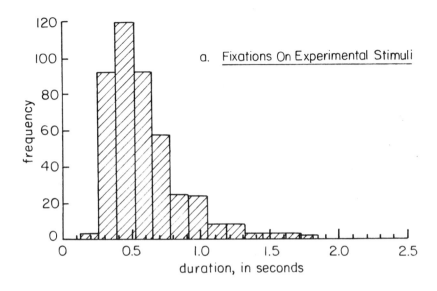

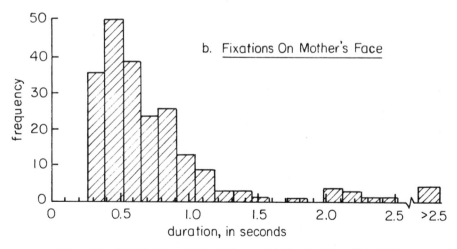

Figure 5.   Distributions of dwell-times. (a) For fixations directed to the experimental stimuli; n = 443. (b) For fixations directed to mother's face; n = 214.

dwell-time of adults when scanning photographs is reported to be .35 seconds; see Macworth & Bruner, 1970).

Consider first the possible significance of the occasional long dwell-times that appear in each of the distributions. To begin, might these merely be measurement artifacts: could they in fact simply be intervals that contained one or more small saccadic shifts that were too fine to be detected by present procedures? A sampling of instances of long fixations which occurred during periods of "optimal" data were examined, and it was possible to conclude that such fixations were in fact steady to within at least 1 degree of visual angle (see Appendix, section iii, regarding the quality of the data). Whether still smaller saccadic shifts might have been occurring within these extended dwell-times cannot be determined. However, if they did occur they were unrelated to stimulus detail: these longer fixations occurred at about the same relative frequency whether infants were attending to the square elements within the stimulus, whose contours were about 1 degree wide; or to the checkerboard, whose contours were spaced 2 degrees apart; or to the homogeneous IR source. In sum, although the longer dwell-times perhaps might have subsumed several closely adjacent fixations, such small saccadic adjustments, if present, were unrelated to stimulus detail. So the question remains: why did the infants, on occasion, dwell for rather long intervals on some limited area of the stimulus?

Two opposing kinds of explanation might be offered. It could be that these longer fixations were indicative of a heightened interest and the assimilation of more detail; on the other hand, they may simply have reflected intervals in which visual processing was not proceeding at its maximum rate, perhaps because attention lapsed momentarily, or shifted to another modality. As a context for considering these alternatives, note first a number of variables which were found *not* to be associated with the occurrence of long fixations. (These various negative findings are drawn from reactions to the experimental stimuli; the data from the single viewing of mother's face were too limited to consider acceptance of the null hypothesis.) Long fixations are defined as those lasting .7 seconds or more; reference to Figure 5 will show that this is a reasonable cutting point.

The relative incidence of long dwell-times proved to be only trivially correlated with infant age (r = .10), so it is unlikely that their relative frequency of occurrence was strongly related to the developmental status of the infant. Frequency of occurrence also was unrelated to amount of previous exposure—that is, the incidence rate showed no regular change across episodes, or between early and later fixations within an episode. Also, they were not associated with the fixation of any particular element within the array. There was, in fact, a rather surprising randomness in the order of occurrence of these longer fixations. Although sometimes they appeared in pairs, and on rare occasions in longer sequences, an analysis of these groupings proved them to be purely fortuitous: overall, 25% of the infants' fixations met the criterion of .7 seconds or more, and it was found that the empirical probability that any given long fixation would immediately be followed by a second was P = .252. Therefore, the occasional groupings were exactly those that would be produced by a purely random process. (Sometimes the second of the pair of long fixations was directed to the same stimulus, and sometimes the intervening saccade had shifted regard to a different feature; illustrative examples can be found in Figures 11 and 12 below.) Furthermore, the average duration of the sets of fixations which immediately preceded and followed the longer dwell-times was .45 seconds, which is almost exactly at the mean of the remaining set of "more typical" dwell-times shown in Figure 5. In brief, the extended dwell-times were isolated events, and in general they seemed to occur at random intervals throughout the entire series of experimental episodes. Moreover, as was reported in the preceding section, their incidence did *not* increase when the infants were devoting particular attention to the periodically changed figure within the stimulus array. All of these negative findings argue against the notion that longer fixations reflect periods of closer attention. Rather, they favor an alternative view that long fixations represent intervals of suboptimal visual processing—perhaps because an infant's attention momentarily waned, or was directed to another modality. If this explanation is correct, then the increased frequency of extra long fixations when viewing mother's face (see Figure 5) could be due either to its greater visual familiarity or to brief lapses in visual interest as the infant attended to, or anticipated, her speaking. (At the anecdotal level, one might find analogues of such effects in adults, who on occasion seem to be looking fixedly but are not in fact examining intently because their attention is directed elsewhere.)

In contrast to the largely negative findings obtained when seeking age-, target-, or exposure-related correlates of the longer dwell-times, individual differences emerged as a significant factor. Across infants, the correlation between incidence rates in the first and second half of the series of experimental episodes was $r = .68$ ($p < .05$). As previously noted, these individual differences were unrelated to the age of the infant; they were, however, correlated with another parameter of infant scanning. In a later section treating the lengths of infant saccades, it will be shown that a sweep across 10 degrees of visual angle is a reasonable criterion for defining a "long saccade." The frequency of such long saccades was positively correlated ($r = .61$; $p < .05$) with a relative *absence* of long dwell-times. It tentatively is suggested that each of these two measures may be a reflection of something akin to arousal level or visual alertness. If this is true, then the reliable individual differences in the incidence of unusually long dwell-times becomes comprehensible as a reflection of infant state: visually alert infants tend to scan more rapidly and more widely over the stimulus. Analyses to be presented in later sections will give added support to this provisional inference.

"Off Contour" Fixations

The distributions shown in Figure 5 represented fixations located on some contoured area, either within the stimulus array or on mother's face. Figure 6 presents similar data for the relatively rare instances in which the locus of regard happened to fall on an open (uncontoured) area of the visual field. Notice the absence, in each distribution, of any of the long fixations that sometimes occurred when fixations were focused on a contour (as in Figure 5). This would be highly unlikely ($p < .001$, $p < .05$, respectively) if such long fixations actually tend to occur with equal frequency in the presence and absence of a fixated contour. Therefore, it can be con-

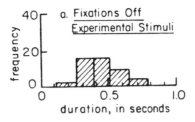

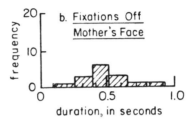

Figure 6. Distributions of dwell-times for fixations that landed on an open (noncontoured) area of the visual field. (a) During presentation of the experimental stimuli; n = 48. (b) When viewing mother's face; n = 15.

cluded that long fixations are unlikely to occur when no contour is present within the central area of the retina—at least not if contours currently are available in peripheral vision.

Two tentative inferences can be drawn from this conclusion. First, if long dwell-times indeed are associated with a momentary lapse in visual attention, then it appears that when attention happens to wane when a fixation is "off contour" some automatic process almost immediately shifts regard to an adjacent contoured area. This assumption—the positing of an automatic "contour centering" mechanism that takes over when saccades are not otherwise guided to specific locations—will find further support from findings to be reported in later sections. Second, for the fixations at issue there was no content within the central area of the retina, and hence there was nothing to be visually assimilated. Therefore, since fixation times could not have been extended by the requirements for content assimilation, the duration of the fixations represented in Figure 6 might be taken as rough estimates of the time required just for the programming and initiation of a coming saccade. This latter inference is basic to the following analysis.

Underlying Processes

Consider again the distributions shown in Figure 5. Two sorts of interpretation might be offered to account for their skewness. It could be argued that this shape reflects some single underlying process which on occasion is considerably extended in time; or the distributions could be viewed as the outcome of two separate processes, one of which is rather narrowly constrained around some modal value while the other is more widely dispersed. Each of the two alternatives has been examined in considerable detail, and the analyses favor the latter interpretation. Notice first that in both distributions there is a central symmetry around the same modal value, suggesting a latent process that is rather narrowly distributed around a mean of about .45 seconds. Second, reference to the distributions in Figure 6 will show that whenever an infant's fixation happened to land in a noncontoured area the mean and dispersion of the resulting dwell-times approximated the values of the hypothesized constrained components of the distributions shown in Figure 5. Third, notice that the frequency of markedly protracted fixations varied with the nature of the visual content (face versus abstract forms), whereas the fixations within the symmetrical and more tightly constrained portion of the curve appear to have been unaffected by the content of the visual field. Finally, the mean value of the hypothesized constrained distribution, .45 seconds, closely approximates the average of .42 seconds estimated from data given by Aslin and Salapatek (1975) to be the average time required to prepare and initiate the forthcoming saccade. (These latter data were from 2-month-old infants, and .42 seconds was the average interval between eye movements when infants employed a series of 10-degree saccades in traversing to a stimulus presented in the periphery of the visual field.)

Together, these various distributional characteristics not only favor the notion of two underlying processes, but also suggest the possible nature of their separate functions. Assume that the observed dwell-time distributions shown in Figure 5 are the result of two simultaneous processes: input falling on the more peripheral areas of the retina is being used to program the coming saccade, while at the same time the central-retina content is being assimilated. An alternative two-process model would posit *sequential* processing: first the current central-retina content is attended and processed, and then the next saccade is programmed in light of this information. Time constraints make this format less probable, however. When no content was available for processing, as for the fixations in Figure 6, infants required an average of around .4 seconds to program and initiate the next saccade; yet when content *was* available, as in the data of Figure 5, and presumably was being assimilated for subsequent processing, the total fixation times often were of no greater duration. By this analysis, the two processes—saccade programming and content assimilation—usually must proceed concurrently. (A possible exception is found in an observation made in the preceding section: when a change was introduced within the stimulus, infants immediately directed their first saccade to this location. In these instances, information from the infant's current fixation must have been used to program the next saccade. It will be shown later in this section, however, that in these instances fixation times were in fact of *about double* the usual duration. Moreover, it also is true for adults—at least sometimes, and perhaps typically—that the next saccade will be initiated before the content of the current fixation has been analyzed. This is illustrated by the frequency of saccadic "returns" to the sought-for target during visual search; see Gould, 1973.) In sum, it will be assumed—for the infant case at least—that the programming of the next saccade does not routinely await a final processing of the content of the current fixation. The remainder of this section will test the plausibility of this parallel-processing hypothesis in the light of additional data, and examine some of its implications.

Assume that the time that typically is required for programming the next saccade varies symmetrically around some mean value, and that this programming time is independent of the temporal requirements of the current content-assimilation process. If the two processes proceed concurrently, then the length of a given fixation must be set by *whichever process is the longer:* the coming saccade cannot be initiated until programming is completed; and, on the other hand, it would be grossly inefficient if an assimilation of content frequently were interrupted by a prematurely executed saccade. Given these assumptions, the probable distributions for the two latent processes can be derived from the data shown in Figures 5 and 6.[3] Figure 7(a) shows the assumed distribution of the saccade-programming process, estimated from the "content-free" dwell-times shown in Figure 6. The mean has been set at .4 seconds—an interval which matches closely the corresponding value inferred above from the Aslin and Salapatek data. Given this distribution, the latent content-related distributions must be as shown in Figure 7(b) and 7(c). Notice that for both types of visual content there is a modal content-assimilation time of around .3 seconds, which accounts for about a third of the infants' fixations. If it is granted that it is most unlikely that infants simply "waste" this moderately large portion of their fixations, then an assimilation of some aspect of visual content often must occur within a period of about a third of a second in infants as young as 2–5 months of age. The longer intervals presumably reflect a variety of additional factors, including, per the earlier analysis of the longer dwell-times, instances in which visual processing simply was not operating at its maximal rate.

So far discussion has centered on averaged values, combining data across infants of different ages. Consider next the values for individual subjects, focusing first on the saccade-programming process. After omitting from an individual record those dwell-times that are greater than .6 seconds, the mean of the remaining values will give a fairly accurate estimate of the average duration of the saccade-programming process for the individual infant.[4] Using this method of estimation, it was found that individual saccade-processing times estimated from the abstract experimental stimuli correlated $r = .69$ ($p < .05$) with individual values derived from the face

[3]If k is the observed duration of a fixation, and z is the longer of the two processes in the given instance, then the probability distribution $P(z=k)$ will follow the shape of the observed distributions reported in Figure 5. Letting x represent the latent saccade-programming process, and y the concurrent content-assimilation process, then $P(z=k) = P(x=k) \times P(y=k) + P(x=k) \times P(y<k) + P(y=k) \times P(x<k)$. Knowing $P(z=k)$, and assuming a plausible distribution for the saccade-programming process $P(x=k)$, then the distribution of $P(y=k)$ can be determined.

[4]The previous cutting point of .7 seconds, selected as optimal for identifying what was an "unusually long fixation," would give less accurate values for the present analysis. Within this present subset of fixations less than .6 seconds, however, the probability is quite small that a content-assimilation process had extended the overall dwell-time: for the experimental data $P = .23$, and for the face data $P = .20$. These probabilities were derived from the distributions of Figure 7; using the notation of footnote 3, $P(y>x) = \sum_{k=.2}^{k=.6} P(y=k) \times P(x<k)$.

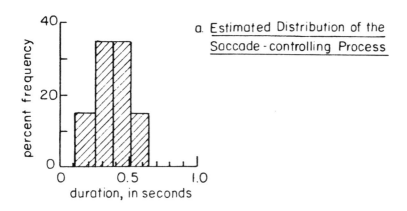

a. Estimated Distribution of the
Saccade-controlling Process

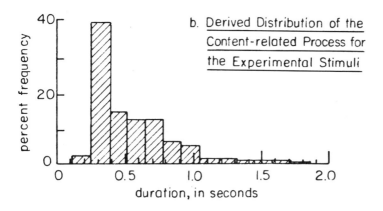

b. Derived Distribution of the
Content-related Process for
the Experimental Stimuli

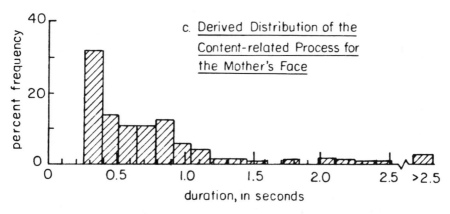

c. Derived Distribution of the
Content-related Process for
the Mother's Face

Figure 7. (a) The estimated distribution of the hypothesized saccade-programming process. (b) and (c) The derived distributions of the hypothesized content-related process.

data—that is, there were reliable individual differences in the rate at which the inferred saccade-programming task was completed. The bulk of this between-infant variation proved to be age-related: for both the experimental stimuli and the face data, the estimated saccade-programming times decreased significantly with the increasing age ($r = -.64$ and $r = -.62$, respectively; each $p < .05$). Mean values dropped from around .5 seconds at 2 months to about .3 seconds at 5 months. (For adults, the comparable value appears to be about .2 seconds, as estimated from the dwell-times when a fixation is made to fall on an open area during a reading task; see Abrams & Zuber, 1972.) In brief, it seems that as individuals grow older they can more rapidly program and initiate the coming saccade.

With regard to the second inferred process—the assimilation of the content of the current fixation—there is little that can be added regarding possible age-related differences in processing times. The difficulty is that for the more typical, relatively brief fixations the content-related processes of individual infants cannot reliably be distinguished from the concurrent saccade-programming times. Individual mean values can be estimated only for instances of unusually long fixations, and it was argued above that these longer fixations probably are not valid measures of required processing times (rather, they appear to be periods of less-than-optimal functioning). All that can be offered here is a speculation: since saccade-programming times seem to decrease with age (as noted, from about .5 to .3 seconds over the 2- to 5-month period), it might be argued that the minimum time required for an assimilation of content should undergo an analogous age-related decrease.

Response Latency to a New Stimulus

There is one further result that should be included while discussing the duration of fixations. The data presented in Figure 6 show that fixations directed toward an uncontoured area will be of relatively brief duration. There is, however, an exception to this. When an infant happens to be fixating an uncontoured area *because the stimulus suddenly has disappeared*, then a relatively long interval will be required before executing a saccade to a contoured area. Consider the evidence for this effect, and some of the implications it carries.

Repeatedly during the course of an experimental series, the small moving target and the experimental figures replaced each other in the visual field (see Figure 1). At each such interchange the infant was left fixating a now empty space, while simultaneously new contours appeared in peripheral vision. The latencies which occurred before an infant shifted regard to the newly presented stimulus are given as a function of age in Figure 8. (Only data from infants shown the Form A stimulus are included here, since in Form B the small spatial separation between the disappearing and replacement stimuli often precluded clear interpretation. Also, since there were no meaningful differences in latency values when the moving target was replaced by the experimental stimulus and vice versa, the data have been combined.) It is evident that the latency to the first saccade decreased significantly with age; the correlation with log age is $r = -.85$ ($p < .05$). Aslin and Salapatek (1975), measuring a similar function in 1- and 2-month-old infants,

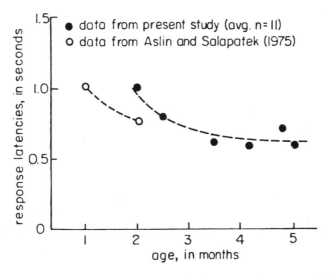

Figure 8.   Average latencies to saccade to a newly appeared stimulus as a function of infant age (standard deviations averaged .14 seconds). The data from the Aslin and Salapatek study are for a stimulus presented 10 degrees in peripheral vision.

have reported an analogous age-related decrease in the latency of the initial saccade directed toward a newly presented peripheral stimulus, and their data are included in the figure. (Just why their average latencies generally were more brief is uncertain, but it might be related to illumination levels, or to an absence of various competing contours within the visual field.)

These latency values are significantly longer than the typical saccade-programming times, which were estimated above to drop from .5 to .3 seconds over this age period ($p < .01$, binomial test). The latter more brief values, however, represent estimated saccade-programming times while surveying an *unchanging* visual array. It seems, therefore, that infants can more rapidly program the coming saccade when the visual field has, for some period, remained constant. This would be the case if infants soon acquire a sense of the relative spatial positions of at least some of the contoured features, and this information is continuously carried forward as the infant moves his regard to each new location. Furthermore, Aslin and Salapatek (1975) observed that when their 1- and 2-month-old infants made a *series* of short saccades in order to reach a newly-presented distant target, the *later* saccades in the series were initiated more quickly than was the first in the series. Again the implication is that when the infant "knows" the target location, the programming of the next saccade proceeds more rapidly. A further analysis gives added support to this proposition.

The Aslin and Salapatek data show that average latency before initiating the first saccade toward a newly presented stimulus will be markedly longer when the stimulus is introduced more than 10 degrees peripherally. In contrast to this, it seems that when infants scan over a *continuously present* array saccades generally can be directed just as quickly to a distant as to a nearby target. This is illustrated in Figures 9(a) and 9(b). (To avoid overly dense plots, only two infants are represented in each figure; the selected cases are typical.) Although the younger infants only occasionally made saccades of greater than 10 degrees, notice that, at either age, the longer saccades typically were initiated just as quickly as were the shorter saccades. Thus when a visual array has for some time *remained stable*, the time required to program a saccade appears to be independent of the eccentricity of the targeted feature. Since the

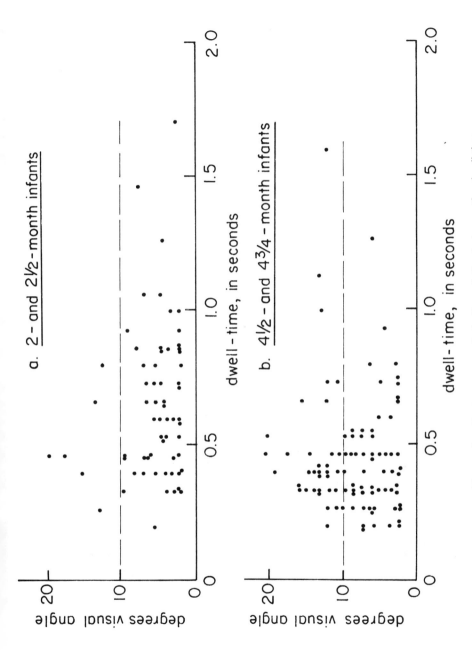

Figure 9. For two age periods, the relation between the dwell-time of a given fixation and the length of the following saccade.

31

Aslin and Salapatek data show this is not true for a *suddenly appearing* stimulus, the inference is again that infants soon gain a sense of the relative locations of continually present contours, and can draw upon this information to facilitate the programming of the next saccade. In an earlier section it was concluded that infants did indeed seem to be learning the spatial location of an element, along with their encoding of its particular shape. The same inference can be drawn from the present set of analyses.

Two rather distinct functions might be served by the ability to encode spatial relationships. First and most obvious, it is basic to the synthesis of data collected by means of a series of discrete fixations—that is, to the learning of organized patterns, rather than just the separate qualities of individually fixated components. Second, knowing something of the relative positions of the features within a stimulus will enable an infant to scan directly to certain selected aspects of a complex array. In a later section it will be shown that infants will use this capacity to re-examine the same features over repeated exposures, and it will be argued that this facilitates the rapid identification of visual regularities in the infant's environment.

Summary

The minimum time required for the assimilation of visual content has been estimated to average about .3 seconds over the 2- to 5-month age period. The value was the same whether infants were examining an abstract figure or mother's face. Fixations rather often lasted for considerably longer than the minimal interval, however, and on present evidence these extended dwell-times seem to reflect instances of suboptimal processing rather than periods of enhanced interest in the content of the particular fixation. The relative incidence of such long fixations was unrelated to the age of the infant; there is provisional evidence, however, that atypically long dwell-times may tend to occur more frequently when an infant is less visually alert.

Concurrently with the assimilation of visual content, retinal input is being utilized to program the direction and distance of the coming saccade. The time required for the latter process seems to decrease as infants grow older, from an average of about .5 seconds at age 2 months to about .3 seconds at 5 months. These estimates assume an unchanging visual field, in which case it seems that infants soon will have acquired a sense of the relative locations of major contoured areas and can use this knowledge to expedite the programming of the next saccade. In contrast, when a saccade is directed toward some new feature that suddenly has appeared in the visual field, the time required to initiate a saccade is about double the above values.

There was evidence indicating that during intervals in which interest wanes, a "contour-centering" mechanism automatically directs an infant's saccades to a nearby contour. By implication, at other times some sort of "higher-level" instruction is guiding saccades to specific locations. The latter notion will gain further support as the nature of such higher-level instructions is examined in the following two sections.

THE LENGTH OF SACCADES

There are several reports in the literature which indicate that during around the third month of life infants will begin to survey rather more broadly over the visual field (e.g., Bergman, Haith, & Mann, 1971; Salapatek, 1975; Uzgiris & Hunt, 1970). The findings of the present study are in accord with this notion—but since the sample extends into older ages the major analysis will focus on a slightly different issue. Granting that the scope of scanning does indeed begin to broaden, should this be viewed as indicating the *rather sudden emergence* of some new capacity, or does the ability to scan to distantly located features show a continued, gradual, development extending over a period of several months? Following an examination of this issue, the implications of the change from a relatively constrained toward a more broadly surveying pattern of scanning will be considered.

Two measures are available for assessing the breadth of scanning. The distributions of the lengths of saccades can be examined; and one also can inquire as to whether infants typically tended to direct the next saccade to the same or to some different feature within the stimulus. Consider first the lengths of saccades.

Age-Related Changes

The distributions shown in Figure 10, as well as the illustrative scatter-plots shown in Figure 9, show that the two youngest infants in the sample rarely made saccades to contours located more than 8 to 10 degrees in peripheral vision—whereas the older babies were, in general, less limited in this regard. Taking 10 degrees as a reasonable cutting point, the relatively lower incidence of long saccades before 3 months of age is marginally significant ($p < .10$, U test). However, it will be shown later in this section that the 3 1/2-month-old infant represented in the bottom left corner of Figure 10 seemed to be *purposefully* limiting his scanning, and, when this atypical case is excluded, the pre- and post-3-months age difference becomes significant at $p = .05$ (U test). As to whether the incidence of long saccades might continue to show a further regular increase beyond the age of 3 months, the distributions shown in Figure 10 appear to indicate that they do not. In fact, over the entire 2- to 5-month age period the correlation of the incidence of long saccades with age is only $r = .35$ (N.S.), and among infants of 3 months and older it becomes $r = -.17$. This initial analysis, therefore, seems to favor somewhat the notion of the relatively sudden emergence of some new capacity, with a subsequent considerable variation in the degree to which the capacity is utilized.

A similar conclusion is reached from an examination of the *targets* of the infants' saccades. Infants less than 3 months of age usually confined attention to some single feature within any given episode, devoting an average of 86% of their saccades simply to a different location within the same figure. In contrast, an average of only 48% of the older infants' saccades were thus confined, the other half being directed to some different feature within the array. The age difference in the incidence of "same-feature" saccades is significant at $p < .05$ (U test). And again, as in the previous analysis, the data do not support the notion of a further increase in the breadth of scanning extending into older ages: for infants aged 3 months and older, the incidence of same-feature saccades was only

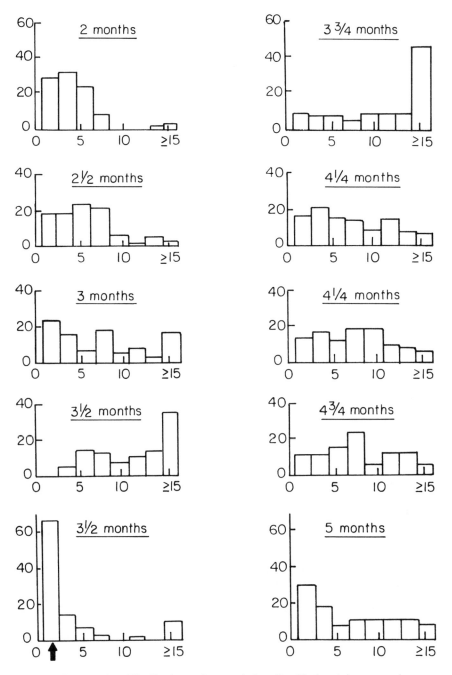

Figure 10. Distributions of saccade lengths. Horizontal axes are in degrees of visual angle; vertical axes represent percentage of saccades. Average n = 50.

trivially related to age (r = .07). In sum, each set of analyses rather favors the notion of a sudden developmental advance in the breadth of scanning occurring during about the third month of life, with little or no further development beyond this period. This position will gain additional support from a further analysis later in the section, but first consider the nature of the constraint that might be limiting the scanning of younger infants.

A certain difficulty in the *execution* of long saccades perhaps somewhat limited the scanning of younger infants, but this would seem not to be a major constraint. Aslin and Salapatek (1975) have shown that, at 1 and 2 months of age, infants typically must instigate a series of 10-degree saccadic steps in order to traverse to distant targets. Nevertheless, by using these "multiple saccades" their infants were able to scan to targets located as far as 30 degrees in peripheral vision. On the other hand, these scannings to targets in the far periphery were observed in conditions where the remote target was the only contour available in extrafoveal vision; also, as was noted earlier, the infants usually delayed for well over a second before initiating the traverse. In contrast, in the present study in which there were numerous closer contours, the younger infants almost never attempted saccades to distant targets, and the typical delay was less than half a second. The constraint that limits the scanning of younger infants, therefore, seems to lie more on the sensory than on the motor side of the system: infants are *able* to traverse to distant locations, but if a nearby contour is present it will more strongly (or more quickly) attract attention, and a single short saccade is rapidly executed to this nearby location. By 3 months of age and beyond, however, infants are no longer so limited. They can on occasion ignore nearby contours in order to scan to distant elements; and, as was demonstrated in the previous section, such long saccades can be initiated without undue delay.

Individual Differences

Earlier in this section it was pointed out that the individual infants of 3 months of age and older differed considerably in their breadth of scanning, and that among these older infants the variation proved unrelated to age. Such individual differences were, however, stable throughout the experiment: the correlation within the 3- to 5-month age group between the proportions of "same-feature" saccades made in the first and the second half of the experiment was r = .80 (p < .01). Although nothing can be inferred regarding the longer-term stability of these individual differences in breadth of scanning, one might inquire about possible correlates within the present experiment. In particular, consider the hypothesis that a disposition to scan relatively broadly over the stimulus was an expression of a heightened visual alertness.

In a previous section it tentatively was suggested that such heightened alertness might be shown by a tendency to examine the stimulus rapidly—that is, to hold each individual fixation for only about the time required for an assimilation of the current retinal content. If scanning widely across the stimulus were, in fact, partly a function of infant age (the full potential emerging by roughly 3 months of age), and then subsequently depended on the level of visual alertness (this determining whether an older infant would exercise the potential), then a combination of the two factors should do well in predicting the overall breadth of scanning of individual infants. This was indeed the case. For the entire sample, the incidence of long saccades was predicted at r = .73 by a regression equation which included as independent variables both infant age and the relative incidence of long dwell-times. This is a significant improvement (F[1, 7] = 6.1, p < .05) over the earlier attempt (r=.35) to predict from age alone. This kind of finding would be expected if underlying these effects was a developing capacity to ignore nearby contours during the programming of a coming saccade. Such a capability would offer the option for a greater flexibility in the guidance of saccades—but this option might or might not be exercised.

A rather different expression of the presumed emerging potential for a more flexible control over the guidance of saccades is illustrated in the lower left-hand distribution shown in Figure 10. In this instance, however, the potential was used to achieve a very *narrow* concentration of attention. This subject was unique among the 10 infants in devoting almost all of his attention to the rather dim checkerboard figure within the stimulus (see Figure 1). In fact, as will be shown in the section to follow, this 3 1/2-month-old baby almost totally ignored the more brightly illuminated square elements that suddenly reappeared at the beginning of each episode, *and* even managed to hold attention to the dim checkerboard through intervals between the episodes when the strongly illuminated moving target traversed the visual field. In brief, during the programming of his saccades this older infant seemed able to override, effectively and consistently, some very strong salience factors. An alternative, that this 3 1/2-month-old infant had simply remained "captured by contour" throughout the entire series of episodes, seems less likely: the four other infants who were of an equal or even younger age never showed this extreme limitation of scanning (see Figure 10), and their attention always was grabbed by the highly salient moving target. It seems probable, therefore, that the infant was exercising his (age-appropriate) ability to override salience effects in order to *avoid attending* to an essentially unpredictable series of visual events. He accomplished this by concentrating his attention on a single stable element within the otherwise changing visual field. In fact, his regard was tightly concentrated even within the checkerboard. Notice in Figure 10 the modal saccade length of slightly under 2 degrees of visual angle; this matches exactly the spacings of the checkerboard elements, so evidently the infant consistency was shifting regard to some just-adjacent contour. If the preceding analysis is correct, then a state of wariness may on occasion be a factor affecting the scope of scanning: once a more flexible guidance of saccades is possible, infants can avoid looking at disturbing features, even though these may be highly salient. A similar kind of controlled avoidance of disturbing stimuli has been documented in the "gaze-avoidant" reactions of 3- and 4-month-old infants confronted by an unfamiliar adult (Bronson, 1972).

The Accuracy of Saccades

Finally, some limited evidence is available on the precision with which infants can program and execute saccades to distant targets. Among infants aged 3 months and older, the saccades made to elements located 10 degrees or more in peripheral vision generally were quite accurate: around 85% ended "on target" (that is, within the 3-degree limit set by the precision of the calibration procedure; see Appendix, section vi). The remainder landed in an open area within the visual field; whether by "intention" is indeterminable.[5] (A somewhat higher incidence of "off-target" fixations was found for the two younger subjects; this perhaps might indicate somewhat less saccadic precision in younger infants, but the total data base of only 6 long saccades made by infants under 3 months of age is too small for firm interpretation. Similarly, the few sample scanpaths that are shown in Figure 6 of the Appendix also seem to indicate less precise saccadic control in younger infants, but here again the sample is of marginal size.)[6] Finding that a large majority of the longer saccades made by older infants landed near some contoured area indicates that, even at somewhat older ages, "salience" continues to play a role in the programming of saccades: although beyond 3 months of age saccades no longer are directed almost exclusively to some strong nearby contour, some sort of salience-related information still must be used if saccades are to avoid landing on noncontoured areas of the visual field.

Summary

In contrast to the behavior of younger infants, it was found that from about 3 months of age onward infants frequently will direct

[5]As was noted earlier, Aslin and Salapatek (1975) found that infants aged 1 and 2 months often made a series of 10-degree saccadic "steps" when shifting attention to a stimulus that was introduced in the far periphery. Similar effects were seen occasionally in the present study when an *older* infant scanned to a distant location. (Under the conditions of the present study the younger infants largely ignored distant targets). These events have been identified, and eliminated from this analysis of saccadic precision. (The 8 instances were identified when an off-contour fixation was followed by a second saccade that continued in the same direction; these saccadic pairs always ended on some contoured feature. The first component averaged 17 degrees, the second 12 degrees [difference significant at p = .06]. The average "pause" was .4 seconds.)

[6]There are, in fact, two different issues relating to saccadic precision, and each calls for systematic longitudinal study. One might inquire about the accuracy of saccades made for differing distances; and one could examine how tightly infants will concentrate a series of short saccades when attempting to "foveate" a small stimulus. Each of these assessments would illuminate the precision with which saccades can be programmed and executed; in addition, the latter type of assessment might support inferences regarding the status of foveal development over the first months of life.

their saccades toward more distantly located features within a stimulus. This appears to reflect the emergence of a new capacity which permits infants to program saccades toward relatively less salient contours. There is some limited evidence that the potential is more likely to be utilized when an infant is visually alert—and also that a state of wariness may occasionally be a factor underlying individual differences in the manner in which the capacity finds expression.

Saccades that span over longer distances generally will land on some contoured area, indicating that although salience effects now may be overridden, salience-related information (that is, the location of areas of nonhomogeneity) continues to be used in the programming of a coming saccade. The general role of salience-related effects in the guidance of infants' saccades will be examined in considerable detail within the Discussion section.

INDIVIDUAL SCANNING PATTERNS

Granting that, beginning around 3 months of age, infants are able to direct saccades to relatively less salient targets, what factors dictate which particular features of a stimulus will be selected? The present section indicates that strength of contour continues to be a factor, but that individual infants also may elect to scan to particular locations under the guidance of memories carried from previous exposures.

Typical and Atypical Patterns

The schematized format of Figure 11 has been adopted to illustrate the rather surprising consistency of an individual's scan-paths over repeated episodes. Represented are the first four episodes for three of the infant subjects; fixations measured to be within 3 degrees of a stimulus contour are assumed to have been directed to the given feature (the criterion reflects the precision of measurement; see Appendix, section vi). The presented cases are typical in their degree of individual across-trial consistency, and in each case a similar consistency continued throughout the remaining episodes

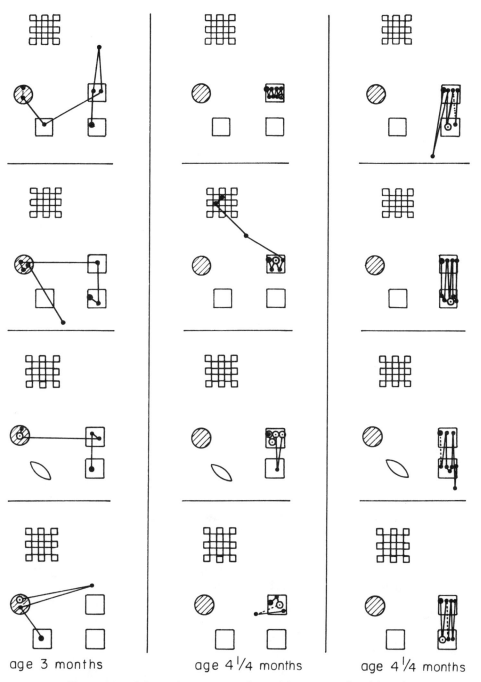

Figure 11. Schematic representations of the scan-paths of three infants over their first four viewings of the experimental stimulus. Fixations measured to be within 3 degrees of a stimulus element are represented as "on target." Larger dots indicate first fixations; circled dots indicate long fixations. Dotted lines are periods of missing data.

in the series. The three records were chosen to illustrate the range of individual differences in scanning patterns. Notice that the record in the middle is marked by repeated re-fixations of the same feature, while the other two infants typically moved to a different target after the single look. The fact that the former baby was not the youngest of the three selected cases illustrates a point developed in the previous section: beyond 3 months of age, the disposition to saccade to the same or to a different feature was not related to age. Notice also that individual subjects tended to re-survey the same particular subset of features over repeated trials. This parameter of individual differences will be examined in a moment. First, however, there were two unusual cases that warrant separate consideration.

Shown in Figure 12 are the schematized scan-paths of two infants who seemed intentionally to disattend to stimulus features which, from the behavior of other infants (and in adult judgment), were by far the most salient components of stimulus: throughout these episodes, both infants usually managed not to look at the suddenly appearing and more brightly illuminated square figures. Furthermore, these two infants also were unique in often disattending to the moving stimulus whose presentation separated the experimental episodes. The 3 1/2-month-old infant focused almost exclusively on the relatively dim but ever-present checkerboard figure, even through the intervening period of motion (this is the infant whose behavior was discussed in the preceding section). The other infant looked about rather erratically (often to open areas between figures) during stimulus presentations, and usually turned away from the stimulus field when the moving target was presented. The latter baby began to cry shortly after the set of episodes represented in the figure (this is the only infant who cried, and since the record was incomplete he has been omitted from other analyses). For both of these infants the inference of purposeful disattention to the most salient stimuli seems fairly clear; and, incidentally, neither of the infants showed any anomalous scanning behavior in the preceding interval when they were viewing mother's face. A combination of the periodic change of the entire visual field, plus the intermittent motion of the bright moving target, seemingly was too intense and unpredictable an experience for these two infants. One

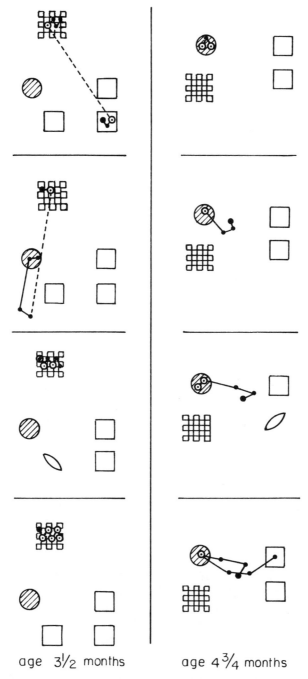

age 3¹/₂ months   age 4³/₄ months

Figure 12. Scan-paths of two atypical infants who seemed to avoid looking at the more visually salient aspects of the stimulus. Conventions are as described for Figure 11.

infant discovered a dim stable feature in the periphery of the field and tightly limited his attention within it; the other generally avoided looking at any contoured targets, and soon began to cry. Although two cases out of 11 subjects is a small data base, the proportion approximates the previously estimated incidence of "highly arousal-prone" infants, who generally tend to be distressed by sudden, intense, or discrepant events (Bronson, 1972).

Determinants of Saccadic Targets

To return to the more typical patterns illustrated in Figure 11, here it appears that each individual infant repeatedly attended to some idiosyncratically selected subset of stimulus features over repeated episodes. To pursue this issue, the analysis will focus on whether or not a given element was fixated during any given episode, ignoring the number of re-fixations within an episode (the latter index would confound the analysis with individual differences in the tendency to make "same-feature" saccades). Table 2 presents the relevant data.

Consider first the overall incidence of fixations directed to the different features, *averaged across subjects*. For the Form A infants it can be seen that less frequent attention was given to the three more peripherally located features, and that among these features the ordering seemed to reflect relative salience: the homogeneous IR source was attended least, the contoured checkerboard was next, and the brighter and suddenly reappearing square (or ellipse) received the most attention. The greatest attention, however, was directed toward the two centrally located, brightly illuminated, and suddenly reappearing square figures; and between these two, the upper figure predominated. A similar ordering can be found in the averaged values for infants who viewed the Form B stimulus. In brief, if one considers only the average reactions of a group of infants, attentional "preferences" seem to be determined by traditionally recognized salience parameters—i.e., proximity, brightness, contour, sudden appearance, and vertical position.

An examination of the individual patterns in Table 2, however, suggests that attention was not guided only by relative salience. Rather, the choice of features to be attended or ignored often was highly idiosyncratic, particularly for subjects shown the more di-

TABLE 2

Percentage of Episodes in Which the Given Infant Looked at the Specified Stimulus Feature (Based on an Average of About 10 Codable Episodes Per Infant).

	Form A Stimulus				
	peripheral elements				
			reappearing elements		
infant age	IR source	checkerboard	square (or ellipse)	lower square	upper square
2	0	0	36	64	9
3-1/2	10	100	0	20	0
3-1/2	91	0	82	82	91
4-1/4	0	0	36	100	100
4-1/4	9	36	0	18	100
4-3/4	0	0	33	56	89
(mean percent)	(18)	(23)	(31)	(57)	(65)

| | **Form B Stimulus** | | | |
| | peripheral elements | | reappearing elements | |
infant age	IR source	checkerboard	lower square (or ellipse)	upper square
2-1/2	0	14	57	71
3	0	25	100	63
3-3/4	0	78	89	78
5	29	14	29	100
mean percent	(7)	(33)	(69)	(78)

versified Form A stimulus. The impression that some relatively unique subset of features was selected for repeated attention by each infant is formalized in Figure 13; the values here are based on the raw data that are summarized in Table 2. When an infant looked at some particular feature during some one episode, one can compute the probability that he or she also looked to the same feature in any other given episode (thus, had the infant also looked at it in each of the remaining episodes, P = 1.0; if the infant never looked at the feature in any other episode, P = 0.0). Reference to Figure 13 will show a marked absence of low probability values—that is, of values which would indicate that an infant had attended intermittently to a variety of different features throughout the series, or that the focus of attention shifted in later episodes. The dotted

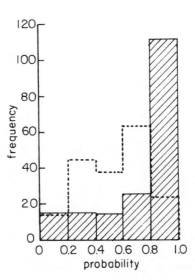

Figure 13. On the horizontal axis, the probability that when an infant looked at a feature in one episode he also looked to the same feature during any other given episode. The vertical axis gives the frequency, across all infants, of fixations having the indicated probability values. The dotted outline shows the frequencies expected by chance. See text for details.

outline in Figure 13 shows the degree of repetition to be expected by chance. It represents the probabilities that would have occurred if infants had merely been following the group-average fixation patterns for the given stimulus set, as represented by the "mean percents" shown in Table 2. The two distributions differ significantly ($p < .01$, X^2 test), showing that the tendency to examine repeatedly the same particular features was *not* simply the result of some of the features being generally more attractive to all infants.

In sum, the individual infants were consistent, as well as idiosyncratic, in directing their attention to particular features within the stimulus. Therefore, although the salience factors were *in general* a predisposing factor in determining infant attention, attentional patterns seem also to have been guided by some additional process—one that produced particular preferences that deviated, sometimes considerably, from infant to infant. Noton and Stark (1971) have found similar patterns showing repetitive but individually differing scanning by adults, and their interpretation of the effect is generally similar to that to be developed in the following paragraphs.

Consider first an interpretation of these idiosyncratic patterns which would posit a set of relatively unique within-infant preferences for particular stimulus characteristics. Such a hypothesis has, in fact, already been suggested for the second infant listed in Table 2. This 3 1/2-month-old infant is one of the two subjects who seemed disturbed by the experimental procedure—the one who chose to look almost exclusively at the ever-present checkerboard. However, beyond this probable instance in which the attentional focus seemingly was dictated by wariness, it has proved difficult to find other plausible forms of infant-specific stimulus preferences that would account for the remaining sets of idiosyncratic patterns illustrated in Table 2. Although this approach cannot be firmly rejected, consider, as an alternative interpretation, one that could explain the individual variation by positing only a single type of infant predisposition that would account for all of the remaining idiosyncratic patterns.

A visual event can be recognized as "familiar" when several successive saccades, directed to a few suitable locations, all produce the expected foveal images. It is not necessary, and probably is not typical, to examine a wide variety of visual details in order to reach this judgment, since, outside of the laboratory, sets of visual features which appear concurrently usually are components of a single relatively unchanging object. Viewed in this light, the infants' characteristic repeated scannings of a limited subset of stimulus features would, in effect, constitute the most efficient approach to the rapid identification of visual regularities within the environment. In brief, it would be adaptive for infants to be disposed toward the recursive scanning of a few selected features within a complex stimulus. Consider the data at issue from this perspective.

Under this hypothesis, the relative saliences of the different stimulus features would set only some general probabilities regarding what was most likely to be attended in the initial episodes; individual deviations from these probabilities could be considered as transient, and perhaps largely fortuitous, effects. The observed cross-episode consistencies now are attributed to a general infant disposition to reexamine previously attended locations on each re-presentation of the stimulus. If one gives weight to its seeming adaptive value, this appears to be a plausible alternative to the positing of a variety of persistent, but differing, infant preferences for particular visual qualities.

The Scanning of Faces

In their scanning of mother's faces, the infants appeared to show a similar variety of idiosyncratic fixation preferences. The clusterings of fixations during about 10 seconds of facial viewing are represented in Figure 14. The data here are less accurate—because facial features are less discrete, and also because at the present viewing distance they were not widely spaced—but it would appear that infants again differed in their attentional focus, and again not in an age-related manner. Here, in contrast to the experimental episodes, the infants were viewing a highly familiar stimulus, but one might again offer the same two alternative types of explanation for the between-infant differences. One might posit a variety of individual preferences (to look mainly at eyes, or mouth, or nose), reflecting perhaps differing maternal reinforcements of infant attentional patterns. Or it might be argued that these latter kinds of determinants provided at most an initial biasing of infant attention, and that subsequently this developed into consistent scanning preferences under the impetus of a general disposition to rapidly confirm familiarity by looking mainly at previously selected locations. Since the tendency to recursive scanning also appeared when the stimulus was relatively unfamiliar, the latter hypothesis carries the greater generality.

Just how long this kind of recursive scanning over the same features might continue if infants were given more lengthy presentations is uncertain. Perhaps they soon would begin to examine additional locations; or perhaps interest in the stimulus would begin to wane, and they might begin simply to stare for relatively long periods at one or two of the more salient features. An argument favoring the latter alternative will be developed in a later section.

One additional observation regarding the data of Figure 14 is of interest. Although as presented here there appear to be no regular age-related differences in scanning patterns, this is not the case when sequence effects are considered. The two patterns in the left-hand panel are the most illustrative: the 2 1/2-month-old infant first directed a series of short saccades in the area of one eye, and then grouped a series of fixations around the other eye; in contrast, the older of the pair of babies shifted between the eyes on nearly every fixation. The difference is similar to that of an earlier analysis, in which it was found that prior to around 3 months of age infants typically directed a series of fixations to a single salient feature within the stimulus, whereas most of the older infants scanned to a different feature of the stimulus on nearly every fixation. (The other younger infant represented in Figure 14 showed the same concentration of successive fixations, while the remaining older infants, as was the case in the earlier analysis of the experimental data, varied somewhat in this regard.)

Summary

When reactions are averaged across infants, it appears that the more salient components of the stimulus were attended more frequently; individually, however, infants often deviated considerably from these norms. Furthermore, the individual infants were highly consistent in their choice of features, looking with surprising regularity to the same individually selected aspects of the stimulus over repeated episodes. It is suggested that this behavior represents a general infant disposition to scan recursively, given repeated presentations of a stimulus. If so, a memory for the relative locations of the previously attended features must soon be guiding saccades—and indeed, it was demonstrated in earlier sections that infants do appear to encode the relative locations of component features. It is argued that this sort of recursive scanning would assist in the rapid identification of periodically recurring visual events within an infant's environment.

CHANGES OVER REPEATED EPISODES

It was suggested earlier that a state of heightened visual alertness is conducive to a broader scanning over the visual display. Given repeated presentations, however, does visual interest then wane and the scope of scanning decrease, or will an infant's attention ultimately shift to previously neglected parts of the visual array? These issues are examined in the present section. Each episode will be considered to constitute a repeated presentation of the same

0 5 10
degrees visual angle

mainly eyes   mainly mouth   mainly nose   left bias   miscellaneous

2 mo.   3 mo.   4¼ mo.   2 mo.

3½ mo.   5 mo.   4¼ mo.   3½ mo.

2½ mo.   3¾ mo.   4¾ mo.

stimulus, despite the fact that a change was introduced in some of the episodes. Since only a few infants (those shown the Form B stimulus) discovered the occasional stimulus change, any effects on the present analyses would, at most, be small; in fact, it will be shown below that they were undetectable.

As was anticipated in designing the stimulus, the two centrally located square figures (brightly illuminated, suddenly appearing) proved to be its most prominent features, attracting overall some 90% of the infants' first fixations within an episode. The following analyses will inquire as to whether there was any regular decline, over the repeated episodes, in the number of successive fixations devoted to these initially dominant features before attention was directed to some different figure. This question will be examined first from the perspective of the serial habituation hypothesis (Bronson, 1974; Jeffrey, 1968), and then in light of the more widely documented general habituation effect.

The Serial Habituation Hypothesis

Following some initial inspection of the square figures, infants did in fact rather often direct attention to other components of the stimulus, but this alone is not a convincing demonstration of serial habituation. The hypothesis requires (a) that the shift in attention be due to the growing familiarity of the first-attended feature, and (b) that attention then be directed to another prominent feature, which in turn is attended until familiar. The hypothesis would find some support, however, if it could be shown that in later trials the shift to another component usually occurred after fewer fixations of the initially attended feature. Since the number of fixations that might be required before a feature would become "familiar" is uncertain, this parameter was allowed to vary from infant to infant. Even with this loose constraint, however, there was no persuasive evidence in support of the serial habituation hypothesis. Examination of the individual episode-by-episode records failed to find, in a majority of infants, the predicted progressive decline in the number of square-figure fixations before attention was shifted to another part of the stimulus. Furthermore, there were no strong regularities in which element would become an infant's second attentional choice, nor was there evidence that this second choice then became the primary focus of attention; it may have been examined closely, or it may have been given only the single glance. In sum, there was no indication that the primary focus of attention changed in a regular manner as a function of number of previous inspections of the stimulus array. (If one wished to argue that the effect will emerge only after longer exposures, or following more repetitions, this would make the hypothesis inapplicable to scanning patterns during an initial period, thereby diluting its explanatory power.) Lasky (1979) recently has infirmed other evidence that has been advanced as supporting the serial habituation hypothesis (i.e., Miller, Ryan, Sinnott, & Wilson, 1976). Depsite its logical appeal, therefore, the notion of an orderly sequencing of attention in the service of efficient total-pattern encoding remains to be demonstrated. In fact, when presentations are rather brief, as in the present study, infants seem inclined merely to establish the identity of a repeated stimulus by scanning consistently to the same locations, rather than to gain further knowledge of the stimulus by extending fixations to new locations. This disposition to scan recursively was documented in the preceding section.

Habituation Effects

Visual habituation *per se* is another issue. Treated purely as a descriptive term, habituation effects have been well documented in a variety of studies. It must be stressed, however, that it is only from grouped data that a regular trial-by-trial decline in total stimulus "inspection times" sometimes can be demonstrated; the inspection time profiles of the individual infants tend to be highly irregular.[7] Despite this individual trial-by-trial irregularity, however, in tradi-

[7]For example, when grouped data are based on a procedure in which testing is terminated as individual infants reach the habituation criterion, total fixation times may show quite regular declines over successive trials (e.g., Cohen & Menton, 1981). On the other hand, McCall (1979), using a fixed number of trials on all subjects, and cluster analyzing the set of individual profiles in order to abstract the various patterns latent in grouped data, found only about half of the subjects falling in the cluster showing a monotonic decline over successive trials. The present study follows the latter format and, as will be seen below, the percentage of infants showing habituation effects is similar to that reported by McCall.

tional habituation studies it usually is found that with enough repetitions most infants eventually will decrease their total viewing time to some fraction of the initial values, and then hold to this pattern over several additional trials. Although the procedures of the present study differed in a number of ways from those of the more usual habituation procedure, it is of interest to see whether such habituation effects can be found in the present data.

Consider the two centrally located and repeatedly reappearing square figures within the array to be the "habituation stimulus"; recall that these were by far the most salient features within the stimulus, attracting some 90% of the infants' first fixations. And let the analogue of an infant's "looking away from the stimulus" be the shifting of regard to any of the remaining peripheral features, or off to the edge of the stimulus field; thus a saccade of some 15 to 20 degrees to a peripheral location would end the "trial." Finally, let the number of sequential fixations devoted to the prominent square figures be the dependent variable. If the criterion for habituation is set at a series of three successive episodes in which the average number of initial square-figure fixations was half or less of the infant's average over the first three episodes, then five of the ten subjects would be considered to have shown habituation effects. The average trial-by-trial profiles for the two groups of infants are shown in Figure 15.

The habituating and nonhabituating groups were not distinguished by age (means of 3.7 and 3.6 months, respectively), nor by stimulus format (an equal number of infants in each group happened to have viewed each stimulus form). A comparison of the two profiles, however, shows two general differences in the averaged reactions. First, members of the nonhabituation group tended to make fewer square-figure fixations during the first two trials, which made it more difficult for these infants later to reach the required criterion. Second, the nonhabituating group continued (on the average) to make a large number of successive square-figure fixations clear through to the end of the series. The analysis here will focus on the latter phenomenon: why did the nonhabituating infants continue to reexamine these relatively simple square figures, when other infants soon began to look elsewhere?

In the discussion of habituation effects, reference often is made to Sokolov's (1960) hypothesis that repeated exposure promotes an

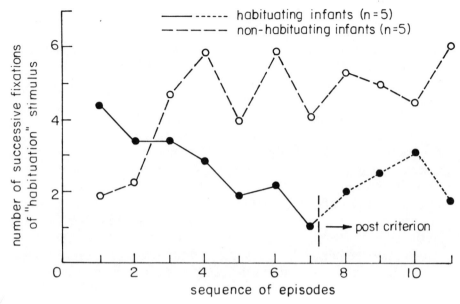

Figure 15.   Averaged habituation curves of "habituating" and "nonhabituating" infants. See text for criterion.

increasingly accurate match between the physical properties of the stimulus and a progressively developing "neuronal model." However, Sokolov reached this position from studies which used very simple types of stimuli, *all of whose properties could be attended in each single exposure.* In contrast, the visual stimuli that typically are used in infant habituation studies would seem too large and diversified to permit such "total pattern" assimilation during each individual trial. For this to be possible, either an infant must be able to assimilate a very large area of the stimulus during each fixation (an unlikely position, as will be argued in the Discussion),or an infant must routinely direct saccades to all pertinent aspects of the stimulus during each exposure (and on present evidence this seems not to occur). In view of such considerations, one might wonder whether Sokolov's formulation can properly be extended to early habituation effects involving complex, nonredundant visual stimuli. As an alternative to the notion that infants continue to attend until an internal "neuronal model" matches the diverse properties of a complex stimulus, consider a modified hypothesis: infants attend until the stimulus is identified as "the same thing again." It was argued in an earlier section that the typically observed recursive scanning over the same subset of features across repeated trials is, in fact, directed toward this end. Latent in this interpretation is a rather different view of the function of early visual scanning: it is adapted to the rapid identification of gross regularities within the infant's visual world, rather than to the full encoding of (often relatively nonsalient) detail. By this hypothesis, infants who soon begin to attend only briefly (that is, who have "habituated"), are demonstrating that with a few selected fixations they now are recognizing the recurrence of the same stimulus—and for this they need have encoded only some few aspects of a complex array. Those infants who do not rapidly habituate, and for whom the later trials in the series often seem marked by large random fluctuations in total inspection times, may in fact recognize the stimulus and yet often continue to attend for relatively extended intervals. Some tentative evidence is available from the present study regarding the characteristics of these latter infants.

In earlier sections, two parameters of infant scanning were advanced as likely indices of alert visual interest: a tendency to direct the next saccade to some different element within the stimulus; and a tendency to hold individual fixations for no longer than required for an assimilation of their content. In brief, aroused or "interested" infants will scan more widely, and more rapidly, over the stimulus. If one examines the *change* in these two parameters for individual infants between the first and second half of the series of episodes, it seems that the nonhabituating infants had in fact begun to be less aroused by the stimulus. For four of the five nonhabituating infants, the incidence of "same-feature" saccades increased in the latter half of the series; in contrast, all five of the habituating infants decreased their incidence of same-feature saccades ($p < .05$, Fisher's exact probability test). With respect to the incidence of extended ($> .7$ seconds) dwell-times, three of the five nonhabituating infants showed a relative increase in the second half of the series, whereas all of the habituating infants decreased in their incidence of extended fixations ($p = .16$, Fisher's exact probability test). Although the findings here are tenuous—both because the first of the two measures is in part confounded with the habituation criterion itself, and because the sample is of marginal size for such comparisons—each approach seems to suggest that the nonhabituating infants perhaps were becoming less visually alert, despite the fact that they tended to maintain a high level of fixations directed to the square elements. Furthermore, of the two nonhabituating infants who happened to view the Form B stimulus, one clearly demonstrated that he had in fact immediately detected the change introduced in the stimulus (per the criterion discussed in an early section; $p < .05$). Therefore, although this finding, like those above, must be regarded as somewhat equivocal, it indicates that infants sometimes may continue to attend to a salient feature beyond the point where an effective encoding has occurred. If one were to generalize from these tentative findings to more traditionally formatted habituation studies, those infants who on later trials often continue to look at the habituation stimulus for extended periods may not be learning much that is new; rather, they may be looking in a disinterested manner (frequent long fixations) at the same salient facets of the stimulus that had largely been encoded during previous exposures. For infants operating in this state, total inspection times might be expected to vary capriciously from one trial to the next, since they no longer are dictated by the time required to survey over selected features of a new and interesting stimulus. Future scanning studies could be designed to pursue issues of this sort in closer detail, and over a wider age range.

Summary

An examination of the relative attention given to the various stimulus components over the sequence of episodes offers no support for the serial habituation hypothesis. At least when the presentations are rather brief, infants of these ages will tend to reexamine the same locations, rather than systematically shift their primary focus of attention to relatively less familiar parts of a stimulus. Habituation effects *per se* were observed, however, for half of the infants in the sample; these infants more quickly disattended to the core components of the stimulus on later presentations. There is some tenuous evidence that the other half of the sample, those who continued to look at the same highly salient elements, were marked by a declining level of visual alertness—and it is argued that there may have been little in the way of additional learning occurring during their feature-limited examinations of the stimulus in these later episodes.

4

Discussion

Most of the results reported in the preceding sections can be considered moderately firm—although the reader will be aware that the interpretations being advanced often are somewhat less certain. The discussion to follow is more speculative: it assumes that the bulk of the preceding interpretations are, in essence, correct, and attempts their synthesis within the context of a developmental model that specifies the determinants of scanning for infants of different ages. The aim is to provide a provisional structure that is of sufficient specificity to be useful in formulating future studies. Many of the issues to be treated are fundamental, yet largely unexplored; by advancing some initial positions, these matters should come into sharper focus.

There are in the current literature a number of information-processing models which consider the mechanisms that might control saccadic sequences (e.g., see the articles in Senders, Fisher, & Monty, 1978). However, these models all have been based upon adult data, and consequently focus on the role played by sophisticated cognitive mechanisms, as in reading, in visual search, etc. They are, at best, only marginally applicable to the infant condition. The following model focuses on the ontogeny of the more simple types of saccadic control mechanisms that might be found in early infancy.

A MODEL OF SACCADIC CONTROL

It was proposed in an earlier section that two kinds of processes are occurring during intervals of stable fixation: a *saccade-programming* process will be setting the parameters for the coming saccade, while a *content-assimilation* process will be taking in central-retina information for subsequent higher level processing. Moreover, from a consideration of temporal parameters it seemed that infants typically must program the coming saccade prior to a final analysis of the visual content of the current fixation. Assuming this to be correct, what then is the source of the information that determines the target of the next saccade? Consider the issue from a developmental perspective, beginning with the options available to the newborn infant. Although the present study did not include subjects of this age, it will be argued that the mechanisms that guide the automatic scanning of early infancy remain as components of the complex saccadic guidance network found at older ages, and hence it is useful to begin with an analysis of the neonatal condition.

At Birth

Let us grant only the most simple type of control during the neonatal period, and posit an automatic "contour-directing" mechanism which, in effect, directs the next saccade toward an area of salient contour. It is well established that newborn infants are indeed able to shift their regard toward contours located in peripheral vision (Harris & MacFarlane, 1974; MacFarlane, Harris, & Barnes, 1976) and, as will be shown below, this mechanism seems sufficient to account for the nonrandom scanning effects that are found at birth. No relatively more complex processes—such as a search for contour (Haith, 1980), or a dependence on memory—are posited for the newborn infant.[8]

---

[8]Haith (1980) has argued that the quality of a newborn's visual scanning implies the presence of rather more complex neocortically-mediated controls, and a comment should be added for those familiar with his position. In his view the neonate is predisposed (a), to *search widely* over the visual field in order to discover contour; and (b), to *scan across* a located contour rather than attempting to center it on the retina. In Haith's view these italicized characteristics imply the presence of something beyond salience-guided reactions. On the other hand, the behavioral data from which these dispositions were inferred might also be attributed, respectively, to the effects of random neural activity, with constraints imposed by eye-muscle tonus; and to a tendency to visually center a nearby contour, together with the assumption that imprecise control often leads infants to "overshoot" the attracting stimulus. The present preference for the latter pair of explanations is

If newborn infants are disposed to move their eyes to center a peripherally located contour, one might wonder why attention is not at times "captured" by some particularly salient element within a contoured stimulus. This can be attributed partly to the immature status of the fovea at birth (Abramov, Gordon, Hendrickson, Hainline, Dobson, & LaBossiere, 1981): the retinal output produced by a foveated contour will be less intense than that from equivalent elements currently located in adjacent areas, resulting in a continual saccadic shifting of regard. In addition, the contour-directing mechanism itself appears to be rather ineffective at the time of birth, making it difficult for the infant to center fixations tightly around the single location. For example, Haith (1980) reports that, when newborns viewed a single vertical contour, on average about half of all fixations landed from 9 to as much as 50 degrees off to one side or the other. In another study using a single vertical bar, the standard deviation of displacements from the stimulus is given as 12 degrees (Mendelson & Haith, 1976), and data from Salapatek (1968) indicate a similar wide dispersion around a small geometrical figure. A study by Salapatek and Kessen (1973) adds some evidence regarding the *optimal* precision with which newborns' fixations can be centered about a prominent contour. From the published illustrations, it appears that on occasions when an infants' fixations remained more or less centered about a single location they still ranged some 5 to 10 degrees around the selected corner of the figure. In sum, at birth (a) an infant's fixations often seem to roam into "empty" areas of the visual field, and (b), even when more effectively constrained they are not very precisely guided to the attracting contour. It will be shown below that there

---

largely aesthetic: they can more easily be reconciled with subsequent developments. As will be shown later, by choosing these modified inferences developments during the following months can be seen as reflecting (a), a decline in randomly directed saccades; and (b), an increase in the precision of saccadic control. The second decision—to discount the possible role of memory-related effects at birth—may perhaps be an oversimplification. Subcortical components within the mammalian visual system may in fact carry some encoding potential (Weiskrantz, 1977)—but it is not clear whether the potential would be present in newborn infants, or whether it would contribute to the guidance of saccades. Given these uncertainties, it seems best to set aside the possibility of early memory-guided effects. The issue is considered again in the closing section of the Discussion.

is a considerable change in each of these attributes by early in the second month; first, however, consider what might be the mediational basis of the scanning patterns found at birth.

Neurological evidence shows the presence of a direct connection from the retina to the subcortical networks concerned with the execution of saccades, and at birth the components of this system are relatively well developed, compared to those of the primary visual system (Bronson, 1982). Since the capacities of the subcortical system seem adequate for the mediation of the various automatic visual reactions found at birth (Bronson, 1974), it will be assumed that neocortical networks initially are not strongly involved in the guidance of saccades. Although it remains in the nature of a hypothesis, formulations which are based upon this cortical/subcortical distinction are congruent with a number of neurophysiological and clinical findings, and have proved able to account for a variety of postnatal advances in visually determined behaviors (see Bronson, 1974; Karmel & Maisel, 1975; Salapatek, 1975).[9] A more simple alternative would be to assume that both cortical and subcortical components of the visual system mediate visual behavior from the time of birth—and then attribute subsequent developmental changes largely to the increasing effectiveness of foveal vision (the latter development is strongly indicated by histological studies; Abramov et al., 1981; Duke-Elder & Cook, 1963). As will be shown below, however, some of the effects to be discussed cannot be subsumed within this less complex model.

In summary, it is hypothesized that at birth an automatic, subcortically mediated mechanism often guides saccades in the gen-

---

[9]Recently, a variant of the cortical/subcortical distinction has been advanced by Maurer and Lewis (1979b), based on the differing anatomical and functional attributes of the retinal x and y ganglion-cell systems. Briefly, x-type cells project only to the neocortex, and seem responsible for the perception of form; y-type cells branch to both cortical and subcortical networks, and seem involved in the directing of attention to sudden changes within the visual field. Maurer and Lewis review evidence indicative of a delayed maturation of the neocortical component of the y-cell system, and attribute a wide range of "2-month" behavioral changes to its subsequent development. However, a number of important advances occur rather prior to age 2 months (see text, below), which suggests that the model needs further elaboration. Maurer and Lewis (1979b, p. 243) note that postnatal developments within the neocortically projecting x-cell system also might account for some behavioral advances, but the possibility is not pursued. The model to be developed here expands on this latter notion.

eral direction of salient contour, but such control initially is rather inaccurate, and also seems to be only intermittently effective—i.e., the distribution of an infant's fixations seem in part a consequence of random activity. Thus, although a newborn infant may at times appear to be surveying over a visual array, in fact the fixations often will land quite far from an attracting contour, and the scanning may not reflect a consistent examination of stimulus features.

Ages 1 and 2 Months

Consider next the situation some 2 months after birth. Two initial issues arise in making behavioral comparisons with the condition at birth: are fixations still widely dispersed, often falling on non-contoured areas of the visual field; and, when directed toward a contour, how accurate is the saccadic control? In the present study it was found that the vast majority of 2-month-olds' fixations remained centered about whichever salient feature of the stimulus happened to be the focus of the first fixation. Therefore it seems that the diffuse, non-target-related eye movements now have disappeared. In addition, saccadic control has become quite precise: on present evidence, fixations rarely will land more than 2 or 3 degrees from the attracting contour. In fact, data from previous infant studies indicate that a more precise control probably begins to appear somewhat prior to age 2 months. Salapatek (1975) has shown that at about 5 weeks of age most infants will concentrate fixations fairly tightly around some small section of contour within an abstract figure, whereas infants tested under similar conditions at birth often showed the widely dispersed pattern that seems to be typical of newborn infants (Salapatek & Kessen, 1966, 1973). In brief, it appears that both the effectiveness and the precision of saccadic control have begun to increase rather dramatically by the beginning of the second month.

Neurological evidence on the organization of the various systems involved in the control of eye movements, together with clinical studies of the consequences of damage to particular components, indicate that a more precise contour-centering ability is mediated by networks within the occipital cortex, and utilizes information from foveal vision (see Bronson, 1974). And, in accord with

the above chronology, there are histological and electrophysiolog-
ical data indicative of rapid developments in both of these components of the visual system beginning soon after birth (Bronson,
1974, 1982). Thus, the onset of enhanced saccadic precision appears
to be associated with concurrent developments occurring within
the central area of the retina and the primary visual system. This
finely articulated component of the primary system draws upon the
output from x-type retinal ganglion cells, and constitutes the initial
stage in the mediation of form perception (e.g., see Fukuda &
Stone, 1974; Stone & Fukuda, 1974).

The Determinants of Stimulus Salience

In a later analysis, it will be argued that just what an infant might
manage to encode during the examination of a diversified stimulus
will depend to a large degree on the manner in which the stimulus is
scanned. Therefore it becomes of considerable importance to be
able to specify, in some detail, just how infant scanning patterns
will be affected by the age of the infant and the physical characteristics of a stimulus. If it is granted that, during the initial postnatal
months, visual attention typically will be directed toward the more
salient features within a stimulus, then a number of recent findings
from the neurosciences become relevant to the prediction of infant
scanning patterns.

Assume that the relative salience of a stimulus feature—that
is, the probability that it will become the target of the next
saccade—depends upon (a), *the intensity of the retinal activity*
which it produces; and (b), *the relative sensitivity of subsequent
saccade-guiding networks* to activity originating within different
retinal areas. With regard to the first of these salience
determinants—the intensity of retinal activity—this is known to be
a function of the difference in brightness levels across a stimulus
contour (strength of contrast) as well as of the spacings between adjacent contours (spatial frequency); and the latter variable will have
different optimal values at different retinal locations (Wilson &
Bergen, 1979). Moreover, it has been shown that optimal spacial
frequency values increase with infant age (Banks & Salapatek,
1981), probably due largely to the growing effectiveness of foveal

vision. This age-related change in salience effects is reflected in the "preferences" at older ages for checkerboard stimuli containing progressively smaller elements (Banks & Salapatek, 1981; Karmel & Maisel, 1975). The second general factor affecting stimulus salience—the relative sensitivities of subsequent networks to outputs from different parts of the retina—also should change as infants grow older. It is known that retinal output projects to both neocortical and subcortical saccade-guiding mechanisms (see Bronson, 1974); furthermore, the neocortical system seems responsive primarily to activity coming from x-type retinal ganglion cells, which are concentrated mainly within the central part of the primate retina, whereas the input to subcortical networks comes from retinal y-cells, and these are distributed widely over the retina (DeMonasterio, 1978). Therefore, as the neocortical system begins to be functionally effective infants should become relatively more responsive to central-retina stimulation. This latter effect can be visualized more clearly if it is represented by a conceptual model.

Figure 16 illustrates the relevant aspects of retinal ganglion-cell distributions. Figure 16(a) symbolizes the distribution of y-type cells, which have collateral fibres feeding into the subcortical saccadic guidance system; and Figure 16(b) represents the x-cell distribution, which feeds into the neocortical system. In each figure, the small arrows reflect the predicted saccade-guiding tendencies that would be induced by small elements of contour falling on various retinal locations; the directions of the arrows indicate that infants will tend to shift any given segment of contour toward the center of the retina. The varying densities of the solid dots symbolize the differences in the relative concentrations of the retinal ganglion cells—both between the x- and y-cell systems, and at different retinal eccentricities within each system.[10] Consider briefly how

[10]A third category of retinal ganglion cells, type w, is not considered, since their (probably varied) functional characteristics remain to be determined (e.g., see Stone & Fukuda, 1974). The parameters of Figures 16(a) and (b) have been estimated from the limited evidence currently available. The relatively large effective field of the left-hand figure and the more limited field of the right-hand figure, as well as the relatively greater density of cells in the right-hand figure, and the intense concentration of cells around the foveal area in this latter case, all reflect the differing dispersions of y- and x-type ganglion cells within the primate retina (DeMonasterio, 1978; DeMonasterio & Gouras, 1975). In the absence of direct evi-

the two illustrations subsume the general effect proposed in the preceding paragraph, before turning to some more complex applications of the conceptual model. At birth only the subcortical component of the saccadic guidance system, represented in Figure 16(a), is assumed to be behaviorally effective—so, during an initial postnatal period, contour centering will be relatively imprecise, since the available system is only grossly organized within the central part of the retina. As the more refined neocortical system illustrated in Figure 16(b) begins to become behaviorally effective, centrally located features will acquire an added salience, enabling infants to concentrate a series of saccades rather precisely around a small segment of contour. The behavioral evidence reviewed above indicates that this latter ability has begun to emerge by the beginning of the second month.

Turn next to the rather more complex issues that arise within the second postnatal month, when both guidance systems (cortical and subcortical) are assumed to be more or less operative, and consider situations in which infants are presented with various types of multiply-contoured stimuli. Imagine the stimuli illustrated in Figure 16(c) superimposed on the ganglion cell distributions of Figures 16(a) and (b); the circles that circumscribe each stimulus represent the "30 degree" eccentricities on the retina, thus providing a scale

---

dence, cell densities for the figure on the right are assumed to decrease at a similar rate in all directions out from the fovea, producing the concentric pattern. The elliptical pattern of the left-hand figure has been inferred from infant behavioral data: during roughly the first month of life, infants will respond to peripheral stimuli at eccentricities of up to 30 to 40 degrees horizontally (Aslin & Salapatek, 1975; MacFarlane et al., 1976), whereas peripheral sensitivity is more limited in the vertical dimension (Aslin & Salapatek, 1975; Kessen, Salapatek, & Haith, 1972).

The effects for the two eyes should combine throughout the limited range of the right-hand figure, whereas for the figure on the left behavioral evidence indicates that such summation could occur during the first month only within a range of some 10 to 15 degrees horizontally (i.e., nasal-side vision initially is severely limited; see Lewis, Maurer, & Milewski, 1979). Also, there is some indication that, in the case of the left-hand figure, a smaller portion of the ganglion cells located in the far periphery actually send axons to the subcortical networks (DeMonasterio, 1978). Each of these two latter effects would further decrease the relative salience of contours falling on the far periphery of the infant retina. Finally, although it will not be stressed in the following analyses, many studies have shown that the y-type ganglion cells (left figure) are relatively more responsive to sudden changes within the visual field (e.g., DeMonasterio & Gouras, 1975).

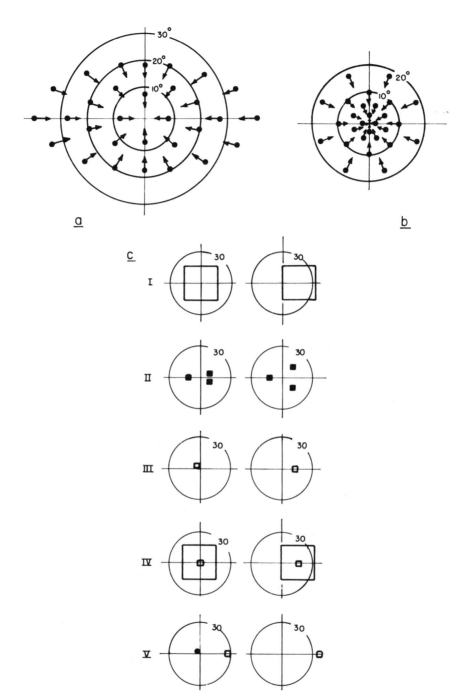

Figure 16. An illustration of factors affecting infant scanning. (a) A representation of the distribution of y-type retinal ganglion cells. (b) A representation of the x-type ganglion cell distribution. (c) Illustrative stimuli. See text for discussion.

for the superpositions. The initial findings to be interpreted come from Salapatek (1975).

An open symmetrical figure of the type shown in illustration C I, when centered on the retina (left illustration), will be in an unstable equilibrium: a small displacement in any direction would move one side into a more densely organized area of the retina, and thus enhance the relative salience of that part of the figure; this should induce a saccade that will center the contour, as is shown in the illustration to the right. Salapatek's data indicate that infants of either 1 or 2 months of age do indeed strongly concentrate fixations about some one side of this sort of open symmetrical figure. When a stimulus is in this location there are, in fact, three effects which diminish the relative salience of the remaining, more peripherally located parts of the figure, thereby stablizing this retinal position. First, much of the disattended contour will fall outside of the effective range of the neocortical contour-centering system of Figure 16(b); second, reference to Figure 16(a) will show that the far side of the stimulus is almost at the limits of the subcortically mediated mechanism; and third, since in Salapatek's figures the contour widths were of about 1 degree of visual angle, their effective salience should be greatest when in near-foveal locations (the effects of contour widths interacting with retinal spacial-frequency sensitivities were discussed earlier).

For this initial analysis it has been sufficient to assume that the salience effects produced by each small section of an extended length of contour would combine to produce the resulting saccade. However, the hypothetical case shown in illustration C II suggests that this must be an oversimplification. For the arrangement shown on the left, one might indeed predict that the next saccade would be directed toward the two closely spaced squares, on the assumption that their individual salience effects would combine. But if they also were to combine for the right-hand illustration in C II, the resulting saccade would in fact land in an open area between the two elements—and the findings of the present study indicate that this kind of "off-contour" fixation rarely occurs. Therefore, it seems that the saccadic guidance systems do not simply combine and then average retinal outputs across wide retinal areas. Rather, *the integrative processes which are guiding successive saccades must pro-*

ceed over circumscribed limits—limits which will result in rather discrete salience nodes that typically will represent contour-dense areas within the stimulus. Furthermore, it is reasonable to assume that the *size* of an integrated area will reflect the degree of precision with which a saccade can be directed toward the chosen target. For example, if the directional precision of a saccade can be controlled within some angle α, and distance to within some percent β, then during the integration of contour elements the inclusion of elements which fall much outside of these spatial limits would impede accuracy, whereas all contour within these limits should be included in order to heighten sensitivity. Two consequences follow from this analysis. First, within either of the saccadic guidance systems illustrated in Figure 16, the areas for contour integration should be relatively large when processing peripherally located features, whereas for near-foveal locations integration should be limited to much smaller retinal areas. Second, the more precise neocortically mediated system of Figure 16(b) should integrate over smaller spatial limits than is the case for the more grossly organized subcortical system of Figure 16(a).[11] As an illustration of such processes, consider the salience effects that might be elicited by a small (4 degree) square when in different locations on the retina. When in a peripheral location (right illustration of C III), it would produce a single salience node. When it is in a more central location, however, the integrative processes would be limited to small subsections of the figure. In effect, therefore, the "contour density" within an integrative area will vary as a function of the size of the given stimulus feature in interaction with its current retinal location.

In summary, it is argued that, during each interval of stable fixation, one or both of the saccade programming mechanisms will

[11]These integrative effects must occur within post-retinal components of the two saccadic guidance networks, since it is ganglion-cell outputs that are being combined. On a much finer scale, analogous integrative effects also occur within the retina itself: (a), y-type retina ganglion cells have larger receptive fields than do x-type cells; and (b), these receptive fields increase in size as a function of retinal eccentricity (DeMonasterio & Gouras, 1975). The scale of these effects, however, is too fine to account for the saccadic guidance phenomenon at issue here—although they may underlie the contrast sensitivity functions discussed by Banks and Salapatek (1981).

derive an array of more or less discrete salience nodes, and their relative intensities will depend upon the spatial characteristics of the various stimulus features in interaction with their current locations on the retina. At ages when relative salience is the major saccadic determinant, the probabilities will favor the next saccade being directed to the most salient among the current nodes.[12] Consider how the available infant scanning data might be interpreted from this perspective.

Some initial evidence regarding the size of the effective area of integration can be deduced from Salapatek's (1969) detailed report of 1- and 2-month-old infants' reactions to stimuli such as shown in illustrations C I and C III of Figure 16. As was noted earlier, at *either age* one side of a large open figure effectively was maintained in a central location on the retina, as is indicated in the right-hand illustration of C I. However, when infants were presented with one (or a pair of) small 4-degree squares such as shown in illustration C III, this smaller stimulus was maintained in central vision by only 55% of the 1-month-old subjects, compared with 97% of the 2-month-old infants (p < .01; X^2). Evidently, at 1 month of age an extended segment of centered contour (right illustration of C I) constitutes a more salient stimulus than does the 4-degree square of illustration C III. Therefore, at this early age the integrative process must span over considerably more than a 4-degree segment of a centrally located contour. By age 2 months, however, the small square of C III seemingly has acquired an additional salience. The developmental change can be attributed to an increasing effectiveness of the more refined guidance system represented in Figure 16(b): since this system integrates over small areas, the component elements of the square now will represent contour-dense, and thus highly salient, features. (An alternative possibility, that the age-

[12]This latter assumption may, on occasion, be incorrect. Recall that two of the older subjects in the present study seemed consistently to direct their saccades to the *relatively less salient* parts of the stimulus, presumably as a defense against heightened arousal ("wariness"). In fact, Gardner and Turkewitz (in press) have reported an analogous phenomenon at around the time of birth. When in a highly aroused state, infants would look to the less salient of a pair of stimuli; only when in a less aroused state did they look at the more salient figure. This possible complication should be considered when interpreting data on scanning patterns, or on "visual preference" effects, with regard to the presumed salience characteristics of various stimuli.

related effect simply reflects the increasing effectiveness of foveal vision, will be infirmed in the following analysis.)

When Salapatek presented both the large and small squares concurrently, infants were faced with competing sets of contoured stimuli. In this circumstance, when parts of one feature were in a central location on the retina, the other figure would be located in peripheral vision, as is shown in illustration C IV. The younger, 1-month-old infants continued to center fixations about a long segment of contour (per the right-hand illustration), which is as might be expected from the preceding analysis. By age 2 months, however, infants not only attended rather often to the smaller square, but frequently *scanned between* the "inner" and "outer" squares. The latter effect is of particular interest, since it seems to indicate that under either of the illustrated conditions there was a rough balance in the relative saliences of stimulus features. For two reasons, this "balance effect" cannot be attributed solely to the emerging effectiveness of foveal vision, and therefore this more simple assumption is not a sufficient explanation of developmental change. First, by age 2 months the salience of the smaller square evidently had increased even when it was in an *extra*-foveal location (right illustration), since it frequently would be the target of a following saccade. Second, if increased foveal effectiveness were the only factor, then once the small square was in a central position (left illustration), it should have remained there. The present more complex model, however, can adequately account for the repeated shifting between inner and outer features. If the effectiveness of the refined system of Figure 16(b) increases by age 2 months, then when the smaller square was in a near-foveal location it would be represented by a number of salience nodes, but would be treated as a single (contour dense) unit when located more peripherally. Similarly, only a rather short segment of an extended "outer" contour would be integrated when it was in a central location, but much or all of its length could be effective when in a peripheral location. In brief, the effective "contour densities" of the stimulus components would change as they were shifted to different retinal locations—leaving them roughly in balance, whether fixation is as shown in the left or the right condition of illustration C IV. For stimuli whose component features were of a different size or spacing, however, one might expect that some single feature within a stimulus could remain dominant. For example, in the present study in which the two square figures were fairly large, the 2- and 2 ½ month-old infants usually continued to locate fixations about whichever square happened to first be attended. Presumably, here the non-attended square was too large to constitute a single (and thus contour dense) unit when in parafoveal vision. In brief, whether 2-month-old infants will tend to scan over a variety of stimulus components, or to concentrate fixations about some single feature, should depend on the spatial arrangements within the stimulus. (Although the presently available scanning data do not permit any more refined analyses, notice that future studies using appropriately designed sets of stimuli should be able to infer from scanning patterns the probable sizes of integrative areas at different retinal locations.)

One further set of experiments will illustrate some additional properties of the model. Studies which were designed to probe the limits of peripheral perception in early infancy (Aslin & Salapatek, 1975; Harris & MacFarlane, 1974; MacFarlane, Harris, & Barnes, 1976) repeatedly have noted that the eccentricity at which a peripheral stimulus would quickly be detected was *reduced* in trials where an initial "gaze-centering" stimulus continued to remain visible to the infant. The salience effects implicit in either Figure 16(a) or 16(b) could account for such effects: given the competing "gaze-centering" stimulus located somewhere in near-foveal vision, as in the left in illustration C V, a newly appearing experimental stimulus might not be sufficiently salient to quickly attract a saccade unless it was introduced in a somewhat less peripheral location. In addition, two of the studies (Harris & MacFarlane, 1974; MacFarlane et al., 1976) provide data regarding the relative *degree* to which the continued presence of the "gaze-centering" stimulus limited peripheral detection at different ages. Both studies found the effect to be markedly stronger during the second month than it was at birth. This would be expected from the present model, since during the second month the increasing effectiveness of the more refined contour-centering system of Figure 16(b) would further enhance the salience of a competing, centrally located, stimulus.

To summarize. The data from a number of scanning studies are consonant with a model which (a), posits two separate salience based saccade-guiding systems that carry different levels of precision and develop at different rates postnatally; and (b), assumes that within each system the effective salience of a contoured feature will, for several reasons, vary as a function of its retinal location. A more simple alternative—that developmental changes in scanning patterns are due only to the increasing effectiveness of foveal vision—failed to account for some of the data under review. Notice, incidentally, that both the complexity and the form of the proposed model were dictated primarily by neurological considerations—and at present its validity rests largely on the correctness of the inferences drawn from such findings. Because of the post hoc nature of the behavioral analyses, they have served more to illustrate the properties of the model than to confirm it.

Finally, it should be noted that, beginning roughly around 2 months of age, infants' saccades may not always be guided by salience effects—that is, attention may on occasion now be attracted by visual discrepancies. This apparently will occur when an altered form happens to fall within the parafoveal area of the retina; on the evidence of the present study, discrepancies located in peripheral vision will remain undetected. The ability to notice and attend to discrepant features might be considered to mark the onset of "directed" saccades, in the sense that programming now may begin to be guided by individual memory, rather than being determined largely by salience effects that are dependent on stimulus characteristics.

At 3 to 5 Months

Findings of the present study indicate that, during around the third month of life, infants begin to direct saccades toward various less salient aspects of a stimulus. This suggests that some additional kind of higher-level control now has become effective—one which can modify salience effects, allowing an infant to direct saccades to more remote, less strongly contrasting, or less densely contoured features within the field. Notice, however, that some form of salience-related information still must be utilized, since it was found that long saccades rarely will land in contour-free locations. To achieve these effects—to scan to remote areas and yet typically land on a contoured target—a simple but adequate form of higher-level instruction need only constrain responses to contours falling beyond some minimum eccentricity within the retina. Assume, as a provisional model for this effect, that instructions imposed from higher levels now modulate the relative sensitivity of the neocortical salience-guided system to inputs coming from different parts of the retina. Thus modulated, the system could then direct the coming saccade toward a contoured target either somewhat remote from or near to the current fixation, and in effect the infant would be oriented either to scan to distant locations or to concentrate attention on the currently centered feature. Notice also that in the *absence* of such "higher-level" instructions, it might be expected that even at older ages successive saccades might simply continue to be directed toward salient, proximally located contours. This could account for indications in the present study that, when older infants began to "lose interest" in the repetitive stimulus, they tended to limit attention to some single feature within the array—a pattern which, for the present stimuli, was *typical* of the younger infants. In a general way, the suggested organization seems reminiscent of arrangements found in other motor systems, where the automatic (reflexive) mechanisms observed in early infancy subsequently come under higher level "volitional" control (e.g., see Curtis, Jacobson, & Marcus, 1972). Here, it is proposed that an automatic, salience-guided system subsequently can be modulated by various higher level "interest dictated" determinants—a format which would permit the accurate guidance of saccades to contours within some selected part of the visual field.

In addition to an emerging ability to scan to relatively less salient features within a visual array, a further type of "higher level" control was observed in older infants: following some initial exposure to the stimulus, infants usually continued, in subsequent episodes, to scan to the same idiosyncratically selected locations that were examined earlier. From such effects it was inferred that a memory-based process was directing saccades toward particular "meaning-related" locations within the stimulus. (Note that some memory for spatial location also seemed to be implied by the "discrepancy" reactions observed in infants of less than 3 months of age; however, since these younger infants did not scan broadly over the stimulus, it is not clear whether they were yet able to utilize memory effects to direct saccades to specific distant locations.)

In summary, it is proposed that, from around age 3 months onward, an automatic "salience guided" scanning disposition may be modulated by any of several "higher-level" determinants. First, saccades can be directed toward areas containing visual discrepancies (an effect that seems to appear by roughly 2 months of age). Second, infants become able to initiate saccades toward less salient, distantly located targets. And third, they can direct saccades to remembered locations. When these options for the more flexible guidance of visual scanning are not invoked, however, saccades seem again to come under the direct control of an automatic salience-guided system.

Summary

The overall arrangement of the saccadic guidance system is assumed to be hierarchical. Initially, an infant's saccades appear to be guided by a broadly responsive but grossly organized subcortical system—a system that seems but intermittently effective at birth, functions without direction from higher-level determinants, and is directly controlled by retinally determined salience variables. Being a y-cell system, it will be most responsive to moving stimuli (see Footnote 10). As infants grow older this initial system appears to be supplemented by a number of more slowly developing but more sophisticated networks. On the basis of the evidence now available, the following chronology has been suggested.

By around the end of the first month, a more precise salience-guided mechanism within the primary visual system begins to rather accurately direct saccades to parafoveally located contours. This x-cell system remains responsive to static (unmoving) contour elements—and also provides the input for form perception. A few weeks later, by roughly 2 months of age, infants can draw upon emerging memory capacities to direct saccades toward nearby discrepant features. From about 3 months onward, the salience-guided system can be modulated by additional higher level determinants, allowing infants to scan to less salient distant features, or toward remembered locations. The class of "interest directed" saccades—those that are guided toward less salient features, or are directed by visual memory—still make use of salience-related information, however, in order to land on contour. This suggests that emerging higher-level mechanisms modulate, rather than simply replace, the salience-guided effects. Also, in the absence of such higher-level instructions salience-related determinants seem again to assume direct control over the guidance of saccades.

A final comment. The proposed model of the determinants of visual scanning has been developed on the basis of infants' reactions to silent, stationary, and relatively unfamiliar stimulus arrays. The typical environment, however, often carries additional properties. Given a sudden sound, the orienting response may include a saccade in the appropriate direction, and subsequent intersensory contingency effects could continue to hold the infant's attention. Similarly, when motion is present within the field it will strongly attract and maintain attention. And given a familiar event that has undergone predictable changes in the past, an infant's saccades may be directed in *anticipation* of a visual change (Watson, 1967). Therefore, although the proposed model of saccadic guidance systems may appear to be rather complex, it does not encompass all determinants. On the other hand, it would not be expected that a parsimonious system would emerge from the evolutionary process: as new adaptations evolved to treat new contingencies, their mediational bases must have been shaped by the functional characteristics of existing networks; a multidetermined, hierarchically organized control system is the most probable consequence. Therefore, although the model at present is both speculative and incomplete, its form and complexity are not inappropriate.

IMPLICATIONS OF THE MODEL
FOR INFANT LEARNING

Consider, finally, the implications of the proposed model for the onset and subsequent development of encoding capabilities. In order to draw inferences regarding the quality of visual learning from a knowledge of infant scanning patterns, one must begin with some assumptions about (a), the number of repeated fixations that might be required for a feature to be encoded; and (b), the size of the visual field that can effectively be encompassed within the single fixation. At present almost nothing is known about these encoding parameters, so what follows is in the nature of an initial exploration of the issues involved in their determination. First some approximate parameter values will be set, mainly from logical considerations regarding what appear to be some probable limitations on infant encoding. Next the data on infant scanning patterns will be interpreted, using these assumed values, to see what implications such scanning data might carry if the encoding parameters are indeed as estimated. Finally, these inferences will be compared with some relevant behavioral data regarding the growth of visual learning capacities. The fit between the implications of the model and the behavioral learning data will show that the initial assumptions regarding encoding parameters appear to at least be tenable.

An adult is able to "encode" (remember) a visual form following but a single fixation. In such circumstances, however, the task requires only *recognition*—that is, a matching of the retinal image with an appropriate form that already is stored in visual memory. In contrast to this, the initial encodings of the visually naive infant must involve the development of the memory structures themselves (e.g., see Hebb, 1949). It seems unlikely that "encoding" in this latter sense could effectively be accomplished by the single look; if this were the case—if the naive infant were capable of effectively storing the content of each single fixation—then recognition phenomena should develop far more rapidly than observation seems to indicate. Assume, therefore, that the initial encodings of early infancy require more than the single unrepeated fixation. If this is the case, then it would also seem likely that a repetition of images which are *successive* would be somewhat more effective than repetitions that have been interspersed among a number of unrelated visual images. Therefore, let us provisionally assume that the initial encodings of early infancy are facilitated by a redundancy, over a set of successive fixations, in the images being transmitted for subsequent processing. This raises a second, related, issue: how large an area of the visual field might contribute to the encoding process during each fixation? If the entire visual field were effective, then successive fixations could in fact be widely dispersed and yet each would contain some common (redundant) form qualities. Again, it seems implausible to attribute an extreme capability—total field encoding—to the very young infant (indeed, it is not available to the adult), so the issue is one of determining where the retinal limits for effective encoding might lie.

Assume that the encoding effects at issue are mediated by the primary visual system; and, furthermore, that the effectiveness of encoding is a function of the intensity of the patterned neural activity that is received by encoding networks. If so, then those forms that are located within the central part of the retina should more readily be encoded, since x-type retinal cells (which presumably are the basis for form perception) are most heavily concentrated within this area (DeMonasterio & Gouras, 1975). There is, in fact, some indirect neurophysiological evidence in support of this proposition. Gross (1973), recording single-unit activity from neurons within the inferotemporal cortex of monkeys, found that an appropriately shaped stimulus elicited heightened activity when it was located anywhere within a radius of about 10 degrees around the fovea, with the strongest effects occurring when the form was within some 5 degrees of the retinal center. The typically wide (20-degree) receptive fields of these form-specific neurons suggest that the potential for *recognition* should be present over a considerable area—and indeed, this seems to be the case for human adults. If, however, one assumes that the initial encodings of early infancy are facilitated by more intense activitation, then contours which are located within a limited area in the central part of the retina should most easily be encoded. If this is the case, then in order to produce effective encoding a visual form should remain in central vision over a number of successive fixations.

In summary, the preceding considerations suggest that the initial encodings of very young infants should develop most rapidly when the infant concentrates a series of successive fixations on some single feature within the visual field. Consider next the implications of this assumption when it is applied to the scanning patterns of infants of different ages.

If an infant is presented with a visual stimulus containing a variety of relatively discrete components, an initial saccade should soon be directed toward some contour-dense area within the stimulus. It is the quality of the saccades which follow, however, that must determine what the infant learns from the visual exposure, and this in turn will depend upon the age of the infant. For the newborn infant, the succeeding series of fixations are likely to be dispersed rather widely around the initially selected area. In fact, even under conditions in which but a single feature is available to attract the infant's saccades—a field containing only a single vertical contour—during the following fixations almost half of the time the contour will be located some 9 degrees or more away from the retinal center (Haith, 1980). Under the present assumption, this would seem not to be a propitious format for an initial encoding of form. Indeed, it previously has been argued, from a juxtaposition of neurological and behavioral evidence, that newborn infants are as yet incapable of encoding visual form in neocortically mediated memory (Bronson, 1974).

On the other hand, notice that the line of argument being developed may not apply to the encoding of the *nonform* attributes of a diversified stimulus. For example, qualities such as contour density might provide fixation-by-fixation redundancies even when successive fixations are rather widely dispersed. Moreover, there may be encoding capabilities for nonform attributes within networks that do not rely on transmission via the primary visual system (see Weiskrantz, 1977)—in which case the argument that central-retina locations will promote more intense neural activation may not apply, and evidence regarding the initially immature status of neocortical memory-related networks would be irrelevant. Therefore, the present analysis must be considered relevant only to the encoding of visual form.[13] With this caveat in mind, consider how age-related changes in scanning patterns might herald the emergencies of form-encoding capabilities.

---

[13]The possibility that different attributes of a visual event might be encoded concurrently within cortical and subcortical networks suggests that the visual experiences of the adult may result from the activation of more than one information-processing system. And if these different encoding capabilities develop at different rates postnatally, then the issue as to when a capacity for "visual memory" first develops may not have a single answer. Indeed, it is possible that findings from habituation studies, which on occasion have been interpreted as early evidence of form discrimination, might merely reflect the detection of changes in contour densities, or in spatial frequencies; see Banks and Salapatek (1981).

Some time early in the second month, it seems that infants often begin to center successive fixations more or less tightly around some single feature, or some limited segment of contour. This should result in a series of near-redundant images, and under the present hypothesis this would support an encoding of the information that is common across images. Also at about this age, one finds what seems to be the earliest evidence of visual memory for form: Wolff (1963) has reported occasional instances of visually elicited smiling as early as 4 to 5 weeks of age, and others report similar responses by around age 6 weeks (Ahrens, cited in Gibson, 1969; Ambrose, 1961). Furthermore, there is reason to believe that the two developments are not merely coincidental. As infants first begin to concentrate fixations around a single facial feature, the eyes are the typical targets (Bergman, Haith, & Mann, 1971; Donnee, 1973; Maurer & Salapatek, 1976). And when social smiles first begin to be elicited by visual stimuli, a schematic face containing only a pair of eyes appears to be the adequate stimulus (Ahrens, cited in Gibson, 1969). Thus the features which presumably are the early targets of redundant fixations do seem to become the core components of the encoded image. Moreover, Ahrens reported that the inclusion of additional features to the schematic face did not enhance smiling until infants were somewhat older (when, on present evidence, they begin to scan more broadly). This finding gives support to the view that the limits for effective encoding do not extend far from the central retina, since, at the age when fixations typically center about the eyes, the infants seem not to be encoding those facial features that would fall in more peripheral locations. A study by Milewski (1976) similarly indicates that only directly fixated stimulus features are encoded. In sum, there is reason to suggest that the developing ability, early in the second month, to concentrate successive fixations about some limited portion of a stimulus heralds the onset of visual form encoding.

During around the third month of life infants become increasingly able to direct their saccades to less salient features, and by 3 months of age they often will survey rather broadly over the stimulus field. Whether a series of near-redundant images still remains a major requirement for effective encoding is uncertain, but there is some evidence which suggests that it does not. If it still were a major requirement, then the serial habituation hypothesis should have found support among the older infants of the present study. The hypothesis predicts that infants will continue to center their fixations about some single feature within the array until it is "familiar," and then move on to another feature—and this kind of sequential focusing of attention was not observed. In fact, it was found that the older infants in the study typically shifted to a different feature in about half of their saccades, a scanning format that largely precludes a series of fixations being directed to the same component. On the other hand, older infants did tend to repeat the same scanning *patterns* over successive presentations of the stimulus (and, when time allowed, sometimes within the single episode). This would produce redundant *groups* of images, which repeat themselves over time blocks of the order of several seconds. Together, these observations might suggest that as infants grow older, (a), the neural activity that results from the single fixation can be maintained for somewhat longer intervals, and thus encoding can proceed when image repetitions are somewhat delayed; and (b), that the "redundancies" which are the basis for encoding now consist of repeating *groups* of images. In brief, the developmental change in scanning patterns might indicate the onset of a capacity to encode gestalts, rather than merely isolated features. Under the present formulation, however, this is more likely to occur when an infant has an alert interest in the visual stimulus. At other times saccadic guidance again will come under the direct control of salience-related determinants, and fixations are likely to be centered about some single feature. In fact, for an older infant the currently-foveated contour could produce retinal output that is more intense than that associated with any contours located elsewhere on the retina; therefore, the present model would predict that when interest is minimal an infant now might hold a foveated contour for a relatively extended period (on present evidence, this occasionally may continue for periods lasting up to several seconds). During such intervals of unchanging visual input, the infant may be learning little that is new about the visual characteristics of the stimulus. In brief, while infants of 3 months and beyond presumably are capable of encoding a number of features as a total gestalt, the exercise of this ability may vary as a function of infant state.

In summary, it could be argued from an analysis of scanning parameters that the newborn infant may be encoding little or nothing of the form qualities of a stimulus; that somewhat before 2 months of age one or two of the most salient features of a stimulus may be encoded; and that beyond 3 months of age infants (if visually alert) will encode a variety of features, together with the spatial relationships among them. All of these analyses, of course, assume that infants are viewing a static stimulus that appears repeatedly for relatively brief intervals. Under such circumstances, the various saccadic control mechanisms seem admirably adapted for the rapid identification of visual regularities within the infant's environment: initially, recognition is achieved through an encoding of one or two more prominent elements, and, later, of multiple features and their interrelationships.

In the preceding analyses it has been assumed that areas of the stimulus that have not been more or less directly fixated will remain largely unrepresented in visual memory. One might wonder, then, just when and by what process the "gaps" in an internal image might ultimately begin to be filled. Day (1975), in reviewing the evidence relating to the scanning characteristics of older children, describes a developmental progression that might illuminate the issue. She concludes that there is a steady improvement, extending throughout early childhood, in the ability to direct saccades to parts of a stimulus that might contain some particular sought-for information. Here, saccades presumably begin to come under *cognitive* guidance; and, equally important, they often may be directed to stimulus areas that are of but minimal salience—an attribute that appears not to be characteristic of the scanning of infants. Such considerations suggest that a combination of the growing contribution of cognitive processes to the guidance of saccades, plus a developing interest in specific visual details, would increase the probability that an internal image will develop into more or less complete representation of the external object.

Appendix

The following sections examine a variety of technical issues in considerable detail. The aim is both to provide support for the interpretations offered in the main text and to foster discussion of the issues involved in applying eye-tracking technologies to infant subjects.

i. DESCRIPTION OF THE EYE-TRACKING UNIT

The system uses infrared (IR) illumination to produce an image of the pupil that appears markedly brighter than other parts of the eye and face, and a still brighter corneal reflection of the IR source (see Appendix Figures 1(a) and 1(b). To preclude the concentration of radiant energy at a small point on the retina should a subject's eye happen to accommodate for distant vision, the light source is not collimated. The calulated maximum intensity at the cornea is about .1 mW/cm^2, which is roughly one-third the value from a comparable commercial system. The differences between the x,y coordinates of the pupil center and those of the corneal "spot" indicate the momentary direction of visual regard (Appendix Figure 1(c)). Hard-copy output from the system is in two formats. Providing the basic data for experimental analysis is the output from a 4-channel strip recorder, which reports at 30 times per second the x and y changes in direction of regard, together with index markers showing experimental time and moments of stimulus change. The

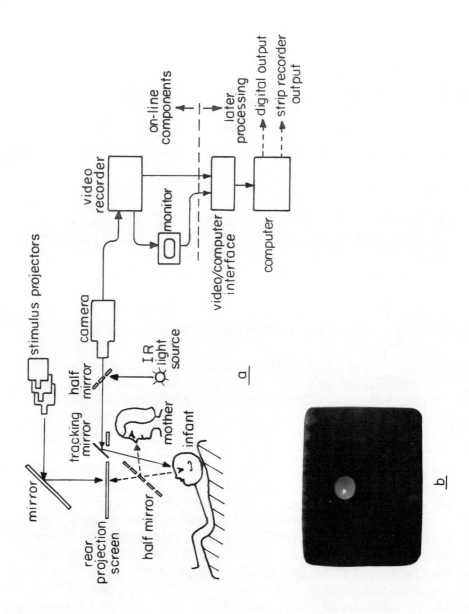

stimulus projectors

mirror

rear projection screen

tracking mirror

half mirror

half mirror

mother

infant

IR light source

camera

video recorder

monitor

on-line components

later processing

video/computer interface

computer

digital output

strip recorder output

a

b

84

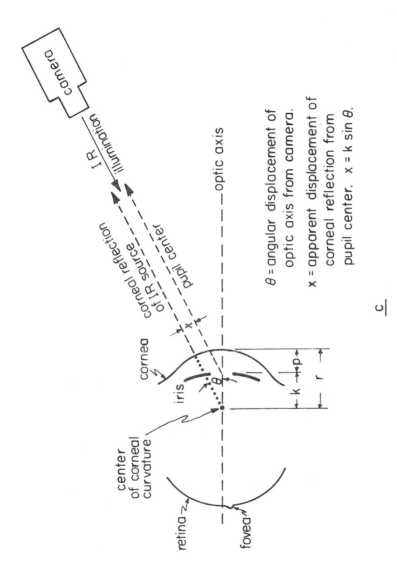

camera

IR illumination

corneal reflection
of IR source

pupil center

cornea

iris

x

center
of corneal
curvature

retina

fovea

optic axis

p

r

k

θ

θ = angular displacement of
optic axis from camera.

x = apparent displacement of
corneal reflection from
pupil center. x = k sin θ.

c

Figure 1. (a) Experimental arrangement. (b) Typical image of a subject's eye. (c) Determinants of observed pupil-spot displacements.

latter are based upon the outputs of photocells located in the paths of the stimulus projectors. Supplementing the data from the strip-recorder is a more detailed output in digital format, which includes various indices for assessing the validity of the strip-recorder data.

ii. QUALITY CONTROL

When a computerized system is used for the automatic determination of pupil- and spot-centers, techniques must be introduced to identify intervals of questionable data. Before beginning computation on data from a given video frame, the present computer program examines line-by-line consistencies and discards any obviously erroneous "periphery of pupil" (or spot) data points. The digital output shows, for each frame, the number of video lines initially "read" as containing potential pupil (or spot) information, and the number finally selected as carrying valid data. A large discrepancy between the two values indicates an excessively "noisy" section of the video record; and an unusually small value in the second index means that only part of the pupil was visible—typically due to partial covering by an eyelid. Extreme values, on either measure, indicate that the corresponding scanning data are of doubtful validity. The estimated coordinates of the pupil center are those of the center of the circle which shows the "best fit" to the array of digitized data points marking the outline of the pupil. After computation of the best fit circle, a "goodness of fit" index is calculated; this is the standard deviation of the differences between the 60 to 80 pupil-periphery datums and corresponding best-fit-circle values. Again, extreme values indicate doubtful data. For acceptable records, the index varies from about .8 when the locus of regard is near to the camera axis to about 1.2 when the pupil becomes elliptical as the subject looks some 30 degrees away from the camera axis. For values within this range, about two-thirds of the discrepancies are less than 3% of the pupil diameter—indicating that imprecisions in determining the pupil center usually will not be the limiting factor in overall system accuracy. On occasions when the "fit" index reaches higher values, this means that the data points defining the pupil periphery are markedly irregular; this usually is due to marginal levels of contour contrast in the video image (see below). Questionable sections of the strip-recorder record are routinely discarded, prior to beginning data analyses, on the basis of the several quality-control indices described above.

A more simple algorithm is used for determining the position of the corneal spot within each video frame. The y value is the average of the (usually 2 to 4) video lines that carry spot infomation, while the x position is the mean of the beginning video-line locations of the spot signal. (Here, and for pupil data, a horizontal video line is divided into 256 equal units.) Nominally 512-line video systems are in fact composed of alternating 256-line frames, with one set displaced vertically by a distance of ½ line. If direction-of-regard data were sampled at the full 60 times/second, a frame-by-frame "jiggle" would appear in the strip-recorder output whenever the corneal spot falls in a location where alternate frames just catch or just miss an upper or lower boundary of the spot. To eliminate this, as well as to minimize random imprecisions, the x-y coordinates are averaged over pairs of adjacent video frames, providing a sampling rate of 30 times/second. Even with this averaging, however, the spot-location coordinates remain the limiting factor setting the ultimate precision of the system. The minimum detectable change is ¼ line in the vertical dimension, and resolution is about the same along the horizontal axis. In the geometry of the present system, this translates into a theoretical minimum detectable change in direction of regard of about ¾ degree of visual angle.

iii. PRECISION OF MEASUREMENT

Two samples of "Optimal" data are shown in Appendix Figure 2(a); roughly two-thirds of the output was of this quality. It can be seen that, by averaging the record over a series of data points, a change in direction of regard of around 1 degree could be distinguished from background noise—a precision that approaches the maximum theoretical resolution of the system. Fairly often, however, successive datums may show variations of the order of 2 degrees of visual angle, as shown in Appendix Figure 2(b). Although it is possible that infant fixations may perhaps be characterized by some form of

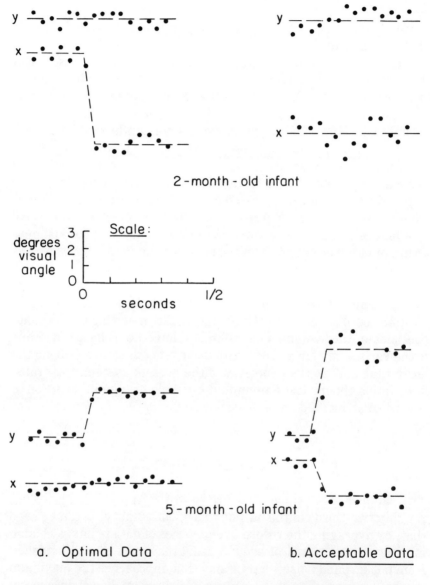

2-month-old infant

Scale:

degrees
visual
angle

3
2
1
0

0   seconds   1/2

5-month-old infant

a. Optimal Data   b. Acceptable Data

Figure 2.   One-half-second samples of typical output data. Horizontal locations are shown by the x values, vertical positions by the y values. Dashed lines show how the outputs would be interpreted.

moment-to-moment imprecision, it is not immediately evident just when these rapid changes in the data might indeed be reflecting true shifts in the locus of fixation. For the purposes of the present study this issue has been set aside, and, in translating an ongoing data record into a series of discrete fixations, a change in locus of regard usually was inferred only when values that have been *averaged over a number of data points* clearly differed by at least 1 to 2 degrees from the mean of the preceding set of averaged values. The typical result of this averaging procedure is illustrated by the dashed lines in Appendix Figure 2. This routine analysis was done by a research assistant who, while skilled in the procedure, was uninformed as to the implications of her coding decisions.

iv. SOURCES OF INACCURATE
OR ERRONEOUS DATA

The mechanism for automatic computer-processing of the video record involves distinguishing among three "brightness" levels—those of the general background of face and eye, of the pupil, and of the corneal spot, (see Appendix Figure 1(b)). Problems arise when pupil-brightness values change sufficiently within an experiment to impede these electronic discriminations. Two major sources of varying pupil brightness have been reduced by present experimental procedures. Pupil dimming can be severe if the IR light falls mainly on the optic disk within the retina—an area of relatively lower reflectance. To minimize such occurrences, positions of stimulus elements were located with respect to the camera axis so that infants rarely looked in the undesired direction. Also, any marked change in pupil diameter will produce a variation in pupil brightness. Minimizing changes in the average brightness of the stimulus field during the course of the experiment considerably reduced such effects. Despite these two types of experimental control, however, the automatic discrimination of valid pupil data at times became marginal, producing strip-recorder direction-of-regard output that could be grossly erroneous. The routine examination of the quality-control indices described above was used to eliminate such intervals of questionable data. Most instances of

"missing data" were a result of this screening process; in the remaining cases the infant's eye was off camera. A review of the
videotapes showed that in these latter instances the infant had
turned away from the stimulus area.

Parallax effects constitute a rather different source of potential error. If the center of the camera lens system lies in the plane of
the experimental stimulus, no parallax effects will occur—but this
ideal condition is precluded when a tracking mirror is included in
the system. In the latter case the best solution, adopted here, is
placement of the tracking mirror in the plane of the stimulus
display. Minor errors now result whenever the subject's eye shifts
from the center-line of the camera axis—that is, when
compensating movements of the experimenter-controlled tracking
mirror do not immediately and accurately keep pace with infant
head movements. Given the geometry of the present system, the
maximum parallax error would be about 1 ½ degrees of visual angle. Use of a single (gimballed) tracking mirror to follow head
movements along either dimension carries a further source of potential error: tracking-mirror adjustments made in one of the two
dimensions inevitably must produce some degree of torsion of the
image reflected to the video camera. In the present study, the image was on occasion rotated as much as 8 degrees. About three-
quarters of the variability introduced by torsion effects, however,
was associated with initial adjustments of the tracking mirror made
to compensate for the slightly differing placements of babies in the
apparatus; being constant through the experiment, these were
identified and corrected on the basis of the calibration data (see below). Effects due to minor tracking-mirror adjustments made
within the course of an experiment remain as a source of error; the
estimated maximum effect here is of the order of 1 ½ degrees of visual angle.

v. CALIBRATION PROCEDURE

Two questions arise in the mapping of the stimulus figures onto the
record of x and y (horizontal and vertical) changes in the direction of
regard: what is the relative *size* of the stimulus configuration, and

what is its *position* in the x,y coordinate system? In the present study these mapping parameters have been estimated by determining the x,y coordinates of the end-points of subjects' eye movements as they tracked a stimulus of about 2 degrees in diameter that moved horizontally through about 20 degrees of visual angle (see Figure 1 in the main text). Motion was at about 4 seconds per cycle, and the stimulus remained at the end-points of travel for about ½ second. Appendix Figure 3 shows typical tracking patterns for three of the infant subjects.[1] Knowing the horizontal distance through which the stimulus has moved, and the associated change in the x-coordinate values on the strip-recorder output, it is possible to estimate the parameter linking change in angle of visual regard with the strip-recorder values (which in turn reflect the difference between spot and pupil centers). Appendix Figure 4 represents the estimated values of this parameter for a number of infants and for two adults; each value is the mean of 6-10 trials. Initially it may seem surprising to find that the infant and the adult values represented in Appendix Figure 4 seem highly similar, since the overall dimensions of the eye increase considerably over this age period. Closer analysis, however, shows that the empirical results might have been anticipated. Reference to Appendix Figure 1(c) shows the value of k to be the critical variable, and that this in turn is the difference between distances r and p. Aslin and Jackson (1979) have examined the literature regarding the value of p, and conclude that it increases by about .90 mm from infancy to adulthood; the radius of corneal curvature, r, increases by about .75 mm during this same period (Mandell, 1967; Mandell & St. Helen, 1968). The net over-

---

[1]Note, incidentally, that facility in smooth tracking seems to be only marginally present at the age where this study begins: at the youngest ages, tracking consisted largely of saccadic "catch-up" motions. Periods of smooth tracking usually began to appear more frequently in older-aged subjects, and, by age 5 months, smooth tracking was nearly continuous, although notice (Figure 3) that it lagged considerably behind the target. Aslin (1981) has carefully documented this development, and both he and Bronson (1974) have argued that the change reflects the emergence of a new functional capacity beginning around 2 months of age, rather than the progressive improvement of a tracking capability that is present from birth. Kremenitzer, Vaughan, Kurtzberg, and Dowling (1979) have reported finding very brief intervals of smooth pursuit in newborn infants, but from the nature of the effect they concluded that at this early age it is mediated by peripheral, rather than foveal, input.

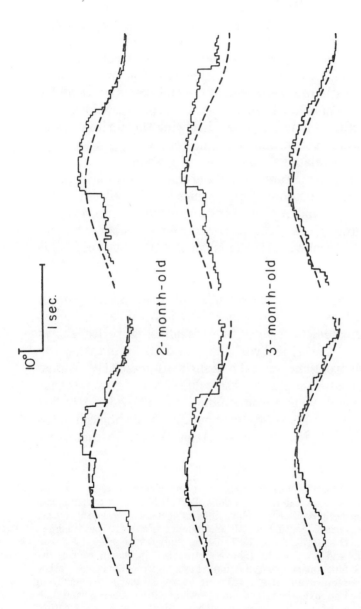

Figure 3. Tracking of a horizontally moving target over two separate trials by infants of different ages. Small steps in the records reflect the sampling of locations at 30 times per second. Dashed lines indicate the stimulus location. Data begin when the vertical direction-of-regard index (not shown) indicated that the infant had made a saccade to the line of stimulus motion.

92

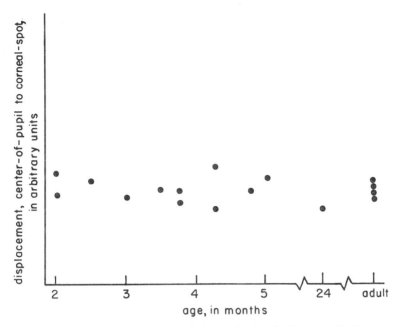

Figure 4. Relative amount of change in the displacement between the pupil center and the corneal spot produced by a 20-degree shift in the direction of regard, for subjects of different ages.

age change in r minus p of .15 mm would produce only an estimated 3% increase in the typical value of k (which is about 4.6 mm in infancy), and this is less than would be detected in the present data.

Since the above variations among the infants proved to be minor, an average of the values derived from all infants in the sample has been used for determining stimulus size in mapping it onto the x,y fixation data points. Assuming the stimulus to be properly *positioned* in the x,y space (see below), the maximum error, should the small individual differences illustrated in Appendix Figure 4 be real, would be about 1 ½ degrees of visual angle at the far edges of a typical stimulus subtending an angle of roughly 20 degrees. No measurements were made for stimuli located at various intermediate eccentricities from the camera axis, to see whether there might be *nonlinear* changes in the present parameter as a function of eccentricity; nor were the parameter values determined for eye movements along the vertical axis. However, calculations based on Mandell's (1967) measurements (in newborn infants) of changes in the radius of corneal curvature between 0 and 30 degrees eccentricity, and on differences in corneal curvature between the horizontal and vertical axes of the eye (York & Mandell, 1969), indicate that the effects of either type of variation in corneal curvature on the presently estimated parameter should be trivial compared to the current precision of measurement. If future calibration procedures permit greater accuracy, however, the effects of variations in corneal curvature must be examined more closely.

With stimulus *size* determined by the above procedure, the *positioning* of the set of stimulus figures can be calculated from the known x,y coordinates of the ends of motion of the calibration stimulus, together with the known location of the experimental figures relative to the moving calibration stimulus. In practice, the positioning of the experimental figures was a two-step process. First, the general location of the stimulus figures was determined using the x,y ends-of-motion coordinates averaged across infants. Then minor readjustments were made for each infant to maximize the match between figure positions and the roughly 60 to 80 stimulus fixations made by the individual infant in the course of an entire experiment. No subsequent adjustments were made to "improve" the fit of fixations within individual episodes (or on mothers' faces). Typically these individual readjustments from group-average placements ranged between ½ and 1 ½ degrees of visual angle, but for two infants they reached 4 degrees. The more typical minor adjustments are comprehensible as reflections of various measurement errors—including the fact that the moving calibration stimulus was itself about 2 degrees in diameter.

Just why two infants required larger readjustments from the group-average determinations is uncertain, but one seemingly plausible explanation can tentatively be ruled out. It is known that the locus of the human fovea is not in line with the optic axis—see Appendix Figure 1(c). For adults the average displacement is estimated to be about 4 degrees to the temporal side and 1 ½ degrees below the optic axis; for infants in the present study the corresponding average values were estimated to be 8 and 6 degrees, respectively (see below). The former value fits well with Slater and Findlay's (1975) estimate of an 8 ½ degree horizontal displacement (they made no estimate of vertical displacement). It is possible, however, that individual infants might vary appreciably in the amount of foveal displacement, in which case the above "first-step" positioning of the stimulus figures using averaged calibration data sometimes could introduce a considerable error for the individual infant.

The calibration data for individual infants were examined closely from this perspective. The x,y coordinate values were available for fixations when the moving stimulus halted briefly at the far end of its trajectory and again when it returned to its beginning location (the midpoints, and right ends, respectively, of the tracking patterns presented in Appendix Figure 3). Selecting the four or five best tracking records for each infant, the *within-infant* variation over repeated trials in the x,y coordinates at each end-of-motion location was found to be of the order of 1 to 3 degrees around the individual's mean for the set of measurements. (It is evident, therefore, that repeated measurement is essential when using this approach to the calibration of infant data.) The *average* values for each individual, derived from each of the two ends of the stimulus motion, are shown in Appendix Figure 5. The figure was constructed by first locating the infants' coordinate values with respect to those of an adult viewing the same moving target, and then locating the entire set with respect to the optic axis, on the assumption that this adult had a typical foveal displacement of 4 degrees temporally and 1 ½ degrees below the optic axis. It can be seen that foveal displacement in infancy indeed appears to be greater than in adulthood. The critical issue, however, is whether the apparent differences among the various infants are real; if so, then variations in foveal displacement may be of sufficient magnitude to require the use of individual (rather than infant-average) values in calibration procedures. Here the present evidence, unfortunately, is divided. Indicating that the differences are, in fact, non-chance, is the finding of significant individual consistencies. Correlating across infants, the foveal displacements estimated from the two end-of-motion locations indicate that there are indeed reliable individual differences in degree of estimated horizontal displacement ($r = .67$; $p = .05$), and in estimated vertical displacement ($r = .90$; $p < .01$). Neither variation was related to infant age. Arguing against regarding such possibly differing foveal displacements as a

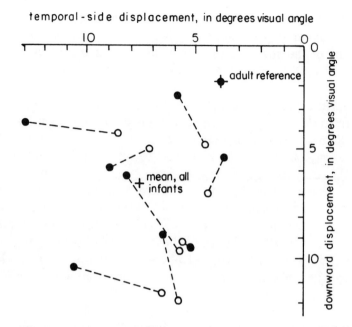

Figure 5.   From calibration data, estimated locations of each infant's fovea with respect to the optic axis of the eye (for infants' left eyes). Solid circles represent locations estimated from the left end-of-motion tracking data; open circles, locations from right end-of-motion data. Dashed lines connect values from the same infant. The origin of the graph is on the optic axis of the eye, see Appendix Figure 1(c).

meaningful effect, however, is the fact that using the individually derived values did not improve the fit of the sets of individual fixations to the stimulus figures; and, in particular, it did not explain why two of the infants required the relatively large 4-degree "readjustments" from the group-determined locations—which was the phenomenon that motivated this rather lengthy analysis. In sum, pending further study it remains uncertain whether possible infant differences in amount of foveal displacement need to be recognized as a factor in calibrating eye-movement data, although in the present instance an attempt in this direction proved unsuccessful.

Future studies designed to resolve the issue should recognize a possible source of bias that has been built into the preceding analysis. Since smooth tracking capabilities are just emerging over the present age period, accuracy may vary among infants—for example, in the amount of "lag" behind the stimulus; and if such constant errors should happen to vary among infants, then the seemingly reliable individual differences shown in Appendix Figure 5 *may indeed be real*, and yet not always affect the placement of saccades which are aimed at components of a *static* array. Future studies using a moving target for calibration purposes should let the target remain motionless for something on the order of a full second at each end of its travel, thus allowing time for the infants to make a final saccadic adjustment. (For a somewhat different approach to the calibration of infant data see Hainline, 1981.)

vi. SUMMARY OF MEASUREMENT ISSUES

After the records have been surveyed to eliminate sections of questionable data, and after averaging over a number of video frames, a change in the locus of fixation of between 1 and 2 degrees of visual angle can consistently and reliably be detected (see Appendix Figure 2). Therefore, those analyses in the present study that required only the measurement of a change in the locus of fixation (e.g., analyses of dwell-times) have utilized this criterion.

When analyses also required specifying the *targets* of each fixation, precision was further limited by the accuracy of the calibration procedures. An estimated maximum error of 1 ½ degrees was associated with procedures for mapping stimulus size, and possible errors associated with the placement of stimulus figures, or due to parallax effects, were of a similar magnitude. Therefore, the criterion for deciding whether or not a given fixation was in fact directed at a nearby stimulus element has been set at a *discrepancy of 3 degrees or less*. Two considerations contributed in setting this limit. First, there is the possibility that sources of error at times may cumulate. Second, it must be recognized that, in addition to various measurement errors, deviations from a targeted stimulus also may reflect *infant-based* inaccuracies. Some limited evidence regarding the accuracy of foveation in infants of different ages is given in Appendix Figure 6. Represented are the locations of successive fixations during 4- to 5-second intervals spent regarding a small neon bulb. Given this small static stimulus in a dark field, the

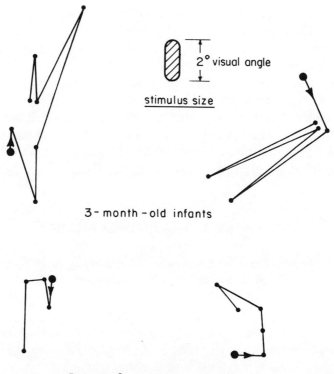

stimulus size

3- month – old infants

5 - and - 6 - month old infants

Figure 6.   Successive fixations during 4- to 5-second presentations of a single small illuminated stimulus presented against a dark background. The heavy dot indicates first fixation; the illustration of the stimulus shows the scale. Upper figures are from two 3-month-old infants; bottom figures are from a 5- and a 6-month-old infant.

uncertainties of calibration can be set aside: the infants must have been responding only to the single stimulus. The apparent dispersion of fixations shown by the two 3-month-old infants, together with the signs of improvement by 5 to 6 months of age, is indeed suggestive of an initial imprecision in saccadic control. These limited data were drawn from optimal records selected from a pilot study; a more systematic pursuit of the issue clearly would be of interest.

References

Abramov, I., Gordon, J., Hendrickson, A., Hainline, L., Dobson, V., & LaBossiere, E. Postnatal development of the infant retina. *Supplement to Investigative Ophthalmology and Visual Science*, 1981, *20* (3), 46.

Abrams, S. G., & Zuber, B. L. Some temporal characteristics of information processing during reading. *Reading Research Quarterly*, 1972, *8*, 42–51.

Ambrose, J. A. The development of the smiling response in early infancy. In B. M. Foss (Ed.), *Determinants of infant behaviour* (Vol. 1). New York: Wiley, 1961.

Aslin, R. N. Development of smooth pursuit in human infants. In D. F. Fisher, R. A. Monty, & J. W. Senders (Eds.), *Eye movements: Cognition and visual perception*. Hillsdale, New Jersey: Lawrence Erlbaum Associates, 1981.

Aslin, R. N., & Jackson, R. W. Accommodative-convergence in young infants: Development of a synergistic sensory-motor system. *Canadian Journal of Psychology*, 1979, *33*, 222–231.

Aslin, R. N., & Salapatek, P. Saccadic localization of visual targets by very young human infants. *Perception and Psychophysics*, 1975, *17* (3), 293–302.

Banks, M. S., & Salapatek, P. Infant pattern vision: A new approach based on the contrast sensitivity function. *Journal of Experimental Child Psychology*, 1981, *31*, 1–45.

Bergman, T., Haith, M. M., & Mann, L. *Development of eye contact and facial scanning in infants*. Paper presented at the meeting of the Society for Research in Child Development, Minneapolis, April 1971.

Bronson, G. W. Infants' reactions to unfamiliar persons and novel objects. *Monographs of the Society for Research in Child Development*, 1972, *37* (3), 1–46.

Bronson, G. W. The postnatal growth of visual capacity. *Child Development*, 1974, *45*, 873–890.

Bronson, G. W. The structure, status, and characteristics of the nervous system at birth. In P. M. Stratton (Ed.), *The Psychobiology of the Human Newborn*. London: Wiley, 1982.

Cohen, L. B., & Gelber, E. R. Infant visual memory. In L. B. Cohen & P. Salapatek (Eds.), *Infant perception: From sensation to cognition* (Vol. 1). New York: Academic Press, 1975.

Cohen, L. B., & Menton, T. G. The rise and fall of infant habituation. *Infant Behavior and Development*, 1981, *4*, 293–304.

Curtis, B. A., Jacobson, S., & Marcus, E. M. *An introduction to the neurosciences*. Saunders: Philadelphia, 1972.

Day, M. C. Developmental trends in visual scanning. In H. W. Reese (Ed.), *Advances in child development and behavior* (Vol. 10). New York: Academic Press, 1975.

DeMonasterio, F. M. Properties of concentrically organized x and y ganglion cells of macaque retina. *Journal of Neurophysiology*, 1978, *41*, 1394–1417.

DeMonasterio, F. M., & Gouras, P. Functional properties of ganglion cells of the rhesus monkey retina. *Journal of Physiology* (London), 1975, *251*, 167–195.

Donnee, L. H. *Infants' developmental scanning patterns to face and nonface stimuli under various auditory conditions*. Paper presented at the meeting of the Society for Research in Child Development, Philadelphia, March 1973.

Duke-Elder, S., & Cook, C. *System of ophthalmology* (Vol. 3, pt. 1). Saint Louis: Mosby, 1963.

Fantz, R. L., Fagan, J. F., & Miranda, S. B. Early visual selectivity. In L. B. Cohen & P. Salapatek (Eds.), *Infant perception: From sensation to cognition* (Vol. 1). New York: Academic Press, 1975.

Fukuda, Y., & Stone, J. Retinal distribution and central projections of y-, x-, and w-cells of the cat's retina. *Journal of Neurophysiology*, 1974, *37*, 749–772.

Gardner, J. M., & Turkewitz, G. Effect of arousal level on visual preferences in preterm infants. *Infant Behavior and Development*, in press.

Gibson, E. J. *Principles of perceptual learning and development*. New York: Appleton-Century-Crofts, 1969.

Gould, J. D. Eye movements during visual search and memory search. *Journal of Experimental Psychology*, 1973, *98*, 184–195.

Gross, C. G. Visual functions of inferotemporal cortex. In R. Jung (Ed.), *Handbook of sensory physiology* (Vol. 7). New York: Springer-Verlag, 1973.

Hainline, L. Eye movements and form perception in human infants. In D. F. Fisher, R. A. Monty, & J. W. Senders (Eds.), *Eye movements: Cognition and visual perception*. New Jersey: Lawrence Erlbaum Associates, 1981.

Haith, M. M. *Rules that babies look by*. Hillsdale, New Jersey: Lawrence Erlbaum Associates, 1980.

Harris, P., & MacFarlane, A. The growth of effective visual field from birth to seven weeks. *Journal of Experimental Child Psychology*, 1974, *18*, 340–348.

Hebb, D. O. *The organization of behavior*. New York: Wiley, 1949.

Jeffrey, W. E. The orienting reflex and attention in cognitive development. *Psychological Review*, 1968, *75*, 323–334.

Karmel, B. Z. The effect of age, complexity, and amount of contour on pattern preferences in human infants. *Journal of Experimental Child Psychology*, 1969, *7*, 339–354.

Karmel, B. Z., & Maisel, E. B. A neuronal activity model for infant visual attention. In L. B. Cohen & P. Salapatek (Eds.), *Infant perception: From sensation to cognition* (Vol. 1). New York: Academic Press, 1975.

Kessen, W., Salapatek, P., & Haith, M. The visual response of the human newborn to linear contour. *Journal of Experimental Child Psychology*, 1972, *13*, 9–20.

Kremenitzer, J. P., Vaughan, H. G., Jr., Kurtzberg, D., & Dowling, K. Smooth-pursuit eye movements in the newborn infant. *Child Development*, 1979, *50*, 442–448.

Lasky, R. E. Serial habituation or regression to the mean? *Child Development*, 1979, *50*, 568–570.

Lewis, T., Maurer, D., & Milewski, A. E. *The development of nasal detection in young infants*. Paper presented at the Association for Research in Vision and Ophthalmology, Sarasota, May 1979.

MacFarlane, A., Harris, P., & Barnes, I. Central and peripheral vision in early infancy. *Journal of Experimental Child Psychology*, 1976, *21*, 532–538,

Macworth, N. H., & Bruner, J. S. How adults and children search and recognize pictures. *Human Development*, 1970, *13*, 149–177.

Mandell, R. B. Corneal contour of the human infant. *Archives of Ophthalmology*, 1967, *77*, 345–348.

Mandell, R. B., & St. Helen, R. Stability of the corneal contour. *American Journal of Optometry and Archives of American Academy of Optometry*, 1968, *45*, 797–806.

Maurer, D., & Lewis, T. L. Peripheral discrimination by three-month-old infants. *Child Development*, 1979, *50*, 276–279. (a)

Maurer, D., & Lewis, T. L. A physiological explanation of infants' early visual development. *Candian Journal of Psychology*, 1979, *33*, 232–252. (b)

Maurer, D., & Salapatek, P. Developmental changes in the scanning of faces by young infants. *Child Development*, 1976, *47*, 523–527.

McCall, R. B. Individual differences in pattern of habituation at 5 and 10 months of age. *Developmental Psychology*, 1979, *15*, 559–569.

Mendelson, M. J., & Haith, M. M. The relation between audition and vision in human infants. *Monographs of the Society for Research in Child Development*, 1976, *41*, 1–61.

Milewski, A. E. Infants' discrimination of internal and external pattern elements. *Journal of Experimental Child Psychology*, 1976, *22*, 229–246.

Miller, D., Ryan, E. B., Sinnott, J. P., & Wilson, M. A. Serial habituation in two-, three-, and four-month-old infants. *Child Development*, 1976, *47*, 341–349.

Noton, D., & Stark, L. Scanpaths in saccadic eye movements while viewing and recognizing patterns. *Vision Research*, 1971, *11*, 929–942.

Salapatek, P. Visual scanning of geometric figures by the human newborn. *Journal of Comparative and Physiological Psychology*, 1968, *66*, 247–258.

Salapatek, P. *The visual investigation of geometric pattern by the one and two month old infant*. Paper presented at the meeting of the American Association for the Advancement of Science, Boston, December 1969.

Salapatek, P. Pattern perception in early infancy. In L. B. Cohen & P. Salapatek (Eds.), *Infant perception: From sensation to cognition* (Vol. 1). New York: Academic Press, 1975.

Salapatek, P., & Kessen, W. Visual scanning of triangles by the human newborn. *Journal of Experimental Child Psychology*, 1966, *3*, 155–167.

Salapatek, P., & Kessen, W. Prolonged investigation of a plane geometric triangle by the human newborn. *Journal of Experimental Child Psychology*, 1973, *15*, 22–29.

Senders, J. W., Fisher, D. F., & Monty, R. A. (Eds.) *Eye movements and the higher psychological functions*. Hillsdale, New Jersey: Lawrence Erlbaum Associates, 1978.

Slater, A. M., & Findlay, J. M. The corneal reflection technique and the visual preference method: Sources of error. *Journal of Experimental Child Psychology*, 1975, *20*, 240–247.

Sokolov, E. N. Neuronal models and the orienting influence. In M. A. B. Brazier (Ed.), *The central nervous system and behavior:* V. III New York: Macy Foundation, 1960.

Stone, J., & Fukuda, Y. Properties of retinal ganglion cells: Comparison of 'w' cells with 'x' and 'y' cells. *Journal of Neurophysiology*, 1974, *37*, 722–748.

Uzgiris, I. C., & Hunt, J. McV. Attentional preference and experience, II: An exploratory longitudinal study of the effect of visual familiarity and responsiveness. *Journal of Genetic Psychology*, 1970, *117*, 109–121.

Watson, J. S. Memory and "contingency analysis" in infant learning. *Merrill-Palmer Quarterly*, 1967, *13*, 55–76.

Weiskrantz, L. Hindsight and blindsight. In E. Pöppel, R. Held, & J. E. Dowling (Eds.), *Neuronal mechanisms in visual perception, Neurosciences Research Program Bulletin*, 1977, *15*, 344–345.

Wilson, H. R., and Bergen, J. R. A four-mechanism model for spacial vision. *Vision Research*, 1979, *19*, 19–31.

Wolff, P. H. Observations on the early development of smiling. In B. M. Foss (Ed.), *Determinants of infant behaviour* (Vol. 2). New York: Wiley, 1963.

York, M. A., & Mandell, R. B. A new calibration system for photokeratoscopy. Part II: Corneal contour measurements. *American Journal of Optometry and Archives of American Academy of Optometry*, 1969, *46*, 818–825.

A
Commentary

Richard N. Aslin
Indiana University

This monograph by Gordon Bronson offers a unique blend of new empirical findings and theoretical insights on visual scanning in young infants. Despite a surge of interest in scanning during the mid-1960's, primarily under the tutelage of William Kessen at Yale, studies of scanning in infants have been rare in the past decade. This diminished interest resulted in part from the methodological difficulties involved in recording and scoring individual fixations that occur at rates as high as four per second. In addition, it became apparent after several initial studies that additional scanning data might not clarify basic questions about visual perception in infants. These initial studies of scanning (e.g., Salapatek & Kessen, 1966) described the location on a stationary visual pattern to which infants directed their gaze. Scanning data from these studies demonstrated quite clearly that even newborns fixate contours, thereby indicating the presence of a rudimentary visuomotor processing system. However, scanning data did not indicate the quality of visual processing in young infants. For example, if an infant only directed fixations to a limited region of a complex pattern, it seemed reasonable to conclude that other regions were not processed (or processed less accurately). Unfortunately, this reasonable conclu-

* Preparation of this article was supported in part by a Research Career Development Award (HD-00309) and a grant from NSF (BNS 80-13075). The helpful comments provided by Sandra Shea are gratefully acknowledged.

sion is contradicted by the fact that adults can detect patterns on the peripheral retina and make reasonably good judgments about the size and shape of extrafoveal targets (see Day, 1957). Thus, if infants could perform even elementary peripheral processing, the usefulness of scanning as a measure of visual perception would depend on an accurate estimate of the size of the retinal area surrounding the center of gaze that could perform pattern perception operations.

Given the complexity involved in recording and scoring infant scanning data, it was not surprising that most researchers interested in infant pattern perception focused their efforts on more global aspects of fixational behavior. Two such techniques emerged as standards for infant vision research in the 1970's: pattern preference (paired comparison), and habituation-dishabituation (response to novelty). Both techniques had the advantage of allowing the presentation of many stimulus contrasts to the infant in a short period of time. Thus, with appropriately controlled stimulus manipulations, many interesting questions could be addressed, even though the accuracy of fixational measurements was quite crude compared to scanning methods. The impasse reached after widespread use of these more global measures of visual fixation was that without a comprehensive description of critical stimulus parameters, an infinite number of stimulus manipulations was required to characterize the infant's visual processing powers.

One avenue for describing general characteristics of all visual stimuli is the linear systems approach employing Fourier analysis (see Banks & Salapatek, 1981, for a general review). Although this approach provides a superior scheme for organizing complex stimuli into a few relatively manageable parameters, it also suffers currently from a dependence on global fixation measures. For example, if an infant shows a preference for one of two stimuli, or shows dishabituation to a stimulus change, it is often unclear whether the basis for discrimination was the global configuration of contours or a local contour difference. Evidence of discrimination could be attributed to the presence of linear versus curvilinear line detectors, detection of amplitude differences in the two dimensional Fourier transform of the stimuli, or, as shown in Figure 1, the ability to fixate a local pattern region and detect differences in luminance or contour density. Perhaps more importantly, a *failure*

LOCAL "FEATURE" HYPOTHESIS

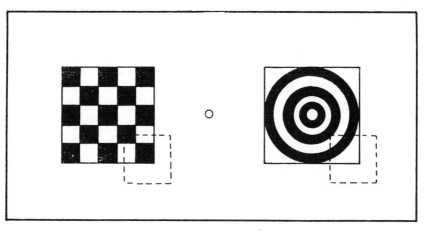

Figure 1. A schematized pattern preference display, illustrating how the fixation of a local region of pattern (the two dashed squares) could account for discrimination based only on differences in luminance or contour density.

to show evidence of discrimination using a global fixation measure results in an ambiguous conclusion regarding discriminative abilities. Such a discriminative failure could be due to low level sensory processing limitations such as acuity, high level configurational limitations such as feature integration, or the simple failure to fixate critical regions of the two patterns. Thus, scanning data can clarify both the presence and absence of pattern discrimination by ruling out the possibility that the infant failed to fixate regions of visual patterns that contained differential information.

Recent dissatisfaction with the primary dependence on global fixation measures, particularly those associated with preferential behaviors (see Haith, 1980, for a critical review of preference techniques), in addition to the availiability of microprocessor-based systems for analyzing video signals, has enabled both on-line and off-line automated scoring of scanning data (see Sheena, 1976). As a result, many of the time consuming aspects of collecting, scoring and analyzing scanning data have been reduced. Bronson (1982) has accomplished here a methodological synthesis of global fixation measures and more detailed scanning measures of individual fixations. By presenting infants with patterns that change, while recordings are made of the location of individual fixations, he has begun to investigate the mechanisms underlying positive and negative instances of pattern discrimination in young infants.

In this commentary, I hope to point out several important aspects of Bronson's monograph and the general approach he proposes for the study of visual processing in infants. First, I will review some of the major findings of Bronson's work, paying particular attention to the implications of these findings for past and future research in visual development and pattern perception. Second, I will relate some of Bronson's findings to work on scanning in adults. The purpose here is to provide analogies with those mechanisms thought to underlie adult pattern processing, as well as to clarify alternative models of adult visual processing by considering *developmental* aspects of scanning. Finally, I will evaluate Bronson's methods for collecting and analyzing scanning data from infants.

THEORETICAL IMPLICATIONS
OF BRONSON'S DATA

In this section, I will address three questions: (1) what aspects of visual stimuli influence or control scanning behavior, (2) what aspects of scanning behavior are important for or indicative of visual processing, and (3) what generalizations can be drawn from Bronson's data and his developmental model of scanning? The first question actually involves two separate processes: the effect that peripheral stimuli have on *changes* in fixation, and the effect that foveated stimuli have on the *maintenance* of fixation. Obviously, if one of these complementary processes were dominant, the infant would either maintain fixation on the first stimulus that was foveated, or rapidly saccade from stimulus to stimulus after a minimal fixation duration.

Bronson has proposed a three-level model for the development of scanning, incorporating the two processes of peripheral elicitation (change) and central fixation (maintenance). For the first level (newborn), all retinal locations appear to be equipotential, in that any stimulus located within the visual field is equally likely to elicit an attentional response. The central retina is primary only in that it coincides with the preferred line of sight. Large fixational variances are present while attempting to fixate a portion of a complex pattern, indicating both poor sensory processing and inaccurate motor control. Any tendency to show evidence of "capture" by a given feature is the result of multiple peripheral stimuli "pulling" attention in all directions at once.

The second level (1–2 months) is characterized by an increasingly effective control of individual fixations and saccadic movements, as well as a bias to process central stimulation more completely or more accurately than peripheral stimulation. In addition, initial examples of attention to visual discrepancies become evident, signalling the beginnings of a reduced dependence on stimulus salience to elicit saccadic re-fixations.

The third level (3–5 months) is dominated by the ability to override salience effects, even though stimulus salience is still important if only a single target is present (saccades rarely land on contour-free locations). Infants are now able to move their next fixation beyond a region of high stimulus salience (e.g., high contour density), indicating that saccadic control has progressed to a higher level. Finally, infants show a tendency, when repeatedly presented with the same stimulus, to scan the components of the stimulus in the same manner. This recursive scan indicates that infants can use remembered locations within a complex stimulus to guide subsequent fixations. Such a scanning strategy may also indicate that infants attempt to verify the identity (or non-identity) of the stimulus on subsequent presentations.

The general developmental trend in this model is toward a more flexible *control* over the balance between peripheral elicitation and central fixation. Of course, the validity of the model depends on a precise specification of stimulus attributes that modulate the complementary processes of peripheral elicitation and central fixation. This task of specifying effective stimulus parameters will require a psychophysical approach—varying the number and size of stimulus elements, their spatial arrangement and eccentricity, their relative salience (contrast and spatial frequency), and their familiarity. Obviously, this is a task that will require a systematic research effort by several investigators.

The second question—what aspects of scanning behavior are important for visual processing?—involves a series of inferences based on a somewhat limited set of dependent measures. These measures include:

(1) The frequency with which a stimulus is fixated.
(2) The duration of all fixations to a stimulus.
(3) The duration of individual fixations (called dwell-times by Bronson).
(4) The ordering or pattern of successive fixation locations, including their dispersion at each location.

Bronson has employed each of these measures to their fullest in his attempt to infer whether the infant has processed a visual pattern during an episode of scanning.

The first two measures—fixation frequency and duration—appeared to provide reliable indices of detecting a change in a peripherally presented stimulus (see Bronson's Figure 2). Moreover, only stimulus changes located in the near periphery resulted in increased fixation frequencies and durations (see Bronson's Figure 3). As Bronson correctly noted, there is some ambiguity associated with the absence of increased fixation frequencies and durations to stimuli located in the far periphery. It is possible (although improbable according to Bronson) that stimuli in the far periphery were in fact processed, but for some reason they did not elicit a saccade and subsequent fixation. Bronson's data do not provide a definitive resolution of this issue, particularly since the size of the central retinal area used by infants in processing stimuli during a given fixation is presently unknown. Clearly, scanning data alone cannot provide an answer to this question. Instead, the answer requires a dependent measure that provides an assessment of visual processing while fixation position is treated as an independent variable. At present, such a dependent measure is not available.

In contrast to the measure of total fixation duration to a stimulus during a trial, increases in individual fixation durations or dwell-times did not provide a good index of increases in visual processing. In fact, Bronson presented a very convincing argument that long dwell-times indicate *poor* visual processing, either because of attentional lapses or slow rates of content assimilation (as in a "blank" stare). Not only were initial dwell-times to a changed stimulus *not* longer in duration, but longer dwell-times were unrelated to infant age, sequencing within a trial, or stimulus characteristics. Finally, when a fixation landed on a region containing no contour, the distribution of dwell-times was very narrow and was centered at a shorter duration than dwell-times on contoured areas.

This distribution of dwell-times to contour-free regions allowed Bronson to infer the operation of a two-process model to account for the duration of dwell-times during scanning: (1) a *programming* process that computes the size and direction of the next saccade, and (2) an *assimilation* process that analyzes and encodes the stimulus attributes located on the central retina during the current fixation. This dual process, although conceivably operating in a *serial* manner, most likely operates in *parallel*, with the subsequent saccade occurring only after both processes are completed. Although this parallel processing model seems well-justified by Bronson (e.g., the minimum dwell-time with or without contour fixation is equivalent), there are several assumptions that may be in error and essentially untestable.

The first of these assumptions is based on Bronson's estimate of saccadic programming time from fixations that landed on contour-free areas of the stimulus. It is assumed that the absence of stimulus information at these regions provides a base line for inferring the absence of the content assimilation process. However, some portion of the content assimilation process may operate even for contour-free regions, since the absence of contours may still carry some information (e.g., "nothing is there"). Thus, the programming time may have been overestimated by this assumption that no assimilation occurred when a contour-free region was fixated. Moreover, the age change in inferred programming time (from .5 to .2 seconds between 2-month-olds and adults) is confounded with possible developmental changes in content assimilation times when contour-free regions are fixated. In fact, if the informational impact of the absence of contours were to decrease with age, the estimated saccadic programming time could remain constant during development.

The second assumption of Bronson's model of dwell-times is that the termination of both the programming and content assimila-

if the stimulus array has remained spatially invariant (at least for global aspects of the array) for some time prior to saccade programming.

There are some empirical data on infant saccades that appear to contradict Bronson's spatial invariance model. Salapatek, Aslin, Simonson and Pulos (1980) recorded saccades to a single peripheral target that disappeared after the first localizing movement. In this disappearing stimulus situation, infants typically continued to make saccades in the direction of the target's initial location. Of particular importance is the fact that saccadic latencies subsequent to the disappearance of the peripheral target were indentical to latencies on trials in which the target did *not* disappear. Thus, there was not an increase in saccadic latency following the disappearance of a target. In this case, however, the target was already in the process of being localized prior to its disappearance, whereas in Bronson's case the target disappeared while it was being fixated. Could this difference provide an alternative interpretation of Bronson's spatial invariance model?

Models of saccadic programming to a single peripheral target are typically quite different from models of scanning movements to a continuously presented, multiple-element stimulus array. At least four processes usually are proposed to account for saccadic localization of a single peripheral target:

1. Detection of the target via the peripheral retina.
2. Deployment of attention from the central retina (current fixation) to the peripheral target.
3. Computation of the required direction and angular extent of the eye movement required to foveate the peripheral target.
4. Execution of the saccadic movement itself.

In the typical case of localizing a single target that appears suddenly in the periphery, the first two processes (detection and attention) are required only prior to the initial saccade. Any failure to accurately fixate the target after this initial saccade simply results in a re-calculation of the fixational error and execution of a subsequent corrective saccade. Similarly, in the case of a single peripheral target that disappears after the initial saccade, the first two processes

need only occur once. Either the subsequent re-calculations and
corrective saccades continue in the same direction as the initial saccade, or the system terminates the attempt at localization for lack
of a peripheral target (this occurred on approximately 20% of the
trials in the Salapatek et al. study). Finally, in the case of a stable,
multiple-element stimulus, the first two processes presumably occur "online" in parallel with the content assimilation process during
each fixation. A sudden change in the stimulus that is currently fixated presumably interrupts the content assimilation process, and in
turn "resets" the four steps involved in programming the next saccade. Thus, when the stimulus change occurs, there is a longer delay at the current fixation location.

    This alternative account of the differences in dwell-time re-
ported by Bronson does not require an assumption that infants
have knowledge of the spatial invariance of stimulus elements in
the array. Rather, it postulates a simple "interrupt" mechanism
that is responsive to changes in the content currently undergoing
assimilation, and a "reset" mechanism that starts the four processes of saccade programming over again. Note that this alternative model predicts a similar increase in dwell-time, not only for
sudden changes in the currently fixated stimulus, but also for sudden changes in non-fixated stimuli. If a peripherally located stimulus element were to undergo a sudden *gross* change in salience
(rather than the subtle change from square to ellipse employed by
Bronson), the detection and attention processes involved in
saccadic programming would: (1) interrupt the content assimilation
process at the current fixation location, (2) reset the saccadic parameters, and (3) initiate a saccade toward the location of the
changed stimulus element. As a result, there would be an increase
in dwell-time at the current fixation location when the sudden
change in the peripheral stimulus occurred.

    Another aspect of Bronson's spatial invariance model is his
contention that the ability to encode spatial relationships among
stimulus elements "is basic to the synthesis of data collected by
means of a series of discrete fixations—that is, to the learning of organized patterns, rather than just the separate qualities of individually fixated components" (p. 32). The question raised by this statement is how scanning behavior contributes to this spatial
knowledge. Certainly, Bronson does not believe that the direction

and extent of saccadic movements actively structure the stimulus array into a spatial coordinate system. This Hebbian notion of the motor movements themselves constructing spatial knowledge is contradicted by the fact that saccadic movements are programmed with peripheral retinal information that existed *prior* to the saccadic movement. Thus, the spatial knowledge required to move the line of sight and to fixate a particular stimulus element is available before the movement, arguing against a strict motor theory of visual pattern perception.

Bronson's statement more likely reflects the view that the resolution of central or foveal vision is superior to peripheral vision. Given this constraint, saccadic movements function to provide clarity of detail to initially indeterminate patches of visual pattern. Thus, scanning movements may be essential in initially specifying and subsequently verifying that a specific portion of visual pattern is located in a specific spatial position relative to other pattern elements. The global nature of this pattern arrangement was probably known prior to any saccadic movements, but the details of visual pattern ("*what* is located there") probably were not.

The final aspect of scanning behavior discussed by Bronson is the recursive nature of scanning during repeated presentations of the same stimulus array. Bronson hypothesized that upon first encountering a complex stimulus, the infant's fixations are "drawn" to specific locations by a combination of stimulus salience and random error. However, subsequent presentations of a similar stimulus array (presumably wildly different arrays would not engage recursive scanning) are scanned in a manner that seems to compare the identity of the current array to the previous array. The infant appears to fixate a limited subset of the possible stimulus elements, presumably as a check on the expected content of these fixations, and with an apparent goal of judging familiarity or non-familiarity. As Bronson stated, "It is not necessary, and probably not typical, to examine a wide variety of visual details in order to reach this judgment, since outside the laboratory sets of visual features which appear concurrently usually are components of a single relatively unchanging object" (p. 47). A test of this model of recursive scanning might consist of systematic variations in the amount of stimulus change required to alter the repetitive scanpath on subsequent stimulus presentations. Such a program of research would be

quite laborious, but the model certainly provides a unique and test-
able approach for studying the influence of memory for visual pattern and spatial arrangement on scanning behavior.

The third and final question in this section—what generalizations can be drawn from Bronson's data?—involves a consideration
of other methods for assessing pattern perception in infants.
Bronson's findings have shown that when infants fixate a novel
stimulus element (e.g., when the square changes to an ellipse),
there is little evidence of a comparison process in the scanning behavior. Thus, a "back and forth" pattern of fixations between the
stable element and the novel element did not occur, at least in the
5-sec. presentation period. Certainly, there were instances in
which both stimulus elements were fixated, but no direct comparison process was apparent. If infants continued to show little evidence of pattern comparison during longer presentaton periods,
then how might we view data on overall fixation behavior to pattern
preference displays such as the one shown in Figure 1? Presumably, the stimulus panel that was fixated initially was more salient.
But if the infant's initial fixation location was between the two panels, the initial saccadic movement to one of the two stimulus panels
must have been guided by peripheral retinal information. Once the
stimulus panel was fixated, would the overall duration of fixation
indicate anything about visual processing? Bronson's data imply
that such a global fixation measure may be confounded by a tendency to shun comparison looking between the stimulus panels and a
tendency to "look away" from the panel *not* because the entire pattern has been encoded, but because the identity of gross details and
their spatial arrangement within the pattern have been encoded.
Scanning data would certainly assist in clarifying what specific regions of the stimulus were fixated and how those fixated regions
were related to global measures of fixational behavior.

Another aspect of Bronson's data that is related to the pattern
preference technique is his finding that *across* subjects, the frequency of fixation to stimulus elements was determined by traditional salience parameters (e.g., proximity, contour density, luminance, movement, etc.). However, fixational frequency data from
individual subjects indicated that this salience effect did not hold
for all infants. Some infants consistently fixated stimulus elements

tion processes occurs prior to the next saccade. Although Bronson believes that subsequent fixations will interfere with the assimilation of information from the preceding fixation, such an assumption may be unwarranted. The process of assimilation may in fact build *across* successive fixations, particularly if several fixations are located on a particular attribute, element, or feature of a complex visual pattern (an integrative process Bronson favors in his summary section). Thus, part of the content assimilation process may occur during the actual saccadic movement itself (approximately 10–40 msec.), the initial portion of the subsequent dwell-time as the oculomotor system "settles" into a new fixation position, and/or across several successive fixations for integrative aspects of visual processing.

Unfortunately, this alternative to Bronson's assumption that content assimilation terminates at the onset of the next saccade is quite cumbersome and nearly impossible to model without knowledge of *what* the infant has processed during the sequence of scanning movements. Such knowledge may be impossible to gather from infants (although probe or masking techniques may work) without a non-fixational measure of visual processing. Again, inferences about visual processing will eventually require multiple measures, and not just data on scanning or just global fixation preferences.

The fourth measure of scanning behavior involves an assessment of the pattern or spatial distribution of fixations. Bronson presented several lines of evidence to support his contention that, for older infants, a stable stimulus field facilitates the programming of saccades. When the stimulus array underwent a sudden change (from the moving target to the multiple-element stimulus display), the infant's fixation was temporarily located on a contour-free area (where the moving target had been located). The latency to shift fixation from this contour-free region to one of the contours in the stimulus array was twice as long as the latency to shift fixation (the dwell-time) during continuous scanning of an unchanging stimulus field. A similar latency effect was shown by Aslin and Salapatek (1975) for saccades to single peripheral targets; the latency to the initial saccade was much longer than subsequent intersaccadic intervals during a series of localizing saccades. Bronson's interpretation of these findings is that saccadic programming is more rapid

that did not conform to group salience parameters. These individual tendencies to fixate different stimulus elements (e.g., the dim red IR light versus the square or ellipse) could have been the result of idiosyncratic stimulus preferences. However, Bronson argued convincingly that his model of recursive scanning can account for these individual differences in frequently fixated stimulus elements. The first presentation of the stimulus array will lead to a scanpath that in general is determined by the salience of the stimulus elements, as well as random fluctuations in saccadic programming. Some infants, therefore, will most frequently fixate one or several salient elements, and a few infants will fixate non-salient elements. If the recursive scanning model is operative, subsequent stimulus presentations will result in a repetition of the initial scanpath, and in turn a continuation of frequent fixations to specific stimulus elements (some of which may be non-salient in a general sense).

The arrangement of pattern preference displays may also influence the presence of discriminative behaviors. Infants in a pattern preference study are typically presented with two widely-spaced stimulus panels. Regardless of the specific measure used (overall fixation duration, frequency of fixation, duration of first fixation), the infant will initially fixate one of the stimulus panels and eventually look away from that panel. If the subsequent fixation after this first look returns to the initially fixated stimulus panel, a recursive scan would presumably occur. However, if the opposite stimulus panel were fixated after looking away from the initial panel, the novelty of the new stimulus would lead to a longer period of scanning (more fixations and an overall longer period of fixation). Thus, the tendency to switch fixation from one stimulus panel to the other, independently of underlying discriminative abilities, may partially determine overall fixation preferences. Moreover, the duration of stimulus presentation would be expected to interact with the frequency of fixational switching between the two panels. Thus, if only one panel could be fixated before termination of the trial, the measure of fixational preference would be determined by visual processing via the peripheral retina. If many switches were possible, the *sequencing* of fixational switches would influence measures of fixational preferences. For example, concentrated same-panel viewing followed by a switch would lead to a single novelty effect as evidenced by a longer fixation, whereas an alternation of scanpaths between the two panels would lead to a novelty effect on each alternation. Thus, the interplay between recursive scanning patterns and the tendency to switch gaze from one stimulus panel to the other could partially determine the outcome of global measures of fixational preference. Given the general developmental shift toward a broader distribution of scanning patterns, developmental changes in pattern discrimination abilities inferred from global measures of preference may indicate a more effective control of scanning behavior, rather than improved processing powers.

Finally, Bronson's data have implications for another widely used measure of visual processing in infants—the habituation-dishabituation technique. Although Bronson presented group data on the habituation of fixation to the initially fixated stimulus element (typically a high salience element), he noted that this group trend was actually composed of two subgroups: habituators and non-habituators. In addition, Bronson presented an argument to support his contention that infants in the non-habituator group failed to show a decrement in fixation because they were not alert. Thus, on repeated presentations of the stimulus array, these non-habituating infants continued to fixate the same stimulus elements that they had fixated on the initial presentation, whereas the habituating infants switched their fixation to other stimulus elements on subsequent presentations. As a measure of encoding, therefore, individual fixations within a scanning episode may be inaccurate because some infants become less attentive, and inattention is associated with a high frequency of long dwell-times. Thus, measures of fixation duration, unless described in detail by scanning techniques, may indicate either high levels of processing (the novelty effect) or low levels of processing (inattentiveness).

Finally, inattentive infants may show highly variable fixation times. This high variance, even though unrelated to encoding, may be sufficient to satisfy a preset criterion of habituation using a global measure of fixation. Those inattentive infants who meet this habituation criterion without encoding the details of the visual pattern are likely to show highly variable dishabituation effects to a "novel" pattern. In fact, some backward habituation curves (see

Cohen & Gelber, 1975) exhibit an *increase* in fixation duration, prior to reaching a criterion of habituation. This increase may reflect a transient influx of long dwell-times that are due to inattention. The subsequent habituation criterion may be met by a shift in attentiveness that leads to fewer long fixations. However, this decrement in long fixations may be related only to the encoding of gross aspects of the stimulus and not stimulus details. If the stimulus details had not been encoded, a post-criterion change in the stimulus would not lead to dishabituation on the global fixation measure. In summary, the use of global measures of fixation in habituation studies may partially obscure underlying differences in individual fixations, which in turn are sometimes poor measures of visual processing.

Given Bronson's weak evidence for serial habituation, as indicated by several measures of scanning behavior, one might ask whether habituation of scanning would result if the stimulus presentation times were increased from 5 sec. to a longer duration. Bronson claimed that such an increase would not allow one to address the *initial* pattern of changes in fixation frequency that might accompany repeated presentations of the same stimulus. Yet, if the infant is ever to encode the details of a complex stimulus (assuming such an encoding process ever occurs in infants younger than 6 months), one must ask when the recursive scanning strategy is abandoned and replaced by a more detailed search for *all* the information contained in the pattern. If, in fact, an increase in stimulus presentation time does not lead to a change in the recursive scanpath, one might question the utility of scanning as a measure of visual information processing. Are infants actually using the most sensitive region of the retina to encode details of the stimulus, or is the directing of gaze an epiphenomenon until some later point in development when the visual system is capable of detailed pattern encoding? Unfortunately, these questions must await the development of new measures of visual processing that can assess encoding during scanning of complex patterns. In this way, the effective size of the information processing area surrounding the line of sight will become known. In addition, one may detect the occurrence of any developmental shift in the quantity of detail encoded during a series of fixations. The spontaneous nature of scanning movements, in contrast to "forced" visual processing measures (e.g., conditioning), may indicate that scanning measures are limited in what they can reveal about visual processing.

COMPARISONS OF INFANT
AND ADULT SCANNING DATA

The literature on infant scanning, although somewhat limited, stands in marked contrast to the literature on eye movements in adults. On the one hand, there are numerous studies, beginning with Dodge's work at the turn of the century (Dodge & Cline, 1901), on eye movements by adults toward single visual targets (see reviews in the three-volume series: Monty & Senders, 1976; Senders, Monty, & Fisher, 1978; Fisher, Monty, & Senders, 1981). Given this rich empirical tradition, one might expect the literature on adults' scanning of complex visual patterns to be far advanced over its developmental counterpart. However, the adult scanning literature has been forced to confront many of the same interpretive issues facing researchers of scanning in infants. One advantage associated with the study of adults, however, is the ability to document in some detail the amount of information actually processed during a scanning episode. Despite this advantage, little significant progress has been made in defining the *relation* between scanning behaviors and visual processing. The major exception to this trend has been the recent research on detailed fixational measures during reading (see review by Rayner, 1978). The advantage of studying eye movements during a reading task is that the fixations proceed across the text in a very stereotyped manner, which is a logical and strategic result of the constraints placed on the spatial arrangement of words in sentences. Scanning of visual patterns containing non-text material does not appear to require a specific ordering of fixations for visual information to be encoded. In general, then, we know that scanning behavior differs dramatically as one varies the content presented to adults in a visual display, as well as the subject's task-specific instructions (see Yarbus, 1967). Without constraints on the spatial or semantic ordering of fixations, adults show large individual differences in the pattern of scanning over complex visual patterns.

At the interpretive level, one might ask if adult models of scanning are similar to the model of infant scanning raised by Bronson (1982). First, consider the relation between fixation position and visual processing. As Stark and Ellis (1981) have noted, there are three possible levels of processing during scanning:

1. Scanning without seeing (a random-like scanpath perhaps controlled by the physical or sensory attributes of the stimulus).
2. Seeing without scanning (perception of the structure of the visual pattern's attributes without an extensive scanpath).
3. Scanning and seeing (a tightly organized scanpath to check for invariant aspects of the visual pattern).

Under certain circumstances, certain stimulus patterns are scanned by some adults in a consistent manner (e.g., Noton & Stark, 1971a,b). However, there is no universal metric for describing the stimulus parameters that influence consistent scanning (a problem similar to the one discussed earlier for studies of infant pattern perception), and no clear hypotheses to explain why scanpaths are sometimes consistent and other times not. This latter issue is particularly puzzling because two subjects may extract the same information from a stimulus but show wildly different scanpaths (Nodine, Carmody, & Kundel, 1978), or they may extract different information (recall vs. recognition) but show quite similar scanpaths (Tversky, 1974). These inconsistencies imply that either (1) the ordering of fixations on a complex (non-alphanumeric) visual pattern is at least partially independent of visual processing, or (2) currently used dependent measures of scanning behavior do not capture the critical aspects of information sampling and encoding required for visual processing.

A second important issue for adult-infant comparisons between models of scanning is the size and location of the retinal area that performs visual processing during scanning. In the case of a reading task, Rayner, Well and Pollatsek (1980) have shown that a limited parafoveal area is used to process letter information during each fixation, and that this area is asymmetrical (skewed rightward from the central fovea). Thus, the size of the effective retinal area for detailed processing during reading is based largely on sensory limitations, plus an acquired attentional asymmetry that facilitates processing of letters located in the direction of the subsequent fixation.

This example from reading, however, may not be representative of information processing during scanning of other, non-text, visual displays. Reading is a highly practiced skill involving many stimulus constraints and semantic relations that may override sensory processing limitations. For non-text displays, more global aspects of the stimulus may be processed during scanning without the necessity of fixating each specific region of the stimulus. In fact, the control of gaze in reading is partially determined by global stimulus attributes, as shown by the predominance of fixations at the beginning of words and the frequent "skipping over" of words that contain only a few letters (e.g., *of, to, a, the*, etc.; see O'Regan, 1979).

The processing of global stimulus attributes by the peripheral retina during a fixation has generated two views of peripheral processing (see discussion by Findlay, 1981). One view of peripheral processing is that attention, presumably under voluntary control, can be deployed from the central retina to a specific peripheral location. Thus, the attentional process acts like a searchlight, selecting out the location and gross features of the subsequently fixated stimulus region. An alternative view of peripheral processing is that attention is elicited involuntarily by the relative salience of peripheral stimuli. In the adult, both of these processes may occur during scanning, depending on the type of stimulus and the instructions to the subject. In the infant, it is not clear how one would determine the relative contribution of these two processes without experimental control of the infant's attentional state to specific stimulus attributes. However, the greater apparent control with which older infants scan various stimulus regions, particularly the ability to saccade beyond a region of high salience, argues that voluntary control of gaze improves with age.

Data from adults reported by Findlay (1981) suggest a tentative hypothesis regarding the level of peripheral processing during infant scanning. Findlay showed that saccadic amplitudes are correlated in an interesting way with saccadic latencies. For long latencies, the saccade is directed to the details of the eliciting target, whereas for short latencies, the saccadic amplitude is determined by global stimulus attributes. Bronson (1982) found that, across infants, longer dwell-times were associated with small saccadic amplitudes, whereas shorter dwell-times were associated with larger saccadic amplitudes. Thus, the majority of infants (short dwell-times and long saccades) may have been guided primarily by *global* stimulus attributes, and only a limited processing of stimulus detail may have occurred during the brief fixations. Other infants (showing longer dwell-times and shorter saccades), characterized by Bronson as inattentive, may in fact have been guided by the *details* of peripheral stimuli. Thus, these infants may have made smaller saccades to fixate nearby regions of the stimulus (regions that can be processed by near-foveal areas), and they may have fixated each region longer in an attempt to process this detailed information, rather than just the more global stimulus attributes. This alternative to Bronson's model is also consistent with his findings on habituation of fixations. Non-habituating infants returned their gaze to the same stimulus elements on repeated trials, perhaps in an attempt to encode stimulus detail, whereas habituating infants altered their fixational patterns on successive trials, perhaps because only global attributes were encoded. Variation in the trial presentation time (beyond the constant 5 sec. used by Bronson) might clarify the amount of processing engaged in by infants during longer dwell-times, particularly if detailed scanning measures could be combined with a measure of the level of visual processing.

Other aspects of Bronson's data from infants are closely related to findings from adults. Antes and Penland (1981) have shown that when adults expect to find specific stimulus objects in a multiple-object display, they fixate these expected objects first. This finding is directly analogous to Bronson's data from infants as they view stimulus elements on repeated (expected) presentations. In addition, adults show briefer fixations (shorter dwell-times) to expected objects when the objects are embedded in a consistent context or conceptual frame. Antes and Penland interpreted this finding as support for a context-driven process that facilitates the encoding of expected information. Similar arguments have been raised by Friedman (1979). Finally, Antes and Penland found that adults only fixate *un*expected objects if the objects are located in the near periphery. Again, this retinal eccentricity effect for novelty is analogous to Bronson's infant data on the fixation of near versus far stimulus elements that have undergone a change in shape.

Although infants in Bronson's study did not show differential dwell-times to repeated (unchanging) versus novel stimulus elements, Friedman and Liebelt (1981) have shown that adults have longer individual fixation durations to unexpected objects. However, the adults in their study were specifically instructed to look for details in the stimulus display and to scan over the entire array. Thus, if non-detailed instructions (or spontaneous scanning) had been in effect, one might expect adults to show little or no differential dwell-time effect for global aspects of the display, regardless of expectations about the objects in the display. This hypothesis is supported by Friedman and Liebelt's data on fixation of expected objects. They found that adults initially had brief dwell-times to expected objects, followed by a gradual increase in dwell-times over the course of the 30-sec. presentation period. This finding suggests that global information was encoded first, followed by a systematic increase in the encoding of stimulus details. In marked contrast, dwell-times for unexpected objects were longer initially, and failed to increase or decrease during the 30-sec. trial. These findings support Navon's (1977) model of the primacy of processing global over local stimulus attributes, at least for displays containing numerous stimulus elements (see Martin, 1979).

Findings from adults on dwell-times to expected and unexpected objects are consistent with Bronson's hypothesis that infants initially process only general or global stimulus attributes. Alternatively, longer stimulus presentations might lead to a change in infant dwell-times. Moreover, it is possible that the difference between non-habituating and habituating infants resides in their spontaneous tendency to encode either global or detailed stimulus information, respectively. Again, it is unclear whether non-habituators who viewed the stimulus for a longer period would begin to show shorter dwell-times as the stimulus details were encoded, or whether they would continue to be inattentive as Bronson has hypothesized.

Another important aspect of Bronson's infant data that is related to adult scanning is the repeated fixation of the same stimulus elements on subsequent presentations. These recursive scanpaths have received some empirical support in the adult literature (Noton & Stark, 1971a,b; Parker, 1978). However, the algorithms used to determine if two scanpaths were similar have typically been quite subjective (see Stark & Ellis, 1981, for an attempt at an objective scanpath metric). It is quite easy to document that the same element was fixated at the beginning of each stimulus presentation, but it is very difficult to quantify the similarity between two non-identical, multiple-saccadic scanpaths. Bronson's recursive scanning data are similarly non-quantitative in that the first stimulus element fixated on each presentation was unambiguous, but the similarity of later fixation patterns was less compelling. At a minimum, we know that a given infant tended to fixate a particular subset of stimulus elements on repeated trials. However, the *ordering* of these fixations did not appear to be invariant, a fact recognized by Bronson's analysis of habituation effects.

Finally, I suggested in an earlier section that Bronson's spatial invariance model of saccadic programming may require refinement, specifically with regard to his assumption that content assimilation terminates before the next saccade. In the area of reading, some models propose that the visual content of each word is processed completely prior to the next saccade (e.g., Just & Carpenter, 1980). Such an assumption implies that several alternative representations of word meaning are *not* carried in memory until the correct representation is rendered unambiguous by subsequent fixations in the sentence. Our rich knowledge of syntactic and semantic structure prevents the frequent occurrence of "garden path" errors during reading (reaching a later word and finding that the hypothesized meaning of an earlier word was incorrect). However, the assumption that processing is completed before the next saccade is applicable only to low levels of processing. Nearly all models of reading propose that integrative processes (e.g., relating two word meanings at a clause boundary) also occur during the current fixation. Thus, the last dwell-time includes visual processing of the currently fixated stimulus element (or word), as well as higher level or relational processing of previously fixated elements.

A similar integrative process undoubtedly operates during the scanning of non-text displays. For example, Gould (1976) discussed four aspects of information processing related to the integration of information over successive fixations while scanning a complex visual display:

1. The ability to process global and local stimulus information via the peripheral retina.
2. The spatial information available to guide saccades.
3. The short-term memory abilities needed to integrate spatial arrangements and visual details during successive fixations.
4. The knowledge-base of the subject that allows the content of non-fixated regions of the display to be inferred or expected.

Obviously, all of these aspects of information processing are relevant to the understanding of scanning behavior in infants. Visual processing may be constrained by each of these four types of abilities. Bronson's monograph has just begun the exciting process of discovering which of these factors plays an essential role in the infants' visual processing, and how the relative importance of each factor may change during the course of early visual development.

METHODS OF COLLECTING AND ANALYZING SCANNING DATA

The methods of data collection, scoring and analysis employed by Bronson (1982) are superior in many respects to past studies of scanning in infants. There are many trade-offs involved in choosing eye monitoring equipment (see surveys of adult and infant eye movements techniques by Young & Sheena, 1975; and Maurer, 1975, respectively). However, the single overriding issue facing investigators of infant eye movements is how to calibrate the raw eye position signal. Whether one chooses a technique such as electrooculography that measures eye position relative to head position, or a technique such as corneal photography that measures eye position relative to fixed light sources, one must relate the resultant data to the actual line of sight. Since the location of the fovea cannot be visualized online (except by the use of an ophthalmoscope which precludes measurement of eye position), it is necessary to calibrate the eye position signal with reference to known locations in the stimulus display.

In adults, calibration is facilitated by two facts: (1) the line of sight is coincident with the fovea and it does not vary within a subject across time, and (2) the subject can be instructed to foveate known positions on the stimulus display, thereby mapping the recorded eye signal onto a stimulus display coordinate system. In infants, or any nonverbal subject, the first fact may not hold and the second fact certainly does not. As Bronson noted, young infants show considerable variance in their fixation of a small, stationary target. This variance might imply an inaccurate specification of the relative retinal location of the fixation stimulus, or an inability to finely control eye position, or both a sensory and a motor deficit in oculomotor control. In addition, there may be anatomical constraints on fixational accuracy and variance (Abramov, Gordon, Hendrickson, Hainline, Dobson, & LaBossiere, 1981).

Nevertheless, even in the absence of high fixational variance, the calibration issue is of critical concern to the reliability and validity of eye position data gathered from infants. Initial applications of corneal photography (e.g., Salapatek & Kessen, 1966) and subsequent use of infrared video technology (Haith, 1969) employed a set of six or more small lights, aligned with the stimulus display, that created discrete reflections on the corneal surface. Scoring by human observers of the distance from pupil center to each marker light reflection provided an estimate of the line of sight (pupil center) relative to the fixed array of lights (and their known positions relative to the stimulus display). This calibration technique has been criticized for failing to account for the consistent discrepancy between pupil center and the line of sight (up to 8–9 degrees in newborns), as well as various parallax errors (see Slater & Findlay,

1972, 1975; and reply by Salapatek, Haith, Maurer, & Kessen, 1972).

An alternative to this fixed marker light calibration procedure (which may ignore or summate inter-individual differences in line of sight errors) is a more adult-like calibration scheme. One can present infants with a small target in various locations and assess the average change in the eye position signal, thereby mapping this signal onto a stimulus display coordinate system. Harris, Hainline, and Abramov (1981) have argued that although the dispersion of infants' fixations around a small target is large, a statistical treatment of these calibration data can usually generate a likely point (or small region) corresponding to the line of sight. This calibration procedure must assume that the infant actually fixated each target position with the line of sight (or fovea), rather than looking away from the target during the collection of some or all of the calibration data. Unfortunately, such an assumption is impossible to verify given currently available techniques.

A variation of the foregoing calibration technique consists of replacing the stationary calibration target with a moving target. The rationale for this substitution is that infants appear to be more attentive to a moving than to a stationary target, thus opitimizing the likelihood that the line of sight would be directed toward the target during the collection of calibration data. This calibration procedure has been used by Aslin (1981) in a study of smooth pursuit eye movements, as well as Bronson (1982) in the present monograph. The disadvantage of this calibration procedure is the fact that during target movement, the line of sight typically lags behind the actual target position. Thus, both Aslin and Bronson based their calibration data on fixations collected just after cessation of target movement, thereby allowing time for the line of sight to "catch" the target. Again, however, this calibration procedure must assume that the line of sight was actually directed to the position of the target during the collection of calibration data.

Once calibration data have been collected, the raw eye position signal can be re-scaled to estimate fixation locations on the stimulus display. It is important to note that recent video-based systems for recording corneal reflections (e.g., Aslin, 1981; Bronson, 1982; Hainline, 1981) provide a measure of the uncalibrated eye position signal (horizontal and vertical coordinates) at a rate of 30 or 60 Hz. Since saccades typically occur at a rate of up to 4 or 5 Hz in adults, many of these fixations last from 200 msec. to several seconds. For adults, computer programs have been used to collapse these individual data points into a mean fixation position and its dwell-time (e.g., Kliegl & Olson, 1981). Harris et al. (1981) have devised a similar procedure for use with infants. In contrast, Bronson performed much of this fixational analysis by hand, even though the video signal was processed in a preliminary way by a computer program (determining coordinates for individual calibrated data points). This grouping of individual data points into clusters (fixation locations and dwell-times) was further adjusted by an inspection of the stimulus locations. Although one could argue that such a "fitting" process may have been biased by the scorer's expectations, Bronson argued convincingly that these minor adjustments were quite rare and that his conclusions were drawn on the basis of an analysis accuracy well within the tolerances of his scoring procedure.

Bronson's calibration procedures did not, however, include a separate re-scaling of vertical eye positions, since the calibration target only moved horizontally. He assumed that vertical calibrations were similar to the horizontal, based largely on corneal curvature data suggesting the absence of large meridian differences. However, separate vertical calibration data should be collected, particularly in light of Harris et al.'s calibration data which shows horizontal-vertical asymmetries.

Future applications of automated or semi-automated corneal reflection analysis systems will undoubtedly include standardized calibration schemes for use with infants, as well as methods to compensate for shifts in head position. An unfortunate aspect of current systems is their dependence on a very small field of view in the recording camera. As a result, the infant's eye must be positioned within a very small region (approximately 3 cm. square). Increasing the size of the field of view reduces the resolution of the eye position signal. Head tracking options are currently available for use with corneal reflection systems, but the temporal response of these head tracking systems cannot always keep up with sudden head movements. Nevertheless, we can look forward to improved

versions of the corneal reflection technique, particularly those not
dependent on the 60 Hz temporal resolution of video-based
cameras.

SUMMARY AND CONCLUSIONS

Bronson's monograph on infant scanning is a rich source of new empirical data and theoretical insights into the mechanisms underlying fixational behaviors. The general approach of combining detailed measures of scanning with more global measures of visual
processing will assist in the clarification of data gathered with other
measures of visual processing in infants. Moreover, Bronson's initial study raises many interesting questions regarding the control
of scanning and its relation to visual processing. A psychophysics of
peripheral retinal processing and saccadic elicitation is clearly
called for as a result of Bronson's work. The relation between
scanning behavior and visual processing in adults may also benefit
from the thorough approach provided by Bronson, even though the
adult probably carries a much more sophisticated cognitive system
to the scanning situation.

  Finally, Bronson's data and theoretical speculations serve notice to investigators of infant pattern perception that there is no
single measure of visual processing that can hope to capture all aspects of this complex mechanism. Although Bronson's data and
models are important in their own right, his most important contribution may reside in the cautious rigor with which he approached a
complicated problem. Such a treatise is relatively rare in today's
burgeoning literature comprised mainly of terse journal articles.
One can hope that similar monographs will broaden the perspective
with which researchers approach their studies, and foster a rigorous scientific method in areas whose techniques and interpretations
have been less than definitive.

REFERENCES

Abramov, I., Gordon, J., Hendrickson, A., Hainline, L., Dobson, V., &
  LaBossiere, E. Postnatal development of the infant retina. *Supplement to
  Investigative Ophthalmology and Visual Science*, 1981, *20* (3), 46.

Antes, J. R., & Penland, J. G. Picture context effects on eye movement patterns. In D. F. Fisher, R. A. Monty & J. W. Senders (Eds.), *Eye movements: Cognition and visual perception.* Hillsdale, N.J.: Lawrence Erlbaum Associates, 1981.

Aslin, R. N. Development of smooth pursuit in human infants. In D. F. Fisher, R. A. Monty & J. W. Senders, (Eds.), *Eye movements: Cognition and visual perception.* Hillsdale, N.J.: Lawrence Erlbaum Associates, 1981.

Aslin, R. N., & Salapatek, P. Saccadic localization of visual targets by the very young human infant. *Perception and Psychophysics,* 1975, *17,* 293–302.

Banks, M. S., & Salapatek, P. Infant pattern vision: A new approach based on the contrast sensitivity function. *Journal of Experimental Child Psychology,* 1981, *31,* 1–45.

Bronson, G. *The scanning patterns of human infants: Implications for visual learning.* Norwood, N.J.: Ablex Publishing Corp., 1982.

Cohen, L. B., & Gelber, E. R. Infant visual memory. In L. B. Cohen & P. Salapatek (Eds.), *Infant perception: From sensation to cognition.* (Vol. I). New York: Academic Press, 1975.

Day, R. H. The physiological basis of form perception in the peripheral retina. *Psychological Review,* 1957, *64,* 38–48.

Dodge, R., & Cline, T. S. The angle velocity of eye movements. *Psychological Review,* 1901, *8,* 145–157.

Findlay, J. M. Local and global influences on saccadic eye movements. In D. F. Fisher, R. A. Monty & J. W. Senders (Eds.), *Eye movements: Cognition and visual perception.* Hillsdale, N.J.: Lawrence Erlbaum Associates, 1981.

Fisher, D. F., Monty, R. A., & Senders, J. W. *Eye movements: Cognition and visual perception.* Hillsdale, N.J.: Lawrence Erlbaum Associates, 1981.

Friedman, A. Framing pictures: The role of knowledge in automatized encoding and memory for gist. *Journal of Experimental Psychology: General,* 1979, *108,* 316–355.

Friedman, A., & Liebelt, L. S. On the time course of viewing pictures with a view towards remembering. In D. F. Fisher, R. A. Monty & J. W. Senders (Eds.), *Eye movements: Cognition and visual perception.* Hillsdale, N.J.: Lawrence Erlbaum Associates, 1981.

Gould, J. D. Looking at pictures. In R. A. Monty & J. W. Senders (Eds.), *Eye movements and psychological processes.* Hillsdale, N.J.: Lawrence Erlbaum Associates, 1976.

Haith, M. M. Infrared television recording and measurement of ocular behavior in human infants. *American Psychologist,* 1969, *24,* 279–282.

Haith, M. M. *Rules that babies look by.* Hillsdale, N.J.: Lawrence Erlbaum Associates, 1980.

Hainline, L. An automated eye movement recording system for use with human infants. *Behavior Research Methods and Instrumentation,* 1981, *13,* 20–24.

Harris, C. M., Hainline, L., & Abramov, I. A method for calibrating an eye-monitoring system for use with infants. *Behavior Research Methods and Instrumentation,* 1981, *13,* 11–17.

Just, M. A., & Carpenter, P. A. A theory of reading: From eye fixations to comprehension. *Psychological Review,* 1980, *87,* 329–354.

Kliegel, R., & Olson, R. K. Reduction and calibration of eye-monitor data. *Behavior Research Methods and Instrumentation*, 1981, *13*, 107–111.

Martin, M. Local and global processing: The role of sparsity. *Memory and Cognition*, 1979, *7*, 476–484.

Maurer, D. Infant's visual perception. In L. B. Cohen & P. Salapatek (Eds.), *Infant perception: From sensation to cognition*. (Vol. I). New York: Academic Press, 1975.

Monty, R. A., & Senders, J. W. *Eye movements and psychological processes*. Hillsdale, N.J.: Lawrence Erlbaum Associates, 1976.

Navon, D. Forest before trees: The precedence of global features in visual perception. *Cognitive Psychology*, 1977, *9*, 353–383.

Nodine, C. F., Carmody, D. P. & Kundel, H. L. Searching for Nina. In J. W. Senders, R. A. Monty & D. F. Fisher (Eds.), *Eye movements and the higher psychological processes*. Hillsdale, N.J.: Lawrence Erlbaum Associates, 1978.

Noton, D., & Stark, L. Eye movements and visual perception. *Scientific American*, 1971, *224*, 34–43. (a)

Noton, D., & Stark, L. Scanpaths in eye movements during pattern perception. *Science*, 1971, *171*, 308–311. (b)

O'Regan, J. K. Saccadic size control in reading: Evidence for the linguistic control hypothesis. *Perception and Psychophysics*, 1979, *25*, 501–509.

Parker, R. E. Picture processing during recognition. *Journal of Experimental Psychology: Human Perception and Performance*, 1978, *4*, 284–293.

Rayner, K. Eye movements in reading and information processing. *Psychological Bulletin*, 1978, *85*, 618–660.

Rayner, K., Well, A. D., & Pollatsek, A. Asymmetry of the effective visual field in reading. *Perception and Psychophysics*, 1980, *27*, 537–544.

Salapatek, P., Aslin, R. N., Simonson, J., & Pulos, E. Infant saccadic eye movements to visible and previously visible targets. *Child Development*, 1980, *51*, 1090–1094.

Salapatek, P., Haith, M. M., Maurer, D., & Kessen, W. Error in the corneal reflection technique: A note on Slater and Findlay. *Journal of Experimental Child Psychology*, 1972, *14*, 493–497.

Salapatek, P., & Kessen, W. Visual scanning of triangles by the human newborn. *Journal of Experimental Child Psychology*, 1966, *3*, 155–167.

Senders, J. W., Monty, R. A., & Fisher, D. F. *Eye movements and the higher psychological processes*. Hillsdale, N.J.: Lawrence Erlbaum Associates, 1978.

Sheena, D. Pattern-recognition techniques for extraction of features of the eye from a conventional television scan. In R. A. Monty & J. W. Senders (Eds.), *Eye movements and psychological processes*. Hillsdale, N.J.: Lawrence Erlbaum Associates, 1976.

Slater, A. M. & Findlay, J. M. The measurement of fixation position in the newborn baby. *Journal of Experimental Child Psychology*, 1972, *14*, 349–364.

Slater, A. M., & Findlay, J. M. The corneal reflection technique and the visual preference method: Sources of error. *Journal of Experimental Child Psychology*, 1975, *20*, 240–247.

Stark, L., & Ellis, S. R. Scanpaths revisited: Cognitive models direct active looking. In D. F. Fisher, R. A. Monty, & J. W. Senders (Eds.), *Eye movements: Cognition and visual perception.* Hillsdale, N.J.: Lawrence Erlbaum Associates, 1981.

Tversky, B. Eye fixations in prediction of recognition and recall. *Memory and Cognition,* 1974, *2*, 275–278.

Yarbus, A. L. *Eye movements and vision.* New York: Plenum Press, 1967.

Young, L. R., & Sheena, D. Survey of eye movement recording methods. *Behavior Research Methods and Instrumentation,* 1975, *7*, 397–429.

Author Index

133